THE WORLD OF JUBA II AND KLEOPATRA SELENE

THE WORLD OF JUBA II AND KLEOPATRA SELENE

Royal scholarship on Rome's African frontier

Duane W. Roller

Routledge
Taylor & Francis Group

NEW YORK AND LONDON

First published 2003
by Routledge
29 West 35th Street, New York, NY 10001

Simultaneously published in the UK
by Routledge
11 New Fetter Lane, London EC4P 4EE

Routledge is an imprint of the Taylor & Francis Group

© 2003 Duane W. Roller

Typeset in Garamond by Wearset Ltd, Boldon, Tyne and Wear
Printed and bound in Great Britain by St Edmundsbury Press, Bury
St Edmunds, Suffolk

Library of Congress Cataloging in Publication Data
A catalog record for this book has been requested

British Library Cataloguing in Publication Data
A catalogue record for this book is available from the British Library

ISBN 0–415–30596–9

CONTENTS

CONTENTS

ILLUSTRATIONS

Figures

Maps

PREFACE

Juba II (48 BC–AD 23/24) ruled Mauretania – northwestern Africa – as a Roman client king for half a century, from 25 BC until his death. Moreover, he was a notable scholar, a product of the intellectual flourishing of the Augustan world. His extensive literary output exists today only in fragments, but is the basis of modern understanding of the ancient comprehension of the southern half of the known world, the vast stretch from the Atlantic coast of northwest Africa to India. Juba was not alone as a scholarly king but was the exemplar of that unusual blend of talents, and was called in antiquity "rex literatissimus." His scholarship was found significant by successors as diverse as Pliny, Plutarch, and Athenaios.

An essential, yet enigmatic, part of Juba's environment is the personality of his wife, Kleopatra Selene (40–*ca.* 5 BC), the daughter of Marcus Antonius and Kleopatra VII. As queen of Mauretania (and also titular queen of the Kyrenaika) she played a crucial role at the royal court; as heiress of the Ptolemies she brought not only stature but a rich cultural inheritance that was to be a major influence on Juba's research. Yet because of the deficiency of source material and her early death she is often hard to see, although her presence was profound.

Juba was rescued by Julius Caesar from the ruins of his father's kingdom of Numidia and was raised in Rome in the Augustan household. He was then sent with Kleopatra Selene to uphold Roman interests in Mauretania, an outstanding example of the Augustan phenomenon of the client king, more properly the "rex socius amicusque," the friendly and allied king, the sympathetic monarch at the fringes of the empire who could be relied upon to uphold Roman interests, both culturally and politically. Less controversial than his more famous colleague Herod the Great, Juba in his reign brought a flourishing intellectual climate, and above all peace and prosperity, to his territories.

Yet this learned monarch is often remembered today merely as the son-in-law of Marcus Antonius and Kleopatra VII, and as such merely a footnote to history. There has been no extensive study of Juba II, Kleopatra Selene, and their world since French efforts at the time of the First World War.

What follows is not only the first examination of their lives and careers in English but the first analytical critique of the king both as an implementer of the Augustan program and as a notable scholar in his own right. Indeed, within half a century of his death he was commemorated as one whose scholarship was more significant than his kingship. But his writings have largely been ignored – beyond the collecting of the fragments of his works – and he has been considered as little more than yet another ancient author whose output has not survived. Likewise, his role as king, however inferior to his impact as historian, explorer, and geographer, has tended to be analyzed in a colonialist context, the defender of Roman civilization against the barbarians, rather than as a crucial factor in the multiculturalism that was the Roman Empire. Juba was a romanized Numidian married to a wife who was half Greek and half Roman, and this background remains a significant part of his outlook. This is especially apparent in the cultural richness of the court at Mauretanian Caesarea, whose diversity exceeded that of the more restricted ethnic milieus of the other client kingdoms. It is becoming increasingly obvious today that ethnic interaction was one of the most powerful cultural factors in ancient society: this has been dramatically demonstrated by Nikos Kokkinos in his recent study of the Herodian family.[1]

It was Glen Bowersock who many years ago introduced the present author to Juba and Kleopatra Selene. Interest further developed from study of Herod the Great and awareness of the complexity of his world, leading to the comprehension that the Augustan era was one of rich and diverse cultural factors running far beyond the traditional understanding of this period. Even the fragmentary authors of Greco-Roman antiquity deserve analysis, and it became clear that Juban studies needed to move beyond the colonialist perspectives of the first half of the twentieth century. Juba was both scholar and king, and any study of his career must attend to both of these roles. Kleopatra Selene was queen and her mother's heir, and in many ways an implementer of Juba's kingship and scholarship. But what follows is not a biography: rather, it is a cultural analysis of personalities and the world that produced them and upon which they had impact. Individuals cannot be separated from their environment, and truly to understand creativity one must attempt to absorb what the creative individual was thinking, saw, and experienced, during both the crucially formative years of adolescence and the time of productivity. The friends of his youth, his teachers and colleagues, the books in his library, the intellectual background of his spouse, and indeed the view from his study are all components of Juba's intellectual processes and collectively determined the ideas he thought and the words he set down.

1   Kokkinos, *Herodian Dynasty*. Even as early as the fifth century BC, questions were being raised as to the meaning of ethnicity. Herodotos (1.146–7) was well aware that claims of ethnic purity or superiority could be manipulated to create a false impression. See, further, for a good discussion of modern scholarship and its attitude toward ethnicity, Jeremy McInerney, *The Folds of Parnassos: Land and Ethnicity in Ancient Phokis* (Austin: University of Texas Press, 1999), pp. 8–39.

ACKNOWLEDGMENTS

The author would like to thank the Harvard College Library, the Stanford University Library, the Blegen Library of the University of Cincinnati, the Library of the University of California at Berkeley, the Library of the University of Michigan at Ann Arbor, and the Library of the Ohio State University, at which much of the research for this project was completed. Special thanks are due to the Trustees of the British Museum, especially the Department of Coins and Medals. The project was supported by a Fellowship for University Teachers from the National Endowment for the Humanities. Several research grants from the Ohio State University were also of great assistance. Although not originally intended for this purpose, a Fulbright Senior Lecturing Award to India in 1995 helped the author in understanding the relationships between that region and the Mediterranean, an essential part of Juba's environment. Extended visits to Morocco, Algeria, and Tunisia, as well as the Levant, were valuable in comprehending the physical world of the Mauretanian client kingdom: particular appreciation is due to all those who assisted in the May 2001 trip to Mauretanian Caesarea and its environs, especially Nacèra Benseddik. David C. Braund, Charles L. Babcock, John Eadie, David Potter, and A. E. K. Vail graciously read the manuscript in its entirety and made many valuable suggestions. For supplying photographs and the permission to use them, the author would like to thank M. Chuzeville, P. Chuzeville, and Ch. Larrieu (Musée du Louvre), Christa Landwehr, the Ny Carlsberg Glyptotek, Yamouna Rebahi (Musée de Cherchel), E. Kleinefenn (Paris), the Agence Nationale d'Archéologie (Algiers), the British Museum, and the late Duane H. D. Roller. Among the many others who were of aid in bringing the project to completion were Neil Adams, Andrew Meadows, Judith Swaddling, and Susan Walker of the British Museum; Sally-Ann Ashton; Glen Bowersock; Deborah Burks; Donna Distel; Lakhdar Drias, Director of the National Museum of Antiquities, Algiers; Elizabeth Fentress; Sabah Ferdi; Klaus Fittschen; Nikos Kokkinos; Philippe Leveau; Wolf-R. Megow; Krzysztof Nawotka; Letitia K. Roller; Kathy Stedke; Richard Stoneman and many others at Routledge; Kate Toll; Susan Treggiari; the late Jerry Vardaman; and Wendy Watkins and the Ohio State University Center for Epigraphical Studies.

ABBREVIATIONS

AA: *Archäologischer Anzeiger*
AÉpigr: *L'Année épigraphique*
AF: Archäologische Forschungen
AfrIt: *Africa Italiana*
AfrRom: *L'Africa Romana*
AJA: *American Journal of Archaeology*
AJP: *American Journal of Philology*
AncHBull: *Ancient History Bulletin*
AncSoc: *Ancient Society*
AncW: *The Ancient World*
AnnPerugia: *Annali della Facoltà di Lettere e Filosofia, Università degli Studi di Perugia*
AnnSiena: *Annali della Facoltà di Lettere e Filosofia* (Siena)
ANRW: *Aufstieg und Niedergang der römischen Welt*
ANSMN: *American Numismatic Society Museum Notes*
AntAfr: *Antiquités africaines*
AntCl: *L'Antiquité Classique*
AntK: *Antike Kunst*
AnzWien: *Anzeiger.* Österreichische Akademie der Wissenschaften, Wien, Philologisch-historische Klasse
ArchCl: *Archeologia classica*
ArchStorTL: *Archivo storico di Terra di Lavoro*
AttiVen: *Atti dell'Istituto veneto di scienze, lettere ed arti*
BAAlg: *Bulletin d'archéologie algérienne*
BAC: *Bulletin Archéologique du Comité des Travaux Historiques et Scientifiques*
BAGRW: *The Barrington Atlas of the Greek and Roman World*, ed. Richard J. Talbert (Princeton, N.J., 2000)
BAMaroc: *Bulletin d'archéologie marocaine*
BAntFr: *Bulletin de la Société Nationale des Antiquaires de France*
BAR: British Archaeological Reports
BAR-IS: British Archaeological Reports, International Series
BCH: *Bulletin de correspondance hellénique*

BÉFAR: Bibliothèque des Écoles françaises d'Athènes et de Rome

BIALond: *Bulletin of the Institute of Archaeology of the University of London*

BJb: *Bonner Jahrbücher des Rheinischen Landesmuseums in Bonn und des Vereins von Altertumsfreunden im Rheinlande*

BMC: *British Museum Catalogue of Coins*

Braund, *Friendly King*: David C. Braund, *Rome and the Friendly King: The Character of the Client Kingship* (London 1984)

Broughton: T. R. S. Broughton, *The Magistrates of the Roman Republic*, Philological Monographs of the American Philological Association 15 (New York 1951–2, 1986)

CAH: *The Cambridge Ancient History*

CÉFR: Collection de l'École française de Rome

CHJ: *Cambridge Historical Journal*

CHL: Commentationes Humanarum Litterarum

CIL: *Corpus inscriptionum latinarum*

CJ: *Classical Journal*

ClBul: *The Classical Bulletin*

Cleopatra: *Cleopatra of Egypt: From History to Myth*, ed. Susan Walker and Peter Higgs (London 2001)

Coltelloni-Trannoy: Michèle Coltelloni-Trannoy, *Le Royaume de Maurétanie sous Juba II et Ptolémée* (Paris 1997)

CP: *Classical Philology*

CQ: *Classical Quarterly*

CRAI: *Comptes rendus des séances de l'Académie des inscriptions et belles-lettres* (Paris)

CSCA: *University of California Studies in Classical Antiquity*

CW: *The Classical World*

CWHF: *The Cambridge World History of Food*, ed. Kenneth F. Kiple and Kriemhild Coneè Ornelas (Cambridge 2000)

DenkschrWien: Österreichische Akademie der Wissenschaften, Wien, Philosophisch-historische Klasse, Denkschriften

EAA: *Enciclopedia dell'arte antica, classica e orientale*

EB: *Encyclopédie berbere* (Aix-en-Provence 1984–)

EchCl: *Echoes du monde classique*

EntrHardt: Entretiens Hardt

EpSt: Epigraphische Studien

FGrHist: Felix Jacoby, *Die Fragmente der griechischen Historiker* (Leiden 1923–)

FHG: K. Müller, *Fragmenta historicorum graecorum* (Paris 1841–1938)

FolOr: *Folia Orientalia*

GGM: *Geographi graeci minores*, ed. C. Müller (1855)

GLM: *Geographi latini minores*, ed. Alexander Riese (1878)

GRBS: *Greek, Roman, and Byzantine Studies*

Gsell: Stéphane Gsell, *Histoire ancienne de l'Afrique du Nord* (Paris 1914–28)

HA: *Historia Augusta*

HRR: Hermann Peter, *Historicorum romanorum reliquae* (Stuttgart 1967)

HSCP: Harvard Studies in Classical Philology

IDélos: *Inscriptions de Délos*

IG: *Inscriptiones graecae*

IGRR: *Inscriptiones graecae ad res romanas pertinentes*

ILS: *Inscriptiones latinae selectae*, ed. H. Dessau (1892–1916)

IrAnt: *Iranica Antiqua*

IstForsch: Istanbuler Forschungen

Jacoby, *Commentary*: Felix Jacoby, Commentary to *FGrHist* #275 (3a, pp. 317–57)

Jacoby, *RE*: Felix Jacoby, "Iuba II" (#2), *RE* 9, 1916, 2384–95

JAOS: *Journal of the American Oriental Society*

JBerlMus: *Jahrbuch der Berliner Museen*

JdI: *Jahrbuch des Deutschen Archäologischen Instituts*

JEA: *Journal of Egyptian Archaeology*

Jodin, *Volubilis*: André Jodin, *Volubilis, Regia Iubae: contribution à l'étude des civilisations du Maroc antique préclaudien* (Paris 1987)

JRA: *Journal of Roman Archaeology*

JRS: *Journal of Roman Studies*

JSav: *Journal des Savants*

Kokkinos, *Herodian Dynasty*: Nikos Kokkinos, *The Herodian Dynasty: Origins, Role in Society, and Eclipse*, Journal for the Study of the Pseudepigrapha Supplement Series 30 (Sheffield 1998)

LCM: *Liverpool Classical Monthly*

Leveau, *Caesarea*: Philippe Leveau, *Caesarea de Maurétanie: une ville romaine et ses campagnes*, CÉFR 70 (1984)

LibAE: *Libyca Archéologie-Épigraphie*

LIMC: *Lexicon Iconographicum Mythologiae Classicae*

Lixus: *Lixus*, CÉFR 166, 1992

LSJ: H. G. Liddell, R. Scott, and H. Stuart Jones, *Greek–English Lexicon*, ninth edition (Oxford 1940)

MAAR: *Memoirs of the American Academy in Rome*

Mazard: Jean Mazard, *Corpus Nummorum Numidiae Mauretaniaeque* (Paris 1955)

MÉFR: *Mélanges d'archéologie et d'histoire de l'École française de Rome*

MÉFRA: *Mélanges de l'École française de Rome, Antiquité*

MM: *Madrider Mitteilungen*

MusHelv: *Museum Helveticum*

ND: *Numismatic Digest*

NH: Pliny, *Natural History*

NP: *Der neue Pauly: Enzyklopädie der Antike*

NTDAR: L. Richardson, Jr., *A New Topographical Dictionary of Ancient Rome* (Baltimore 1992)

Numider: *Die Numider: Reiter und Könige nördlich der Sahara*, ed. Heinz Günter Horn and Christoph B. Rüger (Cologne 1979)

OCD: *Oxford Classical Dictionary*, third edition (Oxford 1997)

OGIS: *Orientis Graeci inscriptiones selectae*

OJA: *Oxford Journal of Archaeology*

OLD: *Oxford Latin Dictionary* (Oxford 1982)

OxyPap: *The Oxyrhynchus Papyri*, ed. Bernard P. Grenfell and Arthur S. Hunt (London 1898–)

PACA: *Proceedings of the African Classical Associations*

PBSR: *Papers of the British School at Rome*

PCG: *Poetae Comici Graeci*, ed. R. Kassel and C. Austin (Berlin 1983–)

PCPS: *Proceedings of the Cambridge Philological Society*

PECS: *The Princeton Encyclopedia of Classical Sites*

PEQ: *Palestine Exploration Quarterly*

PIR: *Prosopographia imperii romani*

PP: *La parola del passato*

QS: *Quaderni di Storia* (Bari)

RA: *Revue archéologique*

RAfr: *Revue africaine*

RAssyr: *Revue d'assyriologie et d'archéologie orientale*

RE: Pauly-Wissowa, *Real-Encyclopädie der klassischen Altertumswissenschaft*

RÉA: *Revue des études anciennes*

RÉG: *Revue des études grecques*

RÉL: *Revue des études latines*

RGM: *Revue de géographie du Maroc*

RHCM: *Revue d'histoire et de civilisation du Maghreb*

RHist: *Revue historique*

RIDA: *Revue international des droits de l'antiquité*

Ritter, *Rom*: Hans Werner Ritter, *Rom und Numidien: Untersuchungen zur rechtlichen Stellung abhängiger Könige* (Lüneburg 1987)

RM: *Mitteilungen des Deutschen Archäologischen Instituts, Römische Abteilung*

RN: *Revue numismatique*

Roller, *Herod*: Duane W. Roller, *The Building Program of Herod the Great* (Berkeley, Calif., 1998)

Romanelli, *Storia*: Pietro Romanelli, *Storia delle province romane dell'Africa*, Studi pubblicati dall'Istituto Italiano per la Storia Antica 14 (Rome 1959)

SchwMbll: *Schweizer Münzblätter*

SEG: *Supplementum epigraphicum graecum*

SIG: *Sylloge inscriptionum graecarum* (Leipzig 1883–)

StMagr: *Studi Magrebini*

Sullivan, *Near Eastern Royalty*: Richard D. Sullivan, *Near Eastern Royalty and Rome, 100–30 BC*, Phoenix Supplementary Volume 24 (Toronto 1990)

SymbOslo: *Symbolae Osloenses*

TAPA: *Transactions of the American Philological Society*

Thomson: J. Oliver Thomson, *History of Ancient Geography* (Cambridge 1948)

TI: *Terrae Incognitae*

WA: *World Archaeology*

Wrack: *Das Wrack: Der Antike Schiffsfund von Mahdia*, ed. Gisela Hellenkemper Salies *et al.* (Cologne 1994)

ZfN: *Zeitschrift für Numismatik*

ZPE: *Zeitschrift für Papyrologie und Epigraphik*

INTRODUCTION

Juba II[1] was born about 48 BC, the son of King Juba I of Numidia, the territory south and west of Carthage. Within two years he was an orphan and
had been removed to Rome as a captive, displayed in the African triumph of
Julius Caesar in 46 BC. Why this happened is connected with the convoluted
and lengthy history of the Roman relationship with Africa and the impact of
the Roman civil wars. The royalty of Numidia had been involved in Roman
affairs for over 150 years. Juba's great-great-great-grandfather, the erudite
warrior king Massinissa, was a follower of Scipio Africanus and lived to the
age of 90, surviving both the Second and the Third Punic Wars and presid-
ing over a notable and cultured court. Massinissa's grandson – Juba's great-
great-uncle – was the famous Jugurtha, who had his own complex
relationship with Rome. Juba's grandfather Hiempsal was a historian, and
his father, Juba I, had come to Rome on a Numidian embassy in the 80s BC,
only to be insulted and assaulted by the young Julius Caesar, which meant
that when Juba I became king he naturally gravitated toward the faction of
Gaius Pompeius.

---

1 *PIR*² I65. The name is inevitably "Iuba" in Latin, whether in literature or on inscriptions or coins. In
   Greek, Ἰόβας is the usual form (occasionally Ἰόβα), but Strabo and Dio used Ἰούβας. Inscriptions
   are not consistent: *IG* 3¹.555, 936 and 2–3².3436 have Ἰούβας but *OGIS* 198 has Ἰόβας; yet all are
   from Athens and roughly contemporary with the king himself. Despite the general prevalence of
   Ἰόβας in Greek, two sources in personal contact with Juba, Strabo and the commissioners of *IG*
   2–3².3436, used Ἰούβας. This is more in conformity with the Latin and may have been the form
   actually preferred by the king. His father's Punic coin legends have the equivalent of "Iobai" (Figure
   25b, p. 245; Mazard #84–93), perhaps closer to the common Greek Ἰόβας, and all Greek sources
   have this form for Juba I. The spelling Ἰούβας used by Strabo, Dio, and the Athenians for Juba II
   may have been transliterated from Latin.
       It is possible that Juba was not the name given to the son of Juba I by his parents. Unlike many of
   the Greek dynasties, the Numidian royal family did not tend to use the same name. In the ten
   known generations (nearly thirty individuals), names repeat only on two occasions other than Juba I
   and II: the two Hiempsals and the two Massinissas (Appendix 2, Stemma B). In both cases the relationship is not close: the former were cousins (thus Hiempsal II was not a direct descendant of
   Hiempsal I) and the latter five generations apart, Massinissa II being a petty chieftain who probably
   took the name of his illustrious ancestor. Thus it is probable that Juba II, his actual name unknown,
   was given his father's name by the Romans.

1

Juba I had great plans for a North African empire, but these collapsed after the death of Pompeius, and he was defeated by Caesar at Thapsus and committed suicide: hence his infant son appeared in the triumph in the summer of 46 BC. Although some of those in the triumph were executed, a decision was made to spare young Juba, for reasons that are not clear. By the time of Caesar's death two years later, Juba was handed over to one of Caesar's relatives and eventually ended up in the household of his grandniece Octavia. Here he grew up along with the other children of the emergent imperial family, being particularly close to Marcellus and Tiberius, who were near his age. Although as a barbarian Juba did not have the status that the Roman children had, Augustus strongly believed that foreign children within his extended family were to be treated as natural-born ones, and at some time Juba was given Roman citizenship.

As a young man growing up in an aristocratic Roman household, Juba received the best contemporary education, specializing in linguistics, Roman history, natural history, and the arts. It seems likely that he had contact with scholars such as Varro and Dionysios of Halikarnassos. Strabo of Amaseia seems to have been a particularly close teacher or fellow student. Juba also learned about his own ancestral heritage through the Numidian exile communities in Rome. African culture of another sort became available after 30 BC when the children of Marcus Antonius and Kleopatra VII became part of Octavia's family, bringing with them a substantial entourage and much information about the world of the Ptolemies.

By this time Juba would have been nearly 20, and although it is not clear what life was being planned for him, his talents as a scholar were being recognized as he published his first works. His literary career probably began with the *Roman Archaeology*, perhaps reflecting the influence of Dionysios of Halikarnassos. Its two books covered the vast range from the mythological foundation of Italy to at least the Spanish wars of the second century BC, but it seems to have emphasized elements that were of particular relevance to the Augustan era, such as the ancient cults that were being rejuvenated, and the relationship between Rome and Africa. Although the subject of Roman origins was a common one for the period, Juba's version gained respect for reliability, especially in his handling of early material.

Another youthful work is the *Omoiotetes* (*Resemblances* or *Equivalences*), a linguistic composition whose goal was to prove the Greek origin of the Latin language, another topical concern in Augustan Rome. It too seems to have focused on early cultic matters, especially terminology. Fifteen books are known, an incredible length contrasted with the scantiness of the *Archaeology*. It is thus possible that there has been a confusion of titles and that both are the same lengthy work on Roman history, cult, and linguistics.

Juba also wrote *On Painting*, a derivative critique of works visible in contemporary Rome, and a *Theatrical History*, whose emphasis seems to have been on production details, especially musical ones. Although it too was probably derivative, it is one of the major bodies of information on ancient music, since Juba's sources, mostly from Hellenistic south Italy, are even less extant than his treatise. He also wrote a commentary on the voyage of Hanno, the great Carthaginian explorer who had descended to the tropics of West Africa and may have circumnavigated the continent, and it is perhaps through Juba's efforts that Hanno's report survives today. Thus by his early twenties, just as Octavian became Augustus and plans were being made for the future, Juba already had a reputation as a scholar of note, with several published works.

At some time Augustus realized that he had a talent within his household who could play a role in the developing plans for postwar Rome. But Juba needed military experience, so, late in 27 BC, he, along with Marcellus and Tiberius, joined the Princeps in Spain. Augustus resided in Tarraco tending to administration while the young men waged war against various Spanish tribes, remaining there until late 25 BC. It was here that the final part of Juba's education took place – his training as a soldier and leader – and Augustus began to implement the plans for his destiny.

Juba could not be sent back to rule his ancestral territories because those had been provincialized by Caesar twenty years previously. But to the west was an anomalous area loosely called Mauretania, and increasingly of concern to the Romans. It had been ruled by a native dynasty – perhaps related to the Numidian one – that had become somewhat romanized. About the time of Juba's birth Mauretania had been split between two contentious relatives, Bocchus and Bogudes, who tended to take opposite sides in Roman affairs. Yet by 31 BC both were dead with no heirs, and thus at the end of the civil war the status of their territories was uncertain. Moreover, Romans from Spain had long been drifting into northwest Mauretania, largely for commercial reasons, and there were a number of Roman settlements that may have been virtual colonies. Hence it would have seemed to Augustus that some normalization was necessary. Thus in 25 BC he decided to settle the issue by placing Juba in charge of Mauretania as king. Following the loose procedures of client kingship, Juba was available, competent, a protégé of prominent Romans, and even had some vague association with the region. But there was one unsettled matter: the finding of a suitable wife to be Juba's partner, someone who could assist in creating a stable kingship and in bringing Roman ways to North Africa. Augustus did not have to look beyond his extended family for a promising candidate: his stepniece, the 15-year-old Kleopatra Selene, the only surviving child of Antonius and Kleopatra VII. Since Kleopatra Selene had been living with Octavia for the previous five years, she and Juba were doubtless already well acquainted. One can only imagine the vitality and precociousness of this child, who had a legal claim to be the queens of both Libya and Egypt, and thus her own African connection to complement that of Juba. As one of the few remaining children of Antonius, she was too dangerous either to execute or to keep in Rome, and Augustus must have felt that the ideal solution to this problem was to send her to Mauretania as Juba's wife. She brought her rich Ptolemaic heritage to the kingdom, and, presumably, her mother's skill and determination. She married Juba late in 25 BC; Krinagoras of Mytilene wrote an epigram for the occasion. The royal couple then departed for Iol, Bocchus' old capital, which, in the emerging fashion of the era, was promptly renamed Caesarea.

The monarchs ruled together for the next twenty years, and Juba alone for nearly thirty more, controlling a vast territory from Roman Africa to the Atlantic, the largest and probably the most amorphous of the client kingdoms. Much of the time was spent in defending the frontier, not always successfully. Barbarian incursions were a constant threat, part of the never-ending conflicts between populations with different cultures and outlooks; Roman military assistance became an early and constant feature of the reign. But Juba and Kleopatra Selene were also assiduous in bringing Mauretania into the imperial economic sphere: the kingdom produced vast amounts of grain, fish, *garum*, purple dye, and timber for export to Italy. A long series of cornucopia coins shows that Juba saw the kingdom as one of the economic mainstays of the empire. He fostered close relationships with Spain and was even appointed city magistrate at two Spanish cities.

At Caesarea, Juba and Kleopatra Selene developed a rich court that combined Roman, Ptolemaic, and indigenous African elements. Saturn, the *frugifer deus*, seems to have been a chief divinity, along with Herakles (whose last labor was localized in Mauretania and who was said to have been an ancestor of both the monarchs), and of course the imperial cult. Building on his acquisition of the Carthaginian state library from the heirs of the historian Sallust, Juba created one of the best royal libraries and attracted scholars and artists: although the few extant names are obscure, they include the court tragedian Leonteus of Argos, the botanist and physician Euphorbos, the historians Asarubas and Cornelius Bocchus, and the gemcutter Gnaios. Kleopatra Selene brought her own entourage, refugees from her mother's court, which would further have heightened the multiculturalism of Caesarea. There was continuing contact with Augustan Rome and with the developing Augustan intellectual circle: Juba was constantly sending information to Marcus Agrippa for his map of the Roman world. Caesarea was probably a richer, more diverse environment than any of the eastern courts.

Scholar that he was, Juba immediately set out to explore and study his territory. Expeditions were sent into the High Atlas, the Sahara, and the Atlantic. His commentary on Hanno had already interested him in the west coast of Africa, and he became familiar with other explorations, such as the Carthaginian circumnavigation of the continent, and those of Eudoxos of Kyzikos, who had had good reason to believe that India could be reached from West Africa. Juba's explorations resulted in the two most enduring legacies of his scholarship. In the High Atlas he discovered a type of spurge that he named euphorbion after his physician, writing a treatise on it, the basis for the modern botanical family Euphorbiaceae and genus Euphorbia. He also explored islands in the Atlantic noted for their large dogs, which he named in Greek but which are known today from Pliny's Latin as the Canaries.

Juba also began work on a major treatise titled *Libyka* that would examine all of North Africa outside Lower Egypt. It outlined not only the history, geography, and natural history of his territories but also other issues of increasing concern to the king, such as direct access to East Africa and India from Mauretania. Building on Ptolemaic explorations of the upper Nile, he concluded that the river originated in Mauretania, to Juba a politically correct idea, and one that lasted well into the nineteenth century. The surviving fragments of *Libyka* include a diversity of subjects, but one of special importance is the discussion of the North African elephant, the major source of information for this now extinct animal.

Libyka was probably published around 5 BC. Augustus was impressed enough to include Juba as geographical adviser on the eastern expedition of his grandson Gaius Caesar, which set forth in 2 BC. The king was one of several distinguished staff members: his decision to go was made easier by the fact that he had recently become a widower. He traveled with Gaius from Antioch to Gaza and inland to Petra and the fringes of Arabia, and then back to Antioch, all the time gathering material for his next work, *On Arabia*. He had left the expedition before Gaius fatally encountered the Armenians, instead joining his fellow client king Archelaos of Kappadokia at his court city of Elaioussa-Sebaste and completing *On Arabia* in its library. *On Arabia* extended the concept of *Libyka* to the east, and together the two works were an examination of the southern half of the known world, from the Atlantic to India. Although much of the treatise is concerned with Arabia, especially the commercial and trade exports of the peninsula – information obtained in the markets of Gaza and Petra – emphasis is on a related Augustan concern, the routes to India and their economic potential. Juba had long been interested in this topic, both in his search for the Atlantic route to India and in his decision extend the scope of *Libyka* into East Africa, a region even today frequented by Indian merchants. But Augustus' interest in reopening Indian trade had not been paralleled by recent scholarly examination, and there had been little material added since the time of Alexander the Great. Indian trade had flourished under the Ptolemies but had collapsed with the fall of that dynasty, and Juba, with his Ptolemaic contacts, his published knowledge of East Africa, and his general expertise in trade and exploration, was the natural scholar to research the topic.

While he was in residence at the court of Archelaos, Juba's personal life took an unexpected turn. Here he met and married Glaphyra, Archelaos' daughter, another dynamic eastern princess, and recently widowed from a son of Herod the Great. Clearly Archelaos and Juba had grandiose dynastic plans for linking East and West, but for some reason the marriage did not last. Despite Augustus' regular favor of intermarriages between royal families, he might well have disapproved of this sudden connection between the two most powerful client kings, and when major barbarian incursions at home caused Juba to rush back to Mauretania, he divorced Glaphyra and went alone.

When Juba returned home, perhaps around AD 3, he began to show the signs of age, writing no more and embarking on no more expeditions. Approaching 60, he handed over many affairs of state to his son Ptolemaios, the last royal bearer of that illustrious name, who appears on coins from AD 5 and seems to have been raised to virtually equal rule sometime after AD 11. Ptolemaios' regnal years began around AD 17–21; in the former year, the great rebellion of Tacfarinas broke out. This went on for over six years and required major Roman intervention; although Roman Africa was more threatened than Mauretania, Juba and Ptolemaios were also heavily involved. In the midst of the uprising, in AD 23 or 24, Juba died, in his early seventies. Ptolemaios helped bring the rebellion to conclusion and was validated as king by the Roman senate.

Little is known about Ptolemaios' reign, although he clearly did not have the stature and intellect of his father. He may have been educated in Athens and was honored at the Gymnasion of Ptolemaios there, which had been built by an ancestor. But as a grandson of Antonius he fell victim to the power politics within the imperial family. He seems to have lacked his father's diplomacy and incautiously flaunted his power and independence. Eventually his cousin, the emperor Gaius Caligula, summoned him to Rome for an explanation. What happened next is obscure, but the situation deteriorated and Ptolemaios was suddenly executed. At worst, it was another example of the emperor's hostile treatment of his relatives; at best, his erratic reaction to Ptolemaios' seemingly inappropriate behavior as a client king. In any case, this meant the end of the kingdom, as Ptolemaios had no heir, and the territory was provincialized by Claudius.

Ancient and modern sources

The only contemporary literary sources for Juba II are slight, perhaps Horace, *Ode* 1.22, and Krinagoras of Mytilene, *Epigrams* 18 and 25. A number of inscriptions provide some prosopographic information and are especially illustrative about members of the royal court.[2] Velleius Paterculus documented the

---

2 The major inscriptions are collected in Coltelloni-Trannoy, pp. 218–19. Most important is *CIL* 2.3417 (=*ILS* 840), from Carthago Nova in Spain, where Juba held a magistracy, which provides details of his ancestry. Others include *CIL* 3.8927, 9257, 9342; *IG* 3^1.549, 555, 936; and *IG* 2–3^2.3436.

eastern campaign of Gaius Caesar to Arabia in which he and Juba took part, but did not mention Juba.[3] Strabo of Amaseia, a friend and schoolmate of the king, made several casual references, probably written just after Juba's death, but did not seem to have access to his scholarly output.[4] The bulk of the material about the king's life and career comes from standard sources for the Augustan period, especially Appian, Dio, Josephus, Plutarch, and Tacitus,[5] which are enough to construct the basic outline of his life, but all are brief and scattered, and few mention Kleopatra Selene. Another contemporary source is the art and architecture of the royal city of Caesarea and other sites in the Mauretanian kingdom. Further, there is the large number of coins that both Juba and Kleopatra Selene issued, separately and jointly. Kleopatra Selene had autonomous powers of coinage, and occasionally even honored her mother on her coins. These are especially useful in providing contemporary visual portraits of the sovereigns and elements of the material culture of their kingdom, particularly their architecture and royal symbols.[6]

The earliest extant authors to quote Juba's works were Dioskourides and perhaps Pomponius Mela, both in the middle of the first century AC (after Christ).[7] Over 100 fragments of the king's writings survive, some quite lengthy, which also provide a certain amount of information about his life.[8] Nearly half are found in the *Natural History* of Pliny the Elder, written forty to fifty years after Juba's death; much of Pliny's material on northwestern Africa, the upper Nile, the Red Sea, and Arabia originates with Juba.[9] Many of the remaining fragments come from two additional authors: Plutarch, who used Juba's *Roman Archaeology* as a source for early Roman history, and Athenaios, whose interests were in drama, the theater, and linguistics.[10] Other sources for the works of Juba include Aelian, Ammianus Marcellinus, Lucius Ampelius, Avienus, Galen, Harpokration, Philostratos, Photios,

---

3 Velleius 2.101–4.

4 Strabo 6.4.2; 17.3.7, 12, 25.

5 Appian, *Civil War* 2.101; Dio 51.15.6, 53.26.2, 55.28.3–4; Josephus, *Jewish Antiquities* 17.349–50; *Jewish Wars* 2.115; Plutarch, *Antonius* 87; *Caesar* 55.1–2; *Sulla* 16.8; *Sertorius* 9.5; Tacitus, *Annals* 4.5.

6 Much has been written about the coinage, and many of the relevant articles are cited in the following text. The most thorough publication is Jean Mazard, *Corpus Nummorum Numidiae Mauretaniaeque* (Paris: Arts et Métiers Graphiques, 1955); see also Jacques Alexandropoulos, *Les Monnaies de l'Afrique Antique, 400 av. J.-C. – 40 ap. J.-C.* (Toulouse: Presses Universitaires du Mirail, 2000), pp. 213–44, 413–35.

7 Dioskourides 3.82; Pomponius Mela 1.30. The recent suggestion that Vitruvius quoted Juba's *Libyka* is implausible: see further, infra, p. 183, note 2).

8 These are collected as *FGrHist* #275. Because of Felix Jacoby's policy of considering as a fragment only those citations that actually name the author (on this, see *FGrHist* 4a1, pp. xii–xiii), it is probable that the surviving fragments of Juba's works, especially in Books 5 and 6 of Pliny's *Natural History* and Book 4 of the *Deipnosophistai* of Athenaios, are far more extensive than the occasional point at which the king is mentioned.

9 Juba, fr. 1–3, 28–44, 54, 57–60, 62–9, 72–9.

10 The major citations are Plutarch, *Romulus* 14, 15, 17; *Numa* 7, 13; *Roman Questions* 4, 24, 59, 78, 89; and Athenaios 1.15, 3.83, 98, 4.170, 175–85, 8.343, 14.660.

Quintilian, and Tatian.[11] Athenaios and Aelian, both active around AD 200, seem to be the last to have quoted Juba directly and at length. His actual writings were probably lost shortly after that time, and later citations in various Byzantine lexica are derivative.

Modern interest began in the mid-nineteenth century with Konrad Müller's identification and publication of ninety-one fragments of Juba's writings[12] and the appearance of a number of German dissertations,[13] more collations of the fragments than critiques. A slightly more critical attitude was displayed by Hermann Peter in the 1870s,[14] and in 1883 the first French study of Juba appeared.[15] Yet throughout the century, more emphasis was placed on Juba as a fragmentary author than as a cultural figure, although he was early recognized as significant in the history of geography.[16]

When the French colonial presence was established in northern Africa late in the century, interest turned toward the physical remnants of Juba's territories. A museum had been founded at Cherchel in Algeria, Juba's Caesarea, as early as 1856, and rudimentary excavations began in 1876.[17] Much of the early explorations were directed toward the physical evidence for early Christianity, but nonetheless this resulted in the discovery of numerous inscriptions that illuminated the world of Juba II and Kleopatra Selene. Although excavations have continued until recent times, physical remnants of the Roman client kingdom continue to be scant and disputed. A similar situation exists at Volubilis in Morocco, the monarchs' western capital, where excavations have continued since 1884, but where most of the visible remains are from the late flourishing of the city, particularly the Severan period.[18]

Nevertheless, the early years of the twentieth century saw an increasing awareness of Juba in both France and Germany. Felix Jacoby published the first detailed study of the king in 1916.[19] Although still within a narrowly historical context, this approached Juba as more than merely a fragmentary

---

11 Aelian, *On the Characteristics of Animals* 7.23; 9.58; 15.8; Ammianus Marcellius 22.15.8; Lucius Ampelius, *Liber memorialis* 38.1.4; Avienus, *Ora maritima* 275–83; Galen 13.271 (Kühn); Harpokration, "Parrhasios," "Polygnotos"; Philostratos, *Life of Apollonios* 2.13, 16; Photios 161.103a, 104b; Quintilian 6.3.90; Tatian, *Oration to the Greeks* 36.

12 *FHG* 3.465–84.

13 In particular, Wenceslaus Plagge, *De Juba II rege Mauretaniae* (Münster, F. Regensburg, 1849); and L. Keller, *De Juba Appiani Cassiique Dionis auctore* (Marburg: N. G. Elwert, 1872).

14 Hermann Peter, *Ueber den Werth der historichen Schriftstellerei von König Juba II von Mauretanien* (*Jahresbericht über die Fürsten- und Landesschule Meissen* 1878–9, pp. 1–14).

15 Maria-Renatus de la Blanchère, *De rege Juba regis Jubae filio* (Paris: E. Thorin, 1883).

16 E. H. Bunbury, *A History of Ancient Geography* (second edition, London: John Murray, 1883), vol. 2, pp. 174–6.

17 Leveau, *Caesarea*, pp. 1–3.

18 Jodin, *Volubilis*, pp. 10–12.

19 *RE* 9, 1916, 2384–95.

author. Jacoby's work on the fragments,[20] which appeared in 1940, increased Müller's ninety-one to a more reliable 104, eliminating some of the questionable ones, but still limited itself only to citations in which the name "Juba" occurs. The culmination of the French colonial impact on scholarship was Stéphane Gsell's massive *Histoire ancienne de l'Afrique du Nord*, completed in 1928, an exhaustive study in eight volumes that devoted more attention than ever before to Juba, his world, and his ancestors.[21] Although excruciatingly thorough and a necessary reference for any scholar of ancient North Africa, the work is not deeply imaginative and suffers from an inevitable colonialist perspective.[22]

There was little new work on Juba in the years immediately after the Second World War; if he was remembered at all, it was as the son-in-law of Antonius and Kleopatra VII.[23] In recent years, however, a growing awareness of the role of client kingship in the early Empire and evolving postcolonialist views[24] of the fringes of the Roman world have led scholars to the career of Juba II.[25] Yet as recently as 1998 the present author could bemoan the fact that "there is no good recent study of Juba,"[26] and because of a historically lesser interest in the careers of women than those of men, the life of Kleopatra Selene even today remains frustratingly vague.

Transliteration and chronological issues

Transliteration is a vexing problem, especially in the world of Greek, Roman, and indigenous cultures that was the Roman Empire. It becomes difficult to impose a consistency that was itself lacking in antiquity.

20 *FGrHist* #275. It is Jacoby's fragment numbering that is used throughout the present work.

21 See the review of vols. 7–8 (the period after the fall of Carthage) by Jérôme Carcapino, "L'Afrique au dernier siècle de la république romaine," *RHist* 162, 1929, 86–95.

22 On the problems of colonialist interpretations of the history of this region and the attempts to move beyond them, see David J. Mattingly, "From One Colonialism to Another: Imperialism and the Maghreb," in *Roman Imperialism: Post-colonial Perspectives*, ed. Jane Webster and Nicolas J. Cooper, Leicester Archaeological Monographs 3, 1996, pp. 49–69.

23 See, for example, Ronald Syme, *The Roman Revolution*, paperback edition (Oxford: Oxford University Press, 1960), pp. 300, 365–6, which, although written before the Second World War, reflects the attitudes in place in the immediate postwar years.

24 A good recent study of the issues of romanization in the postcolonial context of modern scholarship is Greg Woolf, "Beyond Romans and Natives," *WA* 28, 1996–7, 339–50; see also Jane Webster, "Creolizing the Roman Provinces," *AJA* 105, 2001, 209–25.

25 For example, the work of David Braund, especially his *Rome and the Friendly King*.

26 Roller, *Herod*, p. 252. Michèle Coltelloni-Trannoy's *Le Royaume de Maurétanie sous Juba II et Ptolémée* (Paris: CNRS, 1997), while a significant addition to Juban studies and the most complete treatment since that of Gsell, is narrowly focused on the king within his kingdom, paying no attention to his impact as scholar and explorer. On other limitations (which do not diminish its value), see the review by Brent D. Shaw, *Gnomon* 72, 2000, 422–5. See also the recent examination of Juba's kingdom by Ramsay MacMullen, *Romanization in the Time of Augustus* (New Haven, Conn.: Yale University Press, 2000), pp. 42–4, which, although brief, is an incisive and precise summary.

Dependency on extant sources means that the actual form of the personal name used by its owner may be unfamiliar or even unknown. Nonetheless, proper names are generally transliterated directly from Greek or Latin into English except for a few that have common English forms (e.g. Athens, Egypt). "Ptolemy" is used for the geographer but the more accurate "Ptolemaios" for royal personages, and "Alexander" for Alexander the Great but "Alexandros" for all others. The names of the indigenous royalty of North Africa have been presented in their Greek or Latin forms, since often they are known only through classical sources.

Juba's reign began in the second half of the year,[27] so his dated coins refer to a regnal year that, roughly, runs from autumn to autumn: e.g. Year 1 is from autumn 25 to autumn 24 BC and Juba's death in regnal Year 48 occurred between autumn AD 23 and autumn AD 24. For convenience, only the calendar year in effect at the beginning of the regnal year is used herein.

27 Infra, p. 100.

1

JUBA'S NUMIDIAN ANCESTRY

Juba II was descended from a long line of distinguished ancestors who had been involved in Roman politics for nearly two hundred years prior to his accession to the throne of Mauretania. The family tree can be constructed for at least seven generations before Juba,[1] starting with the tribal chieftain Zilalsan, born perhaps around 300 BC.[2] The family was famous and talented, producing a variety of scholars and political and cultural leaders, attached first to Carthaginian interests and then to Roman, with an increasing amount of Hellenism. This impressive ancestry was certainly a factor in Caesar's decision to save young Juba, and that of Augustus to make him king of Mauretania.

Juba's ancestors were kings of Numidia, the territory south and west of Carthage. Originally nomadic herdsmen, by the fourth century BC they became identifiable as a number of tribal groups, which seem to have begun to coalesce into a single ethnic unit late in the following century.[3] This process was said to have been largely due to the efforts of Massinissa, the first of the Numidian kings to appear prominently in the historical record. His grandfather Zilalsan (the first member of the dynasty whose name is known with certainty) held the title of suffete, indicating the Carthaginian

---

1 One may contrast the Herodians, who cannot be traced beyond the great-grandfather of Herod the Great: see Kokkinos, *Herodian Dynasty*, p. 109.

2 See Appendix 2. Nevertheless, Juba was the upstart within his immediate family. His wife Kleopatra Selene, and thus their children, could trace their ancestry back to Lagos, the father of the first Ptolemaios, born perhaps around 400 BC, and even further through the Antonii into the fifth century BC.

3 Maria R.-Alföldi, "Die Geschichte des numidisichen Königreiches und seiner Nachfolger," in *Numider*, pp. 43–51. On the early history, see Elizabeth W. B. Fentress, *Numidia and the Roman Army: Social, Military and Economic Aspects of the Frontier Zone*, BAR-IS 53, 1979, pp. 43–60; François Decret and Mhamed Fantar, *L'Afrique du Nord dans l'antiquité* (Paris: Payot, 1981), pp. 1–67; and Robert Morstein-Marx, "The Myth of Numidian Origins in Sallust's African Excursus (*Iugurtha* 17.7–18.13)," *AJP* 122, 2001, 179–200.

influence existing by the early third century BC.[4] His son, Gaia or Gala, was the first to carry the title "king," but presumably was king only of his tribal group, the Maesyli.[5] Gaia came to Roman notice during the Second Punic War because he opposed another Numidian chieftain, Syphax, who had revolted from the Carthaginians and sided with Rome, a crucial event of the latter years of the war.[6] For the first time, the Romans began to incorporate the Numidian tribes into their strategic designs against Carthage. Gaia's son Massinissa, who turned 20 the year the war began, fought at the side of his father for Carthage and against Syphax and Rome.

Gaia died in Spain near the end of the war,[7] but Massinissa did not inherit the kingship because custom caused it to revert to his uncle Oezalces, brother-in-law of the famous Hannibal. Oezalces died shortly thereafter and was succeeded by his son Capussa, who was promptly killed by a relative, Mazaetullus, who had married Oezalces' widow and thus had acquired the status appropriate for the brother-in-law of Hannibal. This Numidian civil war now involved three tribal groups, those of Syphax, the brothers Gaia and Oezalces, and Mazaetullus. Moreover, Roman and Carthaginian interests were already polarizing in their support of these families. The way was clear for the rise of Massinissa.

Massinissa was the most famous and notable of the ancestors of Juba II, his great-great-great-grandfather.[8] During his long reign, which extended from the Second Punic War into the Third, he prospered despite being caught between Rome and Carthage, eventually siding with the former and playing a decisive role in the destruction of the latter. Learned and erudite, he presided over a court that attracted both Greeks and Romans, and thus became one of the best early examples of the king allied to Rome and an ideal role model for his descendant.

4 On the predecessors of Massinissa, see J.-B. Chabot, *Recueil des inscriptions libyques* (Paris: Imprimerie Nationale, 1940), #2, a bilingual (Libyan and Punic) inscription from Thugga recording the erection of a temple to Massinissa in the tenth year of his son Micipsa (139 BC); Fentress (supra note 3), pp. 50–2; Coltelloni-Trannoy, p. 107; Gabriel Camps, *Massinissa* (*LibAE* 8.1, 1960), pp. 159–83; P. G. Walsh, "Massinissa," *JRS* 55, 1965, 150. Zilalsan may have been a descendant – perhaps grandson – of Ailymas, "king of Libya," an ally of Agathokles of Syracuse (Diodoros 20.17–18). See Gabriel Camps, "Origines du royaume massyle," *RHCM* 3, July 1967, 32–3.

5 The name is Gala in Greco-Roman sources, but the Thugga inscription (Chabot, supra note 4) has GII, indicating that "Gaia" may be a better transliteration. See also F. Stähelin, "Gaia" (#4), *RE Supp.* 3, 1918, 534–8; Gsell, vol. 3, pp. 177–83. Livy (27.19.9) called him "rex Numidarum," but this seems anachronistic.

6 John Briscoe, "The Second Punic War," *CAH*² 8, 1989, 57–9. The wide and complex issues of the Second Punic War are not the primary concern here. On this, see, most recently, B. D. Hoyos, *Unplanned Wars: The Origins of the First and Second Punic Wars*, Untersuchungen zur antiken Literatur und Geschichte 50 (Berlin 1998).

7 Livy 29.29.6; Gsell, vol. 3, p. 189.

8 The ancient sources are primarily Polybios 14, Livy 25–42, and Appian, *Libyka*. For modern sources, see Camps, *LibAE* (supra note 4); Walsh (supra note 4), pp. 149–60; W. Schur, "Massinissa," *RE* 14, 1930, 2154–65; Gsell, vol. 3, pp. 189–364 (*passim*); R.-Alföldi (supra note 3), pp. 51–7, and the recent study by Elfrieda Storm, *Massinissa: Numidien in Aufbruch* (Stuttgart: Franz Steiner, 2001).

Figure 1 The Numidian marble quarries at Chemtou (Tunisia).

Photograph by Duane W. Roller.

The career of Massinissa was lengthy and complex. He was educated at Carthage and became a protégé of the great Carthaginian leader Hasdrubal.[9] His youth and early maturity coincided with the Second Punic War and the internal power struggles within Numidia. He first fought for Carthage, his operations ranging far west to Tingis, disrupting the supplies from Syphax to the Romans, and eventually crossing to Spain and opposing the Scipio brothers: it was his cavalry that killed P. Cornelius Scipio the elder in 211 BC.[10] But a few years later, when the fortunes of war began to turn in favor of Rome, Massinissa realized that Rome might be of use to him in asserting his position within Numidia. He sought out M. Junius Silanus, one of the Roman commanders[11] – the details of the interview were not preserved by Livy but apparently the result was that he joined the Roman side – and then returned to Africa in order to bolster support among his countrymen for his change of allegiance. This was a wise move, since both Syphax

9 Appian, *Libyka* 10, 37.

10 Livy 24.49, 4–6; 25.34; Briscoe (supra note 6), pp. 56–61.

11 Livy 28.16.11–13. He was propraetor in Spain in 210–206 BC (Broughton, vol. 2, p. 577; F. Münzer, "M. Iunius Silanus" (#167), *RE* 10, 1917, 1092–3. This family may have been traditionally sympathetic toward the indigenous populations of North Africa, since sixty-five years later one Decimus [Junius] Silanus was considered the outstanding contemporary scholar of the Punic language and was given the task of translating Mago's treatise on agriculture (*NH* 18.22–3). He is otherwise unknown (Broughton, vol. 2, p. 577), unless he is mentioned by Cicero, *De finibus* 1.24; see also F. Münzer, "D. (Iunius) Silanus" (#160), *RE* 10, 1917, 1088–9.

and Mazaetullus had reverted to the Carthaginians.[12] With Carthage and most of Numidia against him, Massinissa's prospects were not good, and although initially successful he was eventually wounded and had to hide out in the mountains and await the Romans. Eventually, in 204 BC, the Romans under P. Cornelius Scipio Africanus landed in Africa and soon engaged the Carthaginians. Massinissa's cavalry was decisive in the battle and he was said to have personally captured Syphax.[13] He also eliminated the other claimant to Numidian power, Mazaetullus, so his victory over his countrymen was complete.[14] Thus with Roman support Massinissa was able to claim the kingship of Numidia. Scipio formally addressed him as king and gave him insignia of office, telling him that he was the foreigner most respected by Rome;[15] the Senate confirmed the title and gave him additional honors and gifts.[16]

It is probable that few foreigners had ever been so well treated by Rome. Massinissa was to rule as king of Numidia for the next fifty-five years, skill-fully balancing his interests, precarious because he was geographically adjacent to Carthage but a client of Rome. He became famous for exploiting the agricultural bounty of his kingdom,[17] which led to exports to Rome and the Greek world. He was probably the first Numidian to hellenize his court,[18] which became a center of culture: among the visitors were the historian

---

12 Livy 29.23–32; see also Appian, *Iberika* 37; L. A. Thompson, "Carthage and the Massylian *Coup d'État* of 206 BC," *Historia* 30, 1981, 120–6. Massinissa also solicited aid from Baga, king of the Mauri: this is the earliest reference (in terms of context) to Mauretania in Roman literature. On Baga, see infra, p. 46.

13 Livy 29.34; Polybios 14.3–8; Appian, *Libyka* 26. Syphax was sent into exile in Italy, and died two years later at Tibur or Alba, receiving a state funeral (Livy 30.45.4–5; Zonaras 9.23 [from Dio 17]). His son Vermina, who had been in Italy with his father, seems to have been restored to his father's territory and thus ruled on terms agreeable to Rome as petty king over a small district, but nothing is known about him after the Second Punic War and it is probable that he did not survive long (Livy 31.19.4–6; Zonaras 9.13 [from Dio 17]; Mazard #13–16).

14 Livy 29.30.10–13. The personal combat between Massinissa and Hannibal recorded by Zonaras (9.14, from Dio 17) is probably apocryphal.

15 Livy 30.15.9–14. He seems to have begun his regnal years sometime in 205 BC: see Werner Huss, "Die Datierung nach numidischen Königsjahren," *AntAfr* 26, 1990, 39–42. On some of the problems with the veracity of Scipio's addressing Massinissa as king, see E. Badian, *Foreign Clientelae (264–70 B.C.)* (Oxford: Clarendon Press, 1958), pp. 125–6, 295.

16 Livy 30.17.7–14; Appian, *Libyka* 32. On this as one of the first instances of the Roman process for recognition of the client king, of which Massinissa was an outstanding early example, see Braund, *Friendly King*, p. 24; see also Erich S. Gruen, *The Hellenistic World and the Coming of Rome*, first paperback printing (Berkeley: University of California Press, 1986), pp. 159–64, for some of the difficulties with this view.

17 *IDélos* 442a, line 101; Polybios 36.16; Appian, *Libyka* 106; Strabo 17.3.15; Jehan Desanges, "L'Afrique romaine et libyco-berbère," in *Rome et la conquête du monde méditerranéen, 264–27 avant J.-C.*, ed. Claude Nicolet, *Nouvelle Clio* 8bis (Paris: Presses Universitaires de France, 1978), pp. 651–2; Walsh (supra note 4), pp. 152–6 (who diminished the extent of the Numidian agricultural wealth).

Polybios and King Ptolemaios VIII, who was impressed with its Greco-Roman character.[19] Massinissa's coinage shows Greek qualities in the bearded bust of the king, with royal diadem, and includes the elephant, an early numismatic representation of this ubiquitous symbol of North African royalty.[20] It was perhaps also Massinissa who began to exploit the Numidian marble that was soon to be exported to Rome,[21] and to build in Hellenistic fashion, especially the monumental funerary architecture still conspicuous today.[22] He involved himself in the politics of the eastern Mediterranean, assisting Rome in the Makedonian Wars, and eventually sending his son Misagetes with a substantial force and supplies to Greece.[23] Later he shipped grain to Delos and was honored by that island,[24] and was on friendly terms with eastern royalty, especially Nikomedes II of Bithynia.[25] His sons were sent to Greece, probably Athens, to be educated.[26]

Meanwhile, in order to insure his own survival at home, he initiated a

---

18 Coltelloni-Trannoy, p. 143.

19 Polybios 9.25; Ptolemaios VIII (*FGrHist* #234) fr. 7–8. The contacts between Ptolemaios VIII and Massinissa are discussed by Tadeusz Kotula, "Orientalia Africana. Réflexions sur les contacts Afrique du Nord romaine – Orient hellénistique," *FolOr* 24, 1987, 120–1.

20 Mazard #17; Hans R. Baldus, "Die Münzprägung der Numidischen Königreiche," in *Numider*, pp. 191–4.

21 The marble, yellow with red veins and known today as *giallo antico*, came from the vicinity of Simitthu (modern Chemtou) in the upper Bagradas (modern Mejerda) valley, in what is now northwestern Tunisia, where quarries and workshops are still visible in an impressive setting (Figure 1, p. 12). See Heinz Günter Horn, "Die antiken Steinbrüche von Chemtou/Simitthus," in *Numider*, pp. 173–80; Mustapha Khanoussi, "Les *officiales marmorum numidicorum*," *AfrRom* 12, 1998, 997–8. It was first exported to Egypt and Greece and then to Rome, one of the earliest foreign stones to arrive in the city, where it was used in the Temple of Concord and Forum of Augustus, among other structures. See *NH* 36.49; Hazel Dodge, "Decorative Stones for Architecture in the Roman Empire," *OJA* 7, 1988, 66; *Marble in Antiquity: Collected Papers of J. B. Ward-Perkins*, Archaeological Monographs of the British School at Rome 6, ed. Hazel Dodge and Bryan Ward-Perkins (1992), pp. 15, 24, 116, 157.

22 Infra, p. 130.

23 Livy 36.4.5–8, 42.29.8–9, 43.6.11–14, 45.13.12–17. On the problems and paradoxes this created, see Braund, *Friendly King*, p. 184.

24 *IG* 11.4.1115 (=*SIG*⁴ 652), 1116; *IDélos* 442A, 100–6; 1577ᵇⁱˢ. The Delians may have commissioned the noted local sculptor Polianthes to erect a statue of the king. On the grain shipments, perhaps an attempt to create an eastern market due to the decline of those in Italy, see Lionel Casson, *Ancient Trade and Society* (Detroit: Wayne State University Press, 1984), pp. 76–7; Philippe Gauthier, "Sur le don de grain numide à Délos: un pseudo-Rhodien dans les comptes de hiéropes," in *Comptes et inventaires dans la cité grecque: Actes du colloque international d'épigraphie tenu à Neuchâtel du 23 au 26 septembre 1986 en l'honneur de Jacques Tréheux*, ed. Denis Knoepfler (Neuchâtel: Faculté des Lettres, Université de Neuchâtel, 1986), pp. 61–9. A delegation to Delos in the 170s BC may have been led by Massinissa's son Gulussa: see Marie-Françoise Baslez, "Un Monument de la famille royale de Numidie à Délos," *RÉG* 94, 1981, 160–5.

25 *IDélos* 1577; Arnaldo Momigliano, "I regni indigeni dell'Africa Romana (1)," in *Africa Romana* (Milan: Hoepli, 1935), pp. 94–5.

26 Livy, *Epitome* 50; *IG* 2².2316.41–4.

series of territorial disputes with Carthage.[27] A continuing series of con-
frontations ensued, warily watched by Rome, that lasted until the outbreak
of the Third Punic War.[28] In 151 BC the Carthaginians invaded Numidia (a
violation of the terms of the end of the Second Punic War), and Massinissa,
who was now 87, decisively defeated them, leading his forces personally on
horseback.[29] This Carthaginian incursion gave Rome the pretext for war,
something probably already decided, but the Roman government was
ambivalent about what role the elderly monarch should play. Eventually, in
148 BC, it was decided that he could be of use to Rome, but the envoys
found him dead at the age of 90.[30]

When his great-great-great-grandson Juba II arrived in Rome a century
later, Massinissa's legend was well established.[31] Contemporary Romans
were fascinated with the tale of the witty and cultured barbarian king, who
had lived so long and fathered the last of his forty-four sons at 86, and was
noted for such ability and strength in extreme old age.[32] He had been so
impressed with Rome that he became its greatest friend, evolving, in the
best barbarian tradition, from hostility to alliance.[33] Particularly romantic,
although doubtless elaborated, was the story of his relationship with
Sophoniba, the elegant daughter of his mentor Hasdrubal. Sophoniba was

27 Livy 34.61.16, 42.23; Appian, *Libyka* 67–70. For the legality of Massinissa's actions, see Polybios
15.18.5. See further, Romanelli, *Storia*, pp. 22–42; Ritter, *Rom*, pp. 61–79; W. V. Harris, "Roman
Expansion in the West," *CAH²* 8, 1989, 144–6. Rome may have hoped that Massinissa and
Carthage would weaken each other (I. M. Barton, *Africa in the Roman Empire* [Accra: Ghana Universities Press, 1972], pp. 16–17), or even have feared that Numidia would conquer Carthage if Rome
did not act (F. E. Adcock, "Delenda est Carthago," *CHJ* 8.3, 1946, 118–19).

28 The extent to which Massinissa was the catalyst in Rome's decision to make another war against
Carthage has long been debated, and it is probably best to assume that the Roman concern about
Massinissa's activities was merely one of many contributing factors. See Walsh (supra note 4); Harris
(supra note 27), pp. 149–57; Gruen (supra note 16), pp. 130–1. But the king, because he retained
Carthaginian contacts, became an important source about internal Carthaginian affairs for the
Romans (Livy 41.22.1).

29 Polybios 36.16; Livy, *Epitome* 48; Appian, *Libyka* 70–2.

30 Appian, *Libyka* 105–6; also Polybios 36.16; Livy, *Epitome* 48 (which recorded that the king lived to
92); Valerius Maximus 5.2.Ext4; see also *OxyPap* 4, 1904, p. 668, lines 118–22. On Massinissa's last
days, see F. W. Walbank, *A Historical Commentary on Polybius* (Oxford: Clarendon Press, 1957–79),
vol. 3, pp. 675–8; G. M. Paul, *A Historical Commentary on Sallust's "Bellum Jugurthinum"* [Liverpool
1984] pp. 26–8.

31 See Diodoros 32.16, which, although adapted from Polybios 36.16, recorded the attitude toward the
king in Juba's Rome. Another contemporary portrait is that of Cicero (*Republic* 6.9), who described
the great desire of P. Cornelius Scipio Aemilianus to meet him: "nothing was more important to me
than to meet Massinissa, who was most friendly with our family, for justifiable reasons. When I
came to him, the old man embraced me and wept before me." ("nihil mihi fuit potius, quam ut
Masinissam convenirem regem, familiae nostrae iustis de causis amicissimum. Ad quem ut veni,
conplexus me senex conlacrimavit"). It was after his inspiring conversation with Massinissa that
Scipio had his famous dream. Livy was equally eulogistic: see, for example, 37.53.20–2.

32 An example of his wit was preserved by Ptolemaios VIII in his *Hypomnemata* (*FGrHist* #234, fr.
8 = Athenaios 12.518–19). The citation of 44 sons is from Livy, *Epitome* 50, but the text is unclear.

33 Livy 28.35.8–11, 31.11, 37.53.21–2; see also, somewhat later, Silius Italicus 16.115–17.

the wife of his enemy Syphax, but Massinissa became enamored with her and sent her poison so that she would not be captured alive by the Romans – an episode as much from tragedy as history.[34] Massinissa was a role model for Juba to adopt: the ancestor who embodied all the best qualities of barbarian integrity, Greco-Roman culture, and political astuteness, strongly attached to a particular Roman family, turning from enemy to friend, spending his life balancing the needs of his territory with those of Rome.[35]

Upon his death, Massinissa left his kingdom to three of his sons and made P. Cornelius Scipio Aemilianus the executor of his will,[36] one of the earliest known cases of a royal inheritance involving Rome.[37] Scipio had met the king's heirs and was the adopted grandson of his patron Scipio Africanus. The will, whether oral or written, was executed in perilous times, during the middle of the Third Punic War, in the context of long-standing Carthaginian–Numidian animosity, when the Carthaginians might have been expected to meddle in the succession. Scipio, well known in Numidia and prestigious in Rome, was an obvious choice to supervise this touchy issue. How much the eventual settlement was the work of Scipio and how much was the testament of Massinissa is not certain: Appian, the primary source, is ambiguous, stating only that the sons were to obey (πείθεσθαι) Scipio.[38]

34 The main source is Livy 30.12–15; see also Appian, *Libyka* 10, 27–8; Diodoros 27.7; Zonaras 9.11–13 (from Dio 17); U. Kahrstedt, "Sophoniba," *RE* 2, ser. 3, 1927, 1099–100; T. A. Dorey, "Masinissa, Syphax, and Sophoniba," *PACA* 4, 1961, 1–2; R.-Alföldi (supra note 3), pp. 48–50. On whether Juba discussed this tale, see infra, p. 181. Certain of the elements – especially in Appian's version – seem the details of a tragedy: the encounter between Massinissa and Sophoniba when he brings the poison and tells her either to drink it or be captured, Sophoniba's speech to the nurse before she takes the poison, Massinissa's showing of the body to the Romans, Scipio's final speech to Massinissa, the ironies of a possible former relationship between Massinissa and Sophoniba, and Syphax's subsequent death. The tale also became common in art: see German Hafner, "Das Bildnis des Massinissa," *AA* 1970, pp. 418–20; Karl Schefold, *Die Wände Pompejis* (Berlin: De Gruyter, 1957), pp. 46, 219; G. Bermond Montanari, "Sofonisba," *EAA* 7, 1966, 398–90, figure 489 (a painting from Pompeii showing her taking the poison); *Numider*, pl. 56.

35 Strabo (17.3.9) specifically connected Massinissa and Juba, probably influenced in this comparison by Juba himself, who was acutely aware of his descent from the great king (*CIL* 2.3417 [=*ILS* 840]).

36 Appian, *Libyka* 105–7; Zonaras 9.27 (from Dio 21). Scipio had met Massinissa either in 151 BC when on an elephant-gathering expedition (Appian, *Libyka* 71), or perhaps two years later (Cicero, *Republic* 6.9), and thus was acquainted with his sons, who were to be the heirs.

37 It had been only seven years since the earliest, that of Massinissa's associate Ptolemaios VIII of Egypt, written in 155 BC when he was king of Kyrene (*SEG* 9.7). Although this will was never implemented, because the circumstances under which it was written were no longer in force when the king died nearly forty years later, Ptolemaios may have suggested to Massinissa that Roman supervision of his inheritance was a good idea. See infra, Appendix 3; Braund, *Friendly King*, pp. 129–30. Whether Massinissa had a written will, or just made an oral statement of intent, is not clear.

38 Braund, *Friendly King*, pp. 138–9; Charles Saumagne, *La Numidie et Rome: Massinissa et Jugurtha* (Paris 1966), pp. 100–4; see further, Badian (supra note 15), pp. 137–8. Yet emphasis on the legalities of succession can be futile, as often the rules are of no importance; this was to be demonstrated only a generation later with Jugurtha. For the whole issue of succession to ruling power, see the volume *Succession to High Office*, ed. Jack Goody, Cambridge Papers in Social Anthropology 4, 1966, especially pp. 1–56.

Scipio's decision – whether or not suggested by Massinissa – was to create a regal triumvirate of Massinissa's three oldest sons, Micipsa, Gulussa, and Mastanabal.[39] Yet this three-way rule did not last long, for Gulussa and Mastanabal promptly vanish from the historical record, probably dying soon after their father. Mastanabal is worthy of further note because he was the great-great-grandfather of Juba II, but little is known about him other than that he was educated in Greece and victorious in the Panathenaia in 158 BC.[40] Even his status as the father of the famous Jugurtha[41] did not lead to much comment about his career, and he probably died before his son reached maturity.

Nevertheless, it would be nearly thirty years after Massinissa's death before the Numidian royal line reverted to a direct ancestor of Juba: Micipsa's brothers seem to have left him sole ruler by no later than 139 BC.[42] He survived for another twenty years in control of a territory whose political realities had changed substantially from his father's day. Carthage was no longer an independent state, and, for the time being, no longer a great city, having been burned and destroyed in an event that was compared to the Sack of Troy. Scipio Aemilianus is said to have wept at the destruction and to have told Polybios that Rome would eventually meet the same fate.[43] The Carthaginian territory became the new Roman province of Africa, although the Numidian kings also acquired a substantial portion of it.[44] The material culture of Carthage was dispersed if not destroyed: of particular note was the state library, which was given to Micipsa and his brothers.[45] Carthage being unfit for human habitation, a Roman praetor took up residence at Utica, which had supported Rome in the last stages of the war and was to become the center of romanization in the region.[46]

Little is known about the thirty years of Micipsa's kingship. The oldest surviving son of Massinissa, he adopted his 4-year-old brother Sthembanon, and, it seems, the sons of Gulussa and Mastanabal, including Jugurtha.[47] He

---

39 On the reasons for Scipio's decision, and its possible basis in Greek political theory, see Hervé Trofimoff, "Une préfiguration de la séparation des pouvoirs: le testament de Masinissa," *RIDA* 3rd ser. 35, 1988, 364–84.

40 Diodoros 34/35.35; Livy, *Epitome* 50; *IG* 2^2.2316.41–4. See Stephen V. Tracy and Christian Habicht, "New and Old Panathenaic Victor Lists," *Hesperia* 60, 1991, 232. His father may have commemorated this victory (or another) by commissioning at Kyrene the famous bronze "Berber Head" now in the British Museum (BM Bronze 268): see Duane W. Roller, "A Note on the Berber Head in London," *JHS* 122, 2002, 144–6.

41 Sallust, *Jugurtha* 5.

42 Sallust, *Jugurtha* 5; Chabot (supra note 4) #2; on Micipsa, see F. Schur, "Micipsa," *RE* 15, 1932, 1522–4.

43 Appian, *Libyka* 127–32, supplemented by Diodoros 32.24, probably both from Polybios 38. See also Walbank (supra note 30), vol. 3, pp. 722–5.

44 Romanelli, *Storia*, pp. 43–5.

45 *NH* 18.22–3.

46 Polybios 36.3; Appian, *Libyka* 75.

47 Zonaras 9.27 (from Dio 21); Polybios 36.16; Sallust, *Jugurtha* 5.

further developed his father's capital of Cirta, settling a number of Greeks there[48] and making it a cosmopolitan center that had enough manpower to produce 10,000 cavalry and 20,000 infantry.[49] He may also have begun to favor Iol as a royal city.[50] His Greek education, the Greek settlement at Cirta, and his inheritance of the Carthaginian library (his brothers' portions would have come to him) continued his father's Hellenism, and indeed it was said that he was the most cultured of the Numidian kings and brought many Greeks to his court, becoming a student of philosophy.[51] Hellenistic-style mausolea continued to be built throughout the territory, a further commitment to Greek culture.[52] Micipsa also sponsored the building of a temple to his father in 139 BC at Thugga.[53] He had served his father both diplomatically and militarily during the Third Punic War,[54] and further refined these skills in thirty years of serving Roman interests and protecting his own. He followed the tradition of his father in supplying elephants and horses to Rome, especially to commanders in Spain.[55] When he was supporting the Romans in the Numantine War, which was being prosecuted by his patron Scipio Aemilianus, he seems to have acquired the friendship of Scipio's young relative C. Sempronius Gracchus, and in 126 BC, when Gracchus was quaestor on Sardinia, Micipsa sent a shipment of grain to the island and envoys to Rome announcing his gift. Gracchus, however, was already demonstrating the populism that would soon result in his death, and the envoys were rebuffed by the Senate, a cautionary episode for client kings who might seem to be meddling in Roman internal politics.[56] Regardless of the disposition of the grain, the shipment demonstrates that Micipsa further exploited and developed the wealth and prosperity of the kingdom he had inherited, helped, of course, by his acquisition of substantial amounts of

48 Strabo 17.3.13. There is no explicit evidence as to where these Greeks came from. There would have been a Greek population in Carthage – it had a Pythagorean school in its last years that seems to have had a Greek clientele (Iamblichos 128, 267) – and Greeks were also displaced by the destruction of Corinth in 146 BC. Moreover, the philosopher Kleitomachos, who became head of the Academy in Athens in the 120s BC, was Carthaginian. Originally named Hasdrubal, he went to Athens in the 160s BC to study with Karneades (Diogenes Laertios 4.67). Such an interest presumes the availability of Greek learning at Carthage. Within thirty years Cirta also had an Italian population, probably mercantile (Sallust, *Jugurtha* 21, 26). On Greek culture at Carthage, see Walter Thieling, *Der Hellenismus in Kleinafrika* (Leipzig: Teubner, 1911), pp. 152–3.

49 Appian, *Libyka* 106; Strabo 17.3.13.

50 Leveau, *Caesarea*, p. 11.

51 Diodoros 34/35.35.

52 Friedrich Rakob, "Architecture royale numide," CÉFR 66, 1983, 335–6. These may include Micipsa's own tomb but the evidence is so ambivalent as to make certainty impossible: see J.-G. Février, "L'Inscription funéraire de Micipsa," *RAssyr* 45, 1951, 139–50.

53 Chabot (supra note 4) #2.

54 Appian, *Libyka* 70, 111.

55 Appian, *Iberika* 67; Sallust, *Jugurtha* 7.

56 Plutarch, *C. Gracchus* 2.3; Badian (supra note 15), 181. It may have been Gracchus' association with Micipsa and thus his interest in African matters that led to his abortive attempt to refound Carthage (Appian, *Libyka* 136; *Civil War* 1.24; Plutarch, *C. Gracchus* 11; see Desanges [supra note 17], p. 630).

Carthaginian territory. Nothing further is known about him until his death, which occurred in 118 BC.[57] He too adopted the triumviral method of inheritance, leaving the kingdom to his two sons, Adherbal and Hiempsal (I), and, unfortunately for them, to his nephew and adopted son Jugurtha.

The career of Jugurtha and the Roman war against him are well known. The sharply focused character study by C. Sallustius Crispus, written perhaps seventy years after Jugurtha's death, not only hastened the loss of the more traditional historical analyses by Livy, Dio, and Appian,[58] but created a portrait of Jugurtha formed by Sallust's own era, the collapse of the Republic, when he had served in Africa as Caesar's appointee. Sallust made his emphasis clear in the early chapters of his *Jugurtha*, outlining what was perhaps his primary reason for writing: "This conflict totally mixed up human and divine matters and advanced to such a frenzy that political intensity resulted in war and the desolation of Italy."[59] This chaos and destruction was a world Sallust knew well, as he was one of the players: a protégé of Caesar who was constantly in ethical and legal troubles, especially as a result of his actions as the first Roman governor of the provincialized former Numidian kingdom. He was eventually prosecuted and forced into retirement, leading him to seek (as he himself wrote) the higher goal of becoming a historian,[60] his researches being aided by the former Carthaginian state library, which had passed from the Numidian kings into his hands. Yet the result was a peculiar depiction of Jugurtha less as a Numidian nationalist than as an instigator of the fall of the Republic.[61]

Because of Sallust, the career of Jugurtha is known in great detail.[62] Sallust emphasized his physical and intellectual prowess as a young man, which first impressed his uncle Micipsa but eventually led him to worry

---

57 Livy, *Epitome* 62.

58 Polybios, if he dealt with Jugurtha at all, would have been familiar only with his youth and perhaps his accession in 118 BC, which is the year of the last datable event in his writings. See F. W. Walbank, *Polybius*, first paperback printing (Berkeley: University of California Press, 1990), pp. 12–13.

59 Sallust, *Jugurtha* 5: "Quae contentio divina et humana cuncta permiscuit eoque vecordiae processit, ut studiis civilibus bellum atque vastitas Italiae finem faceret."

60 Sallust, *Catiline* 4; *Jugurtha* 4; on Sallust's career, see Ronald Syme, *Sallust* (Berkeley: University of California Press, 1964), pp. 29–42.

61 On Jugurtha's effect on Roman internal politics, see Badian (supra note 15), pp. 192–4, and Andrew Lintott, "Political History, 145–96 BC," *CAH²* 9, 1994, 88–95.

62 The scant other sources are Plutarch's biographies of Marius and Sulla; Livy, *Epitome* 62–7; Velleius 2.11, and the brief extant fragments of Appian's *Noumidika*. A recent summary is Andrew Lintott, "The Roman Empire and Its Problems in the Late Second Century," *CAH²* 9, 1994, 27–31; see also Fentress (supra note 3), pp. 61–4, and Syme (supra note 60), pp. 138–56 (on the strategy of the war); Romanelli, *Storia*, pp. 72–88; Ritter, *Rom*, pp. 91–119; Saumagne (supra note 38), pp. 183–235; Domenico Siciliani, "La guerra giugurtina," *Africa Romana* (Milan: Hoepli, 1935), pp. 51–82; Gsell, vol. 7, pp. 123–265; Paul (supra note 30); Th. Lenschau, "Iugurtha," *RE* 10, 1917, 1–6; R.-Alföldi (supra note 3), pp. 59–63.

about his ambition and potential as a rival.[63] Micipsa thus decided to place Jugurtha in command of a Numidian contingent sent to aid the Romans in the Numantine War, allegedly hoping that he would be killed. But he had underestimated his nephew, who caught the notice of the family patron, Scipio Aemilianus, who made him part of his entourage. Scipio educated Jugurtha in Roman ways and customs, and after the war sent him home with a most enthusiastic letter of recommendation. This evidently encouraged Micipsa – his worries seemingly forgotten – to adopt him as joint heir with his own sons Adherbal and Hiempsal (I) and to leave an oral testament in which Jugurtha was put forth as the primary heir, not only because of his ability but because he was older than Micipsa's sons, who were enjoined to defer to Jugurtha's superior wisdom and virtue.[64]

This arrangement was an obvious prescription for disaster, and it is interesting that there is no evidence of Roman supervision of the will.[65] Micipsa was allegedly out of his mind when he died in 118 BC, and the two Romans most acquainted with the family, Scipio Aemilianus and C. Gracchus, were already dead; the civil strife that had led to their deaths may have discouraged the Numidians from involving Rome in the succession. There appears to have been enduring animosity among the three heirs. Jugurtha was sensitive about the low status of his mother, and felt that his grandfather had slighted him because of this. The sons of Micipsa lost no opportunity to point this out. Because Jugurtha was the oldest, these insults were acutely felt, especially when the issue erupted at the first meeting of the three after Micipsa's death. This council degenerated into bickering with no agreement as to how to divide the kingdom. Before long, Jugurtha had Hiempsal murdered and civil war erupted between the two survivors.[66] Adherbal soon fled to Rome.[67] Jugurtha sent his own contingent to the city, loaded with presents to be used in lavish bribery of a number of senators, demonstrating the power barbarian kings could wield by spreading their wealth through relatively impoverished Rome.[68] Both were invited to address the Senate. Adherbal invoked his position as a grandson of Massinissa and the inheritor of his friendship and alliance with Rome, emphasizing Jugurtha's generally violent and evil character, which had resulted in the murder of Adherbal's brother. Although Sallust's account is anachronistic and chauvinistic in many ways, as presented it is a powerful summary of the relationship

---

63 Sallust, *Jugurtha* 6. On the difficulties with Micipsa's analysis of Jugurtha as a threat, see Paul (supra note 30) 29.

64 Sallust, *Jugurtha* 7–10.

65 It has been assumed that the otherwise undocumented African command of M. Porcius Cato (consul in 118 BC), recorded by Aulus Gellius (13.20.9–10) but not recognized by Broughton, was to deal with the Numidian succession. See Gsell, vol. 7, pp. 21, 142; Paul (supra note 30), pp. 46–7.

66 Sallust, *Jugurtha* 11–12.

67 Adherbal may have been in Rome previously: see Braund, *Friendly King*, p. 23; *De viris illustribus* 66.

68 Sallust, *Jugurtha* 13–15; Braund, *Friendly King*, pp. 58–9.

between Rome and client kingdoms.[69] Jugurtha's response was brief – although he drew attention to his service at Numantia – for he believed that his bribery was a more powerful weapon.[70] An intense senatorial debate resulted in the sending of a commission to Numidia led by L. Opimius (consul in 121 BC), who had been implicated in the murder of C. Gracchus and thus would have been expected to be ill-disposed toward Jugurtha. But upon his arrival Opimius was well entertained and bribed, and for this reason, Sallust suggested, the commission reported favorably on Jugurtha's claim and divided the kingdom in such a way that he received the better portions.[71]

Although Rome believed that it had settled the dispute, Jugurtha still coveted Adherbal's part of the kingdom, and attacked it in 112 BC. Adherbal asked Rome for help and withdrew to Cirta, where he enlisted the aid of the resident Roman population.[72] Another Roman commission arrived in Numidia and spoke to Jugurtha but was not allowed to approach Adherbal, now besieged in Cirta, who nonetheless managed to send a further message to Rome that resulted in a third but ineffective Roman commission. The siege of Cirta was not lifted, and the Romans in the city urged surrender. Adherbal did surrender, only to be promptly tortured to death; the Romans and many others in the city were also killed.[73]

---

69 But see Gruen (supra note 16), pp. 159–60.

70 This may be when Jugurtha uttered his famous aphorism that anything could be bought in Rome if the price were right (Sallust, *Jugurtha* 20): Appian (*Noumidika*) and Livy (*Epitome* 64) placed this after his second visit to Rome. For a view that diminished the role of bribery, see Walter Allen, Jr., "The Source of Jugurtha's Influence in the Roman Senate," *CP* 33, 1938, pp. 90–2. Allen noted that "a barbarian king would naturally send many gifts with his embassies, and to his old friends in particular," which makes the bribery more perceptual than real. See also Christina Shuttleworth Kraus, "Jugurthine Disorder," in *The Limits of Historiography: Genre and Narrative in Ancient Historical Texts*, ed. Christina Shuttleworth Kraus (Leiden: E. J. Brill, 1999), pp. 231–2.

71 Sallust, *Jugurtha* 16. It must be kept in mind that the bribery does not necessarily mean that the senators acted differently from the way they might have otherwise (see Lintott, "The Roman Empire" [supra note 62], pp. 30–1), and that the membership of the commission was a result of internal politics at Rome, especially the ascendancy of those opposed to C. Gracchus, and only secondarily concerned with issues in Africa (see D. C. Earl, "Sallust and the Senate's Numidian Policy," *Latomus* 24, 1965, 532–6).

72 The existence of this Italian colony at Cirta, certainly mercantile, demonstrates that much of Rome's involvement in Numidian politics at this time was not of territorial but of commercial interest: the merchants and traders at Cirta must have made long and loud complaints to Rome about their inability to do business in Numidia. See also Lintott, "The Roman Empire" (supra note 62), pp. 30–1; Leo Teutsch, *Das Städtewesen in Nordafrika in der Zeit vom C. Gracchus bis zum Tode des Kaisers Augustus* (Berlin: De Gruyter, 1962), pp. 5–6; Paul (supra note 30), p. 86.

73 Sallust, *Jugurtha* 20–6; Livy, *Epitome* 64. The extent of this "massacre" has long been debated, and it should be noted that Sallust was explicit in recording that the *negotiatores* who were killed had taken up arms against Jugurtha. Regardless, the reports that came to Rome assisted in serving as a pretext for war. See R. Morstein-Marx, "The Alleged 'Massacre' at Cirta and Its Consequences (Sallust *Bellum Iugurthinum* 26–27)," *CP* 95, 2000, 468–77.

Needless to say, there was outrage in Rome. Jugurtha felt that bribery would settle the issue and sent ambassadors to the city, but they were told to go home and only return with the king. Meanwhile, Roman forces had moved into Numidia and attacked. Jugurtha seems to have been successful in bribing the Roman commanders into an armistice, but it was repudiated in Rome. He was finally persuaded to come to the city, but refused to reply to the charges against him, although he was able to bring about the murder of his cousin and potential rival Massiva, son of Gulussa, who was resident in Rome. Jugurtha was then ordered to leave Italy, and even though ambivalence persisted in Rome, full-scale war soon resulted.[74]

The details of the Jugurthine War need not be recounted here.[75] It continued for seven years, mostly inconclusively, with a series of Roman commanders promising quick victory and failing to deliver. Jugurtha had learned well his lessons in Spain and was quite capable in Roman tactics, even able to organize the primitive Gaetulians in Roman fashion.[76] The last Roman commander was C. Marius, whose career had been steadily advancing since distinguished service in Numantia. He went to Numidia in 109 BC as aide to Q. Caecilius Metellus (consul in 109 BC), but they soon quarreled, and Marius returned to Rome and was elected consul for 107 BC, forcing through legislation that would give him superior command, although he was no more effective than his predecessors. But Jugurtha's in-law Bocchus I of Mauretania, playing a careful double game, eventually tilted toward Rome and turned Jugurtha over to Marius' quaestor L. Cornelius Sulla.[77] Jugurtha was brought to Rome and appeared in Marius' triumph on 1 January 105 BC, led before the imperial chariot in chains with his two sons. Within a week he was dead, either by suicide or by execution. His sons remained in Italy: the kingship of Numidia passed to his brother Gauda.[78]

As Massinissa had become a paradigm for the ideal barbarian king, his grandson Jugurtha became the opposite model.[79] He was the barbarian who

74 Sallust, *Jugurtha* 27–35.

75 See Sallust, *Jugurtha* 43–114; Livy, *Epitome* 64–7; Plutarch, *Marius* 7–12, *Sulla* 3; Appian, *Noumidika*; Syme (supra note 60), pp. 138–77.

76 Sallust, *Jugurtha* 80.

77 Infra, pp. 48–9.

78 Rome would hardly have wanted a son of Jugurtha to return to the Numidian throne, and thus probably confirmed Gauda as king while keeping Jugurtha's sons in Italy. Gsell's argument (vol. 7, p. 263) that Gauda may never have been king is questionable. A son of Jugurtha named Oxynta or Oxyntas was living under guard at Venusia fifteen years later: an attempt to use him during the Social War to inspire the Numidians in the army of Sextus Caesar backfired badly (Appian, *Civil War* 1.42; Gsell, vol. 7, pp. 261–2; Ritter, *Rom*, pp. 119–20).

79 The name Jugurtha, however, was in vogue in later imperial times, as his memory became idealized (see Elizabeth W. B. Fentress, "Caesarean Reflections," *Opus* 3, 1984, 488, and *CIL* 8.17909). Moreover, Jugurtha also became a modern paradigm for African liberation movements against the European colonial powers: see Jo-Marie Claassen, "Sallust's Jugurtha – Rebel or Freedom Fighter? On Crossing Crocodile-Infested Waters," *CW* 86, 1992–3, 273–97.

did not recognize the importance of good relations with Rome (in contrast to his betrayer, Bocchus of Mauretania), who killed off his rivals and involved Rome in a horrible and fruitless war that resulted in no obvious benefits. It was necessary for the power of Rome totally to crush Jugurtha – at great cost – and Jugurtha died miserable in a Roman prison. This war, it was believed, began a cascading series of destabilizing events that was still in process several generations later. The two Romans who were instrumental in capturing Jugurtha, Marius and Sulla, would come to strenuous disagreement over who was really responsible for ending the war, and this quarrel would have ominous implications for the Republic. One can be certain that Jugurtha's great-great-nephew Juba II – an intimate of the family of Sallust – was as aware of Jugurtha's failings as he was of Massinissa's virtues.[80]

Jugurtha had not only died intestate but had killed many of his potential heirs. His sons were detained in Italy and not available. The only remaining member of his generation was his brother Gauda,[81] the great-grandfather of Juba II, whom his uncle Micipsa had named a secondary heir but who seems – unlike his cousins – to have survived the era of Jugurtha because he was in poor health and perceived as having a weak mind. He remains the most obscure of the Numidian kings.[82] He joined the Roman side during the war against Jugurtha and entered the entourage of Metellus in Utica, eventually requesting royal honors, which were denied.[83] Marius then enlisted Gauda's help by calling him by the title of king and promising that he would become Jugurtha's successor, especially if Marius were allowed to succeed Metellus as commander. Marius then encouraged Gauda to write to friends in Rome asking them to criticize Metellus and to have Marius replace him: Roman equestrians in Utica were also part of this successful effort.[84] Although Sallust implied that Marius was merely manipulating the weak-minded Gauda, it is possible that like the emperor Claudius, Gauda used his apparent infirmities as a survival tactic and that Marius was not totally self-interested but recognized Gauda as the only possible successor to Jugurtha

80 Jugurtha had little time for the arts of civilization, and there is scant information about his reign other than the intrigues and military events. Nevertheless, his coinage shows not only the standard Numidian elephant, but also a clean-shaven portrait of the king, the first Numidian monarch to adopt the Roman custom of shaving (Mazard #73–5). It is perhaps no coincidence that daily shaving among Romans was said to have been instituted by the Roman patron of the Numidian royal family, Scipio Aemilianus (NH 7.211).

81 The name is always Gauda in Latin. Dio, the only Greek literary source, mentioned him twice (fr. 89, from book 26), once as Γαύδας and once as Γναῖος, which, although a Roman name, is closer to the Γάος or Γαῦος of Greek inscriptions. Γάος appears on an inscription from Rhodes erected in honor of his son Hiempsal II, so is perhaps the extant rendering closest to the actual source. See Vassa N. Kontorini, "Le Roi Hiempsal II de Numidie et Rhodes," AntCl 64, 1975, 91.

82 Gsell, vol. 7, pp. 138, 220–1, 262–3, 275–6; Romanelli, Storia, pp. 81–5.

83 Sallust, Jugurtha 65; Dio, fr. 89 (book 26).

84 Plutarch's version (Marius 7–8) makes no mention of Gauda's involvement in the pressure campaign.

and felt that he should be encouraged and supported. Presumably he was confirmed as king after Jugurtha's death, probably at the instigation of Marius.[85] Yet his actual reign remains a total blank, and he had died by 88 BC, when Marius fled to Africa from Sulla and found Gauda's son Hiempsal II on the throne.[86]

Gauda seems to have continued the Numidian custom of dividing his kingdom, giving it to his sons Hiempsal II and Masteabar. The latter is known only through a single highly fragmentary inscription that identifies him as a son of Gauda but provides no further information.[87] Masteabar may have been the grandfather of Arabion, who was still ruling a small portion of western Numidia after the main part had been provincialized in 46 BC, and whose rule lasted until about 41 BC.[88] Thus the sons of Gauda permanently split the Numidian territory. The major portion came to Hiempsal II, who was recognized by the Romans as "rex amicus."[89] Masteabar's territory degenerated into little more than a petty fiefdom.

From the time of the death of Gauda, Roman and Numidian affairs became totally tangled. The scare of Jugurtha and the spread of Roman influence in North Africa meant that the Numidian territories could no longer function separately from Rome, especially as the Roman political structure collapsed, owing to the developing civil war, whose first protagonists, Marius and Sulla, had themselves been deeply involved in Numidian affairs and quarreled over their varying interpretations of their roles.[90] Sulla had placed the scene of Bocchus surrendering Jugurtha to him on his signet ring, which Marius saw as a deliberate provocation,[91] and when Bocchus dedicated a victory memorial on the Capitol in Rome in 91 BC, Marius was outraged at the prominence given Sulla and was about to tear the monument down – and Sulla was about to respond in his own precipitous way – when the Social War intervened, postponing but not eliminating the hostility between the two.[92] Marius was expelled from Rome by Sulla a few years later and went to the Numidian court, only to be detained there and to fear for

---

85 Marius seems also to have given Gauda support by settling Gaetulian cavalry in his territory (Lintott, "The Roman Empire" [supra note 62], p. 30).

86 Plutarch, *Marius* 40; Appian, *Civil War* 1.62; see Broughton, vol. 2, pp. 41–2.

87 Kontorini (supra note 81), pp. 95–8; Gabriel Camps, "Les Derniers Rois numides: Massinissa II et Arabion," *BAC* n.s. 17b1, 1984, 303–6; W. Huss, "Die westmassylischen Könige," *AntSoc*, 20, 1989, 210–12. The inscription is from Syracuse, which raises the possibility of Masteabar's relations with that city.

88 See further, infra, pp. 92–3.

89 Cicero, *De lege agraria* 2.58. Official recognition may have been the work of Marius, if Cicero, *Post reditum ad Quirites* 20, is to be taken literally ("quibus regna ipse dederat"). On Hiempsal II, see Th. Lenschau, "Hiempsal," *RE* 8, 1913, 1393–5.

90 Pietro Romanelli, "Chi fu il vincitore di Giugurta: Mario o Silla?" *ArchStorTL* 2, 1960, 171–3.

91 *NH* 37.9; Valerius Maximus 8.14.4; Plutarch, *Sulla* 3–4, *Marius* 10.5–6.

92 Plutarch, *Sulla* 6, *Marius* 32; on the monument, see Thomas Schäfer, "Das Siegesdenkmal vom Kapitol," in *Numider*, pp. 243–50.

his life before escaping.[93] In this way, Numidian affairs came to be manipulated by Roman political interests of the era.

The Greco-Roman sources, needless to say, give the impression that Numidia was merely one of the theaters of the Roman civil war, and little independent information is available, although a close reading demonstrates that affairs in Numidia were far from stable and in a state of decline, something most obvious in the permanent splitting of the kingdom that Massinissa had unified only a century previously. Moreover, Hiempsal II had to face a revolt in his own region, led by a certain Hiarbas, who seems to have seized control not long after Hiempsal became king.[94] He attracted strong Roman interest: Africa became the refuge of choice of many of Sulla's opponents in the 80s BC, beginning with Marius in 88 BC.[95] Shortly thereafter Hiarbas emerged, and expelled Hiempsal from his throne.[96] Where he came from is a mystery. It is hard to relate him to the reigning family, which had largely been killed or exiled at the time of Jugurtha. There is some merit to the suggestion that he was Gaetulian, the Gaetulians being the indigenous population that lived south of Numidia.[97] Portions of them were beginning a transition toward a sedentary way of life. Jugurtha had organized them in Roman military fashion, and Marius had provided land and recognized their independent status.[98] It was a good time for a Gaetulian to claim the throne of Numidia – knowledge of the instability in Rome would only have made the opportunity seem more fortuitous – and this may have been what happened sometime after 88 BC.[99] Yet when Sulla became dictator in 82 BC, the Numidian situation needed attention, both because its legitimate king (whose rule had probably been ratified by Rome) had been deposed, and because Sullan opponents were involved in the claims of the usurper, since Cn. Domitius Ahenobarbus, who had fled to Africa after being proscribed, had gathered a large force and allied himself with Hiarbas.[100]

Sulla selected a rising young man who had joined his cause the previous year, Cn. Pompeius,[101] who landed with his army at Utica and went to Carthage. After a ludicrous episode when his troops became obsessed with

93 Plutarch, *Marius* 40; Appian, *Civil War* 1.62; Badian (supra note 15), pp. 237–8.

94 Appian, *Civil War* 1.80; Gsell, vol. 7, pp. 281–7.

95 Plutarch, *Crassus* 6; Sallust, *Jugurtha* 64.4; Badian (supra note 15), pp. 266–7.

96 Plutarch, *Pompeius* 12; Th. Lenschau, "Hiarbas" (#2), *RE* 8, 1913, 1388; Romanelli, *Storia*, pp. 93–5.

97 Fentress, *Numidia and the Roman Army* (supra note 3), p. 79.

98 Sallust, *Jugurtha* 80; *De bello africo* 32, 56.

99 A memory of the Gaetulian usurper Hiarbas may have been preserved by Vergil in his Gaetulian Iarbas (*Aeneid* 4.36, 326).

100 Plutarch, *Pompeius* 11–12. He was one of the more obscure members of a family that would remain prominent for the next century. See Broughton 2.560; F. Münzer, "Cn. Domitius Ahenobarbus" (#22), *RE* 5, 1903, 1327–8; Robin Seager, *Pompey: A Political Biography* (Oxford: Blackwell, 1979), p. 10.

101 Plutarch, *Pompeius* 11–13; Appian, *Civil War* 1.80; Seager (supra note 100), pp. 10–12. On the career of Pompeius in North Africa, see Mohamed Majdoub, "Pompeius Magnus et les rois maures," *AfrRom* 12, 1998, 1321–8.

recovering the lost treasures of Carthage and proceeded to dig up the ruins of the city, Pompeius engaged Domitius and Hiarbas, defeating them so totally in a forty-day campaign that he was saluted as *imperator*. Domitius was killed; Hiarbas briefly escaped but was soon captured and also killed.[102] During the next year, Pompeius, in Plutarch's revealing phrase, "arranged the affairs of the kings."[103] Hiempsal was returned to the throne.[104] The Gaetulians were, officially at least, made his subjects,[105] a policy that would cause much trouble for the next century. There seems to have been some recognition of the petty kingdom of Masteabar.[106] Pompeius then returned to Italy to be given a triumph, although still in his twenties and only an equestrian, gaining the title "Magnus" that he would carry for the rest of his life. Like his mentor Sulla, he first achieved fame by settling a Numidian war,[107] but, in a dramatic indication of how things had changed in the quarter-century since the time of Jugurtha, this war had seen Romans die on both sides, with a consul killed by a promagistrate. Ominous precedents were being set.[108]

Once he had been returned to his throne, Hiempsal was honored by the Rhodians, probably for commercial reasons:[109] Rhodes was near the end of its independent identity and had long been in decline, and may have been looking for wealthy allies. He still retained possession of the Carthaginian state library and perhaps wrote on history himself.[110] He appears on his coinage as clean-shaven in the Roman style.[111] But there are no other details about his reign for twenty years after his restoration.[112] Roman interests were elsewhere.

102 Livy, *Epitome* 89; according to Orosius (5.21), he escaped to Bulla Regia and perhaps was heading toward Mauretania: because of this it has been suggested (Romanelli, *Storia*, p. 95) that Bulla Regia was his power base. See also Coltelloni-Trannoy, p. 89.

103 Plutarch, *Pompeius* 12.5: διήτησε τὰ τῶν βασιλέων.

104 Aulus Gellius 9.12.14 (=Sallust, *Histories* 1.45 [ed. McGushin]).

105 *De bello africo* 56.

106 This, presumably, is the meaning of the phrase in *De viris illustribus* (77.2) that Pompeius took Numidia from Hiarbas and gave it to Massinissa. This Massinissa may have been the son of Masteabar and father of Arabion: see Camps, *BAC* (supra note 87), pp. 303–10; Huss (supra note 87), pp. 214–15.

107 The parallel was not lost on Sulla: Plutarch, *Pompeius* 13.

108 This was effectively stressed by Badian (supra note 15), pp. 271–2: "From Hiempsal and Hiarbas the road leads straight to . . . Juba [I] and Cleopatra."

109 Kontorini (supra note 81), pp. 89–99.

110 Sallust, *Jugurtha* 17; Paul (supra note 30), p. 74; Victor Matthews, "The *libri Punici* of King Hiempsal," *AJP* 93, 1972, 330–5; Coltelloni-Trannoy, pp. 137–8. Despite the contrary arguments of Syme (supra note 60), p. 153, and Camps (*LibAE*, supra note 4), pp. 15–16, repeated in his "Hiempsal [Iemsal]," *EB* 23, 2000, 3464), it seems unlikely that Sallust's "libri punici . . . regis Hiempsalis" refers to the short-lived Hiempsal I, who barely had time to be king before tangling fatally with Jugurtha. See, further, Véronique Krings, "Les *libri Punici* de Salluste," *AfrRom* 7, 1989, 109–17; Morstein-Marx, *AJP* (supra note 3), pp. 195–7.

111 Mazard #75–83.

112 At some date the citizens of Thurburbo built a structure in his honor, but the inscription seems imperial and may be from the time of Juba II or Ptolemaios, his grandson and great-grandson. See Stéphane Gsell, *Inscriptiones latines de l'Algérie* 1 (Rome: L'Erma di Bretschneider, 1965), #1242; Gsell, vol. 7, p. 290.

In 63 and 62 BC, however, Numidia again came to the forefront of Roman politics. Initially, there was the matter of a major agrarian bill proposed early in 63 BC by the tribune P. Servilius Rullus, an obscurity who was probably acting for others. The bill is known only through Cicero's speeches against it, which makes interpretation difficult.[113] A detailed discussion of it and its context is not in order here;[114] of interest is that the bill, basically a complex procedure for obtaining and distributing land, not only in Italy but in recently acquired overseas territories, contained a special exemption. Lands owned by King Hiempsal could not be included, even though they were within the boundaries of the province of Africa.[115] The status of these royal estates was ambiguous, and the consul C. Aurelius Cotta in 75 BC had officially asserted Hiempsal's ownership of them. Yet the Senate does not seem to have ratified this, and Hiempsal naturally was concerned and sent his son Juba (I) to state his case in Rome. It seems that Rome had coveted these estates for some time – the Senate had frequently debated the matter – and Cotta's affirmation of Hiempsal's ownership must be placed in the context of other events of his consulship, including problems relating to the official provincialization of Kyrenaika and the related issue of grain shortages in Italy that resulted in riots in the streets.[116] Cotta's recognition of the Numidian claim to rich agricultural lands within Roman territory must have seemed unwise to many, and twelve years later an attempt to legalize the exclusion would only have been worse.

One can thus only speculate at the motives for the exemption: Cicero hinted that it was bribery, and noted deprecatingly the presence of Hiempsal's son. There certainly was a long history of Numidian bribery at Rome, or so it was believed.[117] The bill did not seem to have popular support, and ultimately failed to pass, perhaps killed by the threat of a tribunician veto,[118] so the effect on Hiempsal's estates was moot. But it seems that Rome had begun to look avariciously at the agrarian wealth that the Numidian kings held.[119]

A few months later there was a further incident involving the Numidian royalty. Another claimant to the throne, a certain Masintha, appealed unsuc-

---

113 Cicero, *De lege agraria* 1, 2, 3; the few other sources are derivative.

114 For which see Erich S. Gruen, *The Last Generation of the Roman Republic*, first paperback edition (Berkeley: University of California Press, 1995), pp. 389–94; G. V. Sumner, "Cicero, Pompeius, and Rullus," *TAPA* 97, 1966, 569–82; Ritter, *Rom*, pp. 122–4; E. J. Jonkers, *Social and Economic Commentary on Cicero's* De lege agraria orationes tres (Leiden: E. J. Brill, 1963).

115 Cicero, *De lege agraria* 1.10–11, 2.58; see Fentress, *Numidia and the Roman Army* (supra note 3), pp. 53–4. Pompeius may have been behind the exemption since he had restored Hiempsal to his throne: see Sumner (supra note 114), pp. 569–82; Seager (supra note 100), pp. 63–4.

116 Broughton, vol. 2, p. 96; Sallust, *Histories* 2.44 (McGushin); David C. Braund, "Cicero on Hiempsal II and Juba: *de leg. agr.* 2.58–9," *LCM* 8, 1983, 87–9.

117 Paul (supra note 30), pp. 261–3.

118 *NH* 7.117; Plutarch, *Cicero* 12; Cicero, *Pro Sulla* 65; Gruen, *Last Generation* (supra note 114), p. 394.

119 On this, see Fentress, *Numidia and the Roman Army* (supra note 3), pp. 53–4.

cessfully to Rome to be recognized as an independent king. It is probable that he was a descendant of Jugurtha, perhaps a grandson, since to Suetonius he was "iuvenis" and Jugurtha's sons, if still alive, would be in their mid-forties. A descendant of Jugurtha would have a strong claim to the Numidian kingdom. Whoever Masintha was, his case attracted the notice of one of the most powerful people in Rome: it was put forth by Julius Caesar. The position of the legitimate king, Hiempsal, was articulated by his son Juba, perhaps still in the city after his involvement with the Rullan land bill.[120] The hearings became notorious when Juba was physically assaulted by Caesar. Masintha lost his case and was declared subject to Hiempsal, but Caesar spirited him out of town and to Spain.

At about the same time there was the matter of P. Vatinius, quaestor in 63 BC, who was early in a long and distinguished career as a Caesarean adherent. He was attached to the staff of C. Cosconius, propraetor in Spain in the following year. Vatinius went there, probably early in 62 BC, by a strangely circuitous route: he first visited the court of Hiempsal, and then moved west to that of Mastanesosus, probably the Mauretanian king.[121] Again the only source for these events is Cicero, who cross-examined Vatinius on another matter a number of years later,[122] and who made the journey sound as sinister as possible, especially since Vatinius was not only an adherent but a relative of Caesar's, and his long route to Spain had taken him well outside Roman territory. The actual reason behind Vatinius' actions cannot be explained. Cicero, with the hindsight of several years, saw it all as part of some complex Caesarean scheme. Nevertheless, it is intriguing that these three last glimpses of Hiempsal's kingship – the visit of Vatinius, Caesar's defense of Masintha, and the Rullan land bill – all occurred within a few months of each other. It is impossible to see beyond to the broad policies that inspired the events, but clearly there was a growing, almost obsessive, Roman interest in the Numidian kingdom. Within little more than a decade, in 50 BC, the tribune C. Scribonius Curio was to propose the Roman confiscation of all of Numidia,[123] a move that was effected by other means four years later.

---

120 Suetonius, *Julius* 71; Ritter, *Rom*, pp. 124–5; Gsell, vol. 7, p. 294 (who suggested that "Masintha" was a corruption of Massinissa, perhaps the ally of Caesar mentioned by Vitruvius [8.3.25]); Romanelli, *Storia*, p. 100; Teutsch (supra note 72), pp. 52–3. Caesar's status as the nephew of Marius may have been the reason Masintha asked for his help, as Numidians were to do in Africa fifteen years later (*De bello africo* 32), but there is no hint of this, despite Matthias Gelzer, *Caesar: Politician and Statesman*, sixth edition, translated Peter Needham (Cambridge, Mass.: Harvard University Press, 1968), p. 45.

121 On Mastanesosus, see infra, p. 56.

122 Cicero, *In Vatinium* 12.

123 Caesar, *Bellum Civile* 2.25; Dio 41.41; Lucan, *Pharsalia* 4.689–94.

Nothing further is known about Hiempsal's reign. By 50 BC his son Juba I was on the throne.[124] The enclave ruled by Masteabar had remained independent and passed into the hands of Arabion, probably his grandson, by about the same time.[125] The date of the death of Hiempsal II and accession of Juba I falls between 62 and 50 BC, but the details of the succession have not been preserved. Juba I was born no later than around 80 BC and had spent time in Rome as his father's agent. In early 63 BC when he attended the hearings of the land bill of Rullus, Cicero left a description of the young prince: "Hovering before their eyes is Juba, the son of the king, a young man as rich as he is long-haired."[126] Cicero's polemic words imply that Juba was ready to insure the exemption for his father through abundant monetary resources, and then degenerate into a racial epithet, contrasting the hirsute barbarian with the clean-shaven Romans, and punning on the Latin word *iuba*, which means "mane."[127] The coinage of Juba I shows his rich beard,[128] which plays a role in the only other incident known from his youth: a few months later Julius Caesar, when defending Masintha against Hiempsal, came to blows with the prince and pulled his beard.[129] As Rome degenerated into permanent civil instability, the conspicuous physical differences between Romans and foreigners – especially that implied in the very word *barbarus* – became an element of popular culture and invective.

When Juba I became king, a few years later, his rule was not immediately confirmed by Rome.[130] Yet despite his earlier mistreatment by some Romans, his cultural and political debt to Rome was strong, and he placed his coinage onto the Roman standard and adopted occasional Latin titulature

---

124 On Juba I, see Th. Lenschau, "Iuba" (#1), *RE* 9, 1916, 2381–4; A. Charbonneaux, "Giuba I," *EAA* 3, 1960, 917; Ritter, *Rom*, pp. 126–34.

125 Camps, *BAC* (supra note 87), pp. 303–11.

126 Cicero, *De lege agraria* 2.59: "Volitat enim ante oculos istorum Juba, regis filius, adulescens non minus bene nummatus quam bene capillatus."

127 The word was used by Ennius, *Annals* 520, but other citations are from the time of Cicero and later (see *OLD*), so it came to be definitely associated with the African kings. On this see Braund, *Friendly King*, p. 68; Braund, *LCM* (supra note 116), p. 89.

128 Especially Mazard #88. A portrait bust from Caesarea (Figure 15, p. 140), now in the Louvre (MA 1885), idealized, with full beard and exceedingly luxuriant hair, is generally identified as the king and was probably commissioned by his son: see Gisela M. A. Richter, *The Portraits of the Greeks* (London: Phaidon, 1965), p. 280, figures 2000–2. A stele from Chemtou in Numidia shows a horseman with rich beard and thick hair, carrying a royal diadem and riding on an elaborate saddle and using a bridle. Because of these characteristics, it has also been suggested to be of the king. See Theodor Kraus, "Reiterbild eines Numiderkönigs," in *Praestant Interna: Festschrift für Ulrich Hausmann*, ed. Bettina von Freytag geb. Löringhoff *et al.* (Tübingen: E. Wasmuth, 1982), pp. 146–7; François Bertrandy, "À propos du cavalier de Simitthus (Chemtou)," *AntAfr* 22, 1986, 57–71.

129 Suetonius, *Julius* 71.

130 In 49 BC Pompeius was unsuccessfully to move that he be made "socius and amicus" (Caesar, *Bellum civile* 1.6), a motion blocked by the consul C. Claudius Marcellus, although Pompeius unilaterally confirmed him as king later that year (Dio 41.42.7).

(Figure 25a, p. 245).[131] He also initiated an elaborate building program at his capital of Zama and perhaps elsewhere,[132] influenced by both Greek and Roman forms. Coins show an octostyle temple, perhaps in the Doric or Tuscan style, on a high platform (Figure 25b).[133] The eight columns are divided into two groups separated by a passageway at the head of a stairway leading up to the platform. The building is surmounted by a cupola. One coin has this structure on one side and another on the reverse, positioned on a low stylobate with three Atlas figures alternating with Tuscan Doric columns, and a second, Ionic colonnade above the architrave.[134] The building is stoa-like and has been suggested to be Juba's palace at Zama, which was the site of a major building operation on his part, including a double fortification wall, but the apparent presence of horned altars on the roof may indicate a religious function.[135] Yet it is in the tradition of the great stoas of the Hellenistic world,[136] or even the basilicas that were beginning to become common in Rome, such as the so-called Basilica Aemilia, which had been restored in 78 BC, shortly before Juba's visit to the city, and whose coin representations are remarkably similar to the structure depicted on Juba's coins.[137] The cupola on the octostyle temple is also typically Hellenistic, remindful of the Stoa of Poseidon on Delos.[138]

Although the accounts of Juba I were affected by his position on the losing side of the Roman civil war, he seems to have been an aggressive and vigorous monarch who continued the expansive ambitions of his predecessors.[139] He embarked on a major expedition against unnamed desert tribes

---

131 Mazard p. 49, #84–93. On the coinage, see also François Bertrandy, "Remarques sur l'origine romaine du monnayage en bronze et en argent de Juba Ier, roi de Numidie," *BAC* 12–14, 1976–8 (1980), 9–22.

132 If not at Zama, the building shown on Juba's coins may have been at Mactaris (see *BAGRW*, map 33), modern Makthar, a major pre-Roman city that became a colonia in the second century AC. Located in his ancestral region of the Zama hinterland (for which, infra, note 170), its extensive remains and long history make it a possibility for his architectural efforts. See Collette Charles-Picard and Gilbert Charles-Picard, "Recherches sur l'architecture numide," *Karthago* 19, 1980, 20–31, and A. Ennabli, "Mactaris (Makthar)," *PECS*, pp. 540–1.

133 Mazard #84, 85, 90; Gilbert Charles Picard, "Basilique et palais de Juba I de Numidie," *BAC* 18, 1982 (1988), 165–7.

134 Mazard #91.

135 Vitruvius 8.3.24; Gsell, vol. 7, p. 293; Bluma L. Trell, "Ancient Coins: New Light on North African Architecture," in *Actes du Premier Congrès d'Histoire et de la Civilisation du Maghreb* 1 (Tunis: Université de Tunis, 1979), pp. 83–94.

136 A. W. Lawrence, *Greek Architecture*, fifth edition, revised by R. A. Tomlinson (New Haven, Conn.: Yale University Press, 1996), pp. 197–9.

137 Axel Boethius, *Etruscan and Early Roman Architecture*, second integrated edition (Harmondsworth, U.K.: Penguin Books, 1978), p. 151. In fact, the coin representation may be significant in understanding the enigmatic history of the basilica: see Charles-Picard (supra note 132), p. 19.

138 Lawrence (supra note 136), pp. 200–1. The traditional modern name for this building is the Hypostyle Hall.

139 If Lucan 10.144–6, on luxury goods from Egypt at Juba's court, is not anachronistic, Juba I had commercial relations with the Ptolemies, something not unexpected.

who were in a state of revolt, and if the source, Aelian (who recorded it for natural historical, not political or military reasons), can be taken literally, the campaign lasted a year.[140] It is probable that the insurgents were the Gaetulians, whom Pompeius had ill-advisedly placed under Numidian control and who were resisting, as they were to do for the next century.[141] Juba may also have seized some or all of the territory of Leptis, invited in by a local faction.[142] In attacking the ancient Phoenician city that would become famous in imperial times as Leptis Magna, he had moved far around the southern edge of the Roman province to the east, and into the independent district between Roman Africa and Kyrenaika, a venture perhaps not unusual for one who had spent a year in the desert pursuing the Gaetulians, but probably quite frightening to the Romans. The citizens of Leptis complained to Rome, and the Senate appointed a commission that decided in their favor and forced Juba to withdraw. The taking of Leptis, if nothing else, would have resulted in serious questions in Rome about the future of the Numidian kingdom. Moreover, as the polarization between Caesar and Pompeius intensified, it was obvious that Juba would be on the side of Pompeius, who had restored his father to the throne, not that of Caesar, who had publicly assaulted him in Rome.

It was in this context that a solution to the Numidian question was put forth early in 50 BC by the ambitious tribune Q. Scribonius Curio, who proposed that the kingdom be confiscated.[143] Curio's legislation was agrarian, and the agricultural riches of North Africa had long been envied by Rome, but the singling out of Juba and his kingdom also would have had a narrower political focus. It came to nothing – for complex reasons, Curio eventually withdrew his entire legislative program – but nevertheless it would have fatal consequences, as Juba now knew that certain factions in Rome meant to destroy him.

Perhaps in part seeking to mitigate the damage done by Curio's proposal, and to build his own power base in the face of Caesar's return from Gaul early in 49 BC, Pompeius suggested that Juba be officially recognized as a friend and ally of Rome.[144] But the matter was indefinitely postponed, and when Pompeius left Italy for the East, Juba made plans to support him mili-

---

140 Aelian, *On Animals* 7.23. His interest was an encounter with a lion, for which see infra, p. 204.

141 Gsell, vol. 7, pp. 292–3.

142 *De bello africo* 97; Caesar, *Bellum civile* 2.38. It seems without question that the object of Juba's interest was the future Leptis Magna, not Leptis in Africa, on the coast south of Carthage and later known as Leptis Minor (modern Lamta), which was within Roman territory. An incursion here would have resulted in a response stronger than a senatorial commission, and there would have been no debate in Rome about the legality of Juba's actions.

143 Caesar, *Bellum civile* 2.25; Dio 41.41; Lucan 4.689–95; Cicero, *Ad familiares* 8.11.3 (from M. Caelius Rufus to Cicero, April 50 BC). On the character of Curio and his tribunate, see W. K. Lacey, "The Tribunate of Curio," *Historia* 10, 1961, 318–29; on the legislation and its fate, see Gruen, *Last Generation* (supra note 114), pp. 471–81.

144 Caesar, *Bellum civile* 1.6.

tarily.[145] This emerging alliance between Juba and Pompeius may have been influential in Caesar's decision to send his own troops into Numidia, selecting for command none other than Curio.[146] The wisdom of choosing for this endeavor the Roman whom Juba most hated is not immediately obvious.[147] Curio's primary objective was the Pompeian governor of Africa, P. Attius Varus, who was encamped at Utica. Varus had been governor previously, and since the position was vacant, he had returned and used his familiarity with the district to create a power base that was a center of Pompeian support. In Curio's army was the future historian Asinius Pollio, who is the major source (other than Caesar) for the events that followed.[148]

Curio landed in Africa and eventually took up a position near Utica. He was initially successful in defeating both a Numidian cavalry force and Varus. But Juba sent out his general Saburra to make camp south of the city on the Bagradas (modern Mejerda) River: the king did not appear in force for fear that Curio would merely abandon the expedition and put to sea, implying that, for Juba, personal revenge was a major priority. Curio was soon in serious difficulty: emboldened by Caesar's recent successes in Spain, he was rash and overconfident, ill-prepared for the heat of an African summer. The scant water resources were diminished by local poisoning of wells. But he felt that Saburra's force was defeatable and was taken in by Juba's stratagem to appear to remain uninvolved: Juba even let it be known that domestic problems prevented his appearance. Curio withdrew into the hills, where his troops continued to suffer from the heat, and then attacked Saburra's force, only to find it supplemented by Juba's troops. The unfortunate Curio and his exhausted and demoralized troops were slaughtered, except for Asinius Pollio's detachment, which had retreated to protect Utica.[149]

Pollio attempted to embark his troops on merchant ships, but this turned into disaster and chaos, and those left on shore surrendered to Varus. Juba, over his objections, had them killed, although Pollio escaped to write

---

145 *De bello alexandrino* 51; François Bertrandy, "L'Aide militaire de Juba Ier aux Pompeiens pendant la guerre civile en Afrique du Nord (50–46 avant J.-C.)," in *Histoire et archéologie de l'Afrique du Nord: Actes du IVe Colloque International* 2: *L'Armeé et les affaires militaires* (Paris: CTHS, 1991), pp. 289–97. A few years later, in May of 46 BC, Cicero lamented that the alliance between Pompeius and Juba was a major reason that he had withdrawn from active participation in the war, as he did not want to end up a refugee in Numidia (*Ad familiares* 7.3.3).

146 Caesar, *Bellum civile* 1.30–1. For the chronology, see Erik Wistrand, "The Date of Curio's African Campaign," *Eranos* 61, 1963, 38–44.

147 Dio 41.41; Lucan 4.692–3.

148 The ancient sources are Caesar, *Bellum civile* 2.24–42; Livy, *Epitome* 110; Lucan, 4.666–787; Appian, *Civil War* 2.44–6; Dio 41.41–2; Florus 2.13.26; Orosius 6.15. For an analysis of Lucan's highly literary and allegorial treatment of the events, see Charles Saylor, "Curio and Antaeus: The African Episode of Lucan *Pharsalia* IV," *TAPA* 112, 1982, 169–77.

149 Over a century later, Frontinus considered Juba's tactics worthy of recording in his *Stratagems* (2.5.40).

history.[150] Juba took control of Utica – he was escorted into the city under an armed guard of senators loyal to Pompeius – and immediately sent a message to Greece. Pompeius replied by giving Juba honors and recognition as king (something Rome had never officially granted him).[151] But Caesar's faction declared Juba a public enemy and confirmed the Mauretanians Bocchus II and Bogudes II as kings of their own territories, which would have the effect of opening a second front against Juba.[152]

The autumn and winter of 49–48 BC was the high point of Juba I's career. He had defeated a Roman army led, with tragic irony, by the very man who two years previously had proposed taking his kingdom away from him and who was a deputy of the one who had previously assaulted him in Rome. He had occupied a Roman provincial capital, dictated terms to its inhabitants, and received a senatorial escort. He had been honored and acknowledged as king – something that had so long eluded him – by the most senior Roman alive, who had himself gained the name "Magnus" for restoring Juba's father. Now control of all of the Carthaginian territory – something long desired by the Numidian kings – and expulsion of the upstart and invasive Romans were at hand. Dreams of a Numidian empire stretching from the Atlantic to the Kyrenaika were not unreasonable. It was probably about this time that his son, the future Juba II, was born. Juba I had every reason to be proud of his own accomplishments, and immediately began to further his goals by sending a large force to Pompeius in Greece.[153]

But then came Pharsalos, almost exactly a year after the battle at the Bagradas River. Pompeius after his defeat considered taking refuge at the court of Juba.[154] Yet he was persuaded instead to go to Egypt, which was closer and where he had connections to the Ptolemies, but upon his arrival he was promptly killed.[155] Nonetheless, two of his staff did end up in Africa: his father-in-law Q. Caecilius Metellus Scipio (consul in 52 BC)[156] and M. Porcius Cato, great-grandson of the Cato of the Second Punic War:[157] the

---

150 The history (no longer extant) was commemorated by Horace (*Ode* 2.1), who placed the war in the context of Jugurtha, which avoided issues of dubious morality, a common technique in analyses of the civil war: see Annagabriella Bianchi, "Giugurta e la guerra giugurtina in Orazio," *Miscellanea greca e romana* 18 (Studi pubblicati dall'Istituto Italiano per la Storia Antica 56 [Rome 1994]), pp. 151–66.

151 Dio 41.42.

152 On Bocchus II and Bogudes II, see infra, pp. 55–8, 93–5.

153 *De bello alexandrino* 51. The troops may not have reached Pompeius in time, since they are not listed in the catalog of allies at Pharsalos (Caesar, *Bellum civile* 3.3–5).

154 Velleius 2.53; Plutarch, *Pompeius* 76; Appian, *Civil War* 2.83–4.

155 Several years previously, Pompeius had been the executor of the will of Ptolemaios XII Auletes and thus was legally the guardian of his contentious children and heirs, Ptolemaios XIII and Kleopatra VII (Caesar, *Bellum civile* 3.108). Although he had not actively exercised the role, this may explain his choice of Egypt, as well as his murder by members of the Ptolemaic court circle, who would have feared his potential for meddling. On this see Braund, *Friendly King*, pp. 136–7.

156 F. Münzer, "Q. Caecilius Metellus Pius Scipio" (#99), *RE* 3, 1899, 1224–8.

157 Franz Miltner and W. H. Gross, "M. Porcius Cato Uticensis" (#16), *RE* 22, 1953, 168–213.

names of both indicate their long-standing family connections with Africa. Scipio, as senior officer, quickly became the commander of the growing Pompeian forces in Africa and made a close alliance with Juba.[158]

In early 47 BC a considerable number of Pompeians were gathered in and around Utica.[159] By December (which, because of the unadjusted calendar, was actually early autumn) Caesar, who had returned to Rome after a momentous stopover in Egypt, was ready to move against them. He had six legions to oppose fourteen, which allegedly included 120 elephants.[160] His strategy was to ignore Utica and to land on the coast well to the southeast, perhaps driving a wedge between the Pompeian and Juban forces. Shortly after landing and establishing a camp at Hadrumetum (modern Sousse), he began to be harassed by Juba's cavalry.[161] Juba had moved out of Numidia into Africa, but had been stopped when Bocchus II and his general Sittius[162] arrived from Mauretania. Juba then retreated into his kingdom, leaving thirty elephants with Scipio.[163]

Meanwhile, with Cato remaining in Utica, Scipio advanced toward Caesar's position, and in January of 46 BC a major engagement took place on the coast near Ruspina (modern Monastir).[164] Scipio's troops panicked and were driven from the field with major casualties. He appealed to Juba for help, and, leaving Saburra behind to harass Sittius, the king joined Scipio and forced Caesar into retreat. Yet in a brilliant tactical maneuver Caesar's forces turned and attacked in the midst of their withdrawal, almost capturing Juba. This so demoralized Scipio's troops that massive defections began. Meanwhile, Caesar had been opening contacts with the Gaetulians, invoking the name of his uncle Marius, and they were persuaded to revolt, requiring Juba to defend a third front. Tempers began to run short, and Juba and Scipio started bickering about matters as trivial as each other's battle dress. Juba began to act erratically, crucifying any of his troops who retreated and preempting the imminent Caesarean capture of Vaga (modern Beja) by slaughtering its inhabitants and leveling the town.[165] Although allowances must be made for the Roman desire to portray Juba as viciously and

---

158 Velleius 2.54.

159 The major source for the events that followed is the anonymous *De bello africo*, written by a member of Caesar's staff. Other sources are Livy, *Epitome* 110–14; Suetonius, *Julius* 35, 66; Plutarch, *Cato the Younger, Caesar* 52–5; Appian, *Civil War* 2.44–100; Florus 2.13.64–72; Dio 43.2–13. For modern sources, see Gsell, vol. 8, pp. 1–155; Romanelli, *Storia*, pp. 111–28; Gelzer (supra note 120), pp. 264–71; Rudolf Fehrle, *Cato Uticensis* (Darmstadt: Wissenschaftliche Buchgesellschaft, 1983), pp. 261–78; Elizabeth Rawson, "Caesar: Civil War and Dictatorship," *CAH*² 9, 1994, 434–6.

160 H. H. Scullard, *The Elephant in the Greek and Roman World* (London: Thames and Hudson, 1974), pp. 194–8.

161 *De bello africo* 1–6.

162 On the early career of Sittius, see infra, pp. 56–7.

163 *De bello africo* 25, 36; Appian, *Civil War* 2.96.

164 *De bello africo* 32, 52–5.

165 *De bello africo* 66, 75; on Vaga, see Teutsch (supra note 72), p. 36.

disagreeably as possible,[166] desperation seems to have induced him to act in a highly abnormal way. Casualties and desertions were high, and revolts began within Juba's kingdom: the citizens of Thabena, a coastal city on his northern frontier, rose up and massacred the royal garrison, appealing to Caesar, who sent a force to occupy the town.[167]

In early April the final engagement took place at Thapsus, on the coast southeast of Ruspina, at modern Ras Dinass near Bekalta. Juba's elephants, new to warfare, charged back into the lines.[168] This began a rout in which thousands were killed. Others managed to escape toward Utica, where Cato was in charge. Scipio committed suicide, either on his ship or at Utica, and Cato did the same.[169] Juba fled to his royal city of Zama (Figure 2).[170]

166 De bello africo 57: "a most arrogant and impotent man" ("homini superbissimo inertissimoque"). As early as June of 46 BC, Cicero was complaining to Varro that it was improper for the Pompeian forces to seek protection from a barbarian king and his elephants (Ad familiares 9.6.3; see also Alberto Cossarini, "Cic. Epist. 9, 6, 3 ad bestiarum auxilium," AttiVen 141, 1982–3, 93–103). In one of the Suasoriae (7.14) of the elder Seneca, an unfortunate named Gargonius is thoroughly ridiculed for saying something good about Juba, and half a century after the war Ovid would encounter an aged veteran of the campaign who could still speak of the "perfida arma Iubae" (Fasti 4.380; see also Quintilian 11.1.80). This demonization of Juba I – similar to that which would happen to Kleopatra VII some years later – provided an easy way of ignoring greater moral issues of the war. Interestingly, it did not seem to affect the status of his son, as it did not that of Kleopatra VII's daughter, both of whom were able to assert their distinguished lineage despite their parents' sins.

167 De bello africo 77.

168 Florus 2.13.67–9; see also Dio 43.8.

169 The accounts of the deaths of the two commanders (preserved in De bello africo 88–93; Livy, Epitome 114; Plutarch, Cato the Younger 65–70; Appian, Civil War 2.98–9; Florus 2.13.67–9) have become intermixed and confused, but it seems that both died by suicide at about the same time.

170 Zama Regia was the nearest (i.e. easternmost) of the Numidian royal cities, and thus the most accessible. Its location is in the area west of modern Siliana, a region where toponyms such as "Jemna" and "Jamaa" still exist. Topographical interest in the area has tended to center on the location of the great battle of 204 BC in which P. Cornelius Scipio, with the aid of Massinissa, defeated Hannibal. But Zama Regia is in the same vicinity, near where the hills known as Jebel Massouge come to an end about 20 km southwest of Siliana and drop down to a plain. The westernmost extension of the hills creates a pocket about 2 km across surrounded by ridges on all sides except the southwest, where it leads into a large flat plain, an extension of the valley of the Oued Tessa. Somewhere in this plain, perhaps extending east into the pocket, is Zama Regia: Sallust, a local resident in 46 and 45 BC, explicitly put the city "in campo" (Jugurtha 57.1). Although physical remains are remarkably sparse, Numidian tombs are common around the perimeter of the region, especially to the southwest at modern Elles, which is just north of a modern village named El Jemaa. Inscriptions with "ZAM.REG" have been found throughout the area, and a large masonry structure on a prominent summit to the northeast at Kbor Klib has been suggested to be the tomb of Juba and Petreius, or perhaps Caesar's victory monument (but see infra, note 174). This is placed at the only point where it would be visible, and prominently so, from everywhere in the plain of Zama. See Charles Saumagne, "Zama Regia," CRAI 1941, pp. 445–53; Vitruvius (ed. Callebat), pp. 124–6; Louis Déroche, "Les Fouilles de Ksar Toual Zammel et la question de Zama," MÉFR 60, 1948, 55–104; Francis H. Russell, "The Battlefield of Zama," Archaeology 23, 1970, 120–9. An alternative location is near modern Jamna, 9 km west of Siliana, where there are extensive remains, but it is nowhere near a plain and is probably Zama Minor. See Pliny (ed. Desanges), pp. 321–6 (which includes a thorough discussion of the problem of the location of Zama); BAGRW, map 32.

Figure 2 The site of Zama, looking southwest from Kbor Klib. The town site was
   probably in the middle distance, in the flat area.

Photograph by Duane W. Roller.

Accompanying him was the Roman officer M. Petreius, perhaps the praetor
of 64 BC who had been with Pompeius in Greece.[171] Juba's family was in
Zama, including his infant son, the future Juba II, but the king was refused
entry. The citizens of Zama had no reason to allow him in, since he had previously announced that were he to be defeated he would massacre the
inhabitants, burn all his possessions in the forum, and kill his family and
himself. After long entreaties and an unsuccessful request to be given his
family, he and Petreius withdrew to a country estate,[172] indulged in an
elaborate banquet, and then killed one other.[173] Caesar soon arrived in Zama
in pursuit of Juba and spent several weeks in the vicinity auctioning the
royal possessions, rewarding the citizens, and arranging for the territory to

171 Broughton, vol. 2, p. 600; F. Münzer, "M. Petreius" (#3), *RE* 19, 1937, 1182–9.

172 It has been suggested by Saumagne (supra note 170), p. 453, that this was at Ismuc, 20 miles from
   Zama, the only other toponym mentioned by Vitruvius (8.3.24) in his discussion of the royal city, a
   description distinctly set in the context of Juba I. The location of Ismuc is unknown (Vitruvius [ed.
   Callebat], p. 126; *BAGRW Directory*, p. 506, which cites Vitruvius incorrectly).

173 The details vary: see W. C. McDermott, "M. Petreius and Juba," *Latomus* 28, 1969, 858–62. Juba's
   death became a moral paradigm: see Seneca, *On Providence* 2.10. On the cultural implications of the
   death, see Paul Jal, *Le Guerre civile à Rome: étude littéraire et morale* (Paris: Presses Universitaires de
   France, 1963), pp. 310–15.

be provincialized. He may also have erected a victory monument.[174] He eventually left Sallust in charge and returned to Rome, arriving there in July.[175] Although the sources do not record it at this point, he took Juba's infant son with him, perhaps saving him more as the descendant of the noble Massinissa than as the son of the perfidious Juba I.

In late September of that year Caesar celebrated an elaborate quadruple triumph, one of the great spectacles of the era.[176] Gaul, Pontos, Egypt, and Africa were the four stages, and there was a rich variety of games, shows, and exhibits. Caesar's grandnephew C. Octavius, 16 years of age, made one of his first public appearances in the African portion.[177] There was a flaming model of the Pharos at Alexandria and pictures and portraits of those involved, except for Pompeius, who still had many supporters. The suicides of the leaders were prominently depicted: Scipio jumping wounded into the ocean, Cato disemboweling himself, and Petreius and Juba dueling to the death. Some of this was not well received by the spectators, who remembered that thousands of Romans had also died, but by and large they were thrilled at it all, especially the magnificent procession of elephants carrying torches[178] and that of the notable captives, including the Gallic chieftain Vercingetorix, Arsinoë, the sister of Kleopatra VII and, to some, the legitimate queen of Egypt – her appearance in chains offended many – and, of course, the infant son of Juba I, carried along, "the happiest captive ever captured," Plutarch was to write,[179] since he arrived in Rome as a barbarian prisoner but became a learned Greek historian. Yet the little Juba II would have had slight comprehension of what had happened or what was to come. He could not have remembered much if anything about his family,[180] although he was eventually taught to remember his father's friends and would place in his palace at Volubilis a bronze portrait of Cato.[181]

---

174 This is one interpretation of the masonry monument at Kbor Klib: see Russell (supra note 170), p. 129. It is also suggested to be the tomb of Juba and Petreius (supra note 170), and even a Numidian sanctuary of the first half of the first century BC (Friedrich Rakob, "Numidische Königsarchitektur in Nordafrika," *Numider*, pp. 129–30). Regardless, the monument is significant in locating ancient Zama.

175 *De bello africo* 91–8.

176 The primary sources are Plutarch, *Caesar* 55; Appian, *Civil War* 2.101–2; Florus 2.13.88–9; Dio. 43.19–24; for others, see Jean-Louis Voisin, "Le Triomphe africain de 46 et l'idéologie césarienne," *AntAfr* 19, 1983, 7–33; Ettore Pais, *Fasti triumphales populi romani* (Rome: Nardecchia, 1920), pp. 270–80; Gelzer (supra note 120), pp. 284–6.

177 Suetonius, *Augustus* 8.

178 These elephants, captured from Juba, ended up in the hands of Octavian after Caesar's murder and were used in Italy at that time: Cicero, *Philippic* 5.46; Dio 45.13.4; Scullard (supra note 160), pp. 197–8.

179 Plutarch, *Caesar* 55: μακαριωτάτην ἁλοὺς ἅλωσιν.

180 The fate of the rest of the family of Juba I, including his wives and other children, all at Zama, is not recorded.

181 Infra, pp. 144–5.

2

MAURETANIA

The infant son of Juba I was thus saved to grow up in Rome. Twenty years later he would be named king of Mauretania, a territory that he had never seen and over which he had at most a weak claim, if any at all. Why this happened – and why this was a reasonable decision for Augustus – is due to the history of the Roman relationship with the district of northwest Africa that was loosely called Mauretania.[1] This was a vast, undefined area, over 1,000 miles in extent, stretching from the western limit of Roman territory to the Atlantic.[2] The term "Mauretania" originally applied to the western half of this region, beyond the Muluccha River,[3] but acquisitions by the Mauretanian kings, especially in the late second century BC,

---

1 Although the ethnic Μαυρούσιοι was in use in Greek literature from the second century BC (Polybios 3.33.15), the earliest extant use of the toponym in a contemporary sense is Cicero, *Pro Sulla* 56, from 62 BC, describing the intrigues of P. Sittius (see Cicero, *Pro P. Sulla oratio*, ed. D. H. Berry (Cambridge: Cambridge University Press, 1996), pp. 246–7; on Sittius, see infra, pp. 56–7). Sallust, in *Jugurtha* 16.5, 19.4, and 62.7, writing later than Cicero, used "Mauretania" in the context of the latter part of the second century BC, and Livy (29.30.1) used the term in describing the events of the previous century. On the early use of the toponym, see S. Weinstock, "Mauretania," *RE* 14, 1930, 2348–51. As is so often the case, an original ethnic term became a toponym. "Morocco" is derived from Mauretania, and probably represents direct continuity, but the modern country of Mauretania, to the south in the desert, is a colonial creation of 1904 having no relationship to ancient Mauretania, and indeed its territory, except for its short coastline, was outside the limits of all but the vaguest ancient geographical knowledge.

2 *NH* 5.21. As is made clear at 5.9, this is from the map of Marcus Agrippa. See Pliny (ed. Desanges), pp. 109, 186–8.

3 Sallust, *Jugurtha* 92.5. Although some have suggested that the Muluccha is the modern Kiss, the present boundary between Morocco and Algeria (see Coltelloni-Trannoy, p. 76), it is more likely the Moulouya, the next stream to the west (G. M. Paul, *A Historical Commentary on Sallust's "Bellum Jugurthinum"* [Liverpool 1984, pp. 78–9], which in modern times was the border between Spanish Morocco and Morocco proper. The mouths of the two streams are merely 15 km apart, but because the Kiss flows northwest and the Moulouya flows northeast, the territory between them (the modern Beni Snassan) is substantial. Not only does the Moulouya seem to preserve the ancient name, it is a major stream whose source is in the mountains 300 km inland near modern Midelt. The Kiss, however, is only 25 km in length. See also René Rebuffat, "Notes sur les confins de la Maurétanie Tingitane et de la Maurétanie Césarienne," *StMagr* 4, 1971, 45–6; Raymond Thouvenot, "Le Géographe Ptolémée et la jonction terrestre des deux Maurétanies," *RÉA* 64, 1962, 82–8.

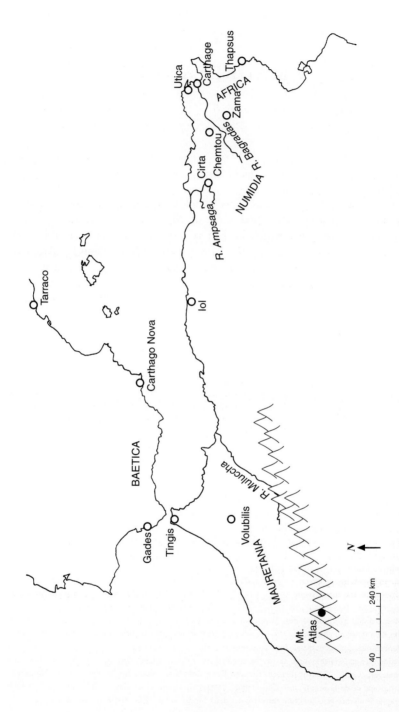

Map 1 Northwest Africa, 146–46 BC

steadily extended the territory to the east. By the time of Juba II, "Mauretania" generally denoted all of coastal North Africa west of the Roman
provinces, although terminology is not consistent and the eastern portions
were historically part of Numidia.[4] Owing to the imprecise frontiers inher-
ent in territories of transient population, Numidia had overlapped both
Carthaginian and Mauretanian territory, but was centered around the
fortress city of Cirta, probably modern Constantine in Algeria, which from
the third to the mid-first century BC was the major seat of the Numidian
kings.[5]

With the fall of Carthage in 146 BC and the making of its territory into a
Roman province, and then with the reduction of the Numidian kingdom
when Jugurtha was defeated in 105 BC, Mauretania came to be defined as
everything west of the Ampsaga River[6] (probably the modern el-Kebir),[7]
although as long as the kingdom survived, it continued to overlap both
eastern Mauretania and western provincial Africa; these ill-defined borders
were a major cause of the wars between Rome and the indigenous population. With the end of an independent Numidia in 46 BC, its lands were
partitioned, the eastern portions becoming Roman and the western Mauretanian. Even at this time the territorial limits of Mauretania remained
imprecise, as scattered Roman enclaves existed both in the east (near the
boundary of Africa) and in the west (across from Spain). Largely because of
the transhumant character of much of its population, northern Africa lacked
the defined frontiers of much of the rest of the Roman world, a continuing
problem for both ancient and modern topographers.

The major city of eastern Mauretania was Iol, originally a Carthaginian
outpost and later a royal seat of a native dynasty.[8] Eventually, as Caesarea, it
was the capital of Juba II and Kleopatra Selene. According to the map of
Marcus Agrippa, it was 322 miles west of the eastern boundary of Mauretania.[9] Far to the west lay the traditional Mauretanian capital, Volubilis. More
isolated and less known than Iol, in large part owing to its inland location,
its origins are obscure but it was to become a major trading center,

---

4 "Numidia" is descriptive rather than toponymic, derived from Greek νομάς, "one who roams
around for pasture" (LSJ), first used by Herodotos (1.15, etc.) to describe a variety of nomadic
peoples including those of North Africa (4.187). Polybios (1.19.3, etc.) used it as an ethnic term;
the first to use it as a toponym was Sallust (*Jugurtha* 8.1).

5 Livy 29.32.14; 30.12.5.

6 Pomponius Mela 1.30; *NH* 5.22. Strabo's placement of the boundary farther west at Salda (17.3.12)
seems an error (Gsell, vol. 8, p. 212) and may reflect the heresay nature of his information, although
he himself noted that the territory was divided in different ways at different times.

7 El-Kebir is the easternmost watercourse in modern Algeria, flowing out of the mountains from a source
near Souk-Ahras and entering the Mediterranean just east of Annaba, ancient Hippo. The modern
Tunisian–Algerian border approximates the Numidian–Mauretanian boundary of 105–46 BC, which
then became the Roman–Mauretanian border.

8 On the early history of Iol, see Leveau, *Caesarea*, pp. 9–13.

9 *NH* 5.21.

especially with Roman Spain, and the western royal city of the client monarchy.[10]

Thus Mauretania was a long, narrow territory – Iol and Volubilis are 800 km apart and population in between was scant – with many unique characteristics. To the Romans it seemed especially arid, home to lions and full of desolate, unpopulated plains where the sun was unusually close to the earth, all of which gave the area an exotic quality.[11] The physical geography

10 On the origins of Volubilis, see Jodin, *Volubilis*, pp. 21–32.
11 Horace, *Ode* 1.22.9–22:

> While I was singing of Lalage, wandering beyond my property in the Sabine woods, free of care and unarmed, a wolf fled from me, not a monster such as that nourished in the broad oaks of martial Daunia or raised in the Juban land, dry nurse of lions. Put me on the wearisome plains where no tree is revived by a summer breeze, and the expanse of the world is oppressed by clouds and an unpleasant sky. Put me under the chariot of the sun where it is too close to an uninhabitable earth.

> namque me silva lupus in Sabina,
> dum meam canto Lalagen et ultra
> terminum curis vagor expeditis,
>   fugit inermem;
> quale portentum neque militaris
> Daunias latis alit aesculetis
> nec Iubae tellus generat, leonum
>   arida nutrix.
> pone me pigris ubi nulla campis
> arbor aestiva recreatur aura,
> quod latus mundi nebulae malusque
>   Iuppiter urget;
> pone sub curru nimium propinqui
> solis in terra domibus negata.

If this refers to Juba II and not his father, and if, as generally assumed, it was published in late 23 BC (see R. G. M. Nisbet and Margaret Hubbard, *A Commentary on Horace: Odes, Book 1* [Oxford: Clarendon Press, 1970], pp. xxxv–xxxvii), this is the earliest mention by name of the king.

Remarkably similar sentiments were expressed by Vitruvius (8.3.24) in his description of the palace of Juba I at Zama:

> Moreover, Zama is a city of Africa, whose fortifications King Juba surrounded with a double wall, and where he chose the site of his palace. . . . Although Africa is the parent and nurse of wild beasts, especially snakes, none grows in the fields of this city.

> Etiamque Zama est civitas Afrorum, cuius moenia rex Iuba duplici muro saepsit ibique regium domum siti constituit. . . . cum esset enim Africa parens et nutrix ferarum bestiarum, maxime serpentium, in eius agris oppidi nulla nascitur.

The similarity between the passages might be an argument for assuming Horace meant Juba I, but it is just as possible that Vitruvius filled out his description by imitating Horace even if the latter referred to Juba II. Regardless of who influenced whom – and it is more likely that the technical writer borrowed from the poet than the reverse – both demonstrate the topicality in the early Augustan period of North African imagery. On the relationship between the two passages, see Erik Wistrand, "Till två Horatiusställen," *Eranos* 39, 1931, 81–6. Snakes became part of the Roman conception of North Africa, most notably in Lucan's description of the epic journey of Cato across Libya after Pharsalos (9.294–949; see Matthew Leigh, *Lucan: Spectacle and Engagement* [Oxford: Clarendon Press, 1997], pp. 265–82).

of Mauretania supports this poetic image,[12] as it is indeed a land of hot, dry plains divided by rugged mountains. Throughout the extent of Mauretania, the Atlas Mountains roughly parallel the coast and cut it off from the desert interior. In the east they are relatively low and close to the coast, rarely rising above 2,000 m. Further west they are more inland (as the coast curves to the north) and become higher and more precipitous, culminating in Mount Atlas, modern Jebel Toubkhal, at 4,167 m the highest point in Africa north of the Sahara. Its precipitous quality is emphasized by its position less than 200 km from the Atlantic.

Another range of mountains, the Rif, lies to the north of the Atlas in eastern Morocco and hugs the coast, curving to the northwest toward the Strait of Gibraltar: Jebel Musa, the southern Pillar of Herakles, is the northernmost point of the range, but the Rif Mountains are effectively continued in Spain by Gibraltar itself and the mountains of Andalusia. The Rif cuts Mauretania into two parts, each more easily in contact with Europe than with each other. To the east is the rugged coast of modern Algeria, in Roman and earlier times centering on Iol–Caesarea and cut off from the interior plateaus by the mountains. To the west, beyond the Rif, and accessible by land only through passes between the southernmost Rif and the Atlas, are the plains of modern Morocco, whose natural communication is north into Spain, since the Rif inhibits movement to the east. In Roman times population was heaviest in a line extending almost due south from Tingis, at the Pillars of Herakles, to Volubilis, a strip of approximately 225 km. To the southwest, the limits of the plain are marked by foothills of the Atlas that reach the coast between modern Rabat and Casablanca.

The Atlas isolates Mauretania from both the interior of Africa and the further Atlantic coast, and thus forces the territory to look toward Europe. South of the mountains is the desert, *deserta ardentia*, as Juba called it,[13] a barrier to travel then as now. Although the Greco-Roman world had long known that it could be crossed, and that great rivers and tropical flora and fauna lay beyond,[14] the desert remained a major obstacle, penetrated regularly only by the camel caravans that brought central African goods to the Mediterranean.[15]

---

12 For the physical geography, see M. Cary, *The Geographic Background of Greek and Roman History* (Oxford: Clarendon Press, 1949), pp. 220–9; A. N. Sherwin-White, "Geographical Factors in Roman Algeria," *JRS* 34, 1944, 1–10; also Weinstock (supra note 1), pp. 2344–86. A general discussion of the region in antiquity is by Jérôme Carcopino, *Le Maroc antique*, third edition (Paris: Gallimard, 1943), although scanty on the period of Juba II; see also Luis A. García Moreno, "La República romana tardía y el conocimiento geográfico y etnográfico de África," *AfrRom* 11, n.d., 319–26; *BAGRW*, maps 28–30.

13 *NH* 5.51 = Juba, fr. 38. Juba's original Greek was translated into Latin by Pliny.

14 Herodotos 2.30–2.

15 These caravans remain the only land transportation across the Sahara, all colonial and later schemes at building railways and highways having failed. A famous sign at Zagora, on the Draa River in southern Morocco at the northern edge of the desert, reports that it is fifty-two days by camel to Timbuctu.

Ancient Mauretania, then, extended over 1,600 km of coastline but with its populated areas never more than 150 km inland, and, especially in the east, was limited to a thin coastal strip and a few small interior valleys. Moreover, because of the nature of the mountains, population was separated into two distinct regions: one on the coast near Iol, in modern Algeria, and the other far to the west along the Tingis–Volubilis axis, in modern Morocco. As might be expected, Iol was influenced by the Carthaginian (subsequently Roman) territories to its east, but the Tingis–Volubilis region, separated from Iol by rugged mountains, became virtually an extension of Roman Spain: even today, Spanish culture remains strong in modern Morocco, as toponyms such as "Casablanca" demonstrate.

The two pockets of historic population are typically Mediterranean in aspect. Iol–Caesarea is situated where the mountains are narrowest: their southern edge is less than 100 km due south of the coast where the high plateaus (averaging around 1,000 m in elevation) of the northern Sahara begin. The terrain is rugged at Iol: the Massif de Dahra rises to 1,415 m less than 20 km south of the city and there is virtually no coastal plain. It is a strange and isolated location for a major city: settlement was perhaps originally due to the presence of a small island just offshore that provided protection for ships, a rare sheltered point along this rugged coast, known today as the Corniche des Dahra. In many ways, Iol was the western outpost of North African civilization: to the east, where the mountains consist of many parallel ranges separating fertile valleys, the traditional heartland of Numidia and Carthage, population density was high in all periods. To the west of Iol, however, the rugged coast continues with few breaks for nearly 300 km until one reaches the Gulf of Arzew and the site near Bettioua traditionally identified as Portus Magnus.[16] Even beyond this point, settlement was limited for nearly another 100 km until Siga,[17] the important regional center of the chieftain Syphax in the late third century BC. Siga, at the mouth of the Tafna, is itself isolated, but to the west, as the coast turns in a more northerly direction, the Atlas Mountains and coast diverge and Mauretania proper begins.

This original territory of Mauretania consists of the area from Tingis at the Pillars of Herakles to Volubilis, 225 km to the south, and west 120 km to Sala on the coast. This creates a triangular region of approximately 15,000 sq. km bounded by the Rif on the east, the Atlas foothills on the south and southwest, and the Atlantic on the northwest, described by modern geographers as a peninsula.[18] The district is a fertile coastal plain

---

16 Jean Lassus, "Le Site de Saint-Leu, *Portus Magnus* (Oran)," *CRAI* 1956, pp. 285–93; *BAGRW*, map 29.

17 P.-A. Février, "Siga," *PECS*, p. 838.

18 Albert André, "Introduction à le géographie physique de la Peninsule tingitane," *RGM* 19, 1971, 57–75, a good summary of the physical geography of the region.

watered by several rivers flowing toward the Atlantic from sources in the mountains.[19] Although none is particularly lengthy – the longest, the Sebou, originates in the eastern Rif barely 300 km from the Atlantic – all are unusually deep and full, especially at the time of snowmelt. The rivers create lush bottomlands that are almost tropical and were prime places for settlement, especially for Roman veterans' colonies. Between the river bottoms are upland steppes at elevations of up to 1,000 m that are barren today, or occasionally planted with cereals. Volubilis itself lies on one of these, the plain of Jebel Zerhoun, at approximately 500 m elevation, near the source of the Khoumane, one of the southern affluents of the Sebou.

The Mediterranean qualities of the region are less prominent along the Atlantic coast, where cooler temperatures and frequent fogs are common. This made the coast less desirable for settlement, and in Greco-Roman times there were only two major towns along 250 km of Atlantic coastline, Lixos and Sala, each at the mouth of the river of the same name.

To the southwest, broken hills rising to over 1,000 m in elevation mark the end of the populated region. The coastal plain is again in evidence beyond these hills, and continues far to the southwest, eventually to be terminated by the Atlas range itself at modern Agadir. But this region was more barren than that to the east, and was essentially outside the populated limits of Greco-Roman culture, although the coast had been explored since at least Carthaginian times. The only settlement of significance in this vast area was the purple dye works at modern Mogador or Essaouira, probably ancient Kerne, over 400 km from Sala and considered in Hellenistic times to be the limit of Mauretania.[20] Still further – nearly 500 km beyond – are the Canary Islands. The closest to land, modern Fuerteventura, lies less than 100 km offshore and is often visible from the mainland. These too had been vaguely known since early times but were first explored in detail and named by Juba II, his most significant contribution to geographical research. Explorers went farther, and indeed Carthaginians and Greeks circumnavigated Africa, but the Canaries remained the extremity of the Greco-Roman world: they lie closer to South America than to Asia Minor.

Although extreme western Africa had long been famed to Greeks as the location of the Garden of the Hesperides,[21] little specific information on the region existed. The early Carthaginian settlement and exploration[22] was itself not well known to Greeks and Romans until their access to the Carthaginian cultural heritage after that city's destruction: the topographical vagueness of Herodotos' report on Carthaginian exploration in West

---

19 On the agricultural economy of the region, see Enrique Gozalbes, "Las características agrícolas de la Mauretania Tingitana," *AfrRom* 12, 1998, 343–58.

20 *NH* 6.199. On the identification of Kerne, see infra, Chapter 5, note 160.

21 Infra, p. 196.

22 Infra, pp. 187–9.

Africa is typical.[23] Even western Greeks, such as the Massalians, who touched the Mauretanian coast, kept their explorations secret for internal strategic reasons.[24] Greeks from Euboia and Boiotia may also have reached the region, as is demonstrated by toponyms such as Kephisis[25] and even Iol,[26] but their settlement, if it existed at all, was sporadic and almost forgotten.

Occasionally some awareness of Mauretania and its inhabitants penetrated into the Greco-Roman world, usually when Mauretanians became involved in Carthaginian wars with the western Greek states and, later, Rome. Mauretanians were allied with Carthage as early as 406 BC when an expedition was made to Sicily,[27] and during the First Punic War the Mauretanians were punished for their friendliness to M. Atilius Regulus, the Roman commander.[28] A chieftain, Baga – the first Mauretanian known by name – was wealthy enough during the Second Punic War to give Massinissa an escort of 4,000 men across Mauretania to the Numidian border, when Massinissa was in the process of successfully seizing the throne of Numidia.[29] How Baga was related to the later Mauretanian ruling dynasty is not known, but his wealth and power make it clear that he was a prominent leader: Livy called him, perhaps somewhat anachronistically, "rex Maurorum." Yet one can see why Sallust wrote that Mauretania was known by name to the Romans long before there was direct contact,[30] and why it remained a vaguely comprehended extremity of the world until the fall of Carthage opened up the western Mediterranean to Rome. At that time, Italian commercial and mercantile interests flowed into North Africa.[31] For example, at Cirta, the Numidian capital, there came to be a substantial group of Italian *negotiatores*:[32] these were deeply involved in the defense of the city against Jugurtha, and their "massacre" was a major cause of the Jugurthine war. One

---

23 Herodotos 4.42. Hekataios (*FGrHist* #1, fr. 355) may have cited at least one Mauretanian toponym, Λίξας (Lixos), but this is highly speculative (see Jehan Desanges, "Lixos dans les sources littéraires grecques et latines," *Lixus*, p. 3).

24 Infra, pp. 188–9.

25 Skylax (*GGM*) 112m; *NH* 37.37.

26 On these and other possible central Greek toponyms in Mauretania, see Michel Gras, "La Mémoire de Lixus. De la fondation de Lixus aux premiers rapports entre Grecs et Phéniciens en Afrique du Nord," *Lixus*, pp. 37–41.

27 Diodoros 13.80.3.

28 Orosius 4.9.

29 Livy 29.30.1; Gsell, vol. 3, p. 175.

30 Sallust, *Jugurtha* 19.7.

31 L. A. Thompson, "Settler and Native in the Urban Centres of Roman Africa," in *Africa in Classical Antiquity: Nine Studies*, ed. L. A. Thompson and J. Ferguson (Ibadan: Ibadan University Press, 1969, pp. 133–6); see also the apt description of the process of Roman immigration by A. J. N. Wilson, *Emigration from Italy in the Republican Age of Rome* (Manchester: Manchester University Press, 1966), pp. 42–54; and Tenney Frank, "The Inscriptions of the Imperial Domains of Africa," *AJP* 47, 1926, 55–73.

32 Sallust, *Jugurtha* 21, 26. On the term, see Paul (supra note 3), p. 87.

expects that a similar community existed at Iol, whose coastal position made it even more accessible to Italy.

In Mauretania proper, Italian contacts were even more widespread.[33] The Roman acquisition of Spain after the Second Punic War had brought Roman territory to within a short distance. The ancient trading center of Tingis served as the port of entry (Figure 14, p. 136). Famed as a foundation of the giant Antaios,[34] it was actually one of the earliest Phoenician outposts, established by the eighth century BC on the western edge of a sheltered bay facing the southern Pillar of Herakles, immediately opposite the Spanish coast. Its location at the natural crossing between Africa and Europe meant that contact with Spain was early and frequent: by the second century BC, direct trade with Rome was an essential part of the local economy, but the specifics of this trade, and exactly who was involved in it, remain difficult to determine.[35] Trade penetrated to the interior, to Lixos and eventually to Volubilis, no later than the end of the second century BC,[36] although it is probable that there were Roman contacts with western Mauretania well before that time.[37] The primary commodities were olives and fish products, which would become the major exports at the time of Juba II.[38] By the late second century BC, Roman interests were so strong that portions of Mauretania could even be described as Roman territory, although this was clearly a cultural, not a legal, definition.

33 Mohamed Majdoub, "La Maurétanie et ses relations commerciales avec le monde romain jusqu'au Ier s. av. J.-C.," *AfrRom* 11, n.d., 291–302; Laurent Callegarin, "La Maurétanie de l'ouest et Rome au Ier siècle av. J.-C.: approche amphorologique," *AfrRom* 13, 2000, 1333–62.

34 *NH* 5.2.

35 Michel Ponsich, "Tangier antique," *ANRW* 2.10.2, 1982, 788–803; Antoinette Hesnard and Maurice Lenoir, "Les Négociants italiens en Maurétanie avant l'annexion (résumé)," *BAC* n.s. 19b, 1983 (1985), 49–51.

36 Jodin, *Volubilis*, pp. 301–2. In the reverse direction, traders from Volubilis went as far as the Magdalensberg, near Klagenfurt in Austria. The Magdalensberg included an extensive settlement of merchants, established by the early first century BC, who traded with the local Keltic inhabitants of Noricum. It may have been the chief city of the district, Noreia (Caesar, *Bellum gallicum* 1.5; Strabo 5.1.8; *NH* 3.131; on its identification with the Magdalensberg, see Géza Alföldy, *Noricum*, tr. Anthony Birley [London: Routledge and Kegan Paul, 1974], pp. 47–51). The major export product was iron, both raw and worked. Many of the merchants left their names and hometowns as graffiti: all that are extant are Italian (from Aquileia to Lucania) except two from Volubilis, Surulus and Orosius Rullus, who may have visited Noricum several times (Alföldy, pp. 73–4). See Rudolf Egger, *Die Stadt auf dem Magdalensberg: Ein Grosshandelsplatz*, DenkschrWien 79 (Vienna 1961), nos. 67, 69, 81, 127, 141, 215, 218, 237, 332, 334 (nos. 81 and 218 identify them as from Volubilis); Raymond Thouvenot, "Deux commerçants volubilitains dans le Norique," *BCTH* 8b, 1972 (1975), 28–32. The date of the Volubilitan traders is not certain, although it may be as early as the beginning of the first century BC.

37 A Lusitanian incursion into Mauretania in 153 BC and the pursuit and defeat of them by the praetor L. Mummius (consul in 146 BC), for which he gained a triumph, indicates that there were already Roman interests in this region before the fall of Carthage (Appian, *Iberika* 57).

38 Mauretanian foods were on the dinner tables of wealthy Romans by early in the first century BC (Macrobius, *Satires* 3.13 = Sallust, *Histories* 2.59 [ed. McGushin]).

According to Sallust, King Bocchus I ruled all the Mauri at the time of the war with Jugurtha.[39] Yet despite his use of an ethnic rather than a geographical term, Sallust's statement can be taken literally, as in the second century BC. Mauretania was still limited to the territory west of the Muluccha.[40] That Bocchus' capital was originally at Volubilis can be shown from the first known event of his career, his encounter with Eudoxos of Kyzikos, the great explorer who opened up the route between the Mediterranean and India. Shortly after 116 BC Eudoxos attempted to reach India by sailing west into the Atlantic, but he abandoned his voyage somewhere near the kingdom of Bocchus, and then went by foot to the royal court. He was not well received, and fled to Roman territory and then to Spain.[41] Thus the court of Bocchus was inland (eliminating Iol), near Roman-held territory that was near to, but was not, Spain. Volubilis seems the only place that Eudoxos could have encountered Bocchus' court.[42]

As the first powerful ruler of a (theoretically) unified Mauretania,[43] Bocchus was in a position to play a significant role in contemporary events. His date of accession is not known: he was already on the throne before the death of Micipsa of Numidia in 118 BC.[44] Shortly after his hostile reception of Eudoxos, he became entangled in the Roman war with Jugurtha. Sallust's *Jugurtha*, the only significant source, presents a finely drawn portrait of a barbarian king at the threshold of romanization, trying desperately to preserve his own interests in the face of overwhelming Roman power that threatened to submerge his needs. Bocchus was drawn into the war unwillingly and then had to decide how he would proceed and how Rome could be used to his own advantage, yet he needed to ensure that it would not destroy him as it was seeking to destroy Jugurtha.[45]

After an attempt to remain neutral, Bocchus became involved by 109 BC, when refugees and deserters began showing up at his court.[46] Unable to continue ignoring circumstances of which he must have been long aware, he began to play a cautious double game, concluding a marriage alliance with

---

39 Sallust, *Jugurtha* 19.7; Eliman Klebs, "Bocchus" (#1), *RE* 3, 1899, 577–8; Gsell, vol. 7, pp. 201–70; Weinstock (supra note 1), pp. 2366–8; Gabriel Camps, "Bocchus," *EB* 10, 1991, 1544–5. On his official relationship with Rome and its ruling elite, see Michèle Coltelloni-Trannoy, "Les Liens de clientèle en Afrique du Nord, du IIe siècle av. J.-C. jusqu'au début du principat," *BAC* n.s. 24b, 1993–5 (1997), 62–4.

40 Sallust, *Jugurtha* 110.8.

41 Strabo 2.3.4–5; see further, infra, pp. 228–30.

42 Jodin, *Volubilis*, pp. 303–4.

43 He described himself to Sulla as "the most important king in this land and of all kings that I have known" ("rex maxumus in hac terra et omnium quos novi"), Sallust, *Jugurtha* 110.1.

44 Sallust, *Jugurtha* 110; Micipsa's death date is provided by Livy, *Epitome* 62.

45 Romanelli, *Storia*, pp. 79–85. On Bocchus and Jugurtha, see Arthur Keaveney, *Sulla: the Last Republican* (London: Croom Helm, 1982), pp. 16–24.

46 Plutarch, *Marius* 10; Sallust, *Jugurtha* 62.7, 74.

Jugurtha[47] and simultaneously sending envoys to Rome. His attempt to establish a relationship with Rome was unsuccessful, allegedly because his ambassadors did not have sufficient bribes. But the affections of Bocchus became the topical issue of the moment: Jugurtha bribed Bocchus' inner circle, promised him Numidian territory, and tried to influence him with anti-Roman rhetoric. The Roman commander, Q. Caecilius Metellus, also sought an alliance with Bocchus. Moreover, the king was sending private messages asserting his loyalty to Metellus' subordinate C. Marius. But before long Jugurtha requested military aid from Bocchus, who agreed and attacked Marius. When Marius defeated both kings near Cirta, Bocchus opened further secret negotiations with the Romans.[48] Marius sent his quaestor L. Cornelius Sulla to cultivate a relationship. Still ambivalent, Bocchus was not certain who to betray to whom, but Sulla kept up subtle pressure, pointing out that Rome would be extremely grateful if Bocchus betrayed Jugurtha, an indication that Roman offers of alliance and friendship carried significant weight among foreign kings.[49] Sulla also held out the powerful temptation of territorial acquisition, once promised somewhat less realistically by Jugurtha.[50] Although still publicly friendly to Jugurtha, Bocchus trapped him and gave him to Sulla.[51] His reward was nominal control of the territory from the Muluccha east to the Roman provincial boundary, although the eastern portions overlapped the continuing and reduced Numidian kingdom.

Sulla felt that his handling of Bocchus was what had made his reputation.[52] He seems to have maintained close contact with the king for many years and probably insured official Roman recognition of his kingship and territorial acquisitions. Bocchus provided Sulla with 100 lions and *iaculatores* for a combat during his praetorship.[53] And it may have been Sulla who encouraged Bocchus to memorialize in sculpture at Rome the surrender of Jugurtha and obtained permission for the monument. Bocchus wanted to show not only favor to the Romans in return for his official designation as an

---

47 Sallust, *Jugurtha* 80; the text, however, is uncertain: either Bocchus married Jugurtha's daughter, or Bocchus' daughter married Jugurtha. Later sources, such as Plutarch (*Marius* 10, *Sulla* 3), explicitly make Bocchus the son-in-law, but they are derived from Sallust's text, and thus the matter remains unresolved. See Weinstock (supra note 1), pp. 2366–7; Gsell, vol. 7, pp. 212–13; Paul (supra note 3), p. 201.

48 Sallust, *Jugurtha* 80–102.

49 On Bocchus' relationship with Rome, see Ritter, *Rom*, pp. 113–16.

50 Paul (supra note 3), p. 246. Bocchus' territory was still limited to west of the Muluccha: in fact, as late as the closing days of the war he was promising Sulla that he would not go east of the river (Sallust, *Jugurtha* 110.8).

51 Sallust, *Jugurtha* 101–13; Livy, *Epitome* 66; Velleius 2.12.1; Plutarch, *Sulla* 3; *Marius* 10; Appian, *Noumidika*; Dio, fr. 89.5.6.

52 Plutarch, *Sulla* 3, where it is clear that the source is the memoirs of Sulla.

53 Seneca, *On the Shortness of Life* 13.6; *NH* 8.53. The date of Sulla's praetorship has long been argued: the most recent study convincingly places it in 97 BC (T. Corey Brennan, "Sulla's Career in the Nineties: Some Reconsiderations," *Chiron* 2, 1992, 132–7).

ally, but also his respect for Sulla, and thus in 91 BC he dedicated on the Roman Capitol both Nikes holding trophies and a scene of gilded figures showing his handing of Jugurtha over to Sulla.[54] The importance of this dedication – and the permission to make it, which had to be granted by the Senate – cannot be overestimated. Such royal dedications had had a sporadic history since Rome first came into contact with barbarian royalty, and their location on the Capitol connected those who made them with the spiritual center of Rome.[55] Massinissa of Numidia well knew this when he requested permission to sacrifice at the Capitoline Temple of Juppiter in 168 BC, something that a nervous Senate declined to authorize.[56] In the late Republic, dedications and ceremonies at the Capitol came to be seen as the ultimate symbol of alliance and friendship between Rome and the kings:[57] it was here that Herod the Great's appointment as king would be officially affirmed.[58] As Bocchus understood perfectly, for a king to have some recognition on the Capitol was the highest level of Roman support. Generally, the physical evidence for these dedications is limited, but some remnants of the Bocchus monument seem to survive,[59] and it probably was the prototype for coins issued by Sulla's son Faustus Cornelius Sulla. These, from 56 BC, show the elder Sulla seated on a raised throne, facing left. To the left is Bocchus, facing right (toward Sulla) and kneeling, raising an olive branch. To the right is Jugurtha, kneeling and facing left, with his hands tied behind his back.[60]

54 Plutarch, *Sulla* 6.1–2; *Marius* 32; E. Badian, *Lucius Sulla, the Deadly Reformer* (Sydney: Sydney University Press, 1970, pp. 11–12). The date is certain because it was just before the outbreak of the Social War. But it also is peculiar, coming fourteen years after the surrender. It may represent the time of a formal treaty of friendship between Rome and Bocchus, or perhaps an event in Bocchus' reign, perhaps his twenty-fifth anniversary, or may simply reflect the fact that it took that long for Sulla, Bocchus' advocate in Rome, to reach a position powerful enough that Senate approval would be granted. The dedication also served Sulla's own purposes in conspicuously slighting his rival Marius.

55 Braund, *Friendly King*, p. 32; David C. Braund, "Client Kings," in *The Administration of the Roman Empire (241 BC–AD 193)*, ed. David C. Braund, Exeter Studies in History 18, 1988, pp. 78–9. Sulla was particularly interested in making the Capitol a monument to Rome's relations with foreign royalty, and may have created a specific precinct for the dedications, as part of the rebuilding necessary after the Temple of Juppiter burned in 83 BC. See Ronald Mellor, "The Dedications on the Capitoline Hill," *Chiron* 8, 1978, 328–30.

56 Livy 45.13.17–14.4.

57 See Cicero, *In Verrem* 2.4.66–7, where the Seleukid prince Antiochos intended to make a dedication on the Capitol; see also Cicero, *Pro C. Rabirio Postumo* 6, for a similar case.

58 Josephus, *Jewish Antiquities* 14.379–89.

59 Th. Schäfer, "Das Siegesdenkmal vom Kapitol," *Numider*, pp. 243–50, pl. 53–5. These are the familiar reliefs of victories and trophies now in the Palazzo dei Conservatori (nos. 2749–52) and in Vienna (Kunsthistorischesmuseum no. 1576).

60 Michael H. Crawford, *Roman Republican Coinage* (Cambridge: Cambridge University Press, 1974), no. 426.1; Lydia H. Lenaghan, "Hercules Melqart on a Coin of Faustus Sulla," *ANSMN* 11, 1964, 131–6; *Numider*, pl. 146. The elder Sulla's signet ring may also have been a prototype.

No further events are known from Bocchus' career, as his affairs dropped from the interest of Roman historians. Even the Capitol memorial was remembered not because of Bocchus or Jugurtha but because of its role in the quarrel between Marius and Sulla. Bocchus' acquisition of western Numidia allowed him to develop Iol as a second capital, creating a territorial duality to Mauretania that has lasted to modern times. He may have remained on the throne until around 81 BC, but this is based on a single late and ambiguous source.[61] Although at least two sons are known, their destinies are uncertain. Volux fought alongside his father in the Jugurthine War, not particularly effectively, and indeed in such a manner that he was almost executed for treason by the Romans.[62] He may not have survived long. Another son, Bogudes (I), was said to have been involved in the defeat of the Numidian usurper Hiarbas in 81 BC but is otherwise unknown.[63]

Mauretanian affairs again entered Roman consciousness with the intrigues of Q. Sertorius.[64] One of the more unusual episodes in his strange career was the time he spent in Mauretania in 81–80 BC[65] hiding from Sulla, who was at the height of his power as dictator of Rome.[66] Sertorius was in command of Hispania Citerior when he learned of Sulla's dictatorship, which made his legal position tenuous and endangered his life. When an army crossed the Pyrenees to oppose him, he embarked from Carthago Nova with three thousand men and fled to Mauretania.[67] Promptly driven out by the Mauretanians and suffering great losses, he was prevented from return-

---

61 Orosius 5.21; Gsell, vol. 7, p. 269; Coltelloni-Trannoy, p. 76.

62 Sallust, *Jugurtha* 101–7; Hans Gundel, "Volux," *RE* 2, ser. 9, 1961, 907–8; Gsell, vol. 7, pp. 253–4. His name may be the same as that of the eponym of Volubilis (Jodin, *Volubilis*, pp. 305–6).

63 Orosius 5.21, the only reference. Bogudes provides a possible connection with the Numidian royal family, since Massinissa had a son of that name: see J.-A. Février, "L'Inscription funéraire de Micipsa," *RAssyr* 45, 1951, 139–50, although for chronological reasons it is almost impossible that the two are the same; see Appendix 2. It is also unlikely that this is the well-known Bogudes II (infra, pp. 57–8): since he survived until 31 BC it would mean an unusually long career, and, moreover, nowhere is he styled as a son of Bocchus, which would be improbable for the son of such a famous father.

64 On Sertorius, see the detailed study by Philip O. Spann, *Quintus Sertorius and the Legacy of Sulla* (Fayetteville: University of Arkansas Press, 1987), which, however, must be used with caution; C. F. Konrad, *Plutarch's Sertorius: A Historical Commentary* (Chapel Hill: University of North Carolina Press, 1994); Piero Treves, "Sertorio," *Athenaeum* n.s. 10, 1932, 127–47; A. Schulten, "Q. Sertorius" (#3), *RE* 2, ser. 2, 1923, 1746–53.

65 Barbara Scardigli, "Sertorio: problemi cronologici," *Athenaeum* n.s. 49, 1971, 244–51. Konrad (supra note 64), p. 111, dated the entire episode to 80 BC. Although the exact dates are of relevance in understanding contemporary Roman history, they add little to the vague knowledge of events in Mauretania.

66 The source is almost entirely Plutarch, *Sertorius* 7–10. A few fragments of the *Histories* of Sallust (1.87–94 McGushin), certainly one of Plutarch's main sources, add some information; see also Strabo 17.3.8 (from Tanusius Geminus, on whom see Konrad [supra note 64], p. xlv); Ronald Syme, *Sallust* (Berkeley: University of California Press, 1964), pp. 193–4.

67 The geographical details of Sertorius' wanderings are detailed by Spann (supra note 64), pp. 48–51.

ing to Spain. Enlisting the aid of Kilikian pirates,[68] he landed on Pityoussa, one of the Balearic islands, from which he was also expelled. Thus finding much of the western Mediterranean closed to him, he sailed with his Kilikian entourage past the Pillars of Herakles and landed on the Atlantic coast of Spain. Here he encountered sailors who told him about the Islands of the Blessed in the Atlantic,[69] describing them in such idyllic terms that Sertorius was strongly tempted to take up a quiet retirement there. The Kilikians, however, had no such ambition and went to Mauretania to involve themselves in a dispute regarding a certain Askalis, son of Iphtha, who had been deposed, allegedly from the Mauretanian throne. Modern ignorance of the contemporary political situation in Mauretania makes it almost impossible to understand why the pirates chose to help restore the king, or why Sertorius soon decided to join the dispute on the side opposing Askalis. But it may be that he saw this as a way to assert his power against his nemesis Sulla, who had sent an army to aid Askalis. Sertorius defeated both Askalis and the Romans, incorporated the survivors into his own force, and besieged and soon captured Tingis, Askalis' base, establishing himself as ruler of that city. The sizable Italian mercantile colony might well have welcomed a compatriot. Sertorius now considered himself in control of all Mauretania (πάντων ἐγκρατής) and ruled wisely and justly, presumably for several months.[70] Then he was summoned by the Lusitanians to be their commander against Rome. Although it was a difficult decision, he saw a

---

68 Kilikian piracy was at its peak in these years, with the collapse of Seleukid control of coastal Kilikia and the failure, as yet, of Rome to deal effectively with the issue: the pirates were always anxious to assist those opposed to Roman power (see Plutarch, *Pompeius* 24, a summary of the effects of piracy at this time). Literary sources, however, often use "Kilikian" generically when discussing pirates: see Konrad (supra note 64), pp. 102–3. A useful, although old, survey of Kilikian piracy is Henry A. Ormerod, *Piracy in the Ancient World*, reprint (Chicago: Argonaut, 1967), pp. 190–247; a good recent bibliography on ancient piracy appears in David C. Braund, "Piracy under the Principate and the Ideology of Imperial Eradication," in *War and Society in the Roman World*, ed. John Rich and Graham Shipley (London: Routledge, 1993), pp. 210–12, supplemented by Philip De Souza, *Piracy in the Graeco-Roman World* (Cambridge: Cambridge University Press, 1999), who stressed (pp. 132–3) that Sertorius' involvement with the pirates was used by Plutarch as a moral paradigm for the decline in his fortunes. Yet the recent memory of piracy in these waters may have influenced Augustus' feeling fifty years later that Mauretania needed a strong Roman presence.

69 See also Sallust, *Histories* 1.90 (McGushin). The description best fits Madeira's two largest islands, Madeira and Porto Santo (Konrad [supra note 64], pp. 106–7; Paul T. Keyser, "From Myth to Map: The Blessed Isles in the First Century BC," *AncW* 26, 1993, 157–61), but one should not be too precise with sailors' tales. Madeira had been known to the Greco-Roman world since at least the third century BC (Timaios [*FGrHist* #566] fr. 164 = Diodoros 5.19–20). For the argument (largely refuted by Konrad) that the Canaries are meant, see Philip O. Spann, "Sallust, Plutarch, and the 'Isles of the Blest,'" *TI* 9, 1977, 75–80.

70 During his stay, Sertorius opened up the tomb of the founder of Tingis, Antaios, and was astonished to find that the body was 60 *peches*, or 9 Greek feet, in length. This is one of several tales scattered through Greek and Roman history of opening the tombs of figures from mythology and discovering their enormous stature: the most famous is the account of the bones of Orestes at Tegea in the Peloponnesos (Herodotos 1.67–8). Such episodes are conventionally explained – if such is necessary – as

chance eventually to be restored to legitimacy within the Roman world, and thus abandoned Mauretania, probably early in 80 BC.[71]

This curious episode is both revealing and puzzling regarding the status of Mauretania around 81 BC. By this time North Africa had had a history of receiving disaffected Romans, so Sertorius' choice of it as a refuge is not surprising. If Bocchus I had still been on the throne, as he seems to have been into that year, an opponent of Sulla would not have expected a good reception in the territory, and hence Sertorius' initial expulsion. His retreat into the Atlantic exposed him to the romanticized tales of the Islands of the Blessed that had been circulating in seamen's lore since at least the time of Homer,[72] and it is not difficult to imagine that one whose life had been as erratic as Sertorius' would find such stories attractive.[73] Some years later, Horace, referring directly to Sertorius, would write of the longing "to go wherever our feet take us, wherever the waves, Notus, or bold Africa calls."[74] The Islands of the Blessed were Horace's ideal refuge for those seeking to escape what (in his day) had become a second generation of civil war: "let us seek the fields, the blessed fields, and the islands of abundance," describing them in terms almost identical to those that the sailors had used to tempt Sertorius.[75] Such was part of the mystique of northwest Africa in the late Republic and the early Augustan period.

The most inscrutable part of Sertorius' escapades is his involvement with the enigmatic Askalis, whose territory was localized in the vicinity of Tingis. Otherwise unknown, he is presented in Plutarch's account as one who had been deposed from the Mauretanian throne and was seeking a restoration.[76] His position was supported by Sulla, which means, given Sulla's personal history, that he was probably a vassal of Bocchus I,[77] whose

the discovery of large animal bones or even fossils (see George Huxley, "Bones for Orestes," *GRBS* 20, 1979, 145–8). The Tomb of Antaios is usually associated with Lixos (Strabo 17.3.8), where Antaios had his palace (*NH* 5.2–3), rather than Tingis, but this is a minor point in what clearly was a event staged by Sertorius to create a heroic context that would enhance his status among the citizens of Tingis. Relevant precedents certainly known to Sertorius include the removal of the bones of Theseus to Athens (Plutarch, *Kimon* 8.5–6), and even the circumstances surrounding the body of Alexander the Great (Aelian, *Historical Miscellany* 12.64).

71 Spann, *Quintus Sertorius* (supra note 64), pp. 54–5.

72 Homer, *Odyssey* 4.563–8.

73 Konrad (supra note 64), pp. 109–10.

74 Horace, *Epode* 16.21–2 ("ire, pedes quocumque ferent, quocumque per undas Notus vocabit aut protervus Africus"). On the poem generally, see Eduard Fraenkel, *Horace* (Oxford: Clarendon Press, 1957), pp. 42–55; Syme (supra note 66), pp. 284–6.

75 Horace, *Epode* 16.41–2: "arva, beata petamus arva divites et insulas." On Juba II and the Islands of the Blessed, see infra, pp. 196–8.

76 On his position, see Coltelloni-Trannoy, p. 107; Scardigli (supra note 65), pp. 246–8; Gabriel Camps, "Ascalis," *EB* 7, 1989, 954.

77 Despite Gsell, vol. 7, p. 271.

recent death may have led to Askalis' overthrow. The issue is complicated by the fact that Askalis is not a North African name, but one that seems Greek, remindful of Askalos, the eponymous founder of the city of Askalon on the coast of Palestine. Although this eponym was known as early as the fifth century BC,[78] it is probably fabricated, but Askalon itself was a center of hellenized Phoenician culture by the late second century BC.[79] It seems plausible that an adventurer from this city could end up as a petty dynast of Tingis at the other end of the Mediterranean.[80] Tingis was itself a city with Hellenic and Phoenician roots, and northwest Africa had become increasingly topical in the Greek world since the second century BC. Thus Askalis was in all likelihood a Levantine adventurer established at Tingis, but subsidiary to Bocchus I. His claim to be king of all Mauretania is exaggerated, but Tingis seems virtually to have been an autonomous petty state.[81] At the time of the death of Bocchus, perhaps midway in 81 BC, Askalis was deposed by his subjects – instability would be a natural result of the death of a king who had been on the throne for at least forty years – and Sulla, indebted to the memory of Bocchus, attempted to restore Askalis to the throne. But like so many situations in North African history it became tangled in the disputes between powerful Romans, and Sertorius, who prevented the restoration, ended up ruler of Tingis itself, the inhabitants already having shown their receptiveness to a foreign ruler.[82] This was hardly "all Mauretania," as he claimed in an exaggeration he had perhaps learned from Askalis, but nevertheless, more than the single city was under his control.[83] Only Sertorius' patriotism kept him from remaining long.

The Askalis episode is demonstrative of the confusion regarding Mauretanian history in the first half of the first century BC. The names of other ruling personalities are known, but it becomes difficult to fit them into a chronologically coherent account, or even to determine the limits of the territory they ruled.[84] Some of this may be due to Roman unfamiliarity with

---

78 Xanthos of Lydia (*FGrHist* #765), fr. 8.

79 Kokkinos, *Herodian Dynasty*, pp. 112–28.

80 By the second century AC there were large numbers of Levantines in Mauretania. Although this was in part due to the freedom of movement in imperial times, it might have been the culmination of a tendency originating in the commercial environment of the late Republic. See Maurice Euzennat, "Grecs et Orientaux in Maurétanie Tingitane," *AntAfr* 5, 1971, 161–78.

81 Carcopino (supra note 12), pp. 174–5. The independent status of Tingis (Tangier) has continued sporadically into modern times.

82 Like modern Tangier, ancient Tingis consisted of a mixed population, perhaps with no dominant ethnic group.

83 Plutarch, *Sertorius* 9.5.

84 An example is the case of Magudulsa. He fled to Rome, seemingly to the household of M. Livius Drusus, plebian tribune in 91 BC and great-grandfather of the emperor Tiberius. But Drusus was said to have betrayed Magudulsa because of a bribe from Bocchus and effected his death by means of an elephant (*De viris illustribus* 66), perhaps a slander by Drusus' enemies (Gsell, vol. 7, p. 269; see also Romanelli, *Storia*, pp. 101–2). This anecdote cannot be connected with any coherent thread in Maure-

the names, many of which are similar.[85] Other problems may result from the uncertain frontiers and isolated population centers of Mauretania, local chieftains who may have called themselves kings, and other attempts by rulers to exaggerate their position and power.

The last years of Bocchus I, after his Capitol dedication of 91 BC, seemingly were ones of decline. The lack of any strong successor – the ephemeral Bogudes I is the probable candidate – and the Mauretanian tolerance of adventurers such as Askalis and Sertorius show that the old king was severely weakened. Even though Askalis seems to have ruled only as petty king of Tingis and its area, and with Bocchus' consent, his very existence, his claim to be king of all Mauretania, and his own weak hold on power indicate the overall instability of the Mauretanian kingdom at that time. Perhaps Bocchus' acquisition of extensive territory after the fall of Jugurtha and his development of Iol as a second royal seat were destabilizing factors. Bogudes I, if the successor, seems not to have lasted long. It is probable that the following years were obscure and unstable ones for Mauretania, although one must not be misled by the failure of Roman historians to write about areas not currently relevant to their interests. A certain Leptasta emerged in the 70s BC, styled "king," sending an unknown person, charged with treason, from Mauretania to an unknown place. He is cited only in a fragment of Book 2 of Sallust's *Histories*, which covered 77–74 BC; the event may be related to the conflicts between Pompeius and Sertorius in those years, but this is purely hypothetical. Whether Leptasta was the legitimate successor of Bocchus I or Bogudes I, or another petty chieftain in the manner of Askalis, cannot be known.[86]

By the latter part of the first half of the first century BC, Mauretania seems to have been partitioned and under the control of two separate but related rulers, Bocchus II and Bogudes II,[87] whose names indicate their descent from Bocchus I, although the lineage is unknown. The division of Mauretania

tanian history. The single source calls Magudulsa "princeps" of Mauretania: he may be the Magdalses mentioned by Appian (*Noumidika*), a member of the court of Bocchus I and involved in the betrayal of Jugurtha. The date of Magudulsa's flight to Rome is often assumed to be that of Drusus' plebian tribunate but may be earlier (Drusus had been military tribune probably in 105 BC, the year of Jugurtha's surrender: see Broughton, vol. 1, pp. 557–8; vol. 2, pp. 21–2). It cannot be later than 91 BC because Drusus was assassinated that year. Nevertheless, he had a sympathy for African royal refugees: he had provided refuge for Adherbal of Numidia when his fatal quarrel erupted with Jugurtha after 118 BC. Magudulsa may have been a son of Bocchus I, a disfavored member of the royal court, or a petty chieftain in the manner of Askalis. See F. Münzer, "M. Livius Drusus" (#18), *RE* 13, 1926, 871.

85 Gsell, vol. 7, pp. 271–2; Coltelloni-Trannoy, p. 83.

86 Sallust, *Histories* 2.93 (McGushin) and p. 12 of the McGushin edition. Leptasta cannot be the same as Iphtha the father of Askalis, despite Gsell, vol. 7, pp. 271–2, Carcopino (supra note 12), pp. 174–5, and Coltelloni-Trannoy, p. 79, since he was king in 77 BC or later and Askalis had been deposed by 80 BC, but he may have been a son.

87 *NH* 5.19; Strabo 17.3.7.

between them – Bocchus ruled from Iol[88] and Bogudes from Volubilis[89] – indicates that they were of equal status, cousins or even brothers. Because Mauretania is so easily divided into separate but equal portions, the split was not difficult to accomplish, avoiding the joint rule that was so often disastrous in Numidia. The father of Bocchus II was Sosus, named by his son on his coins.[90] Although Bocchus II did not indicate whether his father had been king, Sosus may have been the Mastanesosus whom P. Vatinius encountered, probably in 62 BC. Cicero, as he questioned Vatinius, described his passage across North Africa: "Were you not in the kingdom of Hiempsal, and then the kingdom of Mastanesosus, and then did you not go across Mauretania to the Straits?"[91] Thus the route is clear: from the Numidian kingdom ruled by Jugurtha's nephew Hiempsal II to the kingdom of Mastanesosus and then through Mauretania (used in its older, more limiting sense) and across the straits into Spain. Mastanesosus, then, ruled at Iol. He may have been an otherwise unknown son of Bocchus I or Bogudes I, perhaps the ruler who divided the kingdom between his two sons.[92]

The earliest evidence for the reign of Bocchus II[93] is the arrival in eastern Mauretania of yet another dispossessed Roman, P. Sittius.[94] From Nuceria in Campania, he had developed significant commercial interests in Mauretania, probably in the manner of the *negotiatores* who had been in the territory for some time. Before 64 BC he became a trading partner with the king of Mauretania.[95] No name is provided but it is probable that it was Bocchus II, given their later intimacy. His investments seem to have been in African grain, and he ended up heavily in debt[96] and was made a scapegoat for the high import prices of the commodity, standing trial twice, on one occasion being defended by Cicero.[97] His Italian possessions were eventually sold to cover these debts. When the conspiracy of Q. Sergius Catalina was uncovered in 63 BC, Sittius was suspected of complicity, seemingly on little

---

88 Solinus 25.16; Pomponius Mela 1.29.

89 He may also have used Lixos as a royal seat, which flourished with fine art at this time (Jodin, *Volubilis*, p. 312).

90 Infra, p. 94.

91 Cicero, *In Vatinium* 12: "in regno Hiempsalis, fuerisne in regno Mastanesosi, venerisne ad fretum per Mauretaniam?"

92 On the problem of identifying the local rulers at this time, see W. Huss, "Die westmassylischen Könige," *AncSoc* 20, 1989, 209–20.

93 On Bocchus II, see Eliman Klebs, "Bocchus" (#2), *RE* 3, 1899, 578–9; Gabriel Camps, "Bocchus," *EB* 10, 1991, 1545–7.

94 On Sittius, see F. Münzer, "P. Sittius" (#3), *RE* 2, ser. 3, 1927, 409–11; Gsell, vol. 8, pp. 54–6; Wilson (supra note 31), pp. 51–3.

95 Cicero, *Pro Sulla* 56: "important financial dealings with the king of Mauretania" ("magna ratione cum Mauretaniae rege contracta").

96 Wilson (supra note 31), p. 52, suggested that he may even have loaned money to the king of Mauretania.

97 Cicero, *Ad familiares* 5.17; see also *De domo sua* 11. But see Cicero, *Epistulae ad familiares* (ed. Shackleton Bailey), vol. 1, p. 323.

evidence other than that he had been in Mauretania at the time and was said to have been raising an army, an easy charge given the history of Roman adventurers in North Africa.[98] Although it is hard to establish a chronology for Sittius' early career other than this alleged involvement with Catalina,[99] at some undetermined time he abandoned Italy and took up permanent residence in Mauretania. He evidently had an entourage or military force[100] and eventually ended up at the court of Bocchus II.[101] By 46 BC he was commanding part of Bocchus' troops and assisting Julius Caesar in his war against the Pompeians.[102] The intrigues of Sittius provide the only evidence for the early career of Bocchus II, who thus seems to have come to the throne before 64 BC.

Bogudes II's early career is also obscure.[103] At some unspecified date he mounted an expedition along the Atlantic coast, seemingly into the tropics.[104] He returned with gigantic reeds and asparagus; the former he presented to his wife, perhaps the same Eunoë Maura with whom Julius Caesar had an affair.[105] Caesar also lavished presents on both king and queen, which implies that he may have visited the royal court at Volubilis or Lixos. Or he may have encountered Eunoë elsewhere, perhaps if she joined her husband while he campaigned in Spain after Thapsus.[106] Eunoë is a Greek name, and

98 Sallust, *Bellum Catalinae* 21.3; Erich S. Gruen, *The Last Generation of the Roman Republic*, first paperback printing (Berkeley: University of California Press, 1995), p. 285.

99 Cicero's letter to him is undated; commentators have placed it between 57 and 52 BC. It was written shortly after Sittius' second trial, and perhaps in May of 56 BC (Jacques Heurgon, "La Lettre de Cicéron à P. Sittius (Ad Fam., V, 17)," *Latomus* 9, 1950, 369–77), or in the autumn of that year (Cicero, ed. Shackleton Bailey [supra note 97], vol. 1, p. 323).

100 Dio 43.3.1. These may have been remnants of Sertorius' followers (P. A. Brunt, *Italian Manpower, 225 B.C.–A.D. 14*) (Oxford: Oxford University Press, 1971), p. 164. Appian (*Civil War* 4.54) implied that Sittius spent some time in Mauretania with a substantial force and allying with many different parties.

101 The date of his departure from Italy cannot easily be determined. Cicero's letter may have been written at that time – it refers to abandoning the Republic – but this is not explicit. A series of letters by M. Caelius Rufus to Cicero from the summer of 51 BC (*Ad familiares* 8.2, 4, 8, 9) repeatedly refer to a contract with a certain Sittius, perhaps involving the shipment of panthers and other wild animals to Rome. If this is the Sittius in question, it seems reasonable to assume that Sittius was in Africa by that time, but the identity is by no means certain, and since Cicero was proconsul in Kilikia, this Sittius may have been in the East (which does not rule out P. Sittius of Nuceria). See David Magie, *Roman Rule in Asia Minor to the End of the Third Century after Christ* (Princeton, N.J.: Princeton University Press, 1950), p. 1251.

102 *De bello africo* 25; supra, p. 35.

103 Eliman Klebs, "Bogudes" (#2), *RE* 3, 1899, 608–9; Gabriel Camps, "Bogud," *EB* 10, 1991, 1557–8.

104 Strabo 17.3.5; his source is an otherwise unknown "Iphikrates," long emended to Hypsikrates, of Amisos, who wrote on history, perhaps in the first century BC (*FGrHist* #190; see Remo Giomini, "Ipsicrate," *Maia* n.s. 8, 1956, 49–55), although it is difficult to connect the other extant fragments with an interest in West Africa (but see fr. 4, on the Ethiopians). Tatian (*Oration to the Greeks* 37) knew of a Hypsikrates who wrote on Phoenician matters.

105 Suetonius, *Julius* 52.

106 Dio 43.36–8.

she probably was a person of stature not only to marry the Mauretanian king but to receive Caesar's interest (Suetonius mentioned her in the same context as Kleopatra VII), and thus demonstrative of eastern dynastic connections with Mauretania at that time.

In 49 BC, as the struggle with Pompeius intensified, both Bocchus II and Bogudes II were officially recognized as kings by Caesar.[107] Bogudes joined the Caesarean forces in Spain in 47 BC,[108] which resulted in a Pompeian invasion of Mauretania the following year,[109] when a fleet led by Cn. Pompeius the younger attacked Ascurum[110] on the coast but was repulsed. After Thapsus, in which he seems to have taken no part, Bogudes returned to Spain and fought on the Caesarean side at the Battle of Munda in early 45 BC, the final event of this phase of the civil war.[111]

Bocchus II, assisted by Sittius, actively joined the war in Numidia and Roman Africa against the Pompeians and Juba I, occupying the Numidian capital of Cirta.[112] According to Dio,[113] he made an alliance after Thapsus with the son of Pompeius in Spain, sending his own sons there, but otherwise he seems to have been firmly on the Caesarean side, later supporting Octavian. If Dio was correct, it is probable that Bocchus II was briefly playing a double game or that the alliance was to oppose his relative Bogudes II, actually in Spain with Caesar, a glimpse of family rivalry that transcended Roman politics. Yet within a year Caesar was dead and both kings became involved in the further civil war,[114] this time unquestionably on opposite sides. Bogudes eventually left to join Antonius, leaving all Mauretania to Bocchus. By 31 BC both were dead, and Mauretanian affairs and the vacant kingship awaited settlement by the new regime.

---

107 Dio 41.42.7. Faustus Cornelius Sulla, whose coins of a few years previously had depicted the surrender of Jugurtha, was to be sent to Mauretania, but the proposal was vetoed (Caesar, *Bellum civile* 1.6.4). He joined the Pompeian cause, ended up in Africa, and was killed after Thapsus by none other than Sittius (*De bello africo* 95).

108 *De bello alexandrino* 59, 62. On his involvement in the Roman civil war, see Enrique Gozalbes Cravioto, "La intervención de la Mauritania de Bogud en las guerras civiles romanas en la provincia Hispania Ulterior," in *Actas del II Congreso de Historia de Andalucía: Historia Antiqua* (Córdoba: Consejería de Cultura y Medio Ambiente de la Junta de Andalucía, 1994), pp. 287–93.

109 *De bello africo* 23.

110 The location is unknown: Gsell 8.45–6; Romanelli, *Storia*, p. 121. Since it was an attack against Bogudes, it must have been in the west, probably on the coast east of Tingis.

111 Dio 43.36–8.

112 Appian, *Civil War* 2.96; Dio 43.3; *De bello africo* 25.

113 Dio 43.36.

114 Infra, pp. 93–5.

3

JUBA'S YOUTH AND EDUCATION

The infant Juba II arrived in Rome and participated in Caesar's African triumph of 46 BC. He then spent his youth and adolescence in the households of Caesar's heirs, exalted company that exposed him to the most talented military and intellectual leaders of the emergent Augustan regime, eventually accompanying Augustus on campaign, receiving Roman citizenship, and marrying a royal wife. Thus when Augustus eventually placed him on the throne of Mauretania, young Juba was eminently trained both politically and culturally to be the implementer of Augustan policy in northwest Africa.

The exact date of Juba's birth is not known. The first documentation of him is the appearance at Caesar's triumph, at which he was described as a βρέφος[1] or νήπιος,[2] words that imply extreme youth.[3] The failure of the sources to cite a specific age indicates that he might have been only a few months old, and probably at most 2 years of age, which would make him just over 20 when he received the kingship in 25 BC. Thus his birth was perhaps in early 48 BC, when his father was at the peak of his career after the victory at the Bagradas.[4]

---

1 Appian, *Civil War* 2.101.

2 Plutarch, *Caesar* 55. None of the other accounts of Caesar's triumph (for which see supra, Chapter 1, note 176) mentions Juba. Appian and Plutarch probably used the history of Asinius Pollio (consul in 40 BC), who was with Caesar in Africa and was specifically cited by Plutarch (*Caesar* 46) as a source; on Appian's use of Asinius Pollio, see Alain M. Gowing, *The Triumviral Narratives of Appian and Cassius Dio* (Ann Arbor: University of Michigan Press, 1992), pp. 3, 40.

3 Both are standard Greek words for "infancy." They are often used together: see, for example, Euripides, *Ion* 1399, where Kreusa described her son. The words are common in Greek literature from Homer on: βρέφος seems more often to refer to animals, νήπιος to humans. Rarely is there any other definition, and there is no reason to assume that either Appian or Plutarch used these complementary words in any but their most common meaning.

4 There seems no evidence for the specific ages offered by modern commentators, such as 4 (Matthias Gelzer, *Caesar: Politician and Statesman*, trans. Peter Needham [Cambridge, Mass.: Harvard University Press, 1968], p. 284, and Elizabeth Rawson, "Caesar, Civil War and Dictatorship," *CAH*[2] 9, 1994, 436) or about 6 (J. P. D. V. Balsdon, *Romans and Aliens* [London: Duckworth, 1979], pp. 46, 203). Gsell (vol. 8, p. 207) called him "très jeune" at the time of the triumph and stated that he was born "vers 50." None of these suggestions seems consistent with the Greek: ages of 4 to 6 would imply that Juba was a παῖς rather than a βρέφος or νήπιος. See infra, p. 74, for evidence of Juba's birthdate based on his military service.

From the time of the triumph in the summer of 46 BC until his accession to the throne of Mauretania twenty-one years later there is no explicit mention of Juba in the historical record. Yet where he spent those two decades is an issue of crucial importance in his maturation as scholar and future king. They were vital years in Roman history, encompassing the assassination of Caesar, the rise and fall of M. Antonius, the demonization and death of Kleopatra VII, and the transformation of Caesar's heir from the young radical Octavian to the wise and paternal Augustus. Rome was innovatively rebuilt, and Greek and Roman scholars and other literati flourished. Eastern dynasts such as Herod the Great visited the city. Juba, as he grew up, was part of this dynamic environment.

Juba's integration into Roman society continued a policy that had emerged in the second century BC and was to become common in the Augustan period: Augustus himself brought many offspring of barbarian royalty to the city and educated them within his own family.[5] This practice, which allowed the children to become romanized, is first documented as an official practice with the future Ariarathes V of Kappadokia, who was educated in Rome before returning home to assume the kingship in 163 BC.[6] Nevertheless, it was rare during the Republic,[7] being limited to the first half of the second century BC, the period of spreading Roman contacts with the Greek world. After 153/152 BC it died out and was not reinstated for over a century.[8]

As was so often the case, the Romans were implementing a common Hellenistic procedure. Royal children had long been sent to the great cultural centers of the Greek world for their education, especially to Athens.[9] Several of Juba's own ancestors had benefited from this policy. Others had become attached to prominent Romans.[10] These precedents may have assisted Caesar and then Augustus in making education of royal children a policy, and thus Juba was saved to grow up in Rome,[11] although Caesar may have needed no

---

5 Suetonius, *Augustus* 48.

6 Livy 42.19.3–6; Braund, *Friendly King*, pp. 9–10. Livy's phraseology is perhaps significant: "so that from childhood he would be used to Roman customs and men" ("ut iam inde a puero assuesceret moribus Romanis hominibusque").

7 Braund could only find five cases.

8 The last examples are the future Pergamene king Attalos III and the Seleukid king Demetrios II (Polybios 33.18).

9 Braund, *Friendly King*, pp. 11–14.

10 Supra, pp. 14, 17, 18–19, 21.

11 Juba is the only known example of a royal child growing up and being educated in Rome during the 30s BC. Although Suetonius (*Augustus* 48) indicated that this was a regular policy of the Augustan court, instances other than Juba are from the late 20s BC and thereafter, beginning perhaps with the children of Herod the Great and those of Phraates IV of Parthia (Braund, *Friendly King*, pp. 10–12). The children of Antonius and Kleopatra VII, who came to Rome in late 30 or early 29 BC, are peculiar and anomalous instances, since they were half Roman and were not sent by their parents. See infra, pp. 82–3.

other reason than his legendary clemency[12] to spare the child. One is reminded of the scene on the first Boscoreale Cup, of about forty years later, in which a barbarian child (in this case from Gaul) is presented to Augustus and "welcomed to Rome's authority."[13] Yet the fate of others in the triumph of 46 BC varied. Arsinoë (IV), the sister of Kleopatra VII, whom a faction had proclaimed queen of Egypt, was released, spared out of consideration for her brothers, Ptolemaios XIII and Ptolemaios XIV, and perhaps because her sister was Caesar's paramour.[14] Yet the Keltic leader Vercingetorix was executed.[15] Juba's survival may have been in part due to the questionable morality of Caesar's African war, where notable Romans had fallen on both sides: clemency to the survivors might have seemed wise.[16] His distinguished ancestry – he was, as noted, a direct descendant of the great Massinissa, who epitomized (to the Roman mind) barbarian royalty at its best – also played a role. But the sparing of Juba indicated some commitment toward his upbringing (unlike the case of Arsinoë, who seems to have been an adult),[17] and after the triumph some arrangements needed to be made for his care and education.

There is no evidence as to whose household Juba entered. The obvious choice is Caesar's,[18] but one wonders about the suitability of introducing an infant into the home of a childless middle-aged couple, where the atmosphere would soon become tense upon the arrival of Kleopatra and her entourage, including another royal child, Kaisarion.[19] These uncertainties would only increase in the months leading to Caesar's murder, and wherever Caesar's household was from summer 46 to March 44 BC, it was hardly the place to raise an infant. At any rate, it ceased to exist in March 44 BC, and the Horti Caesaris became public property.[20] What happened to Caesar's

12 Suetonius, *Julius* 73–4.

13 Ann L. Kuttner, *Dynasty and Empire in the Age of Augustus: The Case of the Boscoreale Cups* (Berkeley: University of California Press, 1995), p. 112; as Kuttner pointed out, there are similar scenes on the Ara Pacis (pp. 99–111).

14 Dio 42.39; Sullivan, *Near Eastern Royalty*, pp. 258–60, 265. Nonetheless, Kleopatra VII soon was to turn against her and arranged five years later for Antonius to implement her execution: Appian, *Civil War* 5.9; Dio 48.24.

15 Dio 43.19.

16 On the moral problem of the triumph, see Robert Alan Gurval, *Actium and Augustus: The Politics and Emotions of Civil War* (Ann Arbor: University of Michigan Press, 1995), pp. 23–5.

17 Arsinoë's date of birth cannot be determined. She was probably younger than Kleopatra VII, since she was not made queen upon the death of their father Ptolemaios XII, but she was possibly an adult by 48 BC when Caesar made her queen of Cyprus (Dio 42.35.5).

18 So Romanelli, *Storia*, p. 142.

19 Sullivan, *Near Eastern Royalty*, pp. 262–6. Dio (43.27.3) placed her arrival late in 46 BC, after the triumphs but before Caesar's departure for Spain; she went to live in Caesar's own house. Whether Caesar lived there too is not clear. As *pontifex maximus* he was entitled to live in the Domus Publica in the Forum (Suetonius, *Julius* 46), but he does not seem to have been in residence there in May of 45 BC (Cicero, *Atticus* 12.45). After Caesar's murder, Cicero seems to have encountered Kleopatra living in Caesar's estate across the Tiber, the Horti Caesaris (Cicero, *Atticus* 15.15).

20 Suetonius, *Julius* 83.

first house, in the Subura,[21] and his gardens on the Quirinal[22] is unknown, but it may be significant that his widow Calpurnia vanishes from the historical record after the Ides of March.[23]

Assuming Caesar realized that a royal infant might not best be raised in his deteriorating household, potentially in competition with Kaisarion, he might have handed Juba over to one of his closer relatives.[24] Caesar's family, however, is remarkably poorly known. He had two sisters, both named Julia. The sons of one, L. Pinarius and Q. Pedius, were named as Caesar's coheirs along with Octavian;[25] both resigned their inheritance. Pinarius was with Antonius before Philippi but is not known with certainty thereafter,[26] and Pedius was Octavian's colleague in the consulship of 43 BC but died during the year.[27] No children are known of either. Even if Juba had gone to this branch of the family, he could not have stayed long.

Caesar's other sister had a daughter, Atia, who had two children, Octavia and Octavius.[28] Their father, C. Octavius, was dead, and Atia was now

21 Suetonius, *Julius* 46.

22 *NTDAR* 197.

23 The fate of Calpurnia is one of the mysteries of late Republican history. She is last seen handing Caesar's papers and some possessions over to Antonius the night of the Ides of March (Plutarch, *Antonius* 15; Appian, *Civil War* 2.125). As the widow of Caesar she would have been an important player in the months to come, and as the daughter of a consular (L. Calpurnius Piso Caesoninus, consul in 58: Suetonius, *Julius* 21; Erich S. Gruen, *The Last Generation of the Roman Republic*, first paperback printing [Berkeley: University of California Press, 1995], p. 143), who was still alive and would have been active in the political maneuvering of 43 BC (Broughton, vol. 2, pp. 350–1), she would have been an ideal marriage prospect: she would have been at most only in her thirties, as her father could not have been born before the mid-90s BC. Her family remained prominent, as her younger brother, L. Calpurnius Piso (consul in 15 BC), lived to AD 32 and became a patron of literature (Ronald Syme, *The Augustan Aristocracy* [Oxford: Clarendon Press, 1986], pp. 329–45). One can only assume that Calpurnia soon died or completely withdrew from public view immediately after the Ides. Nevertheless, it is another example of the invisible quality of women not attached to men.

24 Another possibility, purely speculative but intriguing, is that the young Juba was handed over to relatives of the supporters of his father. Although over time this might not have been politically expedient, in 46 BC it would have seemed another example of Caesar's clemency. The prominent ally of Juba I, Cato, had close relatives in Rome who were within Caesar's circle: Cato's son-in-law M. Junius Brutus and his young bride Porcia, Cato's daughter (Plutarch, *Brutus* 2, 13). These relatives of Cato may have assisted in forming the Numidian exile community in Rome that was still functioning in early Augustan times (infra, p. 70). The events that soon swept up Brutus and Porcia meant that young Juba could not long remain in this household, which in fact was extinct within four years, but closeness to Cato's relatives may be one of the reasons Juba later commemorated his father's ally at Volubilis (infra, pp. 144–5).

25 Appian, *Civil War* 3.22; Suetonius, *Julius* 83: for their exact relationship to Caesar, see Ronald Syme, *The Roman Revolution*, revised paperback edition (Oxford: Clarendon Press, 1960), pp. 128–9, and Gruen, *Last Generation* (supra note 23), p. 119.

26 Appian, *Civil War* 4.107. It is possible that he is the L. Pinarius Scarpus who was Antonius' agent in Kyrene in 31–30 BC, and who turned the legions there over to Octavian (Syme, *Roman Revolution* [supra note 25], p. 129; Broughton, vol. 2, p. 422).

27 Appian, *Civil War* 3.94, 4.6.

28 Octavius would become Octavian when he accepted Caesar's inheritance in 44 BC, and then Augustus in 27 BC.

married to L. Marcius Philippus (consul in 56 BC). By 44 BC he was living in retirement in Campania and advising his stepson Octavius about his inheritance.[29] Octavius was as yet unmarried and lived with his mother and stepfather;[30] Octavia had been married for some years to C. Claudius Marcellus (consul in 50 BC).[31] Caesar's niece Atia and her descendants seem to have been the dominant side of the Caesarian family and thus this is the most likely place for Juba to have ended up. Less than two years later, however, Caesar was assassinated, and within the year Atia would die.[32] This brought about significant changes to the structure of the family. Octavius – now Caesar's heir and known as Octavian – would briefly marry Claudia,[33] but the marriage was never consummated and they never had a permanent household. Yet at about the same time, Octavia's only male child, M. Claudius Marcellus, would be born.[34] Thus Octavia and the elder Marcellus were starting their own family at the time of Caesar's death, and all signs point to them as the ones most likely to have housed Juba, as Octavia was now the matron of the Julian family.[35]

Yet Octavian's fortunes were changing rapidly. He soon divorced Claudia – conflict with his mother-in-law Fulvia was said to have been the problem[36] – and married Scribonia, whose family was connected to that of Pompeius Magnus.[37] His daughter Julia was born in 39 BC. He also purchased a house originally belonging to the orator and poet C. Licinius Calvus, near the Forum Romanum, perhaps on the north slope of the Palatine.[38]

Meanwhile, Octavia's husband Marcellus had died, perhaps early in 40 BC, leaving her a widow with three small children of her own and probably Juba. Conveniently, at almost the same time, Fulvia, the wife of M. Antonius and Octavian's recent mother-in-law, also died, leaving two young sons, M. Antonius Antyllus and Iullus Antonius. As a result of the accord between M. Antonius and Octavian in autumn 40 BC, commonly known as the Pact of Brundisium,[39] the obvious marriage was made, and now the

---

29 Suetonius, *Augustus* 8; Syme, *Roman Revolution* (supra note 25), p. 128.

30 Cicero, *Atticus* 14.11.

31 J. P. D. V. Balsdon, *Roman Women: Their History and Habits* (London: Bodley Head, 1962), p. 69.

32 Suetonius, *Augustus* 61.

33 Claudia was a daughter of the notorious P. Clodius Pulcher and Fulvia: she was valuable to Octavian because her stepfather was M. Antonius (Suetonius, *Augustus* 62).

34 Propertius 3.18.

35 Plutarch, *Antonius* 31, 57; on Octavia, see M. Hammond, "Octavia" (#96), *RE* 24, 1937, 1859–68; Susan E. Wood, *Imperial Women: A Study in Public Images, 40 B.C.–A.D. 68*, Mnemosyne Supp. 194 (Leiden 1999), pp. 30–5.

36 Suetonius, *Augustus* 62. On the mother-in-law, Fulvia, at this time, see Charles L. Babcock, "The Early Career of Fulvia," *AJP* 86, 1965, 1–32; Diana Delia, "Fulvia Reconsidered," in *Women's History and Ancient History*, ed. Sarah B. Pomeroy (Chapel Hill: University of North Carolina Press, 1991), pp. 197–217.

37 Appian, *Civil War* 5.53; Suetonius, *Augustus* 62; Syme, *Roman Revolution* (supra note 25), p. 213.

38 Suetonius, *Augustus* 72; *NTDAR* 130.

39 Syme, *Roman Revolution* (supra note 25), pp. 216–18.

virtuous and beautiful Octavia and her new husband Antonius had a household of at least six children, all except Juba under 5 years of age.

Soon, however, Octavian himself, after two false starts, began to demonstrate tangible evidence of dynastic thinking. He divorced Scribonia to marry Livia Drusilla, who divorced Tiberius Claudius Nero and brought her infant son Tiberius into Octavian's household; her second son, Drusus, was born at the time of the marriage.[40] Presumably at this time Octavian purchased for his new bride and his suddenly growing family the house of Q. Hortensius Hortalus (consul in 69 BC), one of the greatest orators of the previous generation.[41] Although the house was modest, the neighboring and lavish property that had belonged to Q. Lutatius Catulus (consul in 78 BC) was incorporated into it.[42] Octavia and her brood were next-door neighbors.[43] Thus the imperial court that began to develop as early as 38 BC included a remarkable number of small children, all of whom needed to be educated. Octavian's own relatives included his daughter Julia, approaching 2 years of age; his three nieces, the Marcellae and the elder Antonia (the first child of M. Antonius and Octavia); and his nephew Marcellus. A second Antonia was to follow within two years, and there were also Livia's two sons, Tiberius, approaching 5 years of age, and the infant Drusus, as well as Antonius' two sons. And there was Juba. None of these children was older than 5 except for Juba, who was about 10.

Octavia was to become legendary for raising the children of others.[44] Her reputation in this respect particularly refers to Antonius' children, especially those he was to have by Kleopatra, but also includes the growing family of Octavian, his relatives, in-laws, and foreigners. A dozen children were in this family by the mid-30s BC, mostly Octavia's own children and stepchildren, as well as Juba and another youthful non-Roman member of Caesar's household that Octavian seems to have acquired. This was Hyginos, who had come as a boy to Rome at Caesar's behest from either Alexandria or Spain.[45] He eventually became Octavian's librarian and the teacher of Ovid.[46] This library was part of the Palatine Temple of Apollo, on Octavian's property, probably inaugurated when the temple was dedicated in 28 BC;[47] at this time Octavian may have freed Hyginos, and he became

---

40 Syme, *Roman Revolution* (supra note 25), p. 229.

41 Suetonius, *Augustus* 72: since Hortensius had been dead for a decade, presumably the house was purchased from his heirs.

42 *NH* 17.2; Suetonius, *Grammarians* 17.

43 *NTDAR*, p. 281.

44 Plutarch, *Antonius* 87.

45 Johannes Christes, *Sklaven und Freigelassene als Grammatiker und Philologen im antiken Rom*, Forschungen zur Antiken Sklaverei 10 (Wiesbaden 1979), pp. 72–82.

46 Suetonius, *Grammarians* 20.

47 Dio 53.1.3; *NTDAR*, pp. 14, 58–9.

known as C. Julius Hyginus. A few years older than Juba, he clearly received much of his education in Octavian's household.[48]

Juba's own education, to judge from his scholarly prolificacy, was the best that contemporary Rome could offer. No source specifies his teachers, however, and they can only be presumed from his writings, which show strong interests in geography, exploration, natural history, linguistics, Roman history, Pythagorean philosophy, and the visual and performing arts. Thus these disciplines might be seen as the core of Juba's education.

Many Greek scholars were in Rome by the late 40s BC.[49] Their doyen was Alexandros Polyhistor of Miletos, who had been in the city since 82 BC and was near the end of a long and productive career.[50] He taught at least one member of Octavian's household, Hyginos.[51] A prolific scholar, he wrote extensive ethnographical works, and also on philosophy, cults, and literature. His ethnographies covered most of the Greco-Roman world from Italy east to Mesopotamia and India.[52] There was a treatise on the Delphic oracle[53] and one on the history of philosophy, with particular emphasis on the Pythagoreans.[54] His literary interests seem to have included Greek lyric, since he wrote on Alkman and Korinna:[55] the work on Alkman seems to have had an ethnographic or linguistic basis since it involved the poet's use of toponyms. Alexandros Polyhistor wrote largely to acquaint his Roman audience with a part of the world new to them.[56] This theory of scholarship, as well as his interests, closely paralleled those that Juba would develop, and his presence at some time in the early Augustan court demonstrates the likelihood of contact.

Alexandros Polyhistor may have spent some of the last years of his active career actually in Octavian's household. Others, also now late in their lives, were part of Octavian's coterie of Greek scholars and had been his own teachers. Particularly important insofar as Juba was concerned was the philosopher and historian Athenodoros of Tarsos.[57] His writings emphasized the

---

48 Christes (supra note 45), p. 73, suggested that he was born around 60 BC, but this seems too early to agree with Suetonius' comment that he was a boy when he came to Rome: a birth date of around 55 BC might be better.

49 For the use of Greek scholars in the education of the late republican aristocracy, see Stanley F. Bonner, *Education in Ancient Rome* (Berkeley: University of California Press, 1977), pp. 27–32.

50 *FGrHist* #273; G. Schwartz, "Alexandros von Milet" (#88), *RE* 1, 1884, 1449–52; Elizabeth Rawson, *Intellectual Life in the Late Roman Republic* (London: Duckworth, 1985), see index; Felix Jacoby, commentary on *FGrHist* #273; Christes (supra note 45), pp. 38–42.

51 Suetonius, *Grammarians* 20.

52 Alexandros, fr. 1–81.

53 Alexandros, fr. 83–4.

54 Alexandros, fr. 85–94.

55 Alexandros, fr. 95–7.

56 Felix Jacoby, commentary on *FGrHist* #273, p. 251.

57 *FGrHist* #746; Strabo 14.5.14, 16.4.21; Conrad Cichorius, *Römische Studien* (Leipzig: Teubner, 1922), pp. 279–82; Pierre Grimal, "Auguste et Athénodore," *RÉA* 47, 1945, 261–73; "Auguste et Athénodore (suite et fin)," *RÉA* 48, 1946, 62–79.

history and culture of his native city and Kilikia, although he traveled into interior Nabataea and also wrote on the extremities of the world, to be one of Juba's important interests.[58] Athenodoros seems to have been in Rome from 44 until the late 30s BC,[59] when he returned to Tarsos and lived in respected retirement, but remaining close enough to the imperial family to dedicate a book to Octavia, perhaps a consolation on the death of her son Marcellus in 23 BC.[60] A student of the philosopher, historian, and geographer Poseidonios of Apamea, who was himself interested in the extremities of the world,[61] Athenodoros brought an appreciation of history and geography to Octavian's family.

Another possible tutor for young Juba was Timagenes of Alexandria, who had been in Rome since 55 BC.[62] Originally an intimate of M. Antonius, he moved into Octavian's household no later than 30 BC, still early enough to influence Juba. His protégés included Strabo of Amaseia and Nikolaos of Damaskos. Little of his work is known, but the few fragments that survive show an interest in history and geography, again including the extremities of the earth. Unlike many of his Greek contemporaries, he wrote on the Roman West as well as the Greek East.[63] In one case, Pliny contrasted his and Juba's ideas.[64]

Among other Greek scholars at the early imperial court was Apollodoros of Pergamon, famous for his rhetorical school and numerous pupils. By 45 BC he was elderly, and thus may not have survived long enough to influence Juba directly, although he lived to be 82.[65] In addition to Athenodoros of Tarsos, Octavian's house philosophers were Areios Didymos of Alexandria, a Stoic, and Xenarchos of Kilikian Seleukeia; the latter was one of the many teachers of Strabo and seems to have lived long in Augustus' company, though perhaps too late for Juba.[66] Areios Didymos seems to have come to Rome no later than 30 BC and survived until at least 9 BC, when he wrote a

---

58 Strabo 1.1.9.

59 But see R. Philippson, "Athenodoros," *RE* Supp. 5, 1931, 49.

60 Plutarch, *Publicola* 17.5: for the assumption that it was her son, see Glen Bowersock, *Augustus and the Greek World* (Oxford: Clarendon Press, 1965), p. 34, but it is possible that the occasion was the death of her husband Marcellus in 40 BC, which occurred while Athenodoros was in Rome.

61 *FGrHist* #87; Strabo 2.2 (=Poseidonios, fr. 28); James S. Romm, *The Edges of the Earth in Ancient Thought: Geography, Exploration, and Fiction* (Princeton, N.J.: Princeton University Press, 1992), pp. 198–9. Poseidonios came to Rome in the first century BC and was attached to the Claudii Marcelli (*Souda*, Ποσειδώνιος; Plutarch, *Marcellus* 1.1), so may have been close to Juba's circle, but probably did not live until Juba's time. He was one of Strabo's principal sources.

62 *FGrHist* #88 and commentary thereon; F. Gisinger, "Timagenes" (#2) *RE* 2, ser. 11, 1936, 1063–73; Marta Sordi, "Timagene di Alessandria: uno storico ellenocentrico e filobarbaro," *ANRW* 2.30, 1982–3, 775–97.

63 Strabo 15.1.57; 4.1.13; *NH* 3.132.

64 *NH* 33.118.

65 Suetonius, *Augustus* 89; Lucian, *Makrobioi* 23; Bowersock (supra note 60), pp. 31–2.

66 Paul Moraux, "Xenarchos" (#5), *RE* 2, ser. 9, 1931, 1422–3.

consolation to Livia upon the death of her son Drusus.[67] Juba's later interest in Pythagoreanism may have led him to Pythagorean circles in Rome, represented by Areios Didymos, Alexandros Polyhistor, and the little-known Anaxilaos of Larissa.[68] Aristotelian philosophy may also have been part of Juba's education, since it was popular in the Rome of his youth[69] and part of the course of study of two of his intimates, Strabo of Amaseia and Nikolaos of Damaskos.[70]

Although none of Juba's teachers is named, the teachers of other members of the imperial family are recorded.[71] Octavia's son Marcellus was a student of Athenaios of Kilikian Seleukeia and Nestor of Tarsos (who also taught Tiberius).[72] Athenaios was a military engineer who prepared Marcellus for an expedition to Spain with Augustus in which Juba also participated. A future king would need knowledge about military strategy and tactics, and it seems probable that Athenaios was Juba's teacher in these matters.

Although Greeks largely controlled education in contemporary Rome, Roman scholars also contributed to the intellectual milieu. Two in particular who may have influenced Juba were C. Asinius Pollio and M. Terentius Varro. Both were close to Octavian. As noted, the former had been with Caesar in Africa and then shortly thereafter retired to write a history of the period 60–42 BC, a major source for later scholars. His sense of contemporary history was sharply tuned, and it may have been from Pollio that Juba learned about the career of his own father, Juba I.[73]

Varro, although near the end of his career, was perhaps the greatest Roman scholar of the era. It is inconceivable that Juba was not influenced by this outstanding talent. Juba, to be known as "rex literatissimus," had interests that paralleled Varro's in a number of ways, especially in linguistics and Roman antiquities, and also in the generally polymathic quality of his work. Varro's best-known work, *De lingua latina*, was composed in the 40s BC and dedicated, at least in part, to Cicero.[74] His little-known *Antiquitates rerum humanarum* was the contemporary culmination of the late republican interest in Roman origins.[75] He wrote other treatises on Roman history and culture: *De vita populi Romani* was a brief summary of Roman history, perhaps for a

---

67 Seneca, *Ad Marciam* 3–6; Plutarch, *Antonius* 80; on the life, identification, and philosophical orientation of Areios Didymos, see David Hahm, "The Ethical Doxography of Arius Didymus," *ANRW* 2.36, 1990, 3035–41.

68 On Pythagoreans in Rome at this time, see Rawson (supra note 50), p. 293.

69 Rawson (supra note 50), pp. 289–91.

70 Strabo 16.2.24; *Souda*, Νικόλαος = *FGrHist* #90, fr. 132.

71 Bowersock (supra note 60), pp. 34–7.

72 Lucian, *Makrobioi* 21; Cichorius (supra note 57), pp. 271–9.

73 On Asinius Pollio, see J. André, *La Vie et l'œuvre d'Asinius Pollion* (Paris: C. Klincksieck, 1949); Giuseppe Zecchini, "Asinio Pollione: dall'attività politica alla riflessione storiografica," *ANRW* 30, 1982–3, 1265–96.

74 Rawson (supra note 50), pp. 125–31.

75 Rawson (supra note 50), pp. 236–7.

popular audience; *Aetia* was on Roman customs; and in *De gente populi Romani* he explored Rome's mythical origins.[76] With the possible exception of *Aetia*, these seem to have been written in the 40s BC when Varro was in his seventies,[77] and thus represented the latest in Roman thought and outlook at the time of Juba's education, paralleling his own later output.

Juba's scholarly development would have been further influenced by access to ancestral material, both his own and that of his future wife Kleopatra Selene. There was a scholarly heritage within Juba's own family[78] that he may have learned about through contact with Romans knowledgeable about Africa. About the time Juba came to Rome, Sallust was beginning his researches on North Africa, probably making use of the Carthaginian state library, which had become Roman property when Carthage fell in 146 BC. Some works were translated into Latin and then the books were given to the kings of Numidia. But the library probably returned to Rome, expanded somewhat by the scholarly output of Juba's grandfather Hiempsal, as part of the plunder Sallust removed from his province in 46 BC.[79] Sallust then used it when writing about Juba's ancestor Jugurtha.[80] Juba could not have remained ignorant of the existence of such a library in Rome. He would have studied its volumes enthusiastically, and eventually would commission copies and translations to help create his own royal library.[81] Sallust himself died in 35 BC, too early to have much personal influence on Juba,[82] and Juba's contact in the family was probably the historian's grandnephew and namesake, a man of culture and refinement who was about Juba's age and was the subject of poems by Krinagoras and Horace.[83]

Moreover, Juba would have studied the ancestral knowledge of Kleopatra Selene, perhaps well before their marriage: he was aware of the treatise of her ancestor, Ptolemaios VIII, that discussed his own ancestor Massinissa.[84] Heir to the traditions of the Ptolemies and theoretical queen of the Kyrenaika, at the very least Kleopatra Selene stimulated Juba's interest in northeast Africa and the Nile. She probably retained personal contacts in Egypt; when she and her brothers came to Rome in 30 BC they had an entourage that would have provided information and books for Juba, as would have other Alexandrians at the Augustan court.

76 Rawson (supra note 50), pp. 233–4, 242–5.
77 Varro's prolific output was legendary. By the time he was 78 (38 BC) he had written 490 books (Gellius 3.10.17), and he lived another decade to 27 BC.
78 Supra, p. 27.
79 Dio 43.9.2.
80 Sallust, *Jugurtha* 17–19; Gsell, vol. 7, p. 126. But see G. M. Paul, *A Historical Commentary on Sallust's "Bellum Jugurthinum"* (Liverpool 1984), p. 74, who was dubious about Sallust's access to the books.
81 On this topic, see Victor Matthews, "The *libri Punici* of King Hiempsal," *AJP* 93, 1972, 330–5.
82 Gerhard Perl, "Sallusts Todesjahr," *Klio* 48, 1967, 97–105.
83 Tacitus, *Annals* 3.30; Krinagoras 36; Horace, *Odes* 2.2.
84 *FGrHist* #234; Juba, fr. 87.

The intense scholarly activity in Rome in the late 40s and 30s BC, a foundation laid by Pollio, Varro, and the Greek scholars at the imperial court, had its impact on a new generation of scholars who came to maturity at that time. One of the best examples is Strabo of Amaseia, already mentioned as a pupil of several Augustan intimates. He was in Rome from 44 to 35 BC and then from 29 to 25 BC, as part of a long career that included travel throughout the Roman and Greek East, service with the Roman government in Egypt, a probable visit to the court of Herod the Great, and scholarly retirement in Amaseia at the court of Pythodoris of Pontos.[85] As a historian and especially as a geographer his interests paralleled Juba's. Strabo firmly believed that a king should have a knowledge of geography,[86] and probably encouraged Juba's studies in that discipline, since he was in Rome during the four years prior to Juba assuming his kingship. The almost gratuitous references to Juba scattered throughout his *Geography* seem to indicate some early friendship or association. He is the only explicit source for the death of the king in AD 23 or 24,[87] passages that are themselves evidence for the compositional history of the *Geography* and Strabo's own longevity. It is significant that Strabo, well into his eighties and residing in remote Amaseia, at the other end of the empire from Juba's world, saw fit to comment on the death of one who was a former friend and fellow protégé. Moreover, in his summary of Roman peace and expansion under Augustus,[88] written during AD 14–19, Strabo mentioned only four contemporary personalities: the emperor Tiberius and his two sons, and Juba – a unique emphasis on the Mauretanian king. In the final passage of his *Geography*, Strabo summarized the Augustan world and mentioned no one except the Princeps, Juba, and Juba's son Ptolemaios.[89] Strabo was not familiar with Juba's writings (perhaps they had not yet penetrated into interior Asia Minor) and used the mainstream Hellenistic geographical tradition – Poseidonios, Artemidoros, Eratosthenes, and others – for his description of Juba's world.[90] Yet these exceptional notices of Juba, whom it is unlikely that Strabo would have seen for half a century, indicate a strong friendship that could only have been formed in the days that both were in Rome.

85 Roller, *Herod*, pp. 64–5. But see Aubrey Diller, *The Textual Tradition of Strabo's Geography* (Amsterdam: Hakkert, 1975), pp. 6–7, who placed Strabo's retirement in the Naples area, which seems hard to believe, given the remote tone of his later additions to the *Geography*. On this problem, see, cautiously, Daniela Dueck, *Strabo of Amasia: A Greek Man of Letters in Augustan Rome* (London: Routledge, 2000), pp. 2–3.

86 Strabo 1.1.16.

87 Strabo 17.3.7, 9; François Lasserre, "Strabon devant l'Empire romaine," *ANRW* 30, 1982–3, 880.

88 Strabo 6.4.2.

89 Strabo 17.3.25.

90 Poseidonios: Strabo 17.3.4; Artemidoros and Eratosthenes: Strabo 17.3.2, 8; Jehan Desanges, "Le Regard de Strabon sur l'Afrique du Nord," in *Gli interscambi culturali e socio-economici fra l'Africa settentrionale e l'Europa mediterranea* 1, ed. Luigi Serra (Naples: Istituto Universario Orientale, 1986), pp. 309–19.

The extraordinary cultural environment that was Augustan Rome nurtured and produced an inordinate number of intellectual personalities. Some of these may have been connected to Juba in a variety of ways. For example, Krinagoras of Mytilene, the Augustan poet laureate who seems to have moved freely between the great imperial courts of the day, probably including that of Mauretania, was particularly close to Kleopatra Selene, perhaps reflecting his early association with the Ptolemies.[91] Vitruvius Pollio, the architect, had worked as a military engineer for Caesar and later wrote on architecture.[92] He was a close friend of a Numidian named C. Julius, son of Masinissa, who had fought with Caesar at Zama and who occasionally stayed in Vitruvius' house, providing information about the architecture of Zama, particularly its fortifications and the palace of Juba I.[93] It was perhaps through Vitruvius and Julius that Juba learned about the homeland, family, and distinguished ancestry that he was too young to remember.[94] Vitruvius' architectural theories may also have been of value to Juba in the building of Caesarea.

Juba also may have known the grammarian M. Verrius Flaccus,[95] a noted teacher who moved into the household of Augustus as tutor to his grandsons Gaius and Lucius Caesar. Although this would have been around 10 BC, long after Juba had left, Juba's later contact with C. Caesar and Verrius Flaccus' antiquarian and linguistic interests would make association probable. Other intimates may have been the poet Horace and his friend the grammarian M. Aristius Fuscus.[96] But a special influence on young Juba was the geographical scholarship of M. Vipsanius Agrippa, manifested by a map placed in the

---

91 Krinagoras 18, 25 (*Palatine Anthology* 7.633, 9.235). See further, infra, pp. 87–9. On Krinagoras, see J. S. Phillimore, "Crinagoras of Mytilene," *Dublin Review* 139, 1906, 74–86; J. Geffcken, "Krinagoras," *RE* 11, 1922, 1859–64; David C. Braund, "*Anth. Pal.* 9.235: Juba II, Cleopatra Selene and the Course of the Nile," *CQ* 34, 1984, 175–8; *The Greek Anthology: The Garland of Philip*, vol. 2, ed. A. S. F. Gow and D. L. Page (Cambridge: Cambridge University Press, 1968), pp. 210–13.

92 Vitruvius 2.9.15. On the career and background of Vitruvius, see Barry Baldwin, "The Date, Identity, and Career of Vitruvius," *Latomus* 49, 1990, 425–34.

93 Vitruvius 8.3.24–5; F. Münzer, "C. Iulius" (#22), *RE* 10, 1917, 110. He has hypothetically been equated with Masintha, Caesar's protégé (supra, pp. 28–9), although the incidents are perhaps forty years apart: see Baldwin (supra note 92), p. 432; Vitruvius (ed. Callebat), pp. 127–8.

94 Doubtless there were also those in Rome who remembered the visit of Juba's father and his unfortunate encounter with Caesar (supra, p. 30), and Juba could visit the victory memorial of Bocchus I of Mauretania on the Capitol (supra, pp. 49–50). Many veterans of the late African war could have enlightened him about his family and native land, although perhaps the less said about his father the better, who in public perception remained demonized.

95 Suetonius, *Grammarians* 17, 19.

96 Horace's *Ode* 1.22, addressed to Fuscus, refers to "Iubae tellus ... leonum arida nutrix" (lines 15–16), the only specific reference to Juba in Augustan poetry. The poem seems to have been published in 23 BC, little more than a year after Juba became king, although it is remotely possible that the reference is to his father (supra, Chapter 2, note 11). On Fuscus, see R. G. M. Nisbet and Margaret Hubbard, *A Commentary on Horace: Odes, Book 1* (Oxford: Clarendon Press, 1970), pp. 261–2.

Porticus Vipsania after his death in 12 BC.[97] Pliny recorded that Agrippa was a careful scholar – he was shocked to find a mistake in his material – and the map would have been the product of many years of geographical research, which Agrippa may have published as a geographical commentary before the map was actually created by Augustus.[98] It seems that the project was already in progress before Juba left Rome and that it influenced his geographical interests: Pliny considered Juba's scholarship – at least for parts of the East – superior to that of the map.[99] Juba may also have provided information about Mauretania to Agrippa.[100] Another contact was the historian C. Sulpicius Galba. Roughly Juba's age, he was considered a learned scholar noted for his thoroughness and eye for detail.[101] Galba supplied Juba with information on Romulus and Tarpeius[102] and was one of Pliny's sources[103] but is otherwise virtually unknown. Cornelius Nepos, best known as a biographer but also the author of a wide-ranging geographical work,[104] was at the end of a long if not especially distinguished career at about the time Juba left Rome.[105] Although his geography was not greatly respected by Pliny, and may have been almost totally derivative,[106] his interest in Mauretania may have attracted the attention of young Juba.[107]

Other Greek scholars were active in Rome. Diodoros of Sicily was completing his history in the 30s BC, although remaining aloof from Romans of prominence.[108] Nikolaos of Damaskos, who studied with Timagenes alongside Strabo, was to tutor Kleopatra Selene and then move to the court of Herod the Great and return regularly to Rome as Herod's ambassador,

---

97 *NH* 3.17; J. J. Tierney, "The Map of Agrippa," *Proceedings of the Royal Irish Academy* 63c, 1963, 151–66; Claude Nicolet, *Space, Geography and Politics in the Early Roman Empire* (Ann Arbor: University of Michigan Press, 1991), pp. 95–122.

98 O. A. W. Dilke, *Greek and Roman Maps* (London: Thames and Hudson, 1985), pp. 41–53; Thomson, pp. 332–4.

99 *NH* 6.136–41. If the reading of Pliny's text is correct, he specifically used Juba's material to update the map.

100 Infra, p. 190.

101 *FGrHist* #92; see also *HRR* LVIII; 41. His father, Servius Sulpicius Galba, was one of Caesar's assassins and was executed for the deed; his grandson was the emperor Galba (Suetonius, *Galba* 3).

102 Plutarch, *Romulus* 17 (=Juba, fr. 24).

103 *NH* 1.36.

104 Most commentators on Cornelius Nepos have ignored his geographical writings: see the brief summary by G. Wissowa, "Cornelius Nepos" (#275), *RE* 4, 1900, 1411.

105 His history appeared well before Catullus published his first poem and he survived into the Augustan era (*NH* 9.137). It is not absolutely certain that the historian and geographer are the same person: see Pomponius Mela, *Chorographie*, ed. A. Silberman (Paris: Belles Lettres, 1988), p. 277; K. G. Sallmann, *Die Geographie des älteren Plinius in ihrem Verhältnis zu Varro* (Berlin 1971), pp. 123–5.

106 *NH* 5.4; see also 6.5. Pomponius Mela (3.45) had a somewhat better opinion, but valued him because he was recent.

107 He discussed Tingis (*NH* 5.4) and Kerne (*NH* 6.199), both places of particular interest to Juba.

108 Kenneth S. Sacks, *Diodorus Siculus and the First Century* (Princeton, N.J.: Princeton University Press, 1990), pp. 161–8.

eventually writing the longest of universal histories, recording details about Juba unknown elsewhere.[109] Perhaps more directly influential on Juba was Dionysios of Halikarnassos, a teacher of rhetoric who arrived in Rome about 30 BC and spent at least the next two decades writing his *Roman Archaeology* and other works on rhetoric and linguistics.[110]

Juba's intellectual interests are closely paralleled by those of many other scholars of his era, not all of whom would have been an influence. A constant theme of the Augustan period is the pervasive interest in the history of Rome and in language, representative of the contemporary cultural attitude that produced the unique blend of antiquarianism and innovation that marked the Augustan era. The Roman desire to compete on equal terms with the venerated cities of the Greek East meant that the application of Greek scholarly techniques to analysis of Roman institutions was especially meaningful.[111] Augustus sought to prove the legitimacy of his revolution, in which he destroyed the Republic, by emphasizing his salvation of the republic and the continuity of the new regime with Roman origins, as countless Augustan artifacts from the *Aeneid* to the Ara Pacis demonstrate.[112] This interest in early Rome was complemented by that of the Greek scholars, who were just discovering the new (to them) world of Rome. It had been barely two hundred years since Andronikos of Taras had come to Rome, perhaps the first creative Greek to take up residence there, writing Latin plays under the name of Livius Andronicus.[113] The newness of Rome to the Greeks was matched by the self-conception of the Augustan era, which sought to create a new world by claiming that it was actually ancient. Thus the Greek scholars became the implementation of the Roman, especially Augustan, view of early Rome and its continuity with the present.

Moreover, there were strong reasons why language and linguistics were topical endeavors of the era. The Latin language was still new and thought to be rough and imperfect. Less than thirty years before Juba came to Rome, Lucretius had written that his use of Latin for a philosophical treatise was unprecedented, and that he was destined boldly to go where no one had gone before.[114] Any attempt to elevate the status of the Latin language and

---

109 Nikolaos is probably the source for Josephus' information regarding Juba's marriage to Glaphyra of Kappadokia: see further, infra, pp. 247–9; on Nikolaos, see Ben Zion Wacholder, *Nicolaus of Damascus* (Berkeley: University of California Press, 1962).

110 On Dionysios, see Emilio Gabba, *Dionysius and the History of Archaic Rome* (Berkeley: University of California Press, 1991).

111 On this, see Gabba (supra note 110), pp. 10–12.

112 This issue is explored by Paul Zanker, *The Power of Images in the Age of Augustus*, trans. Alan Shapiro (Ann Arbor: University of Michigan Press, 1988).

113 Eduard Fraenkel, "Livius" (#10a), *RE* Supp. 5, 1931, 598–607; Erich S. Gruen, *Studies in Greek Culture and Roman Policy*, first paperback printing (Berkeley: University of California Press, 1996), pp. 80–2.

114 Lucretius 1.925–7.

to prove its relationship to Greek would be appreciated by the Augustan power elite. These attempts were destined to fail – Juba and so many others wrote on Roman history and even on the Latin language only in Greek – but nonetheless they produced in the latter first century BC a veritable industry of linguistic studies. Juba, with his interests in antiquarianism, linguistics, and art and architecture, was so completely a product of his era.

Another, if less formalized, part of Juba's education would have been his exposure to the Augustan architectural revolution that was transforming Rome from a city of brick to one of marble.[115] Caesar had envisioned a rich building program, partly in competition with Pompeius, and Octavian (and his associates) began to implement this program almost immediately after Caesar's death and continued it unabated for much of the Augustan period. Juba would have been especially observant of the many construction projects in the Rome of his youth, gaining information that would be of use when he became a city founder.

At some time before he became king, Juba accompanied Augustus on campaign. This is documented in a single notice by Dio,[116] who provided no specific details. The context is the aftermath of the death of Antonius and Kleopatra, and the disposition of their children, one of whom was to be married to Juba. Thus it may be that the Actium campaign is the one meant,[117] and that Juba was in the East with Octavian in 31–30 BC, meeting his future wife for the first time. But this seems unlikely, as will be demonstrated.

It was common for aristocratic Roman youths to go into the field at an early age. Octavian himself had joined Caesar in Spain in late 46 BC, when he had just turned 17, immediately after the African triumph.[118] Marcellus, his nephew, began his military career at the same age,[119] as did his stepson Tiberius, the future emperor.[120] Both went with Augustus to Spain in 27–25 BC to engage various troublesome mountain tribes.[121] Dio's account of the settlement of this war is significant:

> When this war ended, Augustus discharged his more elderly soldiers and had them establish a city in Lusitania, called Augusta Emerita. For those who were still of military age he arranged exhibitions in the camps under the direction of Marcellus and Tiberius, since they were aediles. And he gave to Juba, in place of his ancestral lands,

---

115 Suetonius, *Augustus* 28.
116 Dio 51.15.6.
117 So Jacoby, *RE*, p. 2385; J. P. V. D. Balsdon, *Romans and Aliens* (supra note 4), p. 203.
118 Suetonius, *Augustus* 8.
119 Dio 53.26.
120 Suetonius, *Tiberius* 9.
121 The campaign is discussed by Syme, *Roman Revolution* (supra note 25), pp. 331–3.

part of Gaetulia, most of whose inhabitants had been registered in the Roman state, as well as the lands of Bocchus and Bogudes.[122]

This seems proof that Juba was in Spain with his childhood playmates Marcellus and Tiberius, and that it was as a result of his services on this campaign that Augustus made the final decision to give him his kingship.[123]

Seventeen seems to have been the customary age to begin military service. Octavian was considered too young at 16 to join Caesar in Africa, although he did participate in the triumph in the summer of 46 BC.[124] Juba would have been about 21 in 27 BC, a late age to campaign for the first time, but there probably was no alternative. Augustus had not been in the field since Actium. At that time Juba, who probably turned 17 about the time Octavian crossed to Greece on his way to Actium, may have been perceived as not mature enough for battle. It is unlikely that Octavian would have allowed him to campaign at an age at which he himself had been considered too young. Thus the evidence for Juba's first military service suggests strongly that his birth date was no earlier than 48 BC. Regardless, if the Spanish campaign were a test of Juba's abilities as a military leader, it seems to have been successful, for he was promptly sent to rule Mauretania.

A final important step in Juba's upbringing was his acquisition of Roman citizenship. This is only indirectly documented, through the existence of the name Julia and Julius among Mauretanian freedmen and freedwomen.[125] A freedman of Juba's son Ptolemaios, one C. Julius Montanus,[126] provides the link between the Mauretanian royal and Roman imperial families. Yet even if the case of Juba were not documented, it could easily be assumed: Roman

---

122 Dio 53.26.1–2: Παυσαμένου δὲ τοῦ πολέμου τούτου ὁ Αὔγουστος τοὺς μὲν ἀφηλικεστέρους τῶν στρατιωτῶν ἀφῆκε, καὶ πόλιν αὐτοῖς ἐν Λυσιτανίᾳ τὴν Αὔγουσταν Ἡμέριταν καλουμένην κτίσαι ἔδωκε, τοῖς δὲ τὴν στρατεύσιμον ἡλικίαν ἔτ' ἔχουσι θέας τινὰς διά τε τοῦ Μαρκέλλου καὶ διὰ τοῦ Τιβερίου ὡς καὶ ἀγορανομούντων ἐν αὐτοῖς τοῖς στρατοπέδοις ἐποίησε. καὶ τῷ μὲν Ἰούβᾳ τῆς τε Γαιτουλίας τινὰ ἀντὶ τῆς πατρῴας ἀρχῆς, ἐπείπερ ἐς τὸν τῶν Ῥωμαίων κόσμον οἱ πλείους αὐτῶν ἐσεγεγράφατο, καὶ τὰ τοῦ Βόκχου τοῦ τε Βογούου ἔδωκε.

123 On this, see Ritter, *Rom*, pp. 139–40; C. R. Whittaker, "Roman Africa: Augustus to Vespasian," *CAH*² 10, 1996, 590–1. An interesting sidelight is provided by an epigram of Krinagoras (#29 = *Palatine Anthology* 9.419), which describes how Augustus took a cure in the waters of the Pyrenees – an allusion to his illness during the Spanish campaign – perhaps the cold cure prescribed by his physician Antonius Musa (Suetonius, *Augustus* 81). Almost irrelevantly, Krinagoras added mention of Soloeis and the Libyan Hesperides, places that Augustus had not visited but which would become famous if he did. Although both are used metaphorically for the extreme west end of the earth (cf. Herodotos 2.32, 4.43), it seems no coincidence that these places in northwest Africa soon to be part of Juba's kingdom are cited in the context of events that resulted in his receiving of that kingdom. On Soloeis, see Eugen Oberhummer, "Soloeis" (#2) *RE* 2, ser. 3, 1927, 935.

124 Suetonius, *Augustus* 8.

125 *PIR*² I65. Juba's position as *patronus coloniae* at Carthago Nova (infra, pp. 156–7) would also imply citizenship, since a non-Roman would hardly be appointed guardian of Roman institutions (for the term, see *OLD* s.v. *patronus*).

126 *CIL* 8.21093.

citizenship was an expected privilege for foreign notables, especially client kings. Yet the evidence for such grants is astonishingly sparse, and is rarely cited in literature. Josephus' record of Caesar's bestowal of citizenship on Antipatros of Askalon, the father of Herod the Great, is exceptional.[127] Moreover, the foreigners, particularly if they were kings, were often diffident about parading their Roman citizenship before their subjects and may not have felt that it enhanced their prestige.[128]

Such grants were common under Augustus and his immediate successors. Although it is often impossible to tell whether a person with the name C. Julius received citizenship from Caesar or Augustus, it seems that Caesar established the practice, perhaps because of the wartime pressures of the early 40s BC and the need to create support groups in the provinces.[129] The concept existed at least as early as 47 BC when Caesar was received by various eastern notables in Antioch, and gave citizenship to Antipatros of Askalon and others. The policy was continued by M. Antonius, who seems to have favored the royal family of Pontos (in more ways than one, since he also produced offspring within the family):[130] he perhaps began to give citizenship to royalty. Just as Caesar's bestowal on Antipatros was crucial, since it affected Herod the Great, his entire family, and a number of other dynasties into which the Herodians married, Antonius' favor of the Pontic rulers allowed Roman citizenship to spread through Asia Minor.

In the case of Juba, although the evidence seems clear that he and his son Ptolemaios held Roman citizenship, it is impossible to determine when and by whom the grant was made. Caesar is a possible donor, but he was dead before Juba was 5 years of age, and thus Augustus seems the more probable. There is no way to determine the date except to assume that it was before Juba became king in 25 BC.

Thus by 25 BC Juba was almost ready to assume the kingship of Mauretania. He was a Roman citizen, he had been raised in the Augustan household, he had the best education available to a young Roman aristocrat of the era, and he had proved his military prowess in Spain alongside Marcellus, who was rapidly becoming Augustus' heir apparent. Marcellus was to marry Augustus' daughter Julia the year that Juba became king.[131] Juba himself was certainly married before he went to Mauretania. As a young man of promise, upon whom the entire Roman presence in northwest Africa depended, Juba would need to have a wife whose status equaled his own.

127 Josephus, *Jewish Antiquities* 14.137; *Jewish War* 1.194.
128 On this entire issue as it relates to the client kings, see Braund, *Friendly King*, pp. 39–53, who carefully noted that it is impossible to argue from silence on this topic, because of the reasons cited above and because the evidence is so scattered.
129 A. N. Sherwin-White, *The Roman Citizenship*, second edition (Oxford: Clarendon Press, 1973), pp. 309–10.
130 Richard D. Sullivan, "Dynasts in Pontus," *ANRW* 2.7, 1980, 916–18.
131 Suetonius, *Augustus* 63; Dio 53.27.5.

4

KLEOPATRA SELENE

The first two decades of Juba's life were tumultuous times for Rome, as the Republic continued to collapse. Within two years of his arrival in the city, his saviour Julius Caesar was assassinated. The following year, Octavian, Antonius, and M. Aemilius Lepidus were constituted as triumvirs, who placed avenging the murder at the head of their agenda, spending over a year at the task. In October of 42 BC at Philippi their vengeance seemed complete with the deaths of Brutus and Cassius. Antonius had become the dominant member of the triumvirate; Lepidus, already marginalized, was not at Philippi and Octavian's conduct at the battle was less than distinguished.[1] Antonius would have sensed redemption for a personal career that so far had, at best, been mixed: after the battle he was saluted as *imperator* by the victors and the vanquished alike, while Octavian, his status at a low point, was verbally abused after the battle.[2] With the underestimation of him that characterized the era, it might have seemed natural that he return to Italy, possibly to end his brief career, but Antonius would remain in the East to clean up the mess left by the activities of Brutus and Cassius over the previous two years. The eastern provinces had to be stabilized and there were serious internal problems in both Judaea and Egypt, too close to the Roman territories to be ignored. Antonius was the one to settle these difficult issues.[3]

It was Appian who wrote most succinctly about what happened next:

> After the death of Cassius and Brutus, Caesar [Octavian] went to Italy, but Antonius to Asia, where Kleopatra, queen of Egypt, encountered him and immediately subjugated him. This passion brought both of them, and all of Egypt, into extreme difficulty.[4]

1 *NH* 7.148; Kenneth Scott, "The Political Propaganda of 44–30 BC," *MAAR* 11, 1933, 21–2.

2 Suetonius, *Augustus* 13.

3 For the political situation after the Battle of Philippi, see Ronald Syme, *The Roman Revolution* (Oxford: Clarendon Press, 1960), pp. 205–7; Christopher Pelling, "The Triumviral Period," *CAH*² 10, 1996, 8–11.

4 Appian, *Civil War* 5.1: Μετὰ δὲ τὸν Κασσίου καὶ Βρούτου θάνατον ὁ μὲν Καῖσαρ ἐπὶ τῆς Ἰταλίας ᾔει, ὁ δὲ Ἀντώνιος ἐς τὴν Ἀσίαν, ἔνθα αὐτῷ συμβάλλει Κλεοπάτρα βασιλὶς Αἰγύπτου, καὶ εὐθὺς ὀφθεῖσα ἐκράτει. ὁ δὲ ἔρως ὅδε αὐτοῖς τε ἐκείνοις ἐς ἔσχατον ἔληξε κακοῦ καὶ ἐς ὅλην Αἴγυπτου ἐπ᾽ ἐκείνοις.

Actually, they had already met when Antonius was on the staff of Aulus Gabinius (consul in 58 BC) during the latter's Syrian governorship. Gabinius and Antonius had gone to Alexandria in 55 BC to restore Ptolemaios XII, Kleopatra's father, to the throne.[5] If Kleopatra's later life is any indication of what she was like as an adolescent, the 14-year-old princess would have made herself conspicuous to the Roman officers at her father's court. As is well known, Antonius and Kleopatra had a more dramatic meeting fourteen years later, in the autumn of 41 BC, at Tarsos.[6] Eventually he returned with her to Alexandria, to spend the winter in the extravagant series of amusements vividly described by Plutarch.[7] Whether either had any thoughts for the future is not obvious: Antonius was well known for his series of liaisons with eastern royalty. He left in the spring of 40 BC to return to Italy, where the situation was deteriorating again, largely owing to the machinations of his wife Fulvia, who allegedly believed that this would be the best way of forcing him to leave Kleopatra and to return home.[8] Whatever the circumstances under which Antonius and Kleopatra parted that spring, it seems that Kleopatra soon gave birth to twins.

There is no explicit evidence as to exactly when the twins were born. They are not mentioned in extant literature until the context of late 37 BC, when Antonius and Kleopatra met the next time.[9] By this time the triumvirate had been renewed. Antonius had separated from his latest wife, Octavia, and was setting forth on his Parthian campaign. Kleopatra came to meet him en route, probably at Antioch.[10] Antonius acknowledged paternity of Kleopatra's twin children, who would have been 3 years old and would never have seen their father, and seems to have named them Alexandros Helios and Kleopatra (VIII) Selene. The primary source, Plutarch, is somewhat ambiguous, depending on whether προσαγορεύσας here means "named" or "called

5 Plutarch, *Antonius* 3; Appian, *Civil War* 5.8.

6 Plutarch, *Antonius* 25–9; Appian, *Civil War* 5.8–9.

7 Plutarch's source, in part, was not the pro-Augustan historians but a friend of his grandfather Lamprias, who was an intimate of the servants in the Ptolemaic palace, and who described the lavish life that winter, especially its culinary aspects (*Antonius* 28.3–4).

8 Plutarch, *Antonius* 30; Appian, *Civil War* 5.14, 50–9; Dio 48.4–15, 28. After starting and virtually directing the Perusine War, Fulvia was driven out of Italy and met Antonius at Athens, and the two continued together as far as Sikyon, where she became sick and was left behind to die – of a broken heart, it was said, but also an event of great convenience to all, as Appian noted. The almost simultaneous death of Octavia's husband Marcellus led to the marriage between Octavia and Antonius before the end of 40 BC.

9 Plutarch, *Antonius* 36: the meeting is securely dated by the contemporary execution of the Hasmonean Antigonos and the activities of C. Sosius in Judaea on behalf of Herod the Great (Josephus, *Jewish War* 1.357; *Jewish Antiquities* 14.487–91). See also Hermann Bengtson, *Marcus Antonius: Triumvir und Herrscher des Orients* (Munich: Beck, 1977), p. 295.

10 Strabo, *Histories* (FGrHist #91) fr. 18 (=Josephus, *Jewish Antiquities* 15.8–10).

[them] by [their] names."[11] It is hard to believe that these 3-year-olds had no names, and perhaps it is better to assume that Antonius either renamed them or, more likely, gave them their surnames.[12] Kleopatra would have been a reasonable name for the daughter: besides the precedent of her mother, a daughter of the reigning Ptolemaios had been named Kleopatra in each of the past four generations, ever since Ptolemaios V married the Seleukid princess Kleopatra I early in the second century BC. In fact, there even had been a previous Kleopatra Selene, daughter of Ptolemaios VIII and Kleopatra III, and, by the complex intermarriages of the dynasty, Kleopatra VII's great-aunt and step-grandmother.[13] Alexandros was less obvious, appearing only occasionally in dynastic usage. It had never been used as a first name in either the Ptolemaic or the Seleukid main line, and was most common among pretenders and minor dynasts. It is improbable that Antonius would have been influenced by its use among the Hasmoneans, or the Seleukid claimants of the second century BC, Alexandros Balas and Alexandros Zabinas, or even the surnames of two of Kleopatra VII's ancestors, Ptolemaios X Alexandros – her great uncle – and Ptolemaios XI Alexandros, although these did provide a precedent for Ptolemaic usage. It is most likely that the inspiration was the obvious one: Alexander the Great, which also gave the name Kleopatra greater significance, as it was that of his sister.[14] Thus the twins Alexandros and Kleopatra represent their parents' intensive dynastic thought, a response to the similar machinations that were now conspicuous in Rome.

More significant are the children's surnames. The use of Helios fulfills certain contemporary prophetic notions that were current both in Rome and Egypt in the 30s BC.[15] The boy's name linked Alexander the Great to Rome and would bring together East and West, ending the antagonism that had existed since the Trojan War, and thus beginning the golden age.[16] Selene

11 Plutarch, *Antonius* 36; also George Synkellos, *Ekloga* 583. There are numerous examples in LSJ, where προσαγορεύω is used to mean "addressing by name [someone whose name is already known]." Since Antonius had never seen his children before, this would have been the first chance he had to call them by their names, and by doing so formally accept his paternity.

12 Günther Hölbl, *A History of the Ptolemaic Empire*, trans. Tina Saavedra (London: Routledge, 2001), pp. 241–2.

13 Strabo 16.2.3; Josephus, *Jewish Antiquities* 13.420; Appian, *Syrian War* 69; F. Stähelin, "Kleopatra Selene" (#22), *RE* 21, 1921, 782–4; Sullivan, *Near Eastern Royalty*, pp. 83–8. There may have been another, more obscure Kleopatra Selene, the Seleukid princess Kleopatra V, mother of Antiochos XIII, who was one of the last Seleukid kings (cited merely as "Selene" by Cicero [In verrem 2.4.61]). As she was a rival claimant to the Egyptian throne, she was not a good precedent. Sullivan, *Near Eastern Royalty*, Stemma 7, believed, however, that she was the same as the daughter of Ptolemaios VIII.

14 Diodoros 16.91.4; 18.23.1; F. Stähelin, "Kleopatra" (#13), *RE* 11, 1921, 735–8.

15 W. W. Tarn, "Alexander Helios and the Golden Age," *JRS* 22, 1932, 135–60; Michael Grant, *Cleopatra* (London: Weidenfeld and Nicolson, 1972), pp. 142–4.

16 Plutarch, *Life of Antony*, ed. C. B. R. Pelling (Cambridge: Cambridge University Press, 1988), p. 219. Whether any of this thought was reflected in Vergil's *Eclogue* 4 is neither provable nor particularly relevant to the future life of the children.

provided a traditional counterpart to Helios, and, as the children's mother was the new Isis,[17] may have been inspired by that cult. Moreover, there were Parthian connotations, especially relevant with the forthcoming expedition. When a third child was born the following year, he too had a significant name: Ptolemaios (XVI) Philadelphos, after his illustrious ancestor, the first great Greek king of Egypt, Ptolemaios II Philadelphos. Hence all three offspring of Antonius and Kleopatra had names that coupled the great Makedonian past with the glorious present and the ideal future that was to come through the combining of Roman and Greek culture, much as Alexander the Great had joined together Greek and Persian.

Kleopatra Selene's first decade of life is little distinguished in the sources from that of her twin brother.[18] All three of the children made their first recorded public appearance in 34 BC, when Kleopatra Selene was about 6, at the event that has come to be called the Donations of Alexandria. This was the most lavish in a series of territorial gifts from Antonius to Kleopatra and her children, symbolic ceremonies that "donated" land that was either already theirs or never would be theirs, and had more value as contemporary propaganda than political reality.[19] According to Plutarch and Dio, there seem to have been two major donations. The earlier was probably made in 36 BC, perhaps in Antioch at the time of the acknowledgment of the twins,[20] and was followed by a more lavish one in Alexandria two years later.[21] The only additional source, Josephus, is limited to gifts to Kleopatra VII in the Levant.[22] There may have been other donations. Exactly what was given when to whom is not precisely understood. Although one should look at these collectively, only the ceremony in 34 BC in the Gymnasion of Alexandria can properly be called the Donations of Alexandria.

17 Plutarch, *Antonius* 54.6. On this issue, see Hans Volkmann, *Cleopatra: A Study in Politics and Propaganda*, trans. T. J. Cadoux (New York: Sagamore Press, 1958), pp. 148–50. Kleopatra VII was also depicted in contemporary art as Selene (Dio 50.5).

18 In fact, she is often hidden in obscurity: whoever made the summaries of Livy's history did not even seem aware of her, citing only the two boys (*Epitome* 132) – a particular irony, since she was the only one of the three to grow to maturity. This was certainly known to Livy, who probably met and outlived her, and thus demonstrates the caution with which the summaries must be read. On her early life, see generally, Gsell, vol. 8, pp. 217–20, and F. Stähelin, "Kleopatra Selene" (#23), *RE* 21, 1921, 784–5; John Whitehorne, *Cleopatras* (London: Routledge, 1994), pp. 197–202, is superficial.

19 Syme (supra note 3), p. 270; Meyer Reinhold, *From Republic to Principate: An Historical Commentary on Cassius Dio's "Roman History," Books 49–52 (36–29 B.C.)* (American Philological Association Monograph Series 34, Atlanta, 1988), pp. 63–5, 76–7; Plutarch, *Life of Antony* (ed. Pelling, supra note 16), pp. 217–18, 249–52; Bengtson (supra note 9), pp. 218–19; Maria Rosa Cimma, *Reges socii et amici populi romani* (Milan: Giuffre, 1976), pp. 284–8; Grant (supra note 15), pp. 162–75; Hölbl (supra note 12), p. 244.

20 Plutarch, *Antonius* 36; Dio 49.32.4–5; Volkmann (supra note 17), pp. 126–7, 145–50; François Chamoux, *Marc Antoine, dernier prince de l'Orient grec* (Paris: Arthaud, 1986), pp. 313–17.

21 Plutarch, *Antonius* 54; Dio 49.41.

22 Josephus, *Jewish Antiquities* 15.79, 91–5. Velleius did not mention any donations, and no record of any is preserved in the summaries to Livy's history.

The ceremony was perhaps connected with the quasi-triumph Antonius celebrated upon his return from Parthia. The most detailed source, Plutarch, describes with particular attention the thrones on which the participants sat, and the costumes of Alexandros and Ptolemaios. Also present was Kleopatra's other son, Kaisarion, who was now acknowledged, at the age of about 13, as the son of Julius Caesar. He was named king of kings and, by implication, the heir of his mother,[23] who, along with the two younger boys, was given territory, virtually all the districts from Libya in the south to Armenia in the north, including several Roman provinces. But Kleopatra Selene is not mentioned in this account, and only Dio, while not placing her at the ceremony, recorded a gift to her, the Kyrenaika. In his version of the earlier (36 BC?) donation, he also wrote that the children were given parts of Crete. Thus, putting all the information together, it seems that Kleopatra Selene received, in perhaps more than one gift, Crete and the Kyrenaika. Appropriating Crete might have been particularly satisfying to Antonius since the organization of the island as a Roman province had been largely to repair the damage done by his father, M. Antonius, whose attempt to eliminate its use as a pirate base had ended disastrously. The humiliation felt by the family through the ridicule implied in the senior Antonius' posthumous cognomen "Creticus" could now be avenged by the son taking Crete away from Rome and giving it to his daughter.[24]

Roman control of the Kyrenaika had dated from the beginning of the century.[25] Yet traditionally Kyrene had been Ptolemaic: Kleopatra VII's grandfather, Ptolemaios IX, and his uncle, Ptolemaios Apion, had been the last kings of an independent Kyrene, and the death of the latter in 96 BC had soon resulted in Roman control. Hence the bestowal of Crete and Kyrene on Kleopatra Selene, even if the two were not yet unified as a single Roman province,[26] fulfilled dynastic and personal needs of her parents. A certain Crassus[27] may have been sent as royal governor, issuing crocodile coins that

---

23 K. W. Meiklejohn, "Alexander Helios and Caesarion," *JRS* 24, 1934, 192–3.

24 Eleanor Goltz Huzar, *Mark Antony: A Biography* (London: Croom Helm, 1978), pp. 15–16. On the career of Creticus, see Philip De Souza, *Piracy in the Graeco-Roman World* (Cambridge: Cambridge University Press, 1999), pp. 141–8. The cognomen may not originally have been meant to be derisive: see Jerzy Linderski, "The Surname of M. Antonius Creticus and the Cognomina *ex victis gentibus*," *ZPE* 80, 1990, 157–64.

25 Joyce Reynolds and J. A. Lloyd, "Cyrene," *CAH*[2] 10, 1996, 619–21.

26 The evidence for their linkage is clear only in the Augustan period (Reynolds and Lloyd [supra note 25], p. 632). See also André Laronde, *Cyrène et la Libye hellénistique: Libykai Historiai de l'époque républicaine au principat d'Auguste* (Paris: CNRS, 1987), pp. 478–9.

27 The identity of this Crassus is by no means certain. The most likely candidate is the Antonian confidant P. Canidius Crassus (consul suff. in 40 BC), who was to command the land forces at Actium, and died, perhaps by suicide, after the capture of Alexandria, but he was directing Antonius' Armenian campaign from 36 BC, and there seems to have been little opportunity between then and Actium for him to have served in the Kyrenaika. On his career, see Pelling (supra note 3), pp. 31–2, 50–1, 57, 64; for identification of him as royal governor of Kyrene, *BMC Cyrenaica*, ccxxi–ccxxii.

asserted Kleopatra Selene's control of the territory,[28] but there is no evidence of any attempt to expel the Roman government, or even that the people of Crete and Kyrene knew that they were now subjects of a 6-year-old queen.[29] Antonius and Kleopatra VII, at any rate, were almost out of time: Octavian, in Rome, made the most of the Donations of Alexandria, and it was only three years until Actium.

One further item is known about Kleopatra Selene's early life in Alexandria. As royal children needed suitable teachers, Antonius reached back into his Roman circle of Greek intellectuals to call upon Nikolaos of Damaskos, probably on the recommendation of Timagenes of Alexandria, who was serving in the Ptolemaic court when Antonius first came to Egypt in 55 BC.[30] In later years, Nikolaos, now the intimate of both Herod the Great and Augustus, would try to suppress his role as tutor to the royal children at the Alexandrian court. He almost succeeded, since knowledge of this portion of his career rests upon a single obscure notice.[31] Presumably his efforts were most directed toward the eldest, Kaisarion, in his teens, but Kleopatra Selene and her brothers could not have been hurt by the presence in their household of one of the most distinguished scholars of the era.[32] She may have maintained contact in the following decade when she moved to Rome and Nikolaos was visiting the city regularly as ambassador of Herod and biographer of Augustus.

Three other royal tutors are known by name, but none of them seems to have been of particular note. Euphronios played a role in negotiating the disposition of the children after Actium. Theodoros was a tutor of Antyllus, the son of Antonius and Fulvia, who was living in Alexandria at the time, and Rhodon was a tutor of Kaisarion: both were remembered only for betraying their charges when Alexandria fell to Octavian.[33]

The next duty of parents of royal children was to insure that they were properly married. Progress was under way when Alexandros Helios was betrothed to Iopate of Media, daughter of King Artavasdes, whom Antonius had managed to lure away from his Parthian alliance and make king of Armenia Minor.[34] Iotape came to Alexandria in 34 BC, perhaps more as

---

28 *BMC Cyrenaica* ccxxi–ccxxii, p. 117, nos. 24–6. These are remindful of Kleopatra Selene's later crocodile coins from Mauretania (Figure 26c, d, p. 246; Mazard #394, 395).

29 Nonetheless, Augustus in the *Res gestae* (27) would claim to have recovered the territory.

30 Plutarch, *Antonius* 72.

31 Sophronios of Damaskos, *Account of the Miracles of Saints Cyrus and John* 54 (=FGrHist #90, T2). Volkmann (supra note 17), p. 208, believed the tutoring took place in Rome after 29 BC, which seems unlikely, as then there would have been no reason to suppress the episode. See also Ben Zion Wacholder, *Nicolaus of Damascus* (Berkeley: University of California Press, 1962), pp. 21–2, who had Kleopatra VII engage him as tutor around 36 BC when she was in the Levant, a distinct possibility.

32 Glen W. Bowersock, *Augustus and the Greek World* (Oxford: Clarendon Press, 1965), p. 124.

33 Plutarch, *Antonius* 81.

34 Dio 49.44; Hans Buchheim, *Die Orientpolitik des Triumvirn M. Antonius* (Heidelberg: C. Winter, 1960), pp. 81–3.

hostage than bride, and there was the thought that Alexandros Helios might someday become king of Media and Armenia.[35] But there was no chance to make a similar arrangement for his sister, as preparations for war with Rome followed almost immediately.

During the Battle of Actium, the royal children remained in Alexandria, perhaps under the supervision of Euphronios. The following year, as Octavian was advancing toward Egypt, Euphronios, one of the few Antonius and Kleopatra could still trust, was sent to Octavian to negotiate terms, one of which included giving the throne of Egypt to the children. The petition reached Octavian somewhere in Asia Minor and was promptly rejected.[36] When he reached Egypt an attempt was made to remove the children to safety. Kaisarion was sent toward Ethiopia, with India his eventual goal,[37] and the other children were also moved inland, perhaps at least to Thebes.[38] But after the deaths of Antonius and Kleopatra, all were rounded up with the exception of Kaisarion, who was betrayed by Rhodon and killed while en route to Ethiopia, and Antyllus, who was killed in Alexandria at the altar of the Divine Julius.[39] All the others were spared, including the various foreign offspring at the court.[40] Of these, only Iotape is known by name. She was destined not to marry Alexandros Helios but was sent back to her father Artavasdes, since the possibility of handing sensitive Armenia and Media over to a son of Antonius and Kleopatra was too dangerous for Octavian even to

35 Pelling, *CAH*[2] (supra note 3), pp. 39–40. Two bronze statuettes, one in the Metropolitan Museum in New York (Department of Greek and Roman Art #49.11.3) and a companion in the Walters Museum, Baltimore, have recently been suggested to represent Alexandros Helios as Prince of Armenia: Guy Weill Goudchaux, "Cleopatra's Subtle Religious Strategy," *Cleopatra*, p. 139; see also *Cleopatra*, pp. 250–1, no. 270.

36 Plutarch, *Antonius* 72.

37 Plutarch, *Antonius* 81. The monsoon route to India had been discovered less than a century previously and was a Ptolemaic monopoly (infra, pp. 228–30), so India might have seemed an ideal ultimate place of refuge.

38 Synkellos 583.

39 Suetonius, *Augustus* 17.5; Dio 51.15. On the situation with the children after Actium, see Sullivan, *Near Eastern Royalty*, p. 279. The tutors Euphronios and Rhodon disappear from the record at this time. Theodoros was executed for stealing Antyllus' possessions (Plutarch, *Antonius* 81). Conspicuously absent in these last days is Nikolaos of Damaskos, who may have been successful in suppressing his role, or, more likely, had wisely fled to Herod in Judaea, beginning forty years of service to that dynasty, and thus saving both his life and his career. In fact, a number of scholars and intellectuals moved from the Alexandrian court to Judaea at this time (Roller, *Herod*, pp. 55–7).

40 According to Dio (51.15.6), Alexandros Helios and Ptolemaios Philadelphos were spared out of consideration for Kleopatra Selene and Juba, an anachronism that confuses the situation in 30 BC with that of several years later, as Juba would hardly have been a factor in the events of the fall of Alexandria. Dio's statement may reflect Octavian's desire not to kill the boys and eventually to use them in dynastic plans, as he would Kleopatra Selene. On the sparing of the twins, see Meiklejohn (supra note 23), pp. 191–4. It is remotely possible that the boys grew to adulthood and lived out their lives in obscurity (Whitehorne [supra note 18], p. 198) and that this was reflected by Dio, but given the notoriety of their parents this is hard to imagine.

contemplate.[41] Some of the foreign children at the court were married to each other, others returned home, and some, along with the three children of Antonius and Kleopatra, were sent to Rome and Octavia.[42] Thus Octavia's already large household now included the six surviving children of her late husband Antonius: Kleopatra's Kleopatra Selene, Alexandros Helios (both 10), and Ptolemaios Philadelphos (about 6), Fulvia's surviving son Iullus Antonius (aged 13), and Octavia's own two children by Antonius, the two Antoniae, ages 9 and 6. The combined and neighboring families of Octavia and Octavian now contained over a dozen children: these six, Octavian's daughter Julia (aged 9), his stepsons Tiberius and Drusus (aged 12 and 8), Octavia's two Marcellae (of uncertain age but in their mid-teens), and her Marcellus (aged 12), as well as assorted foreigners, some, unknown by name and presumably obscure, brought from Alexandria, as well as Hyginos (about 20 and on the verge of obtaining his freedom) and, of course, Juba, now about 18.

Like that of her future husband, Kleopatra Selene's introduction to Rome was at a triumph, the triple triumph of August 29 BC after Octavian's leisurely return to Rome. The first day was devoted to Illyricum, the second to Actium, and the third to Egypt, on which the twins participated as a symbolic Moon and Sun.[43] Conspicuously absent is Ptolemaios Philadelphos, who had already vanished from the record, and the triumph is the last mention of Alexandros Helios. There is no reason to assume that they were murdered,[44] as this would make little sense, especially in the case of Ptolemaios Philadelphos. Why would he be saved at Alexandria but killed within the year, before the triumph, and why would the younger and less threatening be murdered first? Plutarch explicitly wrote that all Antonius' children

---

41 She married Mithradates III of Kommagene and became the matriarch of the Kommagenian royal line: see Richard D. Sullivan, "The Dynasty of Commagene," *ANRW* 2.8, 1977, 780–98; Sullivan, *Near Eastern Royalty*, p. 297.

42 The children of Antonius and Kleopatra were Octavian's stepnephews and stepniece, which may have been reason to save them. Kaisarion would have been only a cousin. But Octavian may also have felt a sense of obligation because they were the heirs to the Ptolemaic royal line, and Ptolemaios XII Auletes – the children's grandfather – some twenty-five years previously had asked Rome to insure the accession of his own heirs (Ptolemaios XIII and Kleopatra VII), a major reason Pompeius, Caesar, and even Antonius were drawn into Egyptian dynastic politics. It is conceivable that Octavian considered returning one of the children to the throne of Egypt as a way of fulfilling the wishes of Ptolemaios XII, but if he had any such ideas they were soon forgotten. See the discussion in Braund, *Friendly King*, pp. 136–7. On the ambivalent attitude toward the children of Antonius, see Joël Le Gall, "Successeurs d'Auguste mais descendants d'Antoine," *BAntFr* 1987, pp. 223–9.

43 Eusebios, *Chronicle* 2.140 (ed. Schoene); Zonaras 10.31 (531). Kleopatra Selene's participation in this triumph was an ironic reflection of Horace's almost contemporary words about her mother (*Odes* 1.37.30–2): "unwilling to be escorted as a private citizen in savage Liburnians to a proud triumph: she was no humble woman" ("saevis Liburnis scilicet invidens / privata deduci superbo / non humilis mulier triumpho"). On the triumph see Ettore Pais, *Fasti triumphales populi romani* (Rome: Nardecchia, 1920), pp. 305–12.

44 As Pelling (Plutarch, *Life of Antony*, supra note 16), p. 64, believed, following Syme (supra note 3), p. 300.

except Antyllus were saved by Octavian and that they entered Octavia's household,[45] by which time any elimination would have been meaningless. It is better to assume that they died naturally, Ptolemaios Philadelphos in the winter of 30–29 BC (the 6-year-old had known nothing but the mild winters of Egypt), and Alexandros Helios sometime after 29 BC, but before he was old enough to figure in the Augustan dynastic plans implied by Dio.[46] As he was already 11, he died within the next few years, certainly before military and marriageable age.[47]

Kleopatra Selene thus became the only surviving child of Kleopatra VII, growing to maturity amid the Octavian brood. Before long, the matter of her marriage would arise: Augustus was adamant that the foreign children in his extended family be treated as his own.[48] He may have thought Kleopatra Selene a suitable match for Juba when he began to consider placing him on the Mauretanian throne, since it would return her to her native continent and there were long-standing connections between the Ptolemies and northwest Africa. But it was allegedly Octavia who promoted the marriage between these two of her charges.[49] For the marriage to be valid to the Romans, both would have to be of legal age and Roman citizens.[50] Juba was already of marriageable age when Kleopatra Selene arrived in Rome, and she would reach proper age (14–16)[51] in 26–24 BC, roughly the time Juba went to Mauretania. Juba became a Roman citizen, presumably before his marriage, but the status of Kleopatra Selene is uncertain: her father was a Roman citizen,[52] but what of her mother? The Roman

45 Plutarch, *Antonius* 87.1.

46 Dio 51.15.5–7. One is reminded of Lucretius' comments (6.1103–9) on the negative effects of a change of climate on people. Mortality seems to have been the highest in Rome during the summer (Walter Scheidel, *Measuring Sex, Age, and Death in the Roman Empire: Explorations in Ancient Demography* [*JRA* Supplement 21, 1996], pp. 139–63), but it is more likely that the boys were fatally affected by the chilly, damp winters.

47 Grant's suggestion (supra note 15), p. 231, based on a loose reading of Dio 51.15.6, that the boys went to Mauretania with their sister, is intriguing but totally unsupported, and does not account for their complete disappearance from the record. Had these royal children reached maturity, there would be issues of marriage and suitable royal positions, which would certainly have been mentioned by Plutarch in those chapters of his biography of Antonius in which he discussed the destinies of the other children.

48 Suetonius, *Augustus* 48.

49 Plutarch, *Antonius* 87. Octavia appears as a frequent matchmaker among her children, actual and adopted, although Pelling (Plutarch, *Life of Antony*, supra note 16), p. 325, would see this as a consistent tendency by Plutarch to enhance her status.

50 On citizenship and marriage, see Susan Treggiari, *Roman Marriage* (Oxford: Clarendon Press, 1991), pp. 43–9.

51 J. P. D. V. Balsdon, *Roman Women: Their History and Habits* (London: Bodley Head, 1962), p. 173; Treggiari (supra note 50), pp. 39–43. Actual ages of marriage may have been slightly later, in the late teens. See Brent D. Shaw, "The Age of Roman Girls at Marriage: Some Reconsiderations," *JRS* 77, 1987, 30–46.

52 Antonius' Roman citizenship would not have devolved on his offspring if their mother were not also a citizen, unless there were some special arrangement (Treggiari [supra note 50], pp. 45–9).

propaganda machine of the 30s BC had made much of Antonius' illegal "marriage" to a foreign queen,[53] but this does not really address the matter of Kleopatra VII's citizenship.[54] Although no record survives, it is probable that she was a Roman citizen herself.[55] Such a conclusion must remain hypothetical, but citizenship was frequently bestowed in the East during the first century BC, reaching petty dynasts such as Antipatros of Askalon and Polemon I of Pontos. Thus it is difficult to imagine that the major kings were not also recipients.[56] The Ptolemies, one of the oldest eastern allies of Rome, may have received citizenship at the time of the restoral of Ptolemaios XII in 55 BC by Gabinius and Antonius, if not before, or during Julius Caesar's time in Egypt. Or Antonius, always lavish with such bestowals, may have given it directly, either to Kleopatra VII or to her children.[57] If citizenship were not specifically granted to her, Antonius could have bestowed the privilege of *conubium* – legal marriage to a Roman – which, although rare, would have been within his triumviral powers and would have ensured citizenship for the children.[58] If any of these was the case, and

---

53 For the issues and problems, see Syme (supra note 3), pp. 261, 273–4, 277, 280; Reinhold (supra note 19), pp. 220–2; Scott (supra note 1), pp. 36–7.

54 Unless this is the point made by Octavian when he had a public reading of Antonius' will, since it publicized Antonius' large legacy to Kleopatra Selene and Alexandros Helios (Dio 50.3.5; Suetonius, *Augustus* 17.1–2), an outrageous act if their mother were a foreigner, and so foolish even for Antonius that forgery has long been suspected: as Syme (supra note 3), p. 282, pointed out, it was "an opportune discovery." Yet if it were a forgery, one would have expected the forgers to have made a far stronger case against Antonius, as the will only contains provisions that could easily have been predicted from Antonius' known actions. Thus one can argue both ways about the authenticity: see John Crook, "A Legal Point about Mark Antony's Will," *JRS* 47, 1957, 36–8; Scott (supra note 1), pp. 41–3, who believed that it was forged; and John Robert Johnson, "The Authenticity and Validity of Antony's Will," *AntCl* 47, 1978, 494–503, who equally convincingly demonstrated the opposite.

55 This was first proposed by Lily Ross Taylor in her review of *Papers Presented to Hugh Macilwain Last*, *AJP* 80, 1959, 102–3; see also Coltelloni-Trannoy, pp. 39–40, and David C. Braund, "Client Kings," in *The Administration of the Roman Empire (241 BC–AD 193)*, ed. David C. Braund, Exeter Studies in History 18, 1988, pp. 82–3, where it is obliquely hinted. Johnson (supra note 54), p. 503, called it "likely" and noted that such citizenship would solve the questions about Antonius' will.

56 On citizenship for royal foreigners, see Braund, *Friendly King*, pp. 39–53. The commonness of Antonii in the East is one indication of how frequently Antonius bestowed it (A. N. Sherwin-White, *The Roman Citizenship*, second edition [Oxford: Clarendon Press, 1973], pp. 309–10). But nowhere is there any record of citizenship for the Ptolemies, who may not have seen it as an enhancement to their status.

57 At least one freedman with the name Antonius was at the Mauretanian court (*CIL* 8.9344), which implies that Kleopatra Selene may have adopted her father's name, an implication of citizenship directly conferred.

58 The matter of *conubium* is discussed by Treggiari (supra note 50), pp. 43–9. On the legalities of the marriage of Antonius and Kleopatra, see Edoardo Volterra, "Ancora sul matrimonio di Antonio con Cleopatra," in *Festschrift für Werner Flume zum 70. Geburtstag* 1, Cologne: O. Schmidt, 1978, pp. 205–12; David A. Cherry, "The Marriage of Roman Citizens and Non-citizens: Law and Practice" (Ph.D. thesis, University of Ottawa, 1985), pp. 137–41.

there is no documentation, one would not expect the Augustan cleansing of the record to have preserved it. But it is thus probable that Kleopatra Selene was already a Roman citizen when she came to Rome. If not, she received citizenship before her marriage, as did the other foreigners in the imperial family, Juba and Hyginos, and when she came of age there was no legal reason that she and Juba could not marry.

The few sources that mention the marriage give no hint as to the date.[59] It has been assumed that there was a betrothal as early as 29 BC, but this seems based on nothing more than the confused passage of Dio and his assertion that Octavian spared Alexandros Helios and Ptolemaios Philadelphos out of consideration for Kleopatra Selene and Juba, which as previously noted is an unlikely situation.[60] The most probable year for the marriage would be 25 BC, when Kleopatra Selene was of proper age and Juba was sent to rule Mauretania, for to send him with a suitable wife would have been appropriate, even essential.[61] But there is no evidence of the marriage until Juba's sixth regnal year, when the monarchs appear jointly on coins.[62] This was 20–19 BC, when Kleopatra Selene turned 21, and this has been accepted as the date of their marriage by many commentators.[63] But regnal years appear infrequently on Juba's coins, especially (it seems) the earlier ones, so the matter is not certain. Moreover, if the wedding did not occur until 19 BC, this means that Kleopatra Selene and Juba were married at significantly later ages than any of the other imperial children – Julia was married by 16, Tiberius and Drusus by 23 – seemingly violating the Augustan law that stressed marriage for women by age 20 and for men by 25.[64] Kleopatra Selene's future husband left Rome in 25 BC, when she was already of age, and it seems highly improbable that the marriage was postponed beyond this date. The coin of 19 BC provides a *terminus ante quem* but is unlikely to have

59 Plutarch, *Antonius* 87; Dio 51.15.6; *Souda*, Ἰοβάς.

60 Jacoby, *RE* 2385; Balsdon (supra note 51), p. 74. It seems unlikely, as recently argued by Coltelloni-Trannoy (p. 36), that this proves Octavian had decided as soon as the fall of Alexandria to establish a client kingdom in Mauretania. However far-thinking he was, this seems premature in 30 BC.

61 Walter Thieling, *Der Hellenismus in Kleinafrika: Der griechische Kultureinfluss in den römischen Provinzen Nordwestafrikas* (Leipzig: Teubner, 1911), p. 19.

62 Mazard #357.

63 Gsell 8.218; Duncan Fishwick and Brent D. Shaw, "Ptolemy of Mauretania and the Conspiracy of Gaetulicus," *Historia* 25, 1976, 492; Coltelloni-Trannoy, p. 36; Jean Mazard, "Un Denier inédit de Juba II et Cléopâtre-Séléné," *SchwMbll* 31, 1981, 1–2. Other suggested dates are 25 BC (Thieling [supra note 61], p. 19); 23 BC (H. Pavis d'Escurac, "Les Méthodes de l'impérialisme romaine en Maurétanie de 33 avant J.-C. à 40 après J.-C.," *Ktema* 7, 1982, 225); and 20 BC (Balsdon [supra note 51], p. 74 and Stähelin [supra note 13], p. 784). Jacoby (*RE*, p. 2385) would only commit himself to no later than 20 BC.

64 Although the legislation is slightly later (18 BC), it presumably finalizes the maturing of Augustus' thinking over the previous years. On this law, see Susan Treggiari, "Social Status and Social Legislation," *CAH²* 10, 1996, 887–9; Balsdon (supra note 51), pp. 76–7; Treggiari, *Roman Marriage* (supra note 50), pp. 60–80. The exact ages are uncertain (p. 66).

commemorated the marriage; perhaps it was in honor of the fifth anniversary of a wedding at the end of 25 BC, when Kleopatra Selene was about the same age as Livia and Julia at their marriages. But any hypothesis, other than before 19 BC, is questionable because of the lack of dated coins.

Nevertheless, the 20s BC saw marriages throughout the imperial family. Julia and Marcellus, first cousins, were married in 25 BC after Augustus' return from Spain:[65] Marcellus' death within two years saw Julia soon married to M. Vipsanius Agrippa. The elder Antonia married L. Domitius Ahenobarbus, an enigmatic character who made a long career out of inconspicuousness,[66] perhaps around the time of his aedileship in 22 BC. Augustus' stepsons were betrothed – Tiberius to Agrippa's daughter Vipsania, Drusus to the younger Antonia – but the weddings did not occur until 20 and 16 BC. One of the Marcellae married first M. Agrippa and then Antonius' son Iullus Antonius; the other Paullus Aemilius Lepidus (consul in 34 BC), nephew of the triumvir and Octavian's major crony in that family.[67] By 20 BC Octavia's household was depleted. The absence of Alexandros Helios and Ptolemaios Philadelphos from these arrangements is further proof of their demise: everyone else in the extended families of Octavia and Augustus is accounted for.[68]

The marriage of Kleopatra Selene and Juba was commemorated by Krinagoras of Mytilene. He had been a Mytilenean ambassador to Rome and came to the city in 45 BC, when he met Julius Caesar.[69] It is perhaps significant that Kleopatra VII was also there. Krinagoras' exact movements during his long life are not clear, but the fifty-one epigrams ascribed to him show an intimacy with Augustus and his family: mentioned are the Princeps himself, Marcellus, an Antonia, Tiberius, and Germanicus.[70] He may have spent time in Alexandria[71] and even at the court of Herod the Great[72] before coming to Rome in the early 20s BC, perhaps as one of the imperial tutors.[73] He may also have participated, again as a Mytilenean ambassador, in an embassy to Augustus in Spain in 26 or 25 BC,[74] the very time and place Juba was made king. Since he lived to write about Germanicus[75] and could not

65 Dio 53.27.5.

66 Syme (supra note 3), pp. 421–2.

67 Syme (supra note 3), p. 237.

68 The source for these marriages is almost totally Plutarch, *Antonius* 87, excepting only Tiberius and Vipsania (Suetonius, *Tiberius* 7; Velleius 2.96; Tacitus, *Annals* 1.12; Dio 54.31) and Marcella and Lepidus, for which see *PIR*² C1103; see also Balsdon (supra note 51), pp. 71–5.

69 *IG* 12.2.35B.

70 A. S. F. Gow and D. L. Page, *The Greek Anthology: The Garland of Philip and Some Contemporary Epigrams* (Cambridge: Cambridge University Press, 1968), vol. 2, pp. 210–13.

71 #20; Gow and Page (supra note 70), vol. 2, p. 227.

72 Roller, *Herod*, pp. 62–3.

73 J. S. Phillimore, "Crinagoras of Mytilene," *Dublin Review* 139, 1906, 78.

74 *IG* 12.2.35C; Krinagoras #16, 29, 30, 32.

75 Krinagoras #26.

have been born after about 65 BC, he had an especially long life, seemingly still active into his eighties.

The epigram in question is number 25, which tells of a marriage between children of kings, one associated with Egypt, the other with Libya:

> Great neighboring regions of the world, which the Nile, swollen from black Ethiopia, divides, you have created common kings for both through marriage, making one race of Egyptians and Libyans. Let the children of kings in turn hold from their fathers a strong rule over both lands.[76]

Although there are apparent problems with the epigram, mostly geographical, it is generally accepted that the marriage referred to is that of Juba and Kleopatra Selene.[77] Given the status of Egypt in the Augustan era, and the fact that Kleopatra Selene was the sole survivor of the Egyptian royal dynasty, it is almost impossible to suggest any alternative.[78] Unfortunately the date of composition of the epigram is unknown and thus it provides no hint as to the timing of the marriage.[79]

76 ἄγχουροι μεγάλαι κόσμοι χθόνες, ἃς διὰ Νεῖλος

  πιμπλάμενος μελάνων τέμνει ἀπ' Αἰθιόπων

  ἀμφότεραι βασιλῆας ἐκοινώσασθε γάμοισιν,

  ἓν γένος Αἰγύπτου καὶ Λιβύης θέμεναι.

  ἐκ πατέρων εἴη παισὶν πάλι τοῖσιν ἀνάκτων

  ἔμπεδον ἠπείροις σκῆπτρον ἐπ' ἀμφοτέραις.

77 Gsell (vol. 8, p. 218) felt that the epigram was not by Krinagoras, and that it commemorated the marriage of Ptolemaios III and Berenike II of Kyrene, in the mid-third century BC, a view followed by Grace Harriet Macurdy, *Vassal-Queens and Some Contemporary Women in the Roman Empire* (Baltimore: Johns Hopkins University Press, 1937), p. 54. But this seems unnecessary and somewhat convoluted, given the authority of Krinagoras' authorship.

78 Although it is clear that Kleopatra Selene saw her son Ptolemaios as a successor to the Egyptian dynasty – hence his name – the allusions in the poem become even more remote if applied to him.

79 Another epigram of this period may also mention Kleopatra Selene, *Palatine Anthology* 9.752 (=Asklepiades #44, in A. S. F. Gow and D. L. Page, *The Greek Anthology: Hellenistic Epigrams* [Cambridge: Cambridge University Press, 1968], vol. 2, pp. 148–9), which describes a ring cameo of Methe in amethyst belonging to a certain Queen Kleopatra. Two alternative authors are given in the *Palatine Anthology*, Asklepiades and Antipatros of Thessalonika. If it is the former, any connection with Kleopatra Selene can immediately be dismissed, for Asklepiades lived in the early third century BC (see Gow and Page, *Hellenistic Epigrams*, vol. 2, pp. 114–18). But the possibility of authorship by Antipatros means the epigram may be Augustan. The evidence for this date is based on his mention of a number of personalities of the Augustan period, especially L. Calpurnius Piso (#1, 30, 31, 41), perhaps his patron, the consul of 15 BC and the brother of Calpurnia, Julius Caesar's wife. Also mentioned are C. Caesar (#46), grandson of Augustus, and a certain Kotys (#48), the name of several kings of Thrace, Armenia, and Bosporos, in this case probably the son of Rhoimetalkes (*PIR²* C1554) who ruled *ca.* AD 12–19 (Gow and Page, *The Garland of Philip* [supra note 70], vol. 2, p. 59). Thus Antipatros was active in the latter years of Augustus and into the reign of Tiberius. At that time there were few notable women named Kleopatra, and only one who could be called a queen. Kleo-

Assuming that the epigram refers to Kleopatra Selene and Juba, one must allow for a Homeric definition of "Libya" as North Africa west of Egypt.[80] Thus Krinagoras might (subtly) have reminded his readers that in theory Kleopatra Selene had been queen of Kyrenaika. A minor point is that she was not the child of a king – whatever Antonius' pretenses were, no Augustan poet would have validated them – but she was the granddaughter of one and daughter of a queen. The largest problem, however, is geographical, for no one would ever consider that the Nile separated these "neighboring regions." Again one may need to look no further than poetic license, as the Nile was the most conspicuous feature of North Africa, and rivers had a traditional role as a dividing line. But the Nile had long been believed to rise in or near Mauretania, and Juba himself was to address issues regarding its source and course.[81] So to see the river as a crucial factor in the cultural union represented by the marriage of Juba and Kleopatra Selene is quite appropriate: the Nile, the best-known feature of Egypt, had its source in Mauretania, and its upper and lower parts were thus joined through the marriage.[82] Perhaps Krinagoras also used τέμνω in a Homeric sense, to "mark off" or even "cut through."[83]

Thus by 19 BC, and probably several years earlier, Kleopatra Selene had left Octavia's household to join Juba and to become queen of Mauretania. She perhaps retained in her mind at least some feeling of a hereditary claim to her mother's possessions, and even her brief and theoretical rule over Kyrenaika – although such attitudes, bordering on treason, would have been discreetly withheld in the Augustan world. Despite the Augustan negative feeling toward both her parents, there is little doubt that she honored her ancestry as a descendant both of the Ptolemies and of the Antonii, which gave her a longer Roman lineage than the Octavii.[84] She was a conspicuous and early example of the mingling of Roman aristocracy and Greek royalty

patra Selene is the only possibility if the poem reflects the later Augustan period (Conrad Cichorius, *Römische Studien* [Leipzig: Teubner, 1922], pp. 331–2), yet the authorship remains uncertain and cannot be attributed with certainty on the present evidence, although an intriguing connection is the interest in gems at the Mauretanian court (infra, pp. 150–1).

80 *Odyssey* 4.85, essentially the definition used by Juba in his *Libyka* (infra, p. 85).

81 Infra, pp. 192–6.

82 Much of this has been admirably argued by David C. Braund, "*Anth. Pal.* 9.235: Juba II, Cleopatra Selene and the Course of the Nile," *CQ* 34, 1984, 175–8, but it seems unlikely that Juba's fame as a geographer and explorer was already established by the time of his marriage, although the belief that the Nile originated in West Africa long antedated Juba.

83 *Iliad* 6.194, 13.707.

84 Aside from some legendary Octavii of pre-republican times, the family does not seem to be documented before the third century BC (Suetonius, *Augustus* 1–3). In fact, questions about Octavian's ancestry were persistent, and were frequent in the charges made against him by Antonius, especially in the late 40s BC. See Scott (supra note 1), pp. 12–17. The Antonii appear in Roman history as early as the fifth century BC (Livy 3.35.11; Dionysios of Halikarnassos, *Roman Archaeology* 10.58).

that was to become standard during the later empire. Yet she was totally her mother's daughter,[85] as she instilled in her husband – perhaps from the time they were childhood playmates in Octavia's home – a particular interest in her ancestral territory and traditions, which were to have a direct influence on Juba's interests and scholarship. As the daughter of a Greek queen and of one of the most important Romans of the previous generation, she brought greater stature to the Mauretanian court than did Juba, who was unlikely to have had either Greek or Roman ancestry. She was queen of Mauretania and retained her title as queen of Kyrenaika, or even Libya.[86] She could also claim to be queen of Egypt, and thus theoretical ruler of all northern Africa except the Roman province of Africa. However questionable these claims might have seemed in Rome, they gave her immense power and prestige in Africa. One can only imagine that Kleopatra Selene exercised a role at the Mauretanian court much as her surrogate mother Octavia and her step-aunt Livia did in Rome. Octavia and Livia have been identified as two parts of a "triumvirate of exceptional women" who were dynamic as significant players in the creation of Augustan Rome.[87] The third member of this triumvirate is Kleopatra VII. After her death, her daughter must take her place in this exalted company. Unfortunately, Kleopatra Selene virtually vanishes from the extant literature after her marriage. The only further citations are to her children. Even the date of her death is a matter of controversy.[88]

85 Despite contemporary Roman attitudes, Kleopatra Selene was not reluctant to call attention to her mother on her own coins, some of which have the legend ΒΑΣΙ ΚΛΕΟ ΚΛΕΟΠΑ ΘΥΓΑ (Jean Mazard, SchwMbll [supra note 63], pp. 1–2).

86 In addition to Krinagoras' wedding epigram, her retention of her claim as queen of Kyrenaika is supported by the continuation of her crocodile coin types from the time of the Donations of Alexandria to her maturity in Mauretania (Figure 26c, d, p. 246; supra, note 28), Juba's use of the title Libyka for his treatise on North Africa, and the close relations that the Mauretanian kingdom maintained with Kyrene (Dieter Salzmann, "Porträtsiegel aus dem Nomophylakeion in Kyrene," BJ 184, 1984, 152).

87 For the roles of Livia and Octavia, see Diana E. E. Kleiner, "Imperial Women as Patrons of the Arts in the Early Empire," in I Claudia: Women in Ancient Rome, ed. Diana E. E. Kleiner and Susan B. Matheson (New Haven, Conn.: Yale Art Gallery, 1996), pp. 28–41, and on the position of Augustan women generally, Susan Fischler, "Social Stereotypes and Historical Analysis: The Case of the Imperial Women at Rome," in Women in Ancient Societies: An Illusion of the Night, ed. Léonie J. Archer et al. (New York: Routledge, 1994), pp. 127–30.

88 Infra, pp. 249–51. Like the case of Calpurnia (supra, Chapter 3, note 23), her near-invisibility is vivid testimony to the treatment of women in the sources, not of her lack of importance.

5

THE MAURETANIAN CLIENT KINGDOM

Foundation, military history, and economy

Astonishingly little detail is preserved about the sixty-five years of the Mauretanian client kingdom. There is no known royal chronicler in the fashion of Nikolaos of Damaskos at the court of Herod the Great. Understanding relies on casual statements by those recording the periods of Augustus and Tiberius, epigraphical and numismatic material, inferences from Juba's own writings, the physical evidence of the territories, and extrapolation from the political and cultural situation in northwest Africa prior to 25 BC and in the neighboring Roman provinces. Information is most available at times of difficulty, especially along the frontier, when Roman assistance was necessary.

The background

The nature of the kingdom – and indeed its very existence – depended on events of the two decades between the Battle of Thapsus and the appointment of the monarchs as rulers of Mauretania. During these years North Africa was far from quiet.[1] The region continued to be embroiled in the Roman civil war, creating an instability that was paramount in Augustus' mind whenever he began to formulate the idea that Juba II and Kleopatra Selene would best locally represent Roman interests.

After Thapsus, Caesar promptly turned the former territory of Juba I into the new province of Africa Nova.[2] The first governor[3] was Sallust, whose strange, mixed career had not prevented him from somehow gaining Caesar's confidence.[4] Although more experienced men were available, it may have been Sallust's abilities at military logistics that Caesar believed

---

1 The most extensive modern sources for this period are C. R. Whittaker, "Roman Africa: Augustus to Vespasian," *CAH*[2] 10, 1996, 586–93; Gsell, vol. 8, pp. 156–205; Romanelli, *Storia*, pp. 129–64.

2 *De bello africo* 97; Appian, *Civil War* 4.53; Dio 43.9; Leo Teutsch, *Das Städtewesen in Nordafrika in der Zeit von C. Gracchus bis zum Tode des Kaisers Augustus* (Berlin: De Gruyter, 1962), pp. 120–6.

3 On the governors of the African provinces during these years, see W. Sternkopf, "Die Verteilung der römischen Provinzen vor dem mutinensischen Kriege," *Hermes* 47, 1912, 328–39; Yann Le Bohec, "Le Proconsulat d'Afrique d'Auguste à Claude: questions de chronologie," *BAAlg* 7, 1977–9, 223–5; and the relevant magistrates in Broughton.

qualified him to organize a new province. But this proved to be one of Caesar's worst decisions, as Sallust seems to have been disgraceful in his administration, plundering the province. Summoned to trial at the end of 45 BC, he managed to escape prosecution in Caesar's last days and wisely retired from politics to write history.[5] He was replaced by another Caesarean, T. Sextius, who had been with the Dictator in Gaul,[6] and who was to serve in Africa until 40 BC, when he was replaced by M. Aemilius Lepidus.[7] Meanwhile, in the original African province, now called Africa Vetus, whose governorship was vacant owing to the death of Scipio, Caesar chose C. Calvisius Sabinus,[8] who had been with him in Greece in 48 BC. Sabinus was followed by a series of governors who were often at odds with each other and with the governor of Africa Nova, until Lepidus took control of both provinces in 40 BC. In addition to placing loyal men in command, Caesar's policy toward Africa also included settlement. Hence there was a steady stream of Roman emigration into the two Africas continuing into the Augustan period,[9] probably including a significant portion of the 80,000 people Caesar sent from the city of Rome to overseas settlements.[10]

To the west, beyond the Roman provinces, the situation was in flux. Sittius was rewarded for his services at Thapsus with territory in the vicinity of Cirta, which may have been either a discrete enclave, or outside the Roman provincial boundaries.[11] In taking his reward he soon deposed the petty King Arabion, perhaps a descendant of King Gauda of Numidia, whose family had ruled the territory for half a century.[12] Arabion fled to the Pompeius brothers in Spain and waited for his opportunity. Sittius brought his followers to his new territory and briefly ruled as local potentate, perhaps

---

4 Sallust is first noticed as tribune in 52 BC. Implicated in the riots following the death of Clodius that year, he was expelled from the Senate in 50 BC. During the civil war he had been involved in a number of Caesarean operations, most recently a logistical command in the African campaign. See Ronald Syme, *Sallust* (Berkeley: University of California Press, 1964), pp. 29–38.

5 The sources for Sallust's governorship and its aftermath are *De bello africo* 97; Appian, *Civil War* 4.53; Dio 43.9; and the treatise known as *In Sallustium Crispum Oratio* 19–20, a contemporary political invective of uncertain authorship (see Syme [supra note 4], p. 299). On the situation generally, see Syme, pp. 38–40.

6 Caesar, *Bellum gallicum* 6.1.1.

7 Appian, *Civil War* 5.53; Dio 48.20.4, 23.4–5.

8 Cicero, *Philippic* 3.26.

9 See Dio 43.50, regarding Carthage.

10 Suetonius, *Julius* 42.1; on this generally, see Whittaker (supra note 1), pp. 587–9; Teutsch (supra note 2), pp. 99–120.

11 Appian, *Civil War* 4.54; Gsell, vol. 8, pp. 157–9. On Sittius and Cirta, see Teutsch (supra note 2), pp. 65–77; on the eventual status of Cirta and its exclusion from Juba's kingdom, see T. R. S. Broughton, *The Romanization of Africa Proconsularis* (Baltimore: Johns Hopkins University Press, 1929), pp. 71–6.

12 Arabion's father was Massinissa (II) (Appian, *Civil War* 4.54), perhaps a son of Masteabar the son of Gauda; see supra, p. 25; infra, Appendix 2; and Gabriel Camps, "Les Derniers Rois numides: Massinissa II et Arabion," *BAC* n.s. 17b, 1981 (1984), 303–11.

even striking his own coins.[13] Cirta may also have received colonial status, as Italian merchants had been in the city for nearly a century.[14]

Farther west were the territories of Bocchus II and Bogudes II, relatives who regarded each other uneasily. Here too the Roman presence was increasing, and Roman citizenship was soon to be awarded to selected local inhabitants.[15] Bocchus and Bogudes seem to have had their status as virtual client kings confirmed after Thapsus, when they latinized their coin legends.[16] Thus they ruled a vast undefined district from the western edge of the Roman provinces to the Atlantic, nearly 1,000 miles away, including traditional Mauretania and much of western Numidia. Population was centered around Iol, Bocchus' capital, and in the extreme west, from Tingis south to Volubilis, Bogudes' capital. Because of its closeness to Roman territory, this western region had been under Roman influence since the second century BC.[17]

It is not known how Caesar's settlement of North Africa might have evolved, for everything fell apart with his assassination and the renewed civil war. Africa became one of the main theaters of the war between the triumvirs and Sextus Pompeius the Younger, and continued to be a matter of concern to Octavian until after Actium. Immediately after Caesar's death, Arabion was persuaded by his Spanish host Pompeius to return to his ancestral lands and to remove Sittius and Bocchus.[18] He succeeded in killing the former, while Bocchus seems briefly to have gone into exile. Arabion did not long enjoy his restoration, however, as he became involved in the rivalries between the governors of the two African provinces, and was killed by T. Sextius.[19] Violence continued until 40 BC, when Octavian placed his fellow triumvir Lepidus in charge of both provinces.[20] From this time they had a single governor, and official unification may have followed shortly thereafter.[21]

To the west, the festering rivalry between Bocchus and Bogudes reached a peak in 38 BC when Bogudes invaded Spain, allegedly at the initiative of Antonius. His own subjects rose against him, encouraged by Bocchus and

13 Mazard #530–5.
14 Whittaker (supra note 1), pp. 586–7.
15 Dio 48.45.
16 Mazard #103–6, 118–21.
17 Supra, p. 47.
18 Appian, *Civil War* 4.54–6; Cicero, *Atticus* 15.17.1.
19 Dio 48.22; on Arabion's last years, see Camps (supra note 12), pp. 308–10.
20 Appian, *Civil War* 5.53, 65; Dio 48.20.4, 23.4–5, 28.4.
21 Duncan Fishwick, "On the Origins of Africa Proconsularis, I: The Amalgamation of Africa Vetus and Africa Nova," *AntAFr* 29, 1993, 53–62; his "On the Origins of Africa Proconsularis, II: The Administration of Lepidus and the Commission of M. Caelius Phileros," *AntAfr* 30, 1994, 57–80; and his "On the Origins of Africa Proconsularis, III: The Era of the Cereres Again," *AntAfr* 32, 1996, 13–36. He argued that unification took place during the period 40–36 BC, most likely 40/39 BC, but see Michèle Coltelloni-Trannoy, "Les Liens de clientèle en Afrique du Nord, du IIe siècle av. J.-C. jusqu'au début du principat," *BAC* n.s. 24b, 1993–5 (1997), 70, who would argue for the more traditional date of 27 BC.

reinforcements from Spain: Bogudes was unsuccessful in ending the revolt and abandoned his kingdom, joining Antonius in the East. Octavian confirmed Bocchus as king of both his own and Bogudes' territories, and gave the inhabitants of Tingis Roman citizenship.[22] Bocchus now in theory ruled everything west of the province of Africa.[23] Bogudes never returned: he was detailed by Antonius in the months before Actium to defend Methone and was killed there during M. Agrippa's attack.[24] Bocchus, on the other hand, demonstrated his devotion to Rome by adopting a Roman form of numismatic titulature, REX BOCCHUS SOSI F.[25] His use of a bust of Janus on these coins may have been his Roman way of asserting the unification of Mauretania.[26]

Lepidus' command in the provinces, the confirmation of Bocchus as sole king of all territory west thereof, and the spread of Roman citizenship would appear to have stabilized northwest Africa for the first time in a decade. But this apparent stability was illusory. Lepidus was quietly consolidating a strong base of power. By 36 BC he had at his disposal a dozen legions and a thousand ships as well as numerous local forces.[27] His role in the subsequent invasion of Sicily and defeat of Sextus Pompeius is well known, as is Octavian's stripping him of his triumviral power.[28] Lepidus' activities would have seriously weakened the province of Africa, especially their frontier defenses. Octavian planned to investigate and settle affairs personally in late 36 BC, but he never made the journey and instead handed matters over to one of his most talented subordinates, T. Statilius Taurus.[29] He did what was expected of him, but the frequency of triumphs *ex Africa* over the next few years indicates that the work was not easy, owing to repeated incursions by the indigenous tribes.[30]

---

22 Dio 48.45.1–3. On the status of Tingis, see P. A. Brunt, *Italian Manpower 225 B.C.–A.D. 14* (Oxford: Oxford University Press, 1971), p. 251.

23 Whittaker (supra note 1), p. 590. In error is Pliny's statement (*NH* 5.16) that Juba II was the first to rule over all Mauretania, which may be an indication of the confusion among scholars regarding this period.

24 Dio 50.11.3; Strabo 8.4.3.

25 Mazard #118–21; Michel Amandry, "Notes de numismatique africaine, IV," *RN* 6. ser. 31, 1989, 80–5. His father's name, perhaps ZUSN or ZUHSN, might better have been latinized as Sussa.

26 On this, and contrary but unconvincing interpretations of the coins, see J.-G. Février, "Bocchus le Jeune et les Sosii," *Semitica* 11, 1961, 9–15; and M. Euzennat, "Le Roi Sosus et la dynastie maurétanienne," in *Mélanges d'archéologie, d'épigraphie, et d'histoire offerts à Jérôme Carcopino* (Paris: Hachette, 1966), pp. 333–9; Camps (supra note 12), pp. 304–6; Michael Grant, *From Imperium to Auctoritas* (Cambridge: Cambridge University Press, 1946), pp. 174–6.

27 Appian, *Civil War* 5.98.

28 On Lepidus at this point in his career, see Richard D. Weigel, *Lepidus: The Tarnished Triumvir* (London: Routledge, 1992), pp. 81–93.

29 Dio 49.14.6, 49.34.1–2; Suetonius, *Augustus* 47; Appian, *Civil War* 5.129; Broughton, vol. 2, p. 403.

30 Statilius Taurus himself triumphed in 34 BC, and his successors L. Cornificius and L. Autronius Paetus respectively in 33 and 28 BC: see Frederick W. Shipley, "Chronology of the Building Operations in Rome from the Death of Caesar to the Death of Augustus," *MAAR* 9, 1931, 24–5, 30–2, 34; Whittaker (supra note 1), p. 590.

But as things were improving in the province of Africa they were deteriorating in Mauretania. Bocchus died in 33 BC,[31] apparently without an heir, leaving an immense power vacuum. What happened next is uncertain, as the only two sources are unhelpful. Strabo wrote that after the deaths of Bocchus and Bogudes, Juba inherited (παρέλαβε) the kingship.[32] This is too vague to be of much value: Bocchus and Bogudes, as noted, died several years apart, Bogudes had abrogated his kingship (and actually survived his reigning relative by two years), and there is no reason to believe that the 15-year-old Juba was made king on the death of Bocchus. More explicit is the notice by Dio that when Bocchus died, Octavian made his territory a Roman province.[33] This, however, has long been a problem for commentators. The simplest explanation is that Dio somehow skipped over the entire Mauretanian client kingship, conflating the death of Bocchus with the creation of the province of Mauretania seventy years later. Dio's errors of chronology and combining of separate events are notorious – his slips regarding the Donations of Alexandria are typical – but later he picked up the thread and placed Juba in his kingdom,[34] so his statement about the status of Mauretania after 33 BC must be considered seriously. Yet the existence of a provincial Mauretania at this time is unlikely. Such a province is lacking from Augustus' own list of those who had supported him at Actium,[35] and Dio's version of the same list includes among Octavian's allies "those belonging to Bogudes and Bocchus,"[36] which would hardly indicate provincial status. Moreover, Mauretania is conspicuously absent from the lengthy list of provinces in the settlement of 27 BC.[37] No governor or Roman official is known,[38] and the handing over of the territory to Juba eight years later would mean a rare reversion from province to client kingdom that would probably have offended everyone. Thus it seems that the easiest solution is that Dio was in error, at least in his analysis of the contemporary situation. But a coin of Juba II with the double date 48/55 may indicate that late in his reign he felt that although Augustus had given him the kingship in 25 BC, the year of Bocchus' death was also important in the history of the Mauretanian monarchy.[39]

31 Dio 49.43.7.

32 Strabo 17.3.7.

33 Dio 49.43.7.

34 Although aware of Juba's kingship, Dio had little to say about it: see 51.15.6, 53.26.2, 55.28.3, and 59.25.1.

35 Res gestae 25.

36 Dio 50.6.4: οἱ τοῦ Βογούου τοῦ τε Βόκχου γεγονότες.

37 Dio 53.12.4–9.

38 Whittaker (supra note 1), p. 591. It has been suggested that coins of Augustus from Iol with the legend IMP.CAESAR DIVI.F (Mazard #122–4) belong to the period between the death of Bocchus and the accession of Juba. See Coltelloni-Trannoy, p. 25.

39 Jean Mazard, "Nouvel apport à la numismatique de la Numidie et de la Maurétanie," LibAE 4, 1956, #156bis. Year 48 is Juba's last regnal year, beginning in the autumn of AD 23. A date fifty-five years previous would be sometime in 32–31 BC, several months or more after Bocchus' death, and it is thus possible that the fifty-five years refers not to this but to the Battle of Actium.

Regardless of what Juba felt half a century later, the question of the exact status of Bocchus' territory during the period 33–25 BC remains unanswered.[40] Moreover, the issue is complicated by evidence for Roman colonies in Mauretania, some (particularly in the west) bearing the name Colonia Julia, and others (in the east) with the name Colonia Julia Augusta. Most of the latter are reasonably attributed to Claudius, since he was the first to make administrative decisions regarding the province established after the death of King Ptolemaios. But those in the west do not seem to use the name "Augusta" and thus may have been established before 27 BC. There are three: Colonia Julia Constantia Zulil, Colonia Julia Campestris Babba, and Colonia Julia Valentia Banasa.[41] All are in the same region of extreme northwest Africa: according to Pliny, Zulil is 25 miles from Tingis, Babba 75 miles further, in the interior, and Banasa another 75 miles onward, 35 miles from Volubilis.[42] The population of Zulil was exempt from the rule of the local kings and under the legal authority of Baetica – an anachronistic statement for Pliny's day, since there were no local kings any more – and the indigenous Mauretanian population may have been relocated across the strait to Spain in order to clear land for the new colony.[43] Thus it seems that Octavian established Roman colonies in the parts of Mauretania closest to Spain and that the settlements continued to retain some legal attachment to Spain when the territory had become a client kingdom.[44] Volubilis, Bogudes' old capital, may also have had a special arrangement with Rome.[45]

It is worth remembering the Roman political situation at the time of the death of Bocchus, 33 BC. The previous year had seen the Donations of Alexandria, one of the defining moments in the collapse of relations between Antonius and Octavian. The following year would bring Antonius' divorce

40 H. Pavis d'Escurac, "Les Méthodes de l'impérialisme romain en Maurétanie de 33 avant J.-C. à 40 après J.-C.," *Ktema* 7, 1982, 222–5; Brunt (supra note 22), pp. 595–7.

41 *NH* 5.2–5, 20–1; Pliny (ed. Desanges) pp. 79–98; Gsell, vol. 8, pp. 202–4; Nicola K. Mackie, "Augustan Colonies in Mauretania," *Historia* 33, 1983, 333–42; Teutsch (supra note 2), pp. 209–20. For a discussion of the probable location of these sites (with previous bibliography), see J. Boube, "Apropos de *Babba Iulia Campestris*," *BAMaroc* 15, 1983–4, 131–7; also Louis Chatelain, *Le Maroc des Romains*, *BÉFAR* 160, 1944, pp. 46–9, 69–76.

42 On Pliny's distances, see Maurice Euzennat, "Remarques sur la description de la Maurétanie Tingitane dans Pliny, *NH*, V, 2–18," *AntAfr* 25, 1989, 95–109.

43 Strabo 3.1.8. On the problems of reconciling Pliny's Zulil and Strabo's Zelis, which he placed in Spain, see Mackie (supra note 41), pp. 343–8; Pliny (ed. Desanges), pp. 86–7.

44 The strong connection between northwest Mauretania and Spain still existed in AD 69, when some of the territory of Mauretania Tingitana was attached to Baetica (Tacitus, *Histories* 2.58), a situation perhaps reflected in Pliny's statement about Zulil. This was an event in the short reign of the emperor Otho, who was attempting to solidify his rule by restoring an Augustan practice. On the peculiar status of Tingis and other colonies in northwest Mauretania, see Jacques Gascou, "Note sur l'évolution juridique de Tanger entre 38 avant J.-C. et le règne de Claude," *AntAfr* 8, 1974, 67–71, and Christine Hamdoune, "Note sur le statut colonial de Lixus et de Tanger," *AntAfr* 30, 1994, 81–7.

45 Michel Christol and Jacques Gascou, "Volubilis, cité fédérée?" *MÉFRA* 92, 1980, 337–43.

of Octavia and the complete breach between the two triumvirs. Moreover, the triumvirate was on the verge of expiring, which would leave Octavian particularly vulnerable.[46] A new province would require the establishment of an administration, hardly (during this crucial period) the best use of Octavian's time or manpower. It would be easier to create the proper distaste in Rome for the Donations of Alexandria and its juggling around of territory if Octavian were not seen to be doing similar things at the opposite end of the empire. The organization of Africa Nova thirteen years earlier had been assisted by the presence of Roman troops – and even then it had become a pawn in the civil war – but there is no evidence that there were any Roman officials in Mauretania in 33 BC. Octavian may already have been considering using Juba in his final disposition of the territory, but at age 15, Juba was not yet available. The recent accession to client kingship of the far more experienced and crafty Herod in Judaea in 40 BC had resulted in several years of civil war and massive Roman military aid, for which C. Sosius had triumphed *ex Judaea* just a few months before Bocchus' death.[47] Whatever happened to the territory of Bocchus, there was a potential for disaster in those difficult years of 33–32 BC.

The most that Octavian dared do was to establish a handful of colonies in the parts of Mauretania closest to Spain, an informal extension of Roman territory into the adjacent area, which had more in common with Spain, economically, culturally, and geographically, than with the contiguous African territories.[48] Yet probably even this modest effort was not fully implemented until the demobilizations after 30 BC.[49] In a region of sporadic Roman presence, indigenous tribes, and inconsistent rule by both Romans and locals, borders were fluid,[50] and support of long-existing Roman interests was wise. Creating colonies required none of the bureaucratic effort of establishing a province. And presumably there was reason to wait a few years for an ultimate solution involving Juba. It is possible that western Mauretania had some special status from 33 to 25 BC,[51] but what this was cannot be determined. Full provincial recognition seems impossible to accept, as does

---

46 On the intense difficulties Octavian faced at this time, see E. W. Gray, "The Crisis at Rome at the Beginning of 32 BC," *PACA* 13, 1975, 15–29.

47 Shipley (supra note 30), pp. 25–8.

48 On this, see John Spaul, "Across the Frontier in Tingitana," *Roman Frontier Studies 1995: Proceedings of the XVIth International Congress of Roman Frontier Studies*, ed. W. Groenman-Van Waateringe *et al.*, Oxbow Monographs 91 (London: Oxbow, 1997), pp. 253–8; also Mohammed Majdoub, "Octavius et la Maurétanie," *AfrRom* 13, 2000, 1725–37.

49 For the view that the colonies were established only after Juba became king, see E. T. Salmon, *Roman Colonization under the Republic* (Ithaca, N.Y.: Cornell University Press, 1970), p. 144. Yet this seems unlikely, because of the lack of the name "Augusta" and the diminished need for veterans' colonies by 25 BC.

50 Duncan Fishwick and Brent D. Shaw, "Ptolemy of Mauretania and the Conspiracy of Gaeticulus," *Historia* 25, 1976, 492; Romanelli, *Storia*, p. 166.

51 Erich S. Gruen, "The Expansion of the Empire under Augustus," *CAH²* 10, 1996, 168.

the suggestion that Roman legates took up residence in the palaces of Bocchus and Bogudes,[52] or that Juba came by his kingship gradually.[53] It is best to assume that Octavian supported an existing but faint Roman presence as much as feasible, but that his primary concerns (at least through 30 BC) were elsewhere and that he dealt with Mauretania slowly and gradually as the Roman political situation changed.[54] Even at the time of the settlement of 27 BC, Mauretania was still in limbo, as Octavian, now Augustus, departed for Spain, with Juba, now an adult, in tow, soon to make a final disposition of northwest Africa.

Augustus' interests turned to Spain in 27 BC because it was one of the provinces that had been given to him in the settlement in January of that year,[55] festering difficulties with the mountain tribes of Cantabri and Astures,[56] and because his recent preoccupation with the East meant that the West needed his attention. Late in the year he set forth, going first to Gaul and then to Tarraco in Spain (Figure 3), which he made his headquarters.[57] In his entourage were the young men of the imperial household: Marcellus, Tiberius, and Juba. Augustus was in Tarraco before the end of the year, and on 1 January 26 BC he began his eighth consulship in that city. The war against the Spanish tribes was difficult, impacting on Augustus' never strong health, and he spent most of the next two years resident in Tarraco seeking cures and dealing with administrative business while his subordinates conducted the military operations. Embassies came from India, Skythia, Parthia, and Mytilene,[58] knowing that Tarraco, not Rome, was the seat of power. Augustus' forced immobility meant that time could be spent in determining the future, and as he entered his ninth consulship in 25 BC, still in the city, many decisions were made. Colonies were founded, the most famous being Augusta Emerita, modern Mérida. From the East came word

52 Gsell, vol. 8, pp. 200–3; Arnaldo Momigliano, "I regni indigeni dell'Africa Romana," in *Africa Romana* (Milan: Hoepli, 1935), p. 100; Coltelloni-Trannoy, pp. 24–5.

53 Ritter, *Rom*, pp. 139–40.

54 Romanelli, *Storia*, pp. 161–2; Mazard #122–4; Whittaker (supra note 1), p. 590. On his ultimate decision to involve Juba, see Vito Antonio Sirago, "Il contributo di Giuba II alla conoscenza dell'Africa," *AfrRom* 11, 1994, 303–4.

55 Dio 53.12.

56 On the military and political situation, see Géza Alföldy, "Spain," *CAH*[2] 10, 1996, 449–52.

57 The main ancient source for these events is Dio 53.22–8; see also John A. Crook, "Political History, 30 BC to AD 14," *CAH*[2] 10, 1996, 76–83; and, for Augustus' movements, Helmut Halfmann, *Itinera principum*, Heidelberger althistorische Beiträge und epigraphische Studien 2 (Stuttgart 1986), p. 157. Tarraco, which had come to prominence during the Second Punic War, had languished thereafter but in the late Republic had been revitalized as an important mercantile and trade center, and was to be a Roman colonia and provincial capital by the early empire. See Géza Alföldy, "Tarraco" (#1), *RE* Supp. 15, 1978, 584–97. Juba would not have missed the irony of having his future decided in the city that had been the headquarters of P. Cornelius Scipio the Elder (Livy 22.22), who had been killed by the cavalry of his ancestor Massinissa (Livy 25.34).

58 The Indian and Skythian visit is described by Orosius (6.21); for the others, see Halfmann (supra note 57), p. 160.

Figure 3 Tarraco (modern Tarragona), where Juba II was named king.
Photograph by Duane W. Roller.

that Amyntas of Galatia had been killed in wars against mountain tribes, and thus his kingdom was turned into a province.[59] Marcellus married Augustus' daughter Julia during that year, with Agrippa in charge of the ceremonies, since the Princeps, still in poor health, returned to Rome slowly, sending Marcellus on before him. Augustus did not arrive in the city until after the beginning of 24 BC, starting his tenth consulship on the road. The destiny of Juba was also determined at this time: to be sent to rule the territory of Bocchus and Bogudes, Mauretania. The presence of the imperial entourage in Spain would naturally have led Augustus to thoughts of the situation in western Mauretania, at least, which in Roman eyes was virtually part of Spain. Juba, who was now about 23 and had proven himself, returned to Rome in the latter part of 25 BC, probably with Marcellus. He married Kleopatra Selene, perhaps at about the same time that Marcellus married Julia, and then the royal couple set out for Mauretania, probably taking up residence in Bocchus' old palace at Iol before the end of the year.

Limits of the royal territories

Because of the inconsistent and contradictory nature of the sources, which represent different information gathered at different times, there is some difficulty in determining exactly what territory Juba II and Kleopatra Selene ruled.[60] Since the time of the original Punic settlements, the urban population of what came to be called Mauretania had been centered in two major clusters, one around Iol, and the other in the west along a corridor between Tingis and Volubilis. This reflected the realities of topography and eventually led to the dual history of the indigenous Mauretanian monarchy, a situation preserved in the eventual creation of two Roman provinces, and even the modern separation of Morocco and Algeria. Scattered Roman colonies and indigenous cities with Roman population had existed since the latter part of the second century BC, and over the following century there had been an increasing degree of romanization.[61] In the hinterland were various tribes that remained free of the central government – whether indigenous or Roman – although in the later Empire these would drift into and out of

---

59 Sullivan, *Near Eastern Royalty*, pp. 171–4. Amyntas had fought with Antonius at Philippi, who named him king of Pisidia and Lykaonia in 39 BC, and of Galatia three years later. Like many of the eastern kings, he was with Antonius at Actium but managed to win the respect of Octavian, who confirmed his kingship. The reasons Augustus provincialized his territory five years later are not apparent, especially since Amyntas had heirs.

60 On the evidence for the frontiers of Mauretania, much of which postdates the time of the monarchy, see M. Euzennat, "La Frontière romaine d'Afrique," *CRAI* for 1990, pp. 565–80, and René Rebuffat, "Notes sur les confins de la Maurétanie Tingitane et de la Maurétanie Césarienne," *StMagr* 4, 1971, 33–64.

61 On the Roman colonies, see Mackie (supra note 41), pp. 336–50, and Brunt (supra note 22), pp. 595–7.

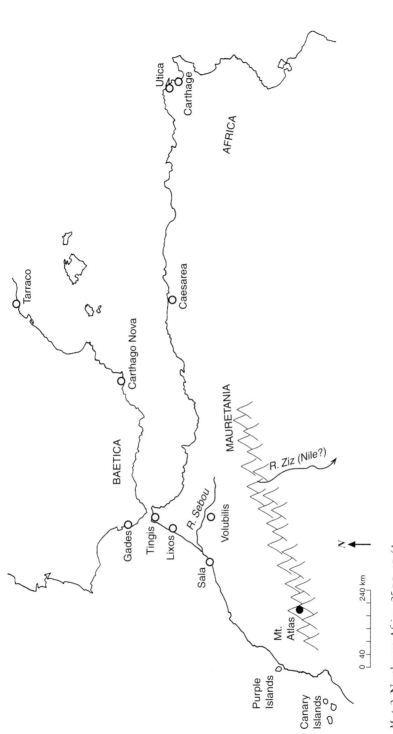

Map 2 Northwest Africa, 25 BC–AD 41

Tarraco

Carthago Nova

BAETICA

Gades

Tingis

Lixos

R. Sebou

Volubilis

Sala

Mt.
Atlas

Purple
Islands

Canary
Islands

MAURETANIA

R. Ziz (Nile?)

Caesarea

Utica

Carthage

AFRICA

N

0   40   240 km

Roman control.[62] Yet there were frequent conflicts, as always when agricul-
turalists and pastoralists live in close proximity, since the increasing agrarian
development in the temperate lowlands conflicted with the winter pasturage
needs of the shepherds. Much of the history of this region concerns such conflicts: Volubilis, which lay close to the effective frontier, was especially
subject to incursions as the transhumant population made its seasonal
moves.[63] A particular problem for Juba and his successors was the Gaetulians,
tribal groups throughout North Africa from the borders of Egypt to the
Atlantic.[64] These were the largest of the African tribes, and were noted for
their warlike character.[65] Their central territory was south of Numidia, and
since the time of Jugurtha they had been in contact with the Romans, having
caused great difficulty for Marius.[66] Yet Marius also incorporated Gaetulians
into his own forces and treated them so well that sixty years later this was the
stated reason that they chose the side of Marius' nephew Julius Caesar. Caesar
made good use of them, especially as cavalry, a determining factor in the
outcome of the African War.[67] It is probable that rewards of land and citizenship followed.[68] Despite this early alliance with certain Roman factions,
the Gaetulians were never reconciled to the central authority and would continue to be a major destabilizing factor. Since they had been opposed to
Juba's father in the African War, they would be predisposed against the son.
Juba II's kingdom included lands also claimed by the Gaetulians, and this
aggravated the long-standing tension between the various populations, as the
settlers blocked the traditional routes of the transhumants.

These issues of pastoralism and agriculturalism have thus caused some
confusion regarding the exact limits of Juba's territories. Unlike the client
kingdoms of the East, which had well-defined borders of ancient origin in
areas of long-standing culture and civilization, Mauretania was an imprecise

---

62 See C. R. Whittaker, "Land and Labour in North Africa," *Klio* 60, 1978, 331–44; and Hugh Elton,
Frontiers of the Roman Empire (Bloomington: Indiana University Press, 1996), pp. 101–4. Issues of
pastoralism in the region are discussed by Philippe Leveau, "Le Pastoralisme dans l'Afrique
antique," in *Pastoral Economies in Classical Antiquity*, Cambridge Philological Society Supp. Vol. 14,
ed. C. R. Whittaker (Cambridge 1988), pp. 177–95.

63 Marlene C. Sigman, "The Romans and the Indigenous Tribes of Mauretania Tingitana," *Historia* 26,
1977, 415–39; Edmond Frézouls, "Rome et la Maurétanie Tingitane: un constat d'échec?" *AntAfr*
16, 1980, 65–93.

64 Strabo 17.3.2–3, 9, 19.

65 Sallust (*Jugurtha* 18) found them "rough and unkempt" ("asperi incultique"). Much of this was perceptual: the "civilized" Romans and the "barbarian" natives – the attitude of colonizer toward
indigenous populations throughout human history. See Brent D. Shaw, "Fear and Loathing: The
Nomad Menace and Roman Africa," in *L'Afrique romaine: les conférences Vanier 1980*, ed. C. M. Wells
(Ottawa: Éditions de l'Université d'Ottawa, 1982), pp. 29–50.

66 Sallust, *Jugurtha* 19, 80, 97, 99, 103.

67 *De bello africo* 32, 35, 56.

68 Marius himself may have made some of these bestowals: see Whittaker, *CAH²* 10 (supra note 1),
p. 608; Jacques Gascou, "Le Cognomen Gaetulus, Gaetulicus en Afrique romaine," *MÉFRA* 82,
1970, 730–1.

area with no lengthy history beyond the Punic settlements on the coast. The only two sources that delineate Juba's kingdom, Strabo and Dio, are themselves in contradiction. According to Strabo, Juba was given not only Mauretania but much of the rest of Libya, and his territory was that of Bocchus and Bogudes with the addition of his ancestral lands.[69] Dio was somewhat more specific: Juba was given the territories of Bocchus and Bogudes and parts of Gaetulia instead of his ancestral lands, which had become romanized.[70] Yet Dio contradicted himself, also writing that Augustus gave Juba his ancestral lands.[71] Hence both sources are in agreement that Juba received the territory of Bocchus and Bogudes – effectively the districts around Iol and Volubilis, and in theory the vast and sparsely populated hinterland from the Ampsaga to the Atlantic – but there is uncertainty as to what additional lands, if any, Juba may have held.

The obvious interpretation of "Juba's ancestral lands" is his father's territory of Numidia. But it seems improbable that this became part of the kingdom. Since 46 BC Numidia had been a Roman province, and just as it is unlikely that a spectral province of Tingitana reverted to royal control in 25 BC, it is even more implausible that Africa Nova, now assimilated with Africa Vetus, was itself deprovincialized, despite Juba's hereditary claim to the territory.[72] In addition to the chaos and instability this would have caused, making uncertain the status of thousands of Roman citizens (not merely a handful in a few small colonies), the economic importance of the province, especially in terms of grain imports, was well established and an essential part of the commercial functioning of the early Empire.[73] Yet one cannot blithely ignore that both Strabo and Dio wrote that Juba received his patrimony, and given the fluidity of the borders and Juba's strong claim to his father's territory, some areas along the fringes of Africa Nova, perhaps with little or no Roman population, were perhaps included in Juba's kingdom, which allowed him to assert – at least to his mentor Strabo – that he had been returned to his ancestral lands.

Strabo's belief that Juba received much of Libya can be easily dismissed as exaggeration, perhaps revealing that Strabo learned about the client kingship of his old protégé through personal sources rather than mainstream geographical and historical scholarship. Strabo may have been using "Libya"

---

69 Strabo 6.4.2, 17.3.7.

70 Dio 53.26.2.

71 Dio 51.15.6.

72 Whittaker, *CAH²* 10 (supra note 1), p. 591. Deprovincialization did occur on occasion – there was a spate of it in the Levant in late Julio-Claudian times – but this was usually a mark of instability both in Rome and in the provinces. See Fergus Millar, *The Roman Near East, 31 B.C.–A.D. 337* (Cambridge, Mass.: Harvard University Press, 1993), pp. 59–64.

73 See Whittaker, *CAH²* 10 (supra note 1), pp. 616–18. As early as 46 BC, Julius Caesar, on his return from Africa, boasted of the large quantities of grain and olive oil that Africa Nova would annually supply to Rome (Plutarch, *Caesar* 55).

in its generalized ancient sense of "Africa," and perhaps he was aware of Krinagoras' wedding epigram and Kleopatra Selene's claim to be queen of the Kyrenaika. Juba's *Libyka* would also have fostered the idea that he ruled Libya, and although Strabo was probably not familiar with the published treatise, he knew the thrust of Juba's scholarship.[74] Despite perceptions to the contrary, there is no evidence that Juba exercised any control over the parts of North Africa that were east of the province of Africa. Nevertheless, it was certainly believed within the royal family that this was part of their natural inheritance, as Kleopatra Selene was not only theoretical queen of the Kyrenaika but the pretender to the Ptolemaic throne in Egypt. Her autonomous powers of coinage may reflect this status.[75]

The final comment on Juba's territory, Dio's statement that he was given parts of Gaetulia, is anachronistic. The more contemporary sources, Strabo and Pliny, use only the ethnic term "Gaetuli,"[76] as would be expected for peoples who had no fixed territory. But by Dio's time this ethnic term had turned into a toponym, Gaetulia.[77] The historical events of Juba's reign make it clear that he and the Gaetulians were continually in dispute over territory, but at that time there was no defined Gaetulia.[78]

Hence Juba's territories certainly included the lands of Bocchus and Bogudes, and perhaps comprised some areas in the frontier region between Mauretania and provincial Africa that had belonged to his father. Since the urbanized districts of the kingdom were limited to the Iol and Tingis–Volubilis regions, there was a vast amount of territory that lacked a permanent population, some of which was claimed by the Gaetulians. Any title to Libya – in the sense of the district between provincial Africa and Egypt – must be seen as hyperbole based on the hereditary interests of Kleopatra Selene. Moreover, Juba had only limited control over the Roman colonies within his kingdom: Tingis and other western colonies remained enclaves governed from Baetica,[79] and Cirta was probably an enclave ruled from Africa. Thus his territory, far more amorphous than that of the eastern client kings,[80] may

---

74 Moreover, Dioskourides, writing not long after the king's death, called him "king of Libya" (Dioskourides 3.82 = Juba, fr. 8b).

75 Mazard #392–5; see also infra, p. 151.

76 Strabo 17.3.2, 9, 23; *NH* 5.17.

77 Despite Gsell, vol. 8, p. 159, it is unlikely that Gaetulia appeared on Agrippa's map. The late geographical works (see *GGM*), the *Divisio orbis terrarum* (26) and the *Dimensuratio provinciarum* (25), that list Gaetulia, although in part derived from the map, probably also reflect later terminology (O. A. D. Dilke, *Greek and Roman Maps* (London: Thames and Hudson, 1985), p. 43); but see J. J. Tierney, "The Map of Agrippa," *Proceedings of the Royal Irish Academy* 63c, 1963, 152–5. Pliny's use of *tota Gaetulia* (*NH* 5.30) is explicitly as an ethnic term.

78 On Juba and the Gaetulian territory, see Jehan Desanges, "Les Territoires gétules de Juba II," *RÉA* 66, 1964, 33–47.

79 Mackie (supra note 41), pp. 350–7.

80 Pavis d'Escurac (supra note 40) described it as "l'emploi parallèle, en Maurétanie, des deux méthodes politiques" (p. 230).

effectively have been limited to the two centers of populations that Bocchus and Bogudes had ruled.

There remains the question of exactly why Augustus sent Juba to rule Mauretania.[81] Although the situation there was unique, given its mixture of Roman colonies and indigenous population, it nonetheless was a perfect example of the type of territory Augustus found suitable for client kingship: a frontier zone with a developing Roman presence. Juba may have had some hereditary claim to the district, since the Mauretanian royal line was connected to the Numidian one.[82] Bocchus II had sons, but since they are not mentioned after 45 BC they may have died in the civil war.[83] It is probable that Bocchus knew that the son of Juba I, perhaps his closest living relative, was growing up in the imperial household, and thus he might have made some arrangement with Rome regarding the disposition of his kingdom, but this is purely hypothetical.[84]

Still, Juba needed no legal claim to the territories of Bocchus, nor to have received any of his father's kingdom, owing to the manipulation of dynastic politics by the Roman ruling elite. Client kings were regularly sent to rule a territory different from that of their ancestors. Herod the Great had only a weak claim to Judaea, whose Hasmonean line was not extinct until Herod, already king, effected the murder of Aristoboulos III:[85] Herod's only connection to the Hasmoneans was through his wife Mariamme. Amyntas of Galatia seems to have been unrelated to the Galatian royal line: like Herod, he married into it, and then succeeded his nephew (by marriage) Kastor II as king, despite the existence of Kastor's son Deiotaros Philadelphos, who became king of Paphlagonia.[86] Archelaos I of Kappadokia had no connection to the ruling dynasty: as with Amyntas, his rise to power was based on the favor of Antonius.[87] Although there were many interconnections between these dynasties, heredity was often a weaker claim than availability or Roman favor, and this seems to have been the case with Juba. He was

---

81 Gsell, vol. 8, pp. 209–15.

82 The families of Bocchus I of Mauretania and Jugurtha were related, but the exact connection is uncertain (Sallust, *Jugurtha* 80), and Sallust hastily pointed out that because polygamy was involved, this did not create a strong connection between the families. Thus it is unlikely that this relationship would allow Mauretania reasonably to be called the ancestral land of Juba. On this, see further, supra, pp. 48–9.

83 Dio 43.36.1. The citation is disputable, for it is unlikely that Bocchus, the supporter of Caesar, would have sent his sons to Pompeius the Younger. See Coltelloni-Trannoy, p. 21.

84 Nevertheless, this has been a favorite argument of modern commentators: see Coltelloni-Trannoy, pp. 19–22; Braund, *Friendly King*, pp. 136, 158. Such arrangements had long been a feature of the relationship between barbarian royalty and Rome, but despite interpretation of Dio 49.43.7 to assume a legacy on the part of Bocchus, the evidence is lacking. See further on royal wills, infra, pp. 272–4.

85 Josephus, *Jewish War* 1.437; *Jewish Antiquities* 15.53–6.

86 Sullivan, *Near Eastern Royalty*, pp. 170–4, stemma 3.

87 Sullivan, *Near Eastern Royalty*, p. 183.

available, competent, had some association with the region, and thus fitted into Augustus' schemes of the creation of client kingships.[88]

Military responsibilities

Foremost among Juba's duties as client king were military responsibilities. Client kings ruled in frontier zones, and thus were inevitably involved in the defense of the empire. Yet the situation was one of anxiety, since the emperor at Rome well knew that the king could represent a threat to the empire as much as forming part of its defense: this was at the heart of the fatal conflict that erupted between the emperor Gaius and Juba's son Ptolemaios. The king had to act within an extremely narrow range of options, so that his defense of his kingdom and the frontier was not seen as dangerous to regional or imperial stability. The late Republic and early Empire are replete with examples of client kings who, wittingly or not, overstepped the limits that were considered proper Roman policy.[89] Some of the best examples come from the Herodians: Herod the Great himself found out that his military duties as client king were almost impossible to reconcile. After receiving permission from Roman officials in Syria, he attacked the Nabataeans, who were destabilizing southern Syria, but he soon received a harsh letter from Augustus terminating their friendship.[90] Some years later Agrippa I was also the recipient of imperial wrath, in this case from his close friend Claudius, because of construction of new fortifications in Jerusalem.[91] Clearly, client kings had little freedom of independent military action, but at the same time were expected to do what the Romans themselves often could not: keep the frontier zone secure and defend their own territories. Thus the kings fell into "a series of traps"[92] that made their position almost impossible.

Given the unstructured nature of Juba's kingdom, his traps were even more pernicious. Presumably it was crucial that he pacify the indigenous

---

88 Although it has been suggested that Juba's claim may have been in part due to a previous visit to Africa, perhaps as a Roman legate, this is unlikely (on the grounds of age if nothing else). See Gsell, vol. 8, pp. 209–10.

89 See the excellent discussion by Braund, *Friendly King*, pp. 91–103.

90 Josephus, *Jewish Antiquities* 16.271–92.

91 Josephus, *Jewish War* 5.147–55; *Jewish Antiquities* 19.326–7.

92 Braund, *Friendly King*, p. 99. Yet the kings were not totally without help from Rome: in at least one case Augustus directed the inhabitants of a district to observe Juba's territorial limits (see Jehan Desanges, "Augustus a-t-il confirmé une decision de Juba II dans l'administration interne du royaume protégé de Maurétanie?" *BAC* n.s. 23b, 1990–2 [1994], 218–19), and in another he confirmed (or perhaps requested) a decision by Juba to give special privileges to a particular district (see Mounir Bouchenaki and Paul-Albert Février, "Un 'castellum' de la region de Tipasa de Juba à Septime Severe," *BAAlg* 7, 1977–9, 193–212. Interestingly, these privileges were eventually forgotten and had to be reinstated by Septimius Severus, who invoked the names of his royal and imperial predecessors, and thereby upheld a royal decision made when a province was still a client kingdom.

population, especially the ever-active Gaetulians.[93] Juba had no lack of competent troops, since Roman military organization had long been a part of the royal administration of the African kings and chieftains. Syphax, during the Second Punic War, had a Roman centurion, a certain Q. Statorius, as his military attaché, who organized his infantry on the Roman model, allowing it to defeat the Carthaginians.[94] Juba I may have structured his army in Roman fashion,[95] and Arabion was able eventually to defeat Sittius because of the Roman training of his forces.[96] Although it is prudent to allow for some chauvinism in these repeated tales of wise barbarians intelligent enough to adopt Roman ways, it is clear that by the time of Juba II there was a history of indigenous rulers in North Africa using Roman military techniques, which was perhaps one of the reasons Augustus felt that a client king could defend the frontiers effectively. Juba himself created a palace guard in the Augustan fashion, *corporis custodes*, uniquely among the client kings,[97] and this overt imitation of a practice otherwise limited to the emperor himself seems to have caused Juba no difficulty, an indication of his unique status as the only client king actually raised by and an in-law of the imperial family, and the only one in the West. Although he lacked the ancient institutions that his eastern colleagues could draw upon, he nonetheless had greater freedom of action, and in military matters he adopted as much of the Roman model as he dared.[98]

Nevertheless, the history of his reign leaves one wondering how effective these preparations were. Although the proclivity for military details in Roman historical writers may have led them to overstate the issue, the known events of northwest Africa during Juba's reign were, for the most part, various military engagements, many with the ever-persistent Gaetulians, and it is obvious that North Africa was far from peaceful. Juba's accession in 25 BC was itself a destabilizing event, since within four years, L. Sempronius Atratinus triumphed *ex Africa*.[99] Even while he was celebrating

---

93 Gsell, vol. 8, pp. 227–30. The military conflicts between Juba and the native population are discussed in detail by Marguerite Rachet, *Rome et les Berbères*, Collection Latomus 110 (Brussels 1970), pp. 69–126.

94 Livy 24.48.

95 David C. Braund, "North African Rulers and the Roman Military Paradigm, *Hermes* 112, 1984, 256.

96 Appian, *Civil War* 4.54.

97 Michael P. Speidel, "An Urban Cohort of the Mauretanian Kings," *AntAfr* 14, 1979, 121–2; Braund, *Hermes* (supra note 95), pp. 255–6.

98 Caesarea also had an urban cohort, seemingly the only one outside actual Roman territory (although there was one at Carthage). See Speidel (supra note 97), pp. 121–2. On the *cohortes urbanae* generally, see Helmut Freis, *Die Cohortes Urbanae*, EpSt 2 (1967).

99 The exact circumstances are unknown. For the triumph, see Shipley (supra note 30), p. 26; it was the last known event in the long career of this officer, who lived 73–7 BC and whose activities included such varied achievements as introduction of Herod the Great to the Roman Senate and service for Antonius as a naval commander (*PIR*² S260).

his triumph, his successor, L. Cornelius Balbus, was hard at work against the Garamantes, whose proficiency at warfare had been known since the fifth century BC.[100] Balbus evidently penetrated far into the desert south of Libya. He triumphed in 19 BC,[101] the final event of a long career.[102] But the Garamantes were not subdued, because a few years later it was necessary to send forth P. Sulpicius Quirinius.[103] A direct result of this decade of instability was the eventual stationing of the *legio III Augusta* in the southern part of the province of Africa.[104]

Although it is unlikely that Juba was involved in any of these expeditions,[105] which tended to occur to the east of his territories, south of Libya, they may be typical of the frontier problems he faced. Some of these disturbances may have been related to the presence of a Roman client king in western North Africa and the increasing threat that Roman expansionism held for traditional ways of life. The peculiar nature of Juba's kingdom – it was greater in extent than all the other client kingdoms combined – meant that it was largely ungovernable. Because of its thin population, frontier pressures were not as threatening as in the north or east, but nonetheless in the long run Juba failed to provide the security that the Romans were seeking. It is significant that incidents became markedly more frequent in the last decades of his reign, and that he died in the midst of a full-scale revolt by the Gaetulian auxilary Tacfarinas. Despite achieving a number of victories, Juba never seems to have mastered the situation. Having a Roman

100 Herodotos 4.174, 183; Charles Daniels, *The Garamantes of Southern Libya* (Stoughton, Wis.: Oleander Press, 1970).

101 *NH* 5.36. Pliny's source was the *acta triumphorum* (*NH* 1.5), which listed the towns that Balbus allegedly captured. The campaign was commemorated by Vergil (*Aeneid* 6.792–5), who saw the Garamantes as counterparts of the Indians at the extremity of the Augustan world. On the expedition, see Jehan Desanges, *Recherches sur l'activité des Méditerranéens aux confins de l'Afrique (VIe siècle avant J.-C.–IVe après J.-C.)*, CÉFR 38 (Paris 1978), pp. 189–95; Andreas Gutsfeld, *Römische Herrschaft und einheimischer Widerstand in Nordafrika*, Heidelberger althistorische Beiträge und epigraphische Studien 8 (Stuttgart 1989), pp. 26–30. For an analysis of Pliny's toponymns, see Pliny (ed. Desanges) pp. 384–415; Pietro Romanelli, "La campagna di Cornelio Balbo nel Sud Africano," in *Mélanges offerts à Léopold Sédar Senghor* (Dakar: Novelles Éditions Africaines, 1977), pp. 429–38; for Balbus' triumph, see Shipley (supra note 30), pp. 37–8.

102 Born in Gades and not originally a Roman citizen, he first appears in the record as a Caesarean in 49 BC and eventually reached the consulship. For his triumph he built the Theater of Balbus in Rome, and then retired to his native city – where Juba was to be *duovir* (infra, pp. 156–7) – endowing further building there: see *PIR²* C1331. He is a fine early example of the assimilation of provincials into the mainstream of Roman politics and culture.

103 Florus 2.31; *PIR²* S732. For the difficulties with the career of Quirinius and the date of his campaign, see Whittaker, *CAH²* 10 (supra note 1), pp. 635–6. He may be the Quirinius who as governor of Syria was involved in the census associated with the birth of Jesus of Nazareth (Luke 2.2).

104 Yann Le Bohec, *La Troisième Légion auguste* (Paris: CNRS, 1989), pp. 335–9. It is not certain when the legion was constituted and posted – certainly by AD 6, and probably after 19 BC: see Dio 54.11.5 and 55.23.2.

105 For a contrary view, see Edward N. Luttwak, *The Grand Strategy of the Roman Empire from the First Century A.D. to the Third* (Baltimore: Johns Hopkins University Press), 1976, p. 25.

legion stationed near the edge of his kingdom must not have been pleasant for the king: this gives a new meaning to Pliny's statement that Juba's scholarship was more memorable than his reign.[106]

The presence of a legion in northern Africa was temporarily effective, for after Quirinius' expedition there were two decades of peace. It was during this interlude that Juba made his trip to the East, and his absence may have been the catalyst for further native incursions. The first hint of renewed activity came around AD 3, when Juba was at the court of Archelaos of Kappadokia, as L. Passienus Rufus received triumphal honors for African victories.[107] Shortly thereafter, the proconsul L. Cornelius Lentulus was killed while on campaign.[108] The date is uncertain, but since Lentulus had been consul in 3 BC, he was probably Passienus Rufus' successor and was killed around AD 3 or slightly later.[109] He too had been on an expedition into the depths of the Libyan desert, since the perpetrators were the Nasamones, that wild tribe that had ranged throughout the interior, and many years previously had crossed the deserts, going perhaps as far south as the Niger and Timbuctu.[110] Clearly, the Roman presence throughout North Africa was being increasingly resented by the indigenous population, and the murder of a Roman proconsul assisted in motivating Juba to abandon his second wife Glaphyra and the scholarly enticements of the court of Archelaos and to hurry back to threatened Mauretania.

Lentulus' death inspired a full-scale operation by the indigenous populations.[111] For the first time, it appears, they demonstrated their objections to Juba's rule by moving into his kingdom[112] and, presumably, into the province of Africa. The reasons are clear: the Gaetulians – the term still used generically for many of the indigenous peoples – had been pressed by over half a century of Roman settlement. Roman expeditions had penetrated deep into the desert. Population was increasing, and the competition between pastoralist and settler was intensifying. Within the Roman territory, taxation of land was particularly offensive.[113] If there were any attempts to conscript the locals into the Roman auxiliaries – and this was certainly an issue

---

106 *NH* 5.16.

107 Velleius 2.116.2; *ILS* 120, 8966; Gutsfeld (supra note 101), p. 31.

108 This is based on an emendation of Ῥέντουλος in the commentary on the *Periegesis* of Dionysios by the twelfth-century scholar Eustathios (*GGM* 2, p. 253, lines 209–10): see Jehan Desanges, "Un Drama africain sous Auguste: le meurtre du proconsul L. Cornelius Lentulus par les Nasamons," in *Hommages à Marcel Renard* 2, ed. Jacqueline Bibauw, Collection Latomus 102 (Brussels 1969), pp. 197–213.

109 *PIR²* C1384; Gutsfeld's date (supra note 101), p. 32, is AD 1–4/5.

110 Herodotos 2.32–3; see Thomson, pp. 70–1.

111 Gsell, vol. 8, pp. 227–30; Gutsfeld (supra note 101), pp. 33–9.

112 Dio 55.28.3–4. Dio, with his customary vagueness, wrote that Juba was king of the Gaetulians, and ascribed the uprising to discontent with his rule and the Roman control it represented.

113 This was to be the cause of a major Nasamonian revolt during the reign of Domitian (Dio 67.4.6; see also Tacitus, *Annals* 3.40).

a decade later at the time of Tacfarinas – this too would have been a source of discontent.[114] Similar circumstances existed in many frontier zones. Elsewhere, stock causes of local dissatisfaction were to be articulately outlined by the British chieftain Galgacus: not only conscription, but taxation, confiscation of commodities, and forced labor.[115]

The Roman response to the Gaetulian uprising was a joint attack by Juba and the proconsul of Africa.[116] Juba took the initiative where his territory had been invaded, and Cossus Cornelius Lentulus moved south from his province. The campaign was not easy – many Roman lives were lost, and most likely Juba had great difficulty – but eventually it was successful. In Years 31 and 32 of his reign (AD 6–7) Juba issued a series of coins with a victory standing on the head of an elephant.[117] Lentulus received triumphal honors and the cognomen Gaetulicus, which his son was also to carry.[118] Juba's coins indicate that he also received triumphal honors. The few that are dated have Year 31 (AD 6) and various triumphal regalia, including a throne and scepter.[119] The conventional explanation has long been that these ornaments were the reward from a grateful Roman Senate,[120] but there is no proof, and Juba may merely have been representing his own triumphal regalia – one would expect him to imitate this Roman practice – perhaps an award made by his own council or people.[121] Regardless, the Gaetulian threat was one that Juba personally helped to repel, and the official view within his kingdom was that this was a significant point of his reign. It seemed to have had the effect of pacifying the region for another decade.

114 Conscription was a cause of the German revolt that occurred early in the reign of Vespasian (Tacitus, *Histories* 4.14). On conscription in Africa, see P. D. A. Garnsey, "Rome's African Empire under the Principate," in *Imperialism in the Ancient World*, ed. P. D. A. Garnsey and C. R. Whittaker (Cambridge: Cambridge University Press, 1978), pp. 241–2.

115 Tacitus, *Agricola* 31. On native revolts generally, and their causes, see Stephen L. Dyson, "Native Revolts in the Roman Empire," *Historia* 20, 1971, 239–74. For particulars about the African situation, see his "Native Revolt Patterns in the Roman Empire," *ANRW* 2.3, 1975, 162–7, and Marcel Benabou, "L'Afrique," in *L'impero romano e le strutture economiche e sociali delle province*, Biblioteca di Athenaeum 4, ed. Michael H. Crawford (Como 1986), pp. 136–41.

116 Dio 55.28.3–5 is the main source, supplemented by Velleius 2.116, Florus 2.31, and Orosios 6.21.18. It is unlikely that *NH* 8.48 reflects Juba's role in this campaign, but see Jehan Desanges, "Un Témoignage masqué sur Juba II et les troubles de Gétulie," *AntAfr* 33, 1997, 111–13.

117 Mazard #196–201; see also #282.

118 Consul in AD 26, the younger Gaetulicus was to be implicated in a plot against the emperor Gaius and executed, which may have been one of the causes of animosity between Gaius and Ptolemaios of Mauretania: see infra, pp. 254–5.

119 Mazard #194–5. Mazard also included a third coin in the series, #193, which shows the ornaments most clearly, but its date is not certain and it may be earlier. All the coins in the series are rare.

120 Gsell, vol. 8, p. 228; see also Braund, *Friendly King*, p. 35.

121 Although the Romans gave triumphal regalia to the client kings, the kings were also known to award it to themselves (Dionysius of Halikarnassos, *Roman Archaeology* 3.61). On the history of Roman awards of such regalia to kings, see Elizabeth Rawson, "Caesar's Heritage: Hellenistic Kings and Their Roman Equals," *JRS* 65, 1975, 155–6.

The next indication of a problem is in Juba's Year 40 (AD 15). The circumstances remain obscure, but that year he issued another victory coin series.[122] It is possible that disturbances broke out upon the death of Augustus, which had occurred in August of AD 14. Whatever happened, it was a preliminary event in the major revolt of Juba's reign, that of Tacfarinas, which erupted within two years and lasted for seven. The sole informative source for this rebellion is the *Annals* of Tacitus.[123] There is no mention of it by Dio or Suetonius, and only the vaguest allusion by Velleius.[124] The Tacfarinas episode was treated in detail by Tacitus because it served his purposes, whether because of his obsession with Tiberius, his bias toward senatorial sources, or his desire to recall the great foreign wars of the past to an era lacking in such heroic exploits.[125] It may not have been as crucial an event in the defense of the empire as Tacitus implied.

Because Tacitus, with his peculiar outlook, is the only effective source, the specific reasons for the uprising are obscure. It belongs in the group of local revolts led by Roman-trained charismatic leaders who used Roman ways to move their people beyond the limitations of Roman control.[126] As Dio succinctly pointed out,[127] barbarians were becoming romanized while retaining ancestral ways, and this caused tensions and contradictions. Certainly there was also direct antagonism between Roman and native; this was bad enough in areas where the natives had become agriculturalist,[128] but worse where it was exacerbated by the historic conflicts between settler and transhumant. The Roman encroachment, tax system, and military obligations all played a role.[129]

As Tacitus recorded it, Tacfarinas,[130] who had been an auxiliary in the

---

122 Mazard #283.

123 Tacitus, *Annals* 2.52; 3.20–1, 32, 73–4; 4.23–6; Rachet (supra note 93), pp. 84–126; Gutsfeld (supra note 101), pp. 39–67.

124 Velleius 2.125.5; the only late epitomizer to record it is Aurelius Victor, an African by birth, and even he was brief (*De Caesaribus* 2.3).

125 Whittaker, *CAH*² 10 (supra note 1), p. 594; Ronald Syme, "Tacfarinas, the Musulamii, and Thuburiscu," in *Studies in Roman Economic and Social History in Honour of Allan Chester Johnson*, ed. P. P. Coleman-Norton *et al.* (Princeton, N.J.: Princeton University Press, 1951), p. 120; see also Olivier Devillers, "Le Rôle des passages relatifs à Tacfarinas dans les *Annales* de Tacite," in *AfrRom* 8, 1991, 203–11; Elizabeth W. B. Fentress, *Numidia and the Roman Army: Social, Military and Economic Aspects of the Frontier Zone* (BAR-IS 53, 1979), pp. 66–8; Gsell, vol. 8, pp. 229–30; Romanelli, Storia, pp. 231–5.

126 The most famous example is that of Arminius in Germany, which had occurred less than a decade previously: see Dyson, *Historia* (supra note 115), pp. 253–8.

127 Dio 56.18.

128 See Tacitus, *Annals* 14.31.

129 Whittaker *CAH*² 10 (supra note 1), pp. 593–6; see Jean-Marie Lassère, "Un Conflit 'routier': observations sur les causes de la guerre de Tacfarinas," *AntAfr* 18, 1982, 11–25; also Vito Antonio Sirago, "Tacfarinas," in *AfrRom* 5, 1988, 199–204.

130 Although Tacitus called him a Numidian, he was actually of the Musulamii, one of the tribes of Gaetulians: see Syme (supra note 125), pp. 115–17.

Roman army, deserted and became a roving brigand, developing into an effective leader of a wide range of discontented peoples whom he organized into a Roman-style military force. By AD 17 his rebellion broke forth, and he waged war on a wide front hundreds of miles long, from Libya into Mauretania. One cannot think of it as a constant attack along this front; rather, it was a series of repeated yet insistent guerrilla actions involving a variety of tribes, with sporadic retreats into the desert to avoid Roman patrols and reprisals. At first Tacfarinas was defeated by the proconsul Furius Camillus – Tacitus was quick to point out that he was a direct descendant of the famous dictator of the early fourth century BC – who was awarded triumphal ornaments and received the acclaim of Tiberius. Juba's victory coins of his Year 43 probably commemorate his own role.[131] But Tacfarinas was not to be eliminated. The following year he again took up the cause, escalating his attacks until he trapped an entire Roman cohort at its outpost on the Pagyda River.[132] The current African proconsul, Lucius Apronius, decimated the disgraced cohort (another of Tacitus' allusions to ancient Roman practices) and engaged Tacfarinas at Thala, but he slipped away into the desert. Apronius received triumphal ornaments and Juba issued another series of victory coins.[133]

Tacfarinas was so encouraged, however, that he sent a letter to Tiberius demanding terms. The emperor was infuriated, and sent Q. Junius Blaesus, the uncle of Sejanus, into the field. Blaesus adopted a divide-and-conquer strategy, providing amnesty to many of Tacfarinas' allies while continuing the operations against the leader himself. He developed a complex method of spreading and separating his forces, largely to defend threatened cities such as Cirta. Blaesus also constructed a line of forts and a number of fortified positions, and did not terminate engagements at the end of the summer campaigning season. Tacfarinas, as usual, fled into the desert, but his brother was captured, and Blaesus was awarded triumphal ornaments and hailed as *imperator*, the last time this ancient honor was conferred on a private citizen.[134] And, for the last time, Juba claimed a victory, in his Year 48,[135] which began in the autumn of AD 23. He did not live to see the final disposal of Tacfarinas, for within the year he was dead. This probably further encouraged Tacfarinas, as did the withdrawal of many Roman forces after

---

131 Mazard #284.

132 The Pagyda River may be the Bagradas (modern Mejerda), the major river of Roman Africa. The engagement would have been along its remote upper reaches, in modern eastern Algeria. On the toponyms, see Syme (supra note 125), pp. 113–30.

133 Year 46 (AD 21): Mazard #285. Apronius and his son L. Apronius Caesianus (who had forced Tacfarinas to retreat into the desert) were honored by a poem set up on a public inscription in Rome (*CIL* 10.7257).

134 This distinction did not save him when his nephew was overthrown, and he committed suicide after having been publicly reviled by Tiberius (Tacitus, *Annals* 5.6–7).

135 Mazard #288.

Blaesus' victory. Tacfarinas seems to have used this as effective propaganda, claiming that it was proof of Roman decline, and an indication that throughout the empire native revolts were becoming increasingly successful. Moreover, at this time there is a hint of rebellion in Mauretania itself, due to the accession of Ptolemaios, who was perceived to be weak.[136] All this incited Rome into more decisive action. The new Roman commander, P. Cornelius Dolabella,[137] grandson of the famous Dolabella of the civil war, embarked on a vigorous campaign that he personally directed in every detail, and before long trapped Tacfarinas at Augea. The Roman forces, angry at the length and violence of the war, showed no mercy and killed Tacfarinas, members of his family, and his bodyguard. Dolabella returned to Rome with prisoners, including some of the elusive and remote Garamantes, rarely seen in the city, but was refused triumphal honors by Tiberius, who did not wish to overshadow Sejanus' uncle Blaesus: Tacitus reported that Tiberius' slight of Dolabella only increased the latter's reputation. But most striking in this last episode of the war was the role of Ptolemaios, in this summer after his father's death, which so impressed the Senate that it sent one of its own to give him an ivory scepter and an embroidered robe, officially recognizing him as king of Mauretania, as well as ally and friend of the Romans.[138] Either he had matured greatly in the first year of his reign or Tacitus' picture of him as an indolent youth is inaccurate.

It is perhaps best to look at the Tacfarinas episode not as a major threat to the empire or as an example of senatorial courage and virtue, as Tacitus did, but as the most detailed account of the almost constant frontier issues Juba, Ptolemaios, and the African proconsuls faced. Ever since the Romans had first set foot in Africa, in the third century BC, this had been a constant issue, not unlike the native-and-settler conflicts at other times and places in world history.[139] There was no ultimate solution beyond total suppression of one side – this usually meant the natives – and this was generally not a feasible possibility.[140]

Disturbances broke out again after the death of Ptolemaios and the annexation of Mauretania,[141] and although the eventual creation of a secure frontier in the second century AC brought about peace, this collapsed in late antiquity, as did the Roman world. Modern colonial governors and

---

136 Tacitus, *Annals* 4.23.
137 *PIR*² C1348.
138 As the sons of Herod the Great learned, being the son of a client king did not mean automatic accession, for Roman validation was necessary.
139 There are many parallels with the history of modern European settlement of North America and Africa: some examples are cited by Dyson, *Historia* (supra note 115), pp. 267–74.
140 Garnsey, "Rome's African Empire" (supra note 114), pp. 232–3.
141 Duncan Fishwick, "The Annexation of Mauretania," *Historia* 20, 1971, 473–80.

armies believed that the same issues continued in their own times and acted accordingly.[142]

Trade and commerce

Overemphasis on the military obsessions of Roman historians may cause one to forget the smooth functioning of the economy and commerce of the Mauretanian monarchy.[143] The wars had little effect on these, although the problem with Tacfarinas seems temporarily to have raised the price of grain in Rome, an increase that Tiberius personally attempted to mitigate by contributing to the cost himself.[144] The foremost commodity was indeed grain,[145] which was the major economic resource of the region in all periods, from the Roman conquest to the end of the Empire. It was alleged that by the time of Nero, African grain could provide the needs of the city of Rome for eight months out of the year.[146] The highly productive soil, reaching almost mythic proportions in some areas, made this possible.[147] Since Republican times Africa had been famous for its large estates, which became a matter of criticism and satire,[148] but probably improved the productivity and lessened the possibility of civic instability provoked by grain shortages

142 One must be cautious about the parallels between modern colonialism and Roman rule, as modern colonial governors often saw themselves as playing the same role as Roman proconsuls, and thereby sought to interpret situations – and their responses – in similar ways. Moreover, the Romans (and modern colonial governors) saw the conflicts as settler against nomad, but the indigenous population away from the coast was not nomadic, but transhumant, which raises a different set of circumstances and conflicts. This failure to understand the true nature of the transhumant population was a major reason the Romans had such difficulty. As has been noted, "rather than conflict, competition, or interaction between two cultures, we have . . . the creation of a new imperial culture that supplanted earlier Roman cultures just as much as it did the earlier cultures of the region." See Greg Woolf, "Beyond Romans and Natives," WA 28, 1996–7, 341. Barry Cunliffe's Greeks, Romans, and Barbarians: Spheres of Interaction (New York: Batsford, 1988) also explores many of these issues, although in the context of western Europe.

143 Most of the economic information comes from the period of Roman provincialization, but similar circumstances existed in the royal period. There is also better information for Africa than for Mauretania, but see Enrique Gozalbes Cravioto, Economía de la Mauritania Tingitana (siglos I A. de C.–II D. de C.) (Ceuta: Instituto de Estudios Ceuties, 1997).

144 Tacitus, Annals 2.87, 4.6; P. D. A. Garnsey, Famine and Food Supply in the Graeco-Roman World: Responses to Risk and Crisis (Cambridge: Cambridge University Press, 1988), pp. 228–9.

145 R. M. Haywood, "Roman Africa," in An Economic Survey of Ancient Rome 4, ed. Tenney Frank (Baltimore: Johns Hopkins University Press, 1938), pp. 39–45; Whittaker, CAH² 10 (supra note 1), pp. 617–18.

146 Josephus, Jewish War 2.383.

147 NH 18.94–5; see also Plutarch, Caesar 55; Columella 1, pr. 24. On the agricultural wealth of Africa proper, see Tenney Frank, "The Inscriptions of the Imperial Domain of Africa," AJP 47, 1926, 67–73.

148 De bello africo 65; NH 18.35; Seneca, Letter 114.26; Petronius 48, 117. On the historic reasons for these large estates, see Garnsey, "Rome's African Empire" (supra note 114), pp. 224–7.

in the capital.[149] Although Mauretania does not seem to have produced the enormous quantity that was grown in Africa proper, grain was nonetheless an important commodity:[150] Juba's cornucopia coins (Figure 25g, p. 245) show that he felt he was contributing to the agricultural richness for which northern Africa was famous.[151]

Perhaps the second most important industry was fishing, as shown by the tridents that appear on many of Juba's cornucopia coins.[152] Little is known about the details of the industry, but it was famous for two of its by-products, *garum* and purple dye.[153] *Garum*, the ubiquitous fish sauce, had long been a staple of Roman cuisine.[154] It may have originated in southern Spain but was one of the renowned products of the region around the Pillars of Herakles and the Atlantic coast of Mauretania (Figure 13, p. 135).[155] More significant within Juba's economy was the purple dye industry, which Pliny, using Juba's *Libyka*, described in detail. Juba discovered islands off the coast, and established a dyeworks there that produced Gaetulian purple, perhaps in an expansion or redevelopment of an ancient Carthaginian industry.[156] The factory was probably placed offshore so as to limit the impact of the intense odors such an establishment would produce. Gaetulian purple was renowned in Augustan times, favored as much as the Tyrian and

149 For the shortages and their civic effects, see Whittaker, *CAH*² 10 (supra note 1), pp. 616–18; one of the most famous examples is when a mob attacked Claudius in the forum when it was learned that there was only a two-week supply of grain (Tacitus, *Annals* 12.43; see also Suetonius, *Claudius* 18). On the importance of grain in the Roman economy, see Peter Garnsey, "Grain for Rome," in *Trade in the Ancient Economy*, ed. Peter Garnsey *et al.* (London: Chatto and Windus, 1983), pp. 118–30.

150 Haywood (supra note 145), pp. 40–1.

151 Mazard #240–58, 265–9. Ironically, the incursions, which Juba seems to have been unable to control and which characterized much of his reign, led to the warfare that may have affected the grain supply, the greatest commodity and economic value (to Rome) of Juba's client kingdom. See further, Garnsey, *Famine* (supra note 144), pp. 227–8.

152 Mazard #253–8; there are also coins with tridents and a fish or, more likely, a dolphin (#260–4). See also Coltelloni-Trannoy, p. 111.

153 See Strabo 17.3.18, for some information.

154 For a discussion of *garum*, see R. Zahn, "Garum," *RE* 7, 1910, 841–9; Pierre Grimal and Th. Monod, "Sur la véritable nature du 'garum'," *RÉA* 54, 1952, 27–38. Martial (13.102) called it "fastosum, munera cara." See further, Andrew Dalby and Sally Grainger, *The Classical Cookbook*, paperback with revisions (London: British Museum Press, 2000), pp. 19–21.

155 Strabo 3.4.2; Horace, *Satires* 2.8.46; *NH* 31.93–4. Many physical remnants of the industrial establishments of the *garum* industry, especially from the period of Juba, have been found along the Moroccan and Spanish coasts: see Michel Ponsich and Miguel Tarradell, *Garum et industries antiques de salaison dans la Méditerranée occidentale* (Paris: Presses Universitaires de France, 1965). On the importation of it to Italy, see Robert Étienne and Françoise Mayet, "Le *garum* a Pompéi. Production et commerce," *RÉA* 100, 1998, 199–215. A descendant of *garum*, anchovy paste, is still a major Moroccan export.

156 Juba, fr. 43 (=*NH* 6.201); Gsell, vol. 8, pp. 233–4. On the significance of purple to the Romans, see Meyer Reinhold, *History of Purple as a Status Symbol in Antiquity*, Collection Latomus 116 (Brussels 1970), pp. 48–70. A popular but nonetheless interesting, and superbly illustrated, account of the use of purple dye throughout history is Gösta Sandberg, *The Red Dyes: Cochineal, Madder, and Murex Purple*, trans. Edith M. Matteson (Asheville, N.C.: Lark Books, 1997).

Lakonian varieties.[157] It was probably *Purpurea haemastoma*, ancient *buccinum*, that was harvested.[158]

It has long been assumed that the Purple Islands lie off the Moroccan coast at Essaouira, approximately 350 km southwest of Casablanca (Figure 21, p. 185).[159] Here there is a cluster of tiny islets about 2 km off the shore; the largest, Mogador, is only a few hundred meters across. Another of similar size was where the promontory of Essaouira is today, but became joined to the coast at some time since antiquity. One of these may be Kerne, which Polybios considered the limit of Mauretania.[160] Excavations on Mogador in the 1950s revealed that the island had been inhabited since the seventh century BC as a port of call for Carthaginian traders: it seems to have been known to Hanno.[161] The Carthaginian settlement was abandoned after

157 Horace, *Epistle* 2.2.181–2; Tibullus 2.3.58; Ovid, *Fasti* 2.319; see also Pomponius Mela 3.104; *NH* 9.127.

158 *NH* 9.125–41; but see Jean Desjacques and Paul Koeberlé, "Mogador et les îles purpuraires," *Hespéris* 42, 1955, 198–9. See also David Herber and J. Herber, "La Pourpre de Gétulie," *Hespéris* 25, 1938, 97–9; Jean Gattefossé, "La Pourpre gétule: invention du roi Juba de Maurétanie," *Hespéris* 44, 1957, 329–33.

159 André Jodin, *Les Établissements du roi Juba II aux Îles Purpuraires (Mogador)* (Tangier: Éditions Marocaines et Internationales, 1967); M. Euzennat, "Mogador ('Cerne')," *PECS*, p. 586; Maria Giulia Amadasi Guzzo, "Notes sur les graffitis phéniciens de Mogador," *Lixus*, pp. 155–73; André Jodin, "Les Rois maures et les Îles Purpuraires (Mogador)," *Ktema* 21, 1996, 203–11. Pliny's failure to provide sailing directions is probably indicative of the islands' closeness to the mainland (*NH* 6.201). It is unlikely that the Purple Islands are the Madeira group, which lie hundreds of kilometers off the coast and are not visible from the mainland, but see F. E. Romer, *Pomponius Mela's Description of the World* (Ann Arbor: University of Michigan Press, 1998), p. 130. Carthaginian explorers may have found the Madeiras and it is possible that early reports of various Atlantic islands became mixed and collected under the rubric of Islands of the Blessed (Thomson, pp. 77–8, 184).

160 *NH* 6.199. The location of Kerne (originally mentioned by Hanno [*GGM*] 8) is far from certain, and it is often placed farther south (a Herne Island on the coast of the Western Sahara at 23° 45′ N is seen to be a survival of the name). But commentators have generally ignored the fact that Kerne was, for Hanno, only three days' sail from the territory of the Lixitai, and if this is Lixos, Kerne cannot be far south: thus Mogador seems more likely, some 450 km beyond Lixos. Yet the issue is complicated by the fact that it is not certain that Hanno's Lixitai are at the site of Lixos: the mouth of the Draa has long been suspected for their location, which would place Kerne three days' farther south, perhaps at the mouth of the Oued Targa (on this, see G. Marcy, "Notes linguistiques: autour du periple d'Hannon," *Hespéris* 20, 1935, 60–6). But Kerne has also been placed as far north as the mouth of the Tensift, just north of Mogador (M. Rousseaux, "Hannon au Maroc," *RAfr* 93, 1949, 213–24). Thus Kerne has been located variously along hundreds of kilometers of coast, and a definitive determination is probably impossible given the present evidence, although Mogador remains a strong possibility. A summary of potential identifications is Raymond Mauny, "Cerné l'Île de Herné (Río de Oro) et la question des navigations antiques sur la côte ouest-africaine," in *Conferencía internacional de Africanistas Occidentales: 4ª Conferencía, Santa Isabel de Fernando Poo 1954*, vol. 2 (Madrid: Dirección General de Marruecos y Colonias, 1954), pp. 73–80. See, further, Michael F. Doran, "The Maritime Provenience of Iron Technology in West Africa," *TI* 9, 1977, 95; John Ferguson, "Classical Contacts with West Africa," in *Africa in Classical Antiquity: Nine Studies*, ed. L. A. Thompson and J. Ferguson (Ibadan: Ibadan University Press, 1969), pp. 5–6; C. F. Konrad, *Plutarch's Sertorius: A Historical Study* (Chapel Hill: University of North Carolina Press, 1994), p. 106.

161 *NH* 6.199–200; Hanno (*GGM*) 8.

the sixth century BC, and there was no significant habitation until the time of Juba, when a villa was constructed that lasted in various forms until the fifth century AC. A large shellmound on the present mainland near Essaouira and basins and tanks on Mogador provide evidence, according to the excavator, that this was the location of Juba's purple factory, since the description by Pliny indicates that such paraphernalia were required.[162]

Other Mauretanian commodities were less important. Olives and olive oil were inferior to cereals as a crop[163] and were primarily cultivated in the easternmost part, near the African border,[164] although there is evidence for their increase in the west at the time of Juba.[165] Strabo spoke highly of the Mauretanian grapevine,[166] but North African wine was sharp in taste and thus was probably not competitive, although at least one type was esteemed.[167] African grapes were of higher quality than the wine they produced, and when smoke-dried were a particular favorite of Tiberius, which increased their popularity.[168] But African figs were said by some to be the best.[169]

Food items were not the only products of Mauretania. Juba believed that his Atlantic coast yielded some of the best pearls.[170] Amber was found in the Electrum Lake, or Lake Kephisis, near the coast.[171] There were copper mines and the harvesting of carbuncular stones.[172] North African elephants were exported for the spectacles in Rome.[173] The furniture industry may have been a royal monopoly, using ivory from south of the Sahara,[174] timber from Mount Atlas, and citrus wood from the lowlands. Mauretanian citrus furniture had been an extravagance even in the late Republic, and came to be

---

162 *NH* 9.133–5; Jodin (*Les Établissements*, supra note 159), pp. 256–7.

163 *NH* 15.8.

164 Haywood (supra note 145), pp. 47–8. Villas in the hinterland of Caesarea, existing during the first three centuries AC, were devoted to oil (and wine) production. See Kevin Greene, *The Archaeology of the Roman Economy* (Berkeley: University of California Press, 1986), pp. 132–3.

165 In later Imperial times Volubilis became a center of olive production, as shown by the fifty-eight known presses on the site, probably from the Severan period: see Aomar Akerraz and Maurice Lenoir, "Les Huileries de *Volubilis*," *BAMaroc* 14, 1981–2, 93–8; Ali Ouahidi, "Nouvelles recherches archéologiques sur les huileries de Volubilis," *AfrRom* 10, 1994, 289–99. This may have been the maturity of an industry originally developed in Juba's day. Moreover, Sala (at modern Rabat) seems to have had an olive oil industry from the mid-first century BC (Jean Boube, "Les Amphores de Sala à l'epoque maurétanienne," *BAMaroc* 17, 1987–8, 183–207).

166 Strabo 17.3.4.

167 *NH* 14.81, 120.

168 *NH* 14.14–17.

169 *NH* 15.69; Columella 5.10.11.

170 *NH* 9.115 (=Juba, fr. 71).

171 *NH* 37.37.

172 Strabo 17.3.11.

173 Hans Roland Baldus, "Eine antike Elefanten-Dressur. Zu einen Münzbild König Jubas II," *Chiron* 20, 1990, 217–20.

174 Juvenal 11.120–7.

prized by the royal and imperial families.[175] In fact the demand was so high that by Pliny's time the supply of the best wood was exhausted.

The commodities of Mauretania led to a brisk trade with Europe, especially through Spain. Tingis, a Roman enclave and the point closest to Europe, became a major trade emporium.[176] From Italy, Arretine pottery began to flow into the kingdom: in the west, because of the route through Tingis, it had appeared as early as 40 BC,[177] but in the east it became common only after 15 BC, when a decade of client kingship had strengthened commercial relations with Italy.[178] Juba's connections with Gades and Carthago Nova – he was *duovir* at both[179] – may have been designed to foster this commerce.

175 *NH* 13.91–5; Lucan 9.426–30; Martial 9.22. See also Russell Meiggs, *Trees and Timber in the Ancient Mediterranean World* (Oxford: Clarendon Press, 1982), pp. 288–92.

176 André Jodin, "Le Commerce maurétanien au temps de Juba II: la céramique arétine de Volubilis (Maroc)," in *Actes du quatre-vingt-onzième Congrès National de Sociétés Savantes, Rennes 1966: Section d'archéologie* (Paris: Bibliothèque Nationale, 1968), pp. 39–40.

177 Gsell 8.232; M. Ponsich, "La Céramique arétine dans le nord de la Maurétanie Tingitane," *BAMaroc* 15, 1983–4, 139–211.

178 Philip M. Kenrick, "The Importation of Italian Sigillata to Algeria," *AntAfr* 32, 1996, 37–44; R. Guery, "Nouvelles marques de potiers sur terre sigillée de Cherchel," *BAAlg* 6, 1975–6 (1980), 61–6.

179 Infra, pp. 156–7.

6

THE ARTISTIC AND CULTURAL PROGRAM OF JUBA AND KLEOPATRA SELENE

It was through the culture of the royal court that a client kingdom could most effectively demonstrate its suitability to be a part of the greater Roman world. The creation of a proper royal city, an artistic program, and support of an intellectual, cultural, and religious life in accordance with Roman standards were the means by which the king, queen, and their kingdom showed their essentially civilized qualities. Royal patronage of the arts and culture had a long and distinguished history in the Mediterranean world, but the most immediate influences on Juba and Kleopatra Selene were the similar activities taking place in Augustan Rome, and their own Numidian and Ptolemaic legacies.

The royal city

An essential part of the Mauretanian kingdom was the development of the court cities. Following the dual history of Mauretania, there were two, Volubilis and Iol, respectively the old capitals of Bogudes II and Bocchus II. Volubilis had been the traditional Mauretanian capital, but the monarchs established Iol as their royal city. The reasons for this are not difficult to determine: although the more isolated in terms of the history and topography of North Africa, Iol was closer to Rome and to Juba's ancestral Numidia. As a coastal settlement it was more connected to the Mediterranean than Volubilis, far in the interior.[1] Volubilis, perhaps because of its distance from the Roman world, had faded in the years since the abdication of Bogudes II, and its rare mention in ancient sources indicates its lesser importance.[2] Iol, on the other hand, was consistently recognized as the capital of Juba and Kleopatra Selene, especially after it became Caesarea early in the reign. The name is first cited in literature by Strabo, but in a passage that seems to have been written after Juba's death.[3] It also appears on Juba's coins

---

1 Brent D. Shaw, review of Coltelloni-Trannoy, *La Royaume de Maurétanie*, *Gnomon* 72, 2000, 423.
2 It was cited only by Pomponius Mela (3.107), Pliny (*NH* 5.5), and Ptolemy the geographer (4.1.14, 8.13.6). All these are lists of cities rather than any discussion of cultural phenomena or their relationship to Juba.
3 Strabo 17.3.12.

119

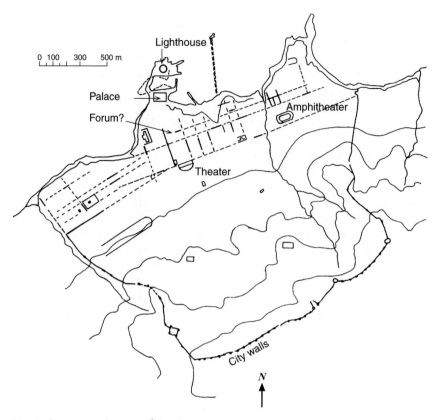

Map 3 Caesarea at the time of the client monarchy

of Year 31 (AD 6),[4] probably the earliest extant use of the name. These coins may commemorate an anniversary of the founding, perhaps either the thirtieth or the twenty-fifth: if so, the city would have been renamed in 24 or 19 BC. Juba was following the trend of the era, as such cities were created by most of the client kings.[5]

---

4 Mazard #188.

5 Suetonius, *Augustus* 60. Whether Juba was the first client king to use the toponym Caesarea cannot be determined, but it is probable. He may have been inspired by Augustus' refounding of Antioch in Pisidia as Colonia Caesarea (Stephen Mitchell and Marc Waelkens, *Pisidian Antioch: The Site and Its Monuments* [London: Duckworth, 1998], p. 8), the first use of the toponym and part of the process of provincializing Galatia in 25 BC, thus an event that took place while Augustus and Juba were in Tarraco. Herod's Caesarea was founded three years later. It seems unlikely that Juba would have waited that long for his foundation, although no precise date is available. Also roughly contemporary was Kappadokian Caesarea, founded by Juba's associate Archelaos of Kappadokia (Roller, *Herod*, pp. 89, 134–5).

Iol may have languished in the years before 25 BC. It seems first to have been established as a royal city by Juba's great-great-great-uncle Micipsa, approximately a century previously,[6] although there had been occupation on the site as early as about 600 BC and fortification from about 200 BC.[7] Yet despite its incorporation into the newly expanded kingdom of Mauretania, the city probably declined in the first century BC: after the defeat of Jugurtha there is no evidence of major activity.[8] It became the royal seat of Bocchus II around the middle of the century, remaining so until his death in 33 BC.

When Juba II and Kleopatra Selene arrived, eight years later, they transformed this decaying petty capital into a proper royal city, the only Caesarea in the western Mediterranean. Although Juba is not to be numbered among the great builder kings of the era, he ensured that Caesarea would have the proper physical attributes appropriate to the Augustan period, and, moreover, that his royal city, like the capitals of his more architecturally vigorous eastern colleagues, would reflect elements of the Augustan architectural revolution that was then spreading through the empire. The royal entourage would have included Roman-trained architects who could implement this policy, using contemporary Roman constructional and decorative techniques, probably including *opus reticulatum*, which is rare outside Italy at this early date.[9]

The physical evidence for the Augustan period at Caesarea is scant. As is so often the case, a long later history of monumental construction, especially in Severan times,[10] has obscured the earlier material, assisted by the continued occupation of the town site as modern Cherchel. Moreover, given the scattered nature of the excavations, it is virtually impossible to make the necessary narrow distinction between the construction program of the client kingdom, before AD 40, and that of the Roman province immediately thereafter. It is also important to avoid the natural tendency to attribute everything impressive from the early Imperial period to royal patronage – a similar problem exists in Herod's territories – and to adopt as minimalist a

---

6 Micipsa seems to have been buried at Iol: see J.-G. Février, "L'Inscription funéraire de Micipsa," *RAssyr* 45, 1951, 139–50. For the early history of the city, see Leveau, *Caesarea*; T. W. Potter, "City and Territory in Roman Algeria: The Case of Iol Caesarea," *JRA* 1, 1988, 190.

7 T. W. Potter, "Models of Urban Growth: The Cherchel Excavations 1977–1981," *BAC* n.s. 19b, 1983 (1985), 458.

8 To Pomponius Mela (1.30) it was unknown before Juba's day.

9 T. W. Potter, *Towns in Late Antiquity: Iol Caesarea and Its Context* (Oxford: Oxbow, 1995), p. 8; Patrizio Pensabene, "La decorazione architettonica di Cherchel: cornice, architravi, soffiti, basi e pilastri," *RM Supp.* 25, 1982, 116–21. The *opus reticulatum* found at Caesarea is no earlier than the time of Ptolemaios (Philippe Leveau, "Trois tombeaux monumentaux à Cherchel," *BAAlg* 4, 1970, 101–48). Yet the technique seems a characteristic of the Augustan client kings (Roller, *Herod*, pp. 99, 181, 256).

10 Potter, *Towns* (supra note 9), pp. 9–10, 32–48.

Figure 4 Caesarea: theater.

Photograph by Duane W. Roller.

view as possible.[11] Nevertheless, there are a number of structures that seem to be from the period of the client monarchy.

Most conspicuous is the theater (Figure 4).[12] Situated directly inland from the harbor and above the forum, it occupies a prominent location within the city. Although built into the side of a hill in the Greek fashion – rather than being freestanding, like a true Roman theater – it generally conforms to Vitruvian rules[13] and was constructed by architects familiar with contemporary Roman theater design, if not actually sent from Augustan Rome.[14] As such, it is an important monument in the architectural dissemination of the building type. Theater building in Rome barely predated Juba's own lifetime, as the first in the city were only built in the 50s BC. The oldest,

11 Potter, "City and Territory" (supra note 6), p. 191.

12 Leveau, *Caesarea*, pp. 33–6; Gilbert Charles Picard, "La Date du théâtre de Cherchel et les débuts de l'architecture théâtrale dans les provinces romaines d'occident," *CRAI* 1975, pp. 386–7; and his "La Date du théâtre de Cherchel," *BAAlg* 6, 1975–6 (1980), 49–54.

13 David B. Small, "Studies in Roman Theater Design," *AJA* 87, 1983, 59–60.

14 Picard, *CRAI* (supra note 12), pp. 390–4. One of the capitals from the theater bears the name of P. Antius Amphio, who was probably a foreman or director of the workshop: see J. B. Ward Perkins, "Tripolitana and the Marble Trade," *JRS* 41, 1951, 93–5. He would have been a slave or freedman, but connected with the Antii, who were somewhat prominent in the late Republic and early Empire (Cicero, *Atticus* 4.17; Appian, *Civil War* 4.40; Tacitus, *Annals* 2.6).

commissioned by M. Aemilius Scaurus in 58 BC, was soon overshadowed by the competing and nearby efforts of Pompeius and Caesar.[15] Juba would have been aware of this architectural competition between the two great personalities of the previous generation, both of whom had been involved in the events that led to his kingship. Moreover, theater construction, especially outside of Rome and by the client kings, was an important priority of the Augustan era: Herod built four, carrying the form to the East.[16] This all may have helped to inspire Juba's own interest in and writings on the theater.[17] It is probable that the Caesarea theater was an early priority of Juba's building program and that the structure was completed about 13 BC, the time of the dedication of Caesar's theater in Rome – whose construction had continued sporadically for thirty years – to one of Juba's childhood playmates, the late Marcellus.

The forum of Caesarea (Figure 5) is to the north of the theater, aligned along a street that runs from its eastern edge toward the harbor. Excavations have demonstrated that the forum is Severan, and that during the client monarchy and early province the district had been an industrial quarter.[18] Thus it is not the site of Juba's forum, but, in fact, numerous examples of Augustan architectural decoration, particularly capitals in Luna marble, were found in this Severan forum, especially in a basilica.[19] These probably had been removed from the Juban forum, which was in the vicinity but whose exact location remains unknown.

In the eastern portion of Caesarea is the amphitheater.[20] Its unusual shape – essentially a rectangle with semicircular ends – demonstrates its early date, preserving a form closer to that implicit in the word ἀμφιθέατρος. In Juba's day, amphitheaters were even a newer building type than the Roman theater: the first permanent one in Rome had been built only four years before he left for Mauretania.[21] The Caesarea amphitheater lacks strong dating controls, but its unusual, seemingly early, form suggests the period

15 *NH* 34.36, 36.113–15; Suetonius, *Julius* 44; Dio 43.49; *NTDAR* pp. 382–5; Ernest Nash, *Pictorial Dictionary of Ancient Rome*, second edition (New York: Prager, 1968), vol. 2, p. 423; L. Richardson, Jr., "A Note on the Architecture of the *Theatrum Pompei* in Rome," *AJA* 91, 1987, 123–6.

16 Roller, *Herod*, pp. 93–4; Alison Cooley, "A New Date for Agrippa's Theatre at Ostia," *PBSR* 67, 1999, 173–82.

17 Leveau, *Caesarea*, p. 35.

18 Potter, *Towns* (supra note 9), pp. 29–48.

19 They were also found elsewhere in the town site. See Patrizio Pensabene, *Les Chapiteaux de Cherchel: étude de la decoration architectonique* (*BAAlg Supp.* 3), 1982, 9–11, especially no. 19, remindful of the capitals of the Temple of Mars Ultor in Rome. See, further, nos. 20–5 and pp. 69–74; Potter, *Towns* (supra note 9), p. 32; D. E. Strong, "Some Observations on Early Roman Corinthian," *JRS* 53, 1963, 80; Klaus Fittschen, "Juba II. und seine Residenz Jol/Caesarea (Cherchel)," *Numider*, p. 242.

20 Leveau, *Caesarea*, pp. 36–9.

21 This is the one built by Statilius Taurus in the Campus Martius in 29 BC, one of the enigmas of Roman topography: see *NTDAR*, p. 11.

Figure 5 Caesarea: site of forum.

Photograph by Duane W. Roller.

of Juba, perhaps 25–15 BC, and it may be the best-preserved example of the earliest phase of amphitheatral typology.[22]

The harbor was another Juban construction (Figure 6). It was mentioned by Strabo in one of the few literary references to Caesarea, and thus was worthy of note: Strabo's personal connections to Juba demonstrate that it was considered one of the important elements of the royal city.[23] A lighthouse stood on a small offshore island, in the style of the Pharos of Alexandria.[24] In addition to that Hellenistic Egyptian precedent, Juba might also have been influenced by the spectacular harbor and lighthouse that Herod began in 22 BC at his own Caesarea.[25] Yet there is little physical evidence at the harbor of Mauretanian Caesarea that can be connected with Juba, and the period of provincialization under Claudius was also a time of major harbor construction in the Roman world.

22 Leveau, *Caesarea*, p. 38; Jean-Claude Golvin and Philippe Leveau, "L'Amphithéâtre et le théâtre-amphithéâtre de Cherchel: monuments à spectacle et histoire urbaine à Caesarea de Maurétanie," *MÉFRA* 91, 1979, 817–32; Jean-Claude Golvin, *L'Amphithéâtre romain: essai sur la théorisation de sa forme et ses fonctions* (Paris: Diffusion de Boccard, 1988), vol. 1, pp. 112–14; David Bomgardner, *The Story of the Roman Amphitheatre* (London: Routledge, 2000), pp. 151–2.

23 Strabo 17.3.12; Leveau, *Caesarea*, pp. 47–50.

24 Jean Lassus, "Les Découvertes récentes de Cherchel," *CRAI* 1959, pp. 222–5. A nearby temple may have been dedicated to Juba's ancestors.

25 Roller, *Herod*, pp. 137–8.

Figure 6 Caesarea: view of offshore island, with site of palace in foreground.

Photograph by Duane W. Roller.

The royal palace and its attendant structures, including the royal library, were probably on the waterfront (Figure 7), inspired almost certainly by the palace and library at Alexandria.[26] Some of the rich sculptural ornamentation found near the harbor, with elaborate decoration remindful of the Third Pompeian style and vegetal reliefs similar to those on the Ara Pacis, may have belonged to the royal residence.[27]

Other elements of the city, especially its orthogonal plan and various baths, may have a Juban origin, but the evidence is lacking beyond reasonable hypothesis.[28] Large public baths are not a feature of Augustan Rome: the modest Baths of Marcus Agrippa were completed around 25 BC, and another was not built until the time of Nero.[29] That Caesarea had baths, probably relatively small public ones, at the time of the client monarchy is a certainty, but the three great bathing establishments visible today – the Western, Central, and Eastern – are products of the later Empire.[30]

26 Fittschen (supra note 19), p. 230.

27 *Numider*, pl. 45–9. The Dionysos themes on these reliefs invoke the memory of Kleopatra Selene's father.

28 Elizabeth Fentress, "Caesarean Reflections," *Opus* 3, 1984, 487.

29 Dio 53.27; *NTDAR*, pp. 386–7, 393–5.

30 Leveau, *Caesarea*, pp. 51–4.

Figure 7 Caesarea: site of palace and view south across city.

Photograph by Duane W. Roller.

An orthogonal plan, although not existent in Rome itself, was nonethe-less a necessity in a newly constructed city, such as Herod's contemporary Caesarea, which was built on essentially abandoned and unpopulated land. Juba, however, was modernizing a city hundreds of years old, and thus his orthogonal plan had to be forced onto the more irregular layout of the Carthaginian and Numidian city, which may have been limited to the area around the harbor. Although many of the monumental constructions at Cae-sarea that fit into its orthogonal plan are much later than Juba's day, the theater and the amphitheater, the two most certain Juban structures, lie several hundred meters apart on opposite sides of the same major street; this and the axis leading at right angles down from the theater past the area of the forum toward the harbor are the best proof of Juba's orthogonal town planning.[31]

An Iseum is known from literature,[32] and there is varying epigraphic and artistic evidence for the expected temples to imperial and dynastic cults.[33] Coins also show the Temple of Augustus (Figure 25f, p. 245), some in

31 Leveau, *Caesarea*, pp. 77–9.
32 *NH* 5.51. It was perhaps on the island at the harbor (Lassus [supra note 24], p. 225).
33 Leveau, *Caesarea*, pp. 16–17.

tetrastyle representation and others in hexastyle, which may be two different temples or two versions of the same temple.[34] Other depictions are remindful of the Curia Julia in Rome, completed in 29 BC.[35] Although this is not exactly an expected precedent for a temple to the imperial cult, there really were no precedents, and since the Curia represented the latest in Roman architecture at the time Juba left Rome, it became a prototype in form if not in function.[36] In building a temple to Augustus, Juba was following the lead of the other client kings, beginning with Herod and his Sebaste of 27 BC. Caesarea also had a site known as the Lucus Augusti, which contained an altar with garlands and trees.[37] A sacred grove commemorating a living person was unusual, but Rome had several groves sacred to deities, many of them obscure.[38] The use of an altar was a distinctly Augustan element – one need only think of the Ara Pacis – and the establishment of altars as the focus of provincial imperial cult in the western provinces is documented at Lugdunum by 12 BC.[39]

The impressive city walls, which extend for 4.46 km, well beyond the urbanized core, may also date from the time of the client monarchy.[40] Although it has been rightly pointed out that these could equally well be from the provincial period,[41] ideologically they fit better into the Juban plan, demonstrating the role of the client king in defending the romanized city from the barbarian exterior,[42] and incidentally creating one of the largest cities – in terms of area – in the Roman West.[43] Their striking position, running high above the town site at the edge of the upper plateau at an elevation of 244 m, contributes to the visual impressiveness of the city.

---

34 Mazard #144–56; Heidi Hänlein-Schäfer, *Veneratio Augusti: Eine Studie zu den Tempeln des ersten Römischen Kaisers*, Archaeologica 39 (Rome 1985), pp. 271–3.

35 Augustus, *Res gestae* 19; Dio 51.22.1–2; *NTDAR*, pp. 103–4.

36 It has been suggested, on the evidence of these coins, that Juba established his own curia and that this was the prototype for the various Roman imperial curias in North Africa: see Bluma L. Trell, "Ancient Coins: New Light on North African Architecture," in *Actes du Premier Congrès d'Histoire et de la Civilisation du Maghreb* 1 (Tunis: Université de Tunis, 1979), pp. 95–6.

37 Mazard #157–61.

38 *NTDAR*, pp. 235–6.

39 Duncan Fishwick, "The Development of Provincial Ruler Worship in the Western Roman Empire," *ANRW* 2.16.2, 1978, 1204–10.

40 Leveau, *Caesarea*, pp. 29–33.

41 Potter, *Towns* (supra note 9), p. 9; Paul-Marie Duval, *Cherchel et Tipasa: Recherches sur deux villes fortes de l'Afrique romaine*, Institut français d'Archéologie de Beyrouth, Bibliothèque Archéologie et Historique 43, 1946, pp. 71–163.

42 On this, see Leveau, *Caesarea*, pp. 32–3; Duane W. Roller, "The Wilfrid Laurier University Survey of Northeastern Caesarea Maritima," *Levant* 14, 1982, 96. The walls of Herod's Caesarea were ideological rather than functional, and this too may have inspired Juba.

43 Philippe Leveau, "L'Urbanisme des princes clients d'Auguste: l'exemple de Caesarea de Maurétanie," in *Architecture et Société de l'archaïsme grec à la fin de la République romaine*, CÉFR 66, 1983, pp. 351–2.

Figure 8 The Oued Bellah aqueduct bridge, east of Caesarea: view south.

Photograph by Duane W. Roller.

Outside the city, the most probable element associated with Juba is the aqueduct system,[44] which runs from the village of Menacer, 30 km southeast of Caesarea. It is most noted for two spectacular bridges over the Oued Ilelouine and the Oued Bellah respectively, the former 137 m long and in the style of the Pont du Gard (Figure 8). Again there is compelling circumstantial evidence that this hydraulic infrastructure dates from the client monarchy, as provision of an adequate water supply was not only an Augustan priority within Rome but an essential part of an important city.[45] The Caesarea aqueduct, especially the Oued Ilelouine bridge, is an expertly crafted piece of innovative architecture and engineering,[46] and its construction fostered the agricultural prosperity and urbanization of the region, as it supplied the rural hinterland as well as the city.[47]

Some 40 km east of Caesarea, near Tipasa, is another construction that may be the work of Juba, or at least an effective part of his vision of the physical aspect of his kingdom. This is the large tomb now known as the

44 Philippe Leveau and Jean-Louis Paillet, *L'Alimentation en eau de Caesarea de Maurétanie et l'aqueduc de Cherchell* (Paris: Harmattan, 1976), which dated the aqueduct to the latter first century AC (pp. 165–7), now superseded by Leveau, *Caesarea*, pp. 57–63.

45 Leveau, *Caesarea*, pp. 61–2; Frontinus, *De aquis urbis Romae* 9; Dio 54.11.7.

46 A. Trevor Hodge, *Roman Aqueducts and Water Supply* (London: Duckworth, 1992), pp. 142–5.

47 Andrew Wilson, "Deliveries *extra urbem*: Aqueducts and the Countryside," *JRA* 12, 1999, 322–3.

Figure 9 The Mauretanian Royal Mausoleum.
Photograph by Duane W. Roller.

Mauretanian Royal Mausoleum (Figure 9).[48] It is an impressive round structure 60.9 m in diameter and 32.4 m high, consisting of an Ionic facade surmounted by a stepped cone. The interior contains various passages and
chambers. This tomb is probably the one described by Pomponius Mela as
the communal mausoleum of the royal family ("monumentum commune
regiae gentis").[49] The context, a discussion of Juba and Iol, makes it reasonable to assume that the royal family is that of Juba and that the extant tomb
is in fact that of the king and Kleopatra Selene, since Pomponius Mela by
his own admission knew nothing of pre-Juban Iol. Such has long been
assumed and was the presumption of the restorer, Marcel Christofle, when
he began work at the site in 1912, and is a view still held by many today.[50]
Others, however, have suggested an earlier date, perhaps of Bocchus I[51] or

48 Its traditional early modern name, still appearing in some publications but totally erroneous, is the
    Tomb of the Christian Woman. Marcel Christofle, *Le Tombeau de la Chrétienne* (Paris: Arts et Métiers
    Graphiques, 1951); Coltelloni-Trannoy, pp. 80–1; see also Pietro Romanelli, "Ancora sull'età della
    Tomba della Cristiana in Algeria," *ArchCl* 24, 1972, 109–11; *Numider*, pp. 452–3; Mounir
    Bouchenaki, *Le Mausolée royal de Maurétanie* (Algiers: Direction des Musées, de l'Archéologie et des
    Monuments et Sites Historiques, 1979).
49 Pomponius Mela 1.31.
50 Most recently, Michael Brett and Elizabeth Fentress, *The Berbers* (Oxford: Blackwell, 1996), pp. 44–5.
51 Friedrich Rakob, "Numidische Königsarchitektur in Nordafrika," *Numider*, p. 142; Filippo Coarelli
    and Yvon Thébert, "Architecture funéraire et pouvoir: réflexions sur l'hellénisme numide," *MÉFRA*
    100, 1988, 766.

Bocchus II.[52] Attribution to Bocchus I seems improbable because his capital was at Volubilis and his association with the Iol area brief and marginal, but Bocchus II, who reigned at Iol, is a definite possibility, as are Juba II and his family. The problem is aggravated by the lack of solid dating controls.

The mausoleum is of a type common in Numidia;[53] at Medracen, in eastern Algeria just north of Timgad, is a similar, and somewhat better built structure, whose decoration has both Egyptian and Greek details with a radiocarbon date of the third century BC.[54] Although it has sometimes been identified as the tomb of Massinissa, the dating implies that his father Gaia was the more probable builder,[55] although there is no reason that Massinissa himself could not also have been buried there. Nevertheless, it demonstrates that the Mauretanian Royal Mausoleum, built one to two centuries later, is an indigenous architectural type whose origins are ultimately in the royal mausolea of the Hellenistic East, such as the Mausoleum of Maussolos at Halikarnassos and perhaps even that of Alexander the Great at Alexandria.[56] In any case, the Mauretanian Royal Mausoleum is strikingly similar to the monumental tomb that Augustus began building in Rome around 27 BC, just before Juba left the city.[57] This is not to suggest that it was derived from the Mausoleum of Augustus, as the similarities are due to the typological origin of both in the royal mausolea of the East. But if the Numidian tomb is that of Juba and Kleopatra Selene, even if inherited from Bocchus II, it served them well politically to have a tomb similar to that of the Princeps and his family in Rome.[58]

Although the full extent of his contribution cannot be determined, at Caesarea Juba created a "showcase city"[59] that would take its impressive place as one of the capitals of the client kingdoms. Caesarea was meant to be seen from the sea approach. The city sits on a plateau approximately 25 m above sea level, which makes the location of the town's site like a stage. The palace of Juba and the public buildings would have been prominent. Behind

---

52 Rakob (supra note 51), p. 142; Coltelloni-Trannoy, pp. 80–1; Gsell, vol. 7, p. 273; Coarelli and Thébert (supra note 51), p. 766.

53 Brett and Fentress (supra note 50), pp. 27–31; Rakob (supra note 51), pp. 170–1; H. Ghazi-Ben Maïssa, "Le Culte royal en Afrique Mineure antique," *Hésperis-Tamuda* 35.2, 1997, 32–41; Gabriel Camps, "Mausolées princiers de Numidie et de Maurétanie," *Archeologia* (Paris) 298, 1994, 50–9.

54 Rakob (supra note 51), pp. 134–8; Gabriel Camps, "Nouvelles observations sur l'architecture et l'âge du Medracen, mausolée royale de Numidie," *CRAI* 1973, pp. 470–517; Friedrich Rakob, "Architecture royale numide," in *Architecture et Société de l'archaïsme grec à la fin de la République romaine*, CÉFR 66, 1983, pp. 325–48; *Numider*, pp. 450–1.

55 Brett and Fentress (supra note 50), pp. 27–9.

56 Coarelli and Thébert (supra note 51), pp. 777–800.

57 Strabo 5.3.8.

58 One might argue that Juba and Kleopatra Selene would build their own tomb, rather than use that of another, but it would have demonstrated a strong and wise continuity with the old regime if the interlopers used its tomb.

59 The phrase "ville-vitrine" is Leveau's (*Caesarea*, p. 24).

Figure 10 Volubilis: view of site from the east.

Photograph by Duane W. Roller.

would be the theater and amphitheater with the land rising to the walls on the ridge. Topography was skillfully used for visual effect in the best tradition of Hellenistic city planning. Upon entering the city, visitors would be impressed by the latest Roman building forms and constructional details and ornamentation, such as the frequent use of Luna marble, and the extensive public sculpture that mirrored Augustan Rome. Like its contemporaries, Herod's Caesarea and Archelaos' Sebaste, Juba's city served as a window onto the kingdom where those approaching from Rome (or elsewhere) could see that they were, in fact, arriving at somewhere important, a version of Rome itself that had all the physical characteristics of the imperial capital. Romans could take comfort that the kings were visibly effective in their romanizing, and the kings in that they were an integral part of the empire and that their kingdoms manifested the latest Roman cultural phenomena.[60]

The dual history of Mauretania was continued in Juba's use of Volubilis as a secondary royal city (Figure 10). It had languished longer than Iol in the years before Juba's arrival, having been abandoned by its ruler Bogudes II in 38 BC, when he left to join Antonius in the East. There is no evidence that

60 Perhaps 25,000–30,000 inhabitants lived in this Roman island of Caesarea (Potter, *Towns* [supra note 9], pp. 15–16).

the city received any attentions from Bocchus II when he acquired it along with the rest of Mauretania. He died five years later, and even after Juba II received the territory, his initial efforts were toward Caesarea.[61]

The physical evidence of Juba's patronage is far more ephemeral at Volubilis than at Caesarea. As with Caesarea, extensive construction in later periods, again especially the Severan, has obscured the earlier material. Literature is of no assistance: the city is not mentioned before the middle of the first century AC.[62] In fact, Volubilis is today a paradox: the extensive and impressive remains encountered by the modern traveler stand in splendid isolation and mark a remote and great Roman city virtually unknown to ancient literature.

Because Volubilis was inhabited continuously from at least the third century BC until late Roman times, it is inevitable that some of the remains date from the period of Juba II. But what is lacking is any strong evidence of royal building, and thus it has long been argued whether or not Volubilis was a royal capital during the time of the client monarchy. That it was, an idea first advanced by Jérôme Carcopino, is based more on reasonable probability than physical evidence.[63] In the years since Carcopino's thesis first appeared, it has been doubted and even attacked by scholars who have raised quite legitimate concerns,[64] especially the failure of excavations to find significant evidence of royal building, and also the failure of the ancient sources that indicate that Caesarea was a royal city to describe Volubilis in the same terms.[65] Yet the arguments against Volubilis as a royal city are weak, the lack of physical evidence notwithstanding, for two separate reasons. First, Juba would have had no credibility as king of Mauretania if he did not bestow patronage on its ancient capital, even if it were far inland and isolated from the Mediterranean, and thus less useful to a romanized kingdom. Second, and the best evidence for royal patronage, are the discoveries of fine art from the period of the monarchy, some of which is specific to the royal family. Yet it is clear that Juba's impact was deliberately restrained and there is no evidence that he provided Volubilis with an Augustan name, such as the "Sebaste" favored by Herod and Archelaos.

Architectural evidence, however, is limited. Augustan period ornamentation, especially Ionic fragments, is found at the site, which is generally assumed to be from the time of Juba. One Ionic capital, in the style of those on the Mauretanian Royal Mausoleum, was found 50 m west of the later

---

61 For the uncertain status of Volubilis between 33 and 25 BC, see Michel Christol and Jacques Gascou, "Volubilis, cité fedérée?" *MÉFRA* 92, 1980, 329–45.

62 The earliest is Pomponius Mela 3.107, followed by *NH* 5.5, neither of which is informative about the history or physical aspect of the city.

63 Jérôme Carcopino, "Volubilis regia Iubae," *Hésperis* 17, 1933, 1–24.

64 The arguments are summarized by Jodin, *Volubilis*, p. 11–13, 86–9; see also H. Ghazi-Ben Maïssa, "Volubilis et le problème de *regia Iubae*," *AfrRom* 10, 1994, 243–61.

65 Pomponius Mela 1.30, 3.107; *NH* 5.5, 20.

forum and may be from a small temple.[66] Some of the lower levels of Temples B and C may also indicate construction during the monarchy.[67] A large residential structure of the third century AC in the northern part of the city, often called the Palace of Gordian[68] and generally believed to be the Roman governor's palace, is thought, on no strong evidence, to be the location of Juba's palace, and, in a slightly circular argument, it is speculated that Juba may have created the entire northern quarter of the city.[69] Yet despite the weakness of the physical evidence – due, as so often, to the sporadic excavations and extensive later building – it seems that Juba favored the ancient Mauretanian capital in a limited way, at the very least doing some building and providing it with a fine collection of art.

Juba bestowed architectural patronage on other Mauretanian cities. Again, however, one must cautiously distinguish royal efforts from incidental building contemporary with the client monarchy. At Sala a monumental quarter was laid out in the center of the city, including a forum with a Capitolium and several temples (Figure 11), making use of imported marbles from Italy and even Greece.[70] Ionic decoration similar to that from Volubilis is also known,[71] and the city had its own collection of Julio-Claudian period sculpture. As one of the major port cities of the Atlantic coast of Mauretania, it was a city worthy of Juba's support, and the importation of Greek marble is the best proof of this.

The other port city on the Atlantic, Lixos, also seems to have received royal patronage (Figure 12). Here there was a specific reason for Juba's interest: it was the alleged site of the Gardens of the Hesperides and thus of the last labor of Herakles, ancestor of both king and queen.[72] In fact, at the time of the monarchy there was extensive reconstruction in the city, especially the building of a large sanctuary at the summit of the akropolis; although specific evidence is lacking, this may have been dedicated to the royal ancestor.[73] There is also a small theater–amphitheater to the east that is generally

66 Jean Boube, "Un Chapiteau ionique de l'époque de Juba II à Volubilis," *BAMaroc* 6, 1966, 109–14; but see Jodin, *Volubilis*, pp. 86–93, who was rightly cautious about the tendency to see Ionic materials as necessarily Juban; see also Jean-Marie Lassère and Gilbert Hallier, "Volubilis préclaudien," *JRA* 2, 1989, 188–90.

67 Jodin, *Volubilis*, 167–70.

68 The name is due to an inscription of the emperor Gordian III (AD 238–44): Louis Chatelain, "Travaux et recherches du Service des Antiquités du Maroc, depuis 1919," *CRAI* 1922, p. 29; Jodin, *Volubilis*, pp. 86–8.

69 Jodin, *Volubilis*, p. 53. The discovery of the bronze bust of Cato in a third-century context (infra, pp. 144–5) may support this argument.

70 M. Euzennat, "Sala," *PECS*, pp. 793–4.

71 Boube (supra note 66), p. 110.

72 On this ancestry, see infra, pp. 154–5.

73 M. Euzennat, "Lixus," *PECS*, p. 521; Mohamed Habibi, "À propos du temple H et du temple de Melkart-Héraclès à Lixus," *AfrRom* 10, 1994, 231–41. On the general rebuilding of Lixos at the time of Juba (which does not necessarily mean royal patronage), see Michel Ponsich, *Lixus: le quartier des temples (étude preliminaire)*, Études et travaux d'archéologie marocaine 9 (Rabat 1981), pp. 134–6.

Figure 11 Sala: view northeast across forum.

Photograph by Duane W. Roller.

Figure 12 Lixos: view south across the center of the site with serpentine Leucos River in the background.

Photograph by Duane W. Roller.

Figure 13 Garum factory on the Atlantic coast of Mauretania, at the site said to be Cotta.
Photograph by Duane W. Roller.

considered to date to the early first century AC.[74] *Garum* factories were
common along this coast (Figure 13), and were an important element of the
royal economy.

Since Juba was not a royal builder in the great sense, there is no significant evidence of patronage outside his kingdom. Even Tingis (Figure 14),
suspended politically between Mauretania and Roman Spain and also heavily
associated with Herakles, does not seem to have benefited.[75] Gades, where
Juba was *duovir* and which was famous for its ancient temple to Herakles, is
a possibility for patronage.[76] Elsewhere, the only place that might have
received his architectural largess was Athens. Support of Athens was virtually a necessity for a client monarch,[77] and it is probable that Juba is among
the kings meant by Suetonius in his description of their cooperative project
to fund the completion of the Olympieion in that city, which was to be

74 Michel Ponsich, "Un Théâtre grec au Maroc?" *BAMaroc* 6, 1966, 317–22; and his "Lixus: informations archéologiques," *ANRW* 2.10.2, 1982, 842–3; Golvin (supra note 22), pp. 230–3; Maurice
   Lenior, "Lixus à l'époque romaine," *Lixus*, pp. 277–8. See further on Lixos, Chapter 6, note 185.

75 Although there is building activity at Tingis during the time of the client monarchy, the evidence is
   industrial and residential, and not in the category of royal patronage. See Michel Ponsich, *Recherches
   archéologiques à Tanger et dans sa région* (Paris: CNRS, 1970), pp. 183–5.

76 Infra, pp. 156–7; see also Habibi (supra note 73), pp. 238–40. The same might be said for the site
   of Juba's other duovirate, Carthago Nova.

77 Infra, p. 271.

Figure 14 Tingis and the view northeast across to Spain.

Photograph by Duane W. Roller.

dedicated to the Genius of Augustus.[78] This was a project that seems never even to have been undertaken – perhaps the implication in Suetonius' use of "destinaverunt" – as there is no evidence of a major construction phase between the time of the Roman architect Cossutius, who worked on it in the first half of the second century BC at the behest of the Seleukid king Antiochos IV,[79] and its final completion by Hadrian in AD 132.[80] Nevertheless, the temple had been plundered by Sulla in 86 BC,[81] and it is possible that the regal contributions merely paid for repairs.[82] Augustan interest in the structure might have been due to the previous Roman involvement, both for better and worse, but the failure of the project to be implemented was probably because Augustus realized the impropriety of (and even encountered Athenian resistance at) appropriating one of the Athenians' ancient shrines for a Roman cult.[83] Juba may also have restored the Gymnasion of

---

78 Suetonius, *Augustus* 60.

79 Vitruvius 7.Pref.17. On the convoluted history of the temple, see Herbert Abramson, "The Olympieion in Athens and Its Connections with Rome," *CSCA* 7, 1974, 1–25.

80 J. B. Ward-Perkins, *Roman Imperial Architecture*, second integrated edition (Harmondsworth, UK: Penguin, 1981), p. 268.

81 *NH* 36.45.

82 Abramson (supra note 79), p. 23.

83 David C. Braund, "Greeks and Barbarians: The Black Sea Region and Hellenism under the Early Empire," in *The Early Roman Empire in the East*, ed. Susan E. Alcock, Oxbow Monograph 95 (Oxford: Oxbow, 1997), pp. 124–5.

Ptolemaios in Athens, built by one of his wife's ancestors.[84] The Athenians may have honored Juba[85] because of either of these structures, but the fact remains that his only documented building project was the royal city of Caesarea.

The artistic program

The cultural diversity of the Mauretanian kingdom was most apparent in its elaborate program of sculpture. The surviving examples from Caesarea and elsewhere demonstrate the care that Juba and Kleopatra Selene took to create a visual record of the complex dimensions of their kingdom in order to honor its three components of Rome, Numidia, and Ptolemaic Egypt.

A repertory of dynastic and political sculpture was a standard feature of the client monarchies.[86] The best early example is the great and indeed excessive monument of Antiochos I of Kommagene at Nemrut Dağ.[87] The Romans had been instrumental in placing him on the throne in 69 BC, and he lasted, styling himself φιλορώμαιος, until around 36 BC; in his last years he tangled with Antonius, although the details are unclear, as are the exact manner and date of his death.[88] The monument at Nemrut Dağ ranks as one of the most spectacular of any dynastic program of antiquity. At the summit of the mountain is an elaborate series of outrageously monumental sculptures arranged on two facing terraces, showing the ancestors of

---

84 Traditionally the gymnasion has been considered the work of Ptolemaios VI in the second century BC, part of the great Hellenistic renewal of the Athenian Agora that also saw the construction of the Stoa of Attalos (Homer A. Thompson, "Excavations in the Athenian Agora: 1949," *Hesperia* 19, 1950, 322–3; R. E. Wycherley, *Agora* 3: *Literary and Epigraphical Testimonia* [Princeton, N.J.: Princeton University Press, 1957], pp. 142–4). More recently, however, it has been suggested that the gymnasion was built by his great-grandfather Ptolemaios III, at the time of his rapprochement with Athens in the 220s BC: see Christian Habicht, *Studien zur Geschichte Athens in hellenistischer Zeit*, Hypomnemata 73 (Göttingen 1982), pp. 112–17; Hildegard Schaaf, *Untersuchungen zu Gebäudestifungen in hellenistischer Zeit* (Cologne: Bohlau, 1992), 73–83. Both Ptolemaios III and Ptolemaios VI were direct ancestors of Kleopatra Selene. The gymnasion was damaged at the time of Sulla but was rebuilt, probably in the Augustan period, becoming the major educational center of Roman Athens. On the possibility that Juba may have paid for the rebuilding, see Stephen G. Miller, "Architecture as Evidence for the Identity of the Early *Polis*," in *Sources for the Ancient Greek City-State*, ed. Mogens Herman Hansen (Copenhagen: Munksgaard, 1995), p. 208.

85 *IG* 2–3².3436.

86 Herod, so proficient in architecture, was confronted with local objections to graven images and thus grudgingly avoided portrait sculpture within his kingdom (Josephus, *Jewish Antiquities* 16.158), although there are a few examples elsewhere (Roller, *Herod*, pp. 272–3). He may have made greater use of painting, a medium more acceptable religiously, but none survives (Josephus, *Jewish Antiquities* 15.25–7; *Jewish War* 1.439).

87 Ekrem Akurgal, *Ancient Civilizations and Ruins of Turkey*, seventh edition, tr. John Whybrow and Molly Emre (Istanbul: Turistik Yayinlar, 1990), pp. 348–52; T. A. Sinclair, *Eastern Turkey: An Architectural and Archaeological Survey* 4 (London: Pindar Press, 1990), pp. 43–50.

88 Richard D. Sullivan, "The Dynasty of Commagene," *ANRW* 2.8, 1977, 763–70.

the king, emphasizing his Achaimenid Persian connections through his father, back to Darayavaush I, and the Seleukid connections of his mother back, perhaps, to Alexander the Great. In addition there are the divine ancestors, Greek and Persian, of these families, including Herakles. Such a monument was of more than passing interest to Juba and Kleopatra Selene since they shared some of the same ancestors. Both claimed descent from Herakles, and Kleopatra Selene had Seleukid ancestry through her great-great-great-grandmother, Kleopatra I, wife of Ptolemaios V. Moreover, Kleopatra Selene's father was, as noted, involved in the affairs of the Kommagenean kingdom. Thus the Nemrut Dağ monument touched the Mauretanian world in a number of ways, although it is unique only in its ostentation, and such programmatic sculpture of Hellenistic monarchs, whose origins lie in Persian and even Assyrian reliefs, would have existed in many places.

Rome had also developed such a tradition. Caesar's Forum Julium was strongly dynastic, including a statue of the dictator himself, and, more significantly, a golden statue of Kleopatra Selene's mother.[89] A dynastic program also existed in Pompeius' theater complex[90] and, somewhat later, in Augustus' Forum[91] and, of course, on the Ara Pacis. Thus there was a complex symbolism of visual imagery in the Rome of Juba's and Kleopatra Selene's youth. How this defined the Augustan era, especially in its creation of a new concept of the Roman past, is well known.[92] Juba's own professional interest in Roman history and the theater was part of this, and in his maturity, when he returned to Rome for visits, he would be able to see the public advancement of Augustus' successors and how they were positioned within the national myth. His later intimacy with Gaius Caesar meant that Juba was uniquely placed both to observe and to participate in the developing self-conception of Augustan Rome.[93] Juba and Kleopatra Selene would have transferred many of these ideas to Mauretania, another way that they created a kingdom that was a reflection of Rome. Juba's *Libyka* was, in part, the literary rendition of Mauretanian and Numidian origins and an affirmation – and legitimizing – of the continued Ptolemaic involvement in northern Africa. This was complemented by the visual program of dynastic and historical sculpture that the monarchs established at their cities.[94]

---

89 Appian, *Civil War* 2.102; Dio 51.22.3.

90 *NH* 36.41.

91 The sources are collected in *NTDAR*, pp. 160–2.

92 Paul Zanker, *The Power of Images in the Age of Augustus*, trans. Alan Shapiro (Ann Arbor: University of Michigan Press, 1988), pp. 210–13.

93 Zanker (supra note 92), pp. 215–23, but he is in error in suggesting that Juba was affected by growing up with Gaius in Rome, as the latter was not born until after Juba left the city.

94 The wealth of Greek household and luxury goods from the Mahdia shipwreck of around 80 BC, found off the Tunisian coast, is a material testimony to how Juba's Caesarea could have been stocked. See *Wrack* and Ramsay MacMullen, *Romanization in the Time of Augustus* (New Haven, Conn.: Yale University Press, 2000), p. 48.

The remains of the Mauretanian sculptural program are fragmentary, but all of the proper elements are extant.[95] The commemoration of Juba's ancestry – which the king stressed as far back as Massinissa[96] – is known through one extant portrait of his father, a heavily bearded head from Caesarea now in the Louvre (Figure 15).[97] The head is indeed "bene capillatus," as Cicero described Juba I, and the only surviving piece of a collection of sculpture that displayed the ancestors of Juba II.[98]

Kleopatra Selene's heritage was also commemorated. A portrait from Caesarea, now in the Cherchel Museum, seems to conform best to existing types of Kleopatra VII, although the evidence is not strong.[99] Another portrait from Caesarea, of a veiled head, may be of either Kleopatra VII or her daughter.[100] But as Kleopatra VII's only surviving child, only Kleopatra Selene could keep alive the memory of her famous mother – especially in such a way as to avoid the demonization of her in contemporary Roman literature – and thus it is probable that she would have commissioned many portraits. Other surviving images of Kleopatra VII, such as the ones in Berlin and the Vatican,[101] may have emanated from the Mauretanian court.

No certain portraits of Kleopatra Selene have been found at Caesarea, although the two pieces noted above may be the queen.[102] A bone counter in the British Museum, 2.8 cm across, shows the left-facing bust of a woman wearing a *sakkos*, with curls remindful of portraits of Kleopatra VII, but the

95 On the program itself, see R. R. R. Smith, *Hellenistic Royal Portraits* (Oxford: Clarendon Press, 1988), pp. 106, 140–1.

96 *CIL* 2.3417 = *ILS* 840, from Carthago Nova.

97 Louvre MA 1885; Gisela M. A. Richter, *The Portraits of the Greeks* (London: Phaidon, 1965), p. 280; Klaus Fittschen, "Bildnisse numidischen Könige," *Numider*, pp. 209–13, pl. 57; Smith (supra note 95), no. 123.

98 Cicero, *De lege agraria* 2.59. Other portraits have unconvincingly been identified as depictions of Juba I: see Richter (supra note 97), p. 280. The rider stele from Chemtou in Numidia has the best chance of being a portrait of him (supra, Chapter 1, note 128), but it may not have been part of the Mauretanian sculpture program. A head of personified Africa (identifiable because of the elephant on it), in the style of the Augustan period, may also be part of Juba's ancestral program (Cherchel Museum no. 34; *Numider*, pp. 542–3).

99 Cherchel Museum no. S66 (31); *Cleopatra*, no. 197; Klaus Fittschen, "Zwei Ptolemäerbildnisse in Cherchel," in *Alessandria e il mondo ellenistico-romano: studi in onore di Achille Adriani*, ed. Nicola Bonacasa and Antonio di Vita (Rome 1983–4), p. 168; Richter (supra note 97), p. 280; German Hafner, "Das Bildniss Massinissa," *AA* 1970, pp. 420–1. It is often identified as Kleopatra VII or even Sophoniba.

100 Cherchel Museum 28 (S65); *Cleopatra*, no. 262.

101 Antikenmuseum 1976.10 (Smith [supra note 95], no. 68); Vatican 179 (Smith [supra note 95], no. 67).

102 On the question of portraits of Kleopatra Selene, see Peter Higgs, "Searching for Cleopatra's Image: Classical Portraits in Stone," *Cleopatra*, pp. 207–8; also Fittschen, "Zwei Ptolemäer-Bildnisse" (supra note 99), pp. 168–70; Klaus Vierneisel, "Die Berliner Kleopatra," *JBerlMus* 22, 1980, 15–16; see also Fittschen, "Bildnesse Numidischen Könige" (supra note 97), p. 222, pl. 74, and J. Charbonneaux, "Un Portrait de Cléopâtre VII au Musée de Cherchel," *LibAE* 2, 1954, 49–63; Richter (supra note 97), p. 280. Smith (supra note 95), no. 69, categorically rejected the other attributions.

Figure 15 Portrait bust of Juba I, from Cherchel (Paris, Louvre MA 1885).
Photograph by M. and P. Chuzeville. Courtesy Musée du Louvre.

Figure 16 Gilded silver dish from Boscoreale, perhaps representing Kleopatra Selene (Paris, Louvre Bj 1969).

Photograph by Ch. Larrieu. Courtesy Musée du Louvre.

piece has been suggested to be her daughter.[103] If this is so, its Egyptian provenience indicates that Kleopatra Selene was still recognized in her homeland well into maturity. More significant is a gilded silver dish in the Louvre, part of the collection found at Boscoreale in 1895 (Figure 16).[104] It is 22.5 cm across and has the figure of a woman depicted in high relief. Her features are remindful of those of Kleopatra VII, but are not the same. On her head is the scalp of an elephant; on one breast is an asp and on the other a panther. To her left is a cornucopia with Helios engraved as a young man.

103 GR 1927.3–18.5; *Cleopatra*, no. 265.
104 Bj 1969; Andreas Linfert, "Die Tochter – Nicht die Mutter. Nochmals zur "Africa"-Schale von Boscoreale," in *Alessandria e il mondo ellenistico-romano: studi in onore di Achille Adriana*, ed. Nicola Bonacasa and Antonino di Vita, Studi e Materiali [Palermo] 4–5 (Rome 1983–4), pp. 351–8.

On her right shoulder is a lion. The piece has a complex visual symbolism that points consistently to a North African context, with the cornucopia and lion especially remindful of the coinage of the Mauretanian monarchs. The suggestion that it is a portrait of Kleopatra Selene has much merit. Perhaps it was commissioned by her son after his mother's death as a gift to his in-laws in the imperial family.[105] If it is the Mauretanian queen, it is the best extant portrait of her.

These presumed representations of Kleopatra Selene are not exactly part of the Mauretanian artistic program and were probably not commissioned by the queen. Yet there is an extensive repertory from Caesarea that demonstrates royal patronage. An example is a male portrait perhaps of Ptolemaios I of Egypt.[106] It has certain similarities to his coins, but even Klaus Fittschen, who proposed the identification, was somewhat hesitant. Yet if this attribution is correct, it is the only remnant of Kleopatra Selene's program of ancestral sculpture other than portraits of her mother, a repertory that thus went back to the founder of her dynasty, and probably included her Seleukid ancestors as well as Alexander the Great.

Her Ptolemaic heritage, however, is more strongly manifested by the Egyptian sculpture that ended up at Caesarea. Most notable is a statue of the priest Petubastes IV (Figure 17).[107] The work is an Egyptian creation in basalt, complete with a hieroglyphic inscription identifying him as a priest of Ptah and giving his age and death date, 31 July 30 BC. This was one of the worst days of a difficult summer in Alexandria, when Dionysos himself – Antonius' alter ego – abandoned the city.[108] The following day Octavian attacked and the city fell; within nine days Kleopatra Selene's parents were dead. Petubastes IV was only 16 when he died as the god was deserting the city: he may have been a favorite of the 10-year-old princess.

Other sculptures of Egyptian origin at Caesarea include one of Tuthmosis I, the great pharoah of the Eighteenth Dynasty, preserved only below the knees,[109] a Uraeus,[110] and a head perhaps of Ammon.[111] All these show the emphasis on things Egyptian – actually imported from Alexandria – at Caesarea.

---

105 *Cleopatra*, no. 324.

106 Cherchel Museum 50; Fittschen, "Zwei Ptolemäerbildnisse" (supra note 99), pp. 165–8; Fittschen, "Bildnisse numidische Könige" (supra note 97), p. 221; Smith (supra note 95), no. 124, tended toward identification as Juba II or Ptolemaios of Mauretania.

107 Cherchel Museum S75 (94); Fittschen, "Juba II. und seine Residenz" (supra note 19), pp. 238–9, pl. 75.

108 Plutarch, *Antonius* 75; on the chronology and meaning of the portents, see Christopher Pelling, "The Triumviral Period," *CAH*² 10, 1996, 63.

109 Cherchel Museum S74 (95); see Nacéra Benseddik *et al.*, *Cherchel* (Algiers: Direction des Musées, de l'archéologique et des monuments et sites historiques, 1983), p. 30.

110 Cherchel Museum 86; Stéphane Gsell, *Cherchel: Antique Iol–Caesarea* (Algiers: Direction de l'Intérieur et des Beaux-Arts, 1952), p. 38.

111 Cherchel Museum 66; see Michelin Fasciato and Jean Leclant, "Une Tête 'ammonienne' du Musée de Cherchel," in *Mélanges d'archéologie et d'histoire offerts à Charles Picard à l'occasion de son 65ᵉ anniversaire* 1 (Paris: Presses Universitaires de France, 1949), pp. 360–75.

Figure 17 Petubastes IV, from Cherchel (Cherchel Museum S75).

Photograph by Duane W. Roller. Courtesy Agence Nationale d'Archéologie, Algiers.

The statue of Tuthmosis I, who reigned *ca.* 1525–1512 BC,[112] was probably the oldest antique at the Caesarea court. A statue of Isis or a priestess of Isis,[113] from the second century AC, shows that the Egyptian orientation of Caesarea outlived Kleopatra Selene and her family, and bronze Alexandrian lamps at Volubilis and in western Mauretania demonstrate that these tastes were not limited to the royal city itself.[114] A bronze Dionysos bust from Volubilis, now in the Rabat Museum,[115] although perfectly acceptable within any program of Greek and Roman mythology, may also have Egyptian connections, given the tendencies of Antonius: it displays similarities to a bronze bust of Juba II also from Volubilis. A relief Sphinx from Caesarea, although of uncertain context, may also be Egyptian in inspiration, although in an Augustan style.[116]

Roman notables, past and present, were part of the Mauretanian program. Central, needless to say, was the Princeps himself, and Caesarea has yielded a cuirass statue second only in quality to the Prima Porta Augustus, found near the theater and perhaps once adorning that structure (Figure 18).[117] The decoration on the breastplate depicts the ultimate avenging of the death of Julius Caesar, culminating in the Battle of Actium, not only a remarkable parallel to the *Aeneid*[118] but an astonishing piece of political pragmatism since this conspicuous public sculpture at Caesarea memorialized the defeat of Kleopatra Selene's parents and necessarily ignored the prominent role of her father in the avenging of Caesar's death. Doing honor to Augustus was a necessity, and the Caesarea statue is the centerpiece of this endeavor.[119]

The Romans depicted in the Mauretanian sculptural program were not limited to the new regime. One of the finest pieces is a bronze portrait of Cato, the famous ally of Juba's father. Discovered in 1944 at Volubilis and now in Rabat, it has the advantage of an undisputed attribution, as it is inscribed "CATO."[120] It was found in a private house of the third century

---

112 For the chronology, see William C. Hayes, "Egypt: Internal Affairs from Tuthmosis I to the Death of Amenophis III," *CAH*³ 2.1, 1973, 315–16.

113 Cherchel Museum 2; Christa Landwehr, *Die römischen Skulpturen von Caesarea Mauretaniae: Denkmäler aus Stein und Bronze 1: Idealplastik Weibliche Figuren Benannt*, AF 18 (1993), no. 50 (pp. 66–70); see also her no. 51 (p. 71); Benseddik *et al.* (supra note 109), p. 19.

114 Charles Picard, "Lampes de bronze alexandrines à Volubilis et Banasa (Maroc)," *RA* 45, 1955, 63–8.

115 Beryl Barr-Sharrar, *The Hellenistic and Early Imperial Decorative Bust* (Mainz: Philipp von Zabern, 1987), C88, p. 98. A maenad, also in bronze, may be part of the same group (Barr-Sharrar C149).

116 Cherchel Museum 45; *Numider*, pp. 544–5.

117 Cherchel Museum S72 (177); Klaus Fittschen, "Zur Panzerstatue in Cherchel," *JdI* 91, 1976, 175–210. For its qualitative comparison to the Prima Porta Augustus, see Ann L. Kuttner, *Dynasty and Empire in the Age of Augustus: The Case of the Boscoreale Cups* (Berkeley: University of California Press, 1995), pp. 29–30. Zanker (supra note 92), p. 223, rather inexplicably, identified the statue as Gaius Caesar. He would have been honored at Caesarea, but no statue has been found.

118 Vergil, *Aeneid* 8.675.

119 Erika Simon, *Augustus: Kunst und Leben in Rom um die Zeitenwende* (Munich: Hirmer, 1986), p. 223.

120 Charles Picard, "La Date du buste en bronze de Caton d'Utique trouvé à Volubilis, Maroc," in *Neue Beiträge zur klassischen Altertumswissenschaft: Festschrift zum 60. Geburtstag von Bernhard Schweitzer*, ed. Reinhard Lullies (Stuttgart: W. Kohlhammer, 1954), pp. 334–40.

Figure 18 Cuirass statue, probably of Augustus, from Cherchel (Cherchel Museum S72).

Photograph by E. Kleinefenn, Paris. Courtesy Christa Landwehr and Agence Nationale d'Archéologie, Algiers.

AC, and this has resulted in unconvincing attempts to date it to later than the time of the client monarchy.[121] Although Cato did retain some popularity in North Africa in later imperial times – a statue of him on the beach at Utica was visible in Plutarch's day[122] – one cannot imagine any time other than that of Juba for his portrait to be commissioned at remote Volubilis, and its third century AC context would represent a dispersal of the king's private collection at that time, perhaps when his palace was rebuilt as the Roman governor's residence.[123] Moreover, its similarity to a youthful bronze of Juba II,[124] which can hardly have been created at any time much later than his assumption of the kingship in 25 BC, indicates that the Cato portrait is from the same era and even the same artist or workshop. Juba may have discreetly chosen to honor him at Volubilis rather than at his more conspicuous royal city. Cato and his family – his daughter Porcia and his son-in-law Brutus – represented the best of the republican tradition Juba's father had supported and thus could be put forth as examples of Roman virtue – certainly a relevant Augustan topic – rather than as proponents of a discredited political system.[125]

Central to the sculptural program were representations of the monarchs themselves. Kleopatra Selene is uncertainly documented: as noted, opinion is divided as to whether the portraits in the Cherchel Museum are of her or her mother. But at least nine portraits of Juba II, in two different types, have been identified.[126] These come from Caesarea,[127] Volubilis,[128] and Sala,[129] as might be expected. Some may have been created after the king's death.[130] One now in Madrid[131] is believed to be of Italian origin and one in Copenhagen (Figure 19),[132] from Rome, may be a wedding portrait. The Volubilis piece, an idealized youthful bronze in the Greek style, is perhaps the official image of the 23-year-old monarch when he assumed office. The others show

121 See, for example, Christiane Boube-Piccot, "Techniques de fabrication des bustes de bronze de Juba II et de Caton d'Utique découverts à Volubilis," *BAMaroc* 7, 1967, 447–75.

122 Plutarch, *Cato the Younger* 71.

123 J. M. C. Toynbee, *Roman Historical Portraits* (London: Thames and Hudson, 1978), pp. 39–41.

124 Rabat Museum 146.

125 Plutarch, *Cato the Younger* 71–3.

126 Klaus Fittschen, "Die Bildnisse der mauretanischen Könige und ihre stadtrömischen Vorbilder," *MM* 15, 1974, 156–73.

127 Cherchel Museum 21, 37, 50; Louvre MA 1886, 3182; see also Fittschen, "Bildnisse numidischen Könige" (supra note 97), pp. 213–17; Richter (supra note 97), p. 280; Smith (supra note 95), pp. 179–80.

128 Rabat Museum 146.

129 Now in Rabat; see Jean Boube, "Un Nouveau Portrait de Juba II découvert à Sala," *BAMaroc* 6, 1966, 91–106.

130 For example, Louvre MA 1886, perhaps a death memorial erected by his son at Caesarea.

131 Prado ABr 963/4; Fittschen, *MM* (supra note 126), p. 157.

132 Ny Carlsberg Glyptotek 1591; *Numider*, pp. 496–7.

Figure 19 Portrait bust of Juba II, from Rome (Copenhagen, Ny Carlsberg Glyptotek 1591).

Courtesy Christa Landwehr and Ny Carlsberg Glyptotek.

him at varying stages of youth, but none in old age, when he may have grown a beard.[133]

As Ptolemaios, the son of Juba and Kleopatra Selene, reached maturity, his portraits were added to the royal collection. At least a dozen are known.[134] But these belong in a different iconographic tradition than those of his father, since unlike Juba, Ptolemaios was a member of the Augustan family, a blood relative of the emperors Gaius Caligula, Claudius, and Nero. Thus his portraiture is somewhat influenced by the iconography of the imperial family, with a hairstyle perhaps derived from that of Gaius Caesar[135] or even Augustus.[136] A portrait in Oslo has been identified as either Ptolemaios[137] or his cousin Nero,[138] demonstrating the similarity between the representations of Ptolemaios and the young men of the Julio-Claudian family.

The assumed portraits of Ptolemaios emanate from both Mauretania and Italy. Several are from Caesarea.[139] From Sala is a full statue in Pentelic marble in the style of the Doryphoros and perhaps of Greek or even Athenian origin,[140] indicative of the close ties that he had with the Greek world, something that may eventually have contributed to his death.[141] Other portraits come from Italy,[142] where, as a direct descendant of Antonius, he would have been popular. Ptolemaios did not live to old age and thus the portraits are youthful, with the one in Uppsala perhaps the youngest, dating to about the time Juba II raised him to a regency, around AD 17–21. Louvre MA 1887 (Figure 20) is a somewhat more mature Ptolemaios, with heavy sideburns, similar to those on his coins.[143] The oldest age represented may be

---

133 Mazard, #355, 356. These coins are not dated and are joint issues with Kleopatra Selene, so they may in fact be earlier rather than later. One would expect Juba II to spend most of his life clean-shaven, given his upbringing in the Augustan household and the ridicule heaped upon his hirsute father.

134 Fittschen, *MM* (supra note 126), pp. 158–60; see also Toynbee (supra note 123), pp. 93–4; Richter (supra note 97), p. 281; Smith (supra note 95), pp. 179–80.

135 This was advanced by Fittschen, *MM* (supra note 126), pp. 170–3; for a critique that finds the idea attractive but specifics lacking, see John Pollini, *The Portraiture of Gaius and Lucius Caesar* (New York: Fordham University Press, 1987), pp. 28–30.

136 Pollini (supra note 135), p. 29.

137 Frederik Poulson, "Porträtkopf eines numidischen Königs," *SymbOslo* 3, 1925, 1–13; Richter (supra note 97), p. 281.

138 Fittschen, *MM* (supra note 126), p. 160.

139 Cherchel Museum 40, 52 (on this, see François Chamoux, "Un Nouveau Portrait de Ptolémée de Maurétanie découvert à Cherchel," in *Mélanges d'archéologie et d'histoire offerts à André Piganiol*, ed. Raymond Chevallier [Paris; SEVPEN, 1966], vol. 1, pp. 395–406), and a third unnumbered (Fittschen, *MM* [supra note 126], D3); Louvre MA 1887, 1888, 3813.

140 Rabat Museum S-2289; Jean Boube, "Une Statue-portrait de Ptolémée de Maurétanie à Sala (Maroc)," *RA* 1990, pp. 331–60; Smith (supra note 95), no. 125, who saw this as an early Juba II or an ancestor.

141 Infra, pp. 253–5.

142 Vatican Braccio Nuovo 65; a piece in the Villa Albani in Rome (Fittschen, *MM* [supra note 126], D4) and one in a private collection in Uppsala, Sweden (Fittschen, *MM* [supra note 126], C1).

143 Mazard, #500, 501, 506–11, some dated to Years 15–17 = AD 32–8.

Figure 20 Ptolemaios of Mauretania, from Cherchel (Louvre MA 1887).
Photograph by M. and P. Chuzeville. Courtesy Musée du Louvre.

Cherchel Museum no. 40, although its poor state of preservation makes analysis difficult.

The Mauretanian program was completed by a vast repertory of Greco-Roman mythological and allegorial sculpture, a direct imitation of similar endeavors in contemporary Rome.[144] No Greek originals have been found, but there are copies of works by famous Greek artists such as Skopas.[145] Especially noteworthy is a Kore of the Villa Albani type.[146] Other copies of Greek originals include a miniature bronze Aphrodite undoing her sandal,[147] and an Artemis or Diana of the Versailles type.[148] There are numerous representations of Herakles or Hercules,[149] and several versions of Apollo.[150] Other gods and goddesses, too numerous to cite, were also part of the program.[151] Three immense heads, 0.86–0.90 m high, perhaps Juppiter (or Neptune), Juno, and Venus, survive from a colossal divine group, part of an elaborate composition in the style of Augustan cultic sculpture.[152]

Only one artist at the royal court is known by name, the distinguished gem-cutter Gnaios, who was part of Kleopatra Selene's entourage and had worked for her father in Alexandria: a signed portrait of Antonius is now in the Ionides Collection in London.[153] Gnaios came to the Mauretanian court and carved portraits of Diomedes (now in Chatsworth, England) and Herakles (now in the British Museum) – both personages of interest to Juba – and of a queenly figure (now in the Metropolitan Museum in New York), probably Kleopatra Selene. He may also have been involved in producing the Mauretanian coin types.[154] Gnaios, who came from a Hellenistic court,

144 Gilbert Charles Picard, "La Sculpture dans l'Afrique romaine," in *150-Jahr-Feier Deutsches Archäologisches Institut Rome, RM Supp.* 25, 1982, 189–90. On the similar activities in Rome, and Juba's direct imitation of them, see Susan Walker, "The Moral Museum: Augustus and the City of Rome," in *Ancient Rome: The Archaeology of the Eternal City,* ed. J. Coulson and H. Dodge, Oxford University School of Archaeology Monograph 54, 2000, pp. 61–75.

145 Cherchel Museum S109; Charles Picard, "Une Réplique oubliée du Pothos scopasique," *RA* 6th ser. 25, 1946, 224–5; Christa Landwehr, *Die römischen Skulpturen von Caesarea Mauretaniae: Denkmäler aus Stein und Bronze 2: Idealplastik: Männliche Figuren* (Mainz: Philipp von Zabern, 2000), no. 112.

146 Cherchel Museum 12 (S10); *Numider,* pp. 534–5; Fittschen, "Juba II. und Seine Residenz" (supra note 19), pp. 234–8.

147 Algiers Musée National 590; Landwehr 1 (supra note 113), no. 6.

148 Cherchel Museum S231; Landwehr 1 (supra note 113), no. 16.

149 Landwehr 2 (supra note 145), nos. 94–101.

150 Landwehr 2 (supra note 145), nos. 67–74.

151 Landwehr's catalogs (vol. 1, supra note 113; vol. 2, supra note 145) include 175 different pieces of Greco-Roman mythological and allegorical sculpture. Although many are from later than the period of the monarchy, they demonstrate the continuing role of Caesarea as a sculptural center.

152 Cherchel Museum 123–5; *Numider,* pp. 538–41.

153 John Boardman, *Greek Gems and Finger Rings, Early Bronze Age to Late Classical* (London: Harry N. Abrams [1970]), pl. 1013, and his *Engraved Gems: The Ionides Collection* (Evanston, Ill.: Northwestern University Press, 1968), p. 27.

154 Marie-Louise Vollenweider, *Die Steinschneidekunst und ihre Künstler in spätrepublikanischer und Augusteischer Zeit* (Baden-Baden: Grimm, 1966), pp. 45–6.

where he had worked for a Roman aristocrat, demonstrates the artistic cross-fertilization of the Mauretanian kingdom. Many of the art works are, to be sure, derivative, but nonetheless the monarchs succeeded in their artistic attempts to create a Caesarea that was a proper image of Rome.

The royal court

The intellectual culture of the court was directed by Juba's own heritage and interests, but especially those of Kleopatra Selene, who honored the memory of her mother and her mother's land, and created a distinct Hellenistic Egyptian tone.[155] By choosing to name her son Ptolemaios – thereby passing over Juba's ancestral names – Kleopatra Selene further emphasized her role as the one who would continue the Ptolemaic dynasty and nullify its deposing in 30 BC. One cannot overemphasize the significance of this nomenclature – a rare example of reaching into the mother's family rather than the father's for the name of the primary male heir – as it conspicuously demonstrates that Kleopatra Selene saw herself as heiress of the Ptolemies and the leader of a Ptolemaic government in exile. This role and her stature are most strikingly manifest in her series of autonomous coins and the depiction of the Nile crocodile on them (Figure 26c, d, p. 246).[156] Her heritage is also commemorated in the Greek legend on her coins, unlike those of her husband, which are almost always in Latin. Unfortunately, none of her autonomous coins is dated, so it is impossible to fit them chronologically into the history of the kingdom.[157]

There is also a long series of joint coins with Juba (Figure 26a, b, p. 246). These are inevitably bilingual and have Egyptian symbols such as the Uraeus, Isis paraphernalia, crocodiles, and perhaps the cult statue of Juppiter Ammon.[158] The only dated one is Juba's Year 6, 19 BC, perhaps an early

155 Although it is likely that the inspiration was directly from Alexandria and Kleopatra Selene's heritage, Hellenistic Egyptian motifs were also acutely topical in contemporary Rome, and thus the egyptianizing of Mauretania could also be seen as romanizing. On the egyptianizing in Augustan Rome, see Sarolta A. Takács, "Alexandria in Rome," *HSCP* 97, 1995, 269–71.

156 Mazard #392–5. The crocodile coins are remindful of those issued in her childhood when she was queen of Kyrene, as well as those of Octavian from 28 BC (Harold Mattingly, *Coins of the Roman Empire in the British Museum* 1: *Augustus to Vitellius* (London: British Museum Publications, 1923, reprinted with revisions 1976), p. 106, nos. 650–5. These have the unfortunate legend "Aegypto capta," and Kleopatra Selene's coins of a few years later may be seen as a response by the true ruler of Egypt.

157 The convoluted theories to explain these coins, involving regencies or divorce and remarriage, are unnecessary; her status is sufficient explanation. Moreover, one need not assume any division of territory between the sovereigns (see Gsell, vol. 8, pp. 219–20): the queen's immense status meant that her personality was more dominant than those of the shadowy queens of many other client kingdoms.

158 Mazard #297–374; Dieter Salzmann, "Zur Münzprägung der mauretanischen Könige Juba II. und Ptolemaios," *MM* 15, 1974, 177–8; but see Gsell, vol. 8, p. 219.

wedding anniversary.[159] Isis symbols also appear on coins of Juba alone,[160] and this and his occasional use of Greek legends[161] indicate that the Egyptian influence at the court transcended the personality of Kleopatra Selene.

Egypt was not the sole cultural influence at Caesarea. The Roman qualities of the court are obvious, in military organization, layout and institutions of the city, and the establishment of an imperial cult, an early and important priority of the kingdom.[162] As usual, numismatic evidence is the most informative. Many coins show the Capricorn,[163] significantly Augustus' own sign and appearing on his coins.[164] Coins also seem to provide evidence for games in honor of the emperor. These have Juba's name, the legend "CAESAREA," and a crown,[165] perhaps a victory crown for the games at Caesarea.[166] Imperial games were a common feature of client kingdoms, such as the Kaisareia, an athletic, music, and dramatic festival, at Herod's Caesarea,[167] and it can be presumed that Juba also inaugurated them.[168]

Another cult of significance was that of Saturn, since worship of the god was another way that Juba could connect the cultures of Rome and Mauretania. The Augustan age was a Golden Age, the new era of Saturn.[169] Greek Kronos, hardly a positive or uplifting figure, was transformed into the ideal Italian agriculturalist, the patron of the Latin people.[170] In Rome, the Temple of Saturn, one of the oldest of the Roman shrines, was splendidly rebuilt beginning in 42 BC by the Caesarean L. Munatius Plancus, who would be one of the most distinguished Augustan loyalists of the following years.[171] There were also indigenous reasons to emphasize the cult of Saturn.[172] The god was

159 Mazard #357; supra, pp. 86–7.
160 Mazard #271–4.
161 Mazard #270.
162 James Rives, "Imperial Cult and Native Tradition in Roman North Africa," *CJ* 96, 2001, 427–9; Coltelloni-Trannoy, pp. 187–94.
163 Mazard, #290–2, 391.
164 Suetonius, *Augustus* 94.12; Salzmann (supra note 158), pp. 174–5; Michèle Coltelloni-Trannoy, "Le Monnayage des rois Juba II et Ptolémée de Maurétanie: image d'une adhésion réitérée à la politique romaine," *Karthago* 22, 1990, 46–7.
165 Mazard #227–35.
166 It may also be a representation of the *corona civica* that Augustus received in 27 BC (Augustus, *Res gestae* 34), or even Juba's own *corona civica*.
167 Josephus, *Jewish Antiquities* 15.268–71.
168 Gsell, vol. 8, pp. 226–7; Coltelloni-Trannoy, pp. 191–2.
169 This is carefully outlined by Karl Galinsky, *Augustan Culture: An Interpretive Introduction* (Princeton, N.J.: Princeton University Press, 1996), pp. 93–7; also, for the historical development of the myth of the Golden Age, see Kenneth J. Reckford, "Some Appearances of the Golden Age," *CJ* 54, 1958–9, 79–87.
170 Vergil, *Georgics* 2.536–40, *Aeneid* 6.791–5.
171 *NTDAR* 343–4; Thomas H. Watkins, *L. Munatius Plancus: Serving and Surviving in the Roman Revolution*, Illinois Classical Studies 7 (Atlanta 1997), pp. 132–3.
172 For a thorough study of Saturn in Africa, see Marcel LeGlay, *Saturne africain, histoire*, BÉFAR 250 (1966), and his *Saturne africain, monuments* (Paris: Arts et Métiers Graphiques, 1966).

associated with the royal ancestor Herakles,[173] and was common in North Africa, often along with Baal-Ammon,[174] who himself was connected with Augustus.[175] Juba I had placed Ammon on his coins,[176] a practice that his son and Kleopatra Selene would follow.[177] All this would encourage Juba II to give prominence to Saturn, the *frugifer deus*,[178] within his agriculturally abundant kingdom, and by AD 30 a sanctuary of the god existed at Caesarea, where prayers were offered for the health of King Ptolemaios.[179] One of those attending, Julia Vitale, came some distance from the city of Rusguniae,[180] indicating that it was an important cult: it would not have assumed the role of guardian of the king's welfare were it not one of the central shrines of the kingdom.[181] Although the cult is not documented before the time of Ptolemaios, the importance of Saturn to the Augustan self-conception and the precedents from Juba's own ancestry are sufficient reason to see it as another example of Juba's blending of indigenous and Roman cultural phenomena. Mauretania, like the world of Saturn, was a region of agricultural abundance, and emphasis on the cult of Saturn could insure the inclusion of Mauretania in the Augustan Golden Age of *Saturnia regna*.[182] It is no accident that Vergil mentioned Saturn and the Garamantes in juxtaposition, implying that it was through the force of Saturn that the African frontier was secure.[183]

173 Dionysios of Halikarnassos, *Roman Archaeology* 1.34; see also LeGlay, *Saturne, histoire* (supra note 172), p. 245.

174 LeGlay, *Saturne, histoire* (supra note 172), pp. 62–7, 215–16, 414–15.

175 L. Müller *et al.*, *Numismatique de l'ancienne Afrique*, vol. 2, reprint (Chicago: OBOL International, 1977), pp. 57–8, #29.

176 Mazard #90, 92.

177 Mazard #355–6.

178 Raymond Thouvenot, "Le Culte de Saturne en Maurétanie Tingitane," *RÉA* 56, 1954, 150–3.

179 Louis Leschi, "Un Sacrifice pour le salut de Ptolémée, roi de Maurétanie," in *Mélanges de géographie et d'orientalisme offerts à E.-F. Gautier* (Tours: Arrault et Cie., 1937), pp. 332–40; LeGlay, *Saturne, histoire* (supra note 172), p. 79. For further evidence for the cult at Caesarea, see LeGlay, *Saturne, monuments* (supra note 172), pp. 315–21.

180 Rusguniae is at Cape Matifou, just east of Algiers, nearly 100 km from Caesarea. See P.-A. Février, "Rusguniae," *PECS*, p. 776; *NH* 5.20; *BAGRW*, map 30. The city seems to have had a special relationship with King Ptolemaios, as is shown by the honor paid to him by the local magistrate L. Caecilius Rufus Agilis (*CIL* 8.9257; *Numider*, pl. 113).

181 In western Mauretania the cult was less common (LeGlay, *Saturne, histoire* [supra note 172], pp. 266–7; Thouvenot [*RÉA*, supra note 172], pp. 150–3). Temple B at Volubilis, a structure of the Severan period but with pre-Roman antecedents, at the east of the city, across the Wadi Fertassa, has been traditionally known as the Temple of Saturn (Michel Ponsich, "Le Temple dit de Saturne à Volubilis," *BAMaroc* 10, 1976, 131–44) but this is purely hypothetical and not generally accepted (Jodin, *Volubilis*, pp. 167–8). Epigraphic evidence from Volubilis for the cult is catalogued by LeGlay, *Saturne, monuments* (supra note 172), pp. 335–6.

182 Vergil, *Eclogues* 6.41–2; William S. Anderson, "Juno and Saturn in the *Aeneid*," *Studies in Philology* 55, 1958, 531–2.

183 Vergil, *Aeneid* 6.794.

In addition to emphasizing the Roman and Ptolemaic nature of his court, Juba did not neglect its indigenous African heritage – as the cult of Saturn shows – although strangely this would have been the least familiar to him. It is probable that members of the Numidian exile community were among the entourage that made the journey from Rome to Iol in 25 BC; these and the existing local elite of Iol would have provided Juba with the information that he needed. Most important was the association with Herakles, because like the cult of Saturn, it also connected indigenous North African history with that of the Greco-Roman world. Some of his labors had long been localized in northwest Africa, and a number of the Mauretanian tribes claimed descent from him.[184] The palace of Antaios and the Gardens of the Hesperides were said to be at Lynx (Lixos).[185] A genealogy was promulgated by the inhabitants of Tingis, in which the civic eponym, Tinga, widow of Antaios, had a child, Sophax, by Herakles, whose son Diodoros was the ancestor of Juba.[186] Although Plutarch was rightly dubious about this, such tales were common in the cities of western Mauretania, which lay close to the Pillars of Herakles.[187] Moreover, Herakles was topical in contemporary Rome. When Augustus returned to the city after his extended Spanish residence that resulted in Juba's kingship, his long time in the west was compared to the labors of Hercules.[188] There were numerous temples and shrines to the god in Rome,[189] one of which, the Temple of Hercules

---

184 *NH* 5.7; Strabo 17.3.7; Pomponius Mela 1.26–7; Paul Corbier, "Hercule africain, divinité indigène?," *Dialogues d'histoire ancienne 1974*, Annales littéraires de l'Université de Besançon 166 (Paris 1974), pp. 95–104.

185 *NH* 5.1–4. Pliny was skeptical about the details of the tale but noted the presence of an altar of Hercules on an island where the famous garden had supposedly been, and reported that the locals felt that the twisting course of the estuary of the Lixos River resembled the serpent that had guarded the apples. He further commented that the grove had been taken over by olive trees. See, further, Sergio Ribichini, "Hercule à Lixus et le Jardin des Hespérides," *Lixus*, pp. 131–6.

   Today the ruins of Lixos (Figure 12, p. 134), the second largest Roman site in Morocco, are located on a high promontory overlooking the distinctly serpentine channel of the Loukas River, which preserves the ancient name. The valley is largely silted in, and where the *garum* factories of antiquity once stood there are extensive salt-making operations: the site is now 4km inland. The estuary is one of the few sheltered places on the Atlantic coast of northern Morocco and was known to Hanno, who landed there and became friends with the local pastoral Lixitai; he was the first to cite the name. On the site of Lixos/Lynx, see Maurice Lenoir, "Lixus à l'époque romaine," *Lixus*, pp. 271–87.

186 Plutarch, *Sertorius* 9. On the Heraklid connections of Juba, see Albert-Marie Denis, "Héraclès et ses cousins de Judée: le syncrétisme d'un historien juif hellénistique," *Hommages à Marie Delcourt*, Collection Latomus 114 (Brussels 1970), pp. 168–78, which, however, must be read with extreme caution; Elizabeth Smadja, "Juba II Hercule sur le monnayage maurétanien," in *Mélanges Pierre Lévêque*, ed. Marie-Madelaine Mactoux and Evelyne Geny, 8: *Religion, anthropologie et société* (Paris: Belles Lettres, 1994), pp. 371–88. Whether young Juba claimed descent from the hero before assuming his kingship is debatable.

187 Coltelloni-Trannoy, pp. 175–6.

188 Horace, *Odes* 3.14.

189 *NTDAR* has a total of seventeen (pp. 185–9).

Musarum, in the southern Campus Martius, had been restored in 29 BC by L. Marcius Philippus, and whose cult had been described by Juba in his *Roman Archaeology*.[190] If the Roman and North African precedents were not sufficient to make Herakles politically correct in Juba's world, both of Juba's wives also claimed descent from the hero.[191] It would be predictable that the king would seek such a heroic genealogy – his status as an orphan might make this more important – and that Herakles, who had also been honored by Juba's father,[192] would be perceived as an appropriate ancestor. No doubt the cult of Herakles was second at Caesarea only to that of Augustus. The strongest physical evidence is again numismatic, coins that show a lion and a club.[193] Although a seemingly obvious representation of the demise of the Nemean lion is ambiguous because of the strong association of Juba I with lions, this could only be an advantage.[194]

Imperial and ancestral cults at Caesarea were eventually supplemented by one of the royal family itself.[195] Although essentially alien to the West,[196] there were the significant precedents of the imperial cult and Ptolemaic traditions from Egypt, and perhaps even those of the Numidian kings.[197] An inscription hints that Juba (or his son Ptolemaios) established a cult of Hiempsal, Juba's grandfather.[198] Two Christian authors of the early third century AC may provide literary evidence for a cult of Juba himself. In his *Octavius*, a dialogue between a Christian and a pagan from Cirta, M. Minucius Felix listed humans who were said to have become divine: Saturn, Juppiter, Romulus, and Juba – part of a Christian argument that divinity is impossible for mortals.[199] His elder contemporary Tertullian, of Carthage,

---

190 Juba, fr. 92.

191 Kleopatra Selene was allegedly descended from Herakles on both sides. Heraklid traditions were endemic in Makedonia (see N. G. L. Hammond and G. T. Griffith, *A History of Macedonia* 2: 550–336 B.C. [Oxford: Clarendon Press, 1979], pp. 3–4, 13), and Antonius also claimed descent (Plutarch, *Antonius* 36.3–4). For Glaphyra, see Josephus, *Jewish War* 1.476, and Denis (supra note 186), pp. 168–73.

192 Gsell, vol. 6, p. 155.

193 Mazard #176–87; Salzmann (supra note 158), pp. 175–6. Some have the club alone (#170–5). Ptolemaios also used the device (#430–9).

194 Aelian, *On the Characteristics of Animals* 7.23. There was also a cult of Tanit-Caelestis at Caesarea by the second century AC, but whether this was established by Juba or previously existed cannot be proven. See Nacéra Benseddik, "Un Nouveau Témoignage du culte de Tanit-Caelestis à Cherchel?" *AntAfr* 20, 1984, 175–81.

195 Coltelloni-Trannoy, pp. 194–9; Ghazi-Ben Maïssa, *Hespéris-Tamuda* 35.2 (supra note 53), pp. 24–9.

196 Fishwick, *ANRW* (supra note 39), p. 1207. See also Braund, *Friendly King*, pp. 114–15.

197 Michèle Coltelloni-Trannoy, "Le Culte royal sous les règnes de Juba II et de Ptolémée de Maurétanie," in *Histoire et archéologie de l'Afrique du Nord (Actes du Ve colloque international: Spectacles, vie portuaire, religions)* (Paris: CTHS, 1992), p. 72.

198 Stéphane Gsell, *Inscriptions latines de l'Algérie* 1 (Rome: L'Erma di Bretschneider, 1965), #1242; Gsell, vol. 7, p. 290.

199 Minucius Felix 21.9–11.

included the Mauretanian *reguli* in a list of local gods, including Astarte and Dushares, who were not Roman but existed within the confines of the empire:[200] whether this refers to Juba and Ptolemaios, or local tribal chieftains, is not clear, as Juba and his son would hardly have considered themselves petty kings. Although both authors were writing Christian tracts, both also had North African connections, and were likely to have been well informed regarding local history. There is also more direct evidence for a cult of Ptolemaios, in particular an inscription dedicated to his *genius*[201] and another expressing wishes for his good health, dated to his tenth regnal year, around AD 30.[202] He may have had greater claim than Juba to divine status because of his mother's ancestors,[203] and it may have been he who actually established the Mauretanian royal cult. Yet it is hard to imagine that Ptolemaios would encourage a cult of himself and not of his father,[204] and thus there is a strong probability that both Juba and Ptolemaios were deified, evidently by local demand.[205]

Regardless, Juba received honors throughout the empire. In Athens his statues were erected in the Gymnasion of Ptolemaios and on the Akropolis,[206] and members of his family were also honored by the city;[207] this respect toward client kings and their families was commonplace in Athens during the Augustan period.[208] Closer to home, Juba was *duovir* in two Spanish cities, Gades[209] and Carthago Nova, where he was also *patronus coloniae*.[210] A *duovir* was the chief magistrate in a Roman colonia or municipium,[211] and although Juba's appointments were probably honorary, they represented the realities of politics and economy in the contemporary western Mediterranean. At Carthago Nova he served a five-year term with

---

200 Tertullian, *Apologeticus* 24.7.

201 *CIL* 8.9342.

202 Leschi (supra note 179), pp. 332–40.

203 Enrique Gozalbes, "El culto indígena a los reyes en Mauritania Tingitana. Surgimiento y pervivencia," in *Paganismo y cristianismo en el occidente del imperio romano*, Memorias de historia antigua 5 (Oviedo 1981), pp. 157–8.

204 For possible cult statues of the kings, see Coltelloni-Trannoy, pp. 198–9; Christa Landwehr, "Juba II. als Diomedes?" *JdI* 107, 1992, 103–24.

205 The role of the locals was mentioned by Minucius Felix. See also *CIL* 8.20627 and Coltelloni-Trannoy, p. 199.

206 *IG* 2–3².3436; Pausanias 1.17.2.

207 Glaphyra: *OGIS* 363; Ptolemaios: *OGIS* 197; an unnamed daughter, *IG* 2².3439.

208 See the list in Braund, *Friendly King*, p. 78.

209 The source is the *Ora maritima* (275–83) of Rufus Festus Avienus, a geographical poem of the latter fourth century AC, based on many earlier but uncertain sources. Some 714 lines are preserved, detailing the coast from Brittany to Massalia. See the Murphy edition; Thomson, pp. 53, 275; on his date, John Matthews, "Continuity in a Roman Family: The Rufii Festi of Volsinii," *Historia* 16, 1967, 485–90; and Rhys Carpenter, *Beyond the Pillars of Heracles* (New York: Delacorte Press, 1966), 199–214. The reference to Juba is perhaps from an inscription.

210 Mazard #397.

211 Christian Gizewski, "Duoviri, Duumviri,' *NP* 3, 1997, 843–5.

one Cn. Attellius, who was also *pontifex*, probably a prominent local citizen. The date was perhaps around AD 9.[212] Ptolemaios eventually inherited his father's office.[213] Carthago Nova, a Carthaginian foundation of the third century BC, became a Roman colony probably under Caesar, and was a rich and prosperous city with an unusually protected harbor.[214] Gades, an ancient Phoenician city, saw its inhabitants receive Roman citizenship from Caesar and became renowned as a cultural center.[215] It was famous for its great sanctuary of Melqart, which had evolved into one of Herakles: this Roman town that retained North African connections and honored Herakles was a suitable environment for his descendant Juba. It would have been natural for Juba to seek recognition in these areas of Europe closest to his territories and to use his position to foster trade.[216]

An essential part of client kingship was the court circle of scholars, artists, and others attending the king. The tradition of king as patron of culture had its origins as early as the Platonic ideals of the philosopher-king[217] and began to flourish at the time of Alexander the Great.[218] It became virtually a requisite of Hellenistic kingship. With the creation of

---

212 Antonio Beltrán, "Juba II y Ptolomeo, de Mauritania, II viri quinquennales de Carthago Nova," *Caesaraugusta* 51–2, 1980, 133–41.

213 Mazard #512–14.

214 *NH* 3.19; P. A. Brunt, *Italian Manpower 225 B.C.–A.D. 14* (Oxford: Oxford University Press, 1971), p. 250; A. Beltrán, "Carthago Nova," *PECS*, pp. 202–3. Interestingly, Pliny connected Carthago Nova with Caesarea by describing the sea route between the two cities.

215 Livy, *Epitome* 110. On Roman Gades, see A. T. Fear, *Rome and Baetica: Urbanization in Southern Spain, c. 50 BC–AD 150* (Oxford: Clarendon Press, 1996), pp. 232–7.

216 On the trade issues, see Beltrán, *Caesaraugusta* (supra note 212), pp. 137–8. Juba may also have had a special relationship with cities in coastal Gaul, particularly Nemausus, as shown by numismatic and ceramic evidence (Romanelli, *Storia*, pp. 168–9). But a coin jointly of Juba and Kleopatra Selene, similar to Mazard #350, found at Assier, in the *département* of Lot, 150 km west-north-west of Nemausus, is probably a casual and recent removal, and not evidence of commercial contact: see M. LeGlay, "Une Monnaie de Juba II," *LibAE* 4, 1956, 149–50; Brigitte Fischer, *Les Monnaies antiques d'Afrique du Nord trouvées en Gaule, Gallia* supp. 36 (Paris 1978), 129–30. Other finds in modern France are probably also casual removals: coins of Juba II have been found under questionable circumstances at Fréjus and Le Mans (Fischer, p. 131). Both were discovered in the nineteenth century; the Le Mans coin has long been lost. Fréjus, ancient Forum Julii, an important commercial center in the Augustan era, might be expected to have had trade contacts with Mauretania: in fact, its economy was similar to that of Mauretania, with *garum* an important commodity (*NH* 31.95–7). On the site, see A. L. F. Rivet, *Gallia Narbonensis* (London: Batsford, 1988), pp. 226–38. Le Mans is more problematic, although as ancient Subdinum it was occupied in the Augustan period (M. Petit, "Subdinum," *PECS*, p. 864). Regardless of how these coins reached the interior of Europe, they are testimony to the value of coinage in defining the ideals and policies of a state, since those who handled the coins would come to know the Mauretanian self-conception of its prosperity and adherence to Augustan ideals, as the coins showed cornucopiae, victories, Herakles, the Capricorn, and many other politically correct images. See Coltelloni-Trannoy, *Karthago* (supra note 164), pp. 45–53.

217 Plato, *Republic* 5.18 (473d).

218 For a good summary, see Claire Préaux, *Le Monde hellénistique* 1, third edition (Paris: Presses Universitaires de France, 1989), pp. 212–20.

the Alexandrian and Pergamene libraries in the third century BC, something again foreseen by Plato,[219] the connection between king and scholarly research was firmly established.[220] Juba would have been part of this tradition merely because he was a Hellenistic king, but his empathy would be further strengthened because of his own credentials as a scholar, which predated even his earliest thoughts of kingship, as well as his eventual role as heir to the Ptolemies. A requisite of any royal court was a fine library, in this case necessary not only for the scholars in residence but for Juba's own researches.[221] According to Elias, the Neoplatonist commentator on Aristotle, Juba's library contained the writings of Pythagoras, but these included forgeries.[222] It is reasonable that Juba would be interested in Pythagoreanism, which had an active following in the Rome of his youth and had come to be connected with Rome's origins,[223] perhaps first gaining popularity through Alexandros Polyhistor, who wrote *On Pythagorean Symbols* and devoted detailed space to Pythagoras and Pythagoreanism in his history of the philosophers.[224] Other scholars, especially at the time of Juba's education, were active Pythagorean writers.[225] Moreover, Juba made extensive use of such authors in his *Theatrical History* and *Roman Archaeology*.[226] The near-mythical status of Pythagoras in the Hellenistic period, culminating in Latin literary accounts such as that by Ovid,[227] means that there is a sharp distinction between the philosopher himself and the vast Pythagorean literature: it was probably the latter that Juba collected and which may, in part, be the origin of Elias' skeptical statement. There was also was a brisk trade

219 Plato, *Republic* 528c.

220 Préaux (supra note 218), pp. 230–8.

221 Stéphane Gsell, "Juba II, savant et écrivain,' *RAfr* 68, 1927, 171–9.

222 Elias, preface to *Commentary on the Categories of Aristotle* (*Commentaria in Aristotelem Graeca* 18 [Berlin 1900] 1.128), which reads Jobata, king of Libya, otherwise unknown, and the emendation to Juba is not difficult: Jacoby, *Commentary*, p. 324. See also the parallel comment by Olympiodoros in his preface, *Commentaria in Aristotelem Graeca* 12 (Berlin 1902) 1.13. Interestingly, Elias and Olympiodoros compared Juba's collecting of the works of Pythagoras to Ptolemaios II's gathering of the works of Aristotle to establish the Alexandria library.

    Forgery of texts had become a growth industry, perhaps orginally developing out of rivalry between the Pergamene and Alexandrian libraries. It was profitable to create forgeries for the increasing number of royal libraries coming into existence in late Hellenistic times, as well as the developing Roman interest in Greek literature. As a result, books were often secreted away to protect them from the rapacious royal library acquisitions staff: the familiar but interesting tale of the burying of the books of Aristotle and Theophrastos by the heirs of Neleus of Skepsis (Theophrastos' student and heir) is the prime example (Strabo 13.1.54). On these issues, see P. M. Fraser, *Ptolemaic Alexandria* (Oxford: Clarendon Press, 1972), vol. 1, pp. 325–6.

223 Elizabeth Rawson, *Intellectual Life in Late Republican Rome* (London: Duckworth, 1985), pp. 291–4.

224 *FGrHist* #273, fr. 94; Diogenes Laertios 8.24–6.

225 Supra, p. 67.

226 Infra, p. 175.

227 Ovid, *Metamorphoses* 15.60–478.

in spurious Pythagorean documents, some of which might well have made their way into Juba's library.[228]

The only other comment on the library is that it had a Punic section:[229] presumably this contained Juba's copies of the works from the Carthaginian state library and the *libri punici* of his grandfather Hiempsal. These would have informed Juba about North Africa, and included authors such as Hanno. One can make obvious presumptions about others represented in the collections: Herodotos, Polybios, Berossos, Ktesias, Eudoxos of Kyzikos, Poseidonios, and Sallust were used by Juba for his geographical and historical researches, and Aristoxenos of Taras for music. Members of the scholarly milieu at Rome in which Juba grew up would also have been included, such as Varro and Alexandros Polyhistor. Assuming that Juba kept his library current during his reign, there would be additions of material published during those years, such as Livy, Dionysios of Halikarnassos, Diodoros of Sicily, Strabo, and Nikolaos of Damaskos. The text of Agrippa's map would be essential. Clearly, this is a minimal list, and any attempt to create a viable royal library would need much more, including the mainstream Greek and Roman authors from Homer through Cicero, although probably with an emphasis on the Hellenistic historical and geographical authors who are little known today. One would also expect that the flowering of Augustan literature, as it became available – Vergil, Horace, Ovid, and others – also found its way to Mauretania.

As was expected of Hellenistic-Roman monarchs, Juba and Kleopatra Selene attracted scholars and artists to their court. Few names are known. The court tragedian was one Leonteus, from Argos.[230] His teacher was Athenion, who may be the same as the author of the comedy *Samothrakians*, which Juba quoted at length, preserved by Athenaios in a discussion of cooks:[231] why and where Juba cited it is not clear, but the play may have been written at the court. The passage – forty-six lines, mostly of a speech by a cook – discusses how cooks have been part of the civilizing process of humanity.[232] The tone of the excerpt, with its emphasis on human origins, is quite Juban.

The other known member of the Mauretanian court is the royal physician Euphorbos. Nothing is known about his career other than his role in Juba's

---

228 On the book trade in late Republican Rome, see Rawson (supra note 223), pp. 41–51. But see also Holger Thesleff, *An Introduction to the Pythagorean Writings of the Hellenistic Period*, Acta Academiae Aboensis, Humaniora 24.3 (Åbo 1961), pp. 54–5, who argued that it was the actual writings of Pythagoras himself that Juba collected.

229 Ammianus Marcellinus 22.15.8; Solinus 32.2.

230 Athenaios 8.343e.

231 Athenaios 14.660–1; *PCG* 4.13–16 (=Juba, fr. 86).

232 Although the obvious place for the passage would be in Juba's *Theatrical History*, its tone of progress of civilization may mean it is from one of his historical works.

natural history researches and his modern botanical legacy,[233] but Pliny commented that he was the brother of Augustus' physician Antonius Musa.[234] The Antonian name makes it probable that the brothers were freedmen of M. Antonius, and perhaps entered Augustus' household in the service of Antonius' wife Octavia, or his daughter. Thus Euphorbos was in all probability part of the entourage that accompanied Juba and Kleopatra Selene to Mauretania in 25 BC. This indicates that some members of the royal court came from the Augustan household, possibly freedmen and freedwomen of Kleopatra Selene inherited from her father.[235] One of these, the gemcutter Gnaios, has already been discussed.[236]

No other member of the intellectual circle is known for certain. Given his closeness to the royal family, it is probable that Krinagoras of Mytilene was at the court, but there is no specific documentation.[237] An Asarubas who wrote on the geography of Mauretania may have been a member of the court.[238] L. Cornelius Bocchus, who wrote on Numidia and the Iberian peninsula, might have been the court historian or geographer.[239] One of the court mimes was named Ecloga.[240] Other freedmen and freedwomen are known by name:[241] some of the ones of Greek ancestry, such as Aischinos[242] and Philodemos,[243] may have been part of the artistic or scholarly presence.

233 Infra, pp. 178–9.

234 *NH* 25.77.

235 Other Antonii in the Juban household were Aischinos Antonianus (*CIL* 8.9344) and Cleopatra, daughter of C. Antonianus, who lived to be 23 years and 7 months of age (Maurice LeGlay, "Notule suivante," *BAC* 1955–6 [1958], 121–2), and was certainly connected to Kleopatra Selene. Julia Selene (*CIL* 8.21248) and Antonia Galatia Caecilia (M. Lenior, "Inscriptions nouvelles de Volubilis," *BAMaroc* 16, 1985–6, 208–9) are probably much later, but nonetheless descendants of members of the royal household that originated with the Antonii or Kleopatra Selene. Yet many of the freedmen and freedwomen at the court may have been indigenous (P. D. A. Garnsey, "Rome's African Empire under the Principate," in *Imperialism in the Ancient World*, ed. P. D. A. Garnsey and C. R. Whittaker [Cambridge: Cambridge University Press, 1978], pp. 247–50).

236 Supra, pp. 150–1.

237 See David M. Jacobson, "Three Roman Client Kings: Herod of Judaea, Archelaus of Cappadocia and Juba of Mauretania," *PEQ* 133, 2001, 31, who stated that Krinagoras was "almost certainly" present.

238 *NH* 37.37.

239 He was a source for Pliny (*NH* 16.216, 37.24, 97, 127) and Solinus (1.97, 2.11, 18), and may have been used by Juba: see *HRR*, CXIII–CXXV, 94–5. This may be the same Cornelius Bocchus who served with the *legio III Augusta* in Lusitania (*PIR*² C1333; Mischa Meier Bochum and Meret Strothmann Bochum, "Cornelius Bocchus," *NP* 3, 1997, 197–8).

240 *CIL* 6.10110. On mime as a literary form, see Nicholas Horsfall, "Prose and Mime," in *The Cambridge History of Classical Literature* 2: *Latin Literature*, ed. E. J. Kenney and W. V. Clausen (Cambridge: Cambridge University Press, 1982), pp. 293–4.

241 See the lists, Coltelloni-Trannoy, pp. 203, 215–17. These are usually from tombstones around Caesarea, and record many who held domestic positions at the court, such as Juba's chef C. Julius Nigeros (Leveau, *Caesarea*, p. 21) or Ptolemaios' valet Julius Narcissus (*AÉpigr* 1971, #519). P. Antius Amphio (supra note 14) may have been director of the royal architectural atelier, and a certain Iacentus perhaps commander of the palace guard (*AÉpigr* 1976, #750).

242 *CIL* 8.9344.

243 *CIL* 8.21089.

Others who are not known by name include the court secretary,[244] and the royal *stichologos*,[245] or poetic reciter.[246]

Ecloga the mime is known because she died in Rome at age 18. This emphasizes another aspect of the royal court: its continued close connections with the imperial family. Ecloga was perhaps sent from Caesarea to Rome as a bequest: others may have been the *structor* Chios Iubatianus[247] and the lady Julia Prima Iubatiana.[248] There were always interactions between the client kings and Rome. Juba and Augustus would have regularly exchanged letters, Juba seeking advice on policy and Augustus providing it. Juba maintained contact with other members of the imperial family – his eventual intimacy with Gaius Caesar, who was not born until after Juba left Rome, demonstrates this – and with the developing circle of Augustan intellectuals. He seems to have retained a friendship with Strabo for over half a century, even when they were at opposite ends of the empire. Juba certainly returned to Rome for visits, and had his own people in Rome who could keep him informed about cultural, political, and architectural activities in the capital. Kleopatra Selene would have had her own circle of correspondents, perhaps centering around her surrogate mother Octavia, and Augustus' daughter Julia, her coeval. The monarchs may even have maintained a home in the city of their upbringing, which would be one explanation for the freedmen and freedwomen who ended up there. It is perhaps unfortunate that many of the conclusions regarding the monarchs' relationship with Rome must be extrapolated from the eastern courts, which are not a good parallel since Mauretania was the only one in the west, and Roman attention tended to be directed more toward the East than the west, given the events of the 30s BC and the continuing Parthian threat. The Mauretanian court was more isolated than the eastern ones, being one of the few parts of the empire Augustus never saw, and with no record of a visit by any prominent Roman.[249]

---

244 *CIL* 8.21097.

245 *AÉpigr* 1952, #100; 1954, #210; Henriette Doisy, "Quelques inscriptions de Caesarea (Cherchel)," *MÉFRA* 64, 1952, 107–8.

246 A Juba who wrote on meter can be neither the king nor someone at his court, as his work is based on the writings of Heliodoros, of the mid–first century AC. This Juba seems to have lived in the Severan period, and may have been a descendant of a member of the royal court. See W. Kroll, "Iuba" (#3), *RE* 9, 1916, 2395–7; H. J. Rose, *A Handbook of Latin Literature from the Earliest Times to the Death of St. Augustine*, reprint of third edition (New York: Methuen, 1967), p. 453; Otto Hense, "De Iuba artigrapho," *Acta Societatis Philologiae Lipsiensis* 4, 1875, 1–320.

247 *CIL* 6.9046; Braund, *Friendly King*, p. 143. A *structor* arranged the table and served the food: Petronius 35.2; Juba, fr. 14 (Athenaios 4.170).

248 *CIL* 6.35602.

249 Suetonius, *Augustus* 47. Although this isolation raises questions as to the degree of intimacy between Augustus and Juba, it perhaps is more of a testimony to Juba's ability to run the internal affairs of his kingdom smoothly and the need for Augustus to keep a closer watch on the more unstable territories of the East, especially Herod's. Unlike that monarch, Juba had no need to make repeated trips to Rome to seek Augustan assistance in untangling his personal problems.

Unique as it was, the royal court of the Mauretanian kingdom was a rich multilingual environment. Coin legends and inscriptions were in both Greek and Latin. The library was trilingual, at least, and was a center of Greek scholarship. The kingdom was residence to a large number of Greeks, Romans, and indigenous Africans,[250] which was only to be expected in the multicultural world that was the Roman Empire, but multilingualism was more prominent at the court of Juba and Kleopatra Selene than at those of the other client monarchies. These latter may have functioned in Greek alone, or Greek and the local language, but never in Latin. The Mauretanian court was a lively and complex environment, the most scholarly of the royal courts of its era. Both the intellectual culture and the visual environment – the art and architecture – reflected this diversity. In addition to its close ties with Augustus and his immediate family, the court was linked to the indigenous African aristocracy, to the oldest of Hellenistic royal dynasties – the Ptolemies – and to an ancient family of republican Rome, the Antonii, and thus had a unique cultural blend not possible in the eastern courts.[251]

250 Gsell, vol. 8, pp. 238–40. On the royal entourage, see, further, Leveau, *Caesarea*, pp. 20–4.
251 A fine summary of the Greek qualities of the royal court is Jehan Desanges, "L'Hellénisme dans le royaume protégé de Maurétanie (25 avant J.-C.–40 après J.-C.)," *BAC* n.s. 20–1b, 1984–5 (1989), 53–61.

7

REX LITERATISSIMUS

Within half a century of Juba's death his scholarly renown was apparent. Pliny wrote that he was "more remembered for the quality of his scholarship even than for his reign,"[1] and Plutarch that "he came to be numbered as one of the most polymathic Greek scholars" and "the most learned of all kings."[2] Pliny so valued his erudition that he believed an apparent error in one of his works was the fault of copyists.[3] Even the Christian scholar Tertullian felt that Juba was one of the great pre-Christian men of learning.[4] He was compared with the famous Didymos Chalkenteros, the first century BC Alexandrian noted for his prolific erudition,[5] and was honored in the academic milieu of the Gymnasion of Ptolemaios in Athens alongside Chrysippos of Soloi, the noted Stoic philosopher of the latter third century BC.[6] At Gades in Spain, which had made Juba *duovir*, an inscription honored his learning.[7] The idea of a literary king was intriguing in antiquity – "rex literatissimus," he was called[8] – although scholarship among kings was not unusual. Archelaos of Kappadokia, Juba's sometime father-in-law and host, wrote on natural history and the regions visited by Alexander the Great, and was a source for Pliny and perhaps Juba.[9] Artavasdes II of Armenia was a tragedian and historian of note before he fatally tangled with Antonius and

---

1 *NH* 5.16: "studiorum claritate memorabilior etiam quam regno." On Juba's scholarship generally, see Stéphane Gsell, "Juba II, savant et écrivain," *RAfr* 68, 1927, 169–97.

2 Plutarch, *Caesar* 55.2: Ἑλλήνων τοῖς πολυμαθεστάτοις ἐναρίθμιος γενέσθαι συγγραφεῦσι, and *Sertorius* 9.5: τοῦ πάντων ἱστορικωτάτου βασιλέων.

3 *NH* 6.170.

4 Tertullian, *Apologeticus* 19.6.

5 Souda, Ἰόβας. On Didymos, see Rudolf Pfeiffer, *History of Classical Scholarship from the Beginnings to the End of the Hellenistic Age* (Oxford: Clarendon Press, 1968), pp. 274–9.

6 Pausanias 1.17.2.

7 Avienus, *Ora maritima* 275–83, and supra, pp. 156–7.

8 The phrase appears only in the *Liber memorialis* (38.1.2) of Lucius Ampelius, dedicated to a certain Macrinus, perhaps the emperor of AD 217–18, who was a native of Mauretania. But it seems proverbial and must have been long in use, perhaps a Latin version of Plutarch's less epigrammatic statement in the *Sertorius* (9.5).

9 *FGrHist* #123; *NH* 37.46, 95, 104, 107; Solinus 52.19; infra, pp. 219–20.

Kleopatra.[10] Herod the Great had literary ambitions.[11] There was a long intellectual tradition among the Ptolemaic kings of Egypt.[12] Juba's ancestors had scholarly inclinations. From as early as the second century BC the Numidian court was known as an intellectual center, and Juba's grandfather Hiempsal seems to have been a historian.[13] Even the Romans had their own scholarly Numa. Thus the Mediterranean world had seen many scholarly kings, but Juba was considered the outstanding exemplar of this combination of talents.

His works were soon and widely accepted.[14] The first to quote Juba seems to have been the medical author Dioskourides, shortly after the middle of the first century AC.[15] By the Flavian period, Pliny was extensively mining Juba's material,[16] and, within a few years, so was Plutarch. Of the

10 *FGrHist* #678; Plutarch, *Crassus* 33.2.

11 *FGrHist* #236.

12 Ptolemaios I (*FGrHist* #138) wrote on Alexander the Great, and Ptolemaios VIII (*FGrHist* #234) composed a wide-ranging historical work that may have discussed Juba's ancestors (Athenaios 6.229d, 12.518f–519a; infra, pp. 191–2).

13 Supra, p. 27.

14 Ironically, they do not seem to have been known to his colleague Strabo, whose remote retirement may have prevented access. His references to Juba are purely political and do not cite him as a literary source. Nevertheless, the contact between the two that seems to have begun in Rome by the 20s BC and that is implicit in Strabo's eulogistic references to the king (supra, p. 69) suggests that they corresponded throughout their lives. Whether or not any material Strabo received from Juba appears in the *Geography* cannot be accurately determined, but a possibility is at 17.3.8, on Sertorius and the tomb of Antaios. Plutarch's discussion of the same material (*Sertorius* 9) cites Juba, but does not contain the typically Juban discursus on elephants found in Strabo's version. Although Strabo's chief source here is the Roman historian Gabinius, Juba himself was mentioned in the previous chapter, and the passage has a Juban flavor and may reflect knowledge received informally from the king. On this, see W. Aly, *Strabon von Amaseia 4: Untersuchungen über Text, Aufbau und Quellen der Geographika* (Bonn: Habelt, 1957), pp. 124–5. Strabo may also have had access to Juba's theories about the source of the Nile (17.3.4, 9).

15 Juba, fr. 8b. On the date of Dioskourides, see infra, p. 178. Pomponius Mela's reference to Juba and Caesarea (1.30), published in AD 43–4 (3.49–52), and thus distinctly earlier than Dioskourides, need not to have been from his writings, especially since he was from Baetica (2.96) and might have had direct knowledge of Juba's world. On his date of publication, see Pomponius Mela (ed. A. Silberman [Paris 1988]), pp. ix–xiii; F. E. Romer, *Pomponius Mela's Description of the World* (Ann Arbor: University of Michigan Press, 1998), pp. 2–3; on his sources, see the Silberman edition, pp. xxx–xliii.

It is impossible to sustain the idea that Vitruvius in his Book 8 was indebted to Juba's *Libyka* (as suggested in the edition of Vitruvius by Ingrid D. Rowland, Thomas Noble Howe, and Michael J. Dewar [Cambridge: Cambridge University Press, 1999], p. 6). Although Juba and Vitruvius were associates, and probably exchanged information (supra p. 70), there is no evidence whatsoever that Vitruvius 8.3.24 (about the palace of Juba I at Zama) is from *Libyka*: a more probable source would be someone who was with Caesar in Africa (perhaps Vitruvius himself, Sallust, or Asinius Pollio). Horace, *Ode* 1.22.15, may also have influenced Vitruvius. Juba may have described his father's palace at Zama in *Libyka*, but his information too would have been derivative: he could not have remembered it. Even if *Libyka* had been published before *De architectura*, which is unlikely, Vitruvius had better sources than Juba.

16 Juba may have been the only Greek author Pliny used extensively and directly: see Klaus Günther Sallmann, *Die Geographie des älteren Plinius und ihrem Verhältnis zu Varro: Versuch einer Quellenanalyse*, Untersuchungen zur antiker Literatur und Geschichte 11 (Berlin 1971), p. 88.

approximately 100 known fragments of Juba's works, nearly half come from the *Natural History*, and half the remainder from the works of Plutarch and one other source, the *Deipnosophistai* of Athenaios. All three of these authors, who account for nearly seventy of the extant fragments, were, like Juba, polymathic in outlook. Athenaios and his contemporary Aelian, both active around AD 200, were probably the last to make extensive use of the actual writings of Juba (although Philostratos, in his *Life of Apollonios of Tyana*, used some of Juba's material on elephants).[17] The few later citations are mostly from Byzantine lexica and probably relied on late-antique summaries.

It is especially notable that Juba, raised in Rome in the imperial household, wrote in Greek.[18] Only *On Arabia*, dedicated to Gaius Caesar, has ever been assumed to have been written in Latin, but there is no reason other than the nationality of the dedicatee and the preservation of almost all of its fragments in Latin to believe that it was composed in that language.[19] Moreover, writing a treatise in Greek for a member of the imperial family, even when authored by another member of that family, is perfectly appropriate. Augustus' discomfort with Greek and his unwillingness to write officially in it were exceptions among the Julio-Claudians.[20] Julius Caesar seems to have written scholarly works in that language, and Tiberius was fluent.[21] The future emperor Claudius was writing his histories in Greek during the latter years of Juba's kingship.[22] There were occasional objections to the use of Greek in Rome for official purposes,[23] but it remained the scholarly language of choice for many, even those whose native language was Latin, which was perhaps natural given the almost total Greek control of education, particularly in the senatorial class in which Juba was raised.[24] Juba was fluent in Latin[25] and had never been in the Greek-speaking world before maturity, yet had grown up in a household with Greek speakers, was educated by them, and married one. He is strong

---

17 Philostratos, *Life of Apollonios* 2.13, 16 = Juba, fr. 50, 52.

18 Plutarch, *Caesar* 55.2; *Comparison of Pelopidas and Marcellus* 1.5. Plutarch, ignoring his ethnicity, classified him as a Greek scholar.

19 *NH* 6.141, 12.55–6 (which seems to make it clear that the work was in Greek), 32.10.

20 Suetonius, *Augustus* 89.

21 Jorma Kaimio, *The Romans and the Greek Language*, Commentationes Humanarum Litterarum 64, 1979, pp. 130–3.

22 *FGrHist* #276. No contact between Claudius and Juba is documented, but since the emperor wrote on Carthage (Suetonius, *Claudius* 42), he might have had interest in the Carthaginian state library that was in Juba's hands, as well as Juba's ancestors, and since the two were cousins (if only by marriage) with similar professional interests, at the very least there may have been correspondence.

23 Suetonius, *Tiberius* 71.

24 Kaimio (supra note 21), pp. 266–71. Cicero (*Pro Archia* 23) drew attention to the far wider acceptance of Greek than Latin.

25 Despite the skepticism of Jacoby, *Commentary*, pp. 318–19.

testimony of the influence of the Greek language on Roman scholarship in early imperial Rome.[26]

It is not possible to create anything more than a speculative chronology of Juba's writings. The only work that has any precise temporal significance is the Arabian treatise dedicated to Gaius Caesar, which was completed – or well under way – before the latter's death in AD 4. The *Libyka* must date to before this time, but after Juba's accession as king, or during the period 25–2 BC, since it not only established Juba's reputation as a geographer and explorer, but also led to his appointment with Gaius. The treatise on euphorbion was also written after he became king, since he or his physician discovered the plant in the Atlas Mountains. No other work of Juba's can be dated with even this vague precision, but some assumptions may be made. It seems that his career as a scholar began before he left Rome. Early works are probably those on Roman history and linguistics: researching natural history, geography, and the remoter regions of the world requires a broader and more mature outlook. The *Roman Archaeology* or *Roman History* and the *Resemblances*, both on early Roman history and culture, parallel contemporary scholarship in Rome and are the type of work an emerging young scholar might write. During Juba's youth, Dionysios of Halikarnassos was writing his own *Roman Archaeology*, and Juba's work of the same name may have been his earliest literary creation.

Roman Archaeology

In writing a *Roman Archaeology*,[27] Juba was continuing a concept that had originated in the third century BC with Hieronymos of Kardia.[28] Roman antiquarianism of the Augustan period increased the popularity of the topic:

26 Kaimio (supra note 21), p. 237. Ironically, Juba may have been least fluent in his native Punic, since he might not have been old enough to retain it when he came to Rome, although contact with the Numidian exile community in Rome (supra, p. 70) may have kept his knowledge alive. It is difficult to credit the view of Jehan Desanges ("L'Hellénisme dans le royaume protégé du Maurétanie [25 avant J.-C.–40 après J.-C.]," *BAC* n.s. 20–1b, 1984–5 [1989], 54) that Juba's reason for writing in Greek was that he had learned it as a child before coming to Rome. Although Numidian royalty certainly knew Greek, Juba was separated from his family at an exceedingly young age – Desanges admitted that knowledge of Greek would make him "très précoce" – and grew up in a Latin-speaking family. The decision to write in Greek would not have been made until many years after he came to Italy, and would have resulted from his education and the contemporary status of scholarship in Rome.

27 Jacoby, *RE*, pp. 2392–4 and his *Commentary*, pp. 330–1. The title is either *Roman Archaeology* (fr. 12) or *Roman History* (fr. 10).

28 Dionysios of Halikarnassos, *Roman Archaeology* 1.6.1. On the *Archaeology* of Hieronymos, which does not seem to have involved autopsy, see Jane Hornblower, *Hieronymus of Cardia* (Oxford: Oxford University Press, 1981), pp. 140–4. His main sources were those who had been in Italy with Pyrrhos of Epeiros, and Italians who came east. On Greek historical attitudes toward Roman origins, see Emilio Gabba, *Dionysios and the History of Archaic Rome* (Berkeley: University of California Press, 1991), pp. 13–15.

Varro produced the definitive Latin version.[29] It was a reasonable field in which a young scholar could first show his talents, a viable and politically correct topic. The arrival of Dionysios in Rome around 30 BC may have been Juba's immediate stimulus.[30] Juba's work need not have been extensive or comprehensive, although the cited length of only two books is remarkably brief, and suggests that it may have been part of a more thorough treatise on Roman origins.[31] The definitive fragments indicate that the chronological scope was from the mythological foundation of Italy to at least the Spanish wars of the second century BC.[32] Since the founding of Ostia was placed in the first book but the Spanish wars in the second, the division between books was perhaps in the third century BC. If Plutarch's citation of Juba regarding Chaironeia in 86 BC[33] is from the *Archaeology*, this is the latest event known to have been included. Other material from the *Archaeology* appears in Plutarch's *Roman Questions*, including information about the Temple of Diana on the Aventine (which Juba may have derived from Varro's *Antiquitates rerum humanarum*),[34] on the cult of Hercules Musarum,[35] and on the Quirinalia.[36] All of these were of particular relevance to the Augustan regime. The Temple of Diana was rebuilt by L. Cornificius, probably the consul of 35 BC.[37] The temple of Hercules Musarum was restored in 29 BC by L. Marcius Philippus, either the stepfather or the half-brother of Octavian.[38] The Quirinalia also gained new importance during the early Empire, since the Temple of Quirinus had burned in 49 BC and was rebuilt by Augustus.[39] It seems no accident that these fragments of Juba's

---

29 On the development of Roman antiquarianism in the late Republic, and into the Augustan period, see Elizabeth Rawson, *Intellectual Life in the Late Roman Republic* (London: Duckworth, 1985), pp. 233–49.

30 Juba and Dionysios have remarkably similar wording in several places, but it is impossible to tell who came first (Juba, fr. 9 = Dionysios 1.9.3; fr. 10 = Dionysios 1.9.2; fr. 11 = Dionysios 1.59.3).

31 Assumption of a length of only two books requires a literal reading of Stephanos of Byzantion (Juba, fr. 10): Jacoby, *RE*, p. 2392; Gsell, vol. 8, p. 264. Dionysios may have referred to Juba's work when he wrote in his preface (*Roman Archaeology* 1.5.4) that only brief and summary works had previously appeared in Greek on Roman history. The remarkable brevity of a two-book composition – remindful of the history of Velleius – makes it possible that the *Archaeology* was merely part of the lengthy (at least fifteen books) *Resemblances*, which also dealt with early Roman culture.

32 Juba, frs. 9, 11, 12.

33 Plutarch, *Sulla* 16.8 = Juba, fr. 27.

34 Plutarch, *Roman Question* 4 = Juba, fr. 91.

35 Plutarch, *Roman Question* 59 = Juba, fr. 92. *Roman Questions* 18, 60, and 90, all dealing with the cult of Hercules, may also have come from the *Archaeology*, as may *Roman Question* 54, which, although not on the cult of Hercules, connects with 59. See H. J. Rose, *The Roman Questions of Plutarch* (Oxford: Clarendon Press, 1924), pp. 22–7.

36 *Roman Question* 89 = Juba, fr. 94. Plutarch, *Romulus* 14.6 (=Juba, fr. 23), on the Rape of the Sabines, may be another fragment, but its linguistic context may place it in the *Resemblances*.

37 Suetonius, *Augustus* 29.5; Broughton, vol. 2, p. 406.

38 Suetonius, *Augustus* 29; *NTDAR*, p. 187.

39 Augustus, *Res gestae* 19; Dio 41.14.3, 54.19.4.

Archaeology focus on elements of early Roman cult and history that enhanced the Augustan image.[40]

It may thus be possible to create a picture of the *Archaeology*. A brief work, it examined matters topical in Rome during the early Augustan period, especially the history of the cults that were in the process of being rejuvenated. In writing on Roman origins, Juba may have felt much as Dionysios: that Roman supremacy far exceeded those of others, something due not to chance but to the moral superiority of the Roman character, and, especially, Rome's Greek origins. Rome, according to Dionysios, had produced countless examples of virtue, piety, and justice, even surpassing the Greeks.[41] Much of the detail of Juba's *Archaeology* was probably on the regal period, although there was a summary of events at least through the time of Sulla. Emphasis was on issues in Roman history that impacted on Juba's ancestors and his ancestral lands, such as the cult of Herakles.[42] Juba's discussion of the Spanish wars of the second century BC examined the destruction of Numantia by Scipio Aemilianus in 133 BC, a campaign involving a family patron and another famous ancestor, Jugurtha.[43] Consideration of the Temple of Diana on the Aventine would have led to comments on its rebuilder Cornificius, and the circumstances under which the rebuilding took place: his triumph *ex Africa* of 32 BC, which 16-year-old Juba probably witnessed.[44] Cornificius had spent two years as proconsul in Africa and would have been a valuable local contact for Juba regarding his ancestral world. Juba may also have emphasized the distinguished ancestors of his close friends, as his enthusiastic praise of M. Claudius Marcellus, the hero of the Second Punic War,[45] may have been inspired by his companionship with Augustus' nephew. Praise of the Claudii Marcelli would certainly have been appreciated in early Augustan Rome, especially by Juba's surrogate mother Octavia, and since the passage is highly eulogistic, it perhaps originated within the family itself, possibly even from Augustus' funeral oration for his nephew.[46]

The *Archaeology* also shows the brashness of youth. Juba dared publicly to disagree with Sulla's own account of the Mithradatic War,[47] writing that

---

40 Plutarch's other citations of Juba's early Roman material are linguistically based, and thus come from the *Resemblances*, even though illustrative of early cult and history: see frs. 88–90, 93, 95.

41 Dionysios, *Roman Archaeology* 1.2–5. Dionysios also wrote to correct the errors of others, who presumably did not understand or respect Roman supremacy: this may also have been one of Juba's goals.

42 On his alleged descent, see supra, pp. 154–5.

43 Juba, fr. 12; Sallust, *Jugurtha* 7–8.

44 Frederick W. Shipley, "Chronology of the Building Operations in Rome from the Death of Caesar to the Death of Augustus," *MAAR* 9, 1931, 30–2.

45 Plutarch, *Comparison of Pelopidas and Marcellus* 1.5–7 = Juba, fr. 25.

46 Augustus, *Operum fragmenti* (ed. Malcovati) 76.

47 Plutarch, *Sulla* 16.8 = Juba, fr. 27. On Sulla's memoirs, see E. Badian, "The Early Historians," in *Latin Historians*, ed. T. A. Dorey (London: Routledge and Kegan Paul, 1966), p. 25.

one Ericius, not Aulus Gabinius, had saved Chaironeia in 86 BC. His source may have been a descendant of Ericius. It seems unlikely that Juba would have made this point unless he believed that he had solid information, for he was elevating the deeds of an obscure family[48] at the expense of a famous one, as a second Aulus Gabinius, perhaps the nephew or son of the newly discredited defender of Chaironeia, had had one of the most distinguished careers of the latest Republic.[49] In replacing the deeds of an immediate ancestor of one of the most famous names of the previous generation with an obscurity, Juba showed daring (or foolishness), but his information was taken seriously by the diligent Plutarch.

Material similar to that in the *Archaeology* appears in the works of Livy, Varro, Dionysios of Halikarnassos, C. Sulpicius Galba, and Verrius Flaccus. Varro died when Juba was about 20, and the others were roughly Juba's contemporaries. Dionysios' *Archaeology* began to be published around 7 BC,[50] and Livy's *Annals* probably began to appear in the 20s BC,[51] but there is no specific information regarding publication dates for Galba and Flaccus. Although in one case Juba quoted Galba,[52] it seems unlikely that he would have made heavy use of authors who were his contemporaries working on the same material. It is more probable that a group of young scholars would have had informal contact and exchange – perhaps this is the "school of Juba" mentioned by Plutarch – expressing similar ideas in their works.[53] Even the identical wording of Juba and Dionysios proves nothing, as it cannot be shown who quoted whom, or whether both took the phrase from a common source, perhaps Varro. The fragments of the *Archaeology* credit no source other than Galba. Varro is perhaps apparent in the discussion of the ritual of Hercules,[54] but not on the cult of Diana, since Plutarch indicated

---

48 The family of Ericius is virtually unknown from the early first century BC until it reemerged in the second century AC: *PIR*² E94–7.

49 Broughton, vol. 2, p. 570.

50 Dionysios of Halikarnassos, *Roman Archaeology* 1.3.4.

51 Livy 1.19 has the name Augustus (not possible before 27 BC) and refers to closings of the Temple of Janus, but only up to 29 BC. He did not mention the subsequent closing in 25 BC (recorded by Dio 53.26.5). Hence it is probable that the earlier part of the work appeared around 27–25 BC.

52 Plutarch, *Romulus* 17.5 = Juba, fr. 24. C. Sulpicius Galba (*PIR*² S720), grandfather of the emperor, is little known. He wrote a history which was "multiplex" and "incuriosa" (Suetonius, *Galba* 3.3), and, in a statement reminiscent of Pliny's on Juba (*NH* 5.16), was said to be "more distinguished in his scholarship than his esteem" ("clarior studiis quam dignitate"). His dates can only be assumed by the careers of his grandson, and his son of the same name, who was consul in AD 22 (*PIR*² S721). The extent and exact subject of his history are unknown, although he was used by Pliny (*NH* 1.36) in his section on stones, sculpture, and building materials. The only extant citation is the discussion of the prosecution of Tarpeius by the Romans, and it is noteworthy that Plutarch, writing somewhat over a century later, did not have a text of Galba at hand, perhaps indicating that the material Juba quoted was never published.

53 Plutarch, *Roman Question* 24.

54 Rose (supra note 35), pp. 21–2.

that Juba's material was more detailed than Varro's.[55] Plutarch's extensive use of Juba's treatise throughout the *Roman Questions* shows that he felt Juba to be a major source, not merely an imitator. In fact, of all the Augustan sources that Plutarch used for early Roman history, Juba is ranked as the most reliable. Varro is criticized more than once. Livy is quoted only once in the *Roman Questions* and is conspicuously absent from the lives of Romulus and Numa.[56] Verrius Flaccus is nowhere mentioned, and Galba only as a source for Juba. Dionysios is cited twice: once where his view is held to be inferior to that of Juba, the other where he is said to be wrong.[57] Only Juba escaped Plutarch's criticism, an indication of the scholarly esteem in which he was held over half a century after his death.[58]

Most of the extant fragments of the *Archaeology* are from the earliest period of Roman history. It seems that Juba quickly gained a reputation as the definitive scholar on at least certain aspects of early Roman history, eclipsing, for a time, his two contemporaries who survive today, Livy and Dionysios. As a member of the imperial family – a status afforded no other historian of the era – Juba may have had access to archival material not used by other scholars. The example of the emperor Claudius indicates that historiography was encouraged – or at least tolerated – within the imperial family,[59] but like Claudius, Juba may have realized that the remote past was the safest topic.

Resemblances

The second work that may be part of Juba's juvenilia is the *Resemblances* (Ὁμοιότητες).[60] Plutarch provided an insight into the composition of this work when he wrote that Juba strove (γλιχόμενος) to derive Latin words from Greek.[61] The Greek origin of all things Roman was a topical sentiment in the early Augustan period, which led naturally to an interest in the origin of various terms in the Latin language and their relationship to Greek.[62] The longer of the two titled fragments of the *Resemblances* makes this function clear, comparing Greek τραπεζοκόμος to Latin *structor*.[63] Unlike the

---

55 Plutarch, *Roman Question* 4; see also *Roman Question* 5, where Plutarch displayed contempt for Varro's interpretation of a strange practice.

56 Plutarch, *Roman Question* 25.

57 Plutarch, *Roman Question* 78; *Romulus* 16.8.

58 Remarkably, this scholarly esteem has not continued to the present, and Juba has tended to be ignored as a source for early Roman history.

59 Suetonius, *Claudius* 41.

60 Jacoby, *RE*, p. 2394; Jacoby, *Commentary*, pp. 331–2; Rose (supra note 35), pp. 20–7.

61 Plutarch, *Numa* 13.6.

62 Dionysios of Halikarnassos, *Roman Archaeology* 1.5.1; Varro, *De lingua latina* 5.21, 77–9 (and elsewhere).

63 Juba, fr. 14 = Athenaios 4.170e.

Archaeology, this was not a brief and superficial work, since it ran to at least fifteen books.[64] As a genre, a study of linguistic resemblances is a product of the Hellenistic period: the earliest known example is that of Sosibios of Sparta, probably of the early second century BC.[65] But the comparative concept was intensely popular in the Augustan period, especially among Greek authors who sought to fit their own Greek heritage into the emergent greatness of Rome and who saw Roman culture as an imitation of that of Greece. This attitude is perhaps most apparent in the *Archaeology* of Dionysios, but also affected Strabo.[66] Juba was no different from his contemporaries. Varro, the preeminent author of the previous generation on the Latin language, was one of Juba's major sources.[67] As with the *Archaeology*, Juba was taking advantage of a topic whose legitimacy had already been established.

Only two fragments mention the *Resemblances* by name.[68] Both are linguistically based. From this it is possible to assume that a number of linguistic comments by Plutarch that are attributed to Juba, both in the *Roman Questions* and the biographies of early Romans, also come from the *Resemblances*. But both it and the *Archaeology* examined early Rome, and it is difficult to separate the two. As an example, one may compare two passages in Plutarch's *Romulus* attributed to Juba.[69] The former concerns the number of Sabine women abducted: Juba's count of 683 is contrasted with the 527 of his predecessor Valerius Antias.[70] There seems nothing linguistic here, but immediately previously Plutarch had noted that some unnamed author recorded that only thirty women were taken, and this was why there were thirty *curiae* in Rome. The discussion of the Sabine women continues, citing but rejecting Zenodotos of Troizen,[71] and then turns to a long examination of the word *talasia* and its meaning in Roman cult and customs.[72] At this point Juba is cited again, which would suggest strongly that he had been the main source all along, others being included merely for Plutarch to disagree with or to reject.

---

64 Juba, fr. 13.

65 *FGrHist* #595. Sosibios is the best-known example of the rebirth of cultural awareness in Hellenistic Sparta. See Paul Cartledge and Antony Spawforth, *Hellenistic and Roman Sparta: A Tale of Two Cities* (London: Routledge, 1989), pp. 176–7.

66 Strabo 3.4.19.

67 For example, compare Juba, fr. 88 with Varro, *De lingua latina* 5.84, and fr. 95 with Varro 6.27.

68 Juba, fr. 13, 14.

69 Plutarch, *Romulus* 14.6 = Juba, fr. 23; 15.3 = fr. 90.

70 *HRR*, CCCV–CCCXXXIII. He seems to have been active around the middle of the first century BC and was a source for Livy.

71 *FGrHist* #821: little known, he probably lived in the second century BC. He was used by Dionysios of Halikarnassos (*Roman Archaeology* 2.49).

72 This topic Plutarch also discussed in *Roman Question* 31, which may also be from Juba. Livy was clearly not a source (see Livy 1.9.12–16), but Varro may have been (Festus 351: see Jacoby, *Commentary*, p. 351).

Another topic of the *Resemblances* was the linguistic origins of the Roman calendar. Again, one might argue that such material could just as easily belong in the *Archaeology*, but the linguistic basis of the arguments makes the former work the more probable source. Plutarch's detailed examination of the structure of the month provides Greek etymologies for the kalends, ides, and nones, and thus is typically Juban.[73] By contrast, *Roman Question* 34, also involving the calendar, is not from Juba, which would be apparent even if Plutarch had not provided the source, Cicero,[74] since there is no linguistic context. These two examples show that Juba's material regarding the calendar was not a general discussion, but about various etymologies. This is reinforced by Athenaios' use of Juba for the origin of the name of the month of February, which parallels the similar but unattributed discussion by Plutarch in the *Romulus*.[75] Thus it seems that Juba used available information about the calendar, probably in part from Varro, to create a linguistic analysis of the origins of calendrical terms.[76] Other topics in the *Resemblances* may include certain cultic terms from the period of Numa,[77] omens,[78] and even household and cooking terminology.[79] A number of obscure etymologies in the Hesychios lexicon may also be from the same work.[80]

The *Resemblances*, then, discussed the origin of Latin historical and cultic terms, and perhaps details of material culture, with a particular emphasis on the similarities between Latin and Greek. Varro may have been a primary source, but it is difficult to imagine how Juba could have filled fifteen books on such a topic.[81] Fifteen (or more) books, essentially the length of Strabo's *Geography*, coupled with the scantiness of the *Archaeology* – only two books – again leads to the conclusion that the *Resemblances*, *Archaeology*, and perhaps even the *Roman History*, if a separate title, were all a single juvenile work on early Roman culture, much like the contemporary efforts of Dionysios and others.

---

73 Plutarch, *Roman Question* 24 = Juba, fr. 95.

74 Cicero, *Laws* 2.21.54.

75 Athenaios 3.98 = Juba, fr. 96; Plutarch, *Romulus* 21.3; see also Livy 1.5.1–2 and Varro, *De lingua latina* 6.13, 33–4.

76 It is perhaps a mistake to assume that every unattributed discussion made by Plutarch on the chronology of the calendar came from the *Resemblances*. *Roman Question* 19, for example, has no linguistic information. More possible is *Numa* 18–19, the names of the months, but even this does not have the comparative tone of the *Resemblances*.

77 Plutarch, *Numa* 7.5 = Juba, fr. 88; 13.5–6 = fr. 89. But Varro (*De lingua latina* 5.84) is also apparent, and it was a topic discussed by Dionysios (*Roman Archaeology* 2.64).

78 Plutarch, *Roman Question* 78 = Juba, fr. 93.

79 Athenaios 6.229c = Juba, fr. 87, perhaps from a Ptolemaic source. Athenaios 14.660e (=Juba, fr. 86), also discussing cooking, is more probably from the *Theatrical History*.

80 The most likely is κυλίκεια (fr. 99), since it is within the category of household terminology. Less probable are Βρίγες (fr. 98), an Asian people (perhaps from one of the geographical works), and λιβυφοίτην (fr. 100), a word elsewhere unknown but most likely from *Libyka*.

81 The number of books rests on a single citation in the Hesychios lexicon (Juba, fr. 13).

Yet on certain topics the *Resemblances* long remained the preferred source. For example, Plutarch's discussion of omens[82] demonstrates how he considered Juba superior to Dionysios, Varro, and Livy, all of whom were available to Plutarch and examined the same topic.[83] Although the descriptions overlap and often have similar wording – this is particularly true of Dionysios and Juba – Varro and Livy were not mentioned and Dionysios, despite his remarkable similarity to Juba, was judged to be inferior.

On Painting

Juba's most obscure work, *On Painting*, may also be a youthful composition. It did not receive the scholarly endorsement that was given the writings on Roman history. It and the *Theatrical History* are Juba's only treatises not used by Pliny or Plutarch, and modern knowledge of *On Painting* rests on skimpy data, none of them earlier than the second century AC. Although at least eight books long,[84] it cannot have been more than derivative, which is another reason to consider it an early work. The only author to cite it was the lexicographer Harpokration of Alexandria, in the second century AC, who provided short biographies of the painters Parrhasios of Ephesos and Polygnotos of Thasos.[85] Neither summary contains any material not cited elsewhere, especially by Pliny,[86] and it is somewhat of a mystery what the value of Juba's work was to Harpokration. Pliny's chapters on painting made no use of Juba as a historical source:[87] he had access to Parrhasios' own writings and many others for the history of the genre.[88]

Certain similarities in the careers of Parrhasios and Polygnotos may indicate the emphasis of Juba's work. Both were foreigners who came to Athens and were greatly honored for their art. Juba might have had particular sympathy for attempts by foreigners to become accepted in the cultural milieu of a new city. More important, both had paintings on display in the Rome of Juba's day. Polygnotos' work was in the Portico of Pompeius, moved there

---

82 Plutarch, *Roman Question* 78.

83 Dionysios, *Roman Archaeology* 2.5; Varro, *De lingua latina* 7.97; Livy 1.18.7–10.

84 Juba, fr. 20.

85 Juba, fr. 20–1. It is also mentioned, without comment, in Photios' *Bibliotheka* (*FGrHist* #275, T15). The title is Περὶ ζωγράφων at fr. 20, and Περὶ γραφικῆς at fr. 21 and in the Photios lexicon. Douris of Samos, the *tyrannos* of that island and polymath in the early Hellenistic period, wrote a Περὶ ζωγραφίας (Diogenes Laertios 1.38; on Douris, see Robert B. Kebric, *In the Shadow of Macedon: Duris of Samos* [*Historia* Supplement 29, 1977], who, however, passed over his work on painting [pp. 10, 24], and Andrew Dalby, "The Curriculum Vitae of Duris of Samos," *CQ* n.s. 41, 1991, 539–41). Anaximenes of Lampsakos, perhaps slightly later, may have written on the same topic: the title is preserved only in Latin (*De picturis antiquis*, *FGrHist* #72, fr. 40). On Harpokration, see Nigel Guy Wilson, "Harpocration, Valerius," *OCD*³, 1996, 667.

86 *NH* 35.60, 67–72 (Parrhasios); 35.58–9 (Polygnotos): see Jacoby, *Commentary*, p. 333.

87 Juba was only cited once, probably from the *Libyka*, on pigments and dyes (*NH* 35.39 = Juba, fr. 74).

88 *NH* 1.35.

from Pompeius' Curia when that structure was closed off after being the site of Julius Caesar's assassination.[89] Parrhasios' painting of Theseus stood in the Temple of Juppiter on the Capitol, and his rendition of the high priest of Kybele was in the possession of the imperial family at least by the time of Tiberius.[90] It seems more than coincidence that the only artists known from the extant fragments of Juba's *On Painting* had works conspicuously visible in Juba's Rome. Hence the treatise may have centered on a discussion of Greek painters whose art was accessible to contemporary Romans, and thus would have been of little importance to future scholars who had far better sources on the history of painting. Although it survived until at least the second century AC, even by the time of Pliny it was of no interest to the scholarly community.

Theatrical History

The *Theatrical History*[91] may also have been a juvenile work, but Juba retained an interest in the theater throughout his life. It was at least seventeen books long.[92] Most of the extant fragments are from the *Deipnosophistai* of Athenaios. Like *On Painting*, it was not used by Pliny or, probably, Plutarch,[93] or any author earlier than Athenaios with the possible exception of the obscure Amarantos of Alexandria, in his Περὶ σκηνῆς.[94] The silence of Plutarch and Pliny is less of a criticism than for *On Painting*, as Pliny's discussion of the theater is limited to the city of Rome and is largely based on architectural details: his sources were Vitruvius and various Roman historians.[95] Plutarch mentioned theaters only in a similar context.[96] Neither showed an interest in the actual production of drama and comedy, the focus of Juba's treatise. Virtually all the known citations of Juba's work concern musical instruments and dance, most coming from a single section of the *Deipnosophistai* that quotes several major authorities on ancient music.[97]

89 *NH* 35.59; *NTDAR* 104. The topic is not known.

90 *NH* 35.69–70.

91 Jacoby, *RE*, p. 2395.

92 This is recorded in the Photios lexicon: *FGrHist* #275, T15.

93 The only possibility that Plutarch might have used the *Theatrical History* is in *Whether Land or Sea Animals Are Wiser* (3, 961e), a discussion of the effect of music on animals. Here the rare word φώτινξ is cited, one of the musical instruments discussed by Juba (Athenaios 4.175e = Juba, fr. 16; also Athenaios 4.182e). Juba was Plutarch's source elsewhere in this essay (17, 25) for elephants, and the conflation of topics seems Juban. See also Aelian, *On the Characteristics of Animals* 6.31, probably from the same source.

94 Juba, fr. 104; for Amarantos, see G. Wentzel, "Amarantos" (#3), *RE* 1, 1894, 1728–9. His dates cannot be fixed any more precisely than between Juba and Galen of Pergamon.

95 *NH* 1.36; 36.5, 50, 102, 113–20, 189.

96 Plutarch, *Pompeius* 42.4; *Marcellus* 30.6.

97 Athenaios 4.175–83 = Juba, frs. 15, 16, 81–4. See the commentary on this passage in Andrew Barker (ed.), *Greek Musical Writings* (Cambridge: Cambridge University Press, 1984–9), vol. 1, pp. 258–303.

Some of these are mainstream scholars such as Plato, Xenophon, and Ephoros, but many are obscure to the modern reader. In particular there is Aristoxenos of Taras, one of the preeminent writers on music, cited repeatedly by Athenaios and perhaps Juba's main source. A member of the Tarantine school that became interested in Roman origins and their possible Pythagorean connections,[98] he studied in Athens with the Pythagorean Xenophilos and then with Aristotle. Polymathic, as would befit his teacher's student, he was best remembered for his writings on harmony and rhythm, although he also wrote about musical instruments.[99]

Other sources include Archytas, also from Taras, a Pythagorean of the early third century BC who wrote Περὶ αὐλῶν,[100] a virtually unknown Aristokles, author of Περὶ χορῶν,[101] probably from the late second century BC, a certain Euphranor, also a Pythagorean, who also wrote a Περὶ αὐλῶν, Douris of Samos, who also wrote on painting,[102] and the Stoic polymath Poseidonios, who wrote in the late second and early first century BC.[103] Not unexpectedly, many of the sources are Pythagorean (a reminder of Juba's own interest in that discipline), some of the same Tarantine Pythagoreans who may have affected Juba's writing of Roman history: Aristoxenos seems to have been the first to put forth the idea that the Roman king Numa had been a disciple of Pythagoras.[104] Thus it seems that Juba's *Theatrical History* was based on a number of Pythagorean authors on music. There was also another Pythagoras, on the staff of Ptolemaios II: Athenaios' use of this Pythagoras was probably through Juba.[105] In fact the entire Athenaian passage on music, citing as it does a variety of Greek and Roman authors and quoting from a number of plays, but mentioning Juba more frequently than any other source, may be almost totally from the *Theatrical History*.[106] Athenaios' banqueters have been discussing their usual topic, cooking, when at 4.174 the conversation took an abrupt turn.[107] The pleasant sounds of an

---

98 This idea was succinctly expressed by Ovid (*Metamorphoses* 15.479–81). On this issue, see Emilio Gabba, "Considerazioni sulla tradizione letteraria sulle origini della Repubblica," in *Les Origines de la République romaine*, EntrHardt 13 (1967), 153–63.

99 On Aristoxenos, see Barker (supra note 97), vol. 2, pp. 119–25.

100 Barker (supra note 97), vol. 2, p. 29.

101 On the identity of this Aristokles, which is not certain, see G. Wentzel, "Aristokles" (#18), *RE* 2, 1895, 935–7.

102 *FGrHist* #76; Kebric (supra note 85), pp. 10, 24.

103 *FGrHist* #87.

104 Gabba (supra note 28), pp. 13–14. On Numa's writings, see Andreas Willi, "Numa's Dangerous Books," *MusHelv* 55, 1998, 139–72.

105 Juba, fr. 76.

106 Heinz-Günther Nesselrath, *Die attische Mittlere Komödie*, Untersuchungen zur antiken Literatur und Geschichte 36 (Berlin 1990), p. 85.

107 On the difficulty of assessing Athenaios' writings on music, see Andrew Barker, "Athenaeus on Music," in *Athenaeus and His World: Reading Greek Culture in the Roman Empire*, ed. David Braund and John Wilkins (Exeter, U.K.: University of Exeter Press, 2000), pp. 434–44.

ὕδραυλις were heard, a water organ of a type invented by Ktesibios of Alexandria, the noted engineer of the third century BC.[108] The musician at the banquet, Alkeides, then launched into a detailed description of the instrument, continuing to a discussion of pipes, citing source after source, including Juba, introduced by name at 4.175d with his account of the τρίγωνον. Comments on other instruments follow, with frequent reference to Juba. The catalogic nature of the material indicates that a significant portion of the *Theatrical History* was a list of instruments and their uses. Over fifty sources are cited, but Juba is mentioned again and again as the primary one upon which Alkeides is dependent. The entire passage on instruments is a long speech by the musician, either a direct quotation or a paraphrase from the *Theatrical History*. Significantly, none of the authors cited by Alkeides is later than Juba – Tryphon of Alexandria, perhaps Juba's contemporary, is the only one close to the king's date – and Athenaios' sources here seem to parallel those used by Juba in other writings. There is a distinct Pythagorean tone to the entire passage. Some of the citations seem more relevant to Juba's type of scholarship than to the issues examined by Athenaios. And then there is an ending as abrupt as the beginning. Alkeides made no conclusion but merely stopped speaking. A sentence of narrative by Athenaios brings the book to a close, and the opening of Book 5 is on an unrelated topic. Juba was not to be mentioned again until Book 6.

The dozen musical instruments recorded from Juba's *Theatrical History* are mostly well known in Greek literature from the classical period onward.[109] Only two are unusual, the λυροφοῖνιξ, the Phoenician lyre,[110] and the ἐπιγόνειον, a stringed instrument named after Epigonos of Sikyon.[111] Neither of these unique citations sheds any light on the composition of the *Theatrical History*. The same can be said for the dances Juba described. He is the only one to use the common word κλωπεία, normally meaning "theft," for a dance,[112] and the meaning of φαινίνδα – whether a dance or game – is

---

108 On Ktesibios, see A. G. Drachmann, *Ktesibios, Philon and Heron: A Study in Ancient Pneumatics*, Acta Historica Scientiarum Naturalium et Medicinalium 4 (Copenhagen 1948), especially pp. 1–16; P. M. Fraser, *Ptolemaic Alexandria* (Oxford: Clarendon Press, 1972), vol. 1, pp. 427–32. The earliest and most detailed source on the engineer is Vitruvius 9.8.2–7, 10.7–8 (who called the water organ a *hydraulus* or *hydraulica machina*), using Ktesibios' own writings. It is not clear whether Juba was one of Athenaios' sources for the water organ: the material from Juba may begin only with the discussion of pipes. Athenaios did not use Ktesibios' own treatise but rather the works of the shadowy Aristokles (used frequently by Juba in the *Theatrical History*) and the Augustan grammarian Tryphon of Alexandria (Athenaios 4.174), yet Juba may have been an intermediate source.

109 Although most of the citations come from the *Deipnosophistai*, some are extant in the Hesychios lexicon (Juba, fr. 15b, 85). One of these, βλίτυρι, the sound made by a harp string, indicates that Juba's focus was as much on music itself as on instruments.

110 Juba, fr. 15a, 84.

111 Juba, fr. 84. On Epigonos, see Barker, *Greek Musical Writings* (supra note 97), vol. 1, p. 270.

112 Juba, fr. 17.

unclear,[113] although he knew the name of the eponymous inventor, one Phainestios, and that the word was used by the fourth century BC comic poet Antiphanes. He also discussed the Persian dance known as the ὄκλασμα, which involved dipping or squatting down and was known to Aristophanes.[114] Other probable citations from the *Theatrical History* are less certain, but it may have included a discussion of the number of actors in plays.[115] The quotations from comic poets in the *Deipnosophistai* that are juxtaposed with quotations from Juba's treatise show that it was heavily slanted toward comedy.[116] Seventeen books is a lengthy work to be centered on the terminology of comedy – although such an emphasis on words is quite Juban – but there is no evidence as to whether the treatise included a discussion of the physical theater itself or the history of the art. Even if it did, Juba's contributions were not profound enough to be used by later scholars.

The Wanderings of Hanno

According to Athenaios,[117] this was a work separate from its expected context, within *Libyka*. It presumably was a commentary and translation of the report of the great Carthaginian explorer Hanno. The original would have been available to Juba in Sallust's library, perhaps already translated into Greek. Although most commentators have ignored this work,[118] it would have been a way for Juba first to approach issues regarding exploration and knowledge of northwest Africa, topics that would be important to him for most of his life, as well as to begin to learn about parts of his ancestral heritage.[119] Except for Athenaios' bald statement and possibly the unique word λιβυφοίτης, "frequenter of Libya," in the Hesychios lexicon,[120] no trace of the work survives unless it is the extant Greek translation of Hanno.

---

113 Juba, fr. 80. Stephen G. Miller ("Architecture as Evidence for the Identity of the Early *Polis*," in *Sources for the Ancient Greek City State*, ed. Mogens Herman Hansen [Copenhagen: Munksgaard, 1995], p. 228) would identify this as a game, and connect it with Juba's probable restoration of the Gymnasion of Ptolemaios in Athens. This is possible, but it seems unlikely to have been part of a separate treatise, and since Juba discussed many dances, it fits better as a part of the *Theatrical History*.

114 Aristophanes, fr. 344b; see also *Thesmophoriazousai* 1175 and the scholiast on that passage (=Juba, fr. 18).

115 Juba, fr. 19.

116 Juba, frs. 17, 80, 86. In particular, there is the lengthy citation (forty-six lines) from the *Samothrakians* of Athenion. See Nesselrath (supra note 106), pp. 71–2.

117 Athenaios 3.83c = Juba, fr. 6.

118 For example, Gsell, vol. 8, p. 262; Jacoby, *Commentary*, pp. 328–9. Exceptions include Victor J. Matthews, "The *libri punici* of King Hiempsal," *AJP* 93, 1972, 333–4; Jehan Desanges, *Recherches sur l'activité des Méditerranéens aux confins de l'Afrique*, CÉFR 38, 1978, 39–85; and Coltelloni-Trannoy, p. 138.

119 For more about Hanno and Juba see infra, Chapter 8, note 22.

120 Juba, fr. 100. This is remindful of, and may even be an error for, Λιβυφοίνικα, "Liby-Phoenicians," used by Hanno in the introduction to his report.

On Euphorbion

One of Juba's minor compositions contains one of his greatest impacts on the modern world. Its title is not known exactly but is approximately Περὶ εὐφορβίου.[121] It was merely a pamphlet that was still in existence in Pliny's day.[122] Pliny's discussion provides the background for this unusual work: during an expedition to the Atlas Mountains (Figure 23, p. 186), Juba or his physician Euphorbos discovered a plant that looked like a thyrsus but with acanthus-like leaves and whose juice was a topical cure for snake bite.[123] It also seemed to improve vision. Highly toxic, the fluid could be gathered only by cutting into the plant with a long pole and catching the juice, for which containers made of goats' stomachs were used. Juba gave this plant the name εὐφόρβιον, devised the means of collection, and wrote a treatise on its discovery and use.[124]

Euphorbion and its uses soon entered standard medical literature. Sometime after the middle of the first century AC. Dioskourides of Anazarbos wrote a treatise called *On the Materials of Medicine*. His date is uncertain, but one of the few contemporaries he mentioned is a certain Laecanius, who may be C. Laecanius Bassus, the suffect consul of AD 40 and the consul of AD 64.[125] Moreover, Dioskourides was not mentioned by Pliny, perhaps indicating that they were contemporaries. Thus Dioskourides may have been writing in the 50s and 60s AC[126] and his discussion of Juba and euphorbion would be the earliest to cite a publication of the king's.[127] Dioskourides' work was a list of the properties of approximately one thousand drugs, mostly plant derived. It became widely disseminated in both the European and the Islamic worlds, was never lost in late antiquity, and remained in use into modern times.[128] Although Dioskourides did not mention Juba's work by title, his text is closely paralleled by that of Pliny, and since Pliny was

---

121 Jacoby in *RE* did not recognize this as an independent work; by the time he wrote *FGrHist* (*Commentary*, p. 329), he admitted the possibility, but still was dubious, believing it to be part of the *Libyka*, despite Galen's assertion. There seems no justification for Müller's assumption (*FHG*, Juba, fr. 27) that the title of the work was Περὶ ὀποῦ: this is based on a loose reading of Galen's text and contradicts the earlier evidence of Dioskourides and Pliny.

122 βιβλίδιον σμικρὸν: Galen, *On the Combining of Drugs According to Place* 1 (13.278 Kühn) = Juba, fr. 8a. See also *NH* 25.77–8 = Juba, fr. 7; *NH* 5.16 = Juba, fr. 42.

123 At *NH* 5.16 Euphorbos discovered the plant; at *NH* 25.77–8 it was Juba himself. As a physician, Euphorbos would have had botanical training.

124 It has been suggested that the plant in question is *Euphorbia canariensis*, the *cardón*, endemic to the Canary Islands (John Mercer, *The Canary Islanders: Their Prehistory, Conquest and Survival* [London: Collings, 1980] p. 21). This is possible, but Juba discovered the plant in the Atlas, not the Canaries.

125 *PIR²* L30, L31.

126 John M. Riddle, *Dioscorides on Pharmacy and Medicine*, History of Science Series 3 (Austin 1985), pp. 13–14.

127 Dioskourides 3.82 (=Juba, fr. 8b), who wrote that Juba discovered the plant.

128 Riddle (supra note 126), pp. xvii–xix.

unaware of Dioskourides but quoted from Juba's treatise, it is certain that Dioskourides was doing the same. He wrote that Juba determined the method of harvesting the plant and extracting its juice, items described by Pliny but not specifically credited to Juba, as his account was limited to the discovery of the plant. Juba's treatise was again quoted by Galen, who also seemed to have it at hand and essentially repeated the information provided by the two earlier authors.

Strangely, Juba's discovery of euphorbion and its medical use is one of his most lasting accomplishments.[129] Because of Dioskourides and Galen, euphorbion entered the mainstream of medical terminology and usage. Contemporary botany still recognizes Euphorbiaceae, a widely distributed family of herbs, shrubs, and trees, including poinsettia and cassava. Most are toxic, but the family also includes a number of medicinal plants such as the castor bean. There is also the genus *Euphorbia*, commonly known as spurge.[130] The physician that Augustus sent to Juba's court, although unknown except for this one event, is the most enduring member of the Mauretanian client kingdom.

Libyka

For a full discussion of this treatise, written between 25 and 2 BC, see Chapter 8.

On Arabia

For a full discussion of this treatise, written between AD 2 and 5, see Chapter 10.

On Assyria

On this enigmatic work, see pp. 237–8.

Spurious or questionable works

A number of alleged Juban works are spurious or questionable. In the Photios lexicon under the word σκομβρίσαι is a reference to the second book of Juba's Περὶ φθορᾶς λέξεως, *On the Deterioration of Words*.[131]

---

129 The other significant survival of Juba's world is his naming of the Canary Islands, for which see infra, pp. 96–8.

130 For modern examples of Euphorbiaceae and *Euphorbia*, see Walter H. Lewis and Memory P. F. Elvin-Lewis, *Medical Botany: Plants Affecting Man's Health* (New York: Wiley, 1977), pp. 37–9.

131 Juba, fr. 22; Jacoby, *RE*, p. 2395; *Commentary*, p. 333. A title Περὶ διεφθορυίας λέξεως is attributed to Didymos Chalkenteros.

The word σκομβρίσαι is not otherwise known, but seems to be a type of marine animal.[132] The failure of anyone earlier than a Byzantine lexicographer to know this work suggests that it may be a late epitome, perhaps from a passage on natural history. Much the same can be said about the title *Fisiologia*. This is found in the *Mythologiae* attributed to the late fifth century AC mythographer Fulgentius in a passage about marine animals, probably from a summary of *On Arabia*.[133] Pliny[134] and Aelian[135] both quoted similar topics from that work.[136]

Other writings

In a less scholarly vein, Juba may have written plays,[137] and is known to have written epigrams, which is perhaps not unexpected given his association with Krinagoras. One epigram is preserved, which Juba wrote after a poor performance of the play *Hypsipyle* by his court tragedian Leonteus of Argos.[138] Whether this was Leonteus' play or the one by Euripides (or someone else) is not known. The epigram runs as follows:

> While looking at me, Leonteus, echo of an artichoke-eating tragedian,
> Do not look into the heart of wretched Hypsipyle.
> For I was once the friend of Bakchos, who admired no voice

132 See σκόμβρος: Aristotle, *History of Animals* 6.17 (571a). There is a parallel entry in the Hesychios lexion for σκομβρίσαι.
133 Fulgentius, *Mythologiae* 2.1 = Juba, fr. 103; Jacoby, *RE*, p. 2395; *Commentary*, p. 357. This may not be a title at all: "Juba in fisiologis" may simply mean "Juba in his physiological writings." See Fulgentius, *Fulgentius the Mythographer*, ed. Leslie George Whitbread (Columbus: Ohio State University Press, 1971), p. 67. On the *Mythologiae*, and the problems regarding its authorship, see F. Skutsch, "Fulgentius" (#3), *RE* 7, 1910, 215–27.
134 *NH* 9.115 = Juba, fr. 71.
135 Aelian, *On the Characteristics of Animals* 15.8 = Juba, fr. 70.
136 A title *De re rustica* was proposed by C. Müller (Juba, *FHG* fr. 69) on the basis of a passage in the *Geoponika* (15.2.21), a late antique compilation of agricultural material, which includes Juba's statement that honey must be stored in wood. But again one must be dubious about creating titles for works cited only in late compendia, and it is better to follow Jacoby (*RE*, p. 2395) in believing that the passage is from the *Libyka* (fr. 61). On the *Geoponika*, see E. Oder, "Geoponika," *RE* 7, 1910, 1221–5.
  On equally dubious testimony is the title Θηριακός. The scholiast to the *Theriaka* of Nikandros attributed such a title to a work by a royal personage whose name is not preserved (Juba, fr. 102); if a reference to Juba's writings, it is more likely from the natural history portions of the *Libyka*. Yet the passage cites the φαλαγγίων, a type of spider (*LSJ*), and there is no other evidence that Juba discussed arachnids in any of his treatises. On the other hand, the word can also mean "spider-wort," a herb that cures spider bites, and Juba was interested in medicinal plants.
137 The evidence for Juba as a playwright is a possible reading of Athenaios 14.634e (cf. *FGrHist* #275, T13, and Jacoby, *Commentary*, pp. 325–6).
138 The source is Athenaios 8.343e–f (Juba, fr. 104), quoting Amarantos. See A.-M. Desrousseux, "Une Épigramme du roi Juba (*FHG*, III, p. 483, fr. 83)," in *Mélanges dédiés à la mémoire de Felix Grat* (Paris; En Dépot Chez Mme. Pecqueur-Grat, 1946), vol. 1, pp. 27–30.

More than mine, listening with gold-lobed ears.
But now earthen pot-stands and dry saucepans
Have deprived me of my voice, because I gratified my stomach.[139]

The language is mock-tragic, expectedly using a number of rare words, notably the unique κιναρηφάγος.

Conclusions

Needless to say, the fragments of Juba's writings do not cover everything that he wrote. There is nothing extant about Sophoniba, the paramour of his ancestor Massinissa, yet parallels between Dio's account of her suicide and his version of that of Kleopatra VII may indicate that Dio was using material that described the earlier death in a fashion similar to the more recent and more famous one.[140] Juba, who had a family connection to both women, is the obvious source: he compared the personal tastes of Massinissa and his mother-in-law.[141] Whether Juba treated his mother-in-law historically is unknown, but she did leave her mark throughout his writings, and he was particularly proud of his descent from Massinissa. Thus there is circumstantial evidence that the death of Sophoniba was a topic examined by Juba, perhaps in the *Roman Archaeology* or the *Libyka*, or even in an autobiography – a literary genre popular in the Augustan era – that would have discussed his ancestry.[142]

Little can be said about Juba's literary style, in part because half the fragments are not in the language in which he wrote. The extant epigram offers little insight into Juba's scholarly prose, and the few direct quotations, such as those cited by Stephanos of Byzantion,[143] are brief and more utilitarian than literary. Perhaps the best glimpse of Juba as stylist comes from the long account of the course of the Nile from its presumed Mauretanian origin

139 Μή με Λεοντῆος τραγικοῦ κιναρηφάγου ἦχος
    λεύσσων Ὑψιπύλης ἐς κακὸν ἦτορ ὅρα.
    ἤμην γάρ ποτ᾽ ἐγὼ Βάκχῳ φίλος, οὐδέ τιν᾽ ὧδε
    γῆρυν χρυσολόβοις οὔασιν ἠγάσατο.
    νῦν δέ με χυτρόποδες κέραμοι καὶ ξηρὰ τάγηνα
    χήρωσαν φωνῆς, γαστρὶ χαριζόμενον.

    Not unexpectedly, the text is corrupt and questionable; that which is used here is the one in the Loeb Classical Library edition of Athenaios. The manuscript tradition reads κεναρηφαγου, printed with a dagger by Jacoby in *FGrHist*; κιναρηφάγου is an emendation of J. Schweighaüser, early in the nineteenth century, but it has a Juban flavor.

140 Zonaras 9.13 (from Dio 17); Dio 51.13–14.

141 Juba, fr. 87 (=Athenaios 6.229d–e).

142 On this, see further, M. James Moscovich, "Cassius Dio on the Death of Sophonisba," *AncHBull* 11, 1997, 25–9.

143 Juba, fr. 9, 10.

to the Mediterranean.[144] Although not in Juba's Greek, Pliny's Latin is still a rich and vivid description that gives the river an animistic quality as it disappears and reappears in the desert, and then divides around islands and crashes through the cataracts, eventually spreading across all Egypt and endowing it with fertility. The style is unlike that of Pliny, and conspicuously lacking in the much-condensed and matter-of-fact parallel description by Ammianus Marcellinus,[145] and thus stands as perhaps the only surviving remnant of the king's literary style.

Juba was typical of polymathic authors of the late Hellenistic period. His presence in the most famous and distinguished Roman household of the era allowed him access to the best education of the times, giving him contact with the aging scholars near the ends of their careers such as Alexandros Polyhistor and Varro as well as with the new generation of younger talents that included Strabo and Nikolaos. His personal evolution as a scholar can easily be followed: from the politically correct treatises of his youth on Roman history, linguistics, and cults to his maturation as geographer and ethnographer writing about his kingdom, to a culmination in his definitive treatment of the southern half of the known world, appearing in the linkage of *Libyka* and *On Arabia*. Certain vestiges of his youthful environment remained throughout his life: he never missed an opportunity to make a linguistic comment or to show interest in the theater. Yet the loss of his writings – at least in direct form – within two centuries of his death testifies not only to the remoteness of his environment but to the sad disappearance of the bulk of ancient literature.

---

144 Juba, fr. 38a (=*NH* 5.51–4).
145 Juba, fr. 38b (=Ammianus Marcellinus 22.15.8–10).

8

LIBYKA

When Juba II and Kleopatra Selene took up residence in Iol late in 25 BC, Juba had been a scholar for a decade. Despite his new duties as king, his research did not diminish. He immediately turned his proven abilities toward writing the definitive monograph about his new kingdom, titled *Libyka*.[1] Completed within the next twenty years, certainly before he joined the entourage of Gaius Caesar in 2 BC,[2] it was based not only on library research but on an extensive amount of exploration. It established his reputation as a geographer and ethnographer, and was instrumental in persuading Augustus to place him on Gaius' staff. As Juba struggled with the military and cultural realities of his kingdom, his active scholarly mind began to plan his study of it. Expeditions were sent forth to the remote extremities, including the desert, the offshore and Atlantic islands (Figures 21 and 22), and the Atlas Mountains (Figure 23). His new royal library, consisting of copies (if not the originals) of the Carthaginian state library and as many contemporary Greek and Latin writings as he had been able to obtain before leaving Rome, provided the academic nucleus of this scholarly endeavor. Kleopatra Selene had introduced Juba to her ancestral Ptolemaic traditions,[3] and the king himself

---

1 Jacoby, *RE*, pp. 2889–91; Gsell, vol. 8, pp. 262–4.

2 Other than within the *termini* of 25–2 BC, and perhaps later in this period rather than earlier, there is no specific evidence as to when the treatise was published. The definitive-sounding statement of recent commentators on Vitruvius, "published in 26/25, or 23," is out of the question. Juba was not even in Africa until the end of 25 BC, and the wide-ranging use of autopsy, exploration, and correlation of data from separate places precludes a publication within two years after his arrival. It remains a mystery how the commentators determined their date. See the edition of Vitruvius by Ingrid D. Rowland, Thomas Noble Howe, and Michael J. Dewar (Cambridge: Cambridge University Press, 1999), p. 6.

3 Her mother Kleopatra VII was said to have been the author of several treatises, on meteorology, cosmetics, and hairdressing. Although the sources are late and obscure (see P. M. Fraser, *Ptolemaic Alexandria* [Oxford: Clarendon Press, 1972], vol. 2, p. 548), and the last two works sound like a formulaic rendering of what she might be thought to have been interested in, her intellectual qualities are beyond dispute (Plutarch, *Antonius* 25–7). Juba might have used a work on cosmetics as a source for *On Arabia* with its emphasis on trade items. Yet if he had made use of his mother-in-law's writings, this could hardly be acknowledged in a work that would be sent to Augustus.

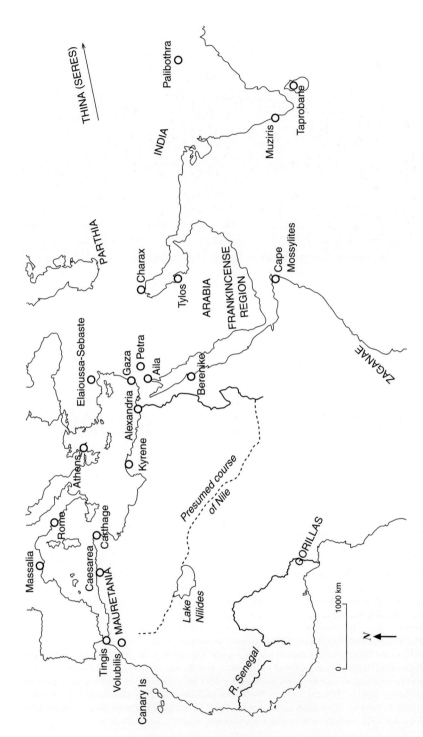

Map 4 The southern half of the known world in the Augustan period

Figure 21 The "Purple Islands" at Mogador (Essaouira): view southeast from one island (now joined to the mainland) to the other.

Photograph by Duane W. Roller.

was now, if only by marriage, a successor to the Ptolemies. This and the Carthaginian material probably led him to conceive of a broad treatise about the southern reaches of the known world, connecting his wife's ancestral kingdom with his new one. The only term that could adequately cover this vast expanse – for which neither "Mauretania," "Africa," nor "Egypt" sufficed – was Libya, a toponym (to Greeks and Romans) as old as Homer[4] but which had long meant the entire continent of Africa.[5] As such, it was somewhat anachronistic in Juba's day, not used in contemporary Greek or Roman politics and thus more remindful of ancient traditions. Most important, it flattered Kleopatra Selene, in theory still its queen.

Widely varying information was available to the king about northern Africa. The eastern portions, Egypt and Libya proper, had been known to Greeks since earliest times and had played a role in Greek mythology. Further west, Greek knowledge diminished, but there was a rich indigenous tradition available to Juba in the Carthaginian library. His own territories were the least known,[6]

---

4 Homer, *Odyssey* 4.85, 14.295.

5 This seems to have been Hekataios' definition: *FGrHist* #1, fr. 333, 342. On early use of the term "Libya," see Ferdinand Strenger, *Strabos Erdkunde von Libyen*, Quellen und Forschungen alte Geschichte und Geographie 28 (Berlin 1913), pp. 1–43.

6 Although the Roman historian Tanusius Geminus had written about Mauretania in his barely known histories, his work seems to have been superficial and anecdotal, centering on Sertorius' brief exile in the district in 81–80 BC (supra, pp. 51–4). Strabo, the single source (17.3.8), dismissed Tanusius' writings as "full of marvelous tales" (τερατολογία). On Tanusius, see *HRR*, LXV–LXVI, 49–51; F. Münzer, "Tanusius Geminus" (#2), *RE* 2, ser. 4, 1932, 2231–3. It is possible that Juba in his youth could have met with some surviving members of Sertorius' entourage.

Figure 22 The Canary Islands: ancient Ninguaria (modern Tenerife).
Photograph by Duane H. D. Roller.

Figure 23 The High Atlas.
Photograph by Duane W. Roller.

and here his own explorations would be most valuable. Yet because the extant fragments of *Libyka* are limited and lack an obvious coherence, it is more difficult to determine their cultural depth than their geographical extent. In fact, there is little surviving about Libya itself, in the narrow sense, and one wonders what Juba could have added to the already extensive literary repertory on Libya and Kyrene, beginning with Hekataios and Herodotos through the Hellenistic geographers such as Eratosthenes and Artemidoros to recent authors such as Alexandros Polyhistor and Sallust.[7] This may explain why the surviving portions of *Libyka* have virtually nothing to do with Libya: the Libyan part of the treatise would necessarily have been derivative and repetitious of other scholarship. But Juba had a greater contribution to make in examining all of northern Africa, from the Atlantic coast to Ethiopia and the Red Sea, and south into the sub-Saharan districts, thereby providing Augustan Rome with its first detailed study of this region.[8] Juba could bring the culture and history of his new territories into the mainstream.[9] He would also serve Kleopatra Selene's interests by connecting their two worlds, as Krinagoras had in his wedding epigram, which wrote of joining the Egyptian and Libyan races, using the Nile as a metaphor for their unification.[10]

Juba could also enlighten his audience about the Atlantic coast of Africa, something that had long been a Roman concern.[11] He was especially interested in the matter of circumnavigation of the continent. Herodotos had reported – although disbelievingly – on the original Carthaginian voyage,[12] and the enigmatic journey of Hanno,[13] about which Juba had written a commentary, demonstrated that from perhaps as early as 500 BC Carthaginian knowledge of coastal West Africa far outstripped

---

7 Hekataios (*FGrHist* #1) fr. 329–57; Herodotos 4.150–205; Strabo 17.3.2; Alexandros Polyhistor (*FGrHist* #273) fr. 32–47; Sallust, *Jugurtha* 17–19.

8 Juba, fr. 35, 37–9, 43–4, 67.

9 Juba, fr. 6, 42.

10 Juba, fr. 38–9.

11 On early knowledge about the Atlantic coast, see W. Aly, "Die Entdeckung des Westens," *Hermes* 62, 1927, 299–341; and, generally, Jehan Desanges, *Recherches sur l'activité des Méditerranéens aux confins de l'Afrique*, CÉFR 38 (1978), pp. 39–85; Rhys Carpenter, *Beyond the Pillars of Heracles* (New York: Delacorte Press, 1966), pp. 68–105; on West Africa, as it was known to Greeks and Romans, see John Ferguson, "Classical Contacts with West Africa," in *Africa in Classical Antiquity: Nine Studies*, ed. L. A. Thompson and J. Ferguson (Ibadan: Ibadan University Press, 1969), pp. 1–25.

12 Herodotos 4.42–5.

13 Jerker Blomqvist, *The Date and Origin of the Greek Version of Hanno's Periplus* (Lund: Liber-Larumedel/Gleerup, 1979); Jacques Ramin, *Le Périple d'Hannon*, BAR Supplementary Series 3 (London 1976); M. Cary and E. H. Warmington, *The Ancient Explorers*, revised edition (Baltimore: Penguin Books, 1963), pp. 63–8; Paul T. Keyser, "From Myth to Map: The Blessed Isles in the First Century BC," *AncW* 24, 1993, 153–4.

that of the Greeks. The extent of Hanno's voyage – even its existence –
has long been debated, but his report implies a descent well into the
tropics,[14] and Pliny felt that he had actually circumnavigated Africa: it may
be that he and Herodotos' unspecified Carthaginians were the same.[15]
The Carthaginian explorations resulted in a Greek reaction,[16] especially
by Massalia, which attempted to dominate trade in the west,[17] sending
out its own explorations, especially those of Euthymenes, who also traveled
down the African coast, perhaps shortly after the time of Hanno.[18] Somewhat later, another Massaliot, Pytheas, went far to the north, reaching the
Arctic and Scandinavia.[19] These explorations were threatening enough to
emergent Rome that P. Cornelius Scipio Aemilianus (consul in 147 BC)
attempted to clarify Carthaginian knowledge about the Atlantic, question-
ing Massaliotes and others but learning nothing: the laconic Massaliotes
seemingly did not even reveal the travels of their compatriots Euthymenes

14 Aly (supra note 11), pp. 317–30; Ramin (supra note 13); Michael F. Doran, "The Maritime
 Provenience of Iron Technology in West Africa," *TI* 9, 1977, 94–7; Jehan Desanges, "Le Point
 sur le 'Périple d'Hannon': controverses et publications récentes," in *Enquêtes et Documents* 6:
 Nantes, Afrique, Amérique (Nantes 1981), pp. 13–29. It was Hanno who first saw what seem to have
 been gorillas, and the modern word was coined from Hanno's text by Thomas S. Savage, who identified the species in the 1840s. See his "Notice of the External Characters and Habits of *Troglodytes
 gorilla*, a New Species of Orang from the Gaboon River," *Boston Journal of Natural History* 5, 1847,
 417–26.

15 *NH* 2.169; see also 5.8; Hanno, ed. Oikonomides and Miller, pp. 5–6. On early voyages to
 West Africa, see D. B. Harden, "The Phoenicians on the West Coast of Africa," *Antiquity* 22,
 1948, 141–50; Keyser (supra note 13), pp. 153–7. It seems difficult to credit the minimalist
 views of Raymond Mauny, "La Navigation sur les côtes du Sahara pendant l'Antiquité," *RÉG* 57,
 1955, 92–101, that only the Carthaginians went beyond Cape Juby (at Tarfaya on the Moroccan
 coast, opposite the Canaries), an argument based largely on the winds. But the Greeks and Romans
 knew too much about tropical West Africa for it all to be based on a single early Carthaginian
 voyage.

16 There was also the voyage of the Persian Sataspes, cousin of Xerxes, who perhaps in the 470s BC
 reached the West African tropics (Herodotos 4.43), presumably with Greek or Carthaginian help:
 see Cary and Warmington (supra note 13), pp. 120–1.

17 A good summary of the effects of Massalia on more primitive peoples in the west is Peter S. Wells,
 Culture Contact and Culture Change: Early Iron Age Europe and the Mediterranean World (Cambridge:
 Cambridge University Press, 1980), pp. 62–70; on Massalian exploration generally, see Paul Fabre,
 "Les Massiliotes et l'Atlantique," in *Océan atlantique et Péninsule armoricaine*, (Actes du 107e Congrès
 National des Sociétés Savantes (Paris: CTHS, 1985), pp. 25–49.

18 Desanges, CÉFR (supra note 11), pp. 17–27; Cary and Warmington (supra note 13), pp. 61–2. The
 sources for Euthymenes are extremely scattered: Seneca, *Natural Questions* 4a.2.22; Aristeides
 36.85–96; Aetius, *Placita* 4.1 (=*FGrHist* #647, fr. 2.2); and the so-called *Anonymus Florentinus*
 (*FGrHist* #647, fr. 1.5). None of these is early, or even pre-Roman. See F. Jacoby, "Euthymenes"
 (#4), *RE* 6, 1907, 1509–11; Richard Hennig, *Terrae Incognitae* 1, second enlarged edition (Leiden:
 E. J. Brill, 1944–56), pp. 80–5.

19 For the date of Pytheas (mid-fourth century BC), see the Roseman edition, pp. 51–2, 155; on Pytheas
 generally, Carpenter (supra note 11), pp. 143–98; F. Gisinger, "Pytheas" (#1), *RE* 24, 1963,
 314–66.

and Pytheas.[20] Thus frustrated, Scipio commissioned his long-time teacher and adviser, the historian Polybios, to investigate the matter personally, and shortly after the fall of Carthage he was provided with a ship to explore the coast.[21] The only source, Pliny, has jumbled material from Polybios himself, Marcus Agrippa, and perhaps even Hanno,[22] but it is probable that Polybios went into the tropics, since he seems to have come to rivers filled with crocodiles and hippopotami.

20 Strabo 4.2.1 (=Polybios 34.10.6). Although it would have been fully within character for the Massaliotes not to reveal the knowledge obtained by their famous explorers (or even their existence), since the data could be considered economic and trade secrets, one must be cautious, since the source tradition is hostile toward early Massaliote exploration, especially the journey of Pytheas. The passage cited, Polybios via Strabo, records that the Massaliotes had nothing worthwhile to say to Scipio (οὐδέν μνήμης ἄξιον), which could mean that Pytheas was mentioned but not considered (by either Polybios or Strabo) as a valid source of information. Neither had much respect for the great explorer but both were aware of him. For Polybios' attitude toward Pytheas, see further, F. W. Walbank, *Polybius* (Berkeley: University of California Press, 1972), pp. 126–7. For Strabo's criticism (best set forth at 1.4.3), see Pytheas, Roseman edition, pp. 25–6. Whether Scipio heard about Pytheas remains an enigma, but it is unlikely, since he was unaware of Euthymenes, whose journeys were more relevant to Scipio's concerns. Neither Polybios nor Strabo knew about Euthymenes, so it is probable that their knowledge of Pytheas came from a source other than the report of the Massaliotes to Scipio. Expectedly, though, Strabo cited the Massaliote diffidence about Pytheas as proof of the explorer's unreliability.

21 *NH* 5.9–10 (=Polybios 34.15.7); F. W. Walbank, *A Historical Commentary on Polybios* (Oxford: Clarendon Press, 1957–79), vol. 3, pp. 633–8; Desanges, CÉFR (supra note 11), pp. 121–47; P. Pédech, "Un Texte discuté de Pline: le voyage de Polybe en Afrique (H.N., V, 9–10)," *RÉL* 33, 1955, 318–32; R. Thouvenot, "Le Témoignage de Pline sur le périple africain de Polybe (V, 1, 8–11)," *RÉL* 34, 1956, 88–92.

22 Pliny (ed. Desanges [Paris: Belles Lettres 1980]), pp. 106–21; Aly (supra note 11), pp. 317–20. The report of Hanno was not yet to enter mainstream scholarship. In fact, its early history has long been vague. Herodotos may have been aware of Hanno's voyage, but did not name the explorer. The treatise may have been quoted, again without attribution, in the Περὶ ἀπίστων (31) of a certain Palaiphatos, perhaps of the later fourth century BC (see Jérôme Carcopino, *Le Maroc antique* [Paris: Gallimard, 1943], pp. 117–19). But Palaiphatos ("Legendary") may be a pseudonym: the author of the *Souda* knew several personalities so named, and it was used proverbially by Juba's court comic poet Athenion (Athenaios 14.660b); thus the date of the quoter of Hanno is highly debatable. The author of the Aristotelian *On Marvellous Things Heard* (37 [833a]), also of uncertain date but perhaps from the early third century BC, was aware of Hanno and may have been the first to cite him by name. Others may also have known about the explorer (Blomqvist [supra note 13], pp. 52–5). But one can easily argue that none of these authors, all of whom are virtually undatable, saw the actual text, having received their information orally. Yet a close stylistic analysis of the Greek text indicates that it may have been composed as early as the fifth century BC (Blomqvist [supra note 13], pp. 50–1). Polybios probably saw the text, but then it seems to have vanished into the Carthaginian library. But, almost suddenly, in the first century AC, Hanno became widely known. Not mentioned by Strabo, he was cited by Pomponius Mela (3.90, 93), who was aware of Juba's world, and then by Pliny (*NH* 2.169, 5.8), an author also heavily dependent on Juba. Thus it seems that Juba recovered the report – whether the original or Greek translation – and made it accessible to the Roman world by writing his own commentary and perhaps reediting the text. Eventually the Greek text itself became attached to the corpus known as the *Minor Greek Geographers*, perhaps after the publication of the *Geography* of Strabo in late Roman times, with which the corpus is associated. See Aubrey Diller, *The Tradition of the Minor Greek Geographers*, Philological Monographs of the American Philological Association 14 (1952).

By Juba's day whatever scattered bits of information of early exploration into the Atlantic that existed were perhaps as inconsistent and little understood as they are today. Strabo, a meticulous if opinionated researcher, was surprisingly vague about the African coast,[23] and displayed no knowledge of the voyages of either Hanno or Polybios.[24] When Juba became king, most reports on the Atlantic coast were over a century old and tended to be ignored, or even to be rejected as mythical.[25] Thus one of his priorities as geographer king was to provide Augustan Rome with definitive information about this portion of his new kingdom. His interest may have been heightened because Polybios, one of the more recent explorers, had been received at the Numidian court in the days of Juba's great-great-great-grandfather Massinissa.[26] Learning that the Atlantic coast was a way to India, the king may also have begun to see the commercial possibilities that this implied.

Connected with the exploration of the West African coast was the problem of the source of the Nile.[27] Study of the peculiarities of this river was as old as Greek intellectualism, as Thales of Miletos was said to have considered its unique properties.[28] At an early date it came to be believed that the river originated in West Africa, a theory seemingly first suggested by Euthymenes of Massalia. He had come to a large river (perhaps the same as that seen by Hanno) that had crocodiles, as did the Nile, and whose waters were driven inland by an onshore wind.[29] Perhaps influenced by Thales' theories regarding winds and the Nile, Euthymenes believed that his river was the Egyptian one. His theory was not accepted – Herodotos, who could find no information on the source of the Nile, seems to have rejected it[30] – and Euthymenes and his voyage were soon forgotten, except perhaps in the western Mediterranean circles in which Juba was to function. But it was a theory that Juba would find attractive since it brought Kleopatra Selene's homeland and new home into contact, a literal geographical fulfillment of Krinagoras' wedding epigram.

23 Strabo 17.3.5–6: see also Thomson, p. 184.

24 Agrippa's map seems to provide information for approximately 1,000 miles along the coast, but some of this may have been received directly from Juba. See *NH* 5.9–10; O. A. W. Dilke, *Greek and Roman Maps* (London: Thames and Hudson, 1985), p. 48.

25 Strabo 1.3.2, 17.3.3. The only recent report would be that of Bogudes II of Mauretania, who seems to have penetrated into the tropics perhaps in the 50s BC (Strabo 17.3.5): Juba might have been able to talk to veterans of the expedition. For the explorations of Eudoxos of Kyzikos, see infra, pp. 228–30.

26 Polybios 31.21, 36.16; Walbank, *Polybius* (supra note 20), p. 11.

27 Albert Rehm, "Nilschwelle," *RE* 17, 1936, 571–90.

28 Seneca, *Natural Questions* 4a.2.22.

29 *FGrHist* #647, fr. 1.5. The river is usually thought to be the Senegal: see Thomson, p. 77, but contrast Desanges, CÉFR (supra note 11), pp. 21–3.

30 Herodotos 2.20.

There are two versions of the title of Juba's treatise, Λιβύκα[31] and Περὶ Λιβύης.[32] There is no way of telling which is correct: the former conforms to the nomenclature of the broad general work Juba seems to have written,[33] while the latter is more Juban in tone. Nevertheless, the two titular citations show that Juba's research on North Africa extended, at least, from the Atlantic to Libya proper, and included both myth and natural history. Three books are known but there were probably many more. The literary sources are varied. Juba's commentary on Hanno demonstrates that he used Carthaginian material, available no doubt through his library: Ammianus Marcellinus explicitly credited Juba's writings on the Nile to Punic texts.[34] The *libri punici* of Juba's grandfather Hiempsal – whatever they were – also would have been a major source. But much of the material, especially about eastern Africa, was Ptolemaic in origin. Ptolemaic connections to Juba's world had existed ever since Ptolemaios VIII (reigned 145–116 BC) had written his lengthy autobiographical *Hypomnata*.[35] This scholarly monarch, a student of the polymath Aristarchos of Samothrake,[36] was Kleopatra Selene's great-great-grandfather and may have visited the court of Massinissa. The extant fragments of the *Hypomnata* suggest a wide-ranging memoir that included material gathered on travels throughout the ancient world, including the Greek mainland, Asia Minor, and Libya. Natural history, political history, and literary criticism were among its topics.[37] Of particular interest to Juba would have been the comments on Libya and Massinissa.[38] Juba made use not only of these memoirs,[39] but of the writings of other Ptolemaic kings, including Ptolemaios II[40] and Ptolemaios IV.[41] In addition, he consulted extensively the reports of the Ptolemaic explorers who had traveled along the Red Sea coast and up the Nile, especially during the time of Ptolemaios II. Juba's access to Ptolemaic sources may have been eased by his wife's contacts and the court retinue she created out of the remnants of her mother's Alexandrian entourage. This wide use of Ptolemaic material – and one suspects that most of the information in the *Libyka* concerning the Red Sea region comes from it[42] – is

---

31 [Plutarch], *Greek and Roman Parallels* 23 (311c) = Juba fr. 5, on Diomedes in Libya. On the date (second century AC) and authorship of the *Parallels*, see Konrat Ziegler, "Plutarchos" (#2), *RE* 2, ser. 21, 1951, 867–70.

32 Athenaios 3.83b = Juba, fr. 6, on flora of Mauretania.

33 The title *Libyka* was in vogue in Hellenistic times, used by a variety of authors (*FGrHist* #759–64).

34 Ammianus Marcellinus 22.15.8; see also Solinus 32.2.

35 *FGrHist* #234; Fraser (supra note 3), vol. 1, p. 515. On the connection between North Africa and the Hellenistic world, see Thadeuz Kotula, "Orientalia africana. Réflexions sur les contacts Afrique du Nord romaine – orient hellénistique," *FolOr* 24, 1987, 117–33.

36 Athenaios 2.71b.

37 Ptolemaios, fr. 1–4, 6–8, 10–12.

38 Ptolemaios, fr. 7, 8.

39 Athenaios 6.229 = Juba, fr. 87.

40 Aelian, *On the Characteristics of Animals* 9.58 = Juba, fr. 49.

41 Plutarch, *Whether Land or Sea Animals Are Wiser* 17 = Juba, fr. 51a, 53.

42 Juba, fr. 34, 38–40, 57, 58, 67, 75–7.

an essential quality of the treatise, indicative of the ancient linkage between the worlds of Juba and Kleopatra Selene that went back at least to the days of Massinissa and Ptolemaios VIII.[43]

Oral information and autopsy also played a role, a technique that Juba would exploit further in *On Arabia*. His explorers ventured into the Atlantic or into and across the Atlas Mountains:[44] some of these expeditions might have included the king himself.[45] The report of twenty-five days' travel to find Ethiopian emeralds shows use of merchants' and traders' reports.[46] Juba had local informants who could remember life under Bocchus II and perhaps even Bocchus I;[47] others, perhaps now part of the new court retinue, could provide information about Juba's father.[48] Anecdotal material about his mother-in-law probably came from similar sources.[49]

It can be seen, then, that central to the *Libyka* was a concept of linking Egypt and West Africa, the Nile and Mauretania. Nowhere can this theoretical structure be better examined than in Juba's researches on the source of the Nile. The Nile was the epitome of the world of Kleopatra Selene's ancestry. Its peculiar properties and mysterious upper reaches had long been a subject of inquiry.[50] Herodotos had been unable to obtain anything but the vaguest information about the river above Elephantine, although he was aware of the Ethiopian city of Meroë, several weeks further upstream.[51] There were rumors about its course beyond Meroë, mostly due to the discovery of a large river in sub-Saharan Africa that was believed to be the Nile, but not surprisingly, there was no known connection between this river and the lower Nile: travelers had simply encountered it and presumed that it was the upper Nile. Euthymenes may have been the first: another instance was the Nasamonians, who came to Etearchos, king of Ammon and reported on their encounter with a large river far to the south, perhaps the Niger near Timbuctu.[52] The Ptolemies were committed to providing more accurate and

---

43 According to Lucan (10.144–6), the palace of Kleopatra VII included Mauretanian furniture. Allowance must be made for the lateness of the source, after Mauretania had been provincialized and when Mauretanian citrus wood furniture was popular in Rome (for which, supra, pp. 117–18), but the citation raises the reasonable possibility of trade and commercial contacts between the later Ptolemaic court and Mauretania.

44 *NH* 6.202–5 = Juba, fr. 44; *NH* 5.16 = Juba, fr. 42; Pliny (ed. Desanges), pp. 141–3.

45 *NH* 25.77 = Juba, fr. 7.

46 *NH* 37.69 = Juba, fr. 77. See also Strabo 17.1.45.

47 *NH* 8.13–15 = Juba, fr. 54.

48 Plutarch, *Whether Land or Sea Animals Are Wiser* 17 = Juba fr. 51a; Aelian, *On the Characteristics of Animals* 7.23 = Juba, fr. 55.

49 Athenaios 6.229 = Juba, fr. 87.

50 On the search for the source of the Nile as a cultural phenomenon, see James S. Romm, *The Edges of the Earth in Ancient Thought* (Princeton, N.J.: Princeton University Press, 1992), pp. 149–56, who, however, did not mention Juba.

51 Herodotos 2.29.

52 Herodotos 2.30–1; Thomson, pp. 70–1. The Niger reaches its northernmost point (and thus is closest to the Mediterranean) some 200 km east of Timbuctu.

connected information about the upper river. During the reign of Ptolemaios II, a certain Dalion was sent above Meroë,[53] the first of a whole line of
Ptolemaic explorers who also learned more about Meroë itself.[54] But
information continued to be vague, with only hints of the basic topographical features beyond Meroë, such as the confluence of the Blue and White
Nile and the more remote lakes and highlands.[55] Where the river originated
was still a mystery.

Romans in the early Augustan period went no farther than the explorers
of Ptolemaios II.[56] But Juba was in a unique position to add new knowledge
and to solve the problem, since it had long been believed that the source of
the Nile was far to the west of its lower course – in other words, near Mauretania. Juba's theory[57] was that the river originated in the mountains of
interior Mauretania not far from the Atlantic, where there was a lake called
Nilides.[58] If Pliny is to be taken literally, Juba had visited it; at any rate, a
crocodile from the lake was brought to Caesarea, proof to Juba that Lake
Nilides was part of the Nile, a reflection of Euthymenes' ideas that similar
fauna meant the same river. Leaving nothing to doubt, Juba put the crocodile in the Caesarea Iseum, where it was still visible in Pliny's day.[59] As
further proof, it was noted that the rise of the lower Nile was related to
excessive precipitation in the Mauretanian mountains: this rather casual
statement shows that Juba correlated data from informants in widely separated areas. From Lake Nilides the river alternatingly flowed underground (at
one place for as much as a twenty-day journey) or passed through lakes.[60]
Eventually it reached Ethiopia and familiar territory: Pliny's account carries
the river to its mouth and thus probably follows a Juban description of the
entire course of the river, which, unlike others, was oriented downstream,

---

53 *FGrHist* #666; *NH* 6.183, 194.

54 All these (Aristokreton, Bion, Basilis, Simonides, and Timosthenes) are listed in a single section of
   NH (6.175–95) and are otherwise largely unknown: see Desanges, CÉFR (supra note 11),
   pp. 258–62; Fraser (supra note 3), vol. 1, p. 176.

55 Strabo 16.4.8, 17.2.2–3, all from Eratosthenes, who collected the reports of the Ptolemaic explorers.

56 The expeditions of C. Petronius, prefect of Egypt, against the Ethiopian queen Kandake in 24–22 BC
   did not extend knowledge further upstream (Strabo 17.1.54; *NH* 6.181; Dio 54.54.6); Hennig
   (supra note 18), pp. 309–11.

57 According to Ammianus Marcellinus (22.15.8), it was based on Punic books, but this was probably
   only a small part of it.

58 *NH* 5.51–4 = Juba, fr. 38a. See Jacoby, *Commentary*, pp. 338–40; Gsell, vol. 8, pp. 254–6; Pliny (ed.
   Desanges), pp. 456–65. On the linguistic basis of "Nilides," which probably has nothing to do with
   "Nile," see G. Marcy, "Notes linguistiques: autour du périple d'Hannon," *Hespéris* 20, 1935, 56–8.

59 The crocodile coins of Juba and Kleopatra Selene (Mazard #339–46) may in part have been inspired
   by this incident (although one need seek no further precedent than Kleopatra Selene's Egyptian heritage). Some crocodile coins were issued by her alone (Figure 26c, d, p. 246; Mazard #394–5). In
   placing the crocodile in the Iseum, Juba was imitating Hanno, who had put gorilla skins in the
   Temple of Hera at Carthage (*NH* 6.200).

60 See the map, Thomson, p. 268.

but included little detail,[61] and Juba may have used informants in Alexandria or within Kleopatra Selene's retinue rather than a geographical source for the lower portions. His sketchy account of the lower river can easily be contrasted with the precise information Eratosthenes collated from Ptolemaic reports.[62]

Varying explanations have been offered for this strange river that flows underground for many days,[63] but it is unlikely to be a total fabrication. More probably it is the result of excessive preconceptions and Juba's desire to prove that the river emanated from a Mauretanian source, thereby leading him to create connections between various southern lakes and watercourses known to him and his informants. The topography of the Atlas Mountains and the extreme northern Sahara would be used to support such a view. The modern visitor to the region can easily see how such a theory might be sustained. The Atlas Mountains, especially in their eastern portions, south of modern Fès, are a series of high, barren ridges rising as much as 1,000 m above the desert. These ridges are cut through by rivers that flow south: a fine example is the Ziz, which twists and turns in a canyon hundreds of meters deep, running all the way through the Atlas (Figure 24). It leaves the mountains near modern Er Rachidia, but remains in a canyon, now approximately 200–300 m wide and 100 m below the surface of the desert, heading southeast, eventually to disappear in a series of generally dry lakes in western Algeria. It is not hard to imagine that such a river could be the upper Nile. The Ziz is one of several rivers with these features, and some of them disappear underground: the best example is the modern Draa, whose source is on the south slopes of Mount Atlas itself and which flows southeast in its own deep canyon through the mountains and into the desert, eventually disappearing underground near modern Mhamid before reemerging hundreds of kilometers to the west (and entering the Atlantic). It seems that either the Ziz or the Draa, or perhaps the Guir, east of the Ziz and with similar features – all three are great rivers that cut through the Atlas and flow into the Sahara – was Juba's Nile. Juba would have coupled his information about these with the earlier reports of great crocodile-bearing rivers emptying into the Atlantic in West Africa, and the vague knowledge of a major sub-Saharan river. An essential part of the thesis is the idea that consistent fauna meant the same river, which, although an old theory, reveals the scanty contemporary knowledge about the nature of the tropics. In fact, Juba should have known better. Onesikritos – a source he used elsewhere – had found fauna in India, including hippopotami, paralleling that in Egypt,[64] and Pliny (probably using information available to Juba) was to

---

61 *NH* 5.59 = Juba, fr. 39.
62 Strabo 17.1.5. See Jacoby, *Commentary*, pp. 338–40.
63 Thomson, pp. 267–78.
64 Strabo 15.1.13.

Figure 24 The canyon of the Ziz River, perhaps Juba's "upper Nile": view southwest from the Atlas toward the Sahara.

Photograph by Duane W. Roller.

undercut Juba's theory by noting that a river called the Niger (probably not the modern river of that name) had the same characteristics and animals as the Nile.[65] Yet Juba's view, however strange geographically and zoologically, became commonplace. The earliest to cite it are Vitruvius and Strabo, who were both personally associated with Juba and may thus have received unpublished information.[66] It long remained the major theory about the upper Nile, even into the third century AC.[67] But sometime around AD 100 a certain Diogenes ended up at Rhapta on the East African coast and either traveled inland or learned about the hinterland: he was the first to report on the central African lakes and mountains where the Nile actually originated. His material was analyzed by the geographer Ptolemy,[68] who, in his own

65 *NH* 5.44. Thomson, p. 268, has drawn attention to the fact that *(n)gir* simply means "water," and similar names occur frequently in writings about sub-Saharan Africa (see *NH* 8.77); see also Ferguson (supra note 11), pp. 20–1. On possibilities for the modern identification of Pliny's Niger, see Pliny (ed. Desanges), pp. 456–61.

66 Vitruvius 8.2.6–7; Strabo 17.3.4.

67 Dio 76.13.3; see also Pausanias 1.33.6.

68 Ptolemy 1.9, 17; 4.6–8; Hennig (supra note 18), pp. 426–33. The explorations of Diogenes were recorded by Ptolemy's primary source, the elusive Marinos of Tyre, whose work seems to have been published shortly before AD 110: see J. Lennart Berggren and Alexander Jones, *Ptolemy's Geography: An Annotated Translation of the Theoretical Chapters* (Princeton, N.J.: Princeton University Press, 2000), pp. 23–4.

confused presentation, became the first to separate the Nile from the Niger and the rivers and lakes of interior Mauretania.[69] Yet as late as the early nineteenth century, explorers were still seeking the upper Nile in West Africa,[70] and it was not until the travels of Richard Burton (1821–90) and John Hanning Speke (1827–64), culminating in Speke's 1862 visit to the lake he named Victoria Nyanza, that the central African lakes and mountains were seen by Europeans and it was possible to trace the Nile's complete course.[71] Juba had been the first to make such an attempt, however erroneous.

The extant fragments of *Libyka* show that its range was across North Africa. In fact, the area of research extended into the Atlantic, dealing not only with the Purple Islands, where Juba established his dying works, but with his attempt to identify the fabled Islands of the Blessed, which had been a mythical repository of various events and adventures known to the Greek imagination from the time of Homer and Hesiod.[72] Tales concerning the home of the dead – especially those chosen for an eternity of bliss – had been localized west of the Pillars of Herakles. Indeed, Herakles' last labor, that of the Apples of the Hesperides, was said to have taken place in this region.[73] These myths came to be mingled with explorers' reports, mostly from Carthaginian sources, about actual islands in the Atlantic, variously identified as the Canaries, Madeira, and the Azores, or even the British Isles.[74] Sailors' tales had described them as a virtual paradise with their rich and temperate climate.[75] The Canaries are near the African coast and would have been known from earliest times; early knowledge of the others is more problematic.[76]

Juba, the descendant of Herakles, was especially interested in the matter of the Garden of the Hesperides.[77] He thus mounted an expedition to locate the Islands of the Blessed, which his explorers identified as a group visible off the coast of extreme southern Mauretania (Figure 22, p. 186).[78] Sailing directions and distances appear in Pliny's recension, converted into miles,

69 See the map, Thomson, p. 269.
70 Thomson, pp. 268–9.
71 Thomson, pp. 275–7.
72 Homer, *Odyssey* 4.562–8; Hesiod, *Works and Days* 169–74.
73 Hesiod, *Theogony* 215–16.
74 Cary and Warmington (supra note 13), pp. 69–71. On the cultural concept of the Islands of the Blessed, and how it has continued to evolve into modern times, see Vincent H. Cassidy, "Other Fortunate Islands and Some That Were Lost," *TI* 1, 1969, 35–9.
75 Plutarch, *Sertorius* 8; Horace, *Epode* 16; C. F. Konrad, *Plutarch's Sertorius: A Historical Commentary* (Chapel Hill: University of North Carolina Press, 1994), pp. 105–9.
76 Thomson, pp. 77–8; Hennig (supra note 18), pp. 40–50.
77 Athenaios 3.83c = Juba, fr. 6.
78 *NH* 6.201–5 = Juba, fr. 43–4; Gsell, vol. 8, pp. 256–60.

although they have become confused.[79] The names preserved are Latin: Junonia, Pluvialia, Capraria, Invallis, Canaria, and Planasia. Pluvialia's original Greek name, Ombrios, is also provided. All the names except Junonia are conspicuously topographic or descriptive, and thus it would not be difficult to recreate Juba's other Greek toponyms. Junonia was probably so named because of ruins perceived to be those of a temple of Hera.[80]

Juba's explorers came first to Ombrios, or Pluvialia, and eventually landed on Junonia, Capraria, and Canaria, the last named after its large dogs, two of which were given to the king. It was by this name that the group came to be called, although probably not until early modern times, and thus the name of the Canary Islands is, along with euphorbion, one of the significant survivals of Juba's world.[81] Also visible, but perhaps not visited, was snowy Ninguaria, by all modern accounts Tenerife.[82] A variety of cultural and natural historical details are provided: in addition to the dogs of Canaria there are comments on the unusual trees and their by-products, the strange lizards, and the rotting remnants of sea creatures on the shore. Some material has a more practical tone, such as the notice taken of the date palms, honey, and papyrus of Canaria. An interest in geology led to observation of the perpetual mountain snows of Ninguaria and the mountain crater lake of Ombrios. Remains of human habitation included a rock-cut temple on Junonia and other ruins on Canaria, but there were no contemporary inhabitants. Nowhere else in the extant fragments of Juba's works is there such a thorough rendering of his range of interests and the type of information that he considered worthy of reporting. On the Canary Islands Juba had no particular bias to promote, unlike in the case of his

79 The material was combined with that of an intermediary, Statius Sebosus, one of Pliny's regular sources on material as varied as India (9.46) and Meroë (6.183), but otherwise unknown unless he is mentioned by Cicero (*Letters to Atticus* 2.14 and 2.15; W. Kroll, "Statius Sebosus" [#28], *RE* 2. ser. 3, 1929, 2223). See further, Jacoby, *Commentary*, pp. 342–3.

80 The single Greek name, Ombrios, is at the beginning of Pliny's excerpt of Juba's description: it is probable that Pliny began by recording Statius Sebosus' Latin list of toponyms and then examined Juba's Greek text, writing the Greek name for the first island. Pliny then corrected himself and reverted to Latin for the remaining names. Two of the islands, Invallis and Planasia, are only in Statius Sebosus' list and seem to be the most remote, perhaps not visited by Juba's team.

81 Juba's original Greek name was perhaps Kynika, interestingly similar to the Kynetes of Herodotos (4.49), the most westerly ethnic group, who may be reflected in the tribe known as the Canarii – so named because their diet was the same as that of dogs – that Suetonius Paulinus found (or heard about) in the tropics during his southern expedition in the 40s AC (*NH* 5.15 and infra, pp. 198–9). Interestingly, the island today called Gran Canaria (the third as one approaches the group from the east) is probably not Juba's Canaria, but Capraria: the name was probably transferred in early modern times from the island today known as Gomera, or just misapplied. Canary birds were named from the islands (not the other way around) in recent times.

82 Thomson, p. 262.

theory of the Nile, nor was he writing as an instrument of Roman government policy, as he would on Arabia and the eastern trade routes. Although economic considerations may have been part of his reason for making the exploration, there was no long-range commercial interest, for there was to be no settlement or exploitation (as these was of the Purple Islands) – this may be why Juba's material is so well preserved – and they remained outside European culture until the early fourteenth century.[83] The report shows Juba's scholarship at its best, displaying a wide-ranging interest in all the phenomena of a place previously unknown.

Despite the focus of *Libyka* on Mauretania, information about Juba's kingdom is rare in the extant fragments, although the account of the discovery of euphorbion hints at a major survey of the interior, perhaps led personally by the king.[84] Mythology tinged with natural history is found in the belief that the apples of the Hesperides, which Herakles brought to Greece, were the κίτρια, or citron.[85] The discussion of the source of the Nile provides some fauna – the alabeta, coracinus, and silurus fish, and crocodiles – from Lake Nilides.[86] The pearls from coastal Mauretania were among the best, but small.[87] Pliny's summary is more catalogic than analytical, yet these fragments show that Juba provided extensive natural and topographical information about his own world.

Yet Pliny did not use Juba's account as his primary source for Mauretania. The reason for this is apparent. In AD 41 the territory became a Roman province. C. Suetonius Paulinus was given a propraetorian command the following year to subdue the territory, and in doing so crossed the Atlas – the first Roman officer to do so – and penetrated far to the south.[88] His published report discussed the interior of Mauretania in detail, with a specific interest in the high-altitude flora of the mountains.[89] He continued into the desert, and seems to have learned about the tropical forests beyond, even if he did not go that far. Much of Pliny's account of Mauretania came from this source and has the context of that

---

83 Cary and Warmington (supra note 13), pp. 69, 260. They appear on a map of 1339; the first extant record of a visit is in 1341 (John Mercer, *The Canary Islanders: Their Prehistory, Conquest and Survival* [London: Collings, 1980], p. 155); see further, infra, p. 259.

84 *NH* 25.77 = Juba, fr. 7 ("invenit . . . Juba").

85 Athenaios 3.83b–c = Juba, fr. 6.

86 *NH* 5.51 = Juba, fr. 38a. The alabeta is otherwise unknown; the name "coracinus" (κορακῖνος) shows that it was dark in color, perhaps a tilapia; the siluris (σίλουρος) is a generic name (LSJ).

87 *NH* 9.115 = Juba, fr. 71.

88 Dio 60.9.

89 *NH* 5.14–15; Pliny (ed. Desanges), pp. 135–41; Hennig (supra note 18), pp. 344–7; P. de la Chapelle, "L'Expédition de Suetonius Paulinus dans le sud-est du Maroc," *Hespéris* 19, 1934, 107–24; Andreas Gutsfeld, *Römische Herrschaft und einheimischer Widerstand in Nordafrika: Militärische Auseinandersetzungen Rom mit den Nomaden*, Heidelberger althistorische Beiträge und epigraphische Studien 8 (Stuttgart 1989), pp. 72–6.

period.[90] Suetonius Paulinus' report would have been at most only thirty years old when Pliny published the *Natural History*. Despite his respect for Juba, he preferred a more recent account, and relegated the king to one of the *celebrati auctores* who had earlier written about the ancient wonders of Mauretania.[91] Only when Juba diverged from Suetonius Paulinus' material was his version used.

The geographical reach of *Libyka* extended across North Africa to the eastern coast of the continent. Its examination of the course of the Nile, down to its mouth, has already been discussed; if Juba's treatise included other material about Egypt proper, this has largely not survived, being ignored by Pliny because of the testimonia that had been added by various Romans up to the time of Nero.[92] But Ethiopia[93] and the routes to the Red Sea were another matter. These were less known to the Romans, and here Juba, always conscious of his Roman audience, could make a more lasting contribution. Yet it is difficult to isolate the various fragments on Ethiopia from those concerned with access to the Red Sea, Arabia, and India; in fact, the question regarding the join between *Libyka* and the later *On Arabia* is a vexing one. It is possible that the geographical limit of *Libyka* was the Nile, which reached Ethiopia after its strange twenty-day underground journey.[94] Juba described the wildlife and islands in the river, and its characteristics down to the Egyptian frontier, but Pliny's version is brief,[95] little more than a long list of toponyms that are contrasted with those from the *Aithiopika* of

---

90 See *NH* 5.20, where there are several references to the emperor Claudius. It also has in places the credulous tone of a Roman officer who had gone far beyond the limits of (to him) the civilized world and was more than a little nervous about being in such remote territory: see *NH* 5.7:

> None of the inhabitants is to be seen in the daytime, and everything is quiet because of the terror of the desert, so that an awesome silence comes over those approaching, and, moreover, a terror at what is raised above the clouds into the neighborhood of the lunar sphere. In the nights it flashes with frequent fires and is filled with the wantonness of Aegipanes and Satyrs, and the music of flutes and pipes and the sound of drums and cymbals.

> Incolarum neminem interdiu cerni, silere omnia haut alio quam solitudinum horrore, sabire tacitam religionem animus propius accendentium praeterque horrorem elati super nubila atque in vicina lunaris circuli; eundem noctibus micare crebris ignibus, Aegipanum Satyrorumque lascivia inpleri, tibiarum ac fistulae cantu typanorum et cymbalorum sonitu strepere.

The modern visitor may not be affected quite the same way as was Suetonius Paulinus, but the Atlas and contiguous northern Sahara are still a mystical place.

91 *NH* 5.7. On Pliny's sources for Africa, see Brent D. Shaw, "The Elder Pliny's African Geography," *Historia* 30, 1981, 424–67.

92 *NH* 6.181.

93 In antiquity the term "Ethiopia" included the regions between the first two cataracts of the Nile, modern Nubia.

94 *NH* 5.52–4 = Juba, fr. 38a.

95 *NH* 5.59 = Juba, fr. 39.

Bion of Soloi,[96] probably one of the explorers of Ptolemaios II. Peculiarly, Juba thought that the people living along the Nile between Syene and Meroë were in fact Arabian and that one Egyptian city, Solis, was an Arabian foundation;[97] this may have been nationalistic propaganda received from Arabian informants. But Juba may have had little to add to previous accounts.

Other comments about Ethiopia fall into the category of mercantile and trade information about the exotic interior of a little-known territory. For example, if one traveled twenty-five days from Koptos, one would find the source of Ethiopian emeralds, which were second in quality only to those from Cyprus.[98] Yet one had to beware of the deadly mantichoras, which had three rows of teeth, the face and ears of a human, the body of a lion, a stinging tail, and a human voice. Its preferred diet was human flesh.[99] There seems no doubt that the mantichoras, or martichoras – Persian for "man-eater"[100] – is the tiger, whose actual characteristics – a leonine body, conspicuous teeth, dangerous tail, and carnivorous tastes – had evolved into a mythical monster.[101] Tigers had been known to the Greeks since the time of Alexander[102] and were brought to Rome in the Augustan period,[103] but had never existed in Ethiopia, or anywhere in Africa.[104] Yet the persistent belief that East Africa was part of India[105] may have led to the idea that Indian tigers were to be found in both areas.[106] But the Ethiopian mantichoras is more a mythical beast of the type known to frequent little-known and remote places.[107]

Juba also discussed the Trogodyte territory, the coastal waters of the Red Sea,[108] although whether in *Libyka* or *On Arabia* is uncertain. The

---

96 *NH* 6.179 = Juba, fr. 37; *FGrHist* #668.

97 *NH* 6.177 = Juba, fr. 36.

98 *NH* 37.69 = Juba, fr. 77.

99 *NH* 8.107 = Juba, fr. 57; *NH* 8.75, from Ktesias (*FGrHist* #688, fr. 45dδ).

100 *LSJ*, μαρτιχόρας.

101 An alternative prototype for the Ethiopian mantichoras is the hyena: see Jacoby, *Commentary*, p. 348.

102 Otto Keller, *Die antike Tierwelt* (Lepizig: W. Engelman, 1909–13), vol. 1, pp. 61–2.

103 *NH* 8.65; Suetonius, *Augustus* 43.4; Dio 54.9.8.

104 Steier, "Tiger," *RE* 2. ser. 6, 1936, 946–7.

105 *NH* 6.175 = Juba, fr. 35.

106 The geographer Ptolemy referred to Ethiopian (i.e. African) tigers (4.8.4), but this does not seem to be supported by the zoological evidence, and may be due to the common confusion of East Africa and India.

107 For the Ethiopian elephant (*NH* 8.35 = Juba, fr. 58; see also *NH* 8.26, 32), see infra, pp. 206–7. A final fragment from *Libyka* about Ethiopia may be #46, Herodian's citation (13.28) of the foreign name Nabomos, remindful of *nabun* (see also ναβοῦς, *IG* 14.1302), an Ethiopian word for the camelopard or giraffe (*NH* 8.69, perhaps also from Juba). But Herodian believed that Nabomos was a proper name, and thus the word may be Babylonian and from Juba's obscure *On Assyria*. On this passage, see Jacoby, *Commentary*, p. 343.

108 *NH* 6.169–75; 13.142; 31.18 = Juba, fr. 34, 35, 67, 40.

Trogodytai[109] had been known to Greeks since Classical times, but came under their detailed scrutiny only with the Ptolemaic development of eastern trade. Ptolemaios II's construction of his Red Sea port of Berenike and the road to it from the Nile[110] brought Greeks into the heart of Trogodytika, and formal relations were established, some Trogodytes eventually serving in the Ptolemaic government.[111] They had been studied by Hellenistic geographers,[112] but Juba believed that he could provide more recent information, since the Hellenistic treatises did not reflect the changing political dynamics of the Augustan period. He listed nine tribal groups,[113] two of whose names, Therothoai ("Beast Hunters") and Ichthyophagoi ("Fish Eaters"), reflect the actual characteristics of the people. Some of the other seven tribes may belong further down the East African coast.[114] Pliny considered Juba's research on the Trogodytes definitive,[115] so much so that what seemed to be Juba's failure to discuss additional towns called Berenike in this region must, he felt, have been a copying error. Juba provided a topographical survey of the coast and its offshore islands, including some of their flora.[116] The most interesting island was Topazos, just southeast of Berenike, generally considered modern St. John's Island or Jazirat Zabarjad, and notable as the only source of peridot, gem olivine, which was especially prized by royalty.[117] In Greek this was χρυσόλιθον,[118] but Pliny called it *topazos* after the island, presumably following Juba. Juba, ever interested in linguistics, noted that *topazin* was Trogodyte for "to seek," because the island was often fogbound and had to be searched for by sailors.[119] This information was based on the work of Philon, an officer of Ptolemaios II who

---

109 This is the correct term (in Greek, Τρογοδύται, Herodotos 4.83), but it was often misspelled (or miscopied) as Troglodytai, "Cave-Dwellers," which is wrong, as there are no cave dwellings in Trogodytika. On this, see G. W. Murray, "Trogodytica: The Red Sea Littoral in Ptolemaic Times," *Geographical Journal* 43, 1967, 24.

110 Strabo 17.1.45; *NH* 6.101–3; on Berenike, see David Meredith, "Berenice Troglodytica" [*sic*], *JEA* 43, 1957, 56–70; Steven E. Sidebotham, "Ports of the Red Sea and the Arabia–India Trade," in *Rome and India: The Ancient Sea Trade*, ed. Vimala Begley and Richard Daniel De Puma (Madison: University of Wisconsin Press, 1979), pp. 20–1.

111 Lionel Casson, *The Periplus Maris Erythraei* (Princeton, N.J.: Princeton University Press, 1989), p. 99.

112 Diodoros 3.32–3; Strabo 16.4.17.

113 *NH* 6.176–7 = Juba, fr. 36.

114 In particular, the Zangenai seem to belong well south, and are often connected with the Azania of the *Periplous of the Erythraian Sea* (15) and Zanzibar: see Casson (supra note 111), p. 136 and H. von Wissman, "Zangenae," *RE* Supp. 11, 1968, 1337–48; also Fraser (supra note 3), vol. 2, p. 780.

115 *NH* 6.170 = Juba, fr. 34; Jehan Desanges, "Les Sources de Pline dans sa description de la Troglodytique [*sic*] et de l'Ethiopie, *NH* 6, 163–97," in *Pline l'Ancien: témoin de son temps*, ed. Iacobus Pigealdus and Iosephus Orozius (Salamanca: Universidad Pontificial, 1987), pp. 277–92.

116 *NH* 13.142 = Juba, fr. 67.

117 *NH* 37.108 = Juba, fr. 75; Casson (supra note 111), p. 94.

118 *Periplous of the Erythraian Sea* 39.

119 *NH* 37.108 = Juba, fr. 75.

wrote on Ethiopia.[120] Other information on the products of Topazos island, such as sandarach and ochre, may also be from Philon's treatise:[121] he was probably Juba's major source for the region. Another nearby Red Sea island, Nekron, produced crystal, which another Ptolemaic explorer, Pythagoras, had exploited.[122] Juba's account of the harvest of coral and other offshore phenomena, such as the descriptively named Χαρίτων βλέφαρον ("Eyelid of the Graces") and Crinis Isidis ("Hair of Isis")[123] almost certainly come from the same Ptolemaic sources, although Pliny may have had Roman information on the latter, since he provided only a Latin name. Juba also recorded the strange lake Insanus (the Greek name is not preserved), which alternated between bitterness and freshness and was full of snakes,[124] perhaps a tale learned from an Arabian or Alexandrian merchant.

A final peculiar incident regarding Trogodytika, although perhaps not reported by Juba, may have stimulated his personal interest in the territory. His mother-in-law Kleopatra VII, an accomplished linguist, spoke the Trogodytic language.[125] After the Battle of Actium, she returned to Egypt ahead of Antonius and proceeded to have the remnants of her fleet dragged across the Isthmus of Suez and into the Red Sea, a distance of 300 stadia. She planned to set forth with her retinue and extensive funds to start a new life somewhere beyond Egypt.[126] But when her ships entered the Red Sea they were burned by the Nabataeans – who were ill-disposed to her for a variety of reasons, not the least of which was their loss of territory under the Donations of Alexandria[127] – and Antonius (whose involvement in or even prior knowledge of this scheme is uncertain) persuaded her to abandon the idea. Her potential destination is unknown, but it is plausible that she had Trogodytika in mind, where she spoke the language and which was easily accessible by her Red Sea fleet, and where she might expect to be welcomed, even as its queen.[128] If this was one of the last things young Kleopatra Selene heard from her mother, Juba would have learned it himself and perhaps have been inspired to find out more about the territory.

Many fragments of *Libyka* are natural historical in context; some of these which also have a geographical basis have already been discussed. The

120 *FGrHist* #670; Strabo 2.1.20.

121 *NH* 35.39 = Juba, fr. 74.

122 *NH* 37.24 = Juba, fr. 76. This Pythagoras may also have been a source for Juba's *Theatrical History* (supra, p. 175).

123 *NH* 13.142 = Juba, fr. 67; see also *NH* 32.21.

124 *NH* 31.18 = Juba, fr. 40; *NH* 2.228, on a spring in Trogodytika, may also be from Juba. For Trogodytes and elephants (*NH* 8.26, 32), see infra, p. 207.

125 Plutarch, *Antonius* 27.

126 Plutarch, *Antonius* 69; see also Dio 51.6.7: on these and other such schemes attributed to Kleopatra at this time, see Plutarch, *Life of Antony*, ed. C. B. R. Pelling (Cambridge: Cambridge University Press, 1988), pp. 288–91.

127 Plutarch, *Antonius* 36.2.

128 Murray (supra note 109), pp. 32–3.

discovery and analysis of euphorbion demonstrates a concern about the medicinal and practical properties of plants; similar is an interest in how to make honey.[129] Juba also mentioned the citron,[130] and may have discussed dates.[131] Precious stones are frequently considered, such as Ethiopian emeralds, topazos, Egyptian alabastrites (perhaps onyx), and the *nilios* stone from the banks of the Nile, perhaps the blue sapphire.[132]

Fauna are an extensive topic. The Nilotic passages include comments on the riverine animals, particularly crocodiles.[133] The Ethiopian mantichoras, whether from myth or natural history, has already been noted. The characteristics of the Mauretanian lynx are also recorded.[134] But of all the animal kingdom, two especially interested Juba: lions and elephants. These were most associated with his world and remained exotic to the Greeks and Romans. Both had an exalted, almost mystical quality that set them apart from other fauna. The lion had been known since Bronze Age times, as is testified in Linear B,[135] by countless references in mythology from Homer onward, and in monuments such as the Lion Gate at Mykenai.[136] The close association of the animal with Herakles made it of special curiosity to Juba. By the beginning of post-Bronze Age Greek society it was already almost mythic, an attitude assisted by its extinction in the Mediterranean coastal areas, although it survived until the fifth century BC in the wilder parts of Thrace.[137] Lions became associated with eastern royalty – one need only think of Assyrian reliefs – which not only contributed to their exoticism but made them suitable for the new royalty of the first century BC. They first came to Rome during the consulship of Q. Scaevola, 95 BC,[138] and became common in the circus thereafter: Juba's father-in-law Antonius was famed as having been the first Roman to yoke them to a chariot.[139] Juba I had a close association with the lion and placed it on his coins,[140] and by the Augustan period they had come to be proverbially associated with the world of Numidian and Mauretanian royalty.[141]

129 It was to be made in a wooden box, as is still done today (*Geoponika* 15.2.21 = Juba, fr. 61). On the questions regarding this passage, see supra, Chapter 7, note 136.
130 Athenaios 3.83bc = Juba, fr. 6, although the participants in the *Deipnosophistai* disputed as to whether Juba had actually discussed the fruit. See also *NH* 13.91.
131 *NH* 13.46–8. This requires an emendation suggested by C. Müller (*FHG*, Juba, fr. 54) but generally not accepted.
132 *NH* 37.73 = Juba, fr. 78; *NH* 37.114 = Juba, fr. 79; John F. Healy, *Pliny the Elder on Science and Technology* (Oxford: Oxford University Press, 1999), p. 268.
133 *NH* 5.51 = Juba, fr. 38a.
134 Aelian, *On the Characteristics of Animals* 14.6.
135 The Linear B is "re-wo" (or "re-wo-pi" when used instrumentally): Michael Ventris and John Chadwick, *Documents in Mycenaean Greek* (Cambridge: Cambridge University Press, 1956), pp. 408, 425.
136 On the lion in antiquity generally, see Keller (supra note 102) 1.24–61.
137 Herodotos 7.125.
138 *NH* 8.53 (although the passage is ambiguous).
139 *NH* 8.55.
140 Mazard #89, 93.
141 Horace, *Ode* 1.22.

Juba II also had his own series of lion coins (Figure 25e, p. 245),[142] continued by his son Ptolemaios,[143] but his surviving discussions of lions remain anecdotal. A story that Juba heard about his father[144] recounted how a member of his entourage had attempted to kill a lion, and that a year later the lion was waiting at the same spot where it had been wounded and identified its attacker from among a large group and killed him. Similar, and perhaps from the same family sources, is the story of a Gaetulian woman who had been attacked by lions, but who escaped following an intense and pathetic verbal plea.[145] These are both folk tales of the Aesopic variety, a type popular in the Hellenistic period. Whether more scientific material was also part of Juba's treatise cannot be determined: a possible example is a brief passage on the social habits of the animal, which in Plutarch's *Whether Land or Sea Animals Are Wiser* follows Juba's account of such characteristics of elephants.[146] Pliny's lengthy discussion of lions is mostly derived from Aristotle but includes later sources, including Polybios and various Romans. Juba is cited once, in the matter of the Gaetulian woman.[147] But the remainder of the paragraph, not otherwise attributed, is also from Juba.[148] It builds on the experience of the Gaetulian woman and discusses the mental state of lions and their method of fighting: so to speak, a psychological profile of the animal. Near the end of the paragraph the reader is told that "when wounded, he familiarizes himself with his attacker through remarkable observation, and makes for him however large the crowd,"[149] the same as the story from the time of Juba I, without the personal details. Thus it is certain that the intervening material on the mental characteristics of lions is part of Juba's treatise. Nevertheless, much of it has a folkish tone ("they are lacking in deceit and suspicion," "when dying he bites the earth and sheds a tear for his death")[150] that reveals its origins as being neither from earlier or Juban scientific analysis but from the anecdotal memory of Numidian royalty and their personal experiences with the animal.

Elephants are the subject of more of the fragments of *Libyka* – over one-third – than any other topic. Juba's area of research – the southern half of the known world – was coterminous with the range of the elephant, which

---

142 Mazard #140–3, 270.
143 Mazard #408–13, 498–502.
144 Aelian, *On the Characteristics of Animals* 7.23 = Juba, fr. 55.
145 *NH* 8.48 = Solinus 27.15 = Juba, fr. 56. On this passage, see Jehan Desanges, "Un Témoignage masqué sur Juba II et les troubles de Gétulie," *AntAfr* 33, 1997, 111–13.
146 Plutarch, *Whether Land or Sea Animals Are Wiser* 17 = Juba, fr. 51a.
147 *NH* 8.42–58. The citation of Juba is in Chapter 48 and requires an emendation, but a reasonable one, since Solinus seems to have read the king's name when he made use of Pliny's text (Solinus 27.15 = Juba, fr. 56).
148 *NH* 8.49–52.
149 *NH* 8.51: "vulneratus observatione mira percussorem novit et in quantalibet multitudine adpetit."
150 *NH* 8.52: "dolis carent et suspicione . . . a moriente humum morderi lacrimamque leto dari."

was originally found from India through Syria and throughout much of Africa, although the Syrian elephant was extinct by the Iron Age. There were several varieties in Africa; Juba's concern was the North African type, found in his territories, and the central African type of Ethiopia and environs.[151]

The Greeks knew about ivory before they encountered the elephant, for this is the original meaning of ἐλέφας, known in the Mediterranean world from the Bronze Age.[152] Herodotos is the first Greek to have mentioned the animal itself. He visited Elephantine on the upper Nile, and wrote of elephants in Ethiopia and in western North Africa.[153] But it is only with Aristotle that Greek literature provides a full account,[154] and by the end of the fourth century BC, as a result of the travels of Alexander the Great, elephants had become familiar in the eastern Mediterranean. Pyrrhos of Epeiros introduced them to Italy, and they were seen in Rome proper in the triumph of M'Curius Dentatus in 275 BC.[155] By Juba's day they were common in the city: at the dedication of the Theater of Pompeius eighteen elephants fought against armored men, which aroused sympathy for the animals among the audience, much to Pompeius' dismay.[156]

Carthaginian knowledge of the animal dates from at least the time of Hanno, who saw them in northwest Africa, half a day's travel from Cape Soloeis.[157] If there is anything to be believed in Juba's statement that he found an elephant in the wilds of the High Atlas with a Carthaginian brand that was four hundred years old,[158] Carthaginians had domesticated them by the latter fifth century BC; by the early third century BC they were an effective part of the Carthaginian military machine.[159] Hannibal's use of them is a legendary part of ancient history: from this time on the elephant was indelibly associated in the Roman mind with North Africa.[160] The Carthaginian facility with the animal and its availability in North Africa meant that domestication soon spread to the petty kings in the region, including Juba's ancestors, and from at least the time of Massinissa the elephant was an important part of the self-conception of Numidian royalty.[161] Jugurtha had

151 Keller (supra note 102), vol. 1, pp. 372–83; H. H. Scullard, *The Elephant in the Greek and Roman World* (London: Thames and Hudson, 1974), pp. 24–31.

152 Linear B "e-re-pa" (Ventris and Chadwick [supra note 135], p. 393); Homer, *Iliad* 4.141, 5.583, and regularly in the *Odyssey*.

153 Herodotos 3.97, 114; 4.191.

154 The citations were collected by Scullard (supra note 151), pp. 37–49.

155 *NH* 8.16; Plutarch, *Pyrrhos* 15; Florus 1.13.28.

156 Dio 39.38.

157 Hanno 4.

158 Philostratos, *Life of Apollonios* 2.13 = Juba, fr. 50.

159 Polybios 1.18–19; Appian, *Libyka* 95.

160 Coltelloni-Trannoy, pp. 169–71.

161 Mazard #17.

an elephant corps, part of which he paid as tribute to the Romans.[162] In his war with Rome his elephants were ineffective on the terrain of the battlefield and scattered, eventually to be captured and killed by the Romans, and he surrendered all his remaining elephants in the peace negotiations.[163] His grandnephew Juba I was also a proponent of elephant warfare, putting their likeness on his coins[164] and capturing them in the forests of Numidia for his ally Scipio.[165] Juba I used them against the Romans, but they were no great help, and Caesar captured sixty-four of them and paraded them before the city of Thapsus, intimidating it into surrender. As a result, the Roman Fifth Legion adopted the figure of an elephant for its standards, and continued to use it as late as the second century AC.[166] Yet however exotic, elephant warfare had been proven ineffective and would not again be a regular part of Roman military tactics until late-antique engagements with the Sassanians,[167] although Juba II may have used them against Tacfarinas.[168] But despite the failure of the animal in military usage, it had become linked with the image of northern Africa and the Roman conception of that part of the world.[169] Still available in the wilds in the second half of the first century BC, the elephant had already become a standard element of the local numismatic iconography (Figure 25d, p. 245),[170] and it is inevitable that Juba would write about it extensively.

Juba's discussion of elephants is almost entirely about those of his own world, northern Africa, with a few comments about the "Ethiopian" variety, the central African type.[171] Ancient writers, including Juba, made no precise zoological distinction between types of elephants,[172] but used a geographical classification. Pliny knew of three varieties, the African, Ethiopian, and Indian, with the home of the African said to be beyond the Syrtic deserts and in Mauretania.[173] The Ethiopian came from Ethiopia proper and

---

162 Mazard #73–5; Appian, *Iberika* 89; Sallust, *Jugurtha* 29.

163 Sallust, *Jugurtha* 49, 53, 62.

164 Mazard #89–93.

165 The use of elephants by Juba I and his allies is described throughout *De bello africo*, especially Chapters 1, 19, 25, 27, and 86; see also Florus 2.13.67.

166 Appian, *Civil War* 2.96.

167 Scullard (supra note 151), pp. 198–207.

168 Mazard #276.

169 J. M. C. Toynbee, *Animals in Roman Life and Art* (Ithaca, N.Y.: Cornell University Press, 1973), pp. 50–3.

170 The elephant not only appears on the coinage of the Numidian kings but on that of Bocchus II (Mazard #119) and the Roman coinage from Iol of perhaps 33–25 BC (Mazard #123–4). Juba II and Ptolemaios were to continue the practice (Mazard #135–9, 276, 403–5).

171 The North African elephant became extinct by late antiquity but the central African type still survives, although heavily endangered (Scullard [supra note 151], pp. 30–1).

172 It was generally recognized that the African and Indian varieties were quite different in size, but this is usually the limit of any ancient zoological taxonomy; see Scullard (supra note 151), p. 24.

173 *NH* 8.32.

Trogodytika; acquisition of Ethiopian elephants was an interest of the earlier Ptolemies.[174] There is no doubt that Pliny's geographical taxonomy is from Juba's account, which always named the Ethiopian[175] – to Juba, the foreign type – but not the African, the indigenous and familiar variety. Juba further classified the African through its tusks, noting that they differed in the elephants of the marshes, mountains, and plains,[176] information he had gained from ivory hunters rather than elephant users. This shows awareness of the three known types of African elephant,[177] but is a distinction limited to their tusks and their ivory, which traveled farther than the elephants themselves.

As with the lion, Juba's material has an anecdotal quality and came largely from ancestral traditions. Hunting of the animal was a major interest. The preferred method was to dig pits covered with brush,[178] which replaced an earlier technique of rounding them up on horseback and herding them into trenches, starving them into docility, the method used by the "kings," presumably Juba's ancestors.[179] It was contrasted to the method used by the Trogodytes (whose interest was in food, not domestication), who would jump onto them from trees and hamstring them, or shoot them with arrows and spears from gigantic bows that it took several people to hold.[180]

But it was the unique habits of the elephant that interested Juba the most. The animals demonstrated a near-human intelligence and social behavior that was particularly fascinating.[181] According to Juba, they would help each other when hunted, organizing their resistance to a party of hunters by placing those with the smallest – and thus least valuable – tusks in the front, thereby protecting those with the best.[182] Most notably, they would rescue their comrades who fell into hunters' pits by using branches and rocks to construct a ramp into the trap, although Plutarch, usually respectful of Juba's scholarship, called this story a monstrosity and claimed that Juba was using his status as a king to impose strange ideas.[183] Juba evidently went further than Plutarch admitted, because Philostratos recorded

---

174 See Steven E. Sidebotham, *Roman Economic Policy in the Erythra Thalassa, 30 B.C.–A.D. 217*, Mnemosyne Supplement 91 (Leiden 1986), p. 4; Murray (supra note 109), pp. 25–7.

175 Juba, fr. 49, 58.

176 Philostratos, *Life of Apollonios* 2.13 = Juba, fr. 50.

177 Scullard (supra note 151), pp. 24–5.

178 Plutarch, *Whether Land or Sea Animals Are Wiser* 17 = Juba, fr. 51a.

179 *NH* 8.24–5.

180 *NH* 8.26.

181 Scullard (supra note 151), pp. 21–3.

182 *NH* 8.7 = Juba, fr. 47.

183 *NH* 8.25; Plutarch, *Whether Land or Sea Animals Are Wiser* 17, 25 = Juba, fr. 51. It must be stressed, however, that Plutarch's criticism of Juba here is part of the structure of the dialogue and so may merely be rhetorical.

that his Apollonios read in Juba's treatise that elephants not only helped each other when hunted but would remove wounded comrades from danger and bathe their wounds in aloe.[184] There are other extreme tales of elephantine social behavior: at the time of the new moon they would ritually purify themselves (the Amilo River in Mauretania was one place this happened) and return home carrying their tired young. They had other religious practices, such as praying and showing obeisance to their trainers and masters. They could understand human speech and even fall in love with humans and recognize specific people after many years.[185] They could link themselves together into a raft to cross the Red Sea.[186] Their great longevity was legendary: in addition to the four-hundred-year-old found in the High Atlas, Juba knew of one of great age that his father had owned and other long-lived ones possessed by the Ptolemaic and Seleukid kings.[187]

Because the ivory trade was an important economic use of the animal,[188] many comments refer to the tusks. Tusks were hunted in Mauretania by magically locating the place where the animals shed them, as water would mysteriously evaporate from skins when near buried tusks.[189] Juba felt that the tusks were the animal's horns, a view rejected by Philostratos, and distinguished types of elephant by the characteristics of their tusks.[190] He described how they were used as digging implements and as weapons and were regularly shed.[191] Certain other anatomical features were also attested, such as their double heart (more a psychological comment) and their trumpeting.[192] Detailed information on their mating habits was also recorded.[193] And, always the linguist, Juba recorded a rare word for their trumpeting, στρηνύζω, "to make a harsh sound."[194]

Juba is an important source for the now extinct North African elephant. Although he has been described as "over-credulous,"[195] his personal familiarity with and devotion to the animal meant that he was able to observe it closely over a long period. He also inherited a vast amount of ancestral anecdotal material. There is much truth in his comments: the social characteristics are credible when interpreted through the humanizing

---

184 Philostratos, *Life of Apollonios* 2.16 = Juba, fr. 52.
185 *NH* 8.1, 13–15: some of these tales came from the court of Bocchus II.
186 *NH* 8.35 = Juba, fr. 58.
187 Philostratos, *Life of Apollonios* 2.13 = Juba, fr. 50; Aelian, *On the Characteristics of Animals* 9.58 = Juba, fr. 49.
188 Scullard (supra note 151), pp. 260–1.
189 Aelian, *On the Characteristics of Animals* 14.5.
190 Philostratos, *Life of Apollonios* 2.13 = Juba, fr. 50.
191 *NH* 8.7–8 = Juba, fr. 47a.
192 Aelian, *On the Characteristics of Animals* 14.6; Juba, fr. 48.
193 *NH* 8.13 = Juba, fr. 54.
194 Juba, fr. 48; for the derivation, see LSJ.
195 Scullard (supra note 151), p. 208.

eyes of those who spent much of their lives around elephants and began to see them as almost human. Some of the anatomical comments, such as the matter of the double heart,[196] imply a quasi-scientific observation of the animal's interior. One may believe less the stories about their religious sensitivity, but nonetheless, the strong social habits of the herd and the other unique qualities of the animal, especially its bulk and the ingenious uses of its trunk, make such interpretation possible within Juba's world. Even today the elephant remains most unusual and mystical, and is used by human beings in ways unimaginable for other animals. Visitors to modern India still feel a deep awe when confronted by elephants and see how they are treated and respected, and their unique integration into human society.[197]

A final characteristic of *Libyka* is its use of myth. Mythology pervades the work, although it is not possible to determine whether there was a special section on the topic. The interest in Herakles and his western localizations has already been noted. Another mythological discussion is the matter of Diomedes on the Libyan coast.[198] He was shipwrecked in Libya after the Trojan War and was about to be sacrificed by the local king, Lykos, to Ares, but was saved by the king's daughter Kallirrhoe, whom Diomedes abandoned when he left for Italy, whereupon she committed suicide.[199] This interesting yet familiar and formulaic tale is not otherwise testified,[200] but it is not difficult to see the source of Juba's interest in its parallel to Dido and Aeneas. Although it is specifically credited to the third book of the *Libyka* (the only book reference to that work preserved), it is connected to early Roman history, a published concern of Juba, and demonstrates his ethnographical research and his awareness of his Roman audience. When Juba moved to North Africa he had just completed his *Roman Archaeology*, which would have investigated the matter of Dido and Aeneas. Moreover, he seems to have had a special interest in Diomedes, since he examined the strange birds associated with that hero, describing their characteristics carefully in

---

196 This is really a characteristic of the shape of the animal's single heart (Scullard [supra note 151], p. 19).

197 There is an exhaustive modern literature on the unique social qualities of the elephant: see, in particular, Jeffrey Moussaieff Masson and Susan McCarthy, *When Elephants Weep* (London: Cape, 1994); Cynthia Moss, *Elephant Memories* (New York: W. Morrow, 1988), especially pp. 121–43; and even the 1948 novel *Elephant Walk* by Robert Standish, one of whose themes is the reaction of a clan of elephants in Sri Lanka to the placement of a tea plantation across one of their traditional routes.

198 [Plutarch], *Greek and Roman Parallels* 23 = Juba, fr. 5.

199 On Diomedes, see Erich Bethe, "Diomedes" (#1), *RE* 5, 1903, 815–26; John Boardman and C. F. Vafopoulou-Richardson, "Diomedes I," *LIMC* 3.1, 1986, 396–409.

200 P. Gunning, "Lykos" (#26), *RE* 13, 1927, 2402–3. It is perhaps not irrelevant that there was also a cult of Odysseus in Libya in Juba's day (Strabo 17.3.17).

one of his more detailed natural historical passages.[201] The fragment also treats some of the mythology of Diomedes, specifically his tomb on the Diomedian Islands (modern Tremiti off the Apulian coast), where birds unique to the area were said to be the metamorphosed comrades of the hero.[202] Diomedes, as one of the early Greek travelers to Italy, was relevant to Juba's historical and cultural interests. He was also of topical concern in Augustan Rome, the negotiator between Aeneas and the Latins and the one who made clear to the indigenous Italian populations the destiny of Aeneas.[203] Juba could make use of this, and just as he had connected Mauretania to the ancestral territories to the east, here he could link North Africa to Italy and to the Roman destiny, and further support Augustan policy by discreetly bypassing the recent unfortunate history of African–Roman relations through withdrawing to the mythological past.

Although written in Greek and thus in the mainstream of Greek ethnological scholarship, *Libyka* was largely designed for a Roman audience, to acquaint Rome with the new world that Juba had been sent to rule. But it also fulfilled the familial self-conception of Juba and Kleopatra Selene as the heir to both Numidian royalty (perhaps even Carthage) and the Ptolemies by linking all these lands in a broad cultural treatise that pushed beyond the boundaries of the known world into the Atlantic, sub-Saharan Africa, and to the east. Much of the information is anecdotal, obtained from the various complex inheritances of which the monarchs were a part. Portions of the treatise did not add to contemporary knowledge and soon vanished.[204] Yet the theory of the course of the Nile was still being considered in the nineteenth century, and information on the North African elephant survived when the animal did not. Moreover, the Ptolemaic and Egyptian connections brought about Juba's interest in

---

201 *NH* 10.126–7 = Juba, fr. 60. It is almost impossible to place this fragment among Juba's works. The obvious source is the *Roman Archaeology*, but its biological thrust is not generally associated with that treatise, even if the topic is early Italy. It more probably comes from the *Libyka*, and is a continuation of fr. 5, providing a fuller treatment of the myth of Diomedes coupled with a digression on the characteristics of the birds. Fauna had become one of Juba's interests after he moved to North Africa.

202 On the birds of Diomedes, see Jean Gagé, "Les Traditions 'diomédiques' dans l'Italie ancienne, de l'Apulie à l'Éturie méridionale, et quelques-unes des origins de la légende de Mézence," *MÉFRA* 84, 1972, 754–66.

203 Vergil, *Aeneid* 8.9, 11.225–33. On some of these issues, and Juba's possible relationship to Diomedes, see Christa Landwehr, "Juba II. als Diomedes?" *JdI* 107, 1992, 103–24.

204 Given the importance of snakes in the Roman conception of North Africa (supra, Chapter 2, note 11), and Juba's documented natural historical interests, it is probable that the treatise contained a section on ophids. Moreover, they had a special connection to his mother-in-law, which may have been part of the Roman interest. Pliny's scant information on snakes (*NH* 8.36–7, 85–8) does have an African context and is intermingled with material from Juba, yet the king is nowhere attributed. He is one of the sources for *NH* 8 (*NH* 1.8), but since this is the book that includes elephants and lions, the debt to Juba is apparent. Books 14, 26, and 28 also credit the king (*NH* 1.14, 26, 28) without citing him specifically in the text: Book 14 is on wine and Books 26 and 28 on drugs, all reasonable Juban topics, whether in *Libyka* or *On Arabia*.

the East African coast, and since this was becoming linked in the contemporary mind with the new route to India and Augustus' policy of developing trade contacts, Juba was led to thoughts in that direction. It is probable that Augustus was sent an early copy of the treatise and approved, seeing Juba as the emerging expert on the southern part of the known world. The Princeps thus encouraged the king to expand his studies to the east by joining the staff of Gaius Caesar and becoming the expert on Arabia.

9

THE EASTERN EXPEDITION WITH
GAIUS CAESAR

By the end of the first century BC, Juba had been on the throne for over twenty years. But the Roman world was changing.[1] Augustus turned 60 in 3 BC, and questions of succession were becoming acute. A new generation of the imperial family was reaching maturity, but events conspired to frustrate any of Augustus' plans concerning who would follow him. Juba's childhood friends did not seem destined to play any role: Marcellus had died in 23 BC, and Tiberius, although granted a five-year Eastern *imperium* beginning in 6 BC, almost simultaneously announced his retirement from politics and withdrawal to Rhodes. Marcus Agrippa, Augustus' closest confidant and an obvious successor, had died in 12 BC, Augustus' sister Octavia the following year, and Tiberius' brother Drusus two years later. Augustus' daughter Julia, successively the wife of Marcellus, Agrippa, and Tiberius, was already involved in the intrigues that resulted in her banishment in 2 BC: a liaison with the only surviving son of Antonius was her ultimate undoing. Any solution to the succession issue would, so it seemed, bypass one generation and turn to the younger one just coming to maturity at the turn of the century.

Moreover, there were external problems Augustus had to face, especially in the East.[2] In 9 or 8 BC the Nabataean king, Obodas, had died, perhaps by poison. His rule had never been strong or stable, and a succession struggle broke out, with various parties appealing to Augustus for arbitration. The Parthians continued to be a threat, and were to meddle in Armenian affairs after the death of the Roman puppet ruler in 7 BC, precipitating a series of crises. In Judaea the situation deteriorated as Herod the Great descended into madness, and after he died in 4 BC erupted into virtual civil war, again resulting in numerous petitions to Augustus. Thus all the non-Roman territories between Syria and Egypt, and well into the eastern interior, were

---

1 For a recent summary of the events of these years, see J. A. Crook, "Political History, 30 BC to AD 14," *CAH²* 10, 1996, 70–112.

2 On the background of Augustan policy in the East, see A. N. Sherwin-White, *Roman Foreign Policy in the East, 168 B.C. to A.D. 1* (London: Duckworth, 1984), pp. 322–41.

in some state of turmoil as Augustus celebrated his sixtieth birthday in September of 3 BC. Both the succession and eastern issues could not be ignored.

Augustus decided to solve both through the medium of his grandson, Gaius Caesar, son of Agrippa and Julia, born in 20 BC and fast approaching the age where he could be brought forth as potential successor. As one would expect from a grandfather, Augustus had shown him favor for many years, and in 5 BC the 15-year-old Gaius started his public career. He was named *princeps iuuentutis*, made a pontifex, and designated consul for AD 1. And Augustus began to see him as the one who could settle the deepening crisis in the East, especially given the recalcitrance of Tiberius, whose Eastern *imperium* was being spent in frustration on Rhodes.

Gaius' first involvement in eastern politics came with the death of Herod the Great. A violent dispute erupted over that succession – or indeed, whether there would be a succession – and appeals were made to Augustus, who convened a commission in Rome in the spring of 4 BC.[3] Sitting on the commission were leading Romans and friends of Augustus, but the only one recorded by name is young Gaius, who, in a prominent place at Augustus' side, heard the testimony of Herod's sons and relatives, members of his royal court including Nikolaos of Damaskos, and an embassy of fifty Jewish leaders. He also read the dispatches from Roman officials in Syria and Judaea. These debates were long and heated, and, because of the large number attending, a second meeting had to be held in the Temple of Apollo Palatinus, near Augustus' residence. There were also public disturbances, as eight thousand members of the local Jewish community agitated for abolition of the monarchy. After the second session, Augustus decided to partition Herod's kingdom and to deny kingship to any of his sons. Presumably Gaius took part in the deliberations and advised Augustus on his final decision; such was this 16-year-old's introduction to the ever-turbulent politics of the Roman East.[4] In placing Gaius on the commission Augustus was testing his grandson's sensitivity and maturity as a politician and diplomat and educating him about the East, and within two years plans were being laid for a major eastern campaign for the young heir apparent. It was becoming increasingly obvious that Tiberius had no interest in exercising the duties of his *imperium*, which would terminate in 2 BC. Gaius, who would turn 18 that year, seemed the natural successor.

Thus plans were formulated for a great eastern expedition led by Gaius that would range far and wide, from the Nabataean territories and Arabia in

---

3 Josephus, *Jewish Wars* 2.25–38, 80–100; *Jewish Antiquities* 17.228–49, 301–20; J. A. Crook, *Consilium Principis: Imperial Councils and Counsellors from Augustus to Diocletian* (Cambridge: Cambridge University Press, 1955), pp. 32–3.

4 The two sessions were perhaps two or three weeks apart in April or May of 4 BC. Gaius was mentioned only in the context of the first; whether he attended the second is perhaps immaterial to the experience he gained by attending at least the first.

the south to Armenia in the north.[5] Most ancient sources tend to emphasize the crisis in Armenia as the primary reason. Yet this had been dormant in the years immediately prior to Gaius' departure and did not resurface until he was already en route, and thus cannot have been the main cause.[6] The most contemporary literary comments, an epigram of Antipatros of Thessalonike and Ovid's *Ars amatoria*, both written as the expedition was setting forth, make little mention of Armenia but emphasize the Parthians, the real focus of Augustus' interest.[7] Ovid took note of Mars, Crassus, and legionary standards, and thus conspicuously connected the departure with the dedication of the Temple of Mars Ultor in the Forum of Augustus, 12 May 2 BC,[8] and the standards M. Licinius Crassus had lost in 53 BC, which were finally to find a permanent home in the temple.[9] Since it was Tiberius who had recovered the standards – in 20 BC, in his first major independent campaign, in the year of Gaius' birth – and Tiberius' little-used *imperium* would expire at the end of the year of the dedication, necessitating a rethinking of Roman policy in the East, from its very initiation Gaius' expedition was in contrast,

---

5 The primary ancient sources are Velleius 2.101–2, Pliny (*NH* 6.141, 160; 12.55–6; 32.10), Tacitus (*Annals* 1.3; 2.4, 42), Suetonius (*Augustus* 65, 67, 93; *Tiberius* 12; *Nero* 5), and Dio 55.10–12, 57.17.3–4. A single surviving letter from Augustus to Gaius, dated 23 September AD 1 (Aulus Gellius 15.7.3), is the sole remnant of a published volume of correspondence between the Princeps and his grandson while the latter was in the East. Although the letter expresses Augustus' expectation that Gaius would succeed him, it sheds no other light on the campaign. There are also numerous inscriptions, many of which record the honors paid to the expedition by cities through which it passed, as well as a memorial to Gaius at Pisa (*ILS* 140), erected in April of AD 4, that records his death date, 21 February of that year. The best modern account remains F. E. Romer, "Gaius Caesar's Military Diplomacy in the East," *TAPA* 109, 1979, 199–214, which includes citations of the relevant inscriptions; supplemented by his "A Numismatic Date for the Departure of C. Caesar," *TAPA* 108, 1978, 187–202; and Frédéric Hurlet, *Les Collègues du prince sous Auguste et Tibère: de la légalité républicaine à la légitimité dynastic*, CÉFR 227, 1997, pp. 127–41; see also Glen Bowersock, "Augustus and the East: The Problem of the Succession," in *Caesar Augustus: Seven Aspects*, ed. Fergus Millar and Erich Segal (Oxford: Clarendon Press, 1984), pp. 170–9; Helmut Halfmann, *Itinera principum*, Heidelberger althistorische Beiträge und epigraphische Studien 2 (Stuttgart 1986), pp. 166–7; Crook, *CAH*[2] 10 (supra note 1), pp. 104–5; David Magie, *Roman Rule in Asia Minor* (Princeton, N.J.: Princeton University Press, 1950), pp. 481–5; Daniela Sidari, "Studi su Gaio e Lucio Cesare," *AttiVen* 138, 1979–80, 275–302. On the iconography of Gaius and its political meaning, see, cautiously, Paul Zanker, *The Power of Images in the Age of Augustus*, translated Alan Shapiro (Ann Arbor: University of Michigan Press, 1988), pp. 215–23. Other modern comments on the campaign are cited infra. Many of the details of the expedition are not germane to the issues of Juba's involvement, on which the following account centers.

6 Romer, *TAPA* 109 (supra note 5), pp. 203–4.

7 Antipatros #47; see also #46; Ovid, *Ars amatoria* 1.177–227 (see Ronald Syme, *History in Ovid* [Oxford: Clarendon Press, 1978], pp. 8–15); Bowersock (supra note 5), p. 171. There is also a fragment of what may be Augustus' own valedictory (pseudo-Plutarch, *Sayings of Kings and Commanders* 207e).

8 The date has been determined by C. J. Simpson, "The Date of Dedication of the Temple of Mars Ultor," *JRS* 67, 1977, 91–4.

9 Romer, *TAPA* 108 (supra note 5), pp. 191–202.

even in contention, with the career of Tiberius. This tension between the two would affect not only affairs in the East but also the careers of prominent Romans for many years to come.[10]

Augustus was well aware of his grandson's youth and inexperience, and thus assembled a strong field staff. Chief of staff was M. Lollius, the consul of 21 BC, who had been the first Roman official in Galatia when it became a province after the death of Amyntas in 25 BC.[11] Literary sources do not remember his association with Gaius favorably: it was said that he took bribes from every king in the East, and that even his earlier military campaigns in Germany had been a disaster.[12] There were indeed problems with the quality of his service, which seem to have resulted in his dismissal from the staff and suicide; this may have brought about the ultimate collapse of the expedition itself. But it is unlikely that Augustus would have chosen a proven incompetent for this sensitive post, and Lollius' real sin may have been in slandering Tiberius to Gaius, and thus becoming a scapegoat for Tiberius' contemporary personal difficulties, leading the literary tradition to assert that he was known for long-standing incompetence and treachery.[13]

Another important staff member was P. Sulpicius Quirinius, who had been consul in 12 BC and who had triumphed for campaigns in Kilikia against the murderers of Amyntas of Galatia.[14] He had also fought against the Garamantes in Africa[15] and may recently have held a position in Syria.[16] It is not certain whether he was with the expedition from the start, or merely joined it in Syria, but he may have succeeded Lollius as chief of staff.[17] Also on the staff was Cn. Domitius Ahenobarbus.[18] Because he did not become consul until AD 32, he may have been no older than Gaius and, as his cousin, was perhaps a childhood friend. He was also having his first overseas experience, and may have been asked to join because of his family

10 Bowersock (supra note 5), pp. 170–1.
11 Suetonius, *Tiberius* 12; *PIR*[2] L311; Ronald Syme, *The Augustan Aristocracy* (Cambridge: Cambridge University Press, 1986), p. 43.
12 *NH* 9.118; see also Velleius 2.97, 102.
13 Tacitus, *Annals* 3.48; Bowersock (supra note 5), p. 183. See also Velleius Paterculus, *The Tiberian Narrative (2.94–131)*, ed. A. J. Woodman (Cambridge: Cambridge University Press, 1977), pp. 110–11, and Syme, *History* (supra note 7), p. 12 for the contradictory evidence as to Lollius' career.
14 Tacitus, *Annals* 3.48; Strabo 12.6.5; Syme, *Augustan Aristocracy* (supra note 11), pp. 338–41.
15 Supra, p. 108.
16 Whether he had been in Syria just before Gaius' campaign depends on whether he is the Κυρήνιος cited at Luke 2.2 who conducted the census associated with the birth of Jesus of Nazareth. He definitely was in Syria by AD 6, as he was involved in the deposing of Archelaos of Judaea that year (Josephus, *Jewish Antiquities* 17.355, 18.1). The Syrian part of his career has been long and inconclusively debated.
17 He was astute enough to show respect to Tiberius, and twenty years later received a magnificent public funeral at which the emperor himself delivered the eulogy, contrasting his distinguished career with that of the perfidious Lollius (Tacitus, *Annals* 3.48).
18 Suetonius, *Nero* 5; *PIR*[2] D127; Syme, *Augustan Aristocracy* (supra note 11), index.

connections, as he was a grandson of Antonius and Octavia and thus one of Augustus' few surviving male blood relatives, perhaps sent forth to redeem the mixed career of his father, the consular L. Domitius Ahenobarbus.[19] Tradition has it that the son did not rise to expectations and that he too was dismissed, degenerating into a life of dishonesty, to be charged with treason in the last days of Tiberius. His reputation may eventually have suffered because he was unfortunate enough to be the father of the emperor Nero. Velleius called him a young man of most noble simplicity and wrote highly of the reputation of the family, comments made before it became tainted with the name of Nero.[20]

Two young men better known for their later careers were on Gaius' military staff. One was the future historian Velleius, unknown except for the autobiographical comments within his history.[21] Coming from a military family, he had recently begun his career in Thrace and Makedonia before being attached to the staff as military tribune. After many years of army service, particularly under Tiberius, he retired to write a history dedicated to M. Vinicius, the consul of AD 30, an old family friend.[22] He thus provided the only extant eyewitness account of any portion of Gaius' campaign, a version that does not have the same biases as the later sources, although as a devotee of Tiberius, Velleius was careful to slander Lollius.

The other known member of the military staff became the most notorious Roman of the following years. This was L. Aelius Sejanus,[23] participating in the first documented event of his infamous career, perhaps because he had been adopted by Aelius Gallus, who had made the only previous Roman expedition into Arabia. A remarkable and impressive youth, he probably first met Tiberius at this time, an event that the future emperor never forgot. Nothing else is known about his time with Gaius.

Although the members of Gaius' political and military staff seem to have had mixed, or even disastrous, later careers, much of this is due to the unforgiving party politics of the post-Augustan era, especially the violent opinions surrounding the principate of Tiberius. Moreover, these men are generally best known to the historical record because of events other than their association with Gaius, usually involving their relationship with Augustus' successor. Augustus would have chosen the best general staff possible for his grandson, and the presence of two consulars, his sister's grandson (himself the son of a consular), and two promising young army officers

---

19 *PIR*² D128; Ronald Syme, *The Roman Revolution*, paperback edition (Oxford: Clarendon Press, 1960), pp. 421–2.

20 Velleius 2.10; see also Josephus, *Jewish Antiquities* 20.148–50.

21 Velleius 2.101–4.

22 *PIR*² V445.

23 Tacitus, *Annals* 4.1; Syme, *Augustan Aristocracy* (supra note 11), p. 302: but see Dieter Hennig, *L. Aelius Seianus: Untersuchungen zur Regierung des Tiberius*, Vestigia 21 (Munich 1975), pp. 14–18.

demonstrates the care with which Augustus made his plans.[24] Moreover, in the fashion of great eastern expeditions since that of Alexander the Great, Augustus insured that Gaius would have advice from scholars. Three members of this contingent are known: Isidoros or Dionysios of Charax; Archelaos, the client king of Kappadokia; and Juba II of Mauretania.

Gaius' first scholarly adviser is recorded in a single notice by Pliny:[25]

> This place [i.e. Charax] was the birthplace of Dionysios, the most recent author on the geography of the world, whom the divine Augustus sent in advance to the East to write a complete commentary when his elder son was to go to Armenia against the Parthians and Arabians.

The problem with this dogmatic statement is that Dionysios of Charax, so notable as to be remembered over half a century later as the most recent writer on world geography, is otherwise unknown. Hence there has been almost universal emendation of "Dionysium" to "Isidorum," and the assumption that Pliny meant the well-known geographer Isidoros of Charax, who seems to date from the Augustan period.[26] Although any major emendation must be regarded cautiously, this is the presumption followed hereinafter.[27]

Charax was a trading emporium on the lower Tigris allegedly founded by Alexander as an Alexandria, but restored by Antiochos IV Epiphanes in the

---

24 Another staff member may have been a certain L. Licinius. Everything that is known about him is from a single fragmentary inscription (*CIL* 6.1442) that seems to identify him as one of the *comites* of Gaius and have a "C" as the first letter of his cognomen, raising the possibility that he was of the Licinii Crassi and perhaps a descendant of the Crassus whose loss of the standards to the Parthians was inexorably part of the context of the expedition.

25 *NH* 6.141: "Hoc in loco genitum Dionysium terrarum orbis situs recentissimum auctorum, quem ad commentanda omnia in Orientem praemiserit divus Augustus ituro in Armeniam ad Parthicas Arabicasque res maiore filio."

26 O. A. W. Dilke's date of around AD 25 for Isidoros' geographical writings is too late, as he needed already to have had a reputation as a geographer before Augustus commissioned him (*Greek and Roman Maps* [Ithaca, N.Y.: Cornell University Press, 1985], p. 124).

27 On Isidoros, see *FGrHist* #781; F. H. Weissbach, "Isidoros Charakenos" (#20), *RE* 9, 1916, 2064–8; Thomson, p. 286; Dilke (supra note 26), p. 124; Klaus Günther Sallmann, *Die Geographie des älteren Plinius in ihrem Verhältnis zu Varro: Versuch einer Quellenanalyse*, Untersuchungen zur antiken Literatur und Geschichte 11 (Berlin 1971), pp. 50–60. There is no certainty that all the fragments attributed to an Isidoros are by the geographer from Charax. The most vigorous proponent of the accuracy of Pliny's text at *NH* 6.141 and an otherwise unknown Dionysios is Sheldon Arthur Nodelman, "A Preliminary History of Characene," *Berytus* 13, 1960, 107, who also dated Isidoros to the latter first century AC, as a younger contemporary of Pliny's, based on the Characene king list in the *Makrobioi* attributed to Lucian. Nodelman's arguments are complex and somewhat circular, and have not been generally accepted. It is an annoying textual problem that will never be solved with the present evidence. See also Sallmann (supra), pp. 50–1; Dilke (supra note 26), p. 71.

early second century BC.[28] Originally at the head of the Persian Gulf, in Isidoros' day it was already 50 miles inland, owing to siltation.[29] Little is known about the author beyond his fragmentary writings and his presumed association with Gaius. His extensive geographical work was used repeatedly by Pliny – especially for latitudes, distances, and circumferences[30] – who often contrasted his measurements with those of the two Hellenistic geographers Eratosthenes and Artemidoros. In Pliny's day he was the most recent writer on the geography of the world, yet in some ways was less accurate than Juba.[31]

The fragments of Isidoros' writings do not reveal whether he wrote a single work, a wide-ranging geographical study, or several different treatises. The only independent text preserved is under the title *Parthian Stations*,[32] a list of places from Zeugma on the Euphrates to Alexandropolis in Arachosia, 838 *schoinoi* to the east, the surviving portion of a land itinerary across Asia. Details become fewer as the route progresses east, and it is unlikely that Isidoros was basing his conclusions on autopsy; perhaps he was using Parthian sources of around 100 BC,[33] although mention of the civil war between Phraates IV and Tiridates means that in some ways the treatise had been updated to the Augustan period.[34] It may have included a general Persian history,[35] probably the *Description of Parthia* which Athenaios quoted regarding pearls that were found on an island in the Persian Gulf.[36] Another fragment, if from the same treatise, refers to Goaisos, king of the Spice-Bearing Omani.[37] Isidoros was taking advantage of the temporary rapprochement between Rome and Parthia after the return of the standards to write about areas of the far East that previously had been known only by tradition.[38] He also wrote about the Nabataeans[39] – although the context is not

---

28 On the history of Charax, see Nodelman (supra note 27), pp. 83–121, and D. T. Potts, "The Roman Relationship with the *Persicus sinus* from the Rise of Spasinou Charax (127 BC) to the Reign of Shapur II (AD 309–79)," in *The Early Roman Empire in the East*, ed. Susan E. Alcock, Oxbow Monograph 95 (Oxford: Oxbow, 1997), pp. 89–107, and, for the location of the site, John Hansman, "Charax and the Karkeh," *IrAnt* 7, 1967, 36–45.

29 *NH* 6.138–40 = Juba, fr. 1.

30 *FGrHist* #781, frs. 6–19.

31 *NH* 6.141.

32 *GGM* 1.244–56; *FGrHist* #781, fr. 2; Isidoros of Charax, *Parthian Stations*, ed. Wilfred H. Schoff (Philadelphia: Commercial Museum, 1914).

33 Thomson, p. 291.

34 Dio 51.18; 53.33.1–2.

35 Lucian, *Makrobioi* 15–17, on the topic of long-lived kings. The several references to Isidoros in this passage indicate that he may have written extensively on the royal history of the Hellenistic East.

36 Athenaios 3.93e–94b = Isidoros, fr. 1.

37 Isidoros, fr. 4; see also *NH* 6.145; D. T. Potts, *The Arabian Gulf in Antiquity 2: From Alexander the Great to the Coming of Islam* (Oxford: Clarendon Press, 1990), p. 325.

38 See Strabo 11.6.4; M. Cary and E. H. Warmington, *The Ancient Explorers*, revised edition (Baltimore: Penguin Books, 1963), p. 194.

39 Hesychios, Δουσάρην = Isidoros, fr. 5.

certain – and is said to have written a *periplous*,[40] part of which may be reflected in the extant material about the Persian Gulf. The fragments that can be most safely attributed to Isidoros of Charax indicate that his geographical knowledge was wide-ranging, from Arachosia to Bithynia – and perhaps Nabataea – to Britain.[41] Although much of his material was derivative, this represents an amazing territorial extent, from the British Isles to Afghanistan, and he may have written more specifically on Persia and the Parthians.

As noted, the sole connection between Isidoros and Gaius is the single disputable notice by Pliny, also the only extant comment on Isidoros' career. The most important point is that Isidoros was the most recent author on geography, which may have been what appealed to Augustus. Isidoros was probably in Rome during his career and attracted the notice of Augustus there, who became familiar with his writings and their emphasis on the far eastern territories, about which there had been little recent information. Yet it is unlikely that Augustus sent him in advance to write about the East for Gaius[42] – the time factor, if nothing else, would make this improbable – and more reasonable that Gaius used published material in his preparations, perhaps consulting with Isidoros if the latter were in Rome or met somewhere en route, perhaps the exact meaning of Pliny's "praemiserit." He may have accompanied the expedition part of the way, perhaps into Nabataea and the fringes of Arabia, and, as a Parthian expert, advised Gaius during his negotiations with the Parthians on the Euphrates.[43]

The second scholar associated with Gaius was the client king of Kappadokia, Archelaos.[44] On the death of Herod the Great he had become the most senior of the client kings and now was a rare survivor from the era of Antonius, who had placed him on the throne. When Gaius came to the East, Archelaos had ruled Kappadokia for nearly forty years, and, as befits a client king, renamed his capitals Caesarea and Sebaste and rebuilt them in Roman fashion.[45] Archelaos took his duties seriously, and was involved in the affairs of much of Asia Minor and the Levant: Augustus relied on him as a regular

---

40 This is cited by the geographer of the third century AC, Marcianus of Herakleia (*FGrHist* #781, T2), but may not be the same Isidoros as the Characene geographer: see Sallmann (supra note 27), p. 51.

41 *NH* 5.150 (=Isodoros, fr. 18); *NH* 4.102 (=Isodoros, fr. 11).

42 Despite the contention of N. J. E. Austin and N. B. Rankov (*Exploratio: Military and Political Intelligence in the Roman World from the Second Punic War to the Battle of Andrianople* [London: Routledge, 1995]), who saw Isidoros' report as a rare example of a "prior strategic reconnaissance" (p. 31).

43 Isidoros perhaps put together Gaius' itinerary, possibly including a visit to Charax, which never occurred. See Robert K. Sherk, "Roman Geographical Exploration and Military Maps," *ANRW* 2.1, 1974, 539; on the topographical responsibilities of Roman military expeditions, see further, p. 543.

44 *FGrHist* #123. On Archelaos, see Sullivan, *Near Eastern Royalty*, pp. 182–5; and his "The Dynasty of Cappadocia," *ANRW* 2.7, 1980, 1149–61; on his role with the expedition, see Mario Pani, *Roma e i re d'Oriente da Augusto a Tiberio*, Pubblicazioni della Facoltà di lettere e filosofia dell'Università di Bari 11 (Bari 1972), pp. 47–9.

45 Roller, *Herod*, pp. 251–3.

informant on the East, and made certain that he was of service to Gaius, although in what exact capacity is uncertain.[46] Archelaos had wide-ranging scholarly interests – he was compared to Juba as a scholarly king[47] – that may have been of value to Gaius. Fragments of his works indicate that he wrote on Alexander the Great, perhaps the source for extant material on India.[48] Several of the citations concern precious stones, which may also be from the work on Alexander, since some are from India, but stones from Carthage and Egypt are also discussed.[49] Archelaos also wrote on cults[50] and agriculture,[51] one of several agricultural manuals written by kings.[52] Two extant titles, *On Rivers* and *On Stones*, by an unspecified Archelaos, cannot be attributed to the king with certainty,[53] as there was another literary Archelaos, author of Ἰδιοφυῆ ("Peculiarities"), whom Diogenes Laertios[54] distinguished from the author on Alexander, and who may have written some of the material on stones and rivers. It is not possible to untangle the authorship of all the material attributed to various writers named Archelaos. At the very least, the king of Kappadokia wrote an agricultural manual and on Alexander the Great, which was a wide-ranging topic that would have included natural history and geography. Although an agricultural manual would have pleased the Roman elite, it was more likely the geographical and historical material that Augustus felt would be useful to Gaius, as well as the king's extensive political expertise.

There is no reason to believe that Archelaos accompanied Gaius, but it is probable that stopovers were made at the Kappadokian court cities and that there was regular contact between the two, the king perhaps even coming to Antioch as adviser. One place Archelaos did not go was to Rhodes, having been warned by "intimi Augusti" not to visit Tiberius, and king and exile had no contact while Gaius was in the East. On the other hand, Archelaos was helpful and solicitous to Gaius. Tiberius never forgot, and shortly after

---

46 Josephus, *Jewish Antiquities* 16.357–60; Sullivan, *ANRW* (supra note 44), pp. 1156–7; Dio 57.17.4: ἐθεράπευσε.

47 Solinus 52.18–23; see also *NH* 37.107–8, where Pliny used both kings simultaneously as sources.

48 Diogenes Laertios 2.17; *NH* 37.46; see also Solinus 52.18–23.

49 *NH* 1.37; 37.95, 104, 107.

50 Archelaos, fr. 6 (*OxyPap* 2, 1899, #118).

51 *NH* 8.202, 218.

52 *NH* 18.22. Pliny's table of contents for Book 18 (*NH* 1.18), which is on agriculture, cites King Archelaos' agricultural manual. A King Archelaos was also one of the sources for Book 37 (*NH* 1.37): the actual citation in this book (*NH* 37.46) makes it clear it is the king of Kappadokia.

53 The citations are in the treatise *On Rivers* (*GGM* 2.637–44), of unknown authorship. The first (*On Rivers* 1.5 = Archelaos fr. 7) quotes *On Rivers* by Archelaos for information about the Hydaspes; the second (8.2 = fr. 8) quotes the same treatise on the Lykormas, in Aitolia; the third (9.3 = fr. 9) is from a work titled *On Stones*, also by Archelaos, and about the Maiandros. The first may be from Archelaos of Kappadokia's Alexander treatises, but authorship of the other two by the king is more questionable. See Felix Atenstädt, "Zwei Quellen des Sogennanten Plutarch *De fluviis*," *Hermes* 57, 1922, 238–9.

54 Diogenes Laertios 2.17.

he became emperor he summoned the elderly and ill monarch to Rome and charged him with treason. Although Archelaos was acquitted (seemingly on grounds of ill health), he died in Rome just after the trial, and his kingdom was turned into a province.[55] He had become dangerously powerful in Asia Minor, which was probably the main reason for his trial, but the issue of his relationship with Gaius many years previously was brought out, demonstrating that Tiberius always remembered who had and had not befriended him at the time of Gaius' eastern trip.

The third of Gaius' scholarly advisers was Juba.[56] Unlike the other two,[57] he produced a major scholarly work as part of his service with the expedition, which Pliny cited by name three times, "the volumes that were written on Arabia for C. Caesar the son of Augustus."[58] Yet it is improbable that the project was commissioned in time to have been completed before departure. Juba had not previously written on the East – except perhaps Egypt and the adjoining Red Sea coast – and *On Arabia* must be seen not as an advance research project but as resulting from the Arabian parts of the expedition, to be completed, in all likelihood, before Gaius' death in early AD 4, and probably written at the court of Archelaos.

Juba, like other members of Gaius' advisory group, was chosen by Augustus for specific reasons. He had known him for nearly half a century and had watched him mature from refugee to scholar and king. Like Archelaos, Juba had the wisdom of a king and the knowledge of a scholar; despite the continual frontier problems he faced, Augustus' selection of him was an affirmation of proven capabilities during his quarter-century of kingship, and, in fact, his experience with frontier issues – however mixed – may have been one of his credentials. But Augustus would have been unlikely to make use of him unless his scholarship had some reference to the expedition, and this is good proof that *Libyka*, probably including material on Egypt and the Red Sea – close to Gaius' concern – had already been published by 4–2 BC. Augustus saw in Juba the type of scholar who would be an asset to Gaius as both adviser and chronicler.

---

55 Tacitus, *Annals* 2.42; Suetonius, *Tiberius* 37.4; Dio 57.17.3–7. On the lengthy poor relationship between Archelaos and Tiberius, see F. E. Romer, "A Case of Client Kingship," *AJP* 106, 1985, 75–100.

56 On Gaius and Juba, see Jacoby, *Commentary*, pp. 326–8.

57 Although it is clear that Isodoros was to produce a commentary on the expedition (*NH* 6.141), there is no evidence of any such treatise, and given the expedition's collapse, especially in the area of Isodoros' expertise, it may never have been written. There is no indication that Archelaos was expected to write anything.

58 *NH* 6.141, 12.56; 32.10 = Juba, fr. 1–3: "voluminibus quae scripsit ad C. Caesarem Aug. f. de Arabia." The wording is from *NH* 32.10: the other two citations are slightly different. Despite the fact that these seem to preserve a Latin title, *NH* 12.55–6 makes it clear that the work was in Greek. On the vagueness of the term "Arabia" – certainly emphasized by the wide range of Juba's work – see Glen Bowersock, *Roman Arabia*, first paperback edition (Cambridge, Mass.: Harvard University Press, 1983), p. 1.

There may also have been personal reasons for the king's inclusion. Gaius's tutor M. Verrius Flaccus may have been one of Juba's teachers or intellectual colleagues.[59] Gaius' mother Julia was a childhood friend of Kleopatra Selene, and the personal difficulties that Julia was facing, which had caused her estrangement from her husband Tiberius and would lead to her banishment as her son set forth, may have increased a natural closeness between Gaius – whose father was dead – and the Mauretanian royal family. Juba, in his mid-forties, would be the closest thing that young Gaius had to a father while on the expedition. Moreover, it would have been to the king's advantage to cultivate as much as possible the presumed future emperor. Juba may also have known another staff member, Quirinius, because of the latter's service in Africa some years previously. He may even have been acquainted, at least by reputation, with Isidoros, who had possibly written about Massinissa.[60] Moreover, in a strange way Juba complemented Isidoros, as they came from the opposite extremities of the Empire, and Juba's presence linked the far west to the ancient East. The three scholars each had a discrete area of expertise: Isidoros on Parthia and the Persian Gulf, Archelaos on Asia Minor and the far East, and Juba on Egypt and coastal Arabia.

As with his two scholarly colleagues, it is uncertain how much Juba traveled with the expedition. His marriage to Glaphyra, which must have occurred at this time, as it is the only time she was available, places him at the court of her father Archelaos, and this is the strongest proof that he took part, and the basis for the common assumption of this by modern commentators.[61] Yet the extent of Juba's participation is unknown. He was at the court of Archelaos, and one expects that he visited Tiberius on Rhodes, as there is no hint that he became one of his later victims, and, moreover, Tiberius was an old friend.[62] It is most probable that Juba accompanied Gaius only in the earlier parts of his tour before returning to the court of Archelaos when the expedition moved beyond his area of expertise, there to marry Glaphyra and to finish his treatise, before new disturbances in Africa, most notably the death of L. Cornelius Lentulus, made it necessary for him to return home.

And so the great expedition set forth,[63] probably in late 2 BC or early the

---

59 Supra, p. 70.
60 Lucian, *Makrobioi* 17 (=Isodoros, fr. 3).
61 Infra, pp. 247–9. That he took part, at least in the earlier portions, seems obvious from *NH* 6.141. See Gsell, vol. 8, pp. 222–3, 266–7; Romanelli, *Storia*, p. 167; Romer, *TAPA* 109 (supra note 5), p. 202; Kokkinos, *Herodian Dynasty*, p. 228. Jacoby, *RE*, p. 2386, was more skeptical.
62 This makes it unlikely that Juba was one of the Augustan intimates who advised Archelaos to keep his distance from Tiberius, despite Romer (*AJP* 106, supra note 55), p. 97.
63 Late in 2 BC, just before Gaius departed, there came the public revelation of the adulteries of his mother, which the sequence of events of Velleius (2.100.3) and Dio (55.10.12) places after the dedication of the Temple of Mars Ultor. Velleius had Gaius depart immediately after Julia's crimes were made known (2.101.1). This too had an effect on the context of the campaign, since adultery might call into question the parentage of the heir apparent, and Julia was still the wife of Tiberius. (On these issues, see W. K. Lacey, "2 BC and Julia's Adultery," *Antichthon* 14, 1980, 127–42.)

following year,[64] making a slow and triumphant progression east, with stopovers in many places.[65] Perhaps attempting to smooth over the growing personal conflict, even Tiberius lowered himself to declare his loyalty to Gaius, coming to either Chios or Samos.[66] The first goal was probably Antioch, reached late in 1 BC, where Gaius could establish his headquarters, assume his consulship, and turn toward his first problem, that for which Juba had been assigned, Arabia.

The exact focus of this first part of the expedition has long been uncertain. According to the cenotaph of Gaius at Pisa, he waged war during his consulship beyond the limits of Roman territory.[67] This cannot mean in Armenia, since the war against the Armenians took place after his consulship,[68] and thus it must refer to an earlier campaign, the first of Gaius' eastern tenure. It has been persuasively demonstrated that it took place in interior Nabataea, near Arabia (this perhaps a more exotic and even poetic term for commemoration),[69] a campaign documented only in a series of allusions by Pliny,[70] whose source was Juba's *On Arabia*. Since Juba had been asked to provide expertise for this region, an Arabian campaign was part of Augustus' original plans, but for some reason it amounted to little, as Gaius only had a glimpse (*prospexit*) of Arabia.[71] Pliny contrasted this brevity with the more thorough efforts of Aelius Gallus twenty-five years previously. In Pliny's time Aelius Gallus was still the only Roman to have gone into Arabia with an army, destroying a number of towns and making a full report, despite the disastrous outcome of the campaign.[72] Gaius, however, only reached the *Arabicus sinus*, presumably at Aila. He found Arabia tantalizing, and sought renown there, but seems to have gone no farther than the

---

64 Romer's date of the latter part of 2 BC (*TAPA* 108 [supra note 5], pp. 187–202) has been disputed by Halfmann (supra note 5), p. 166, who placed the departure on 29 January 1 BC, on the basis of epigraphic evidence.

65 The evidence for the stopovers is mostly epigraphic: see the summary in Romer, *TAPA* 108 (supra note 5), pp. 201–2.

66 Dio 55.10.19; Suetonius, *Tiberius* 12.

67 *ILS* 140, 10–11: "consulatum quem ultra finis extremas populi Romani bellum gerens feliciter peregerat."

68 Dio 55.10a.4–8.

69 G. W. Bowersock, "A Report on Arabia Provincia," *JRS* 61, 1971, 227–8; see also T. D. Barnes, "The Victories of Augustus," *JRS* 64, 1974, 22–3; Romer, *TAPA* 109 (supra note 5), pp. 204–5; Bowersock, *Roman Arabia* (supra note 58), p. 56. Hurlet (supra note 5), p. 135, would merely substitute "Nabataea" for the "Arabia" of the sources, which seems simplistic topographically.

70 *NH* 6.141, 12.56, 32.10 = Juba, frs. 1–3; *NH* 2.168, 6.160.

71 *NH* 6.160. Juba's knowledge of the frankincense trade is no evidence of penetration of the peninsula, despite the arguments of J. Innes Miller (*The Spice Trade of the Roman Empire, 29 B.C. to A.D. 641* [Oxford: Clarendon Press, 1969], p. 15), as he collected his information at Gaza: see infra, pp. 232–4.

72 S. Jameson, "Chronology of the Campaigns of Aelius Gallus and C. Petronius," *JRS* 58, 1968, 71–84.

head of the Arabian Gulf.[73] Yet there could have been no military engagement in Arabia, or Pliny would not have drawn attention to the differences with Aelius Gallus' campaign. The conclusion is that the "bellum gerens" of the Pisa inscription was near Arabia, more in the Nabataean territory, and probably not against the Nabataeans themselves, but perhaps against nomads or bandits from the Arabian peninsula who were threatening the Nabataeans.[74] Stabilizing the Nabataean kingdom in the years after Herod the Great's death would have been an Augustan priority, and Rome may even have placed Nabataea under direct control at this time, and sent Gaius to investigate and to wage war as necessary.[75] Augustus might not have known all the details, or what actions Gaius might need to take, and so he engaged Juba – who had his own knowledge of frontier populations – to advise and chronicle an expected Arabian campaign south of Nabataea.

Gaius probably sailed from the port of Antioch, Seleukia Pieria, to Gaza,[76] and then moved inland to Petra,[77] and on to Aila, where he had his glimpse of Arabia. He dealt with whoever was threatening Nabataea, and terminated direct Roman control, if such had existed, returning the territory to Aretas IV, who then reigned for another forty years.[78] The expedition went no farther than the Arabian Gulf, probably at the port of Aila. Sejanus could warn Gaius of the dangers his own adoptive father had experienced twenty-five years previously in Arabia proper, and there was no reason to penetrate the peninsula, although Gaius was greatly attracted by the idea, and was able to gather some of the first accurate information about the region.[79] Regardless of whether he was waging wars against

---

73 "Gaius ... gloriam petiit" (*NH* 12.55). On this enigmatic phrase, see Jehan Desanges, *Recherches sur l'activité des Méditeranéens aux confins de l'Afrique (VIᵉ siècle avant J.-C.–IVᵉ siècle après J.-C.)*, CÉFR 38 (Paris 1978), pp. 319–20.

74 Bowersock, *JRS* (supra note 69), pp. 227–8 (nomads); Steven E. Sidebotham, *Roman Economic Policy in the Erythra Thalassa, 30 B.C.–A.D. 217* (Leiden 1986), pp. 130–5 (bandits, citing Strabo 4.6.6).

75 See Strabo 16.4.21, where Syria and Nabataea are said to have the same political status. King Aretas IV of Nabataea seems to have stopped minting coins about the time of Herod's death: see Bowersock, *Roman Arabia* (supra note 58), pp. 53–8.

76 *NH* 12.63–5: Juba's familiarity with the markets of Gaza suggests autopsy: see infra, pp. 232–4.

77 A Roman road running from Gaza to Petra has been connected with the expedition: see Benjamin Isaac, "Trade Routes to Arabia and the Roman Army," in *Roman Frontier Studies, 1979: Papers Presented to the 12th International Congress of Roman Frontier Studies*, ed. W. S. Hanson and K. J. F. Keppie, BAR-IS 71, 1980, pp. 889–93.

78 Aretas' coinage had resumed by AD 1, the year Gaius was in the vicinity (and perhaps two years earlier); this has been ingeniously assumed to document a three-year interregnum brought about by Roman control (Bowersock, *Roman Arabia* [supra note 58], pp. 53–8). In contrast, see Fergus Millar, *The Roman Near East, 31 B.C.–A.D. 337* (Cambridge, Mass.: Harvard University Press, 1993), p. 44, and Sidebotham (supra note 74), p. 132, who rightly pointed out the inevitable weakness of such negative evidence, and rejected Roman direct control, while ignoring the evidence of Strabo (16.4.21) regarding the status of Nabataea. Most recently, see Kokkinos, *Herodian Dynasty*, p. 375, who rejected totally any Roman takeover. Regardless, the situation in Nabataea was in flux in the years after Herod's death, part of the context of Gaius' expedition.

79 *NH* 12.56; Potts, *Arabian Gulf* (supra note 37), p. 22.

nomads, bandits, or even the Nabataeans, his presence strengthened both Roman visibility and the Nabataeans themselves as an evolving frontier population.[80]

After settling the Nabataean issue, Gaius was free to return to Antioch. He may have approached the frontier of Egypt but he did not enter the province.[81] Instead, he set sail from Gaza, passing by Judaea,[82] and arrived back in Antioch probably late in AD 1, to deal with the Parthian and Armenian issues, which had now become acute.[83] The brief stability that had existed since 6 BC had degenerated, since Phraates IV had been assassinated about the time Gaius left Rome. He had been on the throne for nearly forty years and had been responsible for the uneasy peace with Rome and the return of the standards. His weak son, Phraates V or Phraatakes, was now king, and had been negotiating for nearly two years with Augustus, who refused to accept his legitimacy. The Parthians were meddling more than ever in the Armenian succession, and Augustus and Phraates were exchanging pointed communiqués. Since a weak king in Parthia was no comfort to Rome, and indeed dangerous, after Gaius landed in Syria he spent the next few months in direct negotiations with Phraates, resulting in a meeting between the two in the late summer of AD 2 on the Euphrates, for which Velleius provided an eyewitness account.[84] Part of this conference was Phraates' betrayal of Lollius, who, he said, had been in his (and others') pay, and who died mysteriously a few days later.

Yet the conference was a failure, because it did not solve the Armenian crisis. Although Phraates agreed to withdraw his claims, the Parthian

---

80 This portion of the campaign may be commemorated by an inscription from Messene: see James E. G. Zetzel, "New Light on Gaius Caesar's Eastern Campaign," *GRBS* 11, 1970, 259–66, on which Gaius is described as having escaped danger when "fighting against the barbarians for the safety of all mankind" (Zetzel's translation).

81 A visit to Egypt is documented only by the Christian writer Orosius (7.3). Given the restrictions on entering Egypt and the furor when Germanicus went there illegally in AD 19, it is highly unlikely that a visit by Gaius would have gone otherwise unrecorded, especially with the contention between him and Tiberius. Orosius' main point was another issue: his distaste that Gaius had not gone to Jerusalem to sacrifice at Herod's Temple, a failure that, according to Orosius, brought a major famine to the Romans. Gaius indeed bypassed Jerusalem and was promptly commended by Augustus for doing so (to Orosius' horror): this incident was recorded by Suetonius (*Augustus* 93) immediately after describing a trip to Egypt by Augustus. In Orosius' account this became an Egyptian visit by Gaius. On this, see Romer, *TAPA* 109 (supra note 5), pp. 205–8.

82 Suetonius, *Augustus* 93 ("praetervehens"). Gaius' father Marcus Agrippa, in the company of Herod the Great, had sacrificed at the Jerusalem Temple fifteen years previously (Roller, *Herod*, pp. 48–9) – in fact, a gate of the complex had been named after him – and Gaius may have been tempted to visit, but perhaps he did not wish to tread in his father's footsteps, and Roman policy may not have desired such a high Roman official to visit the territory of Herod's demoted sons and thereby equate their legitimacy with that of their father.

83 On the remainder of Gaius' campaign, see Romer, *TAPA* 109 (supra note 5), pp. 208–14; Erich S. Gruen, "The Expansion of the Empire under Augustus," *CAH²* 10, 1996, 160–2.

84 Velleius 2.101–2.

faction in Armenia, led by a certain Addon, did not follow his lead and refused to disarm. Since Addon was weakened by Phraates' withdrawal of support, Gaius decided to invade Armenia, and set forth in the spring of AD 3. There were a number of Roman successes, and eventually Addon suggested a conference at Artageira. Precautions were inadequately made – the loss of the experienced Lollius was acutely felt, and Addon distracted Gaius and assaulted him, wounding him – although only slightly, it seemed. Artageira soon fell to the Romans, but the injury had great psychological effect. Discipline suffered as the expedition straggled back to Antioch, collapsing so completely that Augustus eventually had to institute a purge of Gaius' staff. Gaius petitioned Augustus to resign his office. Augustus would agree to this only after his grandson took time to recuperate and then returned to Italy. In early AD 4 he had recovered enough to set sail, and, resigning, did so, but he quickly grew worse, and died on 21 February during a stopover in Limyra in Lykia, where his cenotaph is still visible.[85]

Juba had long since abandoned the expedition. His services as an Arabian expert were no longer required after late AD 1, and he probably did not participate in the Parthian negotiations. He may have taken advantage of being in the vicinity to visit Alexandria: it is inconceivable that the scholar did not spend time in the greatest center of learning in the Greco-Roman world, not only the historic seat of Ptolemaic culture and the source of much of his scholarly information, but his late wife's birthplace. He then moved on to Kappadokia, probably in AD 2, to write his report in Archelaos' library and to marry Glaphyra.[86]

85 Joachim Ganzert, *Das Kenotaph für Gaius Caesar in Limyra: Architektur und Bauornamentik* (*IstForsch* 35, 1984).

86 At Archelaos' court, Juba may have met the mythographer Konon (*FGrHist* #26), who dedicated his *Diegeseis* to the king of Kappadokia (*FGrHist* #26, T1). Konon wrote extensively on foundation myths, including Roman origins (fr. 1.46), a subject of interest to Juba. He may have been the source of Juba's enigmatic information about Semiramis (Juba, fr. 59; Konon, fr. 1.9).

10

ON ARABIA

The most lasting result of Juba's time with Gaius Caesar was his final scholarly work, *On Arabia*. It was written between AD 2, when Juba detached himself from Gaius' expedition and went to Kappadokia and married Glaphyra, and AD 5, when he abandoned her and returned to Mauretania.[1] It represented the culmination both of his scholarly talents and of geographical and natural historical knowledge of the latter Augustan period.[2]

Although *On Arabia* is cited by name only three times,[3] nearly thirty additional fragments survive from this treatise, almost all from Pliny's *Natural History*, and covering a geographical range from the Nile to India.[4] Many are about natural history, but cultural history, trade and commerce, and ethnography are also among the topics. There is no indication of the length of the work. Sources include Ptolemaic explorers, the Alexander historians and chroniclers, Berossos, Poseidonios, and Juba's own autopsy. When *On Arabia* is coupled with *Libyka*, it can be seen that Juba created an extensive and wide-ranging treatise that covered all the southern half of the known world, from West Africa to India. In fact, it is difficult to divide the two works, since material about the Nile, its upper regions, and East Africa blends seamlessly into that about the Red Sea and the Arabian peninsula.

Libyka would have been completed before Augustus commissioned Juba to join his grandson's entourage. Where it left off cannot easily be determined: the source of the Nile was a necessary component[5] that would lack

---

1 Infra, pp. 247–9.

2 Jacoby, *Commentary*, pp. 326–8; *RE*, pp. 2391–2.

3 *NH* 6. 141, 12.56, 32.10 = Juba, frs. 1–3.

4 Juba, frs. 28–37, 41, 46, 62–79. On Pliny's use of Juba as a source, see Klaus Günther Sallmann, *Die Geographie des älteren Plinius und ihrem Verhältnis zu Varro: Versuch einer Quellenanalyse*, Untersuchungen zur antiken Literatur und Geschichte 11 (Berlin 1971), pp. 85–8; on his description of Arabia, see Henry I. MacAdam, "Strabo, Pliny the Elder and Ptolemy of Alexandria: Three Views of Ancient Arabia and Its Peoples," in *L'Arabie préislamique et son environnement historique et culturel*, ed. T. Fahd (Strasbourg: Université des sciences humaines de Strasbourg, 1989), pp. 291–5.

5 Juba, fr. 38a.

meaning without a treatment of Ethiopia and the lower Nile,[6] but material on coastal East Africa and its trade with Alexandria[7] connects more easily with the Red Sea and Arabia. Juba's participation in Gaius' tour provided the opportunity to extend his researches to the east, and perhaps round off some of the issues of *Libyka*.

Central to the thesis of *On Arabia* is the Augustan interest in the routes to India. Although trade between India and the Mediterranean had existed for many years, most of it had been overland until the time of Alexander.[8] But when Alexander's comrades Nearchos of Crete and Onesikritos of Astypalaia returned from India to the Persian Gulf by sea, and, moreover, published their accounts,[9] attention was directed toward the ocean journey. Nevertheless, the parts of the Red Sea–India route were still disconnected. Greeks went no farther than the lower end of the sea, and the Indian seamen they met there kept the way to India secret, as the author of the *Periplous of the Erythraian Sea* made clear.[10]

Circumstances changed dramatically in the late second century BC. Although rumors had long existed that there was a sea connection between the western Mediterranean and India,[11] this was not definitively proven until the striking voyages of Eudoxos of Kyzikos, who came to the court of Ptolemaios VIII and became a prominent adviser noted for his inquiring mind

6 Juba, frs. 35–7, 39.

7 Juba, fr. 75.

8 On this, see M. Cary and E. H. Warmington, *The Ancient Explorers*, revised edition (Baltimore: Penguin Books, 1963), pp. 73–87.

9 *FGrHist* #133, 134. On these, see Lionel Pearson, *The Lost Histories of Alexander the Great*, reprint (Chico, Cal.: Scholars Press, 1983), pp. 83–149.

10 *Periplous of the Erythraian Sea* 26. On this important work, not to be confused with the fragmentary treatise of the similar title by Agatharchides of Knidos (*FGrHist* #86; infra p. 234), see Lionel Casson, *The Periplus Maris Erythraei* (Princeton, N.J.: Princeton University Press, 1989). Its author is unknown, but was someone personally familiar with the places described. The evidence consistently points to a date of composition between AD 40 and 70, as definitively established by Casson (pp. 6–7). More recent scholarship has only strengthened this date, perhaps focusing more on the beginning rather than the end of the period. See Christian Robin, "The Date of the *Periplus of the Erythraean Sea* in the Light of the South Arabian Evidence," in *Crossings: Early Mediterranean Contacts with India*, ed. F. De Romanis and A. Tchernia (New Delhi: Manohar, 1997), pp. 41–65, and especially Gerard Fussman, "The *Periplus* and the Political History of India," *Crossings*, pp. 66–71.

11 Phoenicians or Carthaginians were said to have circumnavigated Africa at an early date, and Skylax of Karyanda (*FGrHist* #709, 1000) in the sixth century BC sailed from India to Africa (Herodotos 4.42–4). Herodotos' linkage of these two journeys created an image of a western Mediterranean–Indian route. Although the evidence is obscure and contradictory, Skylax may have titled his work *Voyage beyond the Pillars of Herakles* (*Souda*, Σκύλαξ = *FGrHist* #709, T1), further evidence of a perceived connection. But this may be a much later work by another Skylax (which does not invalidate the concept that the two regions were long associated); see *FGrHist*, *Commentary* on #1000. A summary of pre-Hellenistic knowledge of the route is given in the important study of J. H. Thiel, *Eudoxus of Cyzicus: A Chapter in the History of the Sea-Route to India and the Route around the Cape in Ancient Times*, Historische Studies 23 (Groningen [n.d.]), pp. 7–11.

and geographical interests.[12] While he was there, a shipwrecked Indian was found in a bay on the Arabian Gulf and brought to the court, where he learned Greek and offered to guide an expedition back to India. Eudoxos was selected as leader, and made a round trip, but on his return Ptolemaios VIII confiscated all his Indian goods. After the king died in 116 BC, his widow Kleopatra III sent Eudoxos forth again. During his return journey he was blown off course and landed somewhere in modern Somalia, where he discovered a shipwreck that the locals said had come from the west. When Eudoxos returned to Alexandria, he showed parts of the wreckage to the port officials, who identified the ship as from Gades and of a type used to sail in the Atlantic off Mauretania.[13] Eudoxos also had his goods confiscated again, so he set out a third time in secret, resolving to circumnavigate Africa in a counter-clockwise direction. He passed by Massalia and Gades, and went into the Atlantic, eventually coming to an area where people spoke a language similar to what he had heard in East Africa. He then reversed direction and landed in Mauretania, going to Volubilis and the court of Bocchus I.[14] He attempted to persuade the Mauretanian king to outfit a new expedition, but the king's advisers suggested it would be better to keep the feasibility of circumnavigating Africa a secret and to dispose of Eudoxos. Eudoxos then fled to Spain and outfitted a fourth expedition, carrying a large contingent with agricultural implements and seeds, planning to spend several years en route, and set forth into the Atlantic never to be heard from again.

12 Strabo 2.3.4–6, from Poseidonios of Apamea (*FGrHist* #87, fr. 28), who was in Gades only a few years after Eudoxos disappeared. Eudoxos' journey was also briefly mentioned by Pomponius Mela (3.90) and Pliny (*NH* 2.170); in both cases the immediate source was Cornelius Nepos, almost certainly derived from Poseidonios. On Eudoxos, and the validity of his tale, see Thiel (supra note 11); Cary and Warmington (supra note 8), pp. 127–8; Manfred C. Raschke, "New Studies in Roman Commerce with the East," *ANRW* 2.9, 1978, 661; Jehan Desanges, *Recherches sur l'activité des Méditerranéens aux confins de l'Afrique (VIe siècle avant J.-C.–IVe siècle après J.-C.*, CÉFR 38 (Paris 1978), pp. 151–73; Posidonius, *II. The Commentary*, ed. I. G. Kidd (Cambridge: Cambridge University Press, 1985), pp. 240–57; P. M. Fraser, *Ptolemaic Alexandria* (Oxford: Clarendon Press, 1972), vol. 1, pp. 182–4; Pomponius Mela, *Chorographie*, ed. A. Silberman (Paris 1988), pp. 316–17.

13 The story of Spanish shipwrecks in eastern waters was also mentioned by Pliny (*NH* 2.168–9), interestingly in the context of Gaius Caesar's expedition. The historian L. Coelius Antipater was said to have met someone who made the journey from Spain to Ethiopia, but this may have been Eudoxos himself, as they were virtual contemporaries (see Cicero, *De divinatione* 1.26.56 = Coelius Antipater, fr. 50 [*HRR*]). It may have become almost a mythic tale by Pliny's day. See Kenneth Wellesley, "The Fable of a Roman Attack on Aden," *PP* 9, 1954, 401–5.

14 The text of Strabo (2.3.5) reads Βόγου, which elsewhere is his form of "Bogudes" (8.4.3, 17.3.5, 7). But no Bogudes is known from the late second century BC, and it is most probable that King Bocchus I is meant: the events are far too early for his son Bogudes I or his contentious descendants Bocchus II and Bogudes II. The problem in the text is due to the vagaries of transliteration and the repertory of similar and repeated names in contemporary Mauretania (Baga, Bogod, and Bokos are among those known [Coltelloni-Trannoy, p. 83; see further, Thiel (supra note 11), pp. 38–41]). The names Bocchus and Bogudes were frequently confused by ancient authors: see, for examples, Appian, *Civil War* 5.26; Plutarch, *Antonius* 61.

Despite Strabo's skepticism toward and even ridicule of the tale,[15] Eudoxos of Kyzikos remains one of the greatest explorers of antiquity, probably covering more miles at sea than anyone from the Mediterranean before Columbus, opening the sea route to India for the Greco-Roman world.[16] His time in Mauretania at the court of Bocchus I would have been indirectly remembered when Juba arrived eighty years later, and Juba, as *duovir* at Gades and married to a descendant of Ptolemaios VIII, thus had several points of contact with Eudoxos' world. This was probably what inspired Juba's interest in the routes to India, and it is possible that early in his reign he conceived of a major scholarly project that would, in an academic way, complete the explorations of Eudoxos by definitively connecting Mauretania and India.[17]

After Eudoxos, the India sea route was traversed regularly. A captain named Hippalos was credited with establishing the practicalities of the trade.[18] Eudoxos' and Hippalos' knowledge was not fully utilized for nearly a century, owing to deteriorating conditions within the Ptolemaic kingdom: only about twenty ships a year sailed beyond the Red Sea in the early- to mid-first century BC.[19] But by the 20s BC, 120 made the trip

15 Strabo's intense rejection of any veracity to the tales came from his vigorous attempt to separate truth from fable in geographical understanding: on this, see James S. Romm, *The Edges of the Earth in Ancient Thought* (Princeton, N.J.: Princeton University Press, 1992), pp. 197–200.

16 In fact, elements of Eudoxos' adventures entered folk mythology and remained current, in a localized version, in Columbus' day, when the Italian explorer was said to have received information while at Madeira about western lands (and the route to them) from a mysterious sailor who died after revealing his secrets. See André Tchernia, "Winds and Coins: From the Supposed Discovery of the Monsoon to the *denarii* of Tiberius," in *Crossings* (supra note 10), pp. 259–60.

17 Kleopatra Selene, as always, was an influence on the direction of Juba's scholarship, and his interest in both Alexander and Ptolemaic history, which are important parts of the treatise (as well as relevant to the earlier *Libyka*), was one of her legacies: she would not forget that her ancestor Ptolemaios I had journeyed with Alexander.

18 *Periplous of the Erythraian Sea* 57. He is otherwise unknown, and may have been one of Eudoxos' officers: see Thiel (supra note 11), p. 18; Casson (supra note 10), p. 224. There is no reason to place him in the Julio-Claudian period, which would require two separate and redundant discoveries of the Indian route. See further, Albrecht Dihle, "Die entdeckungsgeschichtlichen Voraussetzungen des Indienhandels der römischen Kaiserzeit," *ANRW* 2.9, 1978, 547–9. But it is possible, perhaps even probable, that there was no seaman Hippalos but that the word is a corruption of ὕφαλος, a Classical Greek word (Sophokles, *Antigone* 589, etc.) meaning "under the sea" (LSJ), and thus a type of west wind, as indicated by Pliny (*NH* 6.100): see Santo Mazzarino, "On the Name of the *Hipalus* (*Hippalus*) Wind in Pliny," *Crossings* (supra note 10), pp. 72–9. Mazzarino emphasized that as a seaman himself, Pliny would not have confused a wind and a predecessor. But the author of the *Periplous*, the source for the seaman Hippalos, was also a sailor. Regardless, the matter little affects the Greek discovery of the monsoon route to India around 120 BC. See further Tchernia (supra note 16), pp. 250–76.

19 Strabo 17.1.13; the date is uncertain but may be in the time of Ptolemaios XII Auletes. The breakdown of contacts in the unstable first century BC can be conspicuously seen in the lack of casual finds of Greek coins in India from 100 BC to the Augustan period: see Duane W. Roller, "A Note on Greek Coins from Tamilnadu," *ND* 19, 1995, 37–41.

annually.[20] Augustus' personal interest – as well as the stable political conditions under Roman control – resulted in this proliferation of commerce.[21] Contacts between Rome and India became frequent – Juba would have seen the Indian ambassadors who visited Augustus in Spain in 26 BC[22] – and Roman officials were sent down the Red Sea.[23] A Temple of Augustus was even built at or near the southwest Indian trading center of Muziris.[24]

Yet despite the emphasis on the connection between the Mediterranean and India, the intervening territory was still little known. This was especially true of the Arabian peninsula. Greeks had been aware of it from the time of Herodotos,[25] but it was not until the late fourth century BC and the journeys of Alexander the Great that interest in Arabia entered mainstream scholarship. The first to write in detail about Arabia seems to have been one Palaiphatos of Abydos, a student of Aristotle's, who wrote an Ἀραβικά known to the compiler of the *Souda*.[26] The few citations are, with one exception,[27] all from late encyclopedias, and demonstrate that he wrote a broad study of the East, almost certainly as a result of Alexander's travels. There is no record of a later writer on Arabia until Teukros of Kyzikos wrote five books on Arabia in the early first century BC;[28] like Palaiphatos, he is mostly known only from late encyclopedias. He too wrote a general work on the East, perhaps for a Roman audience at the time of increasing Roman

---

20 Strabo 2.5.12: this date is confirmed because Strabo received his information while on the staff of Aelius Gallus in Egypt.

21 Raschke (supra note 12), p. 662. On the commodities traded between India and Rome, see Romila Thapar, "Early Mediterranean Contacts with India: An Overview," *Crossings* (supra note 10), pp. 26–8; see also Vito A. Sirago, "Roma e la via oceanica per l'India," *AfrRom* 13, 2000, 237–48.

22 Orosius 6.21; Cary and Warmington (supra note 8), p. 94.

23 Despite the disastrous result of Aelius Gallus' expedition (see Strabo 16.4.22–4 and Glen Bowersock, *Roman Arabia*, first paperback edition [Cambridge, Mass.: Harvard University Press, 1983], pp. 46–9), its intent was for Rome to become more directly involved in the Indian trade, for which see Raschke (supra note 12), pp. 650–75.

24 It appears on the Peutinger Table, the late antique map that may have been derived from that of Marcus Agrippa. Muziris was a suitable place for such a temple, as it was known as the "primum emporium Indiae" (*NH* 6.104; see also *Periplous of the Erythraian Sea* 54; *BAGRW*, Map 5). Such a structure implies a permanent colony of Roman citizens (Martin P. Charlesworth, "Roman Trade with India: A Resurvey," in *Studies in Roman Economic and Social History in Honor of Allan Chester Johnson*, ed. P. R. Coleman-Norton *et al*. [Princeton, N.J.: Princeton University Press, 1951], p. 142). No physical evidence for the temple has been found. On Muziris (probably at modern Cranganore: see Casson [supra note 10], p. 296), see Federico De Romanis, "Rome and the *Nótia* of India: Relations between Rome and Southern India from 30 BC to the Flavian Period," *Crossings* (supra note 10), pp. 94–8, and, most recently, Rajan Gurukkal and Dick Whittaker, "In Search of Muziris," *JRA* 14, 2001, 334–50, a vigorous attempt to gather all the literary and physical evidence for the site.

25 Herodotos 2.8.

26 *FGrHist* #44, T8; Souda, Παλαίφατος Ἀβυδηνός. On the problems with authors named Palaiphatos, see supra, Chapter 8, note 22.

27 The one earlier quotation (if from the same Palaiphatos) is by Strabo (12.3.22) on the Amazons.

28 *FGrHist* #274; *Souda*, Τεῦκρος ὁ Κυζικηνός.

presence in that region. An *Arabian Archaeology* written by a certain Glaukos, preserved only in a number of toponyms cited by Stephanos of Byzantion, may also belong to this period.[29] The failure of any of these to be used by mainstream Roman imperial authors indicates that they were little known – if at all – until late antiquity and may not have been available to Juba. The geographical writings of Eratosthenes of Kyrene, from the third century BC, were, however, available to Strabo,[30] and thus probably also to Juba. Much of Eratosthenes' information was provided by merchants, in this case those who came to Alexandria. The brevity of his material on Arabia indicates that all in all, there was little written about the district before Roman imperial times. Strabo, the earliest extant detailed author on Arabia, used Hellenistic geographers and the report of Aelius Gallus.[31] But this was limited to the Red Sea littoral, and went no farther south than the trading post of Leuke Kome, only a quarter of the way to the mouth of the sea.[32] Poseidonios seems to have been the most recent general writer on the region, but he was already out of date by the time Gaius set forth. For points east of Arabia it was necessary to rely on material from the period of Alexander. The scarcity of reliable information explains why Augustus wanted an updated and thorough treatise on the southern edge of the inhabited world, and indeed this may have been one of the purposes of Gaius' expedition. His scholarly advisers, particularly Juba, were thus commissioned to bring knowledge of the south up to date. This gave Juba a chance to expand his *Libyka* to the east, and, in a literary parallel to the explorations of Eudoxos, provide the Romans with the latest knowledge of the long southern reach of the world from West Africa to India.

Many portions of *On Arabia* depend upon autopsy, often from merchants at the great trade centers,[33] although, unlike *Libyka*, the later treatise does not seem to have included any exploration commissioned by Juba himself.

---

29 *FGrHist* #674. The most recent evidence suggests that Glaukos is early Hellenistic: see Glen Bowersock, "Jacoby's Fragments and Two Greek Historians of Pre-Islamic Arabia," in *Collecting Fragments*, Aporemata 1, ed. Glenn W. Most (Göttingen 1997), pp. 175–9.

30 Strabo 16.4.2.

31 Hellenistic geographers: Eratosthenes (16.4.2), Artemidoros (16.4.18), and Poseidonios (16.4.20); Aelius Gallus, 16.4.22.

32 The "Caesar" who is said to have sacked Arabia Eudaimon (*Periplous of the Erythraian Sea* 26) remains a mystery, despite the assertion by J. Innis Miller (*The Spice Trade of the Roman Empire, 29 B.C. to A.D. 641* [Oxford: Clarendon Press, 1969], p. 15) that it was Augustus' grandson Gaius. This happened not long before the writing of the *Periplous* in the middle of the first century AC. No such attack is known, and explanations have varied from emending the text to the name of a local king to assuming an exaggerated memory of Aelius Gallus' campaign (Wellesley [supra note 13], p. 405; Casson [supra note 10], p. 160). There is no chance that it is Gaius Caesar, unless the other information about his campaign is in error. Miller's assumption is based on an imprecise reading of *NH* 12.55–6.

33 *NH* 32.10 = Juba, fr. 3. On Juba's merchant contacts, see Heinz Kortenbeutel, *Der ägyptische Süd- und Osthandel in der Politik der Ptolemäer und römischen Kaiser* (Berlin: Gebrüder Hoffmann, 1931), pp. 10–11. He may have been in part inspired by Herodotos' use of the same technique (3.106–13).

The use of autopsy is most apparent in the description of the frankincense shipments arriving at the market of Gaza.[34] Juba described frankincense (λιβανωτός, *tus*) in its natural state,[35] and how it came to the south Arabian city of Sabota and passed through the Gebbanite country, then to be shipped over a thousand miles[36] in sixty-five stages by camel caravan to Gaza. The expenses of the journey, the prices for different grades in Gaza, and the means of testing the quality are all recounted from the perspective of Gaza.[37] It is probable that Pliny's entire section on frankincense is from *On Arabia*.[38] Another passage that has a similar personal tone is on *stobrus*, a tree that was burned to create a soporific scent.[39] Its origin was in Karmania, southeast of Persis, and its route west had been to Carrhae, Gabba (probably in southern Syria or Galilee), and then to the coast, perhaps again at Gaza. But according to Juba, using information perhaps from Isidoros, a new route via Charax had recently been established. Isidoros may also have provided Juba with the details of the Arabian coast of the Persian Gulf, as Juba's description is oriented on Charax.[40] The two scholars may have combined their information, perhaps while at Petra, and created a literary map of the trade routes emanating from the Nabataean capital, to Charax, Gaza, and to Palmyra in Syria, making one of the earliest Greco-Roman literary references to that famous

---

34 *NH* 12.63–5, between Juba's frs. 63 and 64, and part of the same description. On the frankincense trade, see Gus W. Van Beek, "Frankincense and Myrrh in Ancient South Arabia," *JAOS* 78, 1958, 141–51; and Miller (supra note 32), pp. 102–4.

35 *NH* 12.56 = Juba, fr. 2. On where frankincense originated, see Gus W. Van Beek, "Ancient Frankincense-Producing Areas," in *Archaeological Discoveries in South Arabia* (Baltimore: Johns Hopkins University Press, 1958), pp. 139–42.

36 It is unlikely that Juba expressed his distances in miles. Pliny invariably used the Roman measurement in his passages quoting Juba, but miles were not used in Juba's time in any of the regions covered by *On Arabia*, except along the new Roman roads near the coasts. Juba probably used *stadia* (as did the author of the *Periplous of the Erythraian Sea*) or Persian *schoinoi* (as did Isidoros). The camel drivers Juba talked to in Gaza probably thought more in terms of camel-days than any linear measurement. But the world of the ancient Mediterranean would have been no different from today in that many systems of measurement existed side by side: just as the modern era makes use of Anglo-American and metric units almost competitively (with even the survival of such exotics as Spanish colonial *varas* and Turkish imperial *dunams*), in antiquity Greek, Roman, Persian, Egyptian, and other units were used simultaneously. The Peutinger Table has miles, Gallic *leugae*, and Persian parasangs (O. A. W. Dilke, *Greek and Roman Maps* [London: Thames and Hudson, 1985], p. 115). For an interesting discussion of the problem of a world with numerous schemes of measurement (although in this case architectural rather than land), see Mark Wilson Jones, "Doric Measure and Architectural Design 1: The Evidence of the Relief from Salamis," *AJA* 104, 2000, 73–93.

37 *NH* 12.64. On the trade in Roman times, see Alessandra Avanzini, "Le Commerce des aromates et les états de l'Arabie méridionale pré-islamique," in *Parfums d'Orient*, Res Orientales 11 (Bures-sur-Yvette 1998), pp. 85–92.

38 *NH* 12.54–65. In fact, Pliny was thrown into confusion ("incertiora fecerunt") by information that he had personally obtained in Rome from Arabian ambassadors that contradicted Juba.

39 *NH* 2.79–81 = Juba, fr. 65.

40 *NH* 6.144–56 = Juba, frs. 30–3; Jacoby, *Commentary*, pp. 336–7. For a recent critique of the geography and toponyms of this passage, see D. T. Potts, *The Arabian Gulf in Antiquity* 2: *From Alexander the Great to the Coming of Islam* (Oxford: Clarendon Press, 1990), pp. 302–13.

trading center. Charax is frequently mentioned in these chapters of the *Natural History*, where Juba is virtually the only source cited.[41] Pliny felt that he was more reliable than Isidoros, so much so that Pliny was violating his own rule always to use a local source, believing that Juba was better even for Charax. Nevertheless, Juba and Isidoros must have had many profitable conversations while in the retinue of Gaius, and Juba would have learned much about Charax and its network of trade routes.[42]

Other portions of Juba's treatise relied on Ptolemaic material. Since the time of Ptolemaios I, explorers had been examining the Red Sea and the adjacent regions of Arabia.[43] Philon went some distance down the Egyptian side of the Red Sea:[44] he or a like-named successor was the author of *Aithiopika*, Juba's source for his description of the Ethiopian coast.[45] The report of a Pythagoras, an officer of Ptolemaios II, was also used by Juba for the Red Sea.[46] Although Ptolemaic explorers tended to emphasize the African side (something also of value for Juba, but more probably in *Libyka*), the Arabian side was not neglected, particularly by Pythagoras and the little-known explorers Ariston[47] and Simias.[48] These accounts were collected by Agatharchides of Knidos in the second century BC and published as *On the Erythraian Sea*,[49] probably Juba's main source. Juba may also have used the reports of Ptolemaic explorers who examined the Persian Gulf, perhaps in the time of Ptolemaios III.[50] But the Ptolemies never seem to have made the

---

41 The only indication of other sources is at *NH* 6.149 = Juba, fr. 30, Pliny's comment that Juba omitted the Omani town of Batrasavave, which authors earlier ("priores") than Juba had discussed. This eliminates Isidoros, and the *priores* may be Seleukid accounts, since the explorations of an "Epiphanes" are alluded to at 6.147: for whether this is Antiochos III or IV, see Potts (supra note 40), pp. 11–12. On Seleukid exploration in the Persian Gulf, see Jean-François Salles, "The Arab–Persian Gulf under the Seleucids," in *Hellenism in the East*, ed. Amélie Kuhrt and Susan Sherwin-White (London: Duckworth, 1987), pp. 75–109.

42 *NH* 6.141 = Juba, fr. 1. It is possible that Juba visited Isidoros at Charax, but this must remain pure speculation. On Charax and its role in Roman trade, see D. T. Potts, "The Roman Relationships with the *Persicus sinus* from the Rise of Spasinou Charax (127 BC) to the Reign of Shapur (AD 307–79)," in *The Early Roman Empire in the East*, ed. Susan E. Alcock, Oxbow Monograph 95 (Oxford: Oxbow, 1997), pp. 89–107.

43 On Ptolemaic exploration in this region, see Raschke (supra note 12), pp. 657–8; Kortenbeutel (supra note 33), pp. 15–51; Agatharchides, *On the Erythraean Sea*, ed. Stanley M. Burstein (London: Hakluyt Society, 1989), pp. 1–2.

44 *NH* 37.108 = Juba, fr. 75: Kortenbeutel (supra note 33), pp. 15–16.

45 Strabo 2.1.20; *FGrHist* #670.

46 *NH* 37.34 = Juba, fr. 76; Kortenbeutel (supra note 33), p. 28; see also Athenaios 4.183f (where Juba used Pythagoras as the source for information about an indigenous musical instrument), 14.634a; Aelian, *On the Characteristics of Animals* 17.8–9.

47 Diodoros 3.42.1; Kortenbeutel (supra note 33), p. 20.

48 Agatharchides 41b; Diodoros 3.18.4. Simias probably lived during the time of Ptolemaios III: see A. Klotz, "Simias" (#2), *RE* 2, ser. 3, 1927, 142–3.

49 For the meager evidence about Agatharchides, see Agatharchides (ed. Burstein, supra note 43), pp. 12–22.

50 *NH* 9.6, 12.76; Cary and Warmington (supra note 8), p. 89.

connection between the Persian Gulf and the Red Sea, and probably had no direct contact with India before the time of Eudoxos.[51]

Juba's material on the Arabian peninsula falls into two distinct categories. There are the trade routes and the trade items, centering on Charax, Petra, and Gaza, probably information gained personally while with Gaius, and there is coastal material, much of it in the style of a *periplous*,[52] probably from Ptolemaic sources, although Juba's ability to describe the complete sea circuit of Arabia[53] indicates, not unexpectedly, that some of his information was from the time of Eudoxos and later, and probably derived from Poseidonios.[54] Juba's concern with the issues of the circumnavigation of Africa, although more likely from *Libyka*, demonstrates his sense of connection with Eudoxos.[55]

Juba's process for collecting material about India was similar to that for the Arabian peninsula. Information was proliferating at a rapid rate in the Augustan period, and the accounts of Alexander's contemporaries, long the standard and still widely used, were rapidly becoming obsolete. Juba came to be recognized as a new authority on India, and remained so even into the third century AC.[56] With minor exceptions, all that survives of Juba's material on India is preserved in Book 6 of the *Natural History*. Its lengthy passage on the subcontinent[57] cites Juba only once, but in such a way as to make Pliny's thorough and extensive use of the king apparent.[58] The Indian section opens with measurements and distances, based on the geographers Eratosthenes, Poseidonios, and Agrippa, as well as the Greeks who had been in India such as Megasthenes,[59] who lived at the court of Chandragupta in the early third century BC, and Dionysios,[60] a little-known envoy of Ptolemaios II who also lived at Indian courts. The description then passes to the interior of the country. Pliny's knowledge of Palibothra and the Ganges demonstrates that his source material is Megasthenes and perhaps others at

51 Steven E. Sidebotham, *Roman Economic Policy in the Erythra Thalassa, 30 B.C.–A.D. 217*, Mnemosyne Suppl. 91 (Leiden 1986), p. 7.

52 See, especially, Juba, frs. 30–3, mariners' information obtained at Charax by either Isidoros or Juba (Potts, *Arabian Gulf* [supra note 40], p. 303).

53 *NH* 6.149–56 = Juba, frs. 30–3.

54 *FGrHist* #87, fr. 28.

55 Juba, fr. 35; Jacoby, *Commentary*, p. 338.

56 Solinus 52.19 = Juba, fr. 101.

57 *NH* 6.56–112.

58 *NH* 6.96 = Juba, fr. 28. Juba is probably one of the "prisci" at 6.84 (Jacoby, *Commentary*, p. 335). See Pliny the Elder, *Histoire naturelle, livre VI, 2ᵉ partie*, ed. J. André and J. Filliozat (Paris: Belles Lettres, 1980), p. 16. On Pliny's use of sources, see Sallmann (supra note 4), pp. 26–7. His nephew, Pliny the Younger, wrote (*Letter* 3.5) how he had inherited from his uncle 160 notebooks that were filled, in the smallest handwriting possible, with excerpts from earlier scholars. Pliny the Elder's sources on India are discussed by Albrecht Dihle, "The Conception of India in Hellenistic and Roman Literature," *PCPS* 190 n.s. 10, 1964, 19, but Juba is not mentioned.

59 *FGrHist* #715.

60 *FGrHist* #717.

the Mauryan court; indeed, Palibothra, the Mauryan capital, is central to this part of the account.[61] After describing the northern part of India and the territories to the northwest in modern Afghanistan, the description jumps to the island of Taprobane, modern Sri Lanka, but reveals no knowledge of the south of India. One source continues to be Megasthenes, but two new ones are introduced: Alexander's officer Onesikritos, and the data supplied by the Taprobanian ambassadors who came to Rome during the time of the emperor Claudius.[62] There is a hint of a world beyond India, the home of the Silk People (Seres) across the mountains (and thus accessed by overland trade through Tibet rather than by a sea route).[63] After returning to the lands west of India, the thread cut with the description of Taprobane, the account then breaks off again to relate the voyage from India to Persia by Onesikritos and Nearchos, "described most recently by Juba."[64] Noting the vagueness of the information supplied by Alexander's two officers,[65] Pliny outlined it in the style of a *periplous*, ending with their reunion with Alexander at Sousa. Then there are three modifications to the route ("subsequently," "at a later period," and "when a merchant discovered a shorter route"),[66] until Pliny's own era is reached, when the voyage was made every year.

Pliny next described the route in reverse, from Alexandria to India, going up the Nile to Koptos, across to Berenike on the Red Sea, and to India,

---

61 *NH* 6.68.

62 *NH* 6.84.

63 *NH* 6.88: see Pliny (ed. André and Filliozat, supra note 58), pp. 117–18. The name China (Θῖνα) is first cited in the *Periplous of the Erythraian Sea* (64): the author believed that it was a great city at the end of the world. On Roman trade beyond India, see Casson (supra note 10), pp. 238–42; Raschke (supra note 12), pp. 674–6.

64 *NH* 6.96 = fr. 28: "enarrata proxime a Iuba." Whether Juba actually used the treatises of Nearchos and Onesikritos, or was merely a later writer on similar subjects, is far from obvious: see Jacoby, *Commentary* to *FGrHist* #133 (2B, p. 446) and *Commentary* to *FGrHist* #134 (2B, p. 478). On this problem, see further, Truesdell S. Brown, *Onesicritus: A Study in Hellenistic Historiography* (Berkeley: University of California Press, 1949), pp. 105–7, who adopted the view that Pliny did not consult Nearchos and Onesikritos directly but only through Juba, which is simplistic. Moreover, Brown seems unaware that Juba, whatever his use of the earlier travelers, added contemporary material of his own.

65 Brown (supra note 64), pp. 107–9, would attribute this vagueness to the compilations of Juba and Pliny, noting that Nearchos, at least, would have been more precise, because he was reporting from a ship's log. The fact remains, however, that Pliny was more interested in the conditions of his own day than Alexander's, and would call attention to how circumstances had changed in the intervening 375 years. The longest surviving fragments of Nearchos' account (from Arrian's *Anabasis*: see *FGrHist* #133) are more detailed than Pliny's version, but that is because it would have been more relevant to Arrian than Pliny. Although Pliny made use of both Alexander's companions and Juba, Arrian did not consult Juba. This would imply that Juba was not particularly valuable for the conditions of the fourth century BC, Arrian's main concern, but was of interest for Pliny's period of the first century AC. For Arrian's sources, see A. P. Bosworth, *From Arrian to Alexander: Studies in Historical Interpretation* (Oxford: Clarendon Press, 1988), pp. 38–60.

66 *NH* 6.100–1: "postea," "secuta aetas," "donec conpendia invenit mercator." On these, see Jacoby, *Commentary*, p. 336.

reaching it at Muziris. Some of this information is contemporary to Pliny,[67] and thus must postdate Juba and parallel the extant *Periplous of the Erythraian Sea*, which is only a few years earlier than Pliny's account, but it is also emphasized that Juba updated Alexander's officers. Indeed, mention of Muziris, in the south of India, demonstrates a range of knowledge beyond that of Alexander's day and even of Megasthenes. A similar distinction is made in the account of the Euphrates, where there are three sources, first Nearchos and Onesikritos, then "later writers," and finally Juba,[68] the latter two corresponding to the "subsequently" and "at a later period" of the Indian route. Hence it seems that Juba's account of India differed from those of Nearchos and Onesikritos (although probably also making use of them) and thus relied on later information, but was itself superseded somewhat by material from traders and merchants of the type preserved in the *Periplous of the Erythraian Sea*, and roughly contemporary with Pliny. There was, however, a source between Nearchos and Onesikritos and Juba – the "subsequently" of 6.101 and 124 – who may be Poseidonios or another Hellenistic geographer. But Juba's source is nowhere named and is neither Alexander's officers nor the Hellenistic geographers. This would suggest that it too was largely oral information supplied by merchants and tradesmen, another reason to suppose a visit to Alexandria by Juba. Yet information on India increased so dramatically in the sixty-odd years between Juba and Pliny that even Juba's recent material had become somewhat obsolete.

Other sources for *On Arabia* are not so easy to come by, and may have been obtained through traditional library research in Alexandria or Kappadokia.[69] Moreover, other topics that seem part of the work, such as Persia and Mesopotamia, were included only tangentially because of their secondary relevance to Juba's main interest, the axis from the Red Sea (and even Mauretania) to India. His material on the Euphrates is connected with Charax and presumably came from Isidoros.[70] A confusion in recounting the history of Charax shows that Juba was less comfortable as a historian than as a geographer, but presumably this material too was from Isidoros.[71] The Christian author Tatian, active in the latter second century AC, knew of a work by Juba on Assyria in two books that was derived from Berossos.[72] Whether this is a separate work or part of *On Arabia* cannot be determined.

---

67 *NH* 6.104.

68 *NH* 6.124 = Juba, fr. 29. The later writers are "qui postea scripsere."

69 It has been suggested that the material on Tylos in the Persian Gulf (at modern Bahrain) came from Alexander's admiral Androsthenes of Thasos (*FGrHist* #711), which is possible, although much of Juba's material was orally derived. See G. W. Bowersock, "Tylos and Tyre: Bahrain in the Graeco-Roman World," in *Bahrain through the Ages: The Archaeology*, ed. Shaikha Haya Ali Al Khalifa and Michael Rice (London: KPI, 1986), pp. 399–406.

70 *NH* 6.124 = Juba, fr. 29.

71 *NH* 6.129 = Juba, fr. 1.

72 Tatian, *Oration to the Greeks* 36 = Juba, fr. 4.

Tatian's interest was the validity of Berossos as a source for Mesopotamian history, not what use Juba made of him, so he did not record what Juba obtained from Berossos. Berossos,[73] priest of Marduk or Bel at Babylon around and after 300 BC, wrote in Greek a *History of Babylonia*, under commission from the Seleukid king Antiochos I. Only a few fragments survive, but enough to show that the treatise began with the creation of the world and went to his own day, in probably no more than three books. It was less of value for what it said than for its attempt to create a Greek manner of describing the history and culture of a venerable pre-Greek people, one of the earliest examples of a technique to become common in the Hellenistic era. Berossos' treatise does not seem to have survived long, and in Juba's day it may have been available only through quotations by Alexandros Polyhistor.

Yet Juba did use material from Berossos, and by the second century AC this was known to Tatian as two books on Assyria by the king. Writing an independent treatise on Assyria does not seem to fit his style as a mature scholar: in fact, there are remarkably few of Juba's fragments that can be related to that part of the world. He wrote something about the legendary Babylonian queen Semiramis and her love for her horse, but Pliny saw this as concerning horses, not Babylonian history.[74] Berossos too wrote about Semiramis, although to discredit Greek ideas about her.[75] Juba's only other extant reference to Mesopotamia, concerning the course of the Euphrates from Babylon southwards, is Characene in origin.[76]

Juba's *On Assyria* and his dependence on Berossos remain enigmatic. Assyria was not in his area of interest and Babylonia only marginally so. Yet it is difficult to determine a context for the horse of Semiramis, unless it were natural historical. Even if the material on Assyria were part of *On Arabia*, Tatian knew of two books, which would be an extensive discursus, not occasional references. Perhaps it was a Mesopotamian appendix to *On Arabia*, an outgrowth of Juba's interest in Charax and the Euphrates, or a juvenile academic work, derived from Alexandros Polyhistor, with no connection to his later scholarship.[77]

---

73 *FGrHist* #680. On Berossos and his work, see Gerald P. Verbrugghe and John M. Wickersham, *Berossos and Manetho, Introduced and Translated* (Ann Arbor: University of Michigan Press, 1996), pp. 13–91; Amélie Kuhrt, "Berossus' *Babyloniaka* and Seleucid Rule in Babylonia," in *Hellenism in the East*, ed. Amélie Kuhrt and Susan Sherwin-White (London: Duckworth, 1987), pp. 32–56.

74 *NH* 8.155 = Juba, fr. 59.

75 Berossos, fr. 8a.

76 Juba, fr. 29. The word "Nabomos" cited by the grammarian Herodian (Juba, fr. 46) has a Babylonian sound, and may be from *On Assyria*.

77 Verbrugghe and Wickersham (supra note 73), p. 30; Jacoby, *Commentary*, p. 328.

On Arabia covered a wide variety of topics.[78] Yet because of its emphasis on trade and commerce, much of what Pliny and others gleaned from it relates to trade goods.[79] This is especially apparent in the information on Arabia proper. The detailed comments on frankincense have already been noted, and directly following is a similar passage on myrrh (σμύρνα, *myrra*).[80] Myrrh came from a more widespread region than frankincense, and although it is found in Arabia and India, most of that used by the Romans was from East Africa; even Arabians crossed the Red Sea to obtain it there.[81] Pliny emphasized this type and cited Juba as well as other unnamed sources, but, as usual, Juba's material is centered on the trade route, in this case from East Africa to Alexandria. Other trade items from Arabia known in Mediterranean markets were *ledanum* (or *ladanum*, λάδανον), an aromatic tree that was transplanted by the Ptolemies from Karmania to Upper Egypt,[82] and the styptic olive (*Olea enhaemon*), which grew along the coast.[83]

Juba also provided Pliny with material on other flora of Arabia.[84] One trade item was a type of palm, locally called *dablas*, that came from the territory of the Skenitai, the Tent-Dwellers, in south Arabia.[85] Otherwise

---

78 Fr. 97, on the Indian origin of Dionysos, hints at Juba's interest in cultic material, carried over from the *Roman Archaeology*. Whether fr. 45 is part of *On Arabia* cannot easily be determined. It names a city, Terebinthos, and may give Juba as the source, although the name must be emended. The only use of Terebinthos as a toponym is at ancient Mamre, the sacred location of the tent of Abraham in a terebinth grove (Genesis 18). Yet there is no known context in which such a citation can be placed within Juba's works, although he was in the vicinity, since the site lies less than 50 km from the Gaza–Petra road. On Terebinthos, see Yoram Tsafrir *et al.*, *Tabula Imperii Romani: Iudaea Palaestina* (Jerusalem: Israel Academy of Arts and Sciences, 1994), pp. 177–8, and G. Hölscher, "Mamre," *RE* 14, 1928, 962–5.

79 Juba may also have learned from his mercantile informants what was imported into Arabia: see *NH* 12.78.

80 *NH* 12.66–72 = Juba, fr. 64. On the myrrh trade, see Van Beek, *JAOS* (supra note 34), pp. 143–51.

81 Miller (supra note 32), pp. 104–5; Casson (supra note 10), pp. 118–20.

82 *NH* 12.76; Fraser (supra note 12), vol. 1, p. 141. Pliny may have here combined material from *On Arabia* and *Libyka*: "dicunt in Carmania et super Aegyptum."

83 Pliny's information continued to come from Juba, although he was not mentioned by name from 12.67 to 12.80. The only other source cited at this point is the emperor Claudius, on the *bratus* (12.78; *FGrHist* #276, fr. 1), a cypress-like tree from Parthia.

84 Conspicuously lacking, however, as from all other ancient literature, is the Arabian plant best known today, the coffee bean, *Coffea arabica*. Although it no doubt existed in Juba's day, it does not seem to have been brewed into a beverage until the ninth century AC or later: see Stephen C. Topik, "Coffee," *CWHF*, p. 641. Tea (*Camellia sinensis*) was also unknown to the ancient Mediterranean, although tea cultivation is exceedingly ancient – perhaps thousands of years old – and there was extensive Greek and Roman contact with the regions that today produce the world's tea. The growing and brewing of tea was probably institutionalized in the time of the Han Dynasty and thus could have been known to the ancient Mediterranean world. But it does not seem to have spread beyond China until medieval times and did not come to India until the sixteenth century, so it would have been unknown to ancient authors, whose knowledge of China was mostly derivative. See John H. Weisburger and James Comer, "Tea," *CWHF*, pp. 713–16.

85 *NH* 13.34 = Juba, fr. 66.

unknown, it was cultivated to eat. The Arabian strawberry, the arbutus, was unusually large: one senses a trader bragging about the wares of his home-land.[86] Juba also described the gossypinus, or wool-bearing tree, cotton,[87] discussing its prevalence on the island of Tylos in the Persian Gulf,[88] and said it was superior to Indian linen and the Arabian *cynas* (otherwise unknown). Again there is a sense of mercantile pride: one can imagine the merchants in Gaza or Petra asserting the superiority of their products to those imported from India.[89] They told Juba about the unusually large mussels in Arabian rivers, how they cared for their camels and protected them from flies, and the story of a large sea creature (*cetus*) that entered an Arabian river and was 600 feet long and 360 feet across.[90] Another mer-chant's tale was about a man in Arabia who was restored to life by means of a plant,[91] perhaps another sales pitch for superior-quality Arabian goods. The pearl fisheries of both India and the Red Sea were of special interest.[92] Pearl fishing is one of the few subjects where Juba's comparative technique is preserved, for both Pliny and Aelian cited Juba's discussion of pearls throughout the world, some of which (the Mauretanian) he would have known personally, and others (the British) he could only have read about. Whether Juba wrote about Indian pearls is problematic, although Aelian quoted no other source and alluded to pearl fisheries near the Indian city of Perimoula (probably modern Bombay) in the days of the Greco-Baktrian king Eukratides I of the second century BC. If this material is derived from Juba, it is less likely to be contemporary trade information than from a Hel-lenistic geographer.

Cinnabar (κιννάβαρι, *minium*) came from Karmania and was used as a pigment.[93] Sandarach (σανδαράκη) and ochre were products of the Red Sea island of Topazos but were not imported from there to Rome in Pliny's

---

86 *NH* 15.99 = Juba, fr. 68.

87 *NH* 12.38 = Juba, fr. 62. Juba emphasized the unusual fact that "their trees clothe the Indians" ("Indos suae arbores vestiunt").

88 On Tylos at this time, and its relevance to Augustan policy, see Bowersock, "Tylos and Tyre" (supra note 69), pp. 399–406.

89 For the history of cotton in the Persian Gulf, and its probable origin from India, see Potts, *Arabian Gulf* (supra note 40), pp. 133–6.

90 *NH* 32.10 = Juba, fr. 3. In a similar superlative tone is the matter of the Arabian spring whose pres-sure was so strong that anything thrown into it was cast out again, regardless of its weight (*NH* 31.18 = Juba, fr. 41), and perhaps even the account of how elephants link themselves together as a raft, using their heads as sails, to cross the Red Sea (*NH* 8.35 = Juba, fr. 58).

91 *NH* 25.14 = Juba, fr. 69.

92 Aelian, *On the Characteristics of Animals* 15.8 = Juba, fr. 70; *NH* 9.115 = Juba, fr. 71.

93 *NH* 33.118 = Juba, fr. 72. Jacoby (*Commentary*, p. 349) felt that this was from Onesikritos, but this is not necessary, since Juba was familiar with the trade routes from Karmania to the Mediterranean (fr. 65). See also Casson (supra note 10), pp. 168–9. On cinnabar, see J. F. Healy, "Pliny on Mineral-ogy and Minerals," in *Science in the Early Roman Empire*, ed. Roger French and Frank Greenaway (London: Croom Helm, 1986), pp. 129–30.

day.[94] The former, red sulfide of arsenic, or realgar, was a pigment and was used medicinally: the Romans may have preferred the variety from the mining center near Pompeiopolis (Soloi) in southeastern Asia Minor.[95] Merchants also told Juba about the green emerald (σμάραγδος χλωρός) that was used to decorate houses in Arabia.[96] Emeralds as a trade item do not seem to have been known to the author of the *Periplous of the Erythraian Sea*, and the stone, inlaid into walls, is unlikely to have been a gem emerald, but perhaps was a decorative building stone similar to the green porphyry or the *verde antico* used in the decoration of Roman Imperial structures.[97] Arabian architecture was also said to make use of a transparent stone for its windows.[98] The Arabian rock crystals from the Nekron island in the Red Sea were well documented for Juba through Ptolemaic sources and the large mass of rock crystal that Livia had dedicated on the Capitol in Rome, which he probably saw.[99]

Even allowing for mercantile exaggeration, there is no doubt that the southern Arabian peninsula became wealthy as a result of the trade in incense and other exotics.[100] Moreover, Augustus would have been fully aware of the use of scents and perfumes as an implement of royal power.[101] In fact, it was from Gaza, the location of so much of Juba's research, that perfumes reached Makedonia and the notice of Alexander the Great, becoming a "conspicuous symbol of power."[102] Alexander had contemplated conquering Arabia – Pliny wrote, erroneously, that he had done so – and this certainly formed some of the basis of Augustus' interest. Yet the accounts of Juba and others[103] on Arabia have an exaggerated, mythical quality, that of typical travelers' reports of the extreme material wealth of far-off lands, similar to stories of the golden cities of the New World. Arabian informants may also have attempted to persuade Juba about the primacy of their culture, calling his attention to the Arabian populations along the Nile and even the Arabian role in founding cities in Lower Egypt.[104]

94 *NH* 35.39 = Juba, fr. 74.

95 Strabo 12.3.40; Casson (supra note 10), p. 208.

96 *NH* 37.73 = Juba, fr. 78.

97 Filippo Coarelli, *Guide archeologiche Laterza: Roma* (Rome: Giuseppe Laterza e Figli, 1980), p. 372.

98 *NH* 36.163 = Juba, fr. 73. This may be φεγγίτης ("luminary stone"), mentioned by Pliny immediately previously. See John F. Healy, *Pliny the Elder on Science and Technology* (Oxford: Oxford University Press, 1999), pp. 236–7.

99 *NH* 37.24 (=Juba, fr. 76), 27. This was clear quartz, κρύσταλλος (SiO_2): see Healy (supra note 98), pp. 220–1.

100 Van Beek, *JAOS* (supra note 34), pp. 148–9; Raschke (supra note 12), p. 847 (n. 902).

101 On this issue, see Glen Bowersock, "Perfumes and Power," in *Profumi d'Arabia: atti di convegno*, ed. Alessandra Avanzini (Rome: L'Erma di Bretschneider, 1997), pp. 543–6.

102 Bowersock, "Perfumes" (supra note 101), p. 545; *NH* 12.62; Plutarch, *Alexander* 25.4–5; *Sayings of Kings and Commanders* (179 E–F). Pliny's citation is in the context of Juba's description of frankincense, raising the possibility that it was he who preserved the tale about Alexander.

103 In addition to Juba, see Diodoros 3.47.5–7 and Strabo 16.4.19.

104 *NH* 6.176–7 = Juba, fr. 36; see also *NH* 6.167–8.

Like any geographer, Juba was concerned with dimensions. He provided Pliny with an astonishingly accurate distance around Arabia – somewhat less than 4,000 miles – although he erroneously felt that it was widest in the north.[105] But a major interest was the feasibility of reaching Arabia and its wealth from Mauretania without going through the Mediterranean. The voyage of Eudoxos had proven that this was possible, and the court of Bocchus I had attempted to monopolize the knowledge and keep it from the Greek world. Juba believed that the Atlantic began not far south of the Red Sea at Cape Mossylites, presumably the Mossylon known to the author of the *Periplous of the Erythraian Sea*, near modern Cape Guardafui (Ras Asin), where the Somali coast turns sharply southwest, the easternmost point of Africa.[106] Juba felt that this region was more India than Africa, perhaps reflecting the Indian trading presence that even today is still prominent in this area. He was aware of the southern extent of the East African coast, describing it in *periplous* style, with distances, sailing directions, and the ports of call. Although the description is unclear and provides only 1,875 miles of distance, which would not be far beyond Zanzibar, it is based on accurate detail: Juba's informants knew about the Askitai, a piratical tribe that used poisoned arrows.[107] The author of the *Periplous of the Erythraian Sea* knew the East African coast as far south as the emporium of Rhapta, beyond which it was unexplored.[108] This takes one into the vicinity of Dar es Salaam, the most likely candidate for Rhapta, and whose distance south is very close to Juba's 1,875 miles.[109] Juba's connection of this region with Mauretania is as much wishful thinking as accurate information, based on the tradition of Eudoxos and other local reports from northwest Africa, particularly the involvement of the city of Gades in the circumnavigation of

---

105 *NH* 6.156 = Juba, fr. 33.

106 *NH* 6.175 = Juba, fr. 35; *Periplous of the Erythraian Sea* 10; *BAGRW*, Map 4. On Roman (and Hellenistic) knowledge of East Africa, see L. A. Thompson, "Eastern Africa and the Graeco-Roman World (to AD 641)," in *Africa in Classical Antiquity: Nine Studies*, ed. L. A. Thompson and J. Ferguson (Ibadan: Ibadan University Press, 1969), pp. 29–42.

107 It has been argued from *NH* 6.175–6 that Juba knew of Madagascar and the Comoro Islands (H. von Wissmann, "Zanganae," *RE* Supp. 11, 1968, 1340–2: see also Potts, *Arabian Gulf* [supra note 40], pp. 312–13, and Yves Janvier, "La Géographie greco-romaine a-t-elle connu Madagascar?" *Omaly sy Anio (Hier et aujourd'hui)* 1–2 [Tananarive 1975], pp. 11–41, who felt that early Hellenistic knowledge of the island had been lost by Roman times). Desanges (supra note 12), p. 333, was not convinced of any Greco-Roman knowledge that far south, and considered "le problème, à notre avis insoluble." See also Cary and Warmington (supra note 8), pp. 129–30. Hellenistic and Roman coins have been found in Madagascar and southeast Africa, although these may be casual removals and not indicative of specific contacts. See Raymond Mauny, "Monnaies anciennes trouvées en Afrique au Sud du limes de l'empire romaine," in *Conferencía internacional de Africanistas Occidentales: 4ª conferencía, Santa Isabel de Fernando Poo 1951* (Madrid: Dirección General de Marruecos y Colonias, 1954), vol. 2, pp. 64–7.

108 *Periplous of the Erythraian Sea* 14–18.

109 Casson (supra note 10), pp. 141–3; Raschke (supra note 12), p. 656.

Africa,[110] as well as other tales about far-reaching explorations.[111] Such reports were rampant in Juba's world, and some were true. Although an actual circumnavigation, in the sense of an accurately recorded and detailed voyage that had an effect on Mediterranean culture and trade, would not come until the fifteenth century, its possibility was of vital concern to Juba. When Vasco da Gama went from Portugal to India in 1497–9, this journey allowed the trade from India to Europe to bypass the Venetian-controlled eastern Mediterranean and to come directly to Portugal, thus having a profound impact on culture and civilization.[112] Eudoxos, Bocchus I, the traders of Gades, and Juba all had the same idea. If Juba had any specific plans for establishing India–Mauretania trade around Africa, they never came to fruition (and probably would not have been received well in either Rome or Alexandria), but the thought was there, and inspired *On Arabia*.[113]

110 There were repeated rumors that the Gaderenes often made the journey (*NH* 2.169–70), and this is implicit in the story of Eudoxos (Desanges [supra note 12], pp. 164–5). Yet there may have been a tendency to attribute any remote and unexplainable shipwreck to the enigmatic Gaderenes: this was Strabo's feeling about the discovery Eudoxos made off the Somali coast (Strabo 2.3.5). As civic magistrate of Gades, Juba would have had access to local traditions, whether or not true.

111 For example, there is the incident reported by Q. Metellus Celer (consul in 60 BC). While he was in Gaul, a local chieftain presented him with a contingent of Indians who had arrived off the German coast by sea, one of the most egregious examples of a journey gone off course (*NH* 2.170). There are serious doubts as to the veracity of the tale: the "Indians" may only have been remote peoples appearing at the edges of civilization, and the account seems to depend on ancient conceptions of an encircling navigable Ocean (see Pomponius Mela 3.45) and a Caspian Sea (which seems to have been known to Indian merchants, *NH* 6.52) connected to both the Black Sea and the Ocean and thus providing a route to Europe. Nevertheless, the mere existence of such tales, not their factual possibility, is significant in understanding ancient theories of exploring the perimeters of the world: the possibility that Indians might have come around the north to Europe would reinforce the idea that a southern connection to India was also possible. See Pomponius Mela ed. Silberman, pp. 277–8; Hermann Bengtson, "Q. Caecilius Metellus Celer (cos 60) und die Inder," *Historia* 3, 1954–5, 229–36.

112 For a recent detailed study of the great Portuguese explorer and the impact of his voyage, see Sanjay Subrahmanyam, *The Career and Legend of Vasco da Gama* (Cambridge: Cambridge University Press, 1997).

113 It has even been suggested that part of Gaius' commission was to return home around Africa (Cary and Warmington [supra note 8], p. 129). This seems unlikely, although it is interesting that Pliny (*NH* 2.168) mentioned Gaius' expedition in the context of circumnavigations of Africa.

11

THE MAURETANIAN DYNASTY

The later dynastic history of the family of Juba and Kleopatra Selene is difficult to untangle. One feels acutely the lack of a Josephus or Plutarch. The few sources are baffling in obscurity and present incompatible data. Issues include the death date of Kleopatra Selene, Juba's subsequent marriage, and even the number and names of their children. Most clear is the regnal span of Juba and his heir Ptolemaios. Juba's reign lasted until AD 23 or 24, since his coins run only into his forty-eighth year, and Tacitus recorded that the transition from Juba to the "negligent youth" Ptolemaios was in the ninth or tenth year of Tiberius.[1] Coins with both "rex Iuba" and "rex Ptolemaeus" show that they were co-rulers for a number of years, but none of these joint coins has a regnal year.[2] Coins as early as Juba's Year 30 (AD 5) have a youthful bust of Ptolemaios, perhaps when he assumed the *toga virilis*,[3] and coins from Year 36 (AD 11) show a more mature version (Figure 26e, f); thus a birth date of *ca.* 13–9 BC is possible.[4] Ptolemaios' own coins run for twenty regnal years.[5] Since he was executed by the emperor Gaius Caligula,[6] his death occurred between AD 37 and 41 and thus his first regnal year was

---

1 Mazard #386, 387; Tacitus, *Annals* 4.1, 5, 23. The phrase is "iuventa incurioso." *Iuventa* need not mean extreme youth: Tacitus used the word to describe men in their thirties, especially when compared with someone older: Germanicus at age 34 (*Annals* 2.71) and Nero at age 31 (*Histories* 1.7). See François Chamoux, "Un Nouveau Portrait de Ptolémée de Maurétanie découvert à Cherchel," in *Mélanges d'archéologie et d'histoire offerts à André Piganiol*, ed. Raymond Chevallier (Paris: SEVPEN, 1966), vol. 1, p. 404.

2 Mazard #379, 381, 389, 391.

3 Mazard #375. There is no good evidence for a specific year when the *toga virilis* was assumed: known ages vary from 14 to 18 (Johannes Regner, "Tirocinium Fori," *RE* 2, ser. 6, 1937, 1452–3); Alberto Grilli, "Cicerone nell'età della toga virile," *PP* 52, 1997, 161–76).

4 Mazard #383, 387. A birth date of between 19 and 14 BC is preferred by Max Hofmann, "Ptolemaios von Mauretanien" (#62), *RE* 23, 1959, 1770, and has been followed by many commentators. But this seems rather early, and is based on the erroneous assumption that his parents were not married until 20 BC (supra, pp. 86–7).

5 Mazard #496; on Ptolemaios' coins generally, see Dieter Salzmann, "Zur Münzprägung der mauretanischen Könige Juba II. und Ptolemaios," *MM* 15, 1974, 180–2.

6 Seneca, *On the Tranquility of the Mind* 11.12; Pliny, *Natural History* 5.11; Suetonius, *Gaius* 26.

(a)   (b)   (c)

(d)   (e)   (f)

(g)

Figure 25   Numidian and Mauretanian coins: (a) bilingual bronze coin of Juba I with temple on the reverse (Mazard 85); (b) reverse of the same coin; (c) bronze elephant coin of Juba II (Mazard 135); (d) reverse of the same coin; (e) bronze lion coin of Juba II (similar to Mazard 140); (f) bronze coin of Juba II with the Caesarea Temple of Augustus, dated to Year 32 (AD 7) (Mazard 148); (g) bronze coin of Juba II with cornucopia, dated to Year 44 (AD 19) (similar to Mazard 269).

(a) (b) (c)

(d) (e) (f)

(g) (h)

Figure 26 Mauretanian coins: (a) bronze coin jointly of Juba II and Kleopatra Selene (similar to Mazard 369); (b) reverse of the same coin; (c) bronze crocodile coin of Kleopatra Selene (similar to Mazard 395); (d) reverse of the same coin; (e) bronze coin jointly of Juba II and Ptolemaios, dated to Year 36 (AD 11); (f) reverse of the same coin; (g) gold coin of Ptolemaios, with altar (Mazard 429) (published as silver); (h) reverse of the same coin.

© Copyright the British Museum.

between AD 17 and 21, two to six years before his father's death.[7] Ptolemaios is rarely mentioned in literature without reference to the fact that Juba was his father. Strabo and Suetonius recorded that his mother was Kleopatra Selene,[8] which, however, would be obvious from his name. No other sons are known, and his mother would have been about 30 when he was born, having been married for over a decade. Thus despite his dynastic name, he may not have been the first-born son – his grandmother had not used the name for either her first or second son – but he was the oldest still alive in Juba's later years.

A more problematic issue is the date of Kleopatra Selene's death, which, however, must be examined relative to Juba's second marriage, to Glaphyra of Kappadokia, daughter of King Archelaos. This is known solely through a pair of references by Josephus, his only mention of Juba, and an inscription from the Akropolis of Athens.[9] Her marriage to Juba was a brief moment in Glaphyra's short but interesting life.[10] Born perhaps around 36 BC, when Antonius confirmed her father as king, she married Alexandros, the son of Herod the Great, in 17 BC.[11] She immediately became involved in the turbulent intrigues of the Judaean royal family, missing no opportunity to parade her noble ancestry – Persian and Makedonian – before the upstart Judaeans, and maintaining her superiority to all the other women at court.[12] This incurred the wrath of Herod's formidable sister Salome and significantly lowered Glaphyra's status, making inevitable the charges of conspiracy against her in 12 BC, which she successfully deflected, perhaps because Herod himself was said to be interested in her.[13] Her husband was not so

---

7 Mazard #384. The latter year is preferred by most commentators (Mazard, p. 122; Hofmann [supra note 4], pp. 1772–4), but a coin in the El Kasr hoard (infra, p. 249), which seems to be no later than AD 17, has the legend "rex Ptolemaeus" (no. 64).

8 His mother is cited by Strabo (17.3.7) and Suetonius (*Gaius* 26.1); his father at Strabo 17.3.12, 25; Pliny, *Natural History* 5.16; Tacitus, *Annals* 4.23; Dio 59.25.1.

9 Josephus, *Jewish Antiquities* 17.349–53; *Jewish War* 2.114–16; *OGIS* 363. It is possible that the inscription dates from AD 1, an Olympic year, and a natural time for foreign rulers to be in mainland Greece. Both Glaphyra's father and her sometime father-in-law Herod were involved with the games: for Archelaos, see *OGIS* 359; for Herod, Roller, *Herod*, pp. 230–1. This dates the marriage to Juba a year earlier than otherwise suggested, but is plausible nonetheless. See, further, Nikos Kokkinos, "Reassembling the Inscription of Glaphyra from Athens," *ZPE* 68, 1987, 288–90.

10 For her career, see Richard D. Sullivan, "The Dynasty of Cappadocia," *ANRW* 2.7, 1980, 1161–6; Grace Harriet Macurdy, *Vassal Queens and Some Contemporary Women in the Roman Empire* (Baltimore: Johns Hopkins University Press, 1937), pp. 57–60; for the marriage, Mario Pani, *Roma e i re d'Oriente da Augusto a Tiberio*, Pubblicazione della Facoltà di lettere e filosofia dell'Università di Bari 11 (Bari 1972), pp. 132–4, 140.

11 If Josephus' account of events at *Jewish Antiquities* 16.6–11 is in sequence, it was at the time of Herod's second trip to Rome, which was in the spring of that year (Roller, *Herod*, pp. 67–8).

12 Josephus, *Jewish War* 1.476–7.

13 Josephus, *Jewish Antiquities* 16.193, 328–34: again the date is based on a synchronism with a trip to Rome by Herod.

lucky and was executed five years later.[14] Herod returned Glaphyra and her dowry to her father; presumably her children also went to the court of their grandfather.[15]

Juba arrived in the East a few years later in the retinue of Gaius Caesar. Part of his time was spent at Archelaos' court city of Elaioussa-Sebaste, especially after he withdrew from the expedition early in AD 2. Glaphyra, at the Kappadokian court, widowed and available, was a good match for the king of Mauretania, almost certainly a widower himself. Both Archelaos and Juba may have entertained ideas about a linkage of East and West that would be politically advantageous to both, part of the grandiose planning that would eventually contribute to Archelaos' indictment in Rome. Yet interpretation of the circumstances of this marriage is complicated by a major textual issue. In the *Jewish War*, which Josephus wrote first, the text reads that after Juba died (τελευτήσαντος), Glaphyra returned home to her father as a widow (χηρεύουσαν), and then went to Judaea and married Herod's son the ethnarch Archelaos.[16] The text is explicit and unambiguous, but wrong, since Juba lived for nearly two decades after Archelaos lost his ethnarchy in AD 6. In the *Jewish Antiquities*, which Josephus wrote perhaps fifteen years after the *Jewish War*, the wording is slightly different, and may provide a reason for the difficulty.[17] Here Juba is said to have μεταστάντος, which can, although rarely, mean "died," but more usually "changed places" or "went away."[18] Hence Josephus – whose Greek was never fluent[19] – misread his source (probably Nikolaos of Damaskos) and perhaps even confused the events of the terminations of Glaphyra's first and second marriages, and assumed that Juba had died during his marriage to her, whereupon she became a widow. Josephus had no other interest in Juba and thus was not well informed about his career. In the later *Jewish Antiquities* Josephus stayed closer to the diction of his source, and thus ended up with a contradiction: Juba went away and Glaphyra became a widow.[20] The marriage, then, could not have been terminated by Juba's death, and divorce is the only possibility; one wonders if Augustus, nervous at the power base the marriage would create, had the relationship terminated.[21] Yet Glaphyra's marriage to Juba cannot merely have been one of convenience – an eastern fling for the king of

14 Josephus, *Jewish Antiquities* 16.394; 17.11.

15 Josephus, *Jewish Antiquities* 17.12; *Jewish War* 1.552–3; Kokkinos, *Herodian Dynasty*, p. 246.

16 Josephus, *Jewish War* 2.115. On Josephus' dates of writing, see Tessa Rajak, *Josephus: The Historian and His Society* (London: Duckworth, 1983), pp. 195, 237.

17 Josephus, *Jewish Antiquities* 17.349–50.

18 The verb is μεθίστημι. See LSJ for the usage.

19 Rajak (supra note 16), pp. 46–50.

20 Jacoby, *RE*, p. 2386.

21 The Romans repeatedly involved themselves in the marriage arrangements of client monarchs: in addition to that of Juba II and Kleopatra Selene, the most notable is the betrothal between Herod's sister Salome and the Nabataean Syllaios (Josephus, *Jewish War* 1.566; *Jewish Antiquities* 17.10).

Mauretania – since it was validated and honored by the Athenians. Whatever its true status, it lasted at most two years, probably from no earlier than
AD 2 to no later than AD 5, and it is unlikely that she returned to Mauretania
with Juba, as Josephus' μεταστάντος implies that Juba left her, probably
to return home. Glaphyra's third marriage, to the ethnarch Archelaos,
occurred before Augustus deposed him in AD 6 and sent him into forced
retirement in Vienna in Gaul.[22] This marriage was also brief, as Glaphyra
died early in it, after dreaming that her first husband, Alexandros,
reproached her for marrying his half-brother.[23]

It is difficult to imagine Juba's eastern trip and second marriage except in
the context of Kleopatra Selene's previous death. Polygamy, not a Roman
practice, does not seem a possibility.[24] But there is no specific evidence, and
the issue has become confused by publication in 1910 of the finding of a
hoard of coins from El Ksar (Alkasar) that seems to date from around AD 17
and to include joint Juba–Kleopatra Selene coins of that time as well as
undated coins issued by the queen alone.[25] Yet these coins, if from around
AD 17, more likely commemorate the raising of Kleopatra Selene's son Ptolemaios to joint rule at that time, rather than her continued survival and
remarriage to Juba, or participation in a polygamous relationship.[26]

Further evidence as to her earlier date of death comes from an epigram by
Krinagoras, long assumed to eulogize her:

---

22 Josephus, *Jewish Antiquities* 17.342–4.

23 Josephus, *Jewish Antiquities* 17.349–53; *Jewish War* 2.115–16. Glaphyra's only known children are
two sons from her first marriage: one became Tigranes V of Armenia, around AD 10 (David Magie,
Jr., *Roman Rule in Asia Minor to the End of the Third Century after Christ* [Princeton, N.J.: Princeton
University Press, 1950] pp. 485, 1345–6), and the other, Alexandros, was father to Tigranes VI of
Armenia (Magie, pp. 556–8) and grandfather of Alexandros of Kilikia, consul at Rome in the early
second century AC (Richard D. Sullivan, "The Dynasty of Commagene," *ANRW* 2.8, 1977, 794–5;
Kokkinos, *Herodian Dynasty*, pp. 246–63.

24 Hellenistic-Roman dynasts, including Juba's Numidian ancestors (Sallust, *Jugurtha* 80.6–7), regularly made use of polygamy, with Herod the Great and his ten wives the most notorious example.
But it seems highly unlikely that Juba, heavily romanized and married to Kleopatra Selene in Rome
under Roman law, would have indulged in this practice. Juba's father-in-law Antonius had been in
serious trouble because of his bigamous "marriage" to Kleopatra VII, and despite the fact that this
relationship produced Juba's wife, it is improbable that Juba would have made the same error. Moreover, Glaphyra was probably a Roman citizen herself: all her husbands were, and there had long been
a special relationship between Rome and Kappadokia (Strabo 12.2.11; Sullivan, "Cappadocia" [supra
note 10], pp. 1128–9). Polygamy was not the Roman way, but remarriage after the death of a wife
was normal and accepted (Susan Treggiari, *Roman Marriage: iusti coniuges from the Time of Cicero to the
Time of Ulpian* [Oxford: Clarendon Press, 1991], p. 235). Juba's marriage to Glaphyra is the best
proof that Kleopatra Selene was dead.

25 Kurt Regling, "Zum Fund von Iubadenaren in Alkasar," *ZfN* 28, 1910, 9–27; Gsell, vol. 8,
pp. 220–1.

26 The coins issued by Kleopatra Selene alone (Mazard #392–5), all undated, have been presumed to
indicate a regency while Juba was in the East, but they more likely are merely examples of her
autonomous powers of coinage.

The moon herself grew dark, rising at sunset,
Covering her suffering in the night,
Because she saw her beautiful namesake, Selene,
Breathless, descending to Hades,
With her she had had the beauty of her light in common,
And mingled her own darkness with her death.[27]

Selene is not otherwise known as a personal name in the Augustan period. Krinagoras' intimacy with the Augustan family and his commemoration of the wedding of Kleopatra Selene and Juba make it probable that he eulogized the dead queen.

Since Krinagoras lived long enough to write about Germanicus,[28] this eulogy has only a vague *terminus ante quem* of the second decade of the first century AC. But the crucial element that has excited commentators is the lunar eclipse. Interpretation of ancient references to eclipses by resorting to modern astronomical calculations is dangerous,[29] but nonetheless, if one assumes that Krinagoras was not writing allegorically, it may be possible to shed some light on the problem by examining the various data collected on ancient eclipses. Literal interpretation of the poem requires the eclipse to be total and at sunset, and the definitive *Canon der Finsternisse*[30] lists total lunar eclipses in 9, 8, 5, and 1 BC, and AD 3, 7, 10, 11, and 14. The eclipses of AD 7 and later are after the death of Glaphyra. Those of 1 BC and AD 3 can be eliminated on astronomical grounds, as not fitting the description of Krinagoras.[31] Of the remainder (9, 8, and 5 BC), the one of 23 March 5 BC seems to fit best,[32] although certainty is difficult. Thus so far evidence points toward her death no later than 5 BC, and perhaps as early as 9 BC. But the El Ksar hoard has thrown modern scholars into confusion and led to the assumption that Juba and Kleopatra Selene separated and then reunited after his liaison with Glaphyra and that Kleopatra Selene died sometime between

---

27 Krinagoras 18 (=*Palatine Anthology* 7.633):

καὶ αὐτὴ ἤχλυσεν ἀκρέσπερος ἀντέλλουσα
Μένη, πένθος ἑὸν νυκτὶ καλυψαμένη,
οὕνεκα τὴν χαρίεσσαν ὁμώνυμην εἶδε Σελήνην
ἄπνουν εἰς ζοφερὸν δυομένην Ἀΐδην·
κείνη γὰρ καὶ κάλλος ἑοῦ κοινώσατο φωτός
καὶ θάνατον κείνης μῖξεν ἑῷ κνέφεϊ.

28 Krinagoras 26 (=*Palatine Anthology* 9.283).

29 For this problem, see Duane W. Roller, "Some Thoughts on Thales' Eclipse," *LCM* 8, 1983, 58–9.

30 The English edition is Theodor Oppolzer, *Canon of Eclipses*, trans. Owen Gingerich (New York: Dover, 1962). One year has been added to Oppolzer's BC dates because of his use of a Year Zero.

31 Maud Worcester Makemson, "Note on Eclipses," in Macurdy (supra note 10), pp. 60–2.

32 Makemson (supra note 31), pp. 60–2. This may be the eclipse mentioned by Josephus (*Jewish Antiquities* 17.167) that occurred shortly before the death of Herod the Great (Franz Boll, "Finsternisse," *RE* 6, 1909, 2359).

AD 11 and 17, perhaps at the time of the eclipses of AD 11 or 14.[33] Yet this strains credulity, and places everything at the service of a hoard of coins found and described long ago. It is better to assume that Kleopatra Selene had died before Juba went east, probably in 5 BC.

Another puzzling item is the matter of a certain Drusilla, identified by Tacitus as a granddaughter of Antonius and Kleopatra VII.[34] She married Felix,[35] a freedman of the emperor Claudius (or his mother Antonia) and the procurator of Judaea in the 50s AC, well known for his relationship with Paul of Tarsos,[36] and for marrying three queens.[37] Since the male children of Antonius and Kleopatra died well before child-producing age, Kleopatra Selene is the only possibility for Drusilla's parent. Thus Drusilla was one of Felix's three queens, an exaggeration, perhaps, since it is impossible to determine or even imagine where Drusilla was queen. Still, this might not have been an unexpected claim for a freedman who had reached the highest levels of the Roman government and was notorious for his "complete savageness and wantonness, exercising the power of a king with the temperament of a slave."[38] One would expect such a personality to brag about his importance and elevate the status of his marriages. And, inevitably, there are further complications. After Felix became procurator of Judaea, he married another queen, the former wife of King Azizos of Emesa, daughter of King Agrippa I of Judaea and Kypros, grandniece of Herod the Great. Confusingly, her name was also Drusilla. Her marriage to Azizos occurred when she was 14, and was dissolved sometime between AD 52 and 54, not long after it had taken place, evidently because of the persuasiveness of Felix, whom she promptly married.[39]

The existence in the career of Felix of this second Drusilla has led to the obvious possibility that the coincidence of name is an error: one would expect more to be made somewhere in ancient literature of the freedman who married three queens, two of whom were named Drusilla. Moreover, it seems a strange name for a child of Juba and Kleopatra Selene: a Ptolemaic

---

33 Regling (supra note 25), pp. 11–12 ("nach der Scheidung von Glaphyra die Cleopatra wieder als Gattin annahm"); A. S. F. Gow and D. L. Page, *The Greek Anthology: The Garland of Philip and Some Contemporary Epigrams* (Cambridge: Cambridge University Press, 1968), vol. 2, p. 226; see also Gsell, vol. 8, pp. 220–1; also F. Stähelin, "Kleopatra Selene" (#23), *RE* 21, 1921, 785.

34 Tacitus, *Histories* 5.9.

35 On the full name of Felix, which was probably Tiberius Claudius Felix rather than the Antonius Felix generally accepted, see Nikos Kokkinos, "A Fresh Look at the *gentilicium* of Felix Procurator of Judaea," *Latomus* 49, 1990, 126–41, and his *Antonia Augusta: Portrait of a Great Roman Lady* (London: Routledge, 1992), p. 32.

36 Acts 24.

37 Suetonius, *Claudius* 28. Felix and Drusilla may have met in Rome (Kokkinos, *Latomus* [supra note 35], p. 138).

38 Tacitus, *Histories* 5.9: "omnem saevitiam ac libidinem, ius regium servili ingenio exercuit."

39 Josephus, *Jewish Antiquities* 20.141–4; Richard D. Sullivan, "The Dynasty of Emesa," *ANRW* 2.8, 1977, 215–16.

name is more likely, such as Kleopatra, Berenike, or Arsinoë. There is no doubt that the Mauretanian monarchs had a daughter who reached maturity, as she was honored by the Athenians, but her name is not preserved.[40] The name Drusilla suggests that she might have been born just after the death in 9 BC of Augustus' stepson Drusus, a childhood playmate of both Juba and Kleopatra Selene. Or the name may have been in honor of the matriarch of the imperial family, Livia Drusilla. Drusilla would have reached marriageable age around AD 5–9, and might have married Felix at this time, although this would give him an unusually long career. But such chronological discussions are quite hypothetical, and his marriage with the first Drusilla may have been later and perhaps not her first: one would think that the granddaughter of Antonius and Kleopatra could have done better for a husband, at least in her first marriage. This may suggest that the marriage occurred after both her parents' death, and that she and Felix may have been married as late as the 30s AC: such a match would have been highly improbable before Felix was manumitted, an event of uncertain date but probably later rather than earlier.

No further details are known about the daughter of Juba and Kleopatra Selene. Although she seems to have gained enough status to have been honored by the Athenians, perhaps at the same time as her brother Ptolemaios, she probably died by the 30s AC; one need not think that her marriage to Felix was lengthy or produced any children surviving to maturity. Such children would have been great-grandchildren of Antonius and Kleopatra and the last generation of the Ptolemaic line, and as such would be unlikely to have been lost to the record.[41]

Drusilla's brother and Juba's heir, Ptolemaios, ruled for twenty years, but there are few details about his reign.[42] His father's elevation of him to joint rule around AD 17–21 may reflect the difficulties of Juba's last years. The problem with Tacfarinas, which had been festering for some time, and Juba's own advancing age – he was over 60 when the revolt broke out – may have led him to feel that a secure succession was essential. When Ptolemaios became sole ruler in late AD 23 or in AD 24, the war, which had seemed settled, erupted again, perhaps as a result of the new king's inexperience, until Tacfarinas was caught and killed that summer. Ptolemaios seems to have been personally

40 *IG* 2².3439.

41 One need not linger over the "Regina Urania" cited at Caesarea on a tombstone of her freedwoman Julia Bodine (Jérôme Carcopino, "La Reine Urania de Maurétanie," in *Mélanges dédiés à la mémoire de Felix Grat* [Paris: En Depôt Chez Mme. Pecqueur-Grat, 1946], vol. 1, pp. 31–8; Coltelloni-Trannoy, p. 38). Urania may have been a member of the Mauretanian court, perhaps during the rule of Ptolemaios, who was notorious for surrounding himself with freedmen and slaves (Tacitus, *Annals* 4.23). So little is known about the personalities involved that any greater certainty is impossible, but it is probable that Urania was queen in a more informal than legal sense. Urania may be a nickname, giving the name of the Muse to a favored lady of the royal harem, who was then informally called "queen" by her retinue. On this, see Romanelli, *Storia*, p. 254.

42 The best summary of Ptolemaios' reign is that of Hofmann (supra note 4); see also Coltelloni-Trannoy, pp. 47–59.

involved in the latter stages of the operation and was sent honors and titles by the Roman Senate, which also confirmed him as king.[43]

Virtually nothing is known about the rest of Ptolemaios' reign until its very end. He had inherited the territory of his father and his office as *duovir* of Carthago Nova.[44] He seems to have spent time in Greece: like his father, he was honored at the Gymnasion of Ptolemaios in Athens, which had been built by an ancestor and namesake,[45] and was perhaps educated in that city as well as in Rome.[46] He may have first come to Athens when his father was in the East with Gaius Caesar.[47] He was also honored by the Lykian federation at Xanthos,[48] and may have visited the oracle at Lykian Soura.[49] But he does not seem to have had the cultural interests of his father,[50] gaining instead a reputation for immaturity and domination by members of his court.

Yet he came to feel increasingly independent of Rome, amassing great wealth and eventually issuing gold coins (Figure 26g, h), probably an unwise act.[51] One with triumphal regalia appeared in his Year 18, which may have been enough for the emperor Gaius Caligula to summon him to

---

43 Tacitus, *Annals* 4.23–6; C. R. Whittaker, "Roman Africa: Augustus to Vespasian," CAH[2] 10, 1996, 593–6; supra, p. 113.

44 Strabo 17.3.25; Mazard #512–14; Antonio Beltrán, "Iuba II y Ptolomeo, de Mauritania, II viri quinquennales de Carthago Nova," *Caesaraugusta* 51–2, 1980, 136–8.

45 *OGIS* 197. The inscription was found in the late Roman fortification wall, but it specifies that Ptolemaios was a descendant of King Ptolemaios, the builder of the gymnasion, so its origin in that structure is assured. Both Ptolemaios VI and Ptolemaios III, one of whom is presumed to have built the gymnasion (supra, Chapter 6, note 84), were direct ancestors of the Mauretanian king. This inscription is the only one extant that acknowledges his Ptolemaic heritage.

46 This was essentially official policy but is not specifically attested in his case. See David M. Jacobson, "Three Roman Client Kings: Herod of Judaea, Archelaus of Cappadocia and Juba of Mauretania," *PEQ* 133, 2001, 26.

47 Hofmann (supra note 4), pp. 1770–1.

48 *IGRR* 3.612.

49 An inscription from there records the entourage of an otherwise unidentified King Ptolemaios (George E. Bean, "Report on a Journey in Lycia 1960," *AnzWien* 99, 1962, 6–8; *Bulletin épigraphique* 1963, #253). Bean, the original editor of the inscription, dated it to one of the last of the Egyptian Ptolemies, but the editors of the *Bulletin épigraphique*, on the basis of letter style, suggested it was the entourage of Ptolemaios of Mauretania. A problem, however, is the East Greek personal names in the entourage, not what one would expect for the Mauretanian king, unless it were a local committee. Whichever Ptolemaios was being honored, his reason for being at Soura was probably to visit the famous local fish oracle (*NH* 32.17; Athenaios 8.333–4).

50 There are few hints of his cultural tendencies. He had an art collection (*NH* 13.93), and a coin (Mazard #464) shows a hexastyle Temple of Augustus, but it is not known where the temple was or what role Ptolemaios may have had in its construction. He also seems to have retained his father's taste for fine cameo portraits: see Wolf-R. Megow, "Zwei frühkaiserliche Kameen mit Diademträgern," *AntK* 42, 1999, 82–91.

51 Dio 59.25.1. Three gold coins of Ptolemaios are known (Mazard #398, 399 [the only dated one], 429). Coin #429 was published by Mazard as silver (see Braund, *Friendly King*, pp. 127–8). See also Jean-Claude Faur, "Caligula et la Maurétanie: la fin de Ptolémée," *Klio* 55, 1973, 249–71. On the coinage powers of client kings, see Braund, *Friendly King*, pp. 123–8.

Rome, or perhaps even depose him and send him into exile.[52] The fact that emperor and king were cousins was of no advantage to Ptolemaios, given the emperor's consistent hostility toward his relatives.[53] Regardless of the reason Ptolemaios came to the imperial court, the situation, like Gaius' reign generally, deteriorated rapidly, and, for a reason that is still uncertain, suddenly the emperor had Ptolemaios executed while at court.[54] The varying ancient accounts tell that it was because of Gaius' envy at his elaborate dress, especially a purple cloak,[55] or of his wealth,[56] or merely his usual bad treatment of his relatives.[57] However implausible these reasons seem, they may all be connected in that the emperor felt threatened by Ptolemaios: his growing independence (demonstrated by the gold coins), his flaunting of triumphal insignia and wealth and elaborate dress,[58] and his close relations with the Greek world. The recent scare of the conspiracy of Cn. Cornelius Lentulus Gaetulicus, whose father had been Juba's ally thirty-five years previously, had resulted in a wave of reprisals, including banishment of the emperor's own sisters and execution of Gaetulicus himself.[59] The connection between Ptolemaios and Gaetulicus,

52 Seneca (who seems to have witnessed Ptolemaios' arrest), *On the Tranquility of the Mind* 11.12; see also Suetonius, *Gaius* 35, which implies that Ptolemaios was originally summoned to Rome to be honored. This would not be the only time Gaius removed client royalty: Herod the Great's son Antipas, tetrarch of Galilee, was sent into exile in AD 39 (Josephus, *Jewish War* 2.183; *Jewish Antiquities* 18.252), and Mithradates of Armenia was also deposed (Seneca [supra]; Tacitus, *Annals* 11.8; Dio 60.8).

53 Suetonius, *Gaius* 26. Their common ancestor was Ptolemaios' grandfather and Gaius' great-grandfather Marcus Antonius.

54 Where and when this happened is unclear. Gaius was away from Rome from September AD 39 until summer AD 40 (Helmut Halfmann, *Itinera principum*, Heidelberger althistorische Beiträge und epigraphische Studien 2 [Stuttgart 1986], pp. 170–3). If Ptolemaios were executed in Rome, it was thus probably not before late AD 40 (Gsell, vol. 8, pp. 285; J. P. V. D. Balsdon, *The Emperor Gaius (Caligula)* [Oxford: Clarendon Press, 1934], p. 96). But Ptolemaios may have accompanied his cousin north, as did two other client kings, Agrippa I of Judaea and Antiochos IV of Kommagene, perhaps to Lugdunum, and it may have been there that he met his death. The fate of Ptolemaios may be alluded to at Dio 59.21.4. On the issue of where he died, see Jérôme Carcopino, "Sur la mort de Ptolémée roi de Maurétanie," in *Mélanges de philologie, de littérature et de l'histoire anciennes offerts à Alfred Ernout* (Paris: C. Klincksieck, 1940), pp. 39–50; Faur (supra note 51), pp. 267–71.

55 Suetonius, *Gaius* 35. His dress may have been connected with his role as a priest of the cult of Isis (inherited from his mother), and the reconsecration of the worship of Isis in Rome at this time (Hofmann [supra note 4], pp. 1780–2; see also Duncan Fishwick, "The Annexation of Mauretania," *Historia* 20, 1971, 469–71; Faur [supra note 51], pp. 249–53); Giulio Firpo, "L'imperatore Gaio (Caligola), i τυραννοδιδάσκαλοι e Tolomeo di Mauretania," in *Decima miscellanea greca e romana*, Studi pubblicati dall'Istituto Italiano per la Storia Antica 36 (Rome 1986), pp. 246–53.

56 Dio 59.25.1.

57 Ptolemaios' friendship with the Lykian Federation, the only part of Asia Minor that was independent of Roman control, may also have been seen as questionable. On Lykia at this time, see Magie (supra note 23), p. 529.

58 Whittaker (supra note 43), pp. 597–8. The matter of the purple cloak, if not an Isaic element, may fit into the festive atmosphere at Lugdunum (Suetonius, *Gaius* 20; Dio 59.22–5). For an analysis of the situation which gives Gaius more credit for political astuteness than generally accepted, see Tadeusz Kotula, "Encore sur la mort de Ptolémée, roi de Maurétanie," *Archeologia* (Warsaw) 15, 1964, 76–94; Balsdon (supra note 54), pp. 192–3, saw purely political motives for the removal of Ptolemaios.

59 Suetonius, *Gaius* 24; Dio 59.22.5–9.

and the former's residence at the imperial court, perhaps not acting with proper deference, may have been fatal.[60] The erratic Gaius may have become tired of his cousin's presence and acted precipitously.[61]

Nevertheless, a revolt promptly broke out in Mauretania, led by one Aedemon, one of Ptolemaios' freedmen or petty chieftains, perhaps confirming Gaius' fears about the king's excessive independence.[62] Several years of Roman military operations were necessary before the kingdom of Juba and Ptolemaios became the Roman provinces of Mauretania Caesariensis in the east and Mauretania Tingitana in the west – a continuing vestige of the dual history of the territory – and another client kingdom was absorbed into the empire.[63] The sobriquet is usually attached to his grandmother, but Ptolemaios of Mauretania was truly the last of the Ptolemies,[64] although many others were to claim descent from the Hellenistic kings of Egypt.[65]

60 Fishwick (supra note 55), pp. 467–73; Duncan Fishwick and Brent D. Shaw, "Ptolemy of Mauretania and the Conspiracy of Gaetulicus," *Historia* 25, 1976, 491–4.

61 The murder of Ptolemaios was one of the events of Gaius' reign repudiated by his successor Claudius, who was also Ptolemaios' cousin (Marcus Antonius was their common grandfather). Claudius' proconsul of Africa during the 40s AC, the future emperor Servius Sulpicius Galba, dedicated statues of the late king and his father Juba at Caesarea, probably in the temple of Venus. Fragments of the dedicatory inscription survive: see Marcel LeGlay, "Une Dédicace à Venus offerte à 'Caesarea' (Cherchel) par le futur empereur Galba," in *Mélanges d'archéologie, d'épigraphie et d'histoire offerts à Jérôme Carcopino* (Paris: Hachette, 1966), pp. 629–39; Coltelloni-Trannoy, p. 199. Galba also seems to have made a dedication to the Mauretanian dynasty at Tarracina in Italy, his birthplace and sometime residence (Pietro Longo, "Nuova documentazione epigrafica di età romana da Terracina," *AnnPerugia* 21 n.s. 7, 1983–4, 318–19.

62 On the revolt of Aedemon, see Marguerite Rachet, *Rome et les Berbères*, Collection Latomus 110 (Paris 1970), pp. 126–33; Andreas Gutsfeld, *Römische Herrschaft und einheimischer Widerstand in Nordafrika: Militärische Auseinandersetzungen Roms mit den Nomaden*, Heidelberger althistorische Beiträge und epigraphische Studien 8 (Stuttgart 1989), pp. 67–72; Fishwick (supra note 55), pp. 473–80.

63 *NH* 5.11; Dio 60.8–9; Fishwick (supra note 55), pp. 480–4; Coltelloni-Trannoy, pp. 60–5. On the new provinces, see Philippe Leveau, "La Fin du royaume maure et les origines de la province romaine de Maurétanie Césarienne," *BAC* n.s. 17b, 1984, 313–21; Maurice Euzennat, "Les Troubles de Maurétanie," *CRAI* 1984, pp. 372–93.

64 A final episode in the history of the Mauretanian royal dynasty occurred in AD 69, during the civil war that erupted after the death of Nero (Tacitus, *Histories* 2.58). Lucceius Albinus, who had been procurator of Judaea and whose excesses had contributed to the revolt that broke out there in the 60s AC (Josephus, *Jewish Antiquities* 20.197–200; *Jewish War* 2.272), had been moved to Mauretania Caesariensis, and was also assigned Mauretania Tingitana during the brief reign of Galba. When Otho became emperor, Albinus began to build a power base in the former Mauretanian kingdom, threatened Spain, and proclaimed himself King Juba III, adopting the trappings of royalty. This renewed kingdom of Mauretania was of only a few months' duration, however, as the new king was soon murdered by agents of Otho's soon-to-be successor Vitellius, and the shadowy kingdom reverted to provincial status. Nonetheless, the episode demonstrates that the name Juba still had power and authority nearly half a century after Juba II's death. On Albinus and his ephemeral role as Juba III, see René Rebuffat, "Notes sur les confins de la Maurétanie Tingitane et de la Maurétanie Césarienne," *StMagr* 4, 1971, 56–60.

65 In the third century AC the family of Zenobia, the Palmyrene queen, claimed descent from a Kleopatra, but the reference is too vague to connect it with Kleopatra VII or her children, and since the family also claimed as ancestors Dido and Semiramis, it must all be considered skeptically (Trebellius Pollio, *Tyranni trigenta* [HA] 27, 30).

In conclusion, the simplest summary of the evidence for the dynasty of Juba and Kleopatra Selene is as follows: after their marriage they had at least two children: a son, Ptolemaios, born between 13 and 9 BC, and a daughter, Drusilla, born around 8 BC. If there were other children, they are lost in obscurity or died before maturity.[66] At sometime after 9 BC Kleopatra Selene herself died, and although it is impossible to fix the date with certainty, 5 BC is most probable. In late 2 BC Juba embarked on an extensive tour of the East in the retinue of Gaius Caesar, where he met and married Glaphyra, but the marriage was brief, although long enough that Glaphyra received honor from the Athenians and recognition as Juba's spouse. Juba and Glaphyra divorced – she then married Archelaos of Judaea and promptly died – and Juba returned to Mauretania, probably by AD 5, and began to honor his son Ptolemaios, now an adolescent, as well as the memory of Kleopatra Selene. By AD 21 Ptolemaios was raised to joint kingship. Juba died two years later, and Ptolemaios ruled until about AD 40 and his fatal encounter with the emperor Gaius Caligula. Meanwhile, Drusilla of Mauretania had reached marriageable age around AD 5 and sometime thereafter married Felix, but had died or divorced him by AD 52–4 when he married his third wife, Drusilla of Judaea.

The sporadic and often erroneous information on the members of the Mauretanian dynasty does not allow re-creation of the thorough picture available for many of the other families of client kings. Implausibilities and gaps are numerous, and structuring the available material into a sequence that minimizes apparent contradictions may not be the correct interpretation of events. The date of Kleopatra Selene's death remains a puzzle that is more than a matter of curiosity, as it would shed light on Juba's relationship with Glaphyra and the birth dates of Ptolemaios and Drusilla. Scholars have been too driven by the El Kasr coin hoard to analyze this problem dispassionately. One wonders why better marriages, among the eastern dynasties, were not contracted for either of the known children. No wife of Ptolemaios is known, and Drusilla ended up with a disagreeable, arrogant freedman whom ancient sources universally condemn. Yet the information is remarkably sparse: only seven members and in-laws of the royal family are known by name in the sixty-five years of the Mauretanian client kingdom.[67]

---

66 This may be nothing more than the realities of a world where one-third of the children died in their first year, and half in the first decade (Treggiari [supra note 24], p. 398). On this issue generally, see Iiro Kajanto, *On the Problem of the Average Duration of Life in the Roman Empire* (*Annales Academiae Scientiarum Fennicae* ser. B, vol. 153.2 [Helsinki 1968]), whose statistics are somewhat more optimistic than Treggiari's, and on the pitfalls of estimating longevity in antiquity, see Keith Hopkins, "On the Probable Age Structure of the Roman Population," *Population Studies* 20, 1966–7, 245–64.

67 Compare sixty-five years of the other client kingdoms and the contrast is enormous: over the same period (25 BC–AD 40) over fifty Herodians and two dozen Kappadokians can be cited by name.

EPILOGUE

When the emperor Gaius Caligula summoned his cousin Ptolemaios of Mauretania to the imperial court and then had him executed, he ended sixty-five years of client monarchy in Mauretania. This was not a long period in the history of the Roman Empire, but it was one of profound changes. Mauretania became part of Europe, an orientation that lasted until the spread of Islam, and toponyms and political boundaries were established that continue today. Yet the personalities of Juba and Kleopatra Selene faded into footnotes to history. The polymathic authors of the later Empire, Pliny, Plutarch, and Athenaios, so deeply extracted the essence of Juba's writings for their own encyclopedic efforts that the originals were lost, perhaps as early as AD 200.

Kleopatra Selene fared worse than her husband. Although queen of Mauretania and Kyrenaika, and pretender to the Egyptian throne, she became little more than a reflection of her husband and parents. She vanishes from the literary record after her children's birth, and even her death date remains uncertain. Her daughter Drusilla is remembered only because of her grandparents and husband, not her mother. With the possible exception of Krinagoras' obituary epigram, Kleopatra Selene is not mentioned in literature outside the shadow of male relatives, and occasionally is hidden even by them. In fact, she would be even more ephemeral were it not for the less biased evidence of coins and her Egyptian artistic program at Caesarea. Yet a significant survival of her influence, perhaps, was the unusually elevated status of women at Caesarea in the centuries following her death.[1] As late as the third century AC there was a prominent educated female aristocracy at the city, including personalities such as the grammarian Volusia Tertullina. It seems that the legacy of the Ptolemaic queens of Egypt and Mauretania continued long beyond their death.

Moreover, the Mauretanian monarchs have had their impact on the arts in modern times. Kleopatra Selene has figured in modern literature, although

---

1 Nacéra Benseddik, "Être femme dans le Maghreb ancien," *AWAL: Cahiers d'études berbères* 20, 1999, 142–5.

excluded by Shakespeare from *Antony and Cleopatra*.[2] Most notable is the *Cléopâtre* of Gauthier de Costes, seigneur de La Calprènede (died 1663), an epistolary romance published in 1648.[3] Both monarchs have appeared in opera: Johann Mattheson's setting of Friedrich Christian Feustking's libretto *Die unglückselige Cleopatra, Königen von Egypten, oder Die Betrogene Staats-Liebe* (1704) recounts events in Alexandria after the Battle of Actium.[4] One of the earliest modern scholarly references to Juba is in Herman Melville's *Moby Dick* (1851),[5] and the shadow of the king is apparent in Jules Verne's *Vingt-milles lieues sous les mers* (1869). Verne, who was familiar with the major ancient sources on Juba,[6] placed Captain Nemo's base in the Canaries,[7] where the passengers on the *Nautilus* find euphorbion.[8] And the treatises of Juba are a significant factor in Lindsey Davis' mystery novel *Venus in Copper*.[9]

Despite these literary and musical memories of the monarchs, they played a far greater role in the expansion of modern European civilization. The Mauretanian client kingdom completed the process of romanization of the Mediterranean, for it was the last extensive area on its shores to come under direct Roman control. When it was provincialized, only two small coastal areas remained outside the Empire: the Lykian Federation and the Mediterranean shoreline of the Nabataean kingdom. Juba and Kleopatra Selene thus

---

2 Shakespeare's description of the Donations of Alexandria refers to the protagonists' "unlawful issue that their lust since then hath made," and mentions each of the three boys by name (Act 3, Scene 6). His source was Plutarch, *Antonius* 54, where only the boys are cited.

3 This is an incredibly wide-ranging and lengthy tale (1,536 pages in the English translation), which, in the fashion of the time and genre, has layer upon layer of material, including among its characters Herod the Great, Kleopatra VII, Phraates IV of Parthia, and almost every prominent member of the Julio-Claudian family. Kleopatra Selene is wooed by both Marcellus and Tiberius (actually not an unreasonable possibility) but ends up with the king of Mauretania, Coriolanus, son of Juba (I).

4 Following a loose reading of Dio 51.15 (supra, p. 73), Juba (tenor) is present in Alexandria at this time, and is enamored not of Selene (a minor character) but of her sister Candace.

5 Interestingly, Melville did not quote Juba's sole extant reference to whales (fr. 3), although he was intimately familiar with the source, Pliny, but fr. 53a, from Plutarch, about elephants. See Herman Melville, *Moby Dick or the Whale* (New York: Modern Library 2000), pp. 546–7.

6 Dr. Pierre Arronax has read Athenaios (1.209), Pliny, Avienus (2.117) and Poseidonios (2.147). Pliny is used by Verne as a source for sea monsters (1.5), remindful of Juba, fr. 58 (*NH* 8.35). References here and in the following two notes are to Jules Verne, *Vingt milles lieues sous les mers*, 2 vols., sixth edition (Paris: Hetzel, [n.d.]).

7 The published text does not specifically locate the base at the islands, although that is Arronax's assumption (2.154), and the Canaries are obliquely mentioned at 2.163. But the first manuscript of the novel did place it in the Canaries, a detail later excised by Verne. See Jules Verne, *The Extraordinary Journeys: Twenty Thousand Leagues under the Seas*, trans. with intro. and notes by William Butcher (Oxford: Oxford University Press, 1988), p. 426.

8 Verne 2.162. The juxtaposition of the two survivals of Juba's researches, the Canaries and euphorbion (Verne's text has "euphorbia"), is a significant insight into Verne's thinking, since the plant was discovered by Juba in the Atlas, not the Canaries, and the citations are quite separate in *NH*.

9 Lindsey Davis, *Venus in Copper* (London: Hutchinson, 1991). The details cannot be revealed to anyone who has not read the book.

brought the Roman encirclement – typified in the concept of *mare nostrum* – to its fulfillment. Their reach went farther, however, since through their efforts Rome learned much about the African continent, the Atlantic islands, and the routes to India. This laid the pattern for the multicultural world that was the later Empire, manifested in the ethnic diversity of the Mauretanian dynasty itself.

Because Africa was separated from the European world with the rise of Islam, the impact of royal Mauretania on the expansion of European civilization has been severely diminished or even forgotten. But in the fourteenth century, when European exploration started anew in western Africa and the adjacent Atlantic, Europe began to be reacquainted with Juba's world, as Portuguese and Spanish explorers moved down the West African coast and into the Atlantic islands. Their guide was Juba's *Libyka*, but it was now so deeply buried in Pliny's *Natural History* that Juba's authorship was ignored. In 1344 the Castilian Don Luís de la Cerda received papal permission to acquire islands in the Atlantic. He had never seen them, and indeed did not know where they were, but in his petition to Pope Clement VI he listed their names, lifted directly from Pliny's mixed Latin and Greek toponyms for the Canary Islands, themselves taken from *Libyka*. Don Luís never saw the islands that the Pope had granted him, but was responsible for introducing Juba's names to modern Europe.[10] Although the others were eventually changed, Juba's Kynika, which had become Pliny's Canaria, became Gran Canaria in Spanish and the name for the entire group.[11] Soon Juba's Purple Islands would become a Portuguese outpost named Mogador.

During the years 1497–9 Vasco da Gama made it all the way around Africa to India, recreating the connection between northwest Africa and India implicit in Juba's *Libyka* and *On Arabia*. At the same time, Columbus was making his voyages to America. He too was acquainted, unknowingly, with Juba, through Pliny, since he owned Cristoforo Landino's Italian translation of the *Natural History*, published in Venice in 1489.[12] He had previously owned *Tractatus de imagine mundi* by Pierre d'Ailly (1350–1420), published in Louvain between 1480 and 1483, and had underlined a passage that implied that the distance from northwest Africa to India was not great. D'Ailly cited Pliny as his source, and this caused Columbus to purchase his own text of the Roman author. Thus he came to know the tales of circuitous routes to India, and of Indians in strange places and in the farthest corners of

10 For early modern exploration of the Canaries, see John Mercer, *The Canary Islanders: Their Prehistory, Conquest and Survival* (London: Collings, 1980), pp. 155–9.

11 William D. Phillips, Jr., and Carla Rahn Phillips, *The Worlds of Christopher Columbus* (Cambridge: Cambridge University Press, 1992), pp. 56–7. As previously noted (supra, Chapter 8, note 81), the name of Canaria is not now applied to the island with that name in antiquity.

12 Columbus' copy still exists, with its copious marginal notes, in the Biblioteca Colombina, Seville (Paolo Emilio Taviani, *Christopher Columbus: The Grand Design*, trans. William Weaver [London: Orbis, 1985], pp. 174–7).

the earth. To Columbus, it would have been perfectly reasonable to find Indians in the western Atlantic, much as Q. Metellus Celer had found them in the North Sea in the 50s BC. Pliny's description of this encounter would have been an inspiration to Columbus, as it also tells of another half of the world beyond the ocean: "thus the surrounding seas are on all sides, and with the globe divided part of the earth is separated from us."[13] Half a century later, Spanish explorers would be building further on Pliny's summation of *On Arabia* by creating their own myths of fabulous wealth in isolated places, most notably the tale of Cíbola.[14] The impact of Juba was subtle, almost hidden, but profound.

Pliny was prescient when he wrote that Juba was remembered more for his scholarship than his kingship.[15] The political system and world that Juba and Kleopatra Selene represented has long vanished. Kleopatra Selene herself has disappeared almost entirely, and Juba's writings nearly so. Yet they moved European reach beyond the Mediterranean, from northwest Africa to India – the entire southern extent of the world – and thus made possible the ideas that discovered the New World, foretold and indeed named by Pliny's contemporary Seneca in his *Medea*:[16]

> There will come an era in the future when the Ocean will release its chains and the full extent of the earth will be revealed. Tethys will disclose new worlds and Thule will not be the farthest land.

13 *NH* 2.170: "sic maria circumfusa undique dividuo globo partem orbis auferent nobis."

14 The story of Cíbola was first reported by Fray Marcos de Niza in 1539, who wrote of seven large cities whose gates and houses were built with precious stones – strikingly similar to the reports of Arabian houses preserved by Pliny from Juba's *On Arabia* – and which was the center of an area of indescribable riches, larger in population than Mexico City (described in the *Relación* of Fray Marcos de Niza: see Clive Hallenbeck, *The Journey of Fray Marcos de Niza* [Dallas: Southern Methodist University Press, 1987], pp. lviii–lxix). Cíbola is generally agreed to be the Zuñi villages of west-central New Mexico (Hallenback, p. 41), hardly the size of Mexico City or displaying the wealth reported by Fray Marcos, who claimed autopsy. See also Stephen Clissold, *The Seven Cities of Cíbola* (London: Eyre and Spottiswoode, 1961), pp. 103–16.

In the retinue of Fray Marcos as guide was a Moorish slave named Esteban, from Azamor in Morocco (Clissold, p. 39). He owed his presence to having been on the earlier dramatic journey of Cabeza de Vaca, who had gone overland from the Gulf of Mexico to Mexico City in 1527–36, the first to report on the assumed riches of the future American Southwest. Esteban was sent in advance by Fray Marcos to locate Cíbola and was killed there by the natives, adding to its mythic quality, and the reason that Marcos did not enter the city but viewed it only from afar (Fray Marcos, *Relación* [Hallenbeck, pp. lxvi–lxviii]). There is a certain irony that someone who was a descendant of Juba's subjects should play such a role in the dissemination of the myth of wealthy remote cities.

15 *NH* 5.16.

16 Seneca, *Medea* 375–9:

> Venient annis saecula seris
> quibus Oceanus vincula rerum
> laxet, et ingens pateat tellus
> Tethysque; novos detegat orbes,
> nec sit terris ultima Thule.

Appendix 1

THE PUBLISHED WORKS OF
JUBA II

The following catalog lists the known works of Juba II, with the original title, the best evidence as to their length and date of publication, the page numbers of the major discussion in the above text, and the source of the known fragments, with both the actual citation and the fragment numbers in *FGrHist*. A broader view of fragments has been assumed than that of Jacoby, not limited merely to passages where the author is cited by name. Fragments are not always easily attributed to a specific work, and this is especially a problem with *Libyka* and *On Arabia* – as the line of separation between these treatises in the Red Sea area is not certain – and between the *Roman Archaeology* and the *Resemblances*. Spurious or doubtful works are not included, as these are inevitably due to late epitomes of sections of the major works.

Catalog

1   *Roman Archaeology* (Ῥωμαικῆς ἀρχαιολογία [fr. 12] or Ῥωμαικῆς ἱστορία [fr. 9, 10]). Two books (fr. 10), composed *ca.* 30–25 BC. Pp. 166–70. This may be the same as, or overlap with, the *Resemblances*, and in many cases it is not possible to separate the fragments between the two.
    Fragments:
    Pliny, *NH* 10.126–7 (fr. 60).
    Plutarch, *Numa* 7 (fr. 88), 13 (fr. 89); *Romulus* 14 (fr. 23), 15 (fr. 90), 17 (fr. 24); *Sulla* 16 (fr. 27); *Comparison of Pelopidas and Marcellus* 1 (fr. 25); *Roman Question* 4 (fr. 91), 24 (fr. 95), 59 (fr. 92), 78 (fr. 93), 89 (fr. 94).
    Stephanos of Byzantion, Ἀβοριγῖνες (fr. 9), Ἀρβάκη (fr. 26), Νομαντία (fr. 12), Λαβίνιον (fr. 11), Ὠστία (fr. 10).

2   *Resemblances* (Ὁμοιότητες [fr. 14] or Περὶ Ὁμοιοτήτων [fr. 13]). At least fifteen books (fr. 13), composed *ca.* 30–25 BC. Pp. 170–3. Fragments:

Athenaios 3.98 (fr. 96), 4.170 (fr. 14), 6.229 (fr. 87).
Etymologicum Magnum 277.37 (fr. 97).
Hesychios, βρίγες (fr. 98), κάρτη (fr. 13a), κόρτην (fr. 13b), κυλίκ<ε>ια (fr. 99), λιβοφοίτην (fr. 100).
Plutarch, *Numa* 7 (fr. 88), 13 (fr. 89); *Romulus* 14–15 (fr. 23, 90); *Marcellus* 8.4–5; *Roman Question* 24 (fr. 95), 54, 59 (fr. 92), 78 (fr. 93), 89 (fr. 94).

3 *On Painting* (Περὶ ζωγράφων [fr. 20] or Περὶ γραφικῆς [fr. 21; *FGrHist* #275, T15]). At least eight books (fr. 20), composed 30–25 BC. Pp. 173–4.
Fragments:
Harpokration, Παρράσιος (fr. 20), Πολύγνωτος (fr. 21).
Photios, *Bibliotheka* 161 (*FGrHist* #275, T15).

4 *Theatrical History* (Θεατρικῆς ἱστορία [fr. 15]). At least seventeen books (*FGrHist* #275, T15), composed perhaps 30–25 BC, or later. Pp. 174–7.
Fragments:
Athenaios 1.15 (fr. 80), 4.175–85 (fr. 15a, 16, 81–4), 8.343 (fr. 104), 14.660 (fr. 86).
Hesychios, βλίτυρι καὶ σκινδαψός (fr. 85), κλώπεια (fr. 17), σαμβύκη (fr. 15b).
Photios, *Bibliotheka* 161 (*FGrHist* #275, T15).
Scholia on Aristophanes, *Thesmophoriazousai* 1175 (fr. 18).
Scholia on Demosthenes, *On the Embassy* 247 (fr. 19).

5 *The Wanderings of Hanno* (αἱ ῎Αννωνος πλάναι). Composed before 25 BC, perhaps later incorporated into *Libyka*. This may have been merely a translation of Hanno's report. P. 177.
Fragments:
Athenaios 3.83 (fr. 6).
Hesychios, λιβυφοίτην (fr. 100)?
Pliny, *NH* 6.200.

6 *On Euphorbion*. No Greek title preserved; cf. fr. 7. A brief pamphlet, composed after 25 BC. Pp. 178–9.
Fragments:
Dioskourides 3.82 (fr. 8b).
Galen, *On the Combining of Drugs According to Place* 1 (Kühn 13.270–1) (fr. 8a).
Pliny, *NH* 5.16 (fr. 42), 25.77–9 (fr. 7).

7 *Libyka* (Λιβύκα [fr. 5] or Περὶ Λιβύης [fr. 6]). At least three books (fr. 5), composed 25–5 BC. Pp. 183–211.

Fragments:

> Aelian, *On the Characteristics of Animals* 7.23 (fr. 55), 7.44 (fr. 53b), 9.58 (49), 14.6.
>
> Ammianus Marcellinus 22.15.8–11 (fr. 38b).
>
> Athenaios 3.83 (fr. 6), 6.229 (fr. 87).
>
> *Geoponika* 15.2.21 (fr. 61).
>
> Heschyios, Λιβυφοίτην (fr. 100).
>
> Philostratos, *Life of Apollonios* 2.13 (fr. 47b, 50), 2.16 (fr. 52).
>
> Pliny, *NH* 5.16 (fr. 42), 5.51–4 (fr. 38a), 5.59 (fr. 39), 6.175–80 (fr. 35–7), 6.200–5 (fr. 43–4), 8.2–3, 8.7 (fr. 47a), 8.13–15 (fr. 54), 8.24–6, 8.35 (fr. 58), 8.48–52, 8.69, 8.107 (fr. 57), 8.155 (fr. 59), 9.115 (fr. 71), 10.126–7 (fr. 60), 13.47–8, 13.142 (fr. 67), 31.18 (fr. 40–1), 35.39 (fr. 74), 37.23–4 (fr. 76), 37.69 (fr. 77), 37.107–8 (fr. 75), 37.114 (fr. 79).
>
> Plutarch, *Whether Land Or Sea Animals Are Wiser* 17 (fr. 51a, 53a), 25 (fr. 51b).
>
> [Plutarch], *Greek and Roman Parallels* 23 (fr. 5).
>
> Scholia to Pollux 5.88 (fr. 48).
>
> Solinus 27.15 (fr. 56).

8 *On Arabia*. No Greek title preserved; cf. fr. 1–3, esp. fr. 3 ("de Arabia"). Length not preserved; composed 2 BC–AD 5. Pp. 227–43.
Fragments:

> Aelian, *On the Characteristics of Animals* 15.8 (fr. 70).
>
> *Etymologicum Magnum* 277.37 (fr. 97)?
>
> Hesychios, Τερέβινθος (fr. 45)?
>
> Pliny, *NH* 2.168–9, 6.96–106 (fr. 28), 6.124 (fr. 29), 6.136–56 (fr. 1, 30–3), 6.165–71 (fr. 34), 9.115 (fr. 71), 12.38–9 (fr. 62), 12.51–81 (fr. 2, 63–5), 13.34 (fr. 66), 13.142 (fr. 67), 15.99 (fr. 68), 25.14 (fr. 69), 31.18 (fr. 41), 32.10 (fr. 3), 33.118 (fr. 72), 35.39 (fr. 74), 36.163 (fr. 73), 37.24 (fr. 76), 37.73 (fr. 78), 37.107–8 (fr. 75).
>
> Solinus 52.19 (fr. 101).

9 *On Assyria* (Περὶ Ἀσσυρίων [fr. 4]). Two books (fr. 4); date uncertain (perhaps a section of *On Arabia*). Pp. 237–8.
Fragments:

> Herodian (grammarian) 13.28 (fr. 46)?
>
> Pliny, *NH* 8.155 (fr. 59)?
>
> Tatian, *Oration to the Greeks* 36 (fr. 4).

10 Epigrams. One extant (6 lines), written after 25 BC. Pp. 80–1.
Athenaios 8.343 (fr. 104).

Appendix 2

STEMMATA

The family and connections of Juba II and Kleopatra Selene (Stemma A)

All the descendants and connections of Juba II and Kleopatra Selene are shown, but this stemma is highly selective with respect to the relations of Augustus, including only those who are prominent in the text or necessary to show family relations. Birth and death dates of the Mauretanians can be speculative and are discussed in the text. For a more complete Julio-Claudian stemma, see *NP* 2 (1997) 303–4.

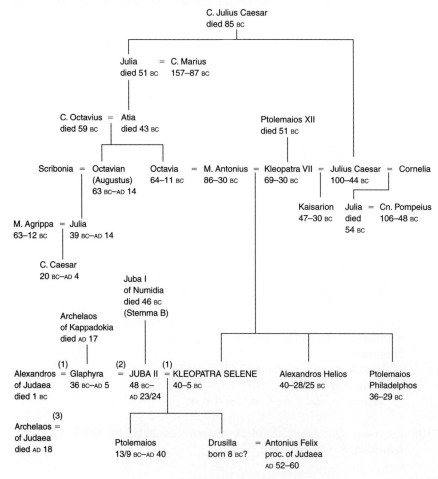

The Numidian royal line (Stemma B)

The connections in the earlier generations are speculative. It is not certain whether Massinissa II was the son of, or even a descendant of, Masteabar. Masteabar and his descendants ruled over a small territory within Numidia while Hiempsal II and then Juba I controlled most of the region.

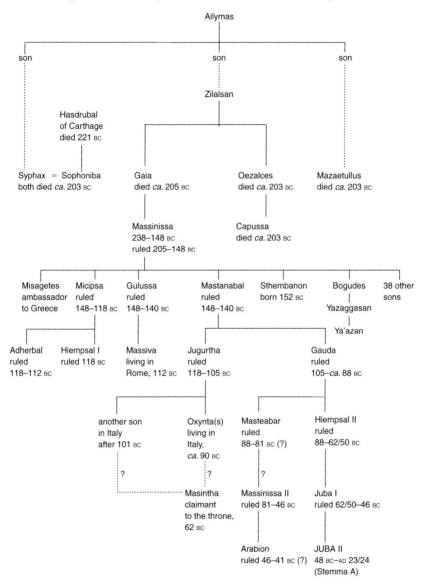

The indigenous Mauretanian royal line (Stemma C)

The connection between Baga and Bocchus I is unknown. It is not certain whether Mastanesosus was the son of Bocchus I, or the exact relationship of Bogudes II to the rest of the family.

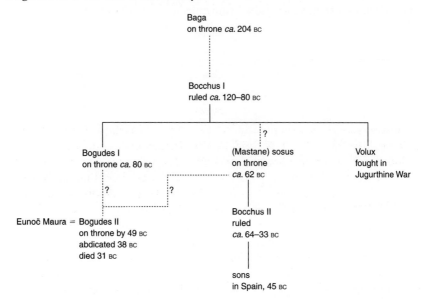

Appendix 3

CLIENT KINGSHIP

The institution that is popularly called "client kingship" pervades any study of Juba II and his Numidian and Mauretanian predecessors.[1] It developed out of Rome's first contacts with royal dynasties in the second century BC, reached its peak in the years of the latest Republic and under Augustus and Tiberius, and faded by the end of the Julio-Claudians, although lasting, to some extent, into the late Empire. The antecedents may be as early as Rome's spreading contacts with chieftains in the remoter areas of Italy, and the concept gained strength during the wars with Carthage, when Rome was in desperate need of allies. The close and lengthy relationships with Hieron II of Syracuse and Massinissa of Numidia epitomized the developing institution. Both kings, after initial alliance with the Carthaginians, became convinced of Roman power and chose to enter into a subordinate relationship, effectively offering loyalty and military support to Rome in return for their own self-preservation and the continued prosperity of their kingdoms.

As the term "client king" implies, the relationship between Rome and king is seen as analogous to that of patron and client in Roman society: the client (or king) shows respect and loyalty in return for favors and benefits. Such was the case with the Spanish allies of C. Pompeius Magnus, who were described as "old and faithful clients."[2] Yet the parallel is not exact. Client kings, in theory, were officially connected to the Roman state, not an individual, although the first contacts that many potential kings had was with a Roman individual of power and authority, and in the imperial period the relationship often had personal ramifications between king and

---

1 The best study on client kingship is Braund, *Friendly King*, the only thorough examination of the phenomenon, with an extensive bibliography, to which the following summary is indebted. Many other works touch on the issue, but in more specific and limited ways, especially E. Badian, *Foreign Clientelae, 264–70 B.C.* (Oxford: Clarendon Press, 1958); Mario Pani, *Roma e i re d'Oriente da Augusto a Tiberio* (Bari 1972); Erich S. Gruen, *The Hellenistic World and the Coming of Rome* (Berkeley: University of California Press, 1984); Sullivan, *Near Eastern Royalty*; and Kokkinos, *Herodian Dynasty*.

2 Sallust, *Bellum Catilinae* 19.5: "Cn. Pompei veteres fidosque clientis."

emperor. Moreover, the term "client king" does not truly exist in ancient literature.[3] What seems a more legitimate phrase, insofar as the Romans had one, was "the friendly and allied king" ("rex amicus sociusque"), which also describes the concept more correctly, as definitively outlined by Suetonius:

> The friendly and allied kings each founded a city called Caesarea in their own kingdom and intended, moreover, to complete together the Athenian temple of Olympian Juppiter – left unfinished since antiquity – using common funds, and to dedicate it to his [Augustus'] Genius. Often, leaving their kingdoms, they would present themselves regularly in the fashion of a client, showing respect, dressed in the toga and without royal insignia, not only in Rome but traveling throughout the provinces.[4]

Crucial here is the assertion that the kings acted "more clientium," a reminder of Sallust's "veteres fidosque clientis." Yet the literature is imprecise and relies more on the actions and characteristics of the kings rather than seeking a strict definition or terminology for them. But there was a procedure by which client kings were created, and the concept served both Rome and king: the king received the prestige and support that came from association with Rome, and Rome obtained the benefits of a sympathetic and powerful person at the dangerous margins of the Empire. Yet the situation was always tense: Rome and king frequently did not see eye to eye about management of the kingdom, and local concerns of high priority to the king might be seen as irrelevant or even threatening to Rome. As most of the Augustan kings found out, it was impossible to do everything right.[5]

The process of becoming a client king was most frequently initiated, in some manner, by the Roman magistrates who were in the vicinity of the kingdom, perhaps acting on a request by the potential king himself.[6] Yet legally only the Senate could actually create a client king, and acceptance of an individual as king was often part of its formal ratification of the acts of its

---

3 Braund, *Friendly King*, pp. 23–4.
4 Suetonius, *Augustus* 60:

> Reges amici atque socii et singuli in suo quisque regno Caesareas urbes condiderent et cuncti simul aedem Iovis Olympii Athenis antiquitus incohatam perficere communi sumptu destinaverunt Genioque eius dedicare; ac saepe regnis relictis non Romae modo sed et provincias peragranti cotidiana officia togati ac sine regio insigne more clientium praestiterunt.

5 Braund, *Friendly King*, pp. 98–9.
6 Braund, *Friendly King*, pp. 23–7.

magistrates in nearby or adjoining provinces. One of the sins Antonius committed during the Donations of Alexandria was that he was creating kings and kingdoms without Senatorial approval. The later history of the Seleukids demonstrates the implications of Senate involvement. Demetrios I was put forth as client king by the elder Tiberius Gracchus but the Senate never ratified the decision,[7] and the kingdom remained independent of Rome for nearly a century longer until Antiochos XIII was similarly nominated by L. Licinius Lucullus but also ignored by the Senate, whereupon he was assassinated, the Seleukid kingdom collapsed, and Pompeius created the province of Syria.[8]

The most complete information on the accession of a client king comes from that of Herod the Great.[9] Josephus, in an essential passage for understanding the establishment of client kingship, recorded the process:

> Because of the memory of the hospitality of Antipatros [Herod's father], and because of the money Herod would give him if he became king, which he had promised before when he had been made tetrarch, but most of all because of his hatred of [the Hasmonean] Antigonos – for he believed him to be seditious and an enemy of the Romans – Antonius was ready to give Herod the assistance that he wanted. Caesar [Octavian], because of the campaigns in Egypt on which Antipatros had assisted his father [Julius Caesar] with hospitality and favor in every way, and because Antonius was exceedingly eager in the matter of Herod, was ready to accept this petition and cooperate in what Herod wished. Thus Messalla, and afterwards Atratinus, convened the Senate and presented Herod, and recounted the good deeds of his father and made mention of his own favor to the Romans. . . . Antonius came forward and told them that because of the forthcoming war against the Parthians it was advantageous that Herod be king. And all agreed and so voted. . . . So great was Antonius' esteem for Herod that not only did he obtain the kingship for him against his expectations (for Herod had come to him not seeking this, not believing that the Romans would give it to him, but rather to one of the ruling family, and thus to make the claim for the brother of his wife [the Hasmonean Aristoboulos III]) . . . but made it all possible in only seven days. . . . When the Senate adjourned, Antonius and Caesar went out with Herod between them, with the consuls and

---

7 Polybios 31.33.3
8 Justin 40.22.3.
9 Roller, *Herod*, pp. 10–17.

other magistrates leading, to make sacrifice and to deposit the decree on the Capitol.[10]

The account is replete with a strong sense of the personal, as Herod's father Antipatros, now dead, was mentioned at every level of the process. Herod had no claim to be king, and, moreover, the matter was implemented without the involvement of those Herod was to rule. This meant serious problems, and it took three years and extensive Roman military intervention before Herod could actually take up his kingship in anything other than theory.

Such conspiring by Rome and king meant that the relationship between ruler and ruled could be difficult: at worst the ruler was seen as a Roman puppet with little concern for the interests of the people, an attitude not eased by the weak claims client kings often had to the territories they came to rule. Thus availability, proven competence, and friendship of prominent Romans were the factors in becoming a client king, not a legal claim. But this meant that there was inevitably tension between ruler and ruled. Roman involvement in these quarrels might aggravate matters without strengthening the king: there are many well-known examples from the Herodians.

As outlined previously, the major responsibilities (to Rome) of the kings were the provision of military aid (often placing the king in an impossible position) and the creation of a suitable Roman environment, both in the personal life of the king and his family and also within his territory. This was again a possible source of tension between king and subjects. In return,

---

10 Josephus, *Jewish Antiquities* 14.381–9:

τὰ μὲν κατὰ μνήμην τῆς Ἀντιπάτρου ξενίας, τὰ δὲ καὶ ὑπὸ χρημάτων ὧν αὐτῷ δώσειν Ἡρώδης, εἰ γένοιτο βασιλεύς, ὑπέσχετο καθὼς καὶ πρότερον ὅτε τετράρχης ἀπεδέδεικτο, πολὺ μέντοι μᾶλλον διὰ τὸ πρὸς Ἀντίγονον μῖσος (στασιαστὴν γὰρ καὶ Ῥωμαίοις ἐχθρὸν αὐτὸν ὑπελάμβανε) πρόθυμος ἦν οἷς Ἡρώδης παρεκάλει συλλαμβάνεσθαι. Καῖσαρ μὲν οὖν καὶ διὰ τὰς Ἀντιπάτρου στρατείας, ἃς κατ᾽ Αἴγυπτον αὐτοῦ τῷ πατρὶ συνδιήνεγκε, καὶ τὴν ξενίαν καὶ τὴν ἐν ἅπασιν εὔνοιαν, χαριζόμενος δὲ καὶ Ἀντωνίῳ σφόδρα περὶ τὸν Ἡρώδην ἐσπουδακότι, πρὸς τὴν ἀξίωσιν καὶ τὴν ὧν ἐβούλετο Ἡρώδης συνεργίαν ἑτοιμότερος ἦν. συναγαγόντες δὲ τὴν βουλὴν Μεσσάλας καὶ μετ᾽ αὐτὸν Ἀτρατῖνος, παραστησάμενοι τὸν Ἡρώδην τάς τε τοῦ πατρὸς εὐεργεσίας αὐτοῦ διεξῆεσαν, καὶ ἦν αὐτὸς πρὸς Ῥωμαίους εἶχεν εὔνοιαν ὑπεμίμνησκον.... Ἀντώνιος ἐδίδασκεν αὐτοὺς ὡς καὶ πρὸς τὸν κατὰ Πάρθων πόλεμον Ἡρώδην βασιλεύειν συμφέρει. καὶ δόξαν τοῦτο πᾶσι ψηφίζονται.

καὶ τοῦτο τὸ μέγιστον ἦν τῆς Ἀντωνίου περὶ τὸν Ἡρώδην σπουδῆς, ὅτι μὴ μόνον αὐτῷ τὴν βασιλείαν οὐκ ἐλπίζοντι περιεποιήσατο (οὐ γὰρ εἰς ἑαυτὸν ἀνέβη ταύτην αἰτησόμενος, οὐ γὰρ ἐνόμιζεν αὐτῷ τοὺς Ῥωμαίους παρέξειν, τοῖς ἐκ τοῦ γένους ἔθος ἔχοντας αὐτὴν διδόναι, ἀλλὰ τῷ τῆς γυναικὸς ἀδελφῷ λαβεῖν).... ἀλλ᾽ ὅτι καὶ ἑπτὰ ταῖς πάσαις ἡμέραις παρέσχεν.... αὐθείσης δὲ τῆς βουλῆς, μέσον ἔχοντες Ἡρώδην Ἀντώνιος καὶ Καῖσαρ ἐξῆεσαν, προαγόντων ἅμα ταῖς ἄλλαις ἀρχαῖς τῶν ὑπάτων, θύσοντές τε καὶ τὸ δόγμα καταθησόμενοι εἰς τὸ Καπετώλιον.

the king and his family might receive an education in Rome, Roman citizenship, the right to Roman ornaments and badges of office (and, from the mid-first century AC, senatorial rank), and at least the theoretical commitment to Roman help in times of difficulty.[11] Thus the client kingdoms became islands of Roman culture, with cities named Caesarea or some form of Sebasteia, Roman festivals and cults, and a Greco-Roman court circle. The king himself might have scholarly tastes, and, in fact, the idea of a scholarly king fitted into the contemporary image of the client king as civilizer, and brought him, in some ways, closer to the Platonic ideal of kingship.

An important expectation of client kingship was to demonstrate honor and respect toward the Greek world and its ancient institutions, and thereby show that the king and his kingdom were truly civilized. This was an old attitude – Maussolos of Halikarnassos and the Attalid kings of Pergamon were famous for it – but became a necessary component of the world of client kingship. Since most of the kingdoms were in or near the Greek world, Hellenism was perhaps neither difficult nor unnatural, yet even the kings remote from Greek territory also adopted it as a conscious policy. Massinissa of Numidia may have been one of the first. Herod the Great began his career of architectural endowment not in his own territories but on Rhodes, which had a lengthy history of royal patronage. Herod could also demonstrate his respect for traditional Greek institutions by rebuilding the bouleterion at the free city of Askalon.[12]

There was no better way for the kings to demonstrate their Hellenism than to honor the most distinguished institution of the Greek world, the Olympic Games, and its most famous city, Athens. At Olympia, Herod was *agonothetes* in 12 BC, and perpetually endowed the games.[13] Archelaos of Kappadokia also lent his prestige and, presumably, provided financial assistance.[14] Support of Athens was virtually a requirement of a client king.[15] The Herodians, Archelaos and his family, and Juba and his family all bestowed their patronage on the city.[16] Needless to say, honoring Athens in particular and Hellenism in general served the kings well, for they were acting with political correctness within the Augustan world.

11 Braund, *Friendly King*, pp. 9–17, 27–9, 39–46.
12 Roller, *Herod*, pp. 233–4, 216–19.
13 Roller, *Herod*, pp. 230–1.
14 *OGIS* 359.
15 Suetonius, *Augustus* 60; see David Braund, "Greeks and Barbarians: The Black Sea Region and Hellenism under the Early Empire," in *The Early Roman Empire in the East*, ed. Susan E. Alcock, *Oxbow Monograph* 95, 1997, pp. 123–5.
16 Herod the Great: Josephus, *Jewish War* 1.425; *OGIS* 414; *IG* 2.2.3441; Roller, *Herod*, pp. 219–20. Herod of Chalkis: *OGIS* 427; Berenike of Judaea: *OGIS* 428. Archelaos of Kappadokia: *OGIS* 357, 360. Glaphyra of Kappadokia: *OGIS* 363. Juba II of Mauretania: *IG* 2–3².3436 (for his possible endowment of the Gymnasion of Ptolemaios, supra, pp. 136–7). Ptolemaios of Mauretania: *OGIS* 197. An unnamed daughter of Juba II: *IG* 2².3439.

But the position of the client king was always precarious, representing a futile attempt to achieve an impossible balance between local and Roman needs. If measured as a step in the process of romanization, the client kings were a success, as kingdom after kingdom became a province, although this was often as destabilizing as the king's accession had been. But in a personal sense the kings were failures, because their rule rarely was totally successful and few died naturally in full possession of their kingdoms. Roman removal of them from office was frequent.

The easiest transition to direct Roman control was for a king to will his territory to Rome.[17] This had antecedents long before the concept of client kingship was formalized: the most famous example is that of Attalos III of Pergamon.[18] The earliest seems to be the case of Ptolemaios VIII, who, as king of Kyrene, published his will on a stele there in 155 BC:

Fifteenth year, month of Loios; with Good Fortune.

This was decreed by king Ptolemaios son of Ptolemaios and queen Kleopatra, gods manifest, the younger. A copy of this has been sent to Rome.

May it be permitted to me, with the benevolence of the gods, to take appropriate vengeance upon those implicated in the impious plot against me who have undertaken to deprive me not only of my kingdom but also of my life. But if something were to happen to me in accordance with mortal men before I have left successors to my kingdom, I leave to the Romans my proper kingdom, with whom, from the beginning, I have truly preserved friendship and alliance. To them I entrust the preservation of affairs, imploring them by all the gods and their own good reputation that if anyone were to attack either the cities or the countryside they would help, according to our friendship and alliance, and with justice, using all their power. As witnesses to this I name Zeus of the Capitol and the Great Gods and the Sun and Founder Apollo, to whom the writings in this matter have been consecrated.

With Good Fortune.[19]

---

17 Braund, *Friendly King*, pp. 129–55.

18 Despite the familiarity of this incident, the sources are scattered: see Braund, *Friendly King*, pp. 131–3.

19 *SEG* 9.7:

Ἔτους πεντεκαιδεκάτου, μηνὸς Λώιου. | Ἀγαθῆι τύχηι. Τάδε διέθετο βασιλεὺς | Πτολεμαῖος βασιλέως Πτολεμαίου | καὶ βασιλίσσης Κλεοπάτρας, θεῶν | Ἐπι-φανῶν, ὁ νεώτερος· ὧν καὶ τὰ ἀντίγραφα | εἰς Ῥώμην ἐξαπέσταλται. – Εἴη μέν μοι | μετὰ τῆς τῶν θεῶν εὐμενείας μετελθεῖν | καταξίως τοὺς συστησαμένους ἐπί με | τὴν ἀνόσιον ἐπιβουλὴν καὶ προελομένους | μὴ μόνον [ον] τῆς βασιλείας, ἀλλὰ καὶ | τοῦ ζῆν στερῆσαι με· ἐὰν δέ τι συμβαίνηι | τῶν

Ptolemaios cited a plot against his life and possible revolts after his death as reasons for bequeathing his kingdom to Rome, invoking Juppiter Capitolinus as witness. He also made it explicit that Rome was to receive the kingdom only if he died without heirs; in fact he ruled another forty years, and when he died, his son Ptolemaios IX was an adult and inherited both Kyrene and Egypt. So the will of Attalos III is the earliest by which Rome actually received territory, and this became embroiled in the legislative reforms of Tiberius Gracchus, who seems to have seen it as offering financial rather than territorial advantages. There are a number of other bequests, especially involving the Ptolemies and their far-flung territories, from the late second and early first centuries BC, but generally, for one reason or another, Rome did not benefit from these, although they might have helped foster the idea that the natural evolution of kingship was Roman acquisition of territory.

In the empire, will-making by kings naturally focused on the imperial family. Herod the Great, with the permission of Augustus, publicly named his successors (although this went through several stages as Herod killed off so many of his heirs), and left large legacies of land and money to members of his family.[20] In addition, he left inheritances to Augustus, Livia, and other members, friends, and freedmen of the imperial family. Augustus was made executor and there was a long and protracted struggle as a variety of parties contested the will. Significantly, Augustus upheld the financial legacies but restructured the territories, denying any of Herod's sons the title of king and dividing up the kingdom into three principalities closely watched by Rome. He also donated money to Herod's heirs and provided dowries for his daughters.[21]

These wills furthered the interests of both king and Rome: they were outstanding examples of loyalty and devotion on the part of the king, and also helped deter the threat of assassination or succession wars. As the object of bequests changed from the Roman state to the emperor, the relationship was

κατ᾽ἄνθρωπον πρότερον ἢ διαδόχους | ἀπολιπεῖν τῆς βασιλείας, καταλείπω | Ῥωμαίοις τὴν καθήκουσάν μοι βασιλείαν, | οἷς ἀπ᾽ἀρχῆς τήν τε φιλίαν καὶ τὴν | συμμαχίαν γνησίως συντετήρηκα· | τοῖς δ᾽αὐτοῖς παρακατατίθεμαι τὰ πράγματα | συντηρεῖν, ἐνευχόμενος κατά τε τῶν θεῶν | πάντων καὶ τῆς ἑαυτῶν εὐδοξίας, ἐάν τινες | ἐπίωσιν ἢ ταῖς πόλεσιν ἢ τῆι χώραι, βοηθεῖν | κατὰ τὴν φιλίαν καὶ συμμαχίαν τὴν [πρὸς] | πρὸς ἀλλήλους ἡμῖν γενομένην καὶ τὸ | δίκαιον παντὶ σθένει. | – Μάρτυρας δέ τούτων ποιοῦμαι Δία τε τὸν | Καπετώλιον καὶ τοὺς Μεγάλους θεοὺς | καὶ τὸν Ἥλιον καὶ τὸν Ἀρχηγέτην Ἀπόλλωνα, | παρ᾽ὧι καὶ τὰ περὶ τούτων ἀνιέρωται γράμματα. | Τύχηι τῆι ἀγαθῆι.

See Günther Hölbl, *A History of the Ptolemaic Empire*, trans. Tina Saavedra (London: Routledge, 2001), p. 187.

20 Josephus, *Jewish Antiquities* 17.188–90, 321.
21 Josephus, *Jewish War* 2.99–100; *Jewish Antiquities* 17.321–3.

again personalized and returned to a closer analogy to that between patron and client, but with greater implications since peoples and territories were involved. But it also provided the basis for evolution from client kingdom to province and thus imperial expansion.

As noted, the king had to tread a narrow path between loyalty to his kingdom and to Rome, duties that could easily become mutually exclusive. Rome had long been a preferred place of refuge for barbarian royalty in difficulty at home: this is, in part, why Herod ended up there in 40 BC and became king. The king might be returned to his territory with Roman support, or, as in the case of Herod, and to some extent Juba II, be made king while in Rome. But this meant that the king's ultimate fate rested with Rome, and as he had been made by Rome, he could easily be unmade.[22] He could be ordered to Rome at any time to explain his actions, potentially with fatal consequences. In extreme cases he could be put on trial at Rome: one early instance that is well documented, because Cicero defended the king, is that of Deiotaros of Galatia, who was accused by his grandson of plotting to murder Julius Caesar in 47 BC.[23] Deiotaros was summoned to Rome and tried in Caesar's house. Either he was acquitted or the case was dismissed because of Caesar's assassination: at any rate he returned to his kingdom. Less fortunate was Archelaos of Kappadokia, who was ordered to Rome by Tiberius around AD 15 and brought to trial before the Senate.[24] Like the case of Deiotaros, this came to an ambivalent conclusion because Archelaos, although probably acquitted, died in Rome and his kingdom was provincialized.

More common was the removal of the king from his kingdom and the sending of him into exile, usually as far away as possible. Often the deposed rulers would then live in wealthy leisure, although less frequently, as in the case of Ptolemaios of Mauretania, they might be imprisoned or even executed. Two of Herod's sons, Archelaos and Antipas, were deposed and sent to Gaul, effectively vanishing from the historical record.[25] The entire royal court might leave the kingdom, providing an obscure yet lavish retirement: this is certainly implied in the case of Antipas, whose wife, the infamous Herodias, accompanied him into exile. But as a final example of the peculiar twists of client kingship, there is the case of Alexandros of Kilikia, great-great-grandson of Herod the Great and one of the last known members of that illustrious dynasty.[26] Son of King Tigranes VI of Armenia, he married into the royal family of Kommagene. The emperor Vespasian

---

22 Jean Gagé, "L'Empereur romain et les rois," *RHist* 22, 1959, 239–41.

23 Cicero, *Pro rege Deiotaro*.

24 Supra, pp. 220–1.

25 Strabo 16.2.46; Josephus, *Jewish War* 2.183; *Jewish Antiquities* 18.252. The case of Antipas is unclear in detail, since *Jewish War* 2.183 records that he died in Spain: see Braund, *Friendly King*, p. 177. On the ultimate fate of Archelaos, see Kokkinos, *Herodian Dynasty*, pp. 228–9.

26 Kokkinos, *Herodian Dynasty*, pp. 250–4.

seems to have arranged the marriage, probably around AD 75, and provided the kingship of Kilikia as a wedding present. After about twenty years on the throne he lost his kingdom, probably because of Domitian, but, invoking the senatorial rights that kings had had since the time of the emperor Gaius, he came to Rome and took up his seat in the Senate, eventually serving as consul, perhaps around AD 100, yet retaining as an honorific the title of king even as he was consul, a blending of roles that even Augustus could never have envisioned.

BIBLIOGRAPHY

Abramson, Herbert, "The Olympieion in Athens and its Connection with Rome," *CSCA* 7, 1974, 1–25.

Adcock, F. E., "'Delenda est Carthago,'" *CHJ* 8.3, 1946, 117–28.

Agatharchides, *On the Erythraean Sea*, tr. and ed. by Stanley M. Burstein, London: Hakluyt Society, 1989.

Akerraz, Aomar, "Volubilis et les royaumes berberes independants," *BAMaroc* 18, 1998, 329–31.

Akerraz, Aomar and Maurice Lenoir, "Les Huileries de Volubilis," *BAMaroc* 14, 1981–2, 69–121.

Akurgal, Ekrem, *Ancient Civilizations and Ruins of Turkey*, seventh edition, tr. John Whybrow and Molly Emre, Istanbul: Turistik Yayinlar, 1990.

Alcock, Susan E., *Graecia Capta: The Landscapes of Roman Greece*, first paperback edition, Cambridge: Cambridge University Press, 1996.

Alexandropoulos, Jacques, "Note sur une monnaie à l'effigie de Juba II," in *Alimenta: Estudios en homenaje al Dr. Michel Ponsich* (*Gerion*, supp. 3, Madrid 1991), pp. 115–18.

——, *Les Monnaies de l'Afrique Antique, 400 av. J.-C.–40 ap. J.-C.*, Toulouse: Presses Universitaires du Mirail, 2000.

Alföldy, Géza, *Noricum*, tr. Anthony Birley, London: Routledge and Kegan Paul, 1974.

——, "Tarraco" (#1), *RE* Supp. 15, 1978, 570–644.

——, "Bellum Mauricum," *Chiron* 15, 1985, 91–109.

——, "Spain," *CAH²* 10, 1996, 449–63.

Allen, Walter, Jr., "The Source of Jugurtha's Influence in the Roman Senate," *CP* 33, 1938, 90–2.

Aly, Wolfgang, "Die Entdeckung des Westens," *Hermes* 62, 1927, 299–341.

——, "Strabon von Amaseia" (#3), *RE* 2, ser. 7, 1931, 76–155.

——, *Strabon von Amaseia* 4: *Untersuchungen über Text, Aufbau und Quellen der Geographika*, Bonn: Habelt, 1957.

Amadasi, Guzzo, Maria Giulia, *Iscrizioni feniche e puniche in Italia*, Rome: Libreria dello Stato, 1990.

Amadasi, Guzzo, Maria Giulia, "Notes sur les graffitis phéniciens de Mogador," *Lixus*, pp. 155–73.

Amandry, Michel, "Notes de numismatique africaine, IV," *RN* 6, ser. 31, 1989, 80–5.

Ancey, Gabriel, "Sur deux épigrammes de Crinagoras," *RA* 15, 1910, 139–41.

Anderson, Graham, "The Banquet of Belles-Lettres: Athenaeus and the Comic Symposium," in *Athenaeus and His World: Reading Greek Culture in the Roman Empire*, ed. David Braund and John Wilkins, Exeter: University of Exeter Press, 2000, pp. 316–26.

Anderson, J. G. C., "Some Questions Bearing on the Date and Place of Composition of Strabo's *Geography*," in *Anatolian Studies Presented to Sir William Mitchell Ramsey*, ed. W. H. Buckler and W. M. Calder, Manchester: Longmans, Green, 1923, pp. 1–13.

Anderson, William S., "Juno and Saturn in the *Aeneid*," *Studies in Philology* 55, 1958, 519–32.

André, Albert, "Introduction à la géographie physique de la Péninsule tingitane," *RGM* 19, 1971, 57–75.

André, J., *La Vie et l'œuvre d'Asinius Pollion*, Paris: C. Klincksieck, 1949.

André, Jean-Marie and Marie Françoise Baslez, *Voyager dans l'Antiquité*, Paris: Fayard, 1993.

Aranegui, Carmen *et al.*, "La Recherche archéologique espagnole à Lixus: bilan et perspectives," *Lixus*, pp. 7–15.

Atenstädt, Felix, "Zwei Quellen des Sogenannten Plutarch *De Fluviis*," *Hermes* 57, 1922, 219–46.

Augustus, *Operum fragmenta*, fifth edition, ed. Henrica Malcovati, Turin: G. B. Paravia, 1969.

Austin, N. J. E. and N. B. Rankov, *Exploratio: Military and Political Intelligence in the Roman World from the Second Punic War to the Battle of Adrianople*, London: Routledge, 1995.

Avanzini, Alessandra, "Le Commerce des aromates et les états de l'Arabie méridionale pré-islamique," in *Parfums d'Orient*, Res Orientales 11, Bures-sur-Yvette 1998, pp. 85–92.

Babcock, Charles L, "The Early Career of Fulvia," *AJP* 86, 1965, 1–32.

Badian, E., *Foreign Clientelae (264–70 B.C.)*, Oxford: Clarendon Press, 1958.

——, "The Early Historians," in *Latin Historians*, ed. T. A. Dorey, London: Routledge and Kegan Paul, 1966, pp. 1–38.

——, *Lucius Sulla, the Deadly Reformer*, Sydney: Sydney University Press, 1970.

Baldus, Hans Roland, "Die Münzprägung der numidischen Königreiche," in *Numider*, pp. 187–208.

——, "Eine antiken Elefanten-Dressur: Zu einem Münzbild König Jubas II," *Chiron* 20, 1990, 217–20.

——, "Die Münzen der numiderkönigen Syphax und Vermina: Prägungen vom Ende des Zweiten punischen Krieges (218/201 v. Chr.)," in *Die Münze: Bild–Botschaft–Bedeuting, Festschrift für Maria R.-Alföldi*, ed. Hans-Christoph Noeske und Helmut Schubert, Frankfurt am Main: P. Lang, 1991, pp. 26–34.

Baldwin, Barry, "The Date, Identity, and Career of Vitruvius," *Latomus* 49, 1990, 425–34.

Balsdon, J. P. V. D., *The Emperor Gaius (Caligula)*, Oxford: Clarendon Press, 1934.

——, *Roman Women: Their History and Habits*, London: Bodley Head, 1962.

——, *Romans and Aliens*, London: Duckworth, 1979.

Baradez, Jean, "Deux missions de recherches sur le *limes* de Tingitane," *CRAI* 1955, pp. 288–98.

——, "Un Grand Bronze de Juba II témoin de l'ascendance mythique de Ptolémée de Maurétanie," *BAMaroc* 4, 1960, 117–32.

Barker, Andrew (ed.), *Greek Musical Writings*, Cambridge: Cambridge University Press, 1984–9.

——, "Athenaeus on Music," in *Athenaeus and His World: Reading Greek Culture in the*

Roman Empire, ed. David Braund and John Wilkins, Exeter: University of Exeter Press, 2000, pp. 434–44.

Barnes, T. D., "The Victories of Augustus," *JRS* 64, 1974, 21–6.

The Barrington Atlas of the Greek and Roman World, ed. Richard J. Talbert, Princeton, N.J.: Princeton University Press, 2000.

Barr-Sharrar, Beryl, *The Hellenistic and Early Imperial Decorative Bust*, Mainz: Philipp von Zabern, 1987.

Barton, I. M., *Africa in the Roman Empire*, Accra: Ghana Universities Press, 1972.

Baslez, Marie-Françoise, "Un Monument de la famille royale de Numidie à Délos," *RÉG* 94, 1981, pp. 160–5.

Beagon, Mary, *Roman Nature: The Thought of Pliny the Elder*, Oxford: Clarendon Press, 1992.

Bean, George E., "Report on a Journey in Lycia 1960," *AnzWien* 99, 1962 (1963), 4–9.

Beltrán, Antonio, "Carthago Nova," *PECS*, pp. 202–3.

——, "Iuba II y Ptolomeo, de Mauritania, II viri quinquennales de Carthago Nova," *Caesaraugusta* 51–2, 1980, 133–41.

Bénabou, Marcel, *La Résistance africaine à la romanisation*, Paris: F. Maspero, 1976.

——, "L'Afrique," in *L'impero romano e le strutture economiche e sociali delle province*, Biblioteca di Athenaeum 4, ed. Michael H. Crawford, Como: New Press, 1986, pp. 127–41.

——, "Les Trois Fidélités du bon roi Juba," in *La Trahison*, Le Genre humain 16–17, Paris 1988, pp. 201–14.

Bencheneb, Saâdeddine, "Massyli = Masila?" *RHCM* 5, July 1968, 12–15.

Bengtson, Hermann, "Q. Caecilius Metellus Celer (cos 60) und die Inder," *Historia* 3, 1954–5, 229–36.

——, *Marcus Antonius: Triumvir und Herrscher des Orients*, Munich: Beck, 1977.

Benseddik, Nacéra, "De Caesarea à Shershel: premiers résultats de la fouille du forum," *BAC* n.s. 19b, 1983 (1985), 451–6.

——, "Un Nouveau Témoignage du culte de Tanit-Caelestis à Cherchel?" *AntAfr* 20, 1984, 175–81.

——, "Être femme dans le Mahgreb ancien," *AWAL: Cahiers d'études berbères* 20, 1999, 113–50.

——, *Fouilles du Forum de Cherchel, 1977–1981*, BAAlg Supp. 6, 1993.

Benseddik, Nacéra and T. W. Potter, *Fouilles du Forum de Cherchel: Rapport preliminaire*, BAAlg Supp. 4, 1986.

Benseddik, Nacéra *et al.*, *Cherchel*, Algiers: Direction des Musées, de l'archéologique et des monuments et sites historiques, 1983.

Berggren, J. Lennart and Alexander Jones, *Ptolemy's Geography: An Annotated Translation of the Theoretical Chapters*, Princeton, N.J.: Princeton University Press: 2000.

Bertrandy, François, "Remarques sur l'origine romaine du monnayage en bronze et en argent de Juba Ier, roi de Numidie," *BAC* 12–14b, 1976–8 (1980), 9–22.

——, "Thiblis (Announa), de Juba Ier au triumvir M. Aemilius Lepidus: les premières étapes de la romanisation d'une cité numide (46–36 av. J.-C.)," *Karthago* 19, 1980, 87–106.

——, "À propos du cavalier de Simmithus (Chemtou)," *AntAfr* 22, 1986, 57–71.

——, "L'aide militaire de Juba Ier aux Pompeiens pendant la guerre civile en Afrique du Nord (50–46 avant J.-C.)," in *Histoire et archéologie de l'Afrique du Nord: Actes du IVe Colloque International* 2: *L'Armée et les affaires militaires*, Paris: CTHS, 1991, pp. 289–97.

Bethe, Erich. "Diomedes" (#1), *RE* 5, 1903, 815–26.

Bianchi, Annagabriella, "Giugurta e la guerra giugurtina in Orazio," in *Miscellanea greca e romana* 18, Studi pubblicati dall'Istituto Italiano per la Storia Antica 56 (Rome 1994), pp. 151–66.

Bieber, Margarete, *The History of the Greek and Roman Theater*, Princeton, N.J.: Princeton University Press, 1961.

Blázquez, J. M., "Tartessos," *PECS*, pp. 884–5.

Blomqvist, Jerker, *The Date and Origin of the Greek Version of Hanno's Periplus*, Lund: LiberLarumedel/Gleerup, 1979.

Boardman, John, *Engraved Gems: The Ionides Collection*, Evanston, Ill.: Northwestern University Press, 1968.

——, *Greek Gems and Finger Rings, Early Bronze Age to Late Classical*, New York: Harry N. Abrams, [1970].

——, *The Greeks Overseas*, new and enlarged edition, London: Thames and Hudson, 1980.

Boardman, John and C. E. Vafopoulou-Richardson, "Diomedes I," *LIMC* 3.1, 1986, 396–409.

Boëthius, Axel, *Etruscan and Early Roman Architecture*, second integrated edition, Harmondsworth, U.K.: Penguin, 1978.

Boll, Franz, "Finsternisse," *RE* 6, 1909, 2329–64.

Bomgardner, D. L., *The Story of the Roman Amphitheatre*, London: Routledge, 2000.

Bonner, Stanley F., *Education in Ancient Rome*, Berkeley: University of California Press, 1977.

Bosworth, A. P., "Asinius Pollio and Augustus," *Historia* 21, 1972, 441–73.

——, *From Arrian to Alexander: Studies in Historical Interpretation*, Oxford: Clarendon Press, 1988.

Boube, Jean, "Un Chapiteau ionique de l'époque de Juba II à Volubilis," *BAMaroc* 6, 1966, 109–14.

——, "Fouilles archéologiques à Sala," *Hésperis-Tamuda* 7, 1966, 25–32.

——, "Un Nouveau Portrait de Juba II découvert à Sala," *BAMaroc* 6, 1966, 91–106.

——, "A propos de *Babba Iulia Campestris*," *BAMaroc* 15, 1983–4, 131–7.

——, "Les Amphores de Sala a l'époque maurétanienne," *BAMaroc* 17, 1987–8, 183–207.

——, "Une Statue-portrait de Ptolémée de Maurétanie à Sala (Maroc)," *RA* 1990, 331–60.

Boube-Piccot, Christine, "Techniques de fabrication des bustes de bronze de Juba II et de Caton d'Utique découverts à Volubilis," *BAMaroc* 7, 1967, 447–75.

Bouchenaki, Mounir, "Relations entre le royaume de Numidie et la république romaine au Ier siècle avant Jésus-Christ," *RHCM* 6–7, 1969, 7–9.

——, *Le Mausolée Royal de Maurétanie*, Algiers: Direction des Musées, de l'archéologique et des monuments et sites historiques, 1979.

Bouchenaki, Mounir and Paul-Albert Février, "Un 'castellum' de la region de Tipasa de Juba à Septime Severe," *BAAlg* 7, 1977–9, 193–212.

Bowersock, Glen W., *Augustus and the Greek World*, Oxford: Clarendon Press, 1965.

——, "A Report on Arabia Provincia," *JRS* 61, 1971, 219–42.

——, *Roman Arabia*, first paperback edition, Cambridge, Mass.: Harvard University Press, 1983.

——, "Augustus and the East: The Problem of the Succession," in *Caesar Augustus: Seven Aspects*, ed. Fergus Millar and Erich Segal, Oxford: Clarendon Press, 1984, pp. 169–88.

——, "Tylos and Tyre: Bahrain in the Graeco-Roman World," in *Bahrain through the Ages: The Archaeology*, ed. Shaikha Haya Ali Al Khalifa and Michael Rice, London: KPI, 1986, pp. 399–406.

——, "Jacoby's Fragments and Two Greek Historians of Pre-Islamic Arabia," in *Collecting Fragments*, Aporemata 1, ed. Glenn W. Most, Göttingen: Vandenhoeck and Ruprecht, 1997, pp. 173–85.

——, "Perfumes and Power," in *Profumi d'Arabia: atti del Convegno*, ed. Alessandra Avanzini, Rome: L'Erma di Bretschneider, 1997, pp. 543–56.

Braund, David C., Review of M. R. Cimma, *Reges socii et amici populi romani*, *JRS* 70, 1980, 203.

——, "Cicero on Hiempsal II and Juba: *De leg. agr.* 2.58–9," *LCM* 8, 1983, 87–9 (author wrongly attributed in *LCM*).

——, "*Anth. Pal.* 9.235: Juba II, Cleopatra Selene and the Course of the Nile," *CQ* 34, 1984, 175–8.

——, "North African Rulers and the Roman Military Paradigm," *Hermes* 112, 1984, 255–6.

——, *Rome and the Friendly King: The Character of the Client Kingship*, London: Croom Helm, 1984.

——, "Client Kings," in *The Administration of the Roman Empire (241 BC–AD 193)*, ed. David C. Braund, Exeter Studies in History 18, 1988, pp. 69–96.

——, "Piracy under the Principate and the Ideology of Imperial Eradication," in *War and Society in the Roman World*, ed. John Rich and Graham Shipley, London: Routledge, 1993, pp. 195–212.

——, "Greeks and Barbarians: The Black Sea Region and Hellenism under the Early Roman Empire," in *The Early Roman Empire in the East*, ed. Susan E. Alcock, Oxbow Monograph 97, Oxford: Oxbow, 1997, pp. 121–36.

Brennen, T. Corey, "Sulla's Career in the Nineties: Some Reconsiderations," *Chiron* 22, 1992, 103–58.

Brett, Michael and Elizabeth Fentress, *The Berbers*, Oxford: Blackwell, 1996.

Briscoe, John, *A Commentary on Livy, Books XXXI–XXXIII*, Oxford: Clarendon Press, 1973.

——, *A Commentary on Livy, Books XXXIV–XXXVII*, Oxford: Clarendon Press, 1981.

——, "The Second Punic War," *CAH²* 8, 1989, pp. 44–80.

Broughton, T. R. S., *The Romanization of Africa Proconsularis*, Baltimore: Johns Hopkins University Press, 1929.

——, *The Magistrates of the Roman Republic*, Philological Monographs of the American Philological Association 15, New York 1951–2, 1986.

Brown, Truesdell S., *Onesicritus: A Study in Hellenistic Historiography*, Berkeley: University of California Press, 1949.

Brunt, P. A., *Italian Manpower, 225 B.C.–A.D. 14*, Oxford: Oxford University Press, 1971.

——, *The Fall of the Roman Republic and Related Essays*, Oxford: Clarendon Press, 1988.

Buchheim, Hans, *Die Orientpolitik des Triumvirn M. Antonius*, Heidelberg: C. Winter, 1960.

Bunbury, E. H., *A History of Ancient Geography*, second edition, London: John Murray, 1883.

Burstein, Stanley M., *Graeco-Africana: Studies in the History of Greek Relations with Egypt and Nubia*, New Rochelle, N.Y.: A. D. Caratzas, 1995.

Callegarin, Laurent, "La Maurétanie de l'ouest et Rome au Ier siècle av. J.-C.: approche amphorologique," *AfrRom* 13, 2000, 1333–62.

Cameron, Alan, "Macrobius, Avienus, and Avianus," *CQ* n.s. 17, 1967, 385–99.

Camps, Gabriel, *Massinissa ou les débuts de l'histoire*, LibAE 8.1, 1960.

——, "Origines du royaume massyle," *RHCM* 3, July 1967, 29–38.

——, "Nouvelles observations sur l'architecture et l'âge du Medracen, mausolée royal de Numidie," *CRAI* 1973, pp. 470–517.

——, "Une Monnaie de Capussa, roi de Numidies Massyles," *BAC* n.s. 15–16b, 1979–80 (1984), 29–32.

——, "Les Derniers Rois numides: Massinissa II et Arabion," *BAC* n.s. 17b, 1981 (1984), 303–11.

——, "Ascalis," *EB* 7, 1989, 954.

——, "Bocchus," *EB* 10, 1991, 1544–7.

——, "Bogud," *EB* 10, 1991, 1557–8.

——, "Mausolees princiers de Numidie et de Maurétanie," *Archeologia* (Paris) 298, 1994, 50–9.

——, "Hiempsal (Iemsal)" *EB* 23, 2000, 3463–4.

Carcopino, Jérôme, "L'Afrique au dernier siècle de la république romaine," *RHist* 162, 1929, 86–95.

——, "Volubilis regia Iubae," *Hésperis* 17, 1933, 1–24.

——, "La Reine Urania de Maurétanie," in *Mélanges dédiés à la memoire de Felix Grat*, Paris: En depôt Chez Mme. Pecqueur-Grat, 1946, vol. 1, pp. 31–8.

——, "Sur la mort de Ptolémée roi de Maurétanie," in *Mélanges de philologie, de littérature et de l'histoire anciennes offerts à Alfred Ernout*, Paris: C. Klincksieck, 1940, 39–50.

——, *Le Maroc antique*, third edition, Paris: Gallimard, 1943.

Carpenter, Rhys, *The Greeks in Spain*, Bryn Mawr Notes 6, London 1925.

——, *Beyond the Pillars of Heracles*, New York: Delacorte Press, 1966.

Cartledge, Paul and Antony Spawforth, *Hellenistic and Roman Sparta: A Tale of Two Cities*, London: Routledge, 1989.

Cary, M., *The Geographic Background of Greek and Roman History*, Oxford: Clarendon Press, 1949.

Cary, M. and E. H. Warmington, *The Ancient Explorers*, revised edition, Baltimore: Penguin Books, 1963.

Cassidy, Vincent H., "Other Fortunate Islands and Some That Were Lost," *TI* 1, 1969, 35–9.

Cassius Dio, *The Augustan Settlement (Roman History 53–55.9)*, ed. J. W. Rich, Warminster: Aris and Phillips, 1990.

Casson, Lionel, "Rome's Trade with the East: The Sea Voyage to Africa and India," *TAPA* 110, 1980, 21–36.

——, *Ancient Trade and Society*, Detroit: Wayne State University Press, 1984.

——, *The Periplus Maris Erythraei*, Princeton, N.J.: Princeton University Press, 1989.

——, "South Arabia's Maritime Trade in the First Century AD," in *L'Arabie préislamique et son environnement historique et culturel*, ed. T. Fahd, Strasbourg: Université des sciences humaines de Strasbourg, 1989, pp. 187–94.

——, "Ancient Naval Technology and the Route to India," in *Rome and India: the Ancient Sea Trade*, ed. Vimala Begley and Richard Daniel De Puma, Madison: University of Wisconsin Press, 1991, pp. 8–11.

Chabot, J.-B., *Recueil des inscriptions libyques* 1, Paris: Imprimerie Nationale, 1940.

Chaisemartin, Nathalie de, "Note sur l'iconographie d'Octave d'après un portrait provenant d'El Jem conservé au Musée de Sousse," *AntAfr* 19, 1983, 35–61.

Chamoux, François, "Gaïus Caesar," *BCH* 74, 1950, 250–64.

——, "Un Nouveau Portrait de Ptolémée de Maurétanie découvert à Cherchel," in *Mélanges d'archéologie et d'histoire offerts à André Piganiol*, ed. Raymond Chevallier, Paris: SEVPEN, 1966, vol. 1, pp. 395–406.

——, *Marc Antoine, dernier prince de l'Orient grec*, Paris: Arthaud, 1986.

Chanler, Beatrice, *Cleopatra's Daughter: The Queen of Mauretania*, New York: Liveright, 1934.

Charbonneaux, J., "Un Portrait de Cléopâtre VII au Musée de Cherchel," *LibAE* 2, 1954, 49–63.

——, "Giuba I," *EAA* 3, 1960, 917.

——, "Giuba II," *EAA* 3, 1960, 917–18.

Charles-Picard, Collette and Gilbert Charles-Picard, "Recherches sur l'architecture numide," *Karthago* 19, 1980, 15–31.

Charlesworth, Martin P., *Trade Routes and Commerce of the Roman Empire*, second edition, Cambridge: Cambridge University Press, 1926.

——, "Roman Trade with India: A Resurvey," in *Studies in Roman Economic and Social History in Honor of Allan Chester Johnson*, ed. P. R. Coleman-Norton, F. C. Bourne, and J. V. A. Fine, Princeton, N.J.: Princeton University Press, 1951, pp. 131–43.

Chatelain, Louis, "Travaux et recherches du Service des Antiquités du Maroc, depuis 1919," *CRAI* 1922, pp. 28–31.

——, *Le Maroc des Romains: étude sur les centres antiques de la Maurétanie Occidentale*, BÉFAR 160, 1944.

Cherry, David A., "The Marriage of Roman Citizens and Non-Citizens: Law and Practice," Ph.D. thesis, University of Ottawa, 1985.

——, *Frontier and Society in Roman North Africa*, Oxford: Clarendon Press, 1998.

Christes, Johannes, *Sklaven und Freigelassene als Grammatiker und Philologen im Antiken Rom*, Forschungen zur antiken Sklaverei 10, Wiesbaden 1979.

Christofle, Marcel, *Le Tombeau de la Chrétienne*, Paris: Arts et Métiers Graphiques, 1951.

Christol, Michel and Jacques Gascou, "Volubilis, cité fédérée?" *MÉFRA* 92, 1980, 329–45.

Ciaceri, Emanuele, "La conquista romana dell'Africa," in *Africa Romana*, Milan: Hoepli, 1935, pp. 29–48.

Cicero, Marcus Tullius, *Epistulae ad familiares*, ed. D. R. Shackleton Bailey, Cambridge: Cambridge University Press, 1977.

——, *Pro P. Sulla Oratio*, ed. with introduction and commentary by D. H. Berry, Cambridge: Cambridge University Press, 1996.

Cichorius, Conrad, *Römische Studien*, Leipzig: Teubner, 1922.

Cimma, Maria Rosa, *Reges socii et amici populi romani*, Milan: Giuffre, 1976.

Claassen, Jo-Marie, "Sallust's Jugurtha – Rebel or Freedom Fighter? On Crossing Crocodile-Infested Waters," *CW* 86, 1992–3, 273–97.

Clarke, G. W., "Minicius Felix *Octavius* 4.6," *CP* 61, 1966, 252–3.

Cleopatra of Egypt: From History to Myth, ed. Susan Walker and Peter Higgs, London: British Museum Press, 2001.

Clissold, Stephen, *The Seven Cities of Cíbola*, London: Eyre and Spottiswoode, 1961.

Cluett, Ronald G., "Roman Women and Triumviral Politics, 43–37 BC," *EchCl* 42 n.s. 17, 1998, 67–84.

Coarelli, Filippo, *Guide archeologiche Laterza: Roma*, Rome: Giuseppe Laterza e Figli, 1980.

Coarelli, Filippo and Yvon Thébert, "Architecture funéraire et pouvoir: réflexions sur l'hellénisme numide," *MÉFRA* 100, 1988, 761–818.

Coltelloni-Trannoy, Michèle, "Le Monnayage des rois Juba II et Ptolémée de Maurétanie: image d'une adhésion réitérée à la politique romaine," *Karthago* 22, 1990, 45–53.

——, "Le Culte royal sous les règnes de Juba II et de Ptolémée de Maurétanie," in *Histoire et Archéologie de l'Afrique du Nord (Actes du Ve Colloque International): Spectacles, Vie Portuaire, Religions*, Paris: CTHS, 1992, pp. 69–81.

——, "Les Liens de clientèle en Afrique du Nord, du IIe siècle av. J.-C. jusqu'au début du principat," *BAC* n.s. 24b, 1993–5 (1997), 59–82.

——, *Le royaume de Maurétanie sous Juba II et Ptolémée*, Paris: CNRS, 1997.

Cooley, Alison, "A New Date for Agrippa's Theatre at Ostia," *PBSR* 67, 1999, 173–82.

Corbier, Paul, "Hercule africain: divinité indigene?" *Dialogues d'histoire ancienne 1974*, Annales littéraires de l'Université de Besançon 166, Paris 1974, pp. 95–104.

Corvisier, Jean-Nicolas and Wiesław Suder, *La Population de l'antiquité classique*, Paris: Presses Universitaires de France, 2000.

Cossarini, Alberto, "Cic. *Epist.* 9,6,3 *ad bestiarum auxilium*," *AttiVen* 146, 1982–3, 93–103.

Crawford, Michael H., *Roman Republican Coinage*, Cambridge: Cambridge University Press, 1974.

——, *Coinage and Money under the Roman Republic: Italy and the Mediterranean Economy*, London: Methuen, 1985.

Crook, John A., *Consilium Principis: Imperial Councils and Counsellors from Augustus to Diocletian*, Cambridge: Cambridge University Press, 1955.

——, "A Legal Point about Mark Antony's Will," *JRS* 47, 1957, 36–8.

——, "Political History, 30 BC to AD 14," *CAH*² 10, 1996, 70–112.

Cunliffe, Barry, *Greeks, Romans, and Barbarians: Spheres of Interaction*, New York: Batsford, 1988.

Dalby, Andrew, "The Curriculum Vitae of Duris of Samos," *CQ* n.s. 41, 1991, 539–41.

Dalby, Andrew and Sally Grainger, *The Classical Cookbook*, paperback with revisions, London: British Museum Press, 2000.

Daniels, Charles, *The Garamantes of Southern Libya*, Stoughton, Wis.: Oleander Press, 1970.

Davis, Lindsey, *Venus in Copper*, London: Hutchinson, 1991.

Decret, François and Mhamad Fantar, *L'Afrique du Nord dans l'antiquité: histoire et civilisation*, Paris: Payot, 1981.

De La Chapelle, F., "L'Expédition de Suetonius Paulinus dans le sud-est du Maroc," *Hespéris* 19, 1934, 107–24.

Delia, Diana, "Fulvia Reconsidered," in *Women's History and Ancient History*, ed. Sarah B. Pomeroy, Chapel Hill: University of North Carolina Press, 1991, pp. 197–217.

Denis, Albert-Marie, "Héraclès et ses cousins de Judée: le syncrétisme d'un historien juif hellénistique," in *Hommages à Marie Delcourt*, Collection Latomus 114, Brussels 1970, pp. 168–78.

Déroche, Louis, "Les Fouilles de Ksar Toual Zammel et la question de Zama," *MÉFR* 60, 1948, 55–104.

De Romanis, Frederico, "Rome and the *Nótia* of India: Relations between Rome and Southern India from 30 BC to the Flavian Period," in *Crossings: Early Mediterranean*

Contacts with India, ed. F. De Romanis and A. Tchernia, New Delhi; Manohar, 1997, pp. 80–160.

Desanges, Jehan, "Le Triomphe de Cornelius Balbus (19 av. J.-C.)," *RAfr* 101, 1957, 5–43.

——, "Les Territoires gétules de Juba II," *RÉA* 66, 1964, 33–47.

——, "Un Drame africain sous Auguste: le meurtre du proconsul L. Cornelius Lentulus par les Nasamons," in *Hommages à Marcel Renard* 2, ed. Jacqueline Bibauw, *Collection Latomus* 102 (Brussels 1969), pp. 197–213.

——, "L'Afrique romaine et libyco-berbère," in *Rome et la conquête du monde méditerranéen, 264–27 avant J.-C.* 2, ed. Claude Nicolet, Nouvelle Clio 8bis (Paris: Presses Universitaires de France, 1978), pp. 627–56.

——, *Recherches sur l'activité des Méditerranéens aux confins de l'Afrique*, CÉFR 38, 1978.

——, "Le Point sur le 'Périple d'Hannon': controverses et publications récentes," in *Enquêtes et Documents 6: Nantes, Afrique, Amérique*, Nantes 1981, 13–29.

——, "Le Regard de Strabon sur l'Afrique du Nord," in *Gli interscambi culturali e socio-economici fra l'Africa settentrionale e l'Europa mediterranea* 1, ed. Luigi Serra, Naples: Istituto Universitario Orientale, 1986, pp. 309–19.

——, "De Timée a Strabon: la polémique sur le climat de l'Afrique du Nord et ses effects," in *Historie et archéologie de l'Afrique du Nord, Actes du IIIe Colloque International*, Paris: CTHS, 1986, pp. 27–34.

——, "Les Sources de Pline dans sa description de la Troglodytique et de l'Ethiopie (*NH* 6, 163–97)," in *Pline l'Ancien: Temoin de son temps*, ed. Iacobus Pigealdus and Iosephus Orozius, Salamanca: Universidad Pontificial, 1987, pp. 277–92.

——, "Arabes et Arabie en terre d'Afrique dans la géographie antique," in *L'Arabie préislamique et son environnement historique et culturel*, ed. T. Fahd, Strasbourg: Université des sciences humaines de Strasbourg, 1989, pp. 413–29.

——, "L'Hellénisme dans le royaume protégé de Maurétanie (25 avant J.-C.–40 après J.-C.)," *BAC* n.s. 20–1b, 1984–5 (1989), 53–61.

——, "Le Sens du terme 'corne' dans le vocabulaire géographique des Grecs et des Romains: à propos du 'Periple d'Hannon,'" *BAC* n.s. 20–1b, 1984–5 (1989), 29–34.

——, "Lixos dans les sources littéraires grecques et latines," *Lixus*, pp. 1–6.

——, "Auguste a-t-il confirmé une décision de Juba II dans l'administration interne du royaume protégé de Maurétanie?" *BAC* n.s. 23b, 1990–2 (1994), 218–20.

——, "The Indigenous Kingdoms and the Hellenization of North Africa," in *From Hannibal to Saint Augustine: Ancient Art of North Africa from the Musée du Louvre*, ed. Monique Seefried Brouillet, Atlanta: Michael C. Carlos Museum, 1994, pp. 68–75.

——, "Un Témoignage masqué sur Juba II et les troubles de Gétulie," *AntAfr* 33, 1997, 111–13.

Desjacques, Jean and Paul Koeberlé, "Mogador et les Îles purpuraires," *Hespéris* 42, 1955, 193–202.

Desmond, Alice Curtis, *Cleopatra's Children*, New York: Dodd, Mead, 1971.

De Souza, Philip, *Piracy in the Graeco-Roman World*, Cambridge: Cambridge University Press, 1999.

Desrousseaux, A.-M., "Une Épigramme du roi Juba (*FHG*, III, p. 483, fr. 83)," in *Mélanges dédiés à la memoire de Felix Grat*, Paris: En Depôt chez Mme. Pecqueur Grat, 1946, vol. 1, pp. 27–30.

Devillers, Olivier, "Le Rôle des passages relatifs à Tacfarinas dans les *Annales* de Tacite," *AfrRom* 8, 1991, 203–11.

Diehl, E., "Leonteus aus Argos" (#4), *RE* 12, 1925, 2040.

Dihle, Albrecht, "The Conception of India in Hellenistic and Roman Literature," *PCPS* 190, n.s. 10, 1964, 15–23.

——, "Die entdeckungsgeschichtlichen Voraussetzungen des Indienhandels der römischen Kaiserzeit," *ANRW* 2.9, 1978, pp. 546–80.

——, *Greek and Latin Literature of the Roman Empire from Augustus to Justinian*, tr. Manfred Malzahn, London: Routledge: 1994.

Dilke, O. A. W., *Greek and Roman Maps*, London: Thames and Hudson, 1985.

Diller, Aubrey, *The Tradition of the Minor Greek Geographers*, Philological Monographs of the American Philological Association 14, 1952.

——, *The Textual Tradition of Strabo's Geography*, Amsterdam: Hakkert, 1975.

Dillon, John, *The Middle Platonists: 80 B.C. to A.D. 220*, Ithaca, N.Y.: Cornell University Press, 1977.

Dodge, Hazel, "Decorative Stones for Architecture in the Roman Empire," *OJA* 7, 1988, 65–80.

Doisy, Henriette, "Quelques inscriptions de Caesarea (Cherchel)," *MÉFRA* 64, 1952, 87–110.

Doran, Michael F., "The Maritime Provenience of Iron Technology in West Africa," *TI* 9, 1977, 89–98.

Dorey, T. A., "Masinissa, Syphax, and Sophoniba," *PACA* 4, 1961, 1–2.

Drachmann, A. G., *Ktesibios, Philon and Heron: A Study in Ancient Pneumatics*, Acta Historia Scientiarum Naturalium et Medicinalium 4, Copenhagen 1948.

Dueck, Daniela, *Strabo of Amasia: A Greek Man of Letters in Augustan Rome*, London: Routledge, 2000.

Duval, Paul-Marie, *Cherchel et Tipasa: recherches sur deux villes fortes de l'Afrique romaine*, Institute français d'Archéologie de Beyrouth, Bibliothèque Archéologique et Historique 43, 1946.

Dyson, Stephen L., "Native Revolts in the Roman Empire," *Historia* 20, 1971, 239–74.

——, "Native Revolt Patterns in the Roman Empire," *ANRW* 2.3, 1975, 138–75.

Eadie, J. W., "Strategies of Economic Development in the Roman East: The Red Sea Trade Revisited," in *The Eastern Frontier of the Roman Empire*, ed. D. H. French and C. S. Lightfoot, BAR-IS 553, 1989, pp. 113–20.

Earl, D. C., "Sallust and the Senate's Numidian Policy," *Latomus* 24, 1965, 532–6.

Edwards, Catharine, *The Politics of Immorality in Ancient Rome*, Cambridge: Cambridge University Press, 1993.

Egger, Rudolf, *Die Stadt auf dem Magdalensberg: Ein Grosshandelsplatz*, DenkschrWien 79, 1961.

el-Houcine, Rahmoune, "L'Afrique du Nord dans ses rapports avec les provinces occidentales de Rome," *AfrRom* 13, 2000, 1147–52.

Elton, Hugh, *Frontiers of the Roman Empire*, Bloomington, Ind.: Indiana University Press, 1996.

Ennabli, A., "Mactaris (Mactar)," *PECS*, pp. 540–1.

Étienne, Robert and Françoise Mayet, "Le *Garum* a Pompéi: production et commerce," *RÉA* 100, 1998, 199–215.

Euzennat, Maurice, "Le Temple C de Volubilis et les origines de la cité," *BAMaroc* 2, 1957, 41–53.

——, "Volubilis: Statuette d'Artemis," *BAMaroc* 2, 1957, 185–6.

——, "Le roi Sosus et la dynastie maurétanienne," in *Mélanges d'archéologie, d'épigraphie et d'histoire offerts à Jérôme Carcopino*, Paris: Hachette, 1966, pp. 333–9.

——, "Grecs et Orientaux en Maurétanie Tingitane," *AntAfr* 5, 1971, 161–78.

——, "Babba Iulia Campestris," *PECS*, p. 133.

——, "Banasa," *PECS*, pp. 140–1.

——, "Lixus," *PECS*, p. 521.

——, "Mogador ('Cerne')," *PECS*, p. 586.

——, "Tingi," *PECS*, p. 923.

——, "Sala," *PECS*, pp. 793–4.

——, "Volubilis," *PECS*, pp. 988–9.

——, "Zilis," *PECS*, p. 1000.

——, "Les Recherches sur la frontière d'Afrique (1974–1976)," in *Limes: Akten des XI. Internationalen Limeskongresses (Székesfehérvár, 30.8–6.9.1976)*, ed. J. Fitz, Budapest: Akademiai Kiado, 1977, pp. 533–43.

——, "Les Troubles de Maurétanie," *CRAI* 1984, pp. 372–93.

——, *Le Limes de Tingitane: la frontière méridionale*, Paris: CNRS, 1989.

——, "Remarques sur la description de la Maurétanie Tingitane dans Pline, *H. N.*, V, 2–18," *AntAfr* 25, 1989, 95–109.

——, "La Frontière romaine d'Afrique," *CRAI* 1990, pp. 565–80.

Fabre, Paul, "Les Massaliotes et l'Atlantique," in *Océan atlantique et Péninsule armoricaine: études archéologiques*, Actes du 107ᵉ Congrès National des Sociétés Savantes, Paris: CTHS, 1985, pp. 25–49.

Farnell, Lewis Richard, *Greek Hero Cults and Ideas of Immortality*, Oxford: Clarendon Press, 1921.

Farrar, Linda, *Gardens of Italy and the Western Provinces of the Roman Empire from the 4th Century BC to the 4th Century AD*, BAR-IS 650, 1996.

Fasciato, Micheline and Jean Leclant, "Une Tête 'Ammoniene' du Musée de Cherchel," in *Mélanges d'archéologie et d'histoire offerts à Charles Picard*, Paris: Presses Universitaires de France, 1949, vol. 1, pp. 360–75.

Faur, Jean-Claude, "Caligula et la Maurétanie: la fin de Ptolémée," *Klio* 55, 1973, 249–71.

Fear, A. T., *Rome and Baetica: Urbanization in Southern Spain, c. 50 B.C.–A.D. 150*, Oxford: Clarendon Press, 1996.

Fehrle, Rudolf, *Cato Uticensis*, Darmstadt: Wissenschaftliche Buchgesellschaft, 1983.

Fentress, Elizabeth W. B., *Numidia and the Roman Army: Social, Military, and Economic Aspects of the Frontier Zone*, BAR-IS 53, 1979.

——, "Forever Berber?" *Opus* 2, 1983, 161–75.

——, "Caesarean Reflections," *Opus* 3, 1984, 487–94.

Ferguson, John, "Classical Contacts with West Africa," in *Africa in Classical Antiquity: Nine Studies*, ed. L. A. Thompson and J. Ferguson, Ibadan: Ibadan University Press, 1969, pp. 1–25.

Février, J.-G., "L'Inscription funéraire de Micipsa," *RAssyr* 45, 1951, 139–50.

——, "Bocchus le Jeune et les Sosii," *Semitica* 11, 1961, 9–15.

Février, Paul-Albert, "Origines de l'habitat urbain en Maurétanie Césarienne," *JSav* 1967, pp. 107–23.

——, "Rusguniae," *PECS*, p. 776.

——, "Siga," *PECS*, p. 838.

——, "Urbanisation et urbanisme de l'Afrique romaine," *ANRW* 2.10.2, 1982, 321–96.

Firpo, Giulio, "L'imperatore Gaio (Caligola), i τυραννοδιδάσκαλοι e Tolomeo di

Mauretania," in *Decima miscellanea greca e romana*, Studi pubblicati dall'Istituto Italiano per la Storia Antica 36, Rome 1986, pp. 185–253.

Fischer, Brigitte, *Les Monnaies antiques d'Afrique du Nord trouvées en Gaule*, Gallia supp. 36, Paris 1978.

Fischler, Susan, "Social Stereotypes and Historical Analysis: The Case of the Imperial Women at Rome," in *Women in Ancient Societies: An Illusion of the Night*, ed. Léonie J. Archer *et al.*, New York: Routledge, 1994, pp. 115–33.

Fishwick, Duncan, "The Annexation of Mauretania," *Historia* 20, 1971, 467–87.

——, "The Institution of the Provincial Cult in Roman Mauretania," *Historia* 21, 1972, 698–711.

——, "The Development of Provincial Ruler Worship in the Western Roman Empire," *ANRW* 2.16.2, 1978, 1201–53.

——, "Le Culte impérial sous Juba II et Ptolémée de Maurétanie: le témoignage des monnaies," *BAC* n.s. 19b, 1983 (1985), 225–34.

——, "On the Origins of Africa Proconsularis, I: The Amalgamation of Africa Vetus and Africa Nova," *AntAfr* 29, 1993, 53–62.

——, "On the Origins of Africa Proconsularis, II: The Administration of Lepidus and the Commission of M. Caelius Phileros," *AntAfr* 30, 1994, 57–80.

——, "On the Origins of Africa Proconsularis, III: The Era of the Cereres Again," *AntAfr* 32, 1996, 13–36.

Fishwick, Duncan and Brent D. Shaw, "Ptolemy of Mauretania and the Conspiracy of Gaetulicus," *Historia* 25, 1976, 491–4.

Fittschen, Klaus, "Die Bildnisse der mauretanischen Könige und ihre stadtrömischen Vorbilder," *MM* 15, 1974, 156–73.

——, "Zur Panzerstatue in Cherchel," *JdI* 91, 1976, 175–210.

——, "Bildnisse numidischer Könige," in *Numider*, pp. 209–25.

——, "Juba II. und seine Residenz Iol/Caesarea," in *Numider*, pp. 227–42.

——, "Zwei Ptolemäerbildnisse in Cherchel," in *Alessandria e il mondo ellenistico-romano: studi in onore di Achille Adriani*, ed. Nicola Bonacasa and Antonino di Vita, Studi e Materiali (Palermo) 4–5, Rome 1983–4, pp. 165–71.

Forrer, Leonard, *Portraits of Royal Ladies on Greek Coins*, reprint, Chicago: Argonaut, 1969.

Fox, Matthew, *Roman Historical Myths: The Regal Period in Augustan Literature*, Oxford: Clarendon Press, 1996.

Fraenkel, Eduard, "Livius" (#10a), *RE* Supp. 5, 1931, 598–607.

——, *Horace*, Oxford: Clarendon Press, 1957.

Frank, Tenney, "The Inscriptions of the Imperial Domains of Africa," *AJP* 47, 1926, 55–73.

Fraser, P. M., *Ptolemaic Alexandria*, Oxford: Clarendon Press, 1972.

Freis, Helmut, *Die Cohortes Urbanae*, EpSt 2, 1967.

Frézouls, Edmond, "Rome et la Maurétanie Tingitane: un constant d'échec?" *AntAfr* 16, 1980, 65–93.

Frier, Bruce, "Roman Life Expectancy: Ulpian's Evidence," *HSCP* 86, 1982, 213–51.

Fritz, K. von, "Neleus" (#4), *RE* 16, 1935, 2280–1.

Fündling, Jörg, "Iuba" (#1), *NP* 5, 1998, 1185.

——, "Iuba" (#2), *NP* 5, 1998, 1185–6.

Fulgentius, *Fulgentius the Mythographer*, tr. and ed. Leslie George Whitbread, Columbus: Ohio State University Press, 1971.

Fussman, Gerard, "The Periplus and the Political History of India," in *Crossings: Early Mediterranean Contacts with India*, ed. F. De Romanis and A. Tchernia, New Delhi: Manohar 1997, pp. 66–71.

Gabba, Emilio, "Considerazioni sulla tradizione letteraria sulle origini della Repubblica," in *Les Origines de la république romaine*, EntrHardt 13, Geneva 1967, pp. 135–69.

——, "The Historians and Augustus," in *Caesar Augustus: Seven Aspects*, ed. Fergus Millar and Erich Segal, Oxford: Clarendon Press, 1984, pp. 61–88.

——, *Dionysius and the History of Archaic Rome*, Berkeley: University of California Press, 1991.

Gagé, Jean, "L'Empereur romain et les rois: politique et protocole," *RHist* 221, 1959, 221–60.

——, "Les Traditions 'diomédiques' dans l'Italie ancienne, de l'Apulie à l'Étrurie méridionale, et quelques-unes des origines de la légende de Mézence," *MÉFRA* 84, 1972, 735–88.

Galinsky, Karl, *Augustan Culture: An Interpretive Introduction*, Princeton, N.J.: Princeton University Press, 1996.

Ganzert, Joachim, *Das Kenotaph für Gaius Caesar in Limyra: Architektur und Bauornamentik*, IstForsch 35, 1984.

Garcia Moreno, Luis A., "Le República romana tardía y el conocimiento geográfico y etnográfico de Africa," *AfrRom* 11 [n.d.], 319–26.

Gardner, Jane F. *Being a Roman Citizen*, London: Routledge, 1993.

Garnsey, P. D. A., "Rome's African Empire under the Principate," in *Imperialism in the Ancient World*, ed. P. D. A. Garnsey and C. R. Whittaker, Cambridge: Cambridge University Press, 1978, pp. 223–54.

——, "Grain for Rome" in *Trade in the Ancient Economy*, ed. P. D. A. Garnsey *et al.*, London: Chatto and Windus, 1983, pp. 118–30.

——, *Famine and Food Supply in the Graeco-Roman World: Responses to Risk and Crisis*, Cambridge: Cambridge University Press, 1988.

Gascou, Jacques, "Le *cognomen Gaetulus, Gaetulicus* en Afrique romaine," *MÉFRA* 82, 1970, 723–36.

——, "Note sur l'évolution du statut juridique de Tanger entre 38 avant J.-C. et le règne de Claude," *AntAfr* 8, 1974, 67–71.

——, "La Politique municipale de Rome en Afrique du Nord I. De la mort d'Auguste au début du IIIe siècle," *ANRW* 2.10.2, 1982, 136–229.

Gattefossé, Jean, "La Pourpre gétule, invention du roi Juba de Maurétanie," *Hespéris* 44, 1957, 329–33.

Gauthier, Philippe, "Sur le don de grain numide à Delos: un pseudo-Rhodien dans les comptes de hiéropes," in *Comptes et inventaires dans la cité grecque: Actes du colloque international d'épigraphie tenu à Neuchâtel du 23 au 26 septembre 1986 en l'honneur de Jacques Tréheux*, ed. Denis Knoepfler, Neuchâtel: Faculté des Lettres, Université de Neuchâtel, 1988, pp. 61–9.

Geffcken, J., "Krinagoras," *RE* 11, 1922, 1859–64.

Gelzer, Matthias, *Caesar: Politician and Statesman*, tr. Peter Needham, Cambridge, Mass.: Harvard University Press, 1968.

Ghazi-ben Maissa, Halima, "Volubilis et le problème de *regia Jubae*," *AfrRom* 10, 1994, 243–61.

——, "Encore et toujours sur la mort de Ptolémée, le roi Amazigh de Maurétanie," *Hésperis-Tamuda* 33, 1995, 21–37.

288

——, "Le Culte royal en Afrique Mineure antique," *Hésperis-Tamuda* 35.2, 1997, 7–42.

Giomini, Remo, "Ipsicrate," *Maia* n.s. 8, 1956, 49–55.

Gisinger, Friedrich, "Timagenes" (#2), *RE* 2, ser 11, 1936, 1063–73.

——, "Promathos," *RE* 23, 1957, 1285–6.

——, "Pytheas" (#1), *RE* 24, 1963, 314–66.

Gizewski, Christian, "Duoviri, Duumviri," *NP* 3, 1997, 843–5.

Gleason, Kathryn L., "The Garden Portico of Pompey the Great," *Expedition* 32.2, 1990, 4–13.

Goette, Hans Rupprecht, "Mulleus–Embas–Calceus: Ikonografische Studien zu römischem Schuhwerk," *JdI* 103, 1988, 401–64.

Golvin, Jean-Claude, *L'Amphithéâtre romain: essai sur la théorisation de sa forme et de ses fonctions*, Paris: Diffusion de Boccard, 1988.

Golvin, Jean-Claude and Philippe Leveau, "L'Amphithéâtre et le théâtre-amphithéâtre de Cherchel: monuments à spectacle et histoire urbaine à Caesarea de Maurétanie," *MÉFRA* 91, 1979, 817–43.

Goody, Jack (ed.), *Succession to High Office*, Cambridge Papers in Social Anthropology 4, 1966.

Goudchaux, Guy Weill, "Cleopatra's Subtle Religious Strategy," in *Cleopatra*, pp. 128–41.

Gow, A. S. F. and D. L. Page, *The Greek Anthology: Hellenistic Epigrams*, Cambridge: Cambridge University Press, 1965.

——, *The Greek Anthology: The Garland of Philip and Some Contemporary Epigrams*, Cambridge: Cambridge University Press, 1968.

Gowing, Alain M., *The Triumviral Narratives of Appian and Cassius Dio*, Ann Arbor: University of Michigan Press, 1992.

Gozalbes, Enrique, "El culto indígena a los reyes en Mauritania Tingitana: surgimiento y pervivencia," in *Paganismo y cristianismo en el occidente del imperio romano*, Memorias de historia antigua 5, Oviedo 1981, pp. 153–64.

——, "Las características agrícolas de la Mauretania Tingitana," *AfrRom* 12, 1998, 343–58.

Gozalbes Cravioto, Enrique, "La intervención de la Mauretania de Bogud en las guerras civiles romanas en la provincia Hispania Ulterior," in *Actas de II Congreso de Historia de Andalucía*, Córdoba: Consejería de Cultura y Medio Ambiente de la Junta de Andalucía, 1994, pp. 287–93.

——, *Economía de la Mauritania Tingitana (siglos I A. de C.–II D. de C.)*, Ceuta: Instituto de Estudios Ceuties, 1997.

Grant, Michael, *From Imperium to Auctoritas: A Historical Study of the Aes Coinage in the Roman Empire, 49 B.C.–A.D. 14*, Cambridge: Cambridge University Press, 1946.

——, *Cleopatra*, New York: Weidenfeld and Nicolson, 1972.

Gras, Michel, "Le Mémoire de Lixus: de la fondation de Lixus aux premiers rapports entre Grecs et Phéniciens en Afrique du Nord," *Lixus*, pp. 27–44.

Gray, E. W., "The Crisis in Rome at the Beginning of 32 BC," *PACA* 13, 1975, 15–29.

Grazioli, Francesco S., "Scipione l'Africano," in *Africa Romana*, Milan: Hoepli, 1935, 3–26.

Green, C. M. C., "De Africa et eius incolis: The Function of Geography and Ethnology in Sallust's History of the Jugurthine War (*BJ* 17–19)," *AncW* 24, 1993, 185–97.

Greene, Kevin, *The Archaeology of the Roman Economy*, Berkeley: University of California Press, 1986.

Grether, Gertrude, "Livia and the Roman Imperial Cult," *AJP* 67, 1946, 222–52.

Grilli, Alberto, "Cicerone nell'età della toga virile," *PP* 52, 1997, 161–76.

Grimal, Pierre, "Auguste et Athénodore," *RÉA* 47, 1945, 261–73.

——, "Auguste et Athénodore (suite et fin)," *RÉA* 48, 1946, 62–79.

Grimal, Pierre and Th. Monod, "Sur la véritable nature du 'garum,'" *RÉA* 54, 1952, 27–38.

Groom, Nigel, *Frankincense and Myrrh: A Study of the Arabian Incense Trade*, London: Longman, 1981.

Gruen, Erich S., *The Hellenistic World and the Coming of Rome*, Berkeley: University of California Press, 1984.

——, *The Last Generation of the Roman Republic*, first paperback printing, Berkeley: University of California Press, 1995.

——, "The Expansion of the Empire under Augustus," *CAH*² 10, 1996, 147–97.

——, *Studies in Greek Culture and Roman Policy*, first paperback printing, Berkeley: University of California Press, 1996.

Gsell, Stéphane, *Histoire ancienne de l'Afrique du Nord*, Paris: Hachette, 1914–28.

——, "Juba II, savant et écrivain," *RAfr* 68, 1927, 169–97.

——, *Cherchel: Antique Iol-Caesarea*, Algiers: Direction de l'Intérieur et des Beaux-Arts, 1952.

——, *Inscriptions latines de l'Algérie* I, Rome: L'Erma di Bretschneider, 1965.

Guery, R., "Nouvelles marques de potiers sur terre sigillée de Cherchel," *BAAlg* 6, 1975–6 (1980), 61–6.

Gundel, Hans, "Volux," *RE* 2, ser. 9, 1961, 907–8.

Gunning, P., "Lykos" (#26), *RE* 13, 1927, 2402–3.

Gurukkal, Rajan and Dick Whittaker, "In Search of Muziris," *JRA* 14, 2001, 334–50.

Gurval, Robert Alan, *Actium and Augustus: The Politics and Emotions of Civil War*, Ann Arbor: University of Michigan Press, 1995.

Gutsfeld, Andreas, *Römische Herrschaft und einheimischer Widerstand in Nordafrika: Militärische Auseinandersetzungen Roms mit den Nomaden*, Heidelberger althistorische Beiträge und epigraphische Studien 8, Stuttgart 1989.

Habibi, Mohamed, "À propos du temple H et du temple de Melkart-Héraclès à *Lixus*," *AfrRom* 10, 1994, 231–41.

Habicht, Christian, *Studien zur Geschichte Athens in hellenistischer Zeit*, Hypomnemata 73, Göttingen 1982.

——, *Athens from Alexander to Antony*, tr. Deborah Lucas Schneider, first paperback edition, Cambridge, Mass.: Harvard University Press, 1999.

Hafner, German, "Das Bildnis des Massinissa," *AA* 1970, pp. 412–21.

Hahm, David, "The Ethical Doxography of Arius Didymus," *ANRW* 2.36, 1990, 2935–3055.

Hahn, Istaván, "Die Politik der Afrikanischen Klientelstaaten im Zeitraum des Bürgerkriege," in *Afrika und Rom in der Antike*, ed. Hans-Joachim Diesner *et al.*, Halle: Martin-Luther-Universität, 1968, pp. 207–28.

Halfmann, Helmut, *Itinera principum*, Heidelberger althistorische Beiträge und epigraphische Studien 2, Stuttgart 1986.

Hallenbeck, Cleve, *The Journey of Fray Marcos de Niza*, Dallas: Southern Methodist University Press, 1987.

Hamdoune, Christine, "Note sur le statut colonial de Lixus et de Tanger," *AntAfr* 30, 1994, 81–7.

Hammond, M., "Octavia" (#96), *RE* 17, 1937, 1859–68.

Hammond, N. G. L. and G. T. Griffith, *A History of Macedonia* 2: *550–336 B.C.*, Oxford: Clarendon Press, 1979.

Hänlein-Schäfer, Heidi, *Veneratio Augusti: Eine Studie zu den Tempeln des ersten römischen Kaisers*, Archaeologica 39, Rome 1985.

Hanno, *Periplus or Circumnavigation {of Africa}*, third edition, ed. Al. N. Oikonomides and M. C. J. Miller, Chicago: Ares, 1995.

Hansman, John, "Charax and the Karkheh," *IrAnt* 7, 1967, 21–58.

Harden, D. B., "The Phoenicians on the West Coast of Africa," *Antiquity* 22, 1948, 141–50.

Harris, W. V., "Roman Expansion in the West," *CAH*² 8, 1989, 107–62.

Hayes, William C., "Egypt: Internal Affairs from Tuthmosis I to the Death of Amenophis III," *CAH*³ 2.1, 1973, 313–416.

Haywood, R. M., "Roman Africa," in *An Economic Survey of Ancient Rome* 4, ed. Tenney Frank, Baltimore: Johns Hopkins University Press, 1938, pp. 1–119.

Head, Barclay V., *Historia Numorum: A Manual of Greek Numismatics*, new enlarged edition, Oxford: Clarendon Press, 1911.

Healy, John F., "Pliny on Mineralogy and Metals," in *Science in the Early Roman Empire: Pliny the Elder, His Sources and Influence*, ed. Roger French and Frank Greenaway, London: Croom Helm, 1986, pp. 111–46.

——, *Pliny the Elder on Science and Technology*, Oxford: Oxford University Press, 1999.

Hennig, Dieter, *L. Aelius Seianus: Untersuchungen zur Regierung des Tiberius*, Vestigia 21, Munich 1975.

Hennig, Richard, *Terrae Incognitae*, second enlarged edition, Leiden: E. J. Brill, 1944–56.

Hense, Otto, "De Iuba artigrapho," *Acta Societatis Philologiae Lipsiensis* 4, 1875, 1–320.

Herber, David and J. Herber, "La Pourpre de Gétulie," *Hésperis* 25, 1938, 97–9.

Hesnard, Antoinette and Maurice Lenoir, "Les Négociants italiens en Maurétanie avant l'annexion (résumé)," *BAC* n.s. 19b, 1983 (1985), 49–51.

Heurgon, Jacques, "La Lettre de Cicéron à P. Sittius (Ad Fam., V, 17)," *Latomus* 9, 1950, 369–77.

Higgs, Peter, "Searching for Cleopatra's Image: Classical Portraits in Stone," in *Cleopatra*, pp. 200–9.

Hillscher, Alfred, *Hominum litteratorum graecorum ante Tiberii mortem in urbe Rome commoratorum*, Leipzig: Teubner, 1891.

Hodge, A. Trevor, *Roman Aqueducts and Water Supply*, London: Duckworth, 1992.

Hölbl, Günther, *A History of the Ptolemaic Empire*, tr. Tina Saavedra, London: Routledge, 2001.

Hölscher, G. "Mamre," *RE* 14, 1928, 962–5.

Hofmann, Max, "Ptolemaios von Mauretanien" (#62), *RE* 23, 1959, 1768–87.

Hopkins, Keith, "On the Probable Age Structure of the Roman Population," *Population Studies* 20, 1966–7, 245–64.

Horn, Heinz Günter, "Die antiken Steinbrüche von Chemtou/Simmitthus," in *Numider*, pp. 173–80.

Hornblower, Jane, *Hieronymus of Cardia*, Oxford: Oxford University Press, 1981.

Horsfall, Nicholas, "Prose and Mime," in *The Cambridge History of Classical Literature* 2: *Latin Literature*, ed. E. J. Kenney and W. V. Clausen, Cambridge 1982, 286–94.

Hoyos, B. D., *Unplanned Wars: The Origins of the First and Second Punic Wars*, Untersuchungen zur antiken Literatur und Geschichte 50, Berlin 1998.

Hurlet, Frédéric, *Les Collègues du prince sous Auguste et Tibère: de la légalité républicaine à la légitimité dynastique*, CÉFR 227, 1997.

Huss, W., "Die westmassylischen Könige," *AntSoc* 20, 1989, 209–20.

——, "Die Datierung nach numidien Königsjahren," *AntAfr* 26, 1990, 39–42.

Huxley, George, "Bones for Orestes," *GRBS* 20, 1979, 145–8.

Huzar, Eleanor Goltz, *Mark Antony: A Biography*, London: Croom Helm, 1978.

Iamblichus, *On the Pythagorean Way of Life*, ed. John Dillon and Jackson Hershbell, *Texts and Translations* 29, Graeco-Roman Religion Series 11, Atlanta 1991.

Imhoof-Blümer, F., "Ein Fund von Iubadenaren," *ZfN* 28, 1910, 1–8.

Isaac, Benjamin, "Trade Routes to Arabia and the Roman Army," in *Roman Frontier Studies, 1979: Papers Presented to the 12th International Congress of Roman Frontier Studies*, ed. W. S. Hanson and L. J. F. Keppie, BAR-IS 71, 1980, pp. 889–901.

——, *The Limits of Empire: The Roman Army in the East*, Oxford: Clarendon Press, 1990.

——, "Trade Routes to Arabia and the Roman Presence in the Desert," in *L'Arabie préislamique et son environnement historique et culturel*, ed. T. Fahd, Strasbourg: Université des Sciences Humaines de Strasbourg, 1989, pp. 241–56.

Isager, Jacob, *Pliny on Art and Society: The Elder Pliny's Chapters on the History of Art*, London: Routledge, 1991.

Isidoros of Charax, *Parthian Stations*, ed. Wilfred H. Schoff, Philadelphia: Commercial Museum, 1914.

Jacobson, David M., "Three Roman Client Kings: Herod of Judaea, Archelaus of Cappadocia and Juba of Mauretania," *PEQ* 133, 2001, 22–38.

Jacoby, Felix, "Euthymenes" (#4), *RE* 6, 1907, 1509–11.

——, "Glaukos" (#37), *RE* 7, 1910, 1420.

——, "Iuba II" (#2), *RE* 9, 1916, 2384–95.

——, *Die Fragmente der griechischen Historiker*, Leiden: E. J. Brill, 1923–.

Jal, Paul, *La Guerre civile à Rome: étude littéraire et morale*, Paris: Presses Universitaires de France, 1963.

Jameson, Shelagh, "Chronology of the Campaigns of Aelius Gallus and C. Petronius," *JRS* 58, 1968, 71–84.

Janvier, Yves, "La Géographie greco-romaine a-t-elle connu Madagascar?" *Omaly sy anio (Hier et aujourd'hui)* 1–2, Tananarive, 1975, 11–41.

Jex-Blake, K. and E. Sellers, *The Elder Pliny's Chapters on the History of Art*, revised reprint, Chicago: Ares, 1976.

Jodin, André, "Note préliminaire sur l'établissement pré-romain de Mogador," *BAMaroc* 2, 1957, 9–39.

——, *Les Établissements du Roi Juba II aux Îles Purpuraires (Mogador)*, Tangier: Éditions Marocaines et Internationales, 1967.

——, "Le Commerce maurétanien au temps de Juba II: la céramique arétine de Volubilis (Maroc)," in *Actes du quatre-vingt-onzième Congrès National de Sociétés Savantes, Rennes 1966: Section d'archéologie*, Paris: Bibliothèque Nationale, 1968, pp. 39–53.

——, *Volubilis, Regia Iubae: contribution à l'étude des civilisations du Maroc antique préclaudien*, Paris: Diffusion de Boccard, 1987.

——, "Les Rois maures et les Îles Purpuraires (Mogador)," *Ktema* 21, 1996, 203–11.

Johnson, John Robert, "The Authenticity and Validity of Antony's Will," *AntCl* 47, 1978, 494–503.

Jones, A. H. M., *The Cities of the Eastern Roman Provinces*, Oxford: Clarendon Press, 1937.

Jonkers, E. J., *Social and Economic Commentary on Cicero's "De lege agraria orationes tres,"* Leiden: E. J. Brill, 1963.

Julien, Ch.-André, *Histoire de l'Afrique du Nord (Tunisie–Algérie–Maroc) des origines à la conquête arabe (647 ap. J.-C.)*, second edition, rev. Christian Courtois, Paris: Payot, 1951.

Kaimio, Jorma, *The Romans and the Greek Language*, CHL 64, Helsinki 1979.

Kahrstedt, Ulrich, "Frauen auf antiken Münzen," *Klio* 10, 1910, 261–314.

——, "Sophoniba," *RE* 2, ser. 3, 1927, 1099–100.

Kajanto, Iiro, *The Latin Cognomina*, CHL 36.2, Helsinki 1965.

——, *On the Problem of the Average Duration of Life in the Roman Empire*, Annales Academiae Scientiarum Fennicae, ser. B, vol. 153.2, Helsinki 1968.

Keaveney, Arthur, *Sulla: The Last Republican*, London: Croom Helm, 1982.

Kebric, Robert B., *In the Shadow of Macedon: Duris of Samos*, Historia Supp. 29, 1977.

Keller, L., *De Juba Appiani Cassiique Dionis auctore*, Marburg: N. G. Elwert, 1872.

Keller, Otto, *Die antike Tierwelt*, Leipzig: W. Engelmann, 1909–13.

Kennedy, George, *A New History of Classical Rhetoric*, Princeton, N.J.: Princeton University Press, 1994.

Kenrick, Philip M., "The Importation of Italian Sigillata to Algeria," *AntAfr* 32, 1996, 37–44.

Keyser, Paul T., "From Myth to Map: The Blessed Isles in the First Century BC," *AncW* 24, 1993, 149–67.

Khanoussi, Mustapha, "Les *officiales marmorum numidicorum*," *AfrRom* 12, 1998, 997–1016.

Klebs, Eliman, "Bocchus" (#1), *RE* 3, 1899, 577–8.

——, "Bocchus" (#2), *RE* 3, 1899, 578–9.

——, "Bogudes" (#1), *RE* 3, 1899, 608.

——, "Bogudes" (#2), *RE* 3, 1899, 608–9.

Kleiner, Diana E. E., "Imperial Women as Patrons of the Arts of the Early Empire," in *I Claudia: Women in Ancient Rome*, ed. Diana E. E. Kleiner and Susan B. Matheson, New Haven, Conn.: Yale Art Gallery, 1996, 28–41.

Klotz, A., "Simias" (#2), *RE* 2, ser. 3, 1927, 142–3.

Kokkinos, Nikos, "Re-assembling the Inscription of Glaphyra from Athens," *ZPE* 68, 1987, 288–90.

——, "A Fresh Look at the *gentilicium* of Felix Procurator of Judaea," *Latomus* 49, 1990, 126–41.

——, *Antonia Augusta: Portrait of a Great Roman Lady*, London: Routledge, 1992.

——, "Which Salome Did Aristobulus Marry?" *PEQ* 118, 1996, 33–50.

——, *The Herodian Dynasty: Origins, Role in Society, and Eclipse, Journal for the Study of the Pseudepigrapha Supplement Series* 30, Sheffield 1998.

Konrad, C. F., *Plutarch's Sertorius: A Historical Commentary*, Chapel Hill: University of North Carolina Press, 1994.

Kontorini, Vassa N, "Le Roi Hiempsal II de Numidie et Rhodes," *AntCl* 64, 1975, 89–99.

Kortenbeutel, Heinz, *Der ägyptische Süd- und Osthandel in der Politik der Ptolemäer und römischen Kaiser*, Berlin: Gebrüder Hoffman, 1931.

Kotula, Tadeusz, "Encore sur la mort de Ptolémée, roi de Maurétanie," *Archeologia* (Warsaw) 15, 1964, 76–94.

——, "*Utraque lingua eruditi*: une page relative à l'histoire de l'éducation dans l'Afrique romaine," in *Hommages à Marcel Renard* 2, ed. Jacqueline Bibauw, Collection Latomus 102, Paris 1969, pp. 386–92.

——, *Masynissa*, Warsaw: Państwowy Instytut Wydawniczy, 1976.

——, "Ósma Kleopatra," *Mówią wieki* 21.12, 1978, 18–21.

——, "Orientalia africana: réflexions sur les contacts Afrique du Nord Romaine–Orient hellénistique," *FolOr* 24, 1987, 117–33.

Kraus, Christina Shuttleworth, "Jugurthine Disorder," in *The Limits of Historiography: Genre and Narrative in Ancient Historical Texts*, ed. Christina Shuttleworth Kraus, Leiden: E. J. Brill, 1999, pp. 217–48.

Kraus, Theodor, "Reiterbild eines Numiderkönigs," in *Praestant interna: Festschrift für Ulrich Hausmann*, ed. Bettina von Freytag geb. Löringhoff *et al.*, Tübingen: E. Wasmuth, 1982, pp. 146–7.

Krings, Véronique, "Les *libri Punici* de Salluste," *AfrRom* 7, 1989, 109–17.

Kroll, W. "Iuba" (#3), *RE*, 1916, 2395–7.

——, "Statius Sebosus" (#28), *RE* 2, ser. 3, 1929, 2223.

——, "Sudines," *RE* 2, ser. 4, 1931, 563.

——, "Cn. Papirius Carbo" (#38), *RE* 18, 1949, 1024–31.

Kuhrt, Amélie, "Berossus' *Babyloniaka* and Seleucid Rule in Babylonia," in *Hellenism in the East*, ed. Amélie Kuhrt and Susan Sherwin-White, London: Duckworth, 1987, pp. 32–56.

Kuttner, Ann L., *Dynasty and Empire in the Age of Augustus: The Case of the Boscoreale Cups*, Berkeley: University of California Press, 1995.

La Blanchère, Maria-Renatus de, *De rege Juba regis Jubae Filio*, Paris: E. Thorin, 1883.

La Calprenède, Gauthier de Costas, Seigneur de, *Hymens Praeludia or Loves Master-Piece, Being That so much admired Romance Entitled Cleopatra*, tr. Robert Loveday, London: A. Mosely and John Crook, 1668.

Lacey, W. K., "The Tribunate of Curio," *Historia* 10, 1961, 318–29.

——, "2 BC and Julia's Adultery," *Antichthon* 14, 1980, 127–42.

Laistner, M. L. W., *The Greater Roman Historians*, Berkeley: University of California Press, 1947.

Landwehr, Christa, "Juba II. als Diomedes?" *JdI* 107, 1992, 103–24.

——, *Die römischen Skulpturen von Caesarea Mauretaniae: Denkmäler aus Stein und Bronze* 1: *Idealplastik weibliche Figuren Bennant* (AF 18, 1993).

——, *Die römischen Skulpturen von Caesarea Mauretaniae* 2: *Idealplastik: Männliche Figuren*, Mainz: Philipp von Zabern, 2000.

Laqueur, Richard, "Nikolaos" (#20), *RE* 17, 1936, 362–424.

Laronde, André, *Cyrène et la Libye hellénistique: Libykai Historiai de l'époque républicaine au principat d'Auguste*, Paris: CNRS, 1987.

Lassère, Jean-Marie, "Onomastica Africana I–IV," *AntAfr* 13, 1979, 227–34.

——, "Un Conflit 'routier': observations sur les causes de le guerre de Tacfarinas," *AntAfr* 18, 1982, 11–25.

——, "L'Organisation des contacts de population dans l'Afrique romaine, sous la République et au Haut-Empire," *ANRW* 2.10.2, 1982, 398–426.

Lassère, Jean-Marie and Gilbert Hallier, "Volubilis préclaudien," *JRA* 2, 1989, 188–90.

Lasserre, François, "Strabon devant l'Empire romain," *ANRW* 30, 1982–3, 867–96.

Lassus, Jean, "Le Site de Saint-Leu, *Portus Magnus* (Oran), *CRAI* 1956, pp. 285–93.

——, "Les Découvertes récentes de Cherchel," *CRAI* 1959, pp. 215–25.

——, "Iol," *PECS*, pp. 413–14.

Lawrence, A. W., *Greek Architecture*, fifth edition, rev. R. A. Tomlinson, New Haven, Conn.: Yale University Press: 1996.

Le Bohec, Yann, "Le Proconsulat d'Afrique d'Auguste à Claude: questions de chronologie," *BAAlg* 7, 1977–9, 223–5.

——, "Onomastique et société à Volubilis," *AfrRom* 6, 1989, 341–56.

——, *La Troisième Légion auguste*, Paris: CNRS, 1989.

LeGall, Joël, "Successeurs d'Auguste mais descendants d'Antoine," *BAntFr* 1987, pp. 223–9.

LeGlay, Marcel, "Une Monnaie de Juba II," *LibAE* 4, 1956, 149–50.

——, "Notule suivante," *BAC* 1955–6 (1958), pp. 121–2.

——, "Une Dédicace à Vénus offerte à 'Caesarea' (Cherchel) par le futur empereur Galba," in *Mélanges d'archéologie, d'épigraphie et d'histoire offerts à Jérôme Carcopino*, Paris: Hachette, 1966, pp. 629–39.

——, *Saturne africain, histoire*, BÉFAR 250, 1966.

——, *Saturne africain, monuments*, Paris: Arts et Métiers Graphiques, 1966.

Leigh, Matthew, *Lucan: Spectacle and Engagement*, Oxford: Clarendon Press, 1997.

Lenaghan, Lydia H., "Hercules-Melqart on a Coin of Faustus Sulla," *ANSMN* 11, 1964, 131–49.

Lenoir, Maurice, "Inscriptions nouvelles de Volubilis," *BAMaroc* 16, 1985–6, 191–233.

——, "Lixus à l'époque romaine," *Lixus*, pp. 271–87.

Lenschau, Th., "Hiarbas" (#2), *RE* 8, 1913, 1388.

——, "Hiempsal," *RE* 8, 1913, 1393–5

——, "Iuba" (#1), *RE* 9, 1916, 2381–4.

——, "Jugurtha," *RE* 10, 1917, 1–6.

Leon, Ernestine F., "One Roman's Family," *ClBul* 35, 1958–9, 61–5.

Leonhardt, Jürgen, "Iuba" (#3), *NP* 5, 1998, 1186–7.

Leschi, Louis, "Un Sacrifice pour le salut de Ptolémée, roi de Maurétanie," in *Mélanges de géographie et d'orientalisme offerts à E.-F. Gautier*, Tours: Arrault et Cie., 1937, pp. 332–40.

Leveau, Philippe. "Trois tombeaux monumentaux à Cherchel," *BAAlg* 4, 1970, 101–48.

——, "Note additionelle à un article paru dans le BAAT IV et à propos de l'opus reticulatum à Cherchel," *BAAlg* 5, 1971–4, 25–34.

——, "Paysans maures et villes romaines en Maurétanie Césarienne centrale," *MÉFRA* 87, 1975, 857–71.

——, "Nouvelles inscriptions de Cherchel," *BAAlg* 6, 1975–6 (1980), 83–165.

——, "Étude de l'évolution d'un paysage agraire d'époque romaine à partir d'une prospection de surface: l'exemple du territoire de Caesarea de Maurétanie," *QS* 13, 1981, 167–85.

——, "Caesarea de Maurétanie," *ANRW* 2.10.2, 1982, 684–738.

——, "L'Urbanisme des princes clients d'Auguste" l'exemple de Caesarea de Maurétanie," in *Architecture et société de l'archaïsme grec à la fin de la République romaine*, CÉFR 66, 1983, pp. 349–54.

——, *Caesarea de Maurétanie: une ville romaine et ses campagnes*, CÉFR 70, Paris 1984.

——, "La Fin du royaume Maure et les origines de la province romaine de Maurétanie Césarienne," *BAC* n.s. 17b, 1984, 313–21.

——, "Le Pastoralisme dans l'Afrique antique," in *Pastoral Economies in Classical Antiquity*, Cambridge Philological Society Supplementary vol. 14, ed. C. R. Whittaker, Cambridge 1988, pp. 177–95.

——, "Caesarea Mauretaniae (Iol)," *EB* 11, 1992, 1698–706.

——, "Quelques réflexions sur Caesarea/Cherchel et Barbegal," *JRA* 12, 1999, 331–2.

Leveau, Philippe and Jean-Louis Paillet, *L'Alimentation en eau de Caesarea de Mauretanie et l'aqueduc de Cherchell*, Paris: Harmattan, [1976].

Lewis, Walter H. and Memory P. F. Elvin-Lewis, *Medical Botany: Plants Affecting Man's Health*, New York: Wiley, 1977.

Lieberman, Samuel, "Who Were Pliny's Blue-Eyed Chinese?" *CP* 52, 1957, 174–7.

Linderski, Jerzy, "The Surname of M. Antonius Creticus and the Cognomina *ex victis gentibus*," *ZPE* 80, 1990, 157–64.

Linfert, Andreas, "Die Tochter–Nicht die Mutter: Nochmals zur 'Africa'-Schale von Boscoreale," in *Alessandria e il mondo ellenistico-romano: studi in onore di Achille Adriani*, ed. Nicola Bonacasa and Antonino di Vita, Studi e Materiali [Palermo] 4–5, Rome: L'Erma di Bretschneider, 1983–4, pp. 351–8.

Lintott, Andrew, "The Capitoline Dedications to Jupiter and the Roman People," *ZPE* 30, 1978, 137–44.

——, "Political History, 146–95 BC," *CAH²* 9, 1994, 40–103.

——, "The Roman Empire and Its Problems in the Late Second Century," *CAH²* 9, 1994, 16–39.

Lixus, CÉFR 166, 1992.

Longo, Pietro, "Nuova documentazione epigraphica di età romana da Terracina," *Ann-Perugia* 21 n.s. 7, 1983–4, 315–41.

Lowrie, Michèle, *Horace's Narrative Odes*, Oxford: Clarendon Press, 1997.

Lullies, Reinhard and Max Hirmer, *Greek Sculpture*, revised and enlarged edition, New York: Harry N. Abrams, 1960.

Luttwak, Edward H., *The Grand Strategy of the Roman Empire from the First Century A.D. to the Third*, Baltimore: Johns Hopkins University Press, 1976.

Maas, Martha and Jane McIntosh Snyder, *Stringed Instruments of Ancient Greece*, New Haven, Conn.: Yale University Press, 1989.

MacAdam, Henry I., "Strabo, Pliny the Elder and Ptolemy of Alexandria: Three Views of Ancient Arabia and Its Peoples," in *L'Arabie préislamique et son environnement historique et culturel*, ed. T. Fahd, Strasbourg: Université des sciences humaines de Strasbourg, 1989, pp. 289–320.

McDermott, W. C., "M. Petreius and Juba," *Latomus* 28, 1989, 858–62.

McInerney, Jeremy, *The Folds of Parnassos: Land and Ethnicity in Ancient Phokis*, Austin: University of Texas Press, 1999.

Mackie, Nicola K., "Augustan Colonies in Mauretania," *Historia* 33, 1983, 332–58.

MacMullen, Ramsay, "Roman Imperial Building in the Provinces," *HSCP* 64, 1959, 207–35.

——, *Romanization in the Time of Augustus*, New Haven, Conn.: Yale University Press, 2000.

Macurdy, Grace Harriet, *Vassal-Queens and Some Contemporary Women in the Roman Empire*, Baltimore: Johns Hopkins University Press, 1937.

Magie, David, Jr., *Roman Rule in Asia Minor to the End of the Third Century after Christ*, Princeton, N.J.: Princeton University Press, 1950.

Majdoub, Mohammed, "La Maurétanie et ses relations commerciales avec le monde romain jusqu'au Iᵉʳ av. J.-C.," *AfrRom* 11, [n.d.], 291–302.

——, "Nouvelles données sur la datation du temple C à Volubilis, *AfrRom* 10, 1994, 283–7.

——, "Les Luttes du début du Iᵉʳ siècle av J.-C. au nord de la Maurétanie," *Lixus*, pp. 235–8.

——, "Pompeius Magnus et les rois maures," *AfrRom* 12, 1998, 1321–8.

——, "Octavius et la Maurétanie," *AfrRom* 13, 2000, 1725–37.

Makdoun, Mohammed, "Encore sur la chronologie du quartier nord-est de Volubilis," *AfrRom* 10, 1994, 263–81.

Makemson, Maud Worcester, "Note on Eclipses," in Grace Harriet Macurdy, *Vassal Queens*, Baltimore: Johns Hopkins University Press, 1937, pp. 60–2.

Mann, John Cecil, "The Frontiers of the Principate," *ANRW* 2.1, 1974, 508–33.

Manton, E. Lennox, *Roman North Africa*, London: Seaby, 1988.

Marble in Antiquity: Collected Papers of J. B. Ward-Perkins, ed. Hazel Dodge and Bryan Ward-Perkins, Archaeological Monographs of the British School at Rome 6, London, 1992.

Marcy, G., "Notes linguistiques: autour du Périple d'Hannon," *Hespéris* 20, 1935, 21–72.

Marion, Jean, "La Population de Volubilis à l'époque romaine," *BAMaroc* 4, 1960, 133–87.

Mariotta, Giuseppe, "Posidonio e Sallustio, *Iug.* 17–19," *AfrRom* 13, 2000, 249–57.

Masson, Jeffrey Moussaieff and Susan McCarthy, *When Elephants Weep: The Emotional Lives of Animals*, London: Cape, 1994.

Matthews, John, "Continuity in a Roman Family: The Rufii Festi of Volsinii," *Historia* 16, 1967, 484–509.

Matthews, Victor, "The *libri Punici* of King Hiempsal," *AJP* 93, 1972, 330–5.

Mattingly, David J., "From One Colonialism to Another: Imperialism and the Maghreb," in *Roman Imperialism: Post-colonial Perspectives*, eds. Jane Webster and Nicolas J. Cooper, Leicester Archaeology Monographs 3, 1996, pp. 49–69.

Mattingly, Harold, *Coins of the Roman Empire in the British Museum*, vol. 1: *Augustus to Vitellius*, London: British Museum Publications, 1923, reprinted with revisions 1976.

Mauny, Raymond. "Cerné l'Île de Herné (Río de Oro) et la question des navigations antiques sur la côte ouest-africaine," in *Conferencia Internacional de Africanistas Occidentales: 4ª Conferencia, Santa Isabel de Fernando Poo 1951*, Madrid: Dirección General de Marruecos y Colonias, 1954, vol. 2, pp. 73–80.

——, "Monnaies anciennes trouvées en Afrique au Sud du limes de l'Empire romaine," in *Conferencia Internacional de Africanistas Occidentales: 4ª Conferencia, Santa Isabel de Fernando Poo 1951*, Madrid: Dirección General de Marruecos y Colonias, 1954, vol. 2, pp. 53–70.

——, "La Navigation sur les côtes du Sahara pendant l'antiquité," *RÉA* 57, 1955, 92–101.

Mazard, Jean, *Corpus Nummorum Numidiae Mauretaniaeque*, Paris: Arts et Métiers Graphiques, 1955.

——, "Nouvel apport à la numismatique de la Numidie et de la Maurétanie," *LibAE* 4, 1956, 57–67.

——, "Deuxième supplément au *Corpus Nummorum Numidiae Mauretaniaque*," *LibAE* 5, 1957, 51–8.

——, "Troisième supplément au *Corpus Nummorum Numidiae Mauretaniaque*," *LibAE* 8.2, 1960, 133–45.

——, "Un Denier Inedit de Juba II et Cléopâtre-Séléné," *SchwMbll* 31, 1981, 1–2.

Mazzarino, Santo, "On the Name of the *Hipalus* (*Hippalos*) Wind in Pliny," in *Crossings: Early Mediterranean Contacts with India*, eds. F. De Romanis and A. Tchernia, New Delhi: Manohar, 1997, pp. 72–9.

Megow, Wolf-R., "Zwei Frühkaiserzeitliche Kameen mit Diademträgern," *AntK* 42, 1999, 82–91.

Meier Bochum, Mischa and Meret Strothmann Bochum, "Cornelius Bocchus," *NP* 3, 1997, 197–8.

Meiggs, Russell, *Trees and Timber in the Ancient Mediterranean World*, Oxford: Clarendon Press, 1982.

Meiklejohn, K. W., "Alexander Helios and Caesarion," *JRS* 24, 1934, 191–5.

Mellor, Ronald, "The Dedications on the Capitoline Hill," *Chiron* 8, 1978, 319–30.

Melville, Herman, *Moby Dick, or The Whale*, New York: Modern Library, 2000.

Mercer, John, *The Canary Islanders: Their Prehistory, Conquest and Survival*, London: Collings, 1980.

Meredith, David, "Berenice Troglodytica," *JEA* 43, 1957, 56–70.

Miles, Gary, *Livy: Reconstructing Early Rome*, Ithaca, N.Y.: Cornell University Press, 1995.

Millar, Fergus, "The Emperor, the Senate, and the Provinces," *JRS* 56, 1966, 156–66.

——, "Local Cultures in the Roman Empire: Libyan, Punic and Latin in Roman Africa," *JRS* 58, 1968, 126–34.

——, *The Roman Near East, 31 B.C.–A.D. 337*, Cambridge, Mass.: Harvard University Press, 1993.

Miller, J. Innes, *The Spice Trade of the Roman Empire, 29 B.C. to A.D. 641*, Oxford: Clarendon Press, 1969.

Miller, Stephen G., "Architecture as Evidence for the Identity of the Early Polis," in *Sources for the Ancient Greek City-State*, ed. Mogens Herman Hansen, Copenhagen: Munksgaard, 1995, pp. 201–44.

Miltner, Franz and W. H. Gross, "M. Porcius Cato Uticensis" (#16), *RE* 22, 1953, 168–213.

Mitchell, Stephen and Marc Waelkens, *Pisidian Antioch: The Site and Its Monuments*, London: Duckworth, 1998.

Montanari, G. Bermond, "Sofonisba," *EAA* 7, 1966, 389–90.

Montero, Santiago, "La conquista de Mauretania y el milagro de la lluvia del año 43 d.c.," *AfrRom* 13, 2000, 1845–51.

Momigliano, Arnaldo, "I regni indigeni dell'Africa Romana," in *Africa Romana*, Milan: Hoepli, 1935, pp. 85–103.

Moraux, Paul "Xenarchos" (#5), *RE* 2, ser. 9, 1931, 1422–35.

Morawiecki, Leslau, "A New Type of Silver Coin of Juba the Second," *SchwMbll* 24, 1974, 105–6.

Morstein-Marx, R., "The Alleged 'Massacre' at Cirta and Its Consequences (Sallust *Bellum Iugurthinum* 26–27)," *CP* 95, 2000, 468–76.

——, "The Myth of Numidian Origins in Sallust's African Excursus (*Iugurtha* 17.7–18.12)," *AJP* 122, 2001, 179–200.

Moscovich, M. James, "Cassius Dio on the Death of Sophonisba," *AncHBull* 11, 1997, 25–9.

Moss, Cynthia, *Elephant Memories: Thirteen Years in the Life of an Elephant Family*, New York: W. Morrow, 1988.

Müller, L., C. T. Falbe and J. Chr. Lindberg, *Numismatique de l'ancienne Afrique*, reprint, Chicago: OBOL International, 1977.

Münzer, F., "Q. Caecilius Metellus Pius Scipio" (#99), *RE* 3, 1899, 1224–8.

——, "Cn. Domitius Ahenobarbas" (#22), *RE* 5, 1903, 1327–8.

——, "C. Iulius" (#22), *RE* 10, 1917, 110.

——, "D. (Iunius) Silanus" (#160), *RE* 10, 1917, 1088–9.

——, "M. Iunius Silanus" (#167), *RE* 10, 1917, 1092–3.

——, "M. Livius Drusus" (#18), *RE* 13, 1926, 859–81.

——, "P. Sittius" (#3), *RE* 2, ser. 3, 1927, 409–11.

——, "Tanusius Geminus" (#2), *RE* 2, ser. 4, 1932, 2231–3.

——, "M. Petreius" (#3), *RE* 19, 1937, 1182–9.

Murray, G. W. "Trogodytica: The Red Sea Litoral in Ptolemaic Times," *Geographical Journal* 133, 1967, 24–33.

Nash, Ernest, *Pictorial Dictionary of Ancient Rome*, second edition, New York: Praeger, 1968.

Nesselrath, Heinz-Günther, *Die attische Mittlere Komödie*, Untersuchungen zur antiken Literatur und Geschichte 36, Berlin 1990.

Nicolet, Claude, *Space, Geography, and Politics in the Early Roman Empire*, Ann Arbor: University of Michigan Press, 1991.

Niese, B. "Gauda," *RE* 7, 1910, 856.

Nisbet, R. G. M. and Margaret Hubbard, *A Commentary on Horace: Odes, Book 1*, Oxford: Clarendon Press, 1970.

Nodelman, Sheldon Arthur, "A Preliminary History of Characene," *Berytus* 13, 1960, 83–121.

Noy, David, *Foreigners at Rome: Citizens and Strangers*, London: Duckworth, 2000.

Die Numider: Reiter und Könige nördlich der Sahara, ed. Heinz Günter Horn and Christoph B. Rüger, Cologne: Rheinland Verlag, 1979.

Oberhummer, Eugen, "Solieis" (#2), *RE* 2, ser. 3, 1927, 935.

Oder, E. "Geoponika," *RE* 7, 1910, 1221–5.

Onrubia-Pintado, J, "Canaries (Îles)," *EB* 11, 1992, 1731–55.

Oppolzer, Theodor, *Canon of Eclipses*, tr. Owen Gingerich, New York: Dover, 1962.

Ormerod, Henry A., *Piracy in the Ancient World: An Essay in Mediterranean History*, reprint, Chicago: Argonaut, 1967.

Ottone, Gabriella, "Problemi relativi alla conoscenza della topografia nord-africana nel Περὶ Λιβύης di Mnasea," *AfrRom* 13, 2000, 177–88.

Ouahidi, Ali, "Nouvelles recherches archéologiques sur les huileries de Volubilis," *AfrRom* 10, 1994, 289–99.

Pais, Ettore, *Fasti triumphales populi romani*, Rome: Nardecchia, 1920.

Paltiel, Eliezer, *Vassals and Rebels in the Roman Empire: Julio-Claudian Policies in Judaea and the Kingdoms of the East*, Collection Latomus 212, Brussels 1991.

Pani, Mario, *Roma e i re d'Oriente da Augusto a Tiberio*, Pubblicazioni della Facoltà di lettere e filosofia dell'Università di Bari 11, Bari 1972.

Paul, G. M., *A Historical Commentary on Sallust's "Bellum Jugurthinum,"* ARCA Classical and Medieval Texts, Papers and Monographs 13, Liverpool 1984.

Pavis d'Escurac, Henriette, "Les Méthodes de l'impérialisme romain en Maurétanie de 33 avant J.-C. à 40 après J.-C.," *Ktema* 7, 1982, 221–33.

Pearson, Lionel, *The Lost Histories of Alexander the Great*, reprint, Chico, Cal.: Scholars Press, 1983.

Pédech, P., "Un Texte discuté de Pline: le voyage de Polybe en Afrique (*H.N.*, V, 9–10)," *RÉL* 33, 1955, 318–32.

Pelling, Christopher, "The Triumviral Period," *CAH²* 10, 1996, 1–69.

Pensabene, Patrizio, *Les Chapiteaux des Cherchel: étude de la décoration architectonique*, *BAAlg Supp.* 3, 1982.

——, "La decorazione architettonica di Cherchel: cornici, architravi, soffitti, basi e pilastri," in *150-Jahr-Feier Deutsches Archäologisches Institut Rom*, RM Supp. 25, 1982, pp. 116–69.

Pera, Rossella, "Monete di Numidia nelle collezioni di Palazzo Rosso a Genova," *AfrRom* 12, 1998, 1329–34.

Perl, Gerhard, "Sallusts Todesjahr," *Klio* 48, 1967, 97–105.

Peter, Hermann, *Ueber den Werth der historischen Schriftstellerei von König Juba II von Mauretanien*, Jahresbericht über die Fürsten- und Landesschule Meissen 1878–9, pp. 1–14.

Petit, M., "Subdinum," *PECS*, p. 864.

Pfeiffer, Rudolf, *History of Classical Scholarship from the Beginnings to the End of the Hellenistic Age*, Oxford: Clarendon Press: 1968.

Philippson, R., "Athenodoros," *RE* Supp. 5, 1931, 47–55.

Phillimore, J. S., "Crinagoras of Mytilene," *Dublin Review* 139, 1906, 74–86.

Phillips, William D., Jr. and Carla Rahn Phillips, *The Worlds of Christopher Columbus*, Cambridge: Cambridge University Press, 1992.

Picard, Charles, "Une Réplique oubliée du Pothos scopasique," *RA* 6th ser. 25, 1946, 224–5.

——, "La Date du buste en bronze de Caton d'Utique trouvé à Volubilis, Maroc," in *Neue Beiträge zur klassischen Altertumswissenschaft: Festschrift zum 60. Geburtstag von Bernhard Schweitzer*, ed. Reinhard Lullies, Stuttgart: W. Kohlhammer, 1954, pp. 334–40.

——, "Lampes de bronze alexandrines à Volubilis et Banasa (Maroc)," *RA* 45, 1955, 63–8.

Picard, Gilbert Charles, "La Date du théâtre de Cherchel et les débuts de l'architecture théâtrale dans les provinces romaines d'occident," *CRAI* 1975, pp. 386–97.

——, "La Date du théâtre de Cherchel," *BAAlg* 6, 1975–6 (1980), 49–54.

——, "La sculpture dans l'Afrique romaine," in *150-Jahr-Feier Deutsches Archäologisches Institut Rom*, RM Supp. 25, 1982, pp. 180–95.

——, "Basilique et palais de Juba I de Numidie," *BAC* n.s. 18b, 1982 (1988), 165–7.

Plagge, Wenceslaus, *De Juba II rege Mauretaniae*, Münster, F. Regensburg, 1849.

Pliny the Elder, *Histoire naturelle, livre V, 1–46: L'Afrique du Nord*, ed. Jehan Desanges, Paris: Belles Lettres, 1980.

——, *Histoire naturelle, livre VI, 2ᵉ partie*, eds. J. André and J. Filliozat, Paris: Belles Lettres, 1980.

Plutarch, *Life of Antony*, ed. C. B. R. Pelling, Cambridge: Cambridge University Press, 1988.

Pollini, John, *The Portraiture of Gaius and Lucius Caesar*, New York: Fordham University Press, 1987.

Pomponius Mela, *Chorographie*, ed. A. Silberman, Paris: Belles Lettres, 1988.

——, *Kreuzfahrt durch die alte Welt*, ed. Kai Brodersen, Darmstadt: Wissenschaftliche Buchgesellschaft, 1994.

Ponsich, Michel, "Un Mosaïque du dieu Océan à Lixus," *BAMaroc* 6, 1966, 323–8.

——, "Un théâtre grec au Maroc?" *BAMaroc* 6, 1966, 317–22.

——, *Recherches archéologiques à Tanger et dans sa région*, Paris: CNRS, 1970.

——, "Le Temple dit de Saturne à Volubilis," *BAMaroc* 10, 1976, 131–44.

——, *Lixus: le quartier des temples (étude preliminaire)*, Études et travaux d'archéologie marocaine 9, Rabat 1981.

——, "Lixus: informations archéologiques," *ANRW* 2.10.2, 1982, 817–49.

——, "Tanger antique," *ANRW* 2.10.2, 1982, 788–816.

——, "La Céramique arétine dans le nord de la Maurétanie Tingitane," *BAMaroc* 15, 1983–4, 139–211.

Ponsich, Michel and Miguel Tarradell, *Garum et industries antiques de salaison dans la Méditerranée occidentale*, Paris: Presses Universitaires de France, 1965.

Poole, Reginald Stuart, *Catalogue of Greek Coins: The Ptolemies, Kings of Egypt* (=BMC Ptolemies), reprint, Bologna: Forni, 1963.

Posidonius, *I. The Fragments*, eds. L. Edelstein and I. G. Kidd, second edition, Cambridge: Cambridge University Press: 1989.

——, *II. The Commentary*, ed. I. G. Kidd, Cambridge: Cambridge University Press, 1988.

Potter, T. W., "Models of Urban Growth: The Cherchel Excavations 1977–81," *BAC* n.s. 19b, 1983 (1985), 457–68.

——, "City and Territory in Roman Algeria: The Case of Iol Caesarea," *JRA* 1, 1988, 190–6.

——, *Towns in Late Antiquity: Iol Caesarea and Its Context*, Oxford: Oxbow, 1995.

Potts, D. T., *The Arabian Gulf in Antiquity* 2: *From Alexander the Great to the Coming of Islam*, Oxford: Clarendon Press, 1990.

——, "The Roman Relationship with the *Persicus sinus* from the Rise of Spasinou Charax (127 BC) to the Reign of Shapur (AD 307–79)," in *The Early Roman Empire in the East*, ed. Susan E. Alcock, Oxbow Monograph 95, London: Oxbow, 1997, pp. 89–107.

Poulsen, Frederik, "Porträtkopf eines numidischen Königs," *SymbOslo* 3, 1925, 1–13.

Préaux, Claire, *Le Monde hellénistique* 1, third edition, Paris: Presses Universitaires de France, 1989.

Pytheas of Massalia, *On the Ocean*, ed. Christina Horst Roseman, Chicago: Ares, 1994.

R.-Alföldi, M., "Die Geschichte des numidischen Königreiches und seiner Nachfolger," in *Die Numider* 43–74.

Rachet, Marguerite, *Rome et les Berbères*, Collection Latomus 110, Brussels 1970.

Rajak, Tessa, *Josephus: The Historian and His Society*, London: Duckworth, 1983.

Rakob, Friedrich, "Numidische Königsarchitektur in Nordafrika," in *Numider*, pp. 119–71.

——, "Römische Architektur in Nordafrika," in *150-Jahr-Feier Deutsches Archäologisches Institut Rom*, RM Supp. 25, 1982, pp. 107–15.

——, "Architecture royale numide," in *Architecture et société de l'archaïsme grec à la fin de la République romaine*, CÉFR 66, 1983, pp. 325–48.

Ramin, Jacques, *Le Périple d'Hannon*, BAR Supplementary Series 3, 1976.

Raschke, Manfred G., "New Studies in Roman Commerce with the East," *ANRW* 2.9, 1978, 604–1361.

Raven, Susan, *Rome in Africa*, third edition, London: Routledge, 1993.

Rawson, Elizabeth, "Caesar's Heritage: Hellenistic Kings and Their Roman Equals," *JRS* 65, 1975, 148–59.

——, *Intellectual Life in the Late Roman Republic*, London: Duckworth, 1985.

——, "Caesar: Civil War and Dictatorship," *CAH*² 9, 1994, 424–67.

Rebuffat, René, "Notes sur les confins de la Maurétanie Tingitane et de la Maurétanie Césarienne," *StMagr* 4, 1971, 33–64.

——, "La Frontière romaine en Afrique Tripolitaine et Tingitane," *Ktema* 4, 1979, 225–47.

Reckford, Kenneth S., "Some Appearances of the Golden Age," *CJ* 54, 1958–9, 79–87.

Regling, Kurt, "Zum Fund von Iubadenaren in Alkasar," *ZfN* 28, 1910, 9–27.

Regner, Johannes, "Tirocinium Fori," *RE* 2, ser. 6, 1937, 1450–3.

Rehm, Albert, "Nilschwelle," *RE* 17, 1936, 571–90.

Reinhold, Meyer, *History of Purple as a Status Symbol in Antiquity*, Collection Latomus 116, Brussels 1970.

——, *From Republic to Principate: An Historical Commentary on Cassius Dio's "Roman History," Books 49–52 (36–29 B.C.)*, American Philological Association Monograph Series 34, Atlanta 1988.

Reuss, Friedrich, "De Jubae regis historia romana a Plutarcho expressa," in *Program des Königlichen Gymnasiums zu Wetzlar* 394, 1880, 1–27.

Rey-Coquais, J.-P., "L'Arabie dans les routes de commerce entre le monde méditerranéen et les côtes indiennes," in *L'Arabie préislamique et son environnement historique et culturel*, ed. T. Fahd, Strasbourg: Université de Sciences Humaines de Strasbourg, 1989, pp. 225–39.

Reynolds, Joyce and J. A. Lloyd, "Cyrene," *CAH*² 10, 1996, 619–40.

Ribichini, Sergio, "Hercule à Lixus et le jardin des Hespérides," *Lixus*, pp. 131–6.

Ricci, Cecilia, "Africani a Roma: testimonianze epigrafiche di età imperiale di personaggi provenienti dal Nordafrica," *AntAfr* 30, 1994, 189–207.

Richardson, L., Jr., "A Note on the Architecture of the *Theatrum Pompei* in Rome," *AJA* 91, 1987, 123–6.

——, *A New Topographical Dictionary of Ancient Rome*, Baltimore: Johns Hopkins University Press, 1992.

Richter, Gisela M. A., *The Portraits of the Greeks*, London: Phaidon, 1965.

Riddle, John M., *Dioscorides on Pharmacy and Medicine*, History of Science Series 3, Austin 1985.

Ritter, Hans Werner, "Iranische Tradition in Numidien," *Chiron* 8, 1978, 313–17.

——, *Rom und Numidien: Untersuchungen zur rechtlichen Stellung abhängiger Könige*, Lüneburg: AL.BE.CH., 1987.

Rives, James, "Imperial Cult and Native Tradition in Roman North Africa," *CJ* 96, 2001, 425–36.

Rivet, A. L. F., *Gallia Narbonensis*, London: Batsford, 1988.

Robin, Christian, "The Date of the *Periplus of the Erythraean Sea* in the Light of South Arabian Evidence," in *Crossings: Early Mediterranean Contacts with India*, ed. F. De Romanis and A. Tchernia, New Delhi: Manohar, 1997, pp. 41–65.

Robinson, E. S. G., *Catalogue of the Greek Coins of Cyrenaica* (=BMC Cyrenaica), reprint, Bologna: Forni, 1965.

Rohden, P. von, "Asarubas," *RE* 2, 1896, 1518.

Roller, Duane W., "The Wilfrid Laurier University Survey of Northeastern Caesarea Maritima," *Levant* 14, 1982, 90–103.

——, "Some Thoughts on Thales' Eclipse," *LCM* 8, 1983, 58–9.

——, "A Note on Greek Coins from Tamilnadu," *ND* 19, 1995, 37–41.

——, *The Building Program of Herod the Great*, Berkeley: University of California Press, 1998.

——, "A Note on the Berber Head in London," *JHS* 122, 2002, 144–6.

Romanelli, Pietro, *Storia delle province romane dell'Africa*, Studi pubblicati dall'Istituto Italiano per la Storia Antica 14, Rome 1959.

——, "Chi fu il vincitore di Giugurta: Mario o Silla?" *ArchStorTL* 2, 1960, 171–3.

——, "Ancora sull'età della Tomba della Cristiana in Algeria," *ArchCl* 24, 1972, 109–11.

——, "La campagna di Cornelio Balbo nel Sud Africano," in *Mélanges offerts a Léopold Sédar Senghor*, Dakar: Novelles Éditions Africaines, 1977, pp. 429–38.

The Roman Empire and Its Neighbours, ed. Fergus Millar, New York: Weidenfeld and Nicolson, 1967.

Romer, F. E., "A Numismatic Date for the Departure of C. Caesar," *TAPA* 108, 1978, 187–202.

——, "Gaius Caesar's Military Diplomacy in the East," *TAPA* 109, 1979, 199–214.

——, "A Case of Client Kingship," *AJP* 106, 1985, 75–100.

——, *Pomponius Mela's Description of the World*, Ann Arbor: University of Michigan Press, 1998.

Romm, James S., *The Edges of the Earth in Ancient Thought: Geography, Exploration, and Fiction*, Princeton, N.J.: Princeton University Press, 1992.

Rose, H. J., *The Roman Questions of Plutarch*, Oxford: Clarendon Press, 1924.

——, *A Handbook of Latin Literature from the Earliest Times to the Death of St. Augustine*, reprint of third edition, London: Methuen, 1967.

Rostovtzeff, M., *The Social and Economic History of the Roman Empire*, second edition revised by P. M. Fraser, Oxford: Clarendon Press, 1957.

Rousseaux, M., "Hannon au Maroc," *RAfr* 93, 1949, 161–232.

Russell, Francis H., "The Battlefield Of Zama," *Archaeology* 23, 1970, 120–9.

Sacks, Kenneth S., *Diodorus Siculus and the First Century*, Princeton, N.J.: Princeton University Press, 1990.

Salama, Pierre, "Vulnérabilité d'une capitale: Caesarea de Maurétanie," *AfrRom* 5, 1988, 253–69.

Salles, Jean-François, "The Arab–Persian Gulf under the Seleucids," in *Hellenism in the East*, ed. Amélie Kuhrt and Susan Sherwin-White, London: Duckworth, 1987, pp. 75–109.

Sallmann, Klaus Günther, *Die Geographie des älteren Plinius und ihrem Verhältnis zu Varro: Versuch einer Quellenanalyse*, Untersuchungen zur antiken Literatur und Geschichte 11, Berlin 1971.

Sallust, *The Histories*, tr. with intro. and comm. by Patrick McGushin, Oxford: Clarendon Press, 1992.

Salmon, E. T., *Roman Colonization under the Republic*, Ithaca, N.Y.: Cornell University Press, 1970.

Salzmann, Dieter, "Zur Münzprägung der mauretanischen Könige Juba II und Ptolemaios, *MM* 15, 1974, 174–83.

——, "Porträtsiegel aus dem Nomophylakeion in Kyrene," *BJb* 184, 1984, 141–66.

Sandberg, Gösta, *The Red Dyes: Cochineal, Madder, and Murex Purple*, tr. Edith M. Matteson, Asheville, N.C.: Lark Books, 1997.

Saumagne, Charles, "Zama Regia," *CRAI* 1941, pp. 445–53.

——, *La Numidie et Rome: Masinissa et Jugurtha*, Publications de l'Université de Tunis, Faculté des Lettres et Sciences Humaines, 4, ser. 4, Paris 1966.

Savage, Thomas S., "Notice of the External Characters and Habits of *Troglodytes gorilla*, a New Species of Orang from the Gaboon River," *Boston Journal of Natural History* 5, 1847, 417–26.

Saylor, Charles. "Curio and Antaeus: The African Episode of Lucan *Pharsalia* IV," *TAPA* 112, 1982, 169–77.

Scanlon, Thomas F. "Textual Geography in Sallust's *The War with Jugurtha*," *Ramus* 17, 1988, 138–75.

Scardigli, Barbara, "Sertorio: problemi chronologici," *Athenaeum* n.s. 49, 1971, 229–70.

——, "La *sacrosanctitas tribunicia* di Ottavia e Livia," *AnnSiena* 3, 1982, 61–4.

——, "Asinius Pollio und Nikolaos von Damaskus,' *Historia* 32, 1983, 121–3.

Schaaf, Hildegard, *Untersuchungen zu Gebäudestiftungen in hellenistischer Zeit*, Cologne: Bohlau, 1992.

Schäfer, Thomas, "Das Siegesdenkmal vom Kapitol," in *Numider*, pp. 243–50.

Schefold, Karl, *Die Wände Pompejis*, Berlin: De Gruyter, 1957.

Scheidel, Walter, *Measuring Sex, Age, and Death in the Roman Empire: Explorations in Ancient Demography*, JRA Supplement 21, Ann Arbor 1996.

Schulten, A., "Q. Sertorius" (#3), *RE* 2, ser. 2, 1923, 1746–53.

Schur, Werner, "Massinissa," *RE* 14, 1930, 2154–65.

——, "Mastanabal," *RE* 14, 1930, 2166–7.

——, "Micipsa," *RE* 15, 1932, 1522–4.

Schwartz, G., "Alexandros von Milet" (#88), *RE* 1, 1884, 1449–52.

Schwartz, Jacques, "Quelques monnaies de Maurétanie," *AntAfr* 14, 1979, 115–19.

Scott, Kenneth, "The Political Propaganda of 44–30 BC," *MAAR* 7, 1933, 7–49.

Scullard, H. H., *The Elephant in the Greek and Roman World*, London: Thames and Hudson, 1974.

Seager, Robin, *Pompey: A Political Biography*, Oxford: Blackwell, 1979.

Shaw, Brent D., "Archaeology and Knowledge: The History of the African Provinces of the Roman Empire," *Florilegium* 2, 1980, 28–60.

——, "The Elder Pliny's African Geography," *Historia* 30, 1981, 424–6.

——, "Fear and Loathing: The Nomad Menace and Roman Africa," in *L'Afrique romaine: les conférences Vanier 1980*, ed. C. M. Wells, Ottawa: Éditions de l'Université d'Ottawa, 1982, pp. 29–50.

——, "Soldiers and Society: The Army in Numidia," *Opus* 2, 1983, 133–57.

——, "The Age of Roman Girls at Marriage: Some Reconsiderations," *JRS* 77, 1987, 30–46.

——, *Rulers, Nomads, and Christians in Roman North Africa*, Aldershot: Varorum, 1995.

——, Review of Michèle Coltelloni-Trannoy, *Le Royaume de Maurétanie sous Juba II et Ptolémée (25 av. J.-C.–40 ap. J.-C.)*, Gnomon 72, 2000, 422–5.

Sherk, Robert K., "Roman Geographical Exploration and Military Maps," *ANRW* 2.1, 1974, 534–62.

Sherwin-White, A. N., "Geographical Factors in Roman Africa," *JRS* 34, 1944, 1–10.

——, *The Roman Citizenship*, second edition, Oxford: Clarendon Press, 1973.

——, *Roman Foreign Policy in the East, 168 B.C. to A.D. 1*, London: Duckworth, 1984.

Sherwin-White, Susan and Amélie Kuhrt, *From Samarkhand to Sardis: A New Approach to the Seleucid Empire*, Berkeley: University of California Press, 1993.

Shipley, Frederick W., "Chronology of the Building Operations in Rome from the Death of Caesar to the Death of Augustus," *MAAR* 9, 1931, 7–60.

Siciliani, Domenico, "La guerra giugurtina," in *Africa Romana*, Milan: Hoepli, 1935, pp. 51–82.

Sidari, Daniela, "Studi su Gaio e Lucio Cesare," *AttiVen* 138, 1979–80, 275–302.

Sidebotham, Steven E., *Roman Economic Policy in the Erythra Thalassa, 30 B.C.–A.D. 217*, Mnemosyne Supplement 91, Leiden 1986.

——, "Ports of the Red Sea and the Arabia–India Trade," in *Rome and India: The Ancient*

Sea Trade, ed. Vimala Begley and Richard Daniel De Puma, Madison: University of Wisconsin Press, 1991, 12–38.

Sigman, Marlene C., "The Role of the Indigenous Tribes in the Roman Occupation of Mauretania Tingitana," Ph.D. thesis, New York University, 1976.

——, "The Romans and the Indigenous Tribes of Mauretania Tingitana," *Historia* 26, 1977, 415–39.

Simon, Erika, *Augustus: Kunst und Leben in Rom um die Zeitenwende*, Munich: Hirmer, 1986.

Simpson, C. J., "The Date of Dedication of the Temple of Mars Ultor," *JRS* 67, 1977, 91–4.

Sinclair, T. A., *Eastern Turkey: An Architectural and Archaeological Survey* 4, London: Pindar Press, 1990.

Singer, Mary White, "Octavia's Mediation at Tarentum," *CJ* 43, 1947–8, 173–7.

Sirago, Vito Antonio, "Tacfarinas," *AfrRom* 5, 1988, 199–204.

——, "Il contributo di Giuba II alla conoscenza dell'Africa," *AfrRom* 11, 1994, 303–17.

——, "Rome e la via oceanica per l'India," *AfrRom* 13, 2000, 237–48.

Skutsch, F., "Fulgentius" (#3), *RE* 7, 1910, 215–27.

Smadja, Elisabeth, "Juba II Hercule sur le monnayage maurétanien," in *Mélanges Pierre Lévêque*, ed. Marie-Madelaine Mactoux and Evelyne Geny, 8: *Religion, anthropologie et société*, Paris: Belles Lettres, 1994, 371–88.

Small, David B., "Studies in Roman Theater Design," *AJA* 87, 1983, 55–68.

Smith, Philip J., *Scipio Africanus and Rome's Invasion of Africa: A Historical Commentary on Titus Livius, Book XXIX*, McGill University Monographs in Classical Archaeology and History 13, 1993.

Smith, R. R. R., *Hellenistic Royal Portraits*, Oxford: Clarendon Press, 1988.

Solin, Heikki, *Beiträge zur Kenntnis der griechischen Personennamen in Rom* 1, CHL 48, Helsinki 1971.

Sordi, Marta, "Timagene di Alessandria: uno storico ellenocentrico e filobarbaro," *ANRW* 2.30, 1982–3, 775–97.

Souville, G., "Volubilis: le collecteur principal du *decumanus maximus*," *BAMaroc* 2, 1957, 175–84.

——, "Volubilis: tête d'Hercule en bronze," *BAMaroc* 2, 1957, 186–7.

Spann, Philip O., "Sallust, Plutarch, and the 'Isles of the Blest,'" *TI* 9, 1977, 75–80.

——, *Quintus Sertorius and the Legacy of Sulla*, Fayetteville: University of Arkansas Press, 1987.

Spaul, John, "The Roman 'Frontier' in Morocco," *BIALond* 30, 1993, 105–19.

——, "Across the Frontier in Tingitana," *Roman Frontier Studies 1995: Proceedings of the XVIth International Congress of Roman Frontier Studies*, ed. W. Groenman-Van Waateringe *et al.*, Oxbow Monograph 91, Oxford: Oxbow, 1997, pp. 253–8.

Speidel, Michael P., "An Urban Cohort of the Mauretanian Kings?" *AntAfr* 14, 1979, 121–2.

Speke, John Hanning, *Journal of the Discovery of the Source of the Nile*, New York: Harper, 1864.

Stähelin, F., "Gaia" (#4), *RE* Supp. 3, 1918, 534–5.

——, "Kleopatra" (#13), *RE* 21, 1921, 735–8.

——, "Kleopatra Selene" (#22), *RE* 21, 1921, 782–4.

——, "Kleopatra Selene" (#23), *RE* 21, 1921, 784–5.

Standish, Robert, *Elephant Walk*, New York: Macmillan, 1949.

Steier, "Tiger," *RE* 2, ser. 6, 1936, 946–52.

Sternkopf, W., "Die Verteilung der römischen Provinzen vor dem mutinensischen Kriege," *Hermes* 47, 1912, 321–401.

Storm, Elfriede, *Massinissa: Numidien im Aufbruch*, Stuttgart: Franz Steiner, 2001.

Strenger, Ferdinand, *Strabos Erdkunde von Libyen*, Quellen und Forschungen zur alten Geschichte und Geographie 28, Berlin 1913.

Strong, D. E., "Some Observations on Early Roman Corinthian," *JRS* 53, 1963, 73–84.

Subrahmanyam, Sanjay, *The Career and Legend of Vasco da Gama*, Cambridge: Cambridge University Press, 1997.

Sullivan, Richard D., "The Dynasty of Commagene," *ANRW* 2.8, 1977, 732–98.

——, "The Dynasty of Emesa," *ANRW* 2.8, 1977, 198–219.

——, "The Dynasty of Judaea in the First Century," *ANRW* 2.8, 1977, 296–354.

——, "Dynasts in Pontus," *ANRW* 2.7, 1980, 913–30.

——, "The Dynasty of Cappadocia," *ANRW* 2.7, 1980, 1125–68.

——, *Near Eastern Royalty and Rome, 100–30 B.C.*, Phoenix Supplementary Volume 24, Toronto 1990.

Sumner, G. V., "Cicero, Pompeius, and Rullus," *TAPA* 97, 1966, 569–82.

Sybel, Ludwig von, "Diomedes," in W. H. Roscher, *Ausführliches Lexicon der griechischen und römischen Mythologie*, Leipzig 1884–6, pp. 1022–7.

Syme, Ronald, "Tacfarinas, the Musulamii and Thubursicu," in *Studies in Roman Economic and Social History in Honor of Allan Chester Johnson*, ed. P. R. Coleman-Norton, F. C. Bourne, and J. V. A. Fine, Princeton, N.J.: Princeton University Press, 1951, pp. 113–30.

——, *The Roman Revolution*, paperback edition, Oxford: Clarendon Press, 1960.

——, *Sallust*, Berkeley: University of California Press, 1964.

——, *History in Ovid*, Oxford: Clarendon Press, 1978.

——, *The Augustan Aristocracy*, Oxford: Clarendon Press, 1986.

Takács, Sarolta A., "Alexandria in Rome," *HSCP* 97, 1995, 263–76.

Tarn, W. W., "Alexander Helios and the Golden Age," *JRS* 22, 1932, 135–60.

Taviani, Paolo Emilio, *Christopher Columbus: The Grand Design*, tr. William Weaver, London: Orbis, 1985.

Taylor, Lily Ross, Review of *Papers Presented to Hugh Macilwain Last*, *AJP* 80, 1959, 102–4.

Tchernia, André, "Winds and Coins: From the Supposed Discovery of the Monsoon to the *denarii* of Tiberius," in *Crossings: Early Mediterranean Contacts with India*, ed. F. De Romanis and A. Tchernia, New Delhi: Manohar, 1997, pp. 250–76.

Teutsch, Leo, *Das Städtewesen in Nordafrika in der Zeit von C. Gracchus bis zum Tode des Kaisers Augustus*, Berlin: De Gruyter, 1962.

Thapar, Romila, "Early Mediterranean Contacts with India: An Overview," in *Crossings: Early Mediterranean Contacts with India*, ed. F. De Romanis and A. Tchernia, New Delhi: Manohar, 1997, pp. 11–40.

Thesleff, Holger, *An Introduction to the Pythagorean Writings of the Hellenistic Period*, Acta Academiae Aboensis, Humaniora 24.3, Åbo 1961.

Thiel, J. N., *Eudoxus of Cyzicus: A Chapter in the History of the Sea-Route to India and the Route around the Cape in Ancient Times*, Historische Studies 23, Groningen [n.d.].

Thieling, Walter, *Der Hellenismus in Kleinafrika: Der griechische Kultureinfluss in den römischen Provinzen Nordwestafrikas*, Leipzig: Teubner, 1911.

Thompson, Dorothy, "Athenaeus in His Egyptian Context," in *Athenaeus and His World:*

Reading Greek Culture in the Roman Empire, ed. David Braund and John Wilkins, Exeter: University of Exeter Press, 2000, pp. 77–84.

Thompson, Homer, "Excavations in the Athenian Agora: 1949," *Hesperia*, 1950, 313–37.

Thompson, L. A., "Eastern Africa and the Graeco–Roman World (to AD 641)," in *Africa in Classical Antiquity: Nine Studies*, eds. L. A. Thompson and J. Ferguson, Ibadan: Ibadan University Press, 1969, pp. 26–61.

——, "Settler and Native in the Urban Centres of Roman Africa," in *Africa in Classical Antiquity: Nine Studies*, ed. L. A. Thompson and J. Ferguson, Ibadan: Ibadan University Press, 1969, pp. 132–81.

——, "Carthage and the Massylian *Coup d'État* of 206 BC," *Historia* 30, 1981, 120–6.

Thomson, J. Oliver, *History of Ancient Geography*, Cambridge: Cambridge University Press, 1948.

Thouvenot, Raymond, "Le Culte de Saturne en Maurétanie Tingitane," *RÉA* 56, 1954, 150–3.

——, "Recherches archéologiques à Mogador," *Hespéris* 41, 1954, 463–7.

——, "Le Témoignage de Pline sur le périple africain de Polybe (V, 1, 8–11)," *RÉL* 34, 1956, 88–92.

——, "Le Géographe Ptolémée et la jonction terrestre des deux Maurétanies," *RÉA* 64, 1962, 82–8.

——, "Deux commerçants volubilitains dans le Norique," *BCTH* 8b, 1972 (1975), 28–32.

Tierney, J. J., "The Map of Agrippa," *Proceedings of the Royal Irish Academy* 63c, 1963, 151–66.

Topik, Stephen C., "Coffee," *CWHF*, pp. 641–53.

Toynbee, J. M. C., *Animals in Roman Life and Art*, Ithaca, N.Y.: Cornell University Press, 1973.

——, *Roman Historical Portraits*, London: Thames and Hudson, 1978.

Tracy, Stephen V. and Christian Habicht, "New and Old Panathenaic Victor Lists," *Hesperia* 60, 1991, 189–236.

Travlos, John, *Pictorial Dictionary of Ancient Athens*, New York: Praeger, 1971.

Treggiari, Susan, *Roman Marriage:* iusti coniuges *from the Time of Cicero to the Time of Ulpian*, Oxford: Clarendon Press, 1991.

——, "Social Status and Social Legislation," *CAH*[2] 10, 1996, 873–904.

Trell, Bluma L., "Ancient Coins: New Light on North African Architecture," in *Actes du Premier Congrès d'Histoire et de la Civilisation du Maghreb* 1, Tunis: Université de Tunis, 1979, pp. 81–97.

Treves, Peiro, "Sertorio," *Athenaeum* n.s. 10, 1932, 127–47.

Trofimoff, Hervé, "Une Préfiguration de la séparation des pouvoirs: le testament de Masinissa," *RIDA* 3rd ser. 35, 1988, 263–84.

Tsafrir, Yoram *et al.*, *Tabula Imperii Romani: Iudaea Palaestina*, Jerusalem: Israel Academy of Sciences and Humanities, 1994.

Tümpel, Karl, "Askalos," *RE* 2, 1896, 1610.

Van Beek, Gus W., "Ancient Frankincense-Producing Areas," in *Archaeological Discoveries in South Arabia*, Baltimore: Johns Hopkins University Press, 1958, pp. 139–42.

——, "Frankincense and Myrrh in Ancient South Arabia," *JAOS* 78, 1958, 141–51.

Velleius Paterculus, *The Tiberian Narrative (2.94–131)*, ed. A. J. Woodman, Cambridge: Cambridge University Press, 1977.

Ventris, Michael and John Chadwick, *Documents in Mycenaean Greek*, Cambridge: Cambridge University Press, 1956.

Verbrugge, Gerald P. and John M. Wickersham, *Berossos and Manetho, Introduced and Translated: Native Traditions in Ancient Mesopotamia and Egypt*, Ann Arbor: University of Michigan Press, 1996.

Verne, Jules, *The Extraordinary Journeys: Twenty Thousand Leagues under the Seas*, tr. with intro. and notes by William Butcher, Oxford: Oxford University Press, 1998.

——, *Vingt mille lieues sous les mers*, 2 vols., sixth edition, Paris: Hetzel, [n.d.].

Vierneisel, Klaus, "Die Berliner Kleopatra," *JBerlMus* 22, 1980, 5–33.

Vitruvius, *De l'architecture, livre viii*, ed. Louis Callebat, Paris: Belles Lettres, 1973.

——, *Ten Books on Architecture*, ed. Ingrid D. Rowland, Thomas Noble Howe and Michael J. Dewar, Cambridge: Cambridge University Press, 1999.

Voisin, Jean-Louis, "Le Triomphe africain de 46 et l'idéologie césarienne," *AntAfr* 19, 1983, 7–33.

Volkmann, Hans, *Cleopatra: A Study in Politics and Propaganda*, tr. T. J. Cadoux, New York: Sagamore Press, 1958.

Vollenweider, Marie-Louise, *Die Steinschneidekunst und ihre Künstler in spätrepublikanischer und Augusteischer Zeit*, Baden-Baden: Grimm, 1966.

Volterra, Edoardo, "Ancora sul matrimonio di Antonio con Cleopatra," in *Festschrift für Werner Flume zum 70. Geburtstag* 1, Cologne: O. Schmidt, 1978, pp. 205–12.

Wacholder, Ben Zion, *Nicolaus of Damascus*, Berkeley: University of California Press, 1962.

Walbank, F. W., *A Historical Commentary on Polybius*, Oxford: Clarendon Press, 1957–79.

——, *Polybius*, first paperback printing, Berkeley: University of California Press, 1990.

Walker, Susan, "The Moral Museum: Augustus and the City of Rome," in *Ancient Rome: The Archaeology of the Eternal City*, ed. J. Coulsen and H. Dodge, Oxford University School of Archaeology Monograph 54, 2000, pp. 61–75.

Walsh, P. G., "Masinissa," *JRS* 55, 1965, 149–60.

Ward-Perkins, J. B., "Tripolitana and the Marble Trade," *JRS* 41, 1951, 89–104.

——, *Roman Imperial Architecture*, second integrated edition, Harmondsworth, U.K.: Penguin Books, 1981.

Warmington, B. H., *Carthage*, London: R. Hale, 1960.

Warmington, E. H., *The Commerce between the Roman Empire and India*, second edition, revised and enlarged, London: Curzon Press, 1974.

Watkins, Thomas H., *L. Munatius Plancus: Serving and Surviving in the Roman Revolution*, Illinois Classical Studies, Supplement 7, Atlanta 1997.

Webster, Jane, "Creolizing the Roman Provinces," *AJA* 105, 2001, 209–25.

Weigel, Richard D., *Lepidus: The Tarnished Triumvir*, London: Routledge, 1992.

Weinstock, S., "Mauretania," *RE* 14, 1930, 2344–86.

Weisburger, John H. and James Comer, "Tea," *CWHF*, pp. 712–20.

Weissbach, F. H., "Isidoros Charakenos" (#20), *RE* 9, 1916, 2064–8.

Welch, Katherine, "The Roman Arena in Late-Republican Italy: A New Interpretation," *JRA* 7, 1994, 59–80.

Wellesley, Kenneth, "The Fable of a Roman Attack on Aden," *PP* 9, 1954, 401–5.

Wells, Peter S., *Culture Contact and Culture Change: Early Iron Age Central Europe and the Mediterranean World*, Cambridge: Cambridge University Press, 1980.

Wentzel, G., "Amarantos" (#3), *RE* 1, 1894, 1728–9.

———, "Aristokles" (#18), *RE* 2, 1895, 935–7.

West, J. M. I., "Uranius," *HSCP* 78, 1974, 282–4.

West, M. L., *Ancient Greek Music*, Oxford: Clarendon Press, 1992.

West, S., "Chalcenteric Negligence," *CQ* n.s. 20, 1970, 288–96.

Wheeler, Mortimer, *Rome beyond the Imperial Frontiers*, London: Bell, 1954.

Whitehorne, John, *Cleopatras*, London: Routledge, 1994.

Whittaker, Charles R., "Land and Labour in North Africa," *Klio* 60, 1978, 331–62.

———, *Frontiers of the Roman Empire: A Social and Economic Study*, Baltimore: Johns Hopkins University Press, 1994.

———, "Roman Africa: Augustus to Vespasian," *CAH*[2] 10, 1996, 586–618.

Willi, Andreas, "Numa's Dangerous Books: The Exegetic History of a Roman Forgery," *MusHelv* 55, 1998, 139–72.

Williams, J. H. C., "'Spoiling the Egyptians': Octavian and Cleopatra," in *Cleopatra*, pp. 190–9.

Wilson, A. J. N., *Emigration from Italy in the Republican Age of Rome*, Manchester: Manchester University Press, 1966.

Wilson, Andrew, "Deliveries *extra urbem*: Aqueducts and the Countryside," *JRA* 12, 1999, 314–31.

Wilson, Nigel Guy, "Harpocration, Valerius," *OCD*[3], 1996, 667.

Wilson Jones, Mark, "Doric Measure and Architectural Design 1: The Evidence of the Relief from Salamis," *AJA* 104, 2000, 73–93.

Wiseman, T. P., "Caesar, Pompey and Rome, 59–50 BC," *CAH*[2] 9, 1994, 368–423.

Wissmann, Hermann von, "Zangenae," *RE* Supp. 11, 1968, 1337–48.

Wissowa, G., "Cornelius Nepos" (#275), *RE* 4, 1900, 1408–17.

Wistrand, Erik, "Till två Horatiusställen," *Eranos* 29, 1931, 81–6.

———, "The Date of Curio's African Campaign," *Eranos* 61, 1963, 38–44.

Wood, Susan E., *Imperial Women: A Study in Public Images, 40 B.C.–A.D. 68*, Mnemosyne Supplement 194, Leiden 1999.

Woodcock, George, *The Greeks in India*, London: Faber, 1966.

Woodhead, A. G., *The Greeks in the West*, New York: Praeger, 1962.

Woolf, Greg, "Beyond Romans and Natives," *WA* 28, 1996–7, 339–50.

Das Wrack: Der Antike Schiffsfund von Mahdia, ed. Gisela Hellenkemper Salies *et al.*, Cologne: Rheinland-Verlag, 1994.

Wycherley, R. E., *Agora 3: Literary and Epigraphical Testimonia*, Princeton, N.J.: Princeton University Press, 1957.

Zahn, R., "Garum," *RE* 7, 1910, 841–9.

Zaminer, Frieder, "Aristoxenos" (#1), *NP* 1, 1996, 1152–4.

Zanker, Paul, *The Power of Images in the Age of Augustus*, tr. Alan Shapiro, Ann Arbor: University of Michigan Press, 1988.

Zecchini, Giuseppe, "Asinio Pollione: dall'attività politica alla riflessione storiografica," *ANRW* 30, 1982–3, 1265–96.

———, *La cultura storica di Ateneo*, Milan: Vita e Pensiero, 1989.

Zetzel, James E. G., "New Light on Gaius Caesar's Eastern Campaign," *GRBS* 11, 1970, 259–66.

Ziegler, Konrat, "Plutarchos" (#2), *RE* 2, ser. 21, 1951, 636–962.

LIST OF PASSAGES CITED

Italicized numbers are citations in ancient texts; romanized numbers are pages in this volume.

GREEK AND LATIN LITERARY SOURCES

Aelian:
  On the Characteristics of Animals 6.31,
    174n; *7.23*, 8n, 32n, 155n, 192n,
    204n, 263; *7.44*, 263; *9.58*, 8n,
    191n, 208n, 263; *14.5*, 208n; *14.6*,
    203n, 208n, 263; *15.8*, 8n, 180n,
    240n, 263; *17.8–9*, 234n
  Historical Miscellany 12.64, 53n
Aetius, *Placita 4.1*, 188n
Agatharchides of Knidos (*FGrHist* #86)
    fr. 41b, 234n
Alexandros Polyhistor (*FGrHist* #273)
    fr. 1–81, 65n; *fr. 32–47*, 187n;
    fr. 83–84, 65n; *fr. 85–94*, 65n; *fr. 94*,
    158n; *fr. 95–7*, 65n
Ammianus Marcellinus *22.15.8–11*, 8n,
    159n, 182n, 191n, 193n, 263
Ampelius, L., *Liber memorialis 38.1*, 8n,
    163n
Anaximenes of Lampsakos (*FGrHist* #72)
    fr. 40, 173n
Anonymus Florentinus, 188n, 190n
Antipatros of Thessalonike *1*, 88n; *30*, 88n;
    31, 88n; *41*, 88n; *46*, 88n, 214n; *47*,
    214n; *48*, 88n
Appian:
  Civil War:
    Book 1: *24*, 19n; *42*, 23n; *62*, 25n,
      26n; *80*, 26n
    Book 2: *44–46*, 33n; *44–100*, 35n;
      83–4, 34n; *96*, 35n, 58n, 206n;

      98–9, 36n; *101*, 7n, 59n; *102*, 138n;
      125, 62n
    Book 3: *22*, 62n; *94*, 62n
    Book 4: *6*, 62n; *40*, 122n; *53*, 91n,
      92n; *54*, 92n, 107n; *54–6*, 93n; *107*,
      62n
    Book 5: *1*, 76n; *8*, 77n; *8–9*, 77n; *9*,
      61n; *14*, 77n; *26*, 229n; *50–9*, 77n;
      53, 63n, 92n, 93n; *65*, 92n; *98*, 94n;
      129, 94n
  Iberika 37, 14n; *67*, 19n; *57*, 47n; *89*,
    206n
  Libyka, *10*, 13n, 17n; *26*, 14n; *27–8*, 17n;
    32, 14n; *37*, 13n; *67–70*, 16n; *70*,
    19n; *70–2*, 16n; *71*, 17n; *75*, 18n;
    95, 205n; *105–6*, 16n; *105–7*, 17n;
    106, 14n, 19n; *111*, 19n; *127–32*,
    18n; *136*, 56n
  Noumidika, 20n, 22n, 23n, 49n, 55n
  Syrian War 69, 78n
Archelaos of Kappadokia (*FGrHist* #123)
    fr. 6, 220n; *fr. 7*, 220n; *fr. 8*, 220n;
    fr. 9, 220n
Aristeides *36.85–96*, 188n
Aristophanes:
  Thesmophoraizousai 1175, 177n
  fr. 344b, 177n
Aristotle, *History of Animals 6.17*, 180n
[Aristotle], *On Marvellous Things Heard 37*,
    189n
Asklepiades *44*, 88n

316

EPIGRAPHIC SOURCES

BIBLICAL SOURCES

INDEX

Romans are generally alphabetized under their *nomen*, but occasionally under the *cognomen* when this is more familiar. Literary figures are not included in the index (see *List of Passages Cited*) unless they were active partipants in the event described.